The New European Central Bank

The New European Central Bank

Taking Stock and Looking Ahead

Edited by
THOMAS BEUKERS, DIANE FROMAGE, AND
GIORGIO MONTI

OXFORD
UNIVERSITY PRESS

OXFORD
UNIVERSITY PRESS

Great Clarendon Street, Oxford, OX2 6DP,
United Kingdom

Oxford University Press is a department of the University of Oxford.
It furthers the University's objective of excellence in research, scholarship, and education by publishing worldwide. Oxford is a registered trade mark of Oxford University Press in the UK and in certain other countries

First Edition published in 2022

Impression: 1

Published in the United States of America by Oxford University Press
198 Madison Avenue, New York, NY 10016, United States of America

British Library Cataloguing in Publication Data
Data available

Library of Congress Control Number: 2022938012

ISBN 978–0–19–887123–1

DOI: 10.1093/oso/9780198871231.001.0001

Printed and bound in the UK by
TJ Books Limited

Foreword

Evolution, not Revolution: The Development of the Role of the European Central Bank since its Establishment

Chiara Zilioli

The European monetary union is the only successful example in history of the voluntary adoption of a single currency by politically and linguistically separate states. The institution that has the mandate to ensure the stability of the currency is one of the world's youngest central banks. In its first twenty-three years of life it has navigated stormy waters, preserved the singleness of the monetary union, maintained the stability of the currency, incorporated several new Member States, and successfully sailed through three very serious financial crises. It is indeed a story that deserves to be carefully studied: '*The "New" European Central Bank: Taking Stock and Looking Ahead*' is a remarkable collection of well-assorted analyses by distinguished scholars on the development of the European Central Bank (ECB) since its establishment. Coming twenty years after euro banknotes and coins were first put in circulation this is a very timely contribution, which presents an opportunity to take stock of the past and look forward into the future.

I have had the great privilege to participate in the monetary union adventure from the beginning and indeed I can see a very different ECB today than in 1998, both from the perspective of the institution's structure and dimensions and in terms of its responsibilities and public presence. At the same time, I see this difference as reflecting the natural evolution of a competent and powerful institution, which has a mandate to achieve, and needs to do so in the most effective and proportionate way, adapting its instruments to the ever-changing reality. Let me go back to the main steps we have gone through in these years.

What is the ECB and what is its role? The natural starting point for any analysis of the ECB's legal framework and the development of its policy action since its establishment is to look into its mandate. The ECB's mandate was codified in the Maastricht Treaty at a time when the prevailing view among economists was in favour of an independent central bank that would deliver on its medium-term price stability objective by setting short-term interest rates, while the role for discretionary, countercyclical fiscal policy would be limited.[1] The 'constitutionalization' of the ECB's mandate and of its legal framework—the Statute of the European System of Central Banks and of

[1] 'Monetary-fiscal policy interactions in the euro area' (2021) ECB Occasional Paper Series No 273 <https://www.ecb.europa.eu/pub/pdf/scpops/ecb.op273~fae24ce432.en.pdf> accessed 12 January 2022 (hereafter 'Monetary-fiscal policy interactions in the euro area').

the European Central Bank (hereinafter the 'Statute'), being a protocol to the Treaty on the Functioning of the European Union (TFEU), is fully part of it and enjoys the same legal ranking—was precisely meant to tie the hands of politicians and avoid shifts in political preferences leading to departures from that optimal model. For this reason, economists and Treaty drafters alike believed that the model needed to be embodied in the Maastricht Treaty. In time, especially after the Great Financial Crisis (GFC), the broader context changed. This has not been a uniquely European development, and comparative analysis shows that other central banks also adapted the way in which their mandates were implemented, while the formal mandates did not change. Based on this trend, some argue that the ECB legal framework deserves to be 'deconstitutionalized' to better withstand the challenges of changing times.[2] On the other hand, the framework has proven to allow for important margins of flexibility, enabling it to cope with a radically different environment than that in which the ECB was established, while protecting the central bank from undue political interference.

There are several instances in which, in the wake of the GFC, the ECB's approach has changed, making use of the flexibility allowed by the law mainly in two ways: either the ECB has used in a new way, or for the first time, the powers that the Treaty drafters had conferred on it from the beginning; or the EU legislator has made use of the flexibility granted to it by the Treaty to confer new powers and tasks on the ECB, within the assigned competences.

Chronologically, the first step in ensuring additional margins of flexibility was the extension of the list of collateral considered adequate for monetary policy operations. In the immediate aftermath of the ECB's establishment, the Eurosystem worked for years to agree on a Single List of eligible collateral to harmonize its financial risk management strategy. Shortly after the Single List was agreed, the inception of the GFC induced the Eurosystem to reconsider its risk management policies and broaden the 'adequate collateral' category, internalizing higher risks than it previously did, in order to increase the amount of collateral counterparties would have available to access monetary policy operations and therefore ultimately the liquidity available to the general economy. National variations were reintroduced in the form of additional collateral claims; a temporary collateral framework was introduced to complement (and derogate from) the general framework at Eurosystem level; and the conditions for collateral to be accepted as eligible were increasingly loosened. This trend has been reinforced during the COVID-19 crisis, when the need for liquidity in the market has further increased. These developments have occurred within the scope of the discretion granted to the ECB to establish what amounts to 'adequate' collateral.[3]

When the financial crisis turned into a sovereign debt crisis, tensions on the national sovereign debt markets and spreads differentials that did not reflect the economic fundamentals started impairing the functioning of the monetary policy

[2] Marco Dani, 'Deconstitutionalising the Economic and Monetary Union' in European Central Bank, 'Continuity and change—how the challenges of today prepare the ground for tomorrow' Proceedings of the ECB Legal Conference 2021, forthcoming. See also, chapter 16 by Marijn van der Sluis, in this volume: 'The analysis that the Maastricht Treaty actually succeeded in structuring the process of European integration, must, in my opinion, lead to the conclusion that the euro and the ECB must be de-constitutionalized'.

[3] Protocol No 4 on the Statute of the European System of Central Banks and of the European Central Bank [2016] OJ C202/230, second indent of art 18.1 (hereafter ESCB Statute).

transmission mechanism. It became clear that much more than the singleness of the collateral policy was at risk: the very singleness of the ECB's monetary policy was at stake. Allowing for national variations in the collateral eligibility criteria had allowed the flow of liquidity in some euro area Member States, albeit only up to a point. The ECB then resorted for the first time to outright purchases, an approach that initially targeted sovereign bonds but was later extended to assets issued by private entities. This option had been part of the toolbox available under the Statute from the outset,[4] but had not been used until then. Outright purchases of sovereign bonds by the ECB became a legally contentious matter and also had a broader impact on the relationship between the Court of Justice of the European Union (CJEU) and national constitutional courts, giving rise to the first referral to the CJEU by the German Federal Constitutional Court, and to the pronouncement by the latter that a CJEU judgment should be considered ultra vires and not applicable in Germany. Without entering into the details of this issue, which would clearly go beyond the scope of this foreword, I would like to highlight that the underlying question is that of the respective scopes of monetary policy and fiscal policy. An expansion of the monetary policy toolkit has been seen by those who oppose the conferral of the monetary policy competence on a supranational institution as an undue interference with national fiscal policy, threatening the application of the national democratic principle in the economic sphere, while at the same time also threatening the principle of central bank independence. The practically difficult separation of monetary policy from economic policy was necessary when the Maastricht Treaty was drafted, not only to protect central bank independence and thereby the objective of price stability, but also to enable the launching of monetary union despite the absence of a political commitment to confer economic competences at supranational level. However, more recent findings and analyses, especially in view of experiences in the context of the COVID-19 pandemic, support the view that monetary policy and fiscal policy are naturally aligned and achieve their respective objectives far more effectively if the two are coordinated and complementary, at least in an environment with structurally low interest rates and persistent downside risks to price stability.[5]

The third development, brought about by the crises (GFC, sovereign debt crisis, pandemic crisis), has been to bring to the forefront the importance of financial stability, the contribution that the central bank can make to achieving it,[6] and the fact that a financially unstable environment jeopardizes the achievement of price stability and therefore a central bank must fight it. An enhanced attention to the financial stability implications in the setting of monetary policy and a more intense dialogue with fiscal authorities seem to have emerged from the crises (and is visible in the analysis carried out by the ECB in its strategic review).[7]

[4] See ESCB Statute (n 3) first indent of art 18.1.

[5] 'Monetary-fiscal policy interactions in the euro area' (n 1).

[6] Consolidated Version of the Treaty on the Functioning of the European Union [2012] OJ C326/47, Art 127(5).

[7] 'Monetary-fiscal policy interactions in the euro area' (n 1); and 'The role of financial stability considerations in monetary policy and the interaction with macroprudential policy in the euro area' (2021) ECB Occasional Paper Series No 272, <https://www.ecb.europa.eu/pub/pdf/scpops/ecb.op272~dd8168a8cc.en.pdf> accessed 12 January 2022.

Another development that has occurred in the last ten years is the conferral on the ECB of new powers and tasks by the legislator. The most eye-catching innovation in this regard was the establishment of the Single Supervisory Mechanism (SSM) and the conferral of banking supervisory tasks on the ECB, on the basis that the ECB's technical expertise would help to deliver on the 'imperative to break the vicious circle between banks and sovereigns'.[8] In this context, the necessary element of flexibility already existed in the Treaty, in the form of the enabling clause to be found in Article 127(6) TFEU (it would not have been possible, otherwise, for the EU legislator to have conferred competences on the ECB). There is no doubt that the conferral of this very important new competence has marked quite profoundly the ECB's evolution into its new role in the euro area and the EU. A central element of the SSM's institutional framework is the relationship between the ECB and the national competent authorities, which is more tilted towards the national level than the relationship between the ECB and the National Central Banks (NCBs) within the Eurosystem has traditionally been. The principal reason for this is that the rulebook of the Banking Union is also composed of directives, and therefore of the national laws implementing them, which are different and which the ECB, an EU institution, needs to apply. Furthermore, the SSM governance does not have the hierarchical structure and the profound integration clearly delineated for the Eurosystem in the Statute.

There are other cases in which the legislator, without conferring new powers, has added tasks for the ECB to perform in close cooperation with other EU institutions and bodies. For example, at the height of the sovereign debt crisis, the ECB was tasked with contributing to the work of the Commission and the European Stability Mechanism (ESM), first in the context of financial assistance programmes[9] and later in the context of the Six-Pack[10] and Two-Pack[11] legislative measures, as part of the

[8] European Council, 'Euro Area Summit statement' (Brussels, 29 June 2012) <https://www.consilium.europa.eu/media/21400/20120629-euro-area-summit-statement-en.pdf> accessed 12 January 2022.

[9] See, eg, Art 13(1) of the Treaty establishing the European Stability Mechanism [2012] T/ESM 2012-LT. For the period before the establishment of the ESM, see the references to the contribution of the ECB in the European Financial Stability Facility Framework Agreement.

[10] 'Six-Pack' is the term used to refer to the following legal instruments: Regulation (EU) No 1173/2011 of the European Parliament and of the Council of 16 November 2011 on the effective enforcement of budgetary surveillance in the euro area [2011] OJ L306/1; Regulation (EU) No 1174/2011 of the European Parliament and of the Council of 16 November 2011 on enforcement measures to correct excessive macroeconomic imbalances in the euro area [2011] OJ L306/8; Regulation (EU) No 1175/2011 of the European Parliament and of the Council of 16 November 2011 amending Council Regulation (EC) No 1466/97 on the strengthening of the surveillance of budgetary positions and the surveillance and coordination of economic policies [2011] OJ L306/12; Regulation (EU) No 1176/2011 of the European Parliament and of the Council of 16 November 2011 on the prevention and correction of macroeconomic imbalances [2011] OJ L306/25; Council Regulation (EU) No 1177/2011 of 8 November 2011 amending Regulation (EC) No 1467/97 on speeding up and clarifying the implementation of the excessive deficit procedure [2011] (OJ L306/33; and Council Directive 2011/85/EU of 8 November 2011 on requirements for budgetary frameworks of the Member States [2011] OJ L306/41.

[11] 'Two-pack' is the term used to refer to the following legal instruments: Regulation (EU) No 472/2013 of the European Parliament and of the Council of 21 May 2013 on the strengthening of economic and budgetary surveillance of Member States in the euro area experiencing or threatened with serious difficulties with respect to their financial stability [2013] OJ L140/1 and Regulation (EU) No 473/2013 of the European Parliament and of the Council of 21 May 2013 on common provisions for monitoring and assessing draft budgetary plans and ensuring the correction of excessive deficit of the Member States in the euro area [2013] OJ L140/11.

new framework for the economic governance of the euro area. The attribution of these new tasks did not stop with the end of the sovereign debt crisis and its most immediate consequences. Additional examples of new tasks can be found, for example, in the Securitisation Regulation[12] and in the European Market Infrastructures Regulation (EMIR),[13] which are anchored to the ECB's competences in the fields of banking supervision and clearing and payment systems respectively. Also, in the field of supervision the ECB is required to cooperate very closely with other EU institutions and bodies, in particular in relation to the failing or likely to fail assessment, which is the 'connection point' between the supervision of a bank and resolution: it is the moment where the ECB as supervisor passes the baton to the Single Resolution Board and the Commission, which are in charge of the resolution of failing banks.

The way in which the ECB's role is perceived by the other institutions and by the public has also fundamentally changed. Strange as it may seem today, in the early days the ECB did not occupy centre stage in EU policies and EU public discourse: it did not formally qualify as an EU institution until the Lisbon Treaty and, because of its perceived technical and sectoral tasks, it was not included by most observers in the inner circle of the most important actors at EU level. Nowadays, the ECB's policies are broadly discussed by the wider public and the ECB as an institution is part of a very dense network of relationships with other institutions and bodies both at EU and at national level, consistently after all with a global trend towards the formalization of what has been defined as 'the natural interest of central banks in financial stability'.[14] What was criticized years ago as isolation arising from an overly radical protection of its independence (the ECB is also geographically isolated from the other EU institutions) has no validity today. Increased dialogue, exchanges, and accountability, and the provision of reasons for adopted policy to other political stakeholders, do not jeopardize independence and are to be welcomed. On the one hand, the risk that independence is undermined for political reasons is always present, and the proper protections and defences need to be applied. On the other hand, as a consequence of the extension of the ECB's scope of action, its independence has warranted increased standards of accountability. This has taken the form of specific arrangements with the Parliament[15] and the Council[16] in relation to its supervisory tasks, but also accountability instruments towards national parliaments and the public at large. In the latter respect, besides explicit accountability obligations it is worth stressing the ECB's move towards more transparency, for example via the disclosure of the agendas and minutes

[12] Regulation (EU) 2017/2402 of the European Parliament and of the Council of 12 December 2017 laying down a general framework for securitization and creating a specific framework for simple, transparent and standardized securitization, and amending Directives 2009/65/EC, 2009/138/EC and 2011/61/EU and Regulations (EC) No 1060/2009 and (EU) No 648/2012 [2017] OJ L347/35.

[13] Regulation (EU) No 648/2012 of the European Parliament and of the Council of 4 July 2012 on OTC derivatives, central counterparties and trade repositories [2012] OJ L201/1.

[14] See chapter 5 by Agnieszka Smoleńska and Thomas Beukers, in this volume.

[15] See Interinstitutional Agreement 2013/694/EU between the European Parliament and the European Central Bank on the practical modalities of the exercise of democratic accountability and oversight over the exercise of the tasks conferred on the ECB within the framework of the Single Supervisory Mechanism [2013] OJ L320/1.

[16] See Memorandum of Understanding MOU/2013/12111 between the Council of the European Union and the ECB on the cooperation on procedures related to the Single Supervisory Mechanism (SSM) [2013] <https://www.ecb.europa.eu/ecb/legal/pdf/mou_between_eucouncil_ecb.pdf> accessed 12 January 2022.

of its decision-making bodies' meetings and more broadly through its communication activity as publicly stated in the outcome of the strategic review.[17] Finally, one should also mention the increased importance of judicial accountability: judicial scrutiny over the ECB's activities has greatly increased over the course of the last decade, including over monetary policy decisions, which are in many other jurisdictions non-justiciable. In a Union of law, judicial control can only be welcome.

To conclude: evolution, not revolution. Looking back, it is true that the ECB as an institution and the application of its mandate(s) look different today than they did at the time of its establishment. This is probably true for many administrative entities observed over a long period (in this case, close to a quarter of a century). In the ECB's case, this period coincides with the beginning of the institution, when many details that at first appear vague on paper are developed and become clearer in practice: an entity called upon to apply the law and adopt legal instruments in a certain field does not do it in a mechanical manner, but in the light of an ever-changing factual context and on the basis of an interpretation of the law that must apply to that context. The development of the ECB's tools and tasks should therefore not be seen as a threat or a danger, but rather as a normal and reassuring sign of its vitality, and necessary to ensure the fulfilment of its mandate. It can be expected therefore that the ECB will continue to change over the next quarter of century (and thereafter) to better achieve its statutory objective(s).

The final question concerns the guiding principles and the limits to the possibility of change. I would focus on three limits. First comes a fundamental principle of EU law: the principle of conferral. Tasks that are not included in the ECB's mandate under the Treaty or which would not serve to achieve—or would even contravene —its objectives cannot be attributed to the ECB or taken over by it. However, as we have seen, the Treaty affords sufficient flexibility in the use of the tools and the construction of the tasks to make them better suited, in view of the needs of the time, to achieve the set objective. Second, the prohibition on a central bank financing the state remains the clear legal limitation in relation to any cooperation with the fiscal authorities: the latter need to finance their actions in the market. Finally, the ECB's independence should be respected: the specific application of the principle of conferral in relation to the ECB (in terms of the fact that, by way of further specification of the competences attributed to the Union as a whole, specific tasks are conferred exclusively on one of its institutions, ie the ECB) is closely connected with the principle of independence 'from any other body', which includes the EU legislator: the increase by the legislator of tasks assigned to the ECB would increase the number of situations where the ECB could be exposed to pressure by other subjects which may seek to exercise undue influence in relation to the ECB's actions. At the same time, the ECB's independence is not an aim in itself, but an institutional device to avoid the pursuit of an objective in the best interest of citizens, price stability, being polluted by short-term considerations. The

[17] The ECB's monetary policy statement (available on the ECB's website, see paragraph 11) explicitly refers to a "monetary policy communication geared towards the wider public, which is essential for ensuring public understanding of and trust in the actions of the ECB". See also 'Clear, consistent and engaging: ECB monetary policy communication in a changing world' (2021) ECB Occasional Paper Series No 274 <https://www.ecb.europa.eu/pub/pdf/scpops/ecb.op274~9aca14e6f6.en.pdf> accessed 12 January 2022.

counterweight to independence is accountability: not only to justify or compensate for derogation from the democratic principle, but also as the best possible remedy to the risk that undue influence that may hamper the ECB's independence is exerted. However, as with independence, accountability is not an aim in itself but a means to ensure that citizens' best interests are achieved.

This is my version of the story of the ECB, seen from a privileged inside point of view. Others might see it differently: this book has the great merit of also enabling critical voices to be heard. Listening to diverse internal and external perspectives and various assessments, both critical and laudatory, is key to broadening and deepening understanding of such a complex, evolutive, and certainly extraordinary, phenomenon as the monetary union. I am sure that readers will find this book very stimulating.

Preface

The idea of this edited volume originates from a workshop on 'The New ECB in Comparative Perspectives' held at the European University Institute on 19–20 September 2017. The workshop was part of the Horizon 2020 ADEMU project (A Dynamic Economic and Monetary Union) funded by the European Commission.

We are happy that so many of the participants in our ADEMU workshop agreed to contribute also to this OUP book project. The focus of the original workshop was on putting the European Central Bank (ECB) in a comparative perspective, something that is still reflected in several chapters of this edited volume. The ambition of this book is rather to give a comprehensive substantive and institutional analysis of the ECB itself, to take stock of the ECB's development around two decades after its creation, and to look ahead at future challenges. To this end, we asked the authors to reflect on whether and, if so, to what extent the developments they consider in their respective chapters lead to the conclusion that we now have a 'new ECB' if compared to the one that started to function in 1999.

To ensure that we have a comprehensive overview of this question, we added a number of topics to the ones originally presented at the workshop in Florence for which we have been able to find excellent authors. We are also grateful for the suggestions for additional topics that were formulated by the external reviewers of our book proposal.

The perspective taken in this edited volume reflects the variety of expertise of the contributing authors. Thus, findings are presented by political scientists, economists, and, predominantly, institutional lawyers. Perspectives are offered by authors from both academia and practice; both leading academics and high-level practitioners from the ECB and the Council of the EU have contributed their knowledge to this endeavour.

This edited volume illustrates how the evolution of the ECB has been affected by several crises, in particular the Great Financial Crisis, the euro area Sovereign Debt Crisis, and the COVID-19 crisis. As is true for many people, the personal and professional lives of the contributors to this edited volume have also been affected by the COVID-19 crisis. We are very grateful for their enthusiasm, patience, and perseverance. We are honoured that Chiara Zilioli has agreed to write the foreword to this edited volume. We also want to thank Imogen Hill, Luise Wilde, and Fiona Tatham from OUP for their great support and patience.

A special word of thanks goes to Carlo Martinoia who has done an excellent job in meticulously bringing all contributions in line with the OUP author guidelines.

Thomas Beukers, Diane Fromage, and Giorgio Monti, June 2022

Contents

List of Contributors xxi
List of Abbreviations xxiii

1. Introduction: The 'New' European Central Bank 1
Thomas Beukers, Diane Fromage, and Giorgio Monti
I. Why Wonder about a 'New' European Central Bank 1
II. The Contributions to this Edited Volume 4
III. Taking Stock of the 'New' European Central Bank 7
A. Perspectives on EMU and ECB change 7
B. The New European Central Bank 9
C. Causes, triggers, and factors of ECB evolution 17
IV. Looking Ahead: Future Developments and Challenges 22

I. THE ECB'S RESPONSE TO THE FINANCIAL AND SOVEREIGN DEBT CRISIS: UNCONVENTIONAL MONETARY POLICY AND THE LENDER OF LAST RESORT FUNCTION

2. The Transformation of the ECB in Sovereign Bond Markets 29
Vestert Borger
I. Introduction 29
II. The ECB in the Original Set-up of the Currency Union 31
A. The stability paradigm 31
B. The narrow conception of stability 33
III. The New Stability Conception 36
A. The Securities Markets Programme 36
B. Outright Monetary Transactions 41
IV. Reconciling the New Stability Conception with the Law 46
A. The mandate 46
B. The prohibition on monetary financing 50
V. Judicial Review of the New ECB 52
VI. Conclusion 58

3. The ECB's Unconventional Quantitative Easing is Turning to Conventional Monetary Policy 59
Klaus Tuori
I. Introduction 59
II. The ECB as a Consensus Model Central Bank—the First Decade 60
III. The ECB Turns to QE—the PSPP 61
A. The main features of the PSPP 63
B. The stated aims of the PSPP 65

IV. QE and PSPP in Economic Theory and Central Bank Practice 66
A. QE in macroeconomics 66
B. QE as a central banking tool 69
V. The PEPP Adds to the ECB's QE Firepower 71
A. PEPP as the pandemic quantitative easing 72
B. Analysing the objectives and effects of PEPP 74
VI. Conclusions: The ECB and New Monetary Policy 75

4. The ECB's Collateral Framework from the 1990s until the Pandemic 80
Jens van 't Klooster
I. Introduction 80
II. ECB Risk Management before 2010 82
III. ECB Risk Management since 2010 89
IV. The Future of ECB Risk Management 94
A. Revising the objectives of risk management 95
B. Market attentiveness instead of market neutrality 97
C. Developing internal credit rating facilities 98
D. Addressing legitimacy concerns by coordinating with EU political institutions 100
V. Conclusion 102

II. MOVING BEYOND MONETARY POLICY: THE ECB, FINANCIAL STABILITY, ECONOMIC INTEGRATION, AND THE (FUTURE OF THE) BANKING UNION

5. The ECB and Financial Stability 105
Agnieszka Smoleńska and Thomas Beukers
I. Introduction 105
II. Financial Stability—the Conventional Use of an Economic Concept 107
III. Financial Stability and the Law of the Economic and Monetary Union 108
IV. Policy Instruments of Financial Stability 110
V. Preventive Policy Instruments of Financial Stability 112
A. Prudential regulation 112
B. Prudential supervision 115
C. Payment systems 118
VI. Remedial Policy Instruments of Financial Stability 123
A. ELA: National Central Banks (NCBs) as Lenders of Last Resort (LOLR) to individual institutions 123
B. Crisis coordination 126
VII. Monetary Policy Tools as Secondary Policy Instrument of Financial Stability 128
A. ECB standard monetary policy 130
B. The ECB's unconventional monetary policy measures 130
C. Unconventional monetary policy and financial stability 132
D. Monetary policy and the distinction between preventive and remedial instruments 134
VIII. Conclusions 135

6. The ECB and Economic Integration 136
Jonathan Bauerschmidt
I. Introduction 136
II. Asymmetry of Competences and Interdependence of Policy Areas 137
III. Delineation of Competences 139
IV. Budgetary Stability: Economic Policy Coordination and Financial Assistance 142
A. Strengthening of the Stability and Growth Pact 142
B. The European Stability Mechanism and the ECB 144
V. Financial Stability: New Forms of Supervision for the Internal Market 147
A. Macroprudential supervision in the European Systemic Risk Board 147
B. Microprudential supervision in the Single Supervisory Mechanism 149
VI. The Cunning of European Integration 153

7. The ECB's Role in the European Banking Union 156
Kern Alexander
I. Introduction 156
II. The Banking Union's Context—the ECB's Mandate 157
A. Price stability 157
B. The ECB's secondary objectives 160
III. The Banking Union and the Single Supervisory Mechanism 163
A. The legal basis of ECB supervision 163
B. ECB competences and tasks as a bank supervisor 164
C. The Supervisory Board 167
D. ECB, banking regulation, and sustainability 170
E. ECB primary task of price stability and new supervisory role 172
IV. Banking Union and the Single Resolution Mechanism 175
A. The Single Resolution Mechanism 176
B. ECB/SSM coordination with the SRB 179
V. Summing Up and Future Challenges 181

8. The Relationship between the ECB and the National Competent Authorities in the Single Supervisory Mechanism: Problems and Perspectives 184
Federico Della Negra and Gianni Lo Schiavo
I. Introduction 184
II. The Role of the ECB and the NCAs within the SSM: An Overview 186
A. The SSM: rationale and organization 186
B. The ECB tasks, powers, and responsibilities 189
C. The NCA tasks, powers, and responsibilities 193
III. The Role of the ECB and the NCAs in Day-to-Day SSM Banking Supervision of Significant Institutions 195
A. The JSTs 195
B. The SEP: off-site and on-site supervision 196
C. The SREP 197

IV. The Role of the ECB and the NCAs in SSM Authorizations 198
A. SSM common procedures (banking licences and qualifying holding authorizations) 199
B. Fit and proper authorizations 202
C. Other SSM authorizations for SIs 202
V. The Role of the ECB in the Oversight of the Functioning of the SSM 204
A. The ECB's responsibility for oversight 204
B. The NCA's duty of assistance 206
VI. Conclusion 207

9. The Role of the ECB in the International Arena and the External Dimension of EMU: A 'New' ECB within a Crippled Legal Framework? 209
Florin Coman-Kund
I. Introduction 209
II. The Legal Framework of the ECB's International Dimension 211
III. The Tricky International Legal Status of the ECB 216
IV. The Evolution of the ECB's International Dimension: The ECB as a Growing Global Player? 220
A. 'Article 219 TFEU' practice 220
B. Relationship with international organizations and fora 221
C. The ECB's international cooperation instruments 224
D. 'Borrowing' of the ECB outside the EU Treaty framework 227
V. A Critical Appraisal of the ECB's International Dimension: A 'New' ECB within a Crippled Legal Framework? 229
VI. Conclusion 233

III. INSTITUTIONAL SETTING: THE ECB'S 'INSTITUTIONAL LOGIC' AND ITS RELATIONSHIP WITH GOVERNMENTS, COURTS, AND PARLIAMENTS

10. The Independence of the ECB: Justification, Challenges, and Possible Threats 237
Alexander Thiele
I. Independence in Times of Crisis 237
II. The Justification of Central Bank Independence 238
A. Economic background 238
B. (German) democratic theory 243
III. Manifestations of Independence 247
IV. Challenges and Threats 250
A. Challenges to independence 250
B. Threats to independent monetary policy 255
V. Conclusion and Outlook 263

11. The Legitimacy and Accountability of the ECB at the Age of Twenty 265
Fabian Amtenbrink and Menelaos Markakis
I. Introduction 265
II. The ECB's Inception 267
III. The Evolution of the ECB's Democratic Legitimacy and Accountability 273
A. The ECB's role as crisis manager 274
B. The ECB's role in the European Banking Union 279
C. The ECB and the COVID-19 pandemic 285
IV. The ECB's Accountability at Twenty and Beyond 287

12. The ECB and the Court of Justice: Old Toolbox, New Problems 292
Takis Tridimas
I. Introduction 292
II. Is there a Role for the CJEU? 295
III. Objectives Versus Effects and the Elusive Quest for the Boundaries of Monetary Policy 296
IV. The Role of Proportionality 302
V. Judicial Scrutiny and Standard of Review 303
A. Principles of judicial review 303
B. Standard of scrutiny 304
C. Process requirements 306
VI. Prudential Supervision: A New Litigation Landscape 308
A. Composite procedures and hybridity 310
VII. Application of National Law by the ECB 313
VIII. Fines 314
IX. Conclusion 316

13. Assessing and (Re-)situating Today's ECB in the EU's Institutional Landscape 318
Diane Fromage
I. Introduction 318
II. The ECB's Institutional Structures: From Maastricht to Lisbon Today 320
A. The ECB's original institutional architecture 320
B. The adaptation of the ECB's institutional design to the EBU: increased national influence in the functioning of the ECB? 324
III. Has the National Component within the Supranational ECB Grown Larger? 328
A. Enhanced representation of national interests in the ECB's institutional structure proper 329
B. The potential reinforcement of the national dimension in practice 331
C. The Eurosystem's and the ECB's supranational character (still) reinforced by recent judicial developments 333

IV. Re-situating the ECB in the EU's Institutional Landscape: How Do the Institutional Logics that Govern Today's ECB Compare to Those of other EU Institutions and Bodies? 335
V. Conclusion 337

14. The ECB in the New Normal: Organizing Fiscal Support for Monetary Policy 340
Ad van Riet
I. Introduction 340
II. The Institutional Loneliness of the ECB 341
III. A Euro Area Fiscal Capacity 343
IV. A Safe Sovereign Asset for the Euro Area 348
V. A Fiscal Backstop for the Eurosystem 351
VI. Conclusion 356

IV. A CONTEXTUAL ANALYSIS OF THE ECB

15. The ECB Mandate—a Comparative Constitutional Perspective 361
Christy Ann Petit
I. Introduction 361
II. Central Bank Mandates: Formal Sources and their Implementation 364
A. Legal sources of central bank mandates, objectives, and tasks 365
B. Implementation of central bank mandates: a purposive and functional approach since the GFC 374
III. Conclusions 388

16. The Role of Constitutional Law for the ECB: Past, Present, and Future 392
Marijn van der Sluis
I. Introduction 392
II. A Constitutional Approach to EMU 394
III. The ECB as a Constitutional Interpreter 397
IV. The ECB during the Euro Area Crisis 402
V. The Judicialization of EMU 405
VI. Conclusion 408

17. The ECB's E-ROAD Ahead 409
René Smits
I. Introduction 409
II. Open Up 414
III. Reform 417
IV. Develop 420
V. Address 425
VI. Europe 427
VII. Final Words 430

Index 433

List of Contributors

Kern Alexander holds the Professorial Chair in Law and Finance and is Professor of Banking Regulation at the University of Zurich

Fabian Amtenbrink is Professor of European Union Law at the Erasmus School of Law of Erasmus University Rotterdam

Jonathan Bauerschmidt is Member of the Legal Service at the Council of the European Union

Thomas Beukers is Senior Legal Advisor at the Dutch Ministry of Foreign Affairs

Vestert Borger is Assistant Professor of European Law at the Europa Institute of Leiden University

Florin Coman-Kund is Assistant Professor in European Union Law at the Erasmus School of Law of Erasmus University Rotterdam

Federico Della Negra is Senior Legal Counsel at the European Central Bank

Diane Fromage is Marie Skłodowska-Curie Individual Fellow at Sciences Po Paris

Gianni Lo Schiavo is Senior Supervisor at the European Central Bank

Menelaos Markakis is Assistant Professor at the Erasmus School of Law of Erasmus University Rotterdam

Giorgio Monti is Professor of Competition Law at Tilburg Law School and part-time Professor at the European University Institute

Christy Ann Petit is Assistant Professor at the School of Law and Government at Dublin City University and the DCU Brexit Institute

René Smits is Professor emeritus of the law of the Economic and Monetary Union at the University of Amsterdam

Agnieszka Smoleńska is Assistant Professor at the Institute of Law Studies, Polish Academy of Sciences, and Associate Researcher at the European Banking Institute

Alexander Thiele is Professor for State Theory and Public Law at the Law Faculty of the BSP Business and Law School in Berlin

Takis Tridimas is Professor of European Law at King's College London

Klaus Tuori is Research Fellow at the University of Luxembourg.

Marijn van der Sluis is Assistant Professor in Constitutional Law at Maastricht University

Ad van Riet is Associate Research Fellow at the United Nations University Institute on Comparative Regional Integration Studies (UNU-CRIS) in Bruges, Belgium

Jens van 't Klooster is FWO Postdoctoral Fellow at the KU Leuven's Institute of Philosophy and member of the research group A New Normative Framework for Financial Debt at the University of Amsterdam

Chiara Zilioli is Director General in the Directorate General Legal Services of the European Central Bank

List of Abbreviations

ABSPP	asset-backed securities purchase programme
ACC	Additional Credit Claims
ADEMU	A Dynamic Economic and Monetary Union
AMICO	Accounting and Monetary Income Committee
AML	anti-money laundering
AMLA	Authority for anti-money laundering and countering the financing of terrorism
APP	Asset Purchase Programme
BANCO	Banknote Committee
BCBS	Basel Committee on Banking Supervision
BICC	Budgetary instrument for convergence and competitiveness
BIS	Bank for International Settlements
BIS CGFS	BIS Committee on the Global Financial System
BIT	Bilateral Investment Treaties
BoC	Bank of Canada
BoE	Bank of England
BRRD	Bank Recovery and Resolution Directive
BUCOM	Budget Committee
CBDC	Central Bank Digital Currency
CBPP3	Third Covered Bond Purchase Programme
CCPs	Central counterparties
CDIC	Canada Deposit Insurance Corporation
CEBS	Committee of European Banking Supervisors
CEPH	Common Eurosystem Pricing Hub
CJEU	Court of Justice of the European Union
CML Rev	Common Market Law Review
CMLR	Common Market Law Reports
COMCO	Committee of Controlling
CQS	credit quality steps
CRD	Capital Requirements Directive
CRR	Capital Requirements Regulation
CSPP	Corporate Sector Purchase Programme
CTF	countering terrorist financing
EAPP	Expanded Asset Purchase Programme
EBA	European Banking Authority
EBLR	European Business Law Review
EBRD	European Bank for Reconstruction and Development
EBU	European Banking Union
ECAF	Eurosystem Credit Assessment Facility
ECB	European Central Bank

ECCO	Eurosystem/ESCB Communications Committee
ECFR	European Company and Financial Law Review
ECOFIN	Economic and Financial Affairs Council
ECON	Committee on Economic and Monetary Affairs
EDIS	European Deposit Insurance System
EDP	Excessive Deficit Procedure
EFAR	European Foreign Affairs Review
EFSF	European Financial Stability Facility
EFSM	European Financial Stability Mechanism
EIB	European Investment Bank
EISF	European Investment Stabilisation Function
EJIL	European Journal of International Law
ELA	emergency liquidity assistance
ELJ	European Law Journal
EL Rev	European Law Review
EMI	European Monetary Institute
EMIR	European Market Infrastructure Regulation
EMU	European Monetary Union
EP	European Parliament
ERM II	Exchange Rate Mechanism
ESA	European Supervisory Authority
ESBies	European Safe Bonds
ESCB	European System of Central Banks
ESFS	European System of Financial Supervision
ESG	environmental, social, and governance
ESM	European Stability Mechanism
ESRB	European Systemic Risk Board
EUConst	European Constitutional Law Review
EURIMF	EU Representatives to the IMF
EuZW	Europäische Zeitschrift für Wirtschaftsrecht
FDIC	Federal Deposit Insurance Corporation
FED	Federal Reserve System
FMIs	financial market infrastructures
FOLTF	failing or likely to fail
FPC	Financial Policy Committee
FRB	Federal Reserve Board
FSB	Financial Stability Board
FSC	Financial stability Committee
FSOC	Financial Stability Oversight Council
GDP	gross domestic product
GFC	Great Financial Crisis
GNI	gross national income
IAC	Internal Auditors Committee
HICP	Harmonised Index of Consumer Prices
HRC	Human Resources Conference
ICON	International Journal of Constitutional Law

IIA	Interinstitutional Agreement
IMF	International Monetary Fund
IMFC	International Monetary Fund Committee
INTERPOL	International Criminal Police Organisation
IRC	International Relations Committee
ITC	Information Technology Committee
JCMS	Journal of Common Market Studies
JEEP	Journal of European Public Policy
JIEL	Journal of International Economic Law
JIMF	Journal of International Money and Finance
JMCB	Journal of Money, Credit and Banking
JSTs	joint supervisory teams
LEGCO	Legal Committee
LIEI	Legal Issues of Economic Integration
LOLR	Lender of Last Resort
LTROs	Longer-Term Refinancing Operations
LSI	less significant institutions
MJ	Maastricht Journal of European and Comparative Law
MIPC	Market Infrastructure and Payments Committee
MOC	Market Operations Committee
MoU	Memorandum of Understanding
MPC	Monetary Policy Committee
MREL	Minimum required eligible liabilities
MRO	Main refinancing operations
NCAs	national competent authorities
NCBs	National Central Banks
NGEU	Next Generation EU
NGFS	Network for Greening the Financial System
NRAs	National resolution authorities
OCA	Optimal Currency Area
OCC	Comptroller of the Currency
ODC	Organisational Development Committee
OECD	Organisation for Economic Cooperation and Development
OJLS	Oxford Journal of Legal Studies
OMT	Outright Monetary Transactions
OOH	owner-occupied housing
OSFI	Office of the Superintendent of Financial Institutions
QE	quantitative easing
PCSA	Payment and Clearing Settlement Act
PELTROs	Pandemic emergency longer-term refinancing operations
PEPP	Pandemic Emergency Purchase Programme
PSI	Private Sector Involvement
PSPP	Public Sector Purchase Programme
PRC	Prudential Regulation Committee
RMC	Risk Management Committee
RRF	Recovery and Resilience Facility

RSP	Reform Support Programme
RTGS	real-time gross settlement system
SCIMF	Sub-committee on IMF-related issues
SDRs	Special Drawings Rights
SEP	Supervisory Examination Programme
SGP	Stability and Growth Pact
SI	significant institution
SIPS	Systemically important payment system regime
SMEs	small and medium enterprises
SMP	Securities Markets Programme
SRB	Single Resolution Board
SREP	Supervisory Review and Evaluation Programme
SRM	Single Resolution Mechanism
SSM	Single Supervisory Mechanism
STC	Statistics Committee
SURE	Support to mitigate Unemployment Risks in an Emergency
TARGET2	Trans-European Automated Real-time Gross Express Transfer System
T2S	TARGET2-Securities
TEU	Treaty on European Union
TFEU	Treaty on the Functioning of the European Union
TIPS	TARGET Instant Payment Settlement
TLAC	total loss absorbing capacity
TLTROs	Targeted longer-term refinancing operations

1

Introduction

The 'New' European Central Bank

Thomas Beukers,[*] Diane Fromage,[**] and Giorgio Monti

I. Why Wonder about a 'New' European Central Bank

The European Central Bank (ECB) was first introduced in the European legal order on the occasion of the Treaty of Maastricht (1992), and it was established when the common currency was launched in 1999. It has existed for over two decades and is thus a relatively young central bank. The question whether and to what extent today's ECB should be qualified as a 'new' ECB if compared to the institution that was originally created is relevant at this moment in time for a variety of reasons.

Firstly, the ECB has undergone remarkable change. The ECB that started to operate twenty years ago was significantly different from the ECB that exists today, which has even been dubbed the 'second European Commission'[1] in view of the large variety of powers it is now called to exercise—including powers that go beyond those typically exercised by a central bank. The many developments to the ECB's substantive mandate and institutional relations, both within and outside the EU legal framework, are extensively covered in this volume, and will be analysed, put into context and critically discussed. It is worth noting at the outset that all these significant changes have largely intervened 'à traités constants', that is, without treaty change.

Secondly, over time, the ECB has become a much more prominent institution with great visibility. The Great Financial Crisis (GFC) that hit Europe in 2008 blatantly showed several weaknesses inherent to the architecture of the Economic and Monetary Union (EMU) as it was designed in the Maastricht Treaty. This put pressure to act on both the Member States and the ECB. In some instances, Member States agreed on measures and the ECB complemented these by exercising its powers. In other instances, the Member States agreed on measures that however were not considered sufficient, meaning that the ECB had to step in. In general, the developments have led to an increase in power for the ECB.

[*] The views expressed by the author are personal and do not necessarily reflect those of the Ministry of Foreign Affairs.

[**] The contribution to this chapter is the outcome of research conducted in the framework of the research project IMPACTEBU, a project that received funding from the European Union's Horizon 2020 research and innovation programme under the Marie Sklodowska-Curie grant agreement No 895841.

[1] Antoine Vauchez, 'La Banque centrale européenne, une institution aux pouvoirs renforcés' (*Vie publique*, 21 January 2020) <https://www.vie-publique.fr/parole-dexpert/271077-la-banque-centrale-europeenne-une-institution-aux-pouvoirs-renforces> accessed 1 December 2021.

Thomas Beukers, Diane Fromage, and Giorgio Monti, *Introduction* In: *The New European Central Bank*. Edited by: Thomas Beukers, Diane Fromage, and Giorgio Monti, Oxford University Press. © Thomas Beukers, Diane Fromage, and Giorgio Monti 2022. DOI: 10.1093/oso/9780198871231.003.0001

The rise to prominence of the ECB within the E(M)U, and the accompanying dynamics between the ECB and the Member States, can be illustrated with the issue of the lack of an EU-wide Lender of Last Resort (LOLR) to sovereigns, a characteristic of the original EMU design highlighted by the GFC and following euro area crisis. The Member States of the euro area tried to fill this gap by creating an emergency fund with the European Financial Stability Facility (EFSF) in 2010 and later also the permanent European Stability Mechanism (ESM) in the first half of 2012. However, only the 'Whatever it takes' message of then ECB President Draghi in July 2012, combined with the September Outright Monetary Transactions (OMT) Press Release,[2] is generally given the credit of sufficiently calming the markets and of convincing these markets that a Lender of Last Resort exists.

The current COVID-19 crisis has not reversed this trend in any way; on the contrary, it has confirmed and even reinforced it. Already at the end of March 2020, the ECB had managed to activate a €750 billion Pandemic Emergency Purchase Programme (PEPP) in reaction to the devastating effects that the health crisis had on European economies.[3] In contrast, the political response to the COVID-19 crisis at the EU level began with a Eurogroup press release on 9 April 2020 including a political agreement on the temporary Support to mitigate Unemployment Risks in an Emergency (SURE)[4] and the idea of a Recovery Fund.[5] It nonetheless still took more than a year for a political programme (the Recovery and Resilience Facility)[6] to be agreed upon and up and running.

Thirdly, the ECB's development and its resulting prominent position in the E(M)U's governance framework have turned the powerful ECB into a highly contested institution. In fact, its greater capacity to act swiftly and autonomously in response to important challenges compared to political actors means that it has come under great pressure to act and that it bears heavy responsibilities. This evolution has also come with some related challenges, linked to the limits to the ECB's Treaty mandate and to its weak democratic legitimacy. As the COVID-19 pandemic is slowly overcome and as inflation is on the rise, the future of the ECB's monetary policy is becoming an increasingly salient and contested issue.

[2] European Central Bank, 'Technical features of Outright Monetary Transactions' (ECB Press Release, 6 September 2012) <https://www.ecb.europa.eu/press/pr/date/2012/html/pr120906_1.en.html> accessed 1 December 2021.

[3] European Central Bank, 'ECB announces €750 billion Pandemic Emergency Purchase Programme (PEPP)' (ECB Press Release, 18 March 2020) <https://www.ecb.europa.eu/press/pr/date/2020/html/ecb.pr200318_1~3949d6f266.en.html> accessed 1 December 2021; Decision (EU) 2020/440 of the European Central Bank of 24 March 2020 on a temporary pandemic emergency purchase programme (ECB/2020/17) [2020] OJ L91/1. See for an updated account of the various adopted measures, European Central Bank, 'Our response to the coronavirus pandemic' <https://www.ecb.europa.eu/home/search/coronavirus/html/index.en.html> accessed 1 December 2021.

[4] Council Regulation (EU) 2020/672 of 19 May 2020 on the establishment of a European instrument for temporary support to mitigate unemployment risks in an emergency (SURE) following the COVID-19 outbreak [2020] OJ L159/1.

[5] Eurogroup, 'Report on the comprehensive economic policy response to the COVID-19 pandemic' (Eurogroup Press Release, 9 April 2020) <https://www.consilium.europa.eu/nl/press/press-releases/2020/04/09/report-on-the-comprehensive-economic-policy-response-to-the-covid-19-pandemic/> accessed 1 December 2021.

[6] In the form of the Recovery and Resilience Facility funded through a new Own Resource Decision that entered into force on 1 June 2021.

Dramatic shifts have happened in a context in which popular support for the ECB has fluctuated,[7] and contestation from the inside (ie from the governors of the National Central Banks that compose the ECB's Governing Council) has also arisen.[8] The ECB's action has furthermore led to an intense and critical academic debate, including from a legal perspective.[9]

Moreover, the ECB's actions have given rise to more frequent contestation in courts, as is visible in the increasing number of challenges before both national courts and the Court of Justice of the EU, and is most evident in the *Weiss* judgment of the German Federal Constitutional Court which, for the first time, led the Constitutional Court to declare that an EU institution had acted ultra vires.[10] At the same time, some parts of the ECB's mandate, such as its new responsibility in prudential supervision, are less contested foundationally than its monetary policy choices.

Fourthly, important developments are still ongoing or foreseen, as illustrated by the ECB's action plan related to climate change[11] and initiatives related to a possible introduction of a digital euro.[12] In fact, there is no reason to suggest that the ECB's impressive development will come to a halt. It is important to understand where we are in terms of ECB development, to be able to delineate what lies ahead. The ECB itself is currently in a phase of intense self-reflection as it has just concluded its second strategy review, which involved active public consultation. The EU more broadly is, too, entering a general period of self-reflection as it has launched the Conference on the Future of Europe.

Summing up, the rise to prominence of the ECB as a powerful and contested EU institution means it is time to reflect both on its past and its future.

It is for all these reasons that this edited volume seeks to determine the extent to which and in which domains we are now confronted with a 'new ECB', how the ECB

[7] Felix Roth and Lars Jonung, 'Public Support for the Euro and Trust in the ECB: The First Two Decades of the Common Currency' in Juan E Castañeda, Alessandro Roselli, and Geoffrey E Wood (eds), *The Economics of Monetary Unions. Past Experiences and the Eurozone* (Routledge 2020); Christel Koop and Christine Reh, 'Europe's Bank and Europe's Citizens: Accountability, Transparency—Legitimacy?' (2019) 26 MJ 63.

[8] For example, Bundesbank Governor Weidmann publicly criticized the ECB's official line in November 2020: Francesco Canepa and Balazs Koranyi, 'Weidmann contradicts ECB on easy policy ahead of December meeting' *Reuters* (Frankfurt am Main, 19 November 2021) <https://www.reuters.com/world/europe/ecb-should-not-react-current-inflation-spike-lagarde-2021-11-19/> accessed 1 December 2021.

[9] See, for instance, the respective chapters included in Fabian Amtenbrink and Christoph Herrmann (eds), *The EU Law of Economic and Monetary Union* (OUP 2020); Mark Dawson, Adina Maricut-Akbik, and Ana Bobić 'Reconciling Independence and Accountability at the European Central Bank: The False Promise of Proceduralism' (2019) 25 ELJ 75; Klaus Tuori, *The ECB and the European Macroeconomic Constitution—From a Central Bank of Stability to a Central Bank of Crisis* (CUP forthcoming).

[10] German Federal Constitutional Court, 'ECB decisions on the Public Sector Purchase Programme exceed EU competences' (German Federal Constitutional Court, Press Release no 32/2020, 5 May 2020) <https://www.bundesverfassungsgericht.de/SharedDocs/Pressemitteilungen/EN/2020/bvg20-032.html> accessed 1 December 2021.

[11] European Central Bank, 'Climate change and the ECB' <https://www.ecb.europa.eu/ecb/climate/html/index.en.html> accessed 1 December 2021; European Central Bank, 'ECB presents action plan to include climate change considerations in its monetary policy strategy' (ECB Press Release, 8 July 2021) <https://www.ecb.europa.eu/press/pr/date/2021/html/ecb.pr210708_1~f104919225.en.html> accessed 1 December 2021 (hereafter ECB, 'Press Release 8 July 2021').

[12] European Central Bank, 'Report on a digital euro' (ECB, 2020) <https://www.ecb.europa.eu/pub/pdf/other/Report_on_a_digital_euro~4d7268b458.en.pdf> accessed 1 December 2021 (hereafter ECB, 'Report on a digital euro').

has evolved or in which ways it may have even transformed, and where future development can be expected. The findings from these interrogations arguably eventually beg the further question of the need for changes to the legal framework that underpins the ECB, and its standing within the EU.

Before taking stock of the 'new' ECB (III), and looking ahead at future development and challenges (IV) the next section presents the contributions included in this edited volume.

II. The Contributions to this Edited Volume

The contributions to this edited volume are divided along four main thematic lines.

Part I focuses on the ECB's response to the euro area sovereign debt crisis, which is arguably the ECB's action that has been most prominently debated in recent times. Vestert Borger first considers whether the ECB may be viewed as having become a 'new entity' based on its activity on the sovereign bond markets and he concludes that indeed, 'the ECB has not simply evolved, it has transformed'. This conclusion derives from his thorough and critical analysis of the ECB's *de facto* (new) role as a Lender of Last Resort following the emergence of the sovereign debt crisis and of the judicial and political reactions to this change. This first substantive chapter in fact paves the way for the specific examination offered by Klaus Tuori of quantitative easing as a form of unconventional monetary policy. He asks to what extent this type of monetary policy instrument is a continuation of, or differs from, the way in which monetary policy had been traditionally conducted by the ECB. This leads him to wonder whether the ECB has passed from being a 'central bank of institutions' to 'a central bank of markets' thus justifying it be considered as a 'new ECB'. Jens van 't Klooster then turns to the issue of the ECB's financial risk management strategy, essentially considering how it has evolved over time. He discusses how developments after 2010 forced the ECB to pay more attention to the financial market impact of its risk management strategy; both to the pro-cyclical dynamics in sovereign bond markets and the climate impact of bond issuers. Asking whether the ECB's strategy is still suitable today, he argues that changes are necessary, and outlines the form that these could take.

The following chapters, which form Part II of this edited volume, consider the ECB's role and actions in areas other than monetary policy. Agnieszka Smoleńska and Thomas Beukers analyse the extent to which several financial stability tools as identified by the leading economist Tommaso Padoa-Schioppa are available to the ECB. They show that the Maastricht Treaty, with its focus on price stability, nonetheless did contain sufficient seeds for the ECB to develop a significant financial stability toolbox over the first two decades of its existence. The natural interest in financial stability of central banks, including the ECB, combined with the events of especially the GFC and euro area crisis, has made their existence as well as their limits clearly visible. Thereafter, Jonathan Bauerschmidt re-situates the ECB, and the monetary policy it is called to conduct, into the broader EU economic integration project, thereby showing the expansive force of monetary policy and how it also 'collides with neighbouring policy areas which apply to all the Member States of the Union'. By considering the ECB's central role in the conduct of these other policies, he wonders whether this poses a threat to its independence and its primary objective of price stability. Kern Alexander subsequently zooms in on the ECB's role in the European Banking Union (EBU) and considers both its first and its second pillars (the Single Supervisory Mechanism and the Single Resolution Mechanism respectively). He additionally examines what future challenges may be, for instance in terms of the further integration of banking markets, or in terms of the role the ECB—in its quality as banking supervisor—can play in addressing emerging risks, such as those posed by environment sustainability. Federico Della Negra and Gianni Lo Schiavo examine the first pillar of the EBU by focusing on the relationship between ECB and National Competent Authorities. They outline the existing problems and future perspectives in this respect and show how judicial decisions have contributed to clarify this relationship. They eventually wonder whether the attribution of new competences to the ECB in the area of prudential supervision has affected its role and standing within the EU, and conclude that administrative integration at the EU level should be further reinforced in this area going forward. In the following chapter, Florin Coman-Kund considers another dimension of the ECB's action by looking at its external role. He highlights that over time, the ECB's international cooperation with other actors, including for instance central banks of third countries or international organizations and forums, has increased. He additionally notes that there is 'an intriguing intra-EU international dimension of the ECB' that has emerged following the adoption of instruments to counter the euro area crisis (European Financial Stability Facility first, and European Stability Mechanism at a later stage). Based on the analysis of these two dimensions of the ECB's international action, he considers that whilst the ECB has indeed become much more active internationally, some constraints exist—both within the EU legal framework and in the norms that govern (some) international organizations and forums—that prevent it from becoming even more active. Moreover, he considers that some adjustments to the existing legal framework could be necessary to ensure that it exercises its powers effectively while ensuring their legitimacy.

Part III, which addresses institutional issues, starts with two chapters that deal with closely interrelated issues, namely the question of the ECB's independence and accountability. Alexander Thiele first (re-)examines the issue of the ECB's independence by explaining what justifies this special status of the bank and defining it through its comparison with other central banks' independence. He also lays out to what extent the ECB's independence may have been and continues to be threatened, but still finds that, overall, it has not been affected. However, he concludes by asking whether such strong independent status should not be amended. Fabian Amtenbrink and Menelaos Markakis examine the 'other side of the coin' of the ECB's independence, namely its accountability and, relatedly, its degree of transparency. They describe the accountability framework as it was designed when the ECB was first established, and outline how it has (not much) evolved since with a view to determining whether it still matches the ECB's responsibilities which undoubtedly have increased over time. Takis Tridimas examines aspects of the judicial accountability of the ECB. He engages with the rationale for judicial review of central bank decisions and discusses the distinction between economic and monetary policy and the role of proportionality. The standard of review and the application of process requirements by the Court of Justice of the EU (CJEU) are also explored. Moreover, he looks at the new litigation landscape of prudential supervision focusing on composite procedures, the application of national law by the ECB, and litigation on the imposition of fines. Diane Fromage analyses the evolution of the ECB's institutional structures and compares them to that of other EU institutions and bodies. She also shows that the dual national and European nature of the National Central Banks and their governors has given rise to tensions and varying dynamics between supranational and national logics. She finds among other things that the institutional logics that govern today's ECB are somewhere between those of the supranational Commission and the intergovernmental Council, although in some ways the Supervisory Board could also be compared to EU agencies.

Ad van Riet explores how euro area governments could mobilize to establish a fiscal framework that resembles that of other currency areas, that is to remedy the imbalance that currently exists in the level of integration between monetary and fiscal policy. He considers several possibilities including the establishment of a central fiscal capacity, the creation of a safe sovereign asset, and the creation of an *ex ante* fiscal backstop to National Central Banks and the ECB. Actions by governments could, in his view, strengthen the EMU and enhance confidence in the euro.

Part IV, the final Part of this edited volume, seeks to resituate the ECB in a broader context. It begins with a chapter by Christy Ann Petit who examines the ECB's mandate. She analyses how it compares to the mandates of other central banks and discusses the relationship between a central bank's mandate, its objectives and tasks, in law and in action. To this end, she offers an overview of both the formal mandate of the ECB, the Federal Reserve, the Bank of Canada, and the Bank of England, and how these formal mandates have been implemented. This allows her to explain what role central banks have assumed during and after the Great Financial Crisis. She shows that statutory sources have remained mostly unchanged whilst policy actions have reshaped the practical scope of central bank mandates in all jurisdictions. Marijn van der Sluis draws a balance on the evolution of the constitutional design of the EMU as it was defined in the Maastricht Treaty, and rebuts the common assumption that it has proven to be a failure. Indeed, in his view, the Maastricht Treaty set both economic and political goals, and in including those defining provisions in primary law, Member States made sure that they—and not the EU institutions—remained in charge. Thus, 'despite the fact that the euro area crisis has led to significant innovations in the day-to-day governance of EMU, the constitutional environment in which the ECB operates has not significantly changed' and Marijn in fact argues 'that the euro and the ECB must be de-constitutionalized'.

The final chapter of this edited volume by René Smits follows a slightly different purpose from the other contributions as it takes a more critical, forward-looking stance. René Smits underlines five developments, which, in his opinion, lead to the conclusion that today's ECB operates in an environment that is radically different from the one in which it was established in 1998. He argues that four main changes have occurred, that represent both threats and opportunities for the future of the ECB: threats to Democracy, Technological developments, the COVID-19 pandemic, and climate change and biodiversity loss. The ECB should, then, Reform, Open Up, Address and Develop to address them and become (or continue to be) a main actor within the EU.

III. Taking Stock of the 'New' European Central Bank

Taking stock of the 'new' ECB is not a matter of simply stating whether or not we are dealing with a new institution. In fact, we argue that attempting to provide a simple yes-or-no answer to this question is neither the most appropriate nor the most pertinent approach. Instead, it is more interesting and insightful to look at the various perspectives one can take in characterizing the ECB's transformation, at the main elements in the evolution of the ECB, and at the main causes, triggers, and factors in the ECB's evolution. These three issues will now be discussed in turn.

A. Perspectives on EMU and ECB change

The focus of this edited volume is on the development of the ECB. There is little doubt that this institution has undergone a considerable and remarkable evolution over the first decades of its existence, as testified by the various chapters in this volume. This evolution is part of a broader context, consisting of the evolution of the EMU, and of the EU more generally, and of developments in central banking across different jurisdictions. As illustrated further below, how one characterizes the ECB's evolution—and whether and to what extent it is considered 'new'—depends on the perspective taken, and it is useful to keep several of the different perspectives in mind.

Taking the perspective of the evolution *of the ECB*, as opposed to that of the EMU or of the broader EU legal order, several authors, also in this volume, convincingly argue that the ECB has undergone a 'constitutional transformation'. Amtenbrink and Markakis, for example, state that 'in the last decade the ECB has undergone a major transformation'.[13] Borger argues that '[f]rom a constitutional perspective, the ECB has not simply evolved, it has transformed ... evidenced by the fact that its mandate has received a new meaning without a corresponding change in the Treaty provisions that make it up'.[14] This already highlights some of the different perspectives that one can take when adopting a specific focus on the ECB's evolution.

In contrast, if only amendments to the Treaties were considered a relevant scale to assess the development of the ECB, there would arguably not be much new under the 'ECB sun' since Maastricht. If one, as we argue is more convincing, takes a broader perspective that takes also secondary instruments, institutional practice and reinterpretation into account, a lot more comes to the surface. Taking the example of the Banking Union, if the only yardstick for measuring what is new were the (constitutional) treaty-making decision of planting a supervisory seed at Maastricht, then one would ignore the tremendous impact of the activation of the enabling clause on supervision—on which basis the EBU could be established—on the functioning, challenges, and internal institutional design of the ECB, as well as on its relationship with National Competent Authorities (NCAs).

[13] See chapter 11 by Fabian Amtenbrink and Menelaos Markakis, in this volume.
[14] See chapter 2 by Vestert Borger, in this volume.

Authors who take a broader perspective in analysing the development of EMU, that is one that includes but is not limited to the ECB, have come to a similar conclusion. Thus, in their analysis of the changes to the macroeconomic constitution of the EU during the euro area crisis years, Tuori and Tuori have posited that there has been a 'constitutional mutation'.[15] According to their analysis, this constitutional mutation has taken place through an innovative and liberal interpretation of individual Treaty provisions, thereby shaking central principles of the Maastricht Treaty. With regard to the ECB in particular,[16] they argue that fundamental principles of the macroeconomic constitution, namely the primacy of the price stability objective, the ECB's independence, and the narrow definition of its mandate, were shaken during the GFC. Price stability has been replaced by financial stability as the overriding objective of the EMU, including in the monetary policy of the ECB.[17]

An even broader perspective has been adopted by de Witte, for example, who has raised the question whether the changes to the EMU that have taken place as a consequence of the euro area crisis have also led to a constitutional mutation of the broader EU legal order as a whole.[18] He concludes that this is not the case. In his analysis, de Witte distinguishes between changes in institutional practice on the one hand and constitutional transformation or mutation on the other. Whereas changes in institutional practice do not alter the meaning of the relevant legal rules but merely complement them, a constitutional transformation or mutation occurs when the meaning of the legal rules is changed compared to how they had previously been understood.[19] De Witte's conclusion is that the euro crisis has deepened the institutional variation existing between EMU law and other areas of EU law but has not led to a profound constitutional mutation of the broader EU legal order.[20] Similarly, Van der Sluis in his chapter argues that the question whether there is a 'new' ECB requires an examination of the constitutional context in which the ECB operates, and as a consequence he considers the process through which change occurs to be more interesting than the substance of the change under consideration.[21]

In addition, it is helpful to utilize a comparative perspective on central banking when characterizing the ECB's development. In this volume, this method is applied in the chapter by Petit. She shows how the development of the ECB's mandate, in terms of the relationship between various objectives and the discretion and trade-offs involved, relates to the development of other prominent central banks.[22] The takeaway might be

[15] Kaarlo Tuori and Klaus Tuori, *The Eurozone Crisis. A Constitutional Analysis* (CUP 2014) 186 (hereafter Tuori and Tuori, *The Eurozone Crisis*).

[16] Their view of a constitutional mutation is not confined to the ECB. Also, the scope of application of the Consolidated Version of the Treaty on the Functioning of the European Union [2012] OJ C326/47, Art 125 (hereafter TFEU) has been restricted; the mutated EU macroeconomic constitution not only allows for prevention, but also for resolution of insolvency crises. Tuori and Tuori, *The Eurozone Crisis* (n 15) 187.

[17] Tuori and Tuori, *The Eurozone Crisis* (n 15) 183.

[18] Bruno de Witte, 'Euro Crisis Responses and the EU Legal Order: Increased Institutional Variation or Constitutional Mutation?' (2015) 11 EuConst 434.

[19] ibid 436.

[20] ibid 457.

[21] See chapter 16 by Marijn van der Sluis, in this volume.

[22] See chapter 15 by Christy Ann Petit, in this volume.

that all central banks have had to undergo comparable transformations to deliver the type of monetary policy rendered necessary by the GFC.

B. The New European Central Bank

The evolution of the ECB that has taken place over the last decades is multifaceted,[23] as the contributions to this volume illustrate. Without doing justice to the many different aspects of this evolution and their detail, we claim that the essence of this evolution can nonetheless be well captured by looking at a few elements that stand out in our view. These elements relate to the main features of the ECB enshrined in the Treaties, namely: (1) the ECB's substantive mandate, to which definition Article 127 TFEU is central; (2) the ECB's relationship to euro area Member States' sovereign debt, in which respect Article 123 TFEU is central; and (3) the ECB's relationship to politics, for which Article 130 TFEU is central. We will now discuss the evolution of these features in turn.

1. The ECB's mandate

Key to the ECB's substantive mandate is Article 127 TFEU, which establishes price stability as the primary objective of the European System of Central Banks. While this Treaty provision has not been significantly amended since Maastricht, its implementation has led to important innovations, and the ECB's tasks have been expanded also beyond those included in this Treaty provision.

A first change in this regard relates to the ECB's evolving interpretation of its monetary policy strategy and to the instruments it has used to achieve its price stability objective. To reach its target of price stability, which has, since July 2021, been quantitatively defined as a year-on-year increase in the Harmonised Index of Consumer Prices (HICP) for the euro area of 2 per cent over the medium run,[24] the ECB traditionally uses a two pillar-approach that consists of an economic analysis and a monetary one. After the first strategy review, which the ECB conducted in 2003, the hierarchy between the two pillars was inverted, and the economic analysis became the first pillar.[25] The standard monetary policy of the ECB uses the setting of three key interest rates (the interest rate on the main refinancing operations, the one on the deposit facility, and the one on the marginal lending facility) to affect financing conditions in the economy.[26]

[23] Brunnermeier and others in their analysis of the ECB strikingly note that: 'In the course of the crisis, the ECB remade itself as an institution.' Markus K Brunnermeier, Harold James, and Jean-Pierre Landau, *The Euro and the Battle of Ideas* (Princeton UP 2018) 316 (hereafter Brunnermeier and others, *The Euro and the Battle of Ideas*).

[24] The ECB's price stability target was originally defined as an increase of below 2 per cent, while the 2003 review led to the addition of the famous 'but close to' formula.

[25] Brunnermeier and others, *The Euro and the Battle of Ideas* (n 23) 321. The new strategy adopted after the second strategy review of 2021 emphasizes the integrated nature of the assessment of the two pillars: see Christine Lagarde and Luis de Guindos, 'Opening Remarks' (ECB Press Conference, 8 July 2021) <https://www.ecb.europa.eu/press/pressconf/2021/html/ecb.sp210708~ab68c3bd9d.en.html> accessed 1 December 2021 (hereafter ECB, 'Press Conference 8 July 2021').

[26] See for a discussion, Paul de Grauwe, *Economics of Monetary Union* (OUP 2012) 173–206 (hereafter de Grauwe, *Economics of Monetary Union*).

This traditional approach to monetary policy has changed through the GFC and the following euro area crisis, leading the ECB to adopt also non-standard or unconventional monetary policy measures. The interest rate indeed hit the zero lower bound, thus forcing the ECB to move into unexplored territory. The ECB has adopted numerous unconventional monetary policy measures, including the Securities and Market Programme (SMP) in 2010, Longer-Term Refinancing Operations (LTROs) in 2011, the Outright Monetary Transactions (OMT) Programme in 2012, the Public Sector Purchase Programme (PSPP) in 2015, and the Pandemic Emergency Purchase Programme (PEPP) in 2020. In his chapter, Tuori argues that with the OMT Programme 'the traditional model of central banking was largely part of ECB history'.[27] Moreover, he claims that six years into quantitative easing (QE), the unconventional is slowly becoming conventional.[28]

The ECB's resort to unconventional monetary policy instruments has given rise to fierce debate about whether these instruments may still be considered to be monetary policy instruments or whether, instead, the ECB is not actually engaging in economic or fiscal policy—which fall beyond the scope of its (exclusive) competence in monetary policy. From the perspective of the categorization of a measure under EU law, this matter has been settled by the CJEU with regard to several of the unconventional instruments, deciding notably in *Gauweiler* and *Weiss* that respectively the OMT Programme and the PSPP are monetary policy measures indeed.[29] In terms of effects, however, these measures have undoubtedly changed the way in which the ECB's policy affects both the economy and government financing (on the latter see below).[30]

A second way in which the ECB's substantive mandate has significantly changed is through the alteration of the relationship between its primary objective of price stability and its secondary objectives. One of these secondary objectives, financial stability, has in fact taken centre stage in the design of the ECB's primary objective of price stability.[31] Considerations directly related to the survival of the currency area have permeated its monetary policy strategy,[32] and an unspoken part of the ECB's mandate—a responsibility for safeguarding the euro area—has thereby become apparent.[33] There is no doubt that the price stability objective is still the ECB's primary

[27] See chapter 3 by Klaus Tuori, in this volume.

[28] ibid.

[29] See chapter 6 by Jonathan Bauerschmidt, in this volume.

[30] cf Case C-62/14 *Gauweiler and Others v Deutscher Bundestag* [2015] EU:C:2015:400, para 100 (hereafter Case C-62/14 *Gauweiler*) and para 110: 'Moreover, the conduct of monetary policy will always entail an impact on interest rates and bank refinancing conditions, which necessarily has consequences for the financing conditions of the public deficit of the Member States.'; Case C-493/17 *Proceedings brought by Heinrich Weiss and Others* [2018] EU:C:2018:1000 paras 57–58 (hereafter Case C-493/17 *Weiss*); Tuori argues that: 'the classification of QE as monetary policy—by the ECB and accepted by the Court of Justice—is not in itself sufficient to affirm that the ECB's PSPP decision at that time and form had a compelling link with the price stability objective', see chapter 3 by Klaus Tuori, in this volume.

[31] See chapter 2 by Vestert Borger, chapter 3 by Klaus Tuori, chapter 5 by Agnieszka Smoleńska and Thomas Beukers, and chapter 7 by Kern Alexander, in this volume.

[32] In the run up to the announcement of the OMT programme, Draghi commented: 'Risk premia that are related to fears of the reversibility of the euro are unacceptable, and they need to be addressed in a fundamental manner. The euro is irreversible'; see Mario Draghi and Vítor Constâncio, 'Introductory statement to the press conference (with Q&A)' (ECB Press Conference, 2 August 2012) <https://www.ecb.europa.eu/press/pressconf/2012/html/is120802.en.html> accessed 1 December 2021.

[33] Brunnermeier and others, *The Euro and the Battle of Ideas* (n 23) 322.

objective, but these developments have led to a significant shift in the balance between the various objectives of the ECB.[34] In fact, in his chapter, Borger outlines as one of the most significant manifestations of this shift the new stability conception of the currency union, which had traditionally been predominantly geared towards price stability, and is now also attributing great importance to financial stability, as is visible in the purchase of government bonds by the ECB.[35]

A third important change to the ECB's mandate results from the assignment of new tasks to it. With the creation of the EBU, the ECB has since 2014 taken up new micro-prudential supervisory responsibilities, conferred to it by the Council on the basis of Article 127(6) TFEU (enabling clause). The impact of the conferral of this new task on the functioning of the ECB can hardly be overstated, not only in terms of substantive responsibilities, but also institutionally: one only needs to think of its internal institutional design—notably the internal 'Chinese wall' established within the ECB between the parts of its governance structure in charge of conducting the single monetary policy, and the parts specifically in charge of banking supervision in Banking Union Member States—or its relationship with NCAs.[36] In addition, the ECB has been given a role, albeit more limited, in the field of resolution and of macro-prudential supervision, both through secondary legislation based on Article 114 TFEU. Moreover, under the ESM, as part of the so-called Troika, the ECB has been given a role in negotiating and monitoring policy conditionality accompanying financial assistance (together with the Commission and the International Monetary Fund).[37] The ECB itself understands this latter role as a way of fulfilling its secondary objective of supporting the general economic policies in the Union contained in Article 127(1) TFEU.[38]

Both the new tasks assigned to the ECB and its new unconventional monetary policy measures have strengthened the ECB's involvement in the definition and the conduct of the economic policies of the Member States. While not directly engaging in the adoption of economic policy measures, the ECB nonetheless, by making liquidity provision conditional on (at times detailed) reform measures, can indirectly intervene in Member State economic policy making.[39] Brunnermeier and others argue that through this conditionality, the ECB has become a quasi-fiscal player during the crisis.[40]

[34] Another secondary objective, environmental sustainability, is recently also taking a more prominent place.

[35] See chapter 2 by Vestert Borger, in this volume.

[36] See chapter 7 by Kern Alexander, chapter 8 by Federico della Negra and Gianni Lo Schiavo, and chapter 13 by Diane Fromage, in this volume.

[37] See chapter 9 by Florin Coman-Kund, in this volume, who presents this as an 'intriguing aspect of the ECB's (intra-EU) international dimension'.

[38] See on this specific role, Paul Dermine, 'Out of the Comfort Zone? The ECB, Financial Assistance, Independence and Accountability' (2019) 26 MJ 108 (hereafter Dermine, 'Out of the Comfort Zone?').

[39] See extensively Thomas Beukers, 'The New ECB and its Relationship with the Eurozone Member States: Between Central Bank Intervention and Central Bank Intervention' (2013) 50 CML Rev 1579 (hereafter Beukers, 'The New ECB').

[40] Brunnermeier and others, *The Euro and the Battle of Ideas* (n 23) 336.

2. The ECB's relationship to sovereign debt

With the evolution of the ECB's substantive mandate described above, the ECB's relationship to euro area Member State sovereign debt has also changed considerably.

The central provision in the Treaties on this relationship is Article 123 TFEU, which prohibits the ECB and the central banks of the Member States from granting overdraft facilities or any other type of credit facility to public authorities and bodies of the Union and of Member States, and from purchasing directly their debt instruments from them. The central aim of the introduction of this provision was to 'encourage the Member States to follow a sound budgetary policy, not allowing monetary financing of public deficits or privileged access by public authorities to the financial markets to lead to excessively high levels of debt or excessive Member State deficits'.[41]

The Court of Justice, in its *Gauweiler* and *Weiss* judgments, has decided that Article 123 TFEU does not only prohibit direct purchases by the ECB on the primary market. The ECB is also barred from purchasing government bonds on secondary markets under conditions which would, in practice, mean that its action has an effect equivalent to that of a direct purchase of government bonds,[42] or if they were such as to lessen the impetus of the Member States concerned to follow a sound budgetary policy.[43] In setting these conditions, and in testing the characteristics of the OMT Programme in particular, the Court of Justice did not follow the German Federal Constitutional Court, which had advocated in favour of setting a limit to the quantity of bonds that could be bought in its request for a preliminary ruling.[44] In these decisions, the Court of Justice has decided that the OMT Programme and the PSPP Programme respectively, are in conformity with this provision. Compatibility is only part of the story though, as the various unconventional monetary policy measures, including these two Programmes, have radically altered the relationship of the ECB with Member States' sovereign debt, and with government financing.

Arguably, this changed relationship has not been accompanied by an explicit legal reinterpretation of Article 123 TFEU, as has been the case with the no-bailout clause of Article 125 TFEU, where the Court has read an implicit higher objective of 'maintaining the financial stability of the monetary union' in the provision in line with the developments on the ground.[45] Nonetheless, it seems fair to say that the ECB's interpretation of what is acceptable under the spirit of Article 123 TFEU has evolved over time, and as a consequence of the euro area crisis.[46]

Sovereign bond purchases, not only under the SMP and (potentially) the OMT Programme, but also under the later QE programmes PSPP and PEPP, provide direct liquidity to the banking system. At the same time, they indirectly provide liquidity to

[41] Case C-62/14 *Gauweiler* (n 30) para 100.
[42] ibid para 97; Case C-493/17 *Weiss* (n 30) para 106.
[43] Case C-62/14 *Gauweiler* (n 30) para 109; Case C-493/17 *Weiss* (n 30) para 107.
[44] Case C-62/14 *Gauweiler* (n 30) para 88.
[45] Case C-370/12 *Pringle v Ireland and Others* [2012] EU:C:2012:756 para 135.
[46] cf the remark by Draghi at the time of his appointment: 'we should not try to circumvent the spirit of the Treaty. No matter what the legal trick is, I think what matters for the people and what matters for the confidence and credibility of the institution is the spirit of this provision of the Treaty.' See Mario Draghi and Vítor Constâncio, 'Introductory statement to the press conference (with Q&A)' (ECB Press Conference, 8 December 2011) <https://www.ecb.europa.eu/press/pressconf/2011/html/is111208.en.html> accessed 1 December 2021.

governments.[47] In their discussion of the SMP and the OMT Programme, Tuori and Tuori note that, from the perspective of the debtors, these Programmes are similar in their effects to government financing.[48] The purchase of sovereign debt, albeit on the secondary market, has also led to the ECB now being seen as a Lender of Last Resort to sovereigns.[49] While the ECB does not recognize this role for itself, it seems fair to say that markets and economists do perceive it to *de facto* act as a Lender of Last Resort to sovereigns, and in this volume both Borger (OMT) and Tuori (QE) argue that this is the case.[50] In any event, the ECB is now the main creditor of the euro area Member States.

Other ECB measures have, too, changed the relationship of the ECB with Member State debt and with government financing. It is no secret that most of the liquidity injected by the ECB in the banking system through measures such as LTROs, which over the past years have made up by far the largest volume of credit to the banking system,[51] has been used by credit institutions to buy sovereign debt of their home country. In so-called carry trade, banks borrow money from the ECB at a low interest rate to then lend it to Member States—by buying government bonds—at a higher rate. LTROs thus have a controversial side effect on government financing, as they improve the fiscal position of Member States by creating demand for government debt.[52] Some analysts therefore consider liquidity provision to the banking system through such refinancing operations as 'implicit monetary financing'.[53] Buiter and Rahbari go even as far as to argue that LTROs are as much about the ECB acting as a Lender of Last Resort to Spanish and Italian sovereigns, as they are about a liquidity crunch of euro area banks.[54]

Another element in the relationship between the ECB and Member State debt that has changed over time is the ECB's treatment of sovereign debt as collateral. The chapter by Van 't Klooster illustrates important elements in the development of this specific relationship. Since 2006, with the introduction of its Single List and harmonizing eligibility criteria, the ECB has used a minimum credit rating requirement for sovereign debt.[55] Before the euro area crisis, the ECB could nonetheless still treat Member State debt equally, meaning that it could be used as collateral without any haircut or safety margin.[56] The euro area crisis has put considerable strain on this approach. Van 't Klooster notes that the conditions under which the ECB Governing Council provided the waivers for the eligibility requirement for Greece in April 2010, Ireland in March 2011, Portugal in July 2011, and Cyprus in July 2013 are vague.[57] At

[47] Brunnermeier and others, *The Euro and the Battle of Ideas* (n 23) 346.

[48] Tuori and Tuori, *The Eurozone Crisis* (n 15) 226.

[49] See for a discussion, chapter 5 by Agnieszka Smoleńska and Thomas Beukers, in this volume.

[50] In this sense, chapter 2 by Vestert Borger and chapter 3 by Klaus Tuori, in this volume. Tuori: 'A slightly less dramatic public finances consequence of the QE programs is that the ECB has arguably become the lender of last resort to the Member States.' And: 'From this perspective, the PEPP could also be seen as a successor of the OMT programme that provided the ECB "guarantee" for Member State financing.'

[51] See chapter 4 by Jens van 't Klooster, in this volume.

[52] Beukers, 'The New ECB' (n 39) 1605–06.

[53] Brunnermeier and others, *The Euro and the Battle of Ideas* (n 23) 348.

[54] Willem Buiter and Ebrahim Rahbari, 'The European Central Bank as Lender of Last Resort for Sovereigns in the Eurozone' (2012) 50 JCMS 6.

[55] See chapter 4 by Jens van 't Klooster, in this volume.

[56] Brunnermeier and others, *The Euro and the Battle of Ideas* (n 23) 102.

[57] See chapter 4 by Jens van 't Klooster, in this volume.

the same time, the impact of a decision by the ECB to either refuse to suspend collateral requirements or not, can be significant, as the case of Cyprus' request for financial assistance in 2013 illustrates.[58]

3. The ECB's relationship with politics

The first two decades of the ECB's existence have shown a remarkable development also in its relationship with politics. The core of this relationship in terms of Treaty rules, that is the independence of the ECB as enshrined in Article 130 TFEU, is arguably still valid. As examined further below, several new threats to the ECB's independence have, though, emerged over time. Moreover, it has become clear that the ECB's relationship with politics is much broader than the sole focus on central bank independence, in all its manifestations, would suggest.

Central bank independence, as prescribed by Article 130 TFEU, means that the ECB and National Central Banks shall not 'seek or take instructions from Union institutions, bodies, offices or agencies, [or] from any government of a Member State or from any other body' and that 'Union institutions, bodies, offices or agencies and the governments of the Member States undertake to respect this principle and not to seek to influence the members of the decision-making bodies of the European Central Bank or of the National Central Banks in the performance of their tasks'. The rationale behind this provision is that keeping the ECB at a distance from politics leads to a better control of price stability, the primary objective of the ECB. Indeed, politicians may be tempted to give priority to measures that would favour their re-election over those that may maintain the inflation rate at the desired (low) level.

During the GFC and the euro area crisis, the ECB has no doubt been under tremendous pressure to act, by both the markets and the Member States. With regard to attempts to influence the ECB, most infamous is the intervention by then French President Sarkozy during a high-level meeting on 7 May 2010, in which he tried to convince then ECB President Trichet that his institution should start buying sovereign bonds: 'Come on, come on, stop hesitating!'[59] We would agree with the assessment of Brunnermeier and others though that '[e]xcept for some brief and mostly rhetorical interventions by French policy makers, the independence of the ECB was never under question during the euro crisis'.[60] If anything, the crisis has illustrated and confirmed that even an independent central bank cannot act without taking its broader political, economic, and financial context into account.

If we look closer at the various components or manifestations of independence, however, the picture that emerges is the following. On the one hand, and from a formal perspective, the independence of the ECB with regard to several of these manifestations has been confirmed. On the other hand, the ECB's independence has in reality come under threat at different levels.

[58] See extensively Beukers, 'The New ECB' (n 39) 1593, 1596.

[59] Quoted in Tony Barber, 'Saving the euro: Dinner on the edge of the abyss' *Financial Times* (Washington, 10 October 2010) <https://www.ft.com/content/190b32ae-d49a-11df-b230-00144feabdc0> accessed 1 December 2021.

[60] Brunnermeier and others, *The Euro and the Battle of Ideas* (n 23) 96.

The ECB's goal independence, that is its autonomy to decide on the definition of its monetary policy objective, has been confirmed by the Court of Justice in *Weiss*,[61] where the Court concluded that the definition chosen by the ECB is not 'vitiated by a manifest error of assessment', indicating that the ECB has broad discretion in deciding on this definition.[62] The same can be said of the ECB's instrument independence, or functional independence,[63] formally confirmed by the Court in *Gauweiler*, where it decided that the ECB has broad discretion in deciding what instruments to choose to attain its objective of price stability.[64]

At the same time, several threats to the ECB's independence have been identified. Thiele in his chapter notes that, under certain circumstances, the ECB might still be acting independently from a formal perspective, but its actual scope of action can, at the same time, be significantly reduced due to certain (external) influences.[65] More specifically, he argues that the ECB's instrumental independence is under threat by the fiscal and the wage policies of the Member States, which may provoke economic consequences that make it more or less impossible for the central bank to fulfil its mandate.[66]

Van Riet in his chapter describes various threats to the financial independence of the ECB[67] that enables the Eurosystem to define monetary policy 'without having to consider the expected profits and losses on its interventions'.[68] These threats, in his view, come from several sources of financial risks to net monetary income, including significant credit risks on the ECB's balance sheet, and its increased exposure to corporate and sovereign defaults.[69] Tuori and Tuori argue that 'through changes in its lending and collateral policy the ECB has risked attaining a stakeholder position vis-à-vis the banking sector, which may cause complications for its role as an independent monetary expert'.[70]

At a different level, threats are identified to the foundations of the ECB's institutional position, including its independence.[71] In his contribution, Thiele extensively discusses the link between the acceptability of independence on the one hand, and a narrow mandate focused on price stability, or the 'justification by task', on the other.[72]

[61] Case C-493/17 *Weiss* (n 30) para 56.

[62] Thiele notes that 'from a normative perspective, the ECB therefore not only has the possibility but the duty to autonomously set its internal inflation target'. See chapter 10 by Alexander Thiele, in this volume.

[63] René Smits, *The European Central Bank. Institutional aspects* (Kluwer Law International 1997) 157 (hereafter Smits, *The European Central Bank*): 'This element refers to the autonomous decision-making in respect of the instruments which the central bank employs to achieve its objective.'

[64] Case C-62/14 *Gauweiler* (n 30) paras 67–68.

[65] See chapter 10 by Alexander Thiele, in this volume.

[66] ibid. The biggest threat in his view would however be a too intensive judicial review not granting the ECB the necessary margin of appreciation it needs to successfully pursue its monetary goals.

[67] This can be understood as the autonomy of the central bank in terms of the funding of its activities and the exercise of its powers; see Smits, *The European Central Bank* (n 63) 157.

[68] See chapter 14 by Ad van Riet, in this volume.

[69] ibid.

[70] Tuori and Tuori, *The Eurozone Crisis* (n 15) 226.

[71] Smits, *The European Central Bank* (n 63) 178: 'Clear-cut tasks and a single ultimate objective are also prerequisites for severing the link with other organs of Government: only for the single purpose of achieving price stability and with its tasks well-defined is it acceptable to take central banking out of the realm of day-to-day politics and entrust the management of monetary affairs to a separate "institution".'

[72] See chapter 10 by Alexander Thiele, in this volume, discussing also the *Bundesverfassungsgericht*'s view on this.

The broad interpretation by the ECB of its mandate has raised concerns over a potential weakening of this justification.[73] Tuori and Tuori claim that the more expert bodies acquire characteristics of a stakeholder and politician,[74] and the 'further away the ECB ventures from a monetary policy focused on price stability and the more active a role it adopts in fiscal rescue operations, the more the original justification for its present institutional status loses pertinence'.[75] As Amtenbrink puts it: 'The ECB is [then] perceived as entering the arena typically reserved for political decision making; an arena where competing (public) interests are balanced and decisions with direct distributional effects are taken', thereby threatening its democratic legitimacy.[76]

Interestingly, the development of the ECB over its first decades of existence has made it clear that the relationship between central banks and politics is not limited to central bank independence and to coordination between a central bank and its fiscal counterpart. In fact, we have also witnessed what has been qualified as 'central bank intervention' in Member State economic policy making.[77] In this context, central bank intervention is being understood not as an ECB act directly affecting Member State economic policy, but as messages from the ECB to individual Member States, with great detail about the necessary fiscal and structural reforms, combined with great and effective pressure.[78] The crisis has, in fact, caused a shift in the ECB's approach from (simply) critically assessing, suggesting, and recommending, to (also) strongly pressuring in favour of a specific course of action by a specific euro area Member State.[79]

Other dimensions of the relationship between the ECB and politics have arguably been subject to only modest developments. Amtenbrink and Markakis argue in this edited volume that 'the accountability framework applicable to the ECB has not evolved sufficiently to match its expanded powers'.[80] The 'institutional loneliness' of the Eurosystem, a weakness of EMU that Padoa-Schioppa pointed to early on, has not been ended.[81] Still, some of the more modest developments are nonetheless worth mentioning here.

In the absence of a euro area treasury or government, the ECB has carefully and closely interacted with the political leaders of the (euro area) Member States collectively, leading to a change in the nature and intensity of this relationship. In his contribution, Van der Sluis contrasts the dynamics between the ECB and the Member

[73] Alicia Hinarejos, '*Gauweiler* and the Outright Monetary Transactions Programme: The Mandate of the European Central Bank and the Changing Nature of Economic and Monetary Union' (2015) 11 EuConst 563, 571–73.

[74] Tuori and Tuori, *The Eurozone Crisis* (n 15) 221.

[75] ibid 187. Similarly at 228. For a critical conceptual discussion of the numerous claims that the ECB has become politicized, see Pier Domenico Tortola, 'The Politicization of the European Central Bank: What is it, and How to Study it?' (2020) 58 JCMS 501.

[76] Fabian Amtenbrink, 'The European Central Bank's Intricate Independence versus Accountability Conundrum in the Post-Crisis Governance Framework' (2019) 26 MJ 165, 178; see also chapter 11 by Fabian Amtenbrink and Menelaos Markakis, in this volume.

[77] Beukers, 'The New ECB' (n 39).

[78] ibid 1602.

[79] ibid 1604.

[80] See chapter 11 by Fabian Amtenbrink and Menelaos Markakis, in this volume. See further on the ECB's accountability at present, Dermine, 'Out of the Comfort Zone?' (n 38).

[81] See for a discussion, chapter 14 by Ad van Riet, in this volume.

States in the reinterpretation of the 'no-bailout' clause of Article 125 TFEU with the dynamics leading to the reinterpretation of the mandate of the ECB outlined above. He highlights that there was no structured interaction between the two actors (ie the ECB and the Member States), and concludes that 'the political consensus that emerged on the actions of the ECB was based on an acquiescence of a new status quo that was tentatively being shaped by the ECB, rather than on compromises that politicians had to publicly defend both in Brussels and in their home state'.[82] Borger instead emphasizes in this respect the close interaction between the Member States, acting in their executive capacity through their heads of state or government, and the ECB in the process that steered the currency union into a different direction, one in which financial stability takes centre stage.[83]

C. Causes, triggers, and factors of ECB evolution

This part discusses several possible causes, triggers, and factors for the ECB's evolution. We evidence that the emergence of a 'new ECB' is not so much a consequence of Treaty change or a change in the underlying ideas, but is very much a reaction to the events that have occurred since the creation of the ECB, and is determined by autonomous action by an ECB, which has used the gaps inherent in its mandate, and by political decision making.

1. Treaty change?

Neither the Treaty of Amsterdam nor the Treaty of Nice have substantively altered the provisions of the Treaty of Maastricht on EMU.[84] Also, the amendments brought about by the Lisbon Treaty are relatively modest. The most notable Treaty change with regard to the ECB is arguably that, with the Lisbon Treaty it has formally become an EU institution (Article 13(1) TEU).[85] This has led to it becoming subject, like the other institutions, to requirements such as the respect for the principle of subsidiarity and proportionality.[86] Other changes include the possibility for the European Council to appoint members of the ECB Executive Board by qualified majority voting, as opposed to common accord, and the procedure to amend the Statute of the European System of Central Banks (Article 129 TFEU), which now partly follows the ordinary legislative procedure. In other words, the new European Central Bank presented in this volume is not a consequence of formal Treaty amendments.

[82] See chapter 16 by Marijn van der Sluis, in this volume.

[83] See chapter 2 by Vestert Borger, in this volume. Beukers similarly points to the central importance that collective (Eurozone) Member State action has played, sometimes with pressure from the ECB, as a condition for ECB action. See Beukers, 'The New ECB' (n 39) 1601.

[84] See Jean-Claude Piris, *The Lisbon Treaty. A Legal and Political Analysis* (CUP 2010) 303 (hereafter Piris, *The Lisbon Treaty*).

[85] See chapter 9 by Florin Coman-Kund, in this volume, for a discussion of the relationship between this change and the ECB's international legal personality.

[86] Piris, *The Lisbon Treaty* (n 84) 234, who also notes that it has not changed the jurisdiction of the Court of Justice over ECB acts, which was already provided for by the Treaties.

2. Changing (underlying) ideas?

The ECB's design at Maastricht was both the product of a political compromise between the Member States and a product of its time.[87] It was the result of a political compromise including France's acceptance of German reunification on the one hand, and Germany's acceptance of the introduction of a single currency under the responsibility of a European Central Bank modelled in close resemblance to the design of the German Bundesbank on the other.[88] It was also a product of the 1990s in the sense that it corresponds to the underlying economic ideas that were dominant at that time. In line with monetarist assumptions, the primary objective that was attributed to the ECB is price stability.[89] In his chapter, Van 't Klooster describes how a set of ideas popularized by the monetarist Milton Friedman—monetary policy cannot make a lasting contribution to the economy's productive capacity—set the background for the ECB's simple objective of price stability.[90] Thiele, in his contribution, illustrates how during the 1990s central bank independence became a central pillar of modern central banking theory.[91] This was supported by empirical findings suggesting that countries with an independent central bank had less of an inflation problem during the 1970s stagflation decade.[92]

For political reasons, and in defiance of the Optimal Currency Area (OCA) theory,[93] the introduction of the euro was not accompanied by a central economic government at euro area level or by political union.[94] Instead, Member States remained in charge of economic and fiscal policy, with only a coordinating role for the EU institutions in this area.[95] Market discipline, several Treaty provisions, and the Stability and Growth Pact were supposed to prevent fiscal crises. Member States also continued to be primarily responsible for the prudential supervision of financial institutions and the stability of the financial system. Borger, in his chapter, explains the little concern for financial stability contained in the Maastricht Treaty by the shift towards monetarism witnessed during that period and the ensuing focus on securing price stability.[96] Tuori and Tuori note that the inter-linkage between financial instability and macroeconomic developments was common knowledge in the 1980s. They find, though, several other (in addition to a focus on price stability) explanations for the absence of concern for financial stability, including moral hazard concerns (leading to a rejection of the attribution of

[87] See Tuori and Tuori, *The Eurozone Crisis* (n 15) 55.

[88] See Andre Szasz, *De Euro* (Schilt Publishing 2001). Close resemblance does not mean the ECB is identical to the *Bundesbank*; see also Tuori and Tuori who refer to the 'adoption' of the Bundesbank model as '*one of the myths surrounding the origins of EMU*': see Tuori and Tuori, *The Eurozone Crisis* (n 15) 29, and chapter 16 by Marijn van der Sluis, in this volume.

[89] Tuori and Tuori, *The Eurozone Crisis* (n 15) 28.

[90] See chapter 4 by Jens van 't Klooster, in this volume.

[91] See chapter 10 by Alexander Thiele, in this volume.

[92] Brunnermeier and others, *The Euro and the Battle of Ideas* (n 23) 95.

[93] See for a (critical) discussion of the OCA theory, de Grauwe, *Economics of Monetary Union* (n 26).

[94] Bauerschmidt recalls how economists such as Friedman voiced concern regarding the feasibility of a monetary union without a political union: see chapter 6 by Jonathan Bauerschmidt, in this volume.

[95] Van der Sluis argues that the relevant rules (TFEU (n 16) Arts 121 and 126) 'in the Treaties had the effect of protecting the Member States from an overly intrusive EU. They aimed to limit European action as much as to promote it.': see chapter 16 by Marijn van der Sluis, in this volume.

[96] See chapter 2 by Vestert Borger, in this volume.

supervisory functions to the ECB) and an intentional obscurity of the function of the Lender of Last Resort.[97]

Have we witnessed changes to the ECB's fundamentals as a consequence of the changes in the underlying (economic) ideas that have happened since Maastricht? That is not the picture that emerges from this edited volume. With regard to the design of the ECB's monetary policy aimed at price stability, it may actually be said, as is argued by Tuori, that the ECB is rather ahead of findings in economic theory to the extent that it decided to engage in so-called quantitative easing (the same would be true for many other central banks).[98] With regard to central bank independence, and although Thiele notes that the last years have seen an increasing number of scholars arguing that central bank independence is not necessary,[99] there does not seem to be a fundamental shift in the importance given to it in the ECB's mandate. Rather, the focus on 'threats' to independence in the recent literature can be read as a confirmation of its importance.

In other areas, we see developments that seem to realign the 'new ECB' more with predominant ideas. For example, the prominent place that financial stability has gained in the application of the ECB's mandate, understood by Borger as part of a changing conception of stability within the EMU,[100] can be seen as a realignment of the ECB with what seems to be a rather stable and dominant view of economists over time, namely that financial stability is a natural interest for any central bank.[101] The same could be said of the Banking Union and early critical writings on the financial trilemma.[102]

There are also examples of areas where we see developments in underlying ideas but only modest ECB development. On the one hand, Amtenbrink and Markakis note, in reference to Cukiermann, that, differently from what held a few decades ago, accountability and transparency have become two buzz words of modern monetary institutions.[103] Still, they consider, on the other hand, that the evolution of the accountability framework applicable to the ECB is rather modest compared to its now expanded powers.[104]

3. Events

The main driver of change for the ECB has no doubt been *events*. They are simply too many to account for here, but they are well accounted for in the various chapters of this volume.

[97] Tuori and Tuori, *The Eurozone Crisis* (n 15) 55–56.

[98] See chapter 3 by Klaus Tuori, in this volume, who argues that the theoretical basis of QE is relatively weak in traditional macroeconomics.

[99] See also for a critical discussion of the positions of these scholars, chapter 10 by Alexander Thiele, in this volume. See also Stiglitz for criticism of specifically ECB independence: Joseph Stiglitz, *The Euro: How a Common Currency Threatens the Future of Europe* (WW Norton & Company 2016) 162.

[100] Including a changing perception of a possible LOLR function of the ECB to sovereigns; see chapter 2 by Vestert Borger, in this volume.

[101] See chapter 5 by Agnieszka Smoleńska and Thomas Beukers, in this volume.

[102] See for an overview and discussion, Dirk Schoenmaker, 'The Financial Trilemma' (2011) 111 Economics Letters 57 <https://papers.ssrn.com/sol3/papers.cfm?abstract_id=1340395> accessed 1 December 2021.

[103] See chapter 11 by Fabian Amtenbrink and Menelaos Markakis, in this volume.

[104] ibid.

The chain of events that led to the Great Financial Crisis, and which originated outside the euro area including the failure of Lehman Brothers in September 2008, was crucial in this respect. Another closely linked chain of events did originate in the euro area, and subsequently provoked the euro area crisis. One of the triggers here was the transparency on the (much worse than officially claimed) state that the Greek public finances were in, which came to light following the rise to power of PASOK in 2010. Many of the developments of the ECB described in this book derive, directly or indirectly, from these two major crises.

The COVID-19 pandemic has, in turn, induced further developments, although many of them, such as LTROs and the asset purchase programmes introduced in response to the pandemic (PEPP) were variations of the instruments adopted during the earlier crisis. It can, in fact, be said that the unconventional monetary policy instruments developed and tested by the ECB during the sovereign debt crisis in a way prepared the ground for the ECB's response to the COVID-19 pandemic.

Other developments of the past decades that have, too, contributed to shape the 'new ECB' include the case of the rise of the climate emergency. This is now perceived by many as a crisis on which also central banks and supervisors may and should have an impact, and in fact is shaping ECB policy making.[105]

4. Discretion in the mandate of an independent institution

A fundamental factor in the development of the ECB has arguably been the fact that the text of the Maastricht Treaty had left many things open and to be decided by the ECB itself autonomously. Thus, often intentionally, the independent ECB has been left with broad discretion to decide how to shape its mandate. Because of this, the ECB's evolution is 'largely the result of the ECB's own understanding of its role and duties.'[106] While Tuori and Tuori have argued that 'the narrow role of central banking, implicit in the Maastricht macroeconomic constitution, presupposed considerable self-restraint in border zones of its constitutional mandate',[107] it seems fair to say that the ECB has not shown considerable self-restraint over the last decade. Arguably, this was not so much the consequence of an intentional power grab by the ECB, but more often rather of lack of sufficient action by political actors leaving a vacuum that needed to be filled by others.

The existence of such broad discretion for the ECB is argued and accounted for by several authors throughout this volume.[108] Van der Sluis generally argues that 'the ECB was given considerable leeway in interpreting the boundaries of its own powers'.[109] Many of the concrete examples given here relate to monetary policy, an area in which the Court of Justice has also confirmed the ECB's broad discretion, and one where it is required 'to make choices of a technical nature and to undertake forecasts and

105 See, eg, European Central Bank, 'Annex: Detailed roadmap of climate change-related actions' (European Central Bank, 8 July 2021) <https://www.ecb.europa.eu/press/pr/date/2021/html/ecb.pr210708_1_annex~f84ab35968.en.pdf> accessed 1 December 2021.

106 See chapter 11 by Fabian Amtenbrink and Menelaos Markakis, in this volume.

107 Tuori and Tuori, *The Eurozone Crisis* (n 15) 227.

108 For an additional example, see ibid: 'A lot was also left to the new institution to meet the requirements of transparency and public accountability.'

109 See chapter 16 by Marijn van der Sluis, in this volume.

complex assessments'.[110] Thiele points to the instrument independence of the ECB including the right to decide autonomously on the methods it uses to measure the inflation rate and the general economic situation of the respective monetary area, and to define its monetary strategy. He also recalls that the price stability objective anchored in Article 127(1) TFEU is a so-called '"undefined legal term" that has to be "filled with life" primarily by the ECB itself'.[111] Van 't Klooster posits, in turn, that the interpretation of 'adequate' in the Treaty requirement that credit transactions with financial market participants are 'based on adequate collateral' is entirely left to the ECB.[112] Finally, Smolenska and Beukers illustrate how discretion in the use of monetary policy instruments has enabled the ECB to also take on roles that have not been explicitly assigned to it, such as the Lender of Last Resort function.[113]

5. Political decisions

As has been seen above, and is also illustrated by Borger in his chapter,[114] political decisions and actions have played an indirect role in various of the autonomous decisions taken by the ECB, such as the introduction of its SMP. Moreover, the new tasks given to the ECB under the ESM Treaty—its role in the Troika—were a consequence of a political decision, in this case by the euro area Member States.[115] Also, the creation of the European Banking Union is an obvious case in point, with the activation by the Council of the dormant provision in Article 127(6) TFEU at its origins.[116]

A further political decision that has led to an evolution of the ECB is the enlargement of the EU and of the euro area. Membership of the common currency went from 12 Member States to 19 Member States between 1 January 2007 and 1 January 2015. Substantively this has increased the number of citizens and consumers directly affected by the monetary policy of the ECB. This has also meant that the 'one size fits all' challenge of a monetary policy with a single interest rate for countries with a different level of inflation became larger. The EU's enlargement did not provoke an institutional development comparable to that triggered by the GFC or euro area crisis. It did, however, lead to an increase in the number of National Central Bank Governors that participate in the ECB Governing Council, and since Lithuania joined the euro area as of 1 January 2015, it has triggered the start of a rotating system in the voting procedure, which has affected the balance between the supranational and the national components within the ECB.[117]

110 Case C-62/14 *Gauweiler* (n 30) para 68; confirmed in Case C-493/17 *Weiss* (n 30) para 73.

111 See chapter 10 by Alexander Thiele, in this volume.

112 See chapter 4 by Jens van 't Klooster, in this volume.

113 See chapter 5 by Agnieszka Smoleńska and Thomas Beukers, in this volume.

114 See chapter 2 by Vestert Borger, in this volume.

115 On which, see chapter 6 by Jonathan Bauerschmidt, chapter 9 by Florin Coman-Kund, and chapter 11 by Fabian Ambtenbrink and Menelaos Markakis, in this volume.

116 On which, see chapter 5 by Agnieszka Smoleńska and Thomas Beukers, chapter 6 by Jonathan Bauerschmidt, chapter 7 by Kern Alexander, chapter 8 by Federico Della Negra and Gianni Lo Schiavo, and chapter 11 by Fabian Ambtenbrink and Menelaos Markakis, in this volume.

117 See chapter 13 by Diane Fromage, in this volume. The voting system is explained here: European Central Bank, 'Rotation of voting rights in the Governing Council of the ECB' (ECB Monthly Bulletin July 2009) <https://www.ecb.europa.eu/pub/pdf/other/mb200907_pp91-99en.pdf> accessed 1 December 2021.

6. Personalities

Personalities matter, also in ECB development. The fact that the mandates and the personalities of ECB presidents are influential factors may be illustrated with the example of ECB President Trichet's fierce opposition to (Greek) debt restructuring. This episode is well documented, and his succession by Draghi is considered by many as having paved the way for the Greek Private Sector Involvement (PSI).[118] Draghi has also used the wriggle room afforded by the Treaties to increase the powers of the ECB and is probably the major figure that accounts for the shape of today's ECB. It remains to be seen how Lagarde's presidency will affect the evolution of the new ECB. In managing the COVID-19 shock, she built on her predecessor's policy stance. Her greater emphasis on transparency and communication of policy choices might help fill the accountability gap noted earlier, and her interest in greening the ECB fits closely to the major economic policy priority of the EU.

7. New relations with (old and new) institutions

A further source and trigger of development of the ECB has been the various new and changed institutional relationships, both with traditional actors through new instruments and with new actors. There are several examples of this phenomenon in the new Banking Union, such as the relationship between the ECB and NCAs,[119] or the new (and unique) accountability relationship the ECB now entertains with national parliaments.[120] Another example is the close interaction between the ECB and political leaders of the (euro area) Member States, both collectively[121] and individually.[122] Litigation before the Court of Justice involving the ECB is not a new phenomenon, but has increased exponentially.[123] While the case law of the Court of Justice in *Gauweiler* and *Weiss* has arguably confirmed rather than shaped ECB development, it is hard to see the recent explicit focus by the ECB on proportionality in isolation from the *Bundesverfassungsgericht*'s decision of 5 May 2020.[124]

IV. Looking Ahead: Future Developments and Challenges

It is impossible to predict what the ECB will look like in another 20 years or so from now. For certain, its development will continue to be triggered by a combination of the

[118] See, eg, the account by former Greek Finance Minister Papaconstantinou in George Papaconstantinou, *Game Over. The Inside Story of the Greek Crisis* (Papadopoulos Publishing 2016) 192–93, 217, 222; Ralph Atkins, 'ECB warns against private role in bail-outs' *Financial Times* (London, 13 October 2011) <https://www.ft.com/content/423dda70-f585-11e0-94b1-00144feab49a> accessed 1 December 2021.

[119] See chapter 8 by Federico Della Negra and Gianni Lo Schiavo, and chapter 13 by Diane Fromage, in this volume.

[120] See chapter 13 by Diane Fromage, in this volume.

[121] See on this interaction, chapter 2 by Vestert Borger and chapter 16 by Marijn van der Sluis, in this volume.

[122] See Beukers, 'The New ECB' (n 39).

[123] See in particular chapter 12 by Takis Tridimas, in this volume.

[124] BVerfG, Judgement of the Second Senate of 5 May 2020 2 BvR 859/15 ECLI:DE:BVerfG:2020:rs20200505085915 and others (hereafter BVerfG 5 May 2020, 2 BvR 859/15).

factors identified above, including the ECB's autonomous interpretation of its mandate, political decision making, and, of course, events.

This section will highlight some of the areas where relevant developments can be expected, and some of the main challenges the ECB will need to address. Without being comprehensive, and without being able to do justice to all the recommendations for future reform formulated by the authors to this edited volume, we will now discuss both substantive and institutional issues as they also emerge from the various chapters.

Looking at the ECB's instruments, it is clear that the new monetary policy toolbox, which is extensively discussed in this volume, is more likely than not to be here to stay. The ECB in fact recognizes that because of the limitations caused by the zero lower bound, monetary policy tools other than the interest rate tool will remain in the ECB's toolbox.[125] This means that the challenges related to these instruments will equally continue to exist and need to be addressed. These include the substantive challenges of: explaining and justifying the effects that ECB monetary policy has on the broader economy, financial stability, and the financing conditions of euro area Member States; addressing the various challenges related to the ECB's unprecedented large balance sheet; and accounting for the redistributive impact of monetary policy measures.[126]

Turning to the ECB's objectives, interesting developments and related challenges may also be expected in this regard. In fact, most of the chapters in this volume in one way or another deal with the question of what role secondary objectives play and/or should play in relation to the primary objective of price stability. A group of prominent economists has advocated in favour of the development of a framework to define the role of secondary objectives such as financial stability or climate change mitigation. This would be necessary because these secondary objectives define the cost of an instrument. Commenting on the outcome of the ECB's recent monetary strategy review, they argue that: 'The ECB has done little to clarify how it plans to address the problem of secondary targets.'[127] Prominent ECB lawyers in their report to the ECB Governing Council have identified several relevant open legal questions, such as whether and to what extent secondary objectives should always be pursued together with the primary objective, or to what extent the ECB can rely on secondary objectives as an explicit legal basis for its monetary policy measures.[128]

Specifically with regard to the secondary objective of financial stability, the ECB's predicament is evident. Will it be able to prevent the potential destabilizing developments of its monetary policy from materializing, in particular those related to

[125] ECB, 'Press Conference 8 July 2021' (n 25).

[126] See on this challenge, chapter 3 by Klaus Tuori, chapter 7 by Kern Alexander, and chapter 11 by Fabian Amtenbrink and Menelaos Markakis, in this volume. See also Fabian Amtenbrink, 'The European Central Bank's Intricate Independence Versus Accountability Conundrum in the Post-Crisis Governance Framework' (2019) 26 MJ 165, 175–76.

[127] Lucrezia Reichlin and others, *The ECB strategy. The 2021 Review and its Future* (CEPR Press 2021) 2.

[128] Michael Ioannidis, Sarah Jane Hlásková Murphy, and Chiara Zilioli, 'The mandate of the ECB: Legal considerations in the ECB's monetary policy strategy review' (2021) ECB Occasional Paper Series No 276 <https://www.ecb.europa.eu/pub/pdf/scpops/ecb.op276~3c53a6755d.en.pdf?34605304c0df6620b17a6a7b32fed3cf> accessed 1 December 2021.

quantitative easing as noted by Tuori?[129] To what extent will financial stability concerns constrain the ECB in pursuing its primary objective of price stability, considering, for example, the effect that a possible interest rate increase can have on the sustainability of euro area Member State public debt? Will the ECB lean against the wind where necessary, as advocated by Alexander and Van 't Klooster?[130]

The greening of the ECB's mandate will be another prominent area of substantive development in the coming years.[131] The ECB published an action plan in July 2021 including a detailed roadmap with concrete actions foreseen until 2024.[132] It emphasizes the direct link with its primary mandate and stresses that central banks are not the main actors in this area. An important responsibility for the ECB will be to clearly communicate to what extent climate change considerations are incorporated in monetary policy measures to pursue price stability on the one hand, and to what extent the ECB is instead pursuing the secondary objective of supporting the relevant economic policies in the Union, with a view to contributing to the achievement of environmental objectives.[133]

The challenges the ECB is facing in the area of Banking Union receive ample attention in this edited volume. In this domain, the ECB is partly in the hands of the political institutions, for example with regard to the stronger, more harmonized and consistent EU regulatory framework advocated by Della Negra and Lo Schiavo.[134] But other challenges can be addressed by the ECB autonomously, such as finding the appropriate level of coordination between monetary policy and banking supervision as highlighted by Alexander.[135]

The possible introduction of a digital euro, which is openly advocated by the ECB, is considered by Smits as 'the primary challenge' facing this institution.[136] All cards remain on the table at the time of writing as the ECB is still in the investigation phase. What form is it to take? And can the ECB autonomously decide on the introduction of a digital currency, as suggested by the ECB itself,[137] or is that decision rather to be taken by the Union legislator?

Van Riet addresses the challenge of creating better conditions for cooperation between monetary and fiscal authorities, potentially increasing the efficacy of monetary policy. In the absence of a fiscal union, his ambitious recommendations for the creation of a fiscal capacity and euro area treasury provide a useful analytical framework for assessing future developments in this area.[138]

[129] 'Without taking a stance on the economic substantive elements of this legal debate, I do find it clear that the ECB's QE has become the most important factor in financial markets and asset prices that contains the possibility of deeply destabilising developments in the future.': chapter 3 by Klaus Touri, in this volume.

[130] See chapter 4 by Jens van 't Klooster and chapter 7 by Kern Alexander, in this volume.

[131] See in particular chapter 4 by Jens van 't Klooster, chapter 7 by Kern Alexander, chapter 11 by Fabian Amtenbrink and Menelaos Markakis, and chapter 17 by René Smits, in this volume.

[132] ECB, 'Press Release 8 July 2021' (n 11).

[133] For a discussion of this distinction, see Francesco Drudi and others, 'Climate change and monetary policy in the euro area' (2021) ECB Occasional Paper Series No 271, 138–40 <https://www.ecb.europa.eu/pub/pdf/scpops/ecb.op271~36775d43c8.en.pdf> accessed 1 December 2021.

[134] See chapter 8 by Federico Della Negra and Gianni Lo Schiavo, in this volume.

[135] See on this, chapter 7 by Kern Alexander, in this volume.

[136] See chapter 17 by René Smits, in this volume.

[137] ECB, 'Report on a digital euro' (n 12) 25.

[138] See chapter 14 by Ad van Riet, in this volume.

Many of the institutional challenges identified in this volume relate to the question of how the independent and powerful ECB—with a large margin of discretion in deciding on the implementation of its mandate—is to be controlled. The main substantive developments of the ECB, including its unconventional monetary policy measures and new Banking Union responsibilities, are expected to be long-lasting. Considering this, there is a momentous challenge of matching the ECB's powers with sufficient democratic accountability. The predominant academic view, including among the various authors in this volume, seems to be that we should not expect too much of legal accountability, or judicial review, in this respect.[139] Although the Court of Justice's deferential approach in the *Gauweiler* and *Weiss* cases has not been exempt from criticism,[140] the main focus of the recommendations formulated with a view to increasing the ECB's accountability and legitimacy is set, also in this volume, on the role played by political institutions, either at the EU or at the national level.

Van der Sluis argues that the ECB (and the EMU more broadly) should be deconstitutionalized, thereby leaving more room for 'ordinary' politics as opposed to constitutional politics to decide the direction of the ECB.[141] Amtenbrink and Markakis advocate an increased involvement of EU political institutions in the setting of the ECB's targeting framework.[142] Van 't Klooster is in favour of increased coordination between the ECB and the EU's political institutions in resolving questions that the Central Bank faces in managing (climate) risk.[143] Having effectively defended its independence even during the turbulent euro area crisis years, there seems to be room for the ECB to increase both its effectiveness and its legitimacy by coordinating with other actors. It is obvious that the ECB is partly in the hands of others in addressing this challenge.

Smits argues that the ECB itself should continue to 'open up'.[144] The ECB's recent approach as part of the 2021 strategy review has been to complement its forward guidance to market participants with proactive stakeholder outreach, including citizens. While the initial focus was in particular on listening,[145] it is now emphasizing that it intends to actively communicate its policy not only to experts but also to ordinary citizens.[146] This should help to explain and justify its actions better, and hopefully bridge the gap that has arisen over the years, leading it to become a *new* albeit more contested EU institution. This is all the more important as it is bound to remain centre-stage in the E(M)U in the coming years.

[139] For an example outside this volume, see Nik de Boer and Jens van 't Klooster, 'The ECB, the Courts and the Issue of Democratic Legitimacy after Weiss' (2020) 57 CML Rev 1689.

[140] See, eg, chapter 16 by Marijn van der Sluis, in this volume. Van der Sluis even believes 'the ECB to be an institution without democratic legitimacy'.

[141] See chapter 16 by Marijn van der Sluis, in this volume.

[142] See chapter 11 by Fabian Amtenbrink and Menelaos Markakis, in this volume.

[143] See chapter 4 by Jens van 't Klooster, in this volume.

[144] See chapter 17 by René Smits, in this volume.

[145] For an overview of the listening events across the euro area organized by the ECB and NCB's during the 2021 strategy review, see European Central Bank, 'Overview of the listening events across the euro area' <https://www.ecb.europa.eu/home/search/review/html/all_events.en.html> accessed 1 December 2021.

[146] For this purpose, since July 2021 the ECB is actively trying to make its regular press conference less technical and more accessible to regular citizens.

PART I

THE ECB'S RESPONSE TO THE FINANCIAL AND SOVEREIGN DEBT CRISIS

Unconventional Monetary Policy and the Lender of Last Resort Function

Part 1 examines the substantive changes to monetary policy introduced by the ECB as a consequence of the financial and sovereign debt crisis by considering their legal basis, the manner in which these measures have been legitimized by the Court of Justice, and their significance for the developing constitutional order of the EU. In particular, it looks at its relationship to the Lender of Last Resort's function within the euro area, and at its pursuit of unconventional monetary policy.

2
The Transformation of the ECB in Sovereign Bond Markets

Vestert Borger[*]

I. Introduction

The central question of this edited volume is whether today's European Central Bank (ECB) constitutes a 'new entity' compared to the one that was founded by the Treaty of Maastricht.[1] It certainly does in as far as its intervention in government bond markets is concerned. When the sovereign debt crisis hit in early 2010, the ECB had little to no instruments at its disposal to address it. It was held back from acting by its narrow mandate in Article 127 of the Treaty on the Functioning of the European Union (TFEU) and by the prohibition on monetary financing in Article 123 TFEU. Yet, by May 2010, only months after the start of the crisis, the ECB had put in place the Securities Markets Programme (SMP), allowing it to purchase government bonds on secondary markets.[2] When the crisis subsequently reached its height in the summer of 2012, the ECB launched the Outright Monetary Transactions Programme (OMT), which equally enabled it to purchase government bonds.[3] The mere announcement of that programme sufficed to pacify markets that until then had been spiralling out of control.

It is right to say that as a result of these actions the ECB constitutes a *new* entity. Terms like 'different' or 'matured' would not do justice to the fundamental nature of the change. From a constitutional perspective, the ECB has not simply evolved, it has *transformed*.[4] Transformation takes place when constitutions change without formal amendment. In the case of the ECB, its transformation is evidenced by the fact that its

[*] This contribution builds on earlier works by the author, in particular Vestert Borger, 'Central Bank Independence, Discretion and Judicial Review' in Joana Mendes (ed), *EU Executive Discretion and the Limits of Law* (OUP 2019); Vestert Borger, *The Currency of Solidarity: Constitutional Transformation During the Euro Crisis* (CUP 2020); Stefaan Van Den Bogaert and Vestert Borger, 'Hoog spel in Karlsruhe: Het Duitse Constitutionele Hof over het Public Sector Asset Purchase Programme' (2020) 95 Nederlands juristenblad 2978. The contribution covers ECB action on sovereign bond markets until July 2021.

[1] Unless indicated otherwise, this contribution simply speaks of the ECB (instead of distinguishing between the ECB, the European System of Central Banks, and the Eurosystem).

[2] Decision of the European Central Bank of 14 May 2010 establishing a securities markets programme (ECB/2010/5) [2010] OJ L 124/8 (hereafter Decision ECB/2010/5).

[3] European Central Bank, 'Technical features of Outright Monetary Transactions' (ECB Press Release, 6 September 2012) <https://www.ecb.europa.eu/press/pr/date/2012/html/pr120906_1.en.html> accessed 13 July 2021.

[4] For an extensive analysis of the transformation of the currency union during the debt crisis, including that of the ECB, see Vestert Borger, *The Currency of Solidarity: Constitutional Transformation during the Euro Crisis* (CUP 2020) (hereafter Borger, *The Currency of Solidarity*).

Vestert Borger, *The Transformation of the ECB in Sovereign Bond Markets* In: *The New European Central Bank*. Edited by: Thomas Beukers, Diane Fromage, and Giorgio Monti, Oxford University Press. © Vestert Borger 2022. DOI: 10.1093/oso/9780198871231.003.0002

mandate has received a new meaning without a corresponding change in the Treaty provisions that constitute it. Key to this transformation is a widening of the currency union's conception of stability. Whereas it used to be predominantly geared towards price stability, it now also attributes great importance to financial stability. The purchase of government bonds by the ECB is one of its most significant manifestations.[5]

In examining the transformation of the ECB, the European Court of Justice is easily put at the centre of attention. Michael Ioannidis, for example, in his analysis of the transformation, states that whereas 'executive and other constitutional actors also play a role in establishing new meaning in textually-unaltered constitutional provisions, it is the constitutional adjudicator that essentially sanctions a constitutional transformation'.[6] In the Union, he argues, 'this is a crucial role of the ECJ'.[7] This attention for the Court is not without reason. By approving the OMT programme in *Gauweiler*, it indeed sealed the transformation. Yet, the fact is that constitutional transformation is just as much about politics as it is about law.[8] To fully understand the ECB's transformation during the sovereign debt crisis, the focus therefore needs to be broadened beyond the Court of Justice, and even beyond the law, to include politics. This chapter does precisely that. It first examines the interaction between law and politics at the origin of the ECB's transformation. On that basis, it subsequently studies its confirmation by the Court of Justice in *Gauweiler* and its consequences for the institutional position of the ECB, notably vis-à-vis courts.

This chapter is divided into six sections. Section II discusses the original legal set-up of the currency union. That set-up was strongly geared towards price stability. This stability conception greatly influenced the constitutional position of the ECB. Price stability takes up a central place in its mandate as primary policy goal. The ECB also enjoys great independence in order to pursue that goal as effectively as possible. One of the safeguards for that independence is the prohibition on monetary financing, which seeks to prevent unsound budgetary policies by the Member States from forcing the ECB to cater for their fiscal needs instead of price stability. During the debt crisis, however, this stability conception proved too narrow as it left another kind of stability exposed: *financial* stability.

Section III of the chapter subsequently shows how the sovereign debt crisis caused the ECB to become a Lender of Last Resort for Member States by purchasing government bonds, first with the Securities Markets Programme in May 2010 and subsequently—and potentially—with Outright Monetary Transactions in September 2012. These bond programmes, however, were only implemented or announced after national political leaders had committed themselves to a different currency union, one with a broader conception of stability. Their commitment set in motion an interaction

[5] See in this respect also chapter 5 by Agnieszka Smoleńska and Thomas Beukers, in this volume.

[6] Michael Ioannidis, 'Europe's New Transformations: How the EU Economic Constitution Changed during the Eurozone Crisis' (2016) 53 CML Rev 1237, 1244 (hereafter Ioannidis, 'Europe's New Transformations').

[7] ibid 1244.

[8] Julian Arato, 'Treaty Interpretation and Constitutional Transformation: Informal Change in International Organizations' (2013) Yale Journal of International Law 289, 303: 'Constitutions do not belong exclusively to the province of pure legal theory; they are not just about law, but also about power. In establishing institutions, rights and obligations, constitutions create and regulate power, and as such they also belong to the realm of politics.'

between political leaders and the ECB leading to a transformed single currency, characterized by greater options to secure financial stability, among which a Lender of Last Resort function for the ECB.

Section IV then discusses how in *Gauweiler* the Court of Justice reconciled this function with the existing set-up of the currency union, in particular that of the ECB. It focuses on two key pillars of that set-up: the ECB's mandate in Article 127 TFEU and the prohibition on monetary financing in Article 123 TFEU. The resulting transformation of the ECB, characterized by its function as a Lender of Last Resort for states, as well as the capacity to conduct substantial interventions in government bond markets more generally, brings with it an institutional repositioning, not least in relation to courts. Section V of the chapter reflects on this on the basis of the case of *Weiss*, concerning the ECB's third government bond instrument, the Public Sector Purchase Programme. Section VI concludes.

II. The ECB in the Original Set-up of the Currency Union

A. The stability paradigm

The original set-up of the currency union, with its great concern for price stability, was truly a product of its time.[9] Two historical developments exercised great influence on the negotiations on the Treaty of Maastricht at the beginning of the 1990s. The first was a change in economic thinking, characterized by a transition from 'Keynesianism' towards 'monetarism', with profound consequences for the ability of governments to control employment.[10] Keynesianism, the dominant school of thought in the first decades after the Second World War, takes the position that there is a 'permanent trade-off' between inflation and employment.[11] The government, in other words, can fight unemployment by boosting demand through 'expansionary' fiscal and monetary policies at the expense of higher inflation.[12] Monetarism, which came into fashion over the course of the 1970s, argues there is no such trade-off.[13] While expansionary monetary and fiscal policies may exert a temporary effect on employment, ultimately they cannot bring it below its 'natural rate'.[14] Instead, the government is better off by focusing its monetary policy on price stability, which contributes to an economic environment supportive of lasting growth. If it does want to target unemployment,

[9] For an extensive discussion of this original legal set-up, on which this one is based, see Borger, *The Currency of Solidarity* (n 4) 81–153.

[10] On this shift, see Peter A Hall, 'From Keynesianism to Monetarism: Institutional Analysis and the British Economic Policy in the 1970s' in Sven Steinmo, Kathleen Telen, and Frank Longstreth (eds), *Structuring Politics: Historical Institutionalism in Comparative Analysis* (CUP 1992) 90 (hereafter Hall, 'From Keynesianism to Monetarism').

[11] Kathleen McNamara, *The Currency of Ideas: Monetary Politics in the European Union* (Cornell University Press 1998) 146 (hereafter McNamara, *The Currency of Ideas*).

[12] Paul De Grauwe, *Economics of Monetary Union* (OUP 2014) 150 (hereafter De Grauwe, *Economics of Monetary Union*). See also Hall, 'From Keynesianism to Monetarism' (n 10) 92.

[13] McNamara, *The Currency of Ideas* (n 11) 146.

[14] ibid 67, 146; De Grauwe, *Economics of Monetary Union* (n 12) 150.

'structural policies', such as labour or tax reforms, are to be preferred over expansionary measures.[15]

The second development concerned German reunification. After the fall of the Wall in November 1989, the reunification of Germany presented itself as a real and urgent possibility. This created fears among West European states that, following reunification, Germany would turn its back to European integration.[16] For Germany, participation in a currency union formed a means to ease these fears. But in exchange for its participation it demanded that a single currency would be 'at least as stable as the D-Mark'.[17] Given its strong negotiating position, not in the least due to its dominance in the European Monetary System,[18] the European Community's instrument for monetary cooperation at the time, Germany managed to force through its focus on price stability on key elements of the negotiations on the Treaty of Maastricht.[19]

Due to these two developments, the original legal set-up for the single currency was built around a 'sound money' or 'stability paradigm'.[20] This means it was primarily concerned about price stability and the ECB's design reflected that concern. The mandate of the ECB in Article 127(1) TFEU determines that its primary goal is to maintain price stability and that it can only support other goals of economic policy to the extent that it does not jeopardize that primary goal.[21] Article 130 TFEU, moreover, makes clear that it pursues that goal in great independence, based on the idea that the more independent a central bank can operate from politics, the better it is at controlling inflation.[22]

The concern for price stability was also visible in the area of economic policy, and in particular fiscal policy. Article 123 TFEU, the so-called prohibition on monetary financing, forbids 'overdraft facilities or any other type of credit facility' with the ECB or National Central Banks in favour of governments or other public bodies of the Member States. It also prohibits the direct purchase of their debt instruments by the ECB or National Central Banks.[23] Together with the prohibitions on privileged access

[15] De Grauwe, *Economics of Monetary Union* (n 12) 150; McNamara, *The Currency of Ideas* (n 11) 147.

[16] André Szász, *The Road to European Monetary Union* (Palgrave Macmillan 1999) 137 ff; Kenneth Dyson and Kevin Featherstone, *The Road to Maastricht: Negotiating Economic and Monetary Union* (OUP 2003) 363–66 (hereafter Dyson and Featherstone, *The Road to Maastricht*).

[17] Dyson and Featherstone, *The Road to Maastricht* (n 16) 718.

[18] On Germany's 'anchor' position within that system, see Dyson and Featherstone, *The Road to Maastricht* (n 16) 25–26; Michele Chang, *Monetary Integration in the European Union* (Palgrave Macmillan 2009) 66–68.

[19] See extensively Andrew Moravcsik, *The Choice for Europe: Social Purpose and State Power from Messina to Maastricht* (Cornell University Press 1998) 440–47, 461–67.

[20] Martin Marcussen, 'The Dynamics of EMU Ideas' (1999) 34 Cooperation and Conflict 383, 402; Kenneth Dyson, *The Politics of the Euro-Zone: Stability or Breakdown?* (OUP 2000) 27; Martin Heipertz and Amy Verdun, *Ruling Europe: The Politics of the Stability and Growth Pact* (CUP 2010) 91–93 (hereafter Heipertz and Verdun, *Ruling Europe*).

[21] See also the Consolidated Version of the Treaty on the Functioning of the European Union [2012] OJ C326/47, Art 282(2) (hereafter TFEU) and Protocol No 4 on the Statute of the European System of Central Banks and of the European Central Bank [2016] OJ C202/230, Art 2.

[22] During the 1980s and 1990s a significant amount of economic research supported that idea. See, eg, Vittorio Grilli, Donato Masciandaro, and Guido Tabellini, 'Political and Monetary Institutions and Public Financial Policies in the Industrial Countries' (1991) 13 Economic Policy 341; Alberto Alesina and Lawrence H Summers, 'Central Bank Independence and Macroeconomic Performance: Some Comparative Evidence' (1993) 25 JMCB 151; Thomas Havrilesky and James Granato, 'Determinants of Inflationary Performance: Corporatist Structures vs Central Bank Autonomy' (1993) 76 Public Choice 249.

[23] The prohibition equally applies to Union institutions, bodies, offices, or agencies.

to financial institutions and bailouts in Articles 124 and 125 TFEU, it promotes fiscal discipline by ensuring that Member States can only (re)finance their debt on the capital markets on similar conditions as private entities.[24] It thereby seeks to avoid that the ECB is put under pressure to take decisions conflicting with the goal of price stability in order to ease the borrowing conditions of Member States, for example by lowering interest rates or, worse even, by 'financing' government debt.[25]

B. The narrow conception of stability

The drafters of the Treaty of Maastricht had been warned that putting so much trust in the virtues of market discipline was a risky strategy.[26] In its report on the possibility of an economic and monetary union of April 1989, the Delors committee had stated:

> To some extent market forces can exert a disciplinary influence ... However, experience suggests that market perceptions do not necessarily provide strong and compelling signals and that access to a large capital market may for some time even facilitate the financing of economic imbalances. Rather than leading to a gradual adaptation of borrowing costs, market views of the creditworthiness of official borrowers tend to change abruptly and result in the closure of access to market financing. The constraints imposed by market forces may either be too slow and weak, or too sudden and disruptive.[27]

During the sovereign debt crisis this scenario materialized. The development of the 'spread', that is to say: the difference in interest rates between the German '*Bund*' and other euro area government bonds, is telling. In the first years following the start of the euro, spreads steadily declined. Markets, in other words, acted as if there were no significant differences in default risk for Member States in the monetary union.[28] Yet, this changed abruptly after the onset of the global financial crisis in 2007–08. Suddenly, markets did start to differentiate between government bonds. And when the financial crisis developed into a sovereign debt crisis at the end of 2009, the situation escalated. Interest rates for bonds of Member States like Greece and Portugal became so high that these States threatened to lose market access.

[24] René Smits, *The European Central Bank: Institutional Aspects* (Kluwer Law International 1997) 75–77 (hereafter Smits, *The European Central Bank*).

[25] Heipertz and Verdun, *Ruling Europe* (n 20) 74–75; Daniel Gros and Niels Thygesen, *European Monetary Integration: From the European Monetary System to Economic and Monetary Union* (2nd edn, Longman 1999) 327; De Grauwe, *Economics of Monetary Union* (n 12) 216.

[26] The following analysis of the narrow stability conception of the currency union's original set-up is based on the one in Borger, *The Currency of Solidarity* (n 4) 158–65, 187–200.

[27] Committee for the Study of Economic and Monetary Union, 'Report on the Economic and Monetary Union in the European Communities' (17 April 1989) <https://ec.europa.eu/economy_finance/publications/pages/publication6161_en.pdf> accessed 13 July 2021, para 30.

[28] European Central Bank, 'The determinants of Euro Area Sovereign Bond Yield Spreads during the Crisis' (2014) ECB Monthly Bulletin May 2014 67, 74 <https://www.ecb.europa.eu/pub/pdf/other/art1_mb201405en_pp67-83en.pdf> accessed 13 July 2021 (the ECB notes in this respect that investors seemed to 'underprice' risk).

At the time, Paul De Grauwe and Yuemei Yi explained this capricious market behaviour by pointing out that euro area Member States issued 'debt in a currency over which they have no control'.[29] Whereas most developed states benefit from a guarantee implicit in their financial systems that they can turn to their central banks to honour their commitments towards creditors in times of financial stress, euro area Member States did not. In fact, the prohibition on monetary financing in Article 123 TFEU was considered to rule out such a guarantee. This made euro area Members States 'susceptible to movements of distrust' on the markets with the potential to result in 'self-fulfilling' crises.[30] This potential resided in the fact that these Member States could experience 'multiple equilibria'.[31] If a Member State found itself in a 'good' equilibrium, it benefitted from market confidence, which translated into modest interest rates and easy access to financing. Yet, in a 'bad' equilibrium, the same Member State lacked the trust of markets and faced high interest rates. This could force it to resort to austerity, which in turn could trigger a recession and negatively affect its fiscal record. In this way, the Member State would end up in a downward spiral. Markets, driven by fear and panic, charged increasingly high interest rates, to the extent that they no longer reflected its true economic position—its 'economic fundamentals' as De Grauwe and Yi call it—[32] ultimately forcing it to default. And in a currency union like the euro area, such problems tend not to limit themselves to one state, but to 'contage' others,[33] pushing them into a downward spiral unrelated to their economic fundamentals as well and destabilizing government bond markets at large.

The meltdown of government bond markets during the euro crisis consequently not only exposed the flaws of the instrument of market discipline, as the Delors report had already predicted, it contested the very conception of stability on which the currency union had been founded. Its original set-up went to great lengths to secure price stability, but in so doing left another kind of stability unprotected: *financial* stability.

Financial stability concerns the stability of the financial system, which comprises all 'financial intermediaries and financial markets and their relations with respect to the flow of funds to and from households, governments, business firms, and foreigners'.[34] Contrary to price stability, which the ECB understands as an inflation rate of 2 per cent over the medium term,[35] financial stability does not lend itself for easy definition. That is why, as the late economist and central banker Tommaso Padoa-Schioppa has

[29] Paul De Grauwe and Yuemei Yi, 'Self-fulfilling Crises in the Eurozone: An Empirical Test' (2013) JIMF 15, 16 (hereafter De Grauwe and Yi, 'Self-fulfilling Crises in the Eurozone').

[30] ibid 16–17.

[31] ibid 17.

[32] ibid 18–19, 26–27.

[33] Paul De Grauwe and Yuemei Yi, 'Mispricing of Sovereign Risk and Macroeconomic Stability in the Eurozone' (2012) 50 JCMS 866, 877–78. See also Vítorio Constâncio, 'Contagion and the European Debt Crisis' (Banque de France, Financial Stability Review no 16, April 2012) 110–11 <https://publications.banque-france.fr/sites/default/files/medias/documents/financial-stability-review-16_2012-04.pdf> accessed 13 July 2021.

[34] Jakob de Haan, Sander Oosterloo, and Dirk Schoenmaker, *Financial Markets and Institutions: A European Perspective* (2nd edn, CUP 2012) 33.

[35] European Central Bank, 'The ECB's monetary policy strategy statement' (ECB, 8 July 2021) <https://www.ecb.europa.eu/home/search/review/html/ecb.strategyreview_monpol_strategy_statement.en.html> accessed 13 July 2021.

explained, economists tend to concentrate on financial *in*stability.[36] Definitions of financial instability often centre around the concept of 'systemic risk', specified by the G10 as 'the risk that an event will trigger a loss of economic value or confidence in, and attendant increases in uncertainties about, a substantial proportion of the financial system that is serious enough to quite probably have significant adverse effects on the real economy'.[37] On the basis of this understanding, as ECB Executive Board Member Yves Mersch has explained, 'financial stability is a state where the build-up of systemic risk is prevented'.[38]

'Traditionally', Dirk Schoenmaker explains, 'central banks have two major objectives: monetary stability and financial stability'.[39] Yet, under the currency union's original stability set-up, the only Treaty provision dealing with financial stability was Article 127(5) TFEU, which determines that, as one of its 'non-basic' tasks, the European System of Central Banks (ESCB) 'shall contribute to the smooth conduct of policies pursued by the competent authorities relating to the prudential supervision of credit institutions and the stability of the financial system'. The provision is repeated in Article 3.3 of the Statute of the ESCB and ECB. Article 25.1 of the Statute subsequently determines that the ECB 'may offer advice to and be consulted by' Union institutions and national competent authorities 'on the scope and implementation of Union legislation relating to the prudential supervision of credit institutions and to the stability of the financial system'.

This little concern for financial stability can be explained by the fact that, due to the shift towards monetarism, the drafters of the Treaty of Maastricht had their eyes mostly on securing price stability.[40] Stronger, they feared that equipping the ECB with greater powers concerning financial stability, could harm its efforts to control inflation.[41] Germany especially had this concern. When the Committee of Central Bank Governors, which was in charge of drafting the Statute of the ESCB and ECB, at first proposed to qualify the stability of the financial system as a 'basic' task and to allow the ESCB to participate in the 'formulation' and 'execution' of policies to protect it,[42]

[36] Tommaso Padoa-Schioppa, 'Central Banks and Financial Stability' (Speech given in Jakarta, 7 July 2003) <https://www.ecb.europa.eu/press/key/date/2003/html/sp030707.en.html> accessed 13 July 2021: 'While monetary stability simply means price stability, no such straightforward definition exists for financial stability. Defining financial stability is notoriously difficult and that is why people find it more convenient to define financial instability.'

[37] Group of Ten, 'Report on Consolidation in the Financial Sector' (January 2001) 126 <https://www.bis.org/publ/gten05.pdf> accessed 13 July 2021.

[38] Yves Mersch, 'Financial stability and the ECB' (Speech at the ESCB Legal Conference, Frankfurt am Main, 6 September 2018) <https://www.ecb.europa.eu/press/key/date/2018/html/ecb.sp180906.en.html> accessed 13 July 2021 (hereafter Mersch, 'Speech at the ESCB Legal Conference of September 2018').

[39] Dirk Schoenmaker, 'Central Banks Role in Financial Stability' in Gerard Caprio Jr (ed), *Handbook of Safeguarding Global Financial Stability: Political, Social, Cultural and Economic Theories and Models, Vol 2* (Elsevier 2013) 272 (hereafter Schoenmaker, 'Central Banks Role in Financial Stability').

[40] ibid 272.

[41] For an inventory of the risks and benefits of making the central bank responsible both for price and financial stability, see Charles Goodhart and Dirk Schoenmaker, 'Should the Functions of Monetary Policy and Banking Supervision Be Separated?' (1995) 47 Oxford Economic Papers 539, 545–49.

[42] Art 3 of the draft stated in this regard that the ESCB should 'participate as necessary in the formulation, co-ordination and execution of policies relating to prudential supervision and the stability of the financial system'. See Committee of Governors of the Central Banks of the Member States, 'Draft Statute of the European System of Central Banks and of the European Central Bank' (Agence Europe Document no 1669/

it made clear it was dead against.[43] The Member States consequently played down the wording, opting for the text that can now be found in Article 127(5) TFEU.[44] As a result, Dirk Schoenmaker explains, the original set-up of the currency union, in particular the position of the ECB, was 'largely modelled after the Bundesbank', which means it followed a 'narrow central banking concept focusing on monetary stability'.[45]

The sovereign debt crisis made clear that, as much as one wants to secure financial stability by *preventing* systemic risk, a mature financial system also requires instruments to deploy once it occurs, instruments that go beyond the 'contributory' powers of the ECB in Article 127(5) TFEU. One such instrument is that of a 'Lender of Last Resort'. In times of severe market unrest, characterized by the risk of a liquidity shortage, such a lender may step in to prevent liquidity problems from turning into solvency problems and secure the financial system at large. It is common knowledge that banks need such a lender.[46] Yet, as De Grauwe and Yi have explained,[47] the debt crisis showed that states also require one.[48] And it is the very need for such a lender that is key to the transformation of the currency union, and with it, of the ECB.

III. The New Stability Conception

A. The Securities Markets Programme

When in early 2010 Greece and other Member States came under heavy fire in the markets, the currency union's toolbox was empty. It had little to no instruments at its disposal to calm down markets that were turning adrift. In fact, the prohibitions on bailout in Article 125 TFEU and on monetary financing in Article 123 TFEU seemed to rule out financial help for distressed Member States. Yet, only months later, in May 2010, the ECB took the unprecedented step to purchase government bonds by putting in place the Securities Markets Programme. And two years later, in September 2012, it decisively changed the path of the crisis by announcing the Outright Monetary

1670, 8 December 1990) <https://www.ecb.europa.eu/ecb/access_to_documents/document/cog_pubaccess/shared/data/ecb.dr.parcg2007_0005draftstatute.en.pdf> accessed 13 July 2021.

[43] Rosa M Lastra, 'The Governance Structure for Financial Regulation and Supervision in Europe' (2003/2004) 10 Colum J Eur L 49, 56.

[44] See also Smits, *The European Central Bank* (n 24) 337–38.

[45] Schoenmaker, 'Central Banks Role in Financial Stability' (n 39) 280.

[46] For discussions of the classical understanding of the Lender of Last Resort and how the concept has developed over time, see Michael D Bordo, 'The Lender of Last Resort: Alternative Views and Historical Experience' in Charles Goodhart and Gerhard Illing (eds), *Financial Crises, Contagion and the Lender of Last Resort: A Reader* (OUP 2002) 109–26; Xavier Freixas and others, 'Lender of Last Resort: A Review of the Literature' in Charles Goodhart and Gerhard Illing (eds), *Financial Crises, Contagion and the Lender of Last Resort: A Reader* (OUP 2002) 27–56; Rosa M Lastra, 'Lender of Last Resort, an International Perspective' (1999) 49 ICLQ 340.

[47] See text to n 29.

[48] See in this respect Paul De Grauwe, 'The European Central Bank as Lender of Last Resort in the Government Bond Markets' (2013) 59 CESifo Economic Studies 520, 520–22; Willem Buiter and Ebrahim Rahbari, 'The European Central Bank as a Lender of Last Resort for Sovereigns in the Eurozone' (2012) 50 JCMS 6, 6–9, 18; Paul Krugman, 'Currency Regimes, Capital Flows, and Crises' (2014) 62 IMF Economic Review 470, 473–75.

Transactions programme. How was that possible?[49] Some argue that actions like these show that, during the crisis, the ECB was 'calling the shots in a situation that is deeply and inherently political',[50] or that it could take the lead because of the 'collective abdication of Eurozone governments'.[51] Such statements, however, misread its actions. Let there be no mistake: the ECB had a pivotal role in overcoming the crisis. Actions like changes to the collateral regime for banks or the approval of Emergency Liquidity Assistance were instrumental to keep the euro afloat. And because of its pivotal role, the ECB held great leverage over the economic policies of Member States, 'individual' and 'collective'.[52]

But when it comes to its most crucial actions—its government bond programmes—the ECB was just as much dependent on the Member States. Only they had the authority to decide on actions that were necessary to preserve the Union, yet that also constituted a departure from the currency union's legal set-up that they had put in place with the Treaty of Maastricht.[53] That is: actions that changed the rules of the game. The resulting picture, then, is that of close interaction between the Member States, acting in their executive capacity through their heads of state or government, and the ECB. To implement its bond programmes, the ECB required the support of the Member States, whereas the Member States themselves needed these programmes to steer the currency union into a different direction, one in which financial stability takes centre stage.

The starting point for this interaction was a meeting of the heads of state or government of all Member States, not just those in the currency union, on 11 February 2010.[54] In the weeks prior to that meeting, Greece had come under severe fire in the markets. It was clear that without help, the Hellenic state would succumb to the pressure, with devastating consequences not only for itself, but for the euro and the Union at large. At the same time, the Treaties did not give the leaders an easy way out. As Herman Van Rompuy, then President of the European Council, recalls: '[W]e could not turn to our joint rule book for answers, but had to invent from scratch. In fact, the EU Treaties explicitly forbid member states to assume each other's financial commitments; this

[49] The following discussion of the interaction between national political leaders and the ECB in the run-up to the launch of the SMP is based on the one in Borger, *The Currency of Solidarity* (n 4) 209–35, 261–71.

[50] Kathleen McNamara, 'Banking on Legitimacy: The ECB and the Euro Zone Crisis' (2012) 13 Georgetown Journal of International Affairs 143, 148.

[51] Henning Deters, 'Deliberative Supranationalism in the Euro Crisis? The European Central Bank and the European Council in Times of Conflict' in Christian Joerges and Carola Glinski (eds), *The European Crisis and the Transformation of Transnational Governance* (Hart Publishing 2014) 261.

[52] See extensively in this regard Thomas Beukers, 'The New ECB and its Relationship with the Eurozone Member States: Between Central Bank Independence and Central Bank Intervention' (2013) 50 CML Rev 1579.

[53] See Borger, *The Currency of Solidarity* (n 4) 216, 362–63; Luuk van Middelaar, *Alarums & Excursions: Improvising Politics on the European Stage* (Agenda Publishing 2019) 30–31; Uwe Puetter, 'Europe's Deliberative Intergovernmentalism: The Role of the Council and the European Council in EU Economic Governance' (2012) 19 JEPP 161, 171; Alicia Hinarejos, *The Euro Area Crisis in Constitutional Perspective* (OUP 2015) 91.

[54] This composition differs from the one of formal European Council meetings, which also includes its own president and that of the Commission. See Consolidated Version of the Treaty on European Union [2012] OJ C326/01, Art 16(2).

so-called "no-bailout-clause" was a founding principle of the Economic and Monetary Union.'[55]

The political leaders, in other words, found themselves in an existential crisis in which they had to choose between the law as it had been understood until then and support for the Union that this law was meant to serve. They chose the latter, and in so doing set in motion a fundamental transformation of the currency union. Their statement after the meeting marked its contours. The first sentence indicated the widening of the stability conception that the currency union would come to experience:

> All euro area members . . . have a shared responsibility for the economic and financial stability in the area.[56]

The final two sentences revealed the implications of this widened conception:

> Euro area Member States will take determined and coordinated action, if needed, to safeguard financial stability in the euro area as a whole. The Greek government has not requested any financial support.[57]

Whereas the statement made clear that Greece had not asked for financial assistance, it was precisely by mentioning this that the leaders showed their willingness to grant assistance if push came to shove. As Van Rompuy puts it: 'Without spelling out that the other EU countries would lend money to Greece, we did touch on the limits of the no-bailout clause by stating that if a Greek bankruptcy threatened the financial stability of the whole eurozone, member states would take action.'[58] It was the first step towards the granting of Lender of Last Resort assistance.

At the beginning of March, Jean-Claude Trichet, then President of the ECB, said at his monthly press conference that he regarded the statement as 'very important' and as 'committing the Heads of State or Government in case we would have to safeguard financial stability in the euro area as a whole'.[59] He thereby made it seem as if responsibility for financial stability should rest solely with the Member States, not with the ECB. A month later, he doubled down on that impression when he was asked to reflect on the necessity of a Lender of Last Resort for the currency union. The ECB, he answered, was already 'fulfilling all the functions of a central bank in any other economy'.[60] Only weeks later, however, it would start buying government bonds.

[55] Herman Van Rompuy, *Europe in the Storm: Promise and Prejudice* (Davidsfonds Uitgeverij 2014) 12 (hereafter Van Rompuy, *Europe in the Storm*).
[56] European Council, 'Statement by the Heads of State or Government of the European Union' (Brussels, 11 February 2010) <https://www.consilium.europa.eu/media/20485/112856.pdf> accessed 13 July 2021.
[57] ibid.
[58] Van Rompuy, *Europe in the Storm* (n 55) 13.
[59] Jean-Claude Trichet and Lucas Papademos, 'Introductory Statement to the Press Conference (with Q&A)' (ECB Press Conference, Frankfurt am Main, 4 March 2010) <https://www.ecb.europa.eu/press/pressconf/2010/html/is100304.en.html> accessed 13 July 2021.
[60] Jean-Claude Trichet and Lucas Papademos, 'Introductory Statement to the Press Conference (with Q&A)' (ECB Press Conference, Frankfurt am Main, 8 April 2010) <https://www.ecb.europa.eu/press/pressconf/2010/html/is100408.en.html> accessed 13 July 2021.

On 2 May 2010, euro area Member States, together with the International Monetary Fund (IMF), put in place an assistance package for Greece of €110 billion.[61] But almost immediately it became clear that the package would not suffice to calm down markets and stop the crisis from spreading to other Member States. During the weekend of 7–9 May, euro area leaders would therefore meet yet again to decide on an assistance fund for the currency union at large. In the run-up to that weekend, on Thursday 6 May, Trichet no longer excluded the possibility that the ECB would purchase government bonds. When asked about it at his monthly press conference, exceptionally held in Lisbon, he said that the Governing Council 'did not discuss this option', thereby indicating that the ECB might resort to bond purchases if the situation called for it.[62]

Only hours later, the members of the Governing Council thought that moment had arrived. In the evening, they met with their spouses at the *Palácio de Bacalhoa*, a fancy estate near Lisbon.[63] Over dinner, their cell phones started ringing: the Dow Jones experienced the greatest 'intraday loss' of all time.[64] Whereas it would ultimately turn out to be a technical glitch, at that time they thought it resulted from the ambiguity about government bond purchases that Trichet had allowed to persist at the press conference earlier that day.[65] During a hastily arranged meeting in the estate's cellar the central bankers agreed to intervene in government bond markets.[66] They tasked the Executive Board to prepare a draft decision the next day in order to enable the Governing Council to take a formal decision on the matter at short notice.

When the following day euro area leaders gathered in Brussels to decide on an assistance fund, they were unaware of this move. All of them, however, were conscious of the fact that they required the ECB to help secure financial stability. Yet, they had different strategies to communicate that to Trichet. French President Sarkozy pressurized him to act: 'Come on, come on, stop hesitating!', he snapped at him.[67] Leaders who were more mindful of the ECB's independence opted for a different approach, especially Chancellor Merkel. She stressed that the ECB had 'a very good record' and that all those sitting around the table had to 'trust' it.[68] Trichet, on his turn, defended the independence of his institution: 'We do not need and we will not ask for your permission. We have a very good track record and you must trust us. If you try to apply pressure, the ECB Council will react negatively with disastrous consequences.'[69] His

[61] Eurogroup, 'Statement by the Eurogroup' (Brussels, 2 May 2010) <https://www.consilium.europa.eu/media/25673/20100502-eurogroup_statement_greece.pdf> accessed 13 July 2021.

[62] Jean-Claude Trichet and Lucas Papademos, 'Introductory Statement to the Press Conference (with Q&A)' (ECB Press Conference, Frankfurt am Main, 6 May 2010) <https://www.ecb.europa.eu/press/pressconf/2010/html/is100506.en.html> accessed 13 July 2021.

[63] For detailed accounts of the events of that evening, see Neil Irwin, *The Alchemists: Three Central Bankers and a World on Fire* (Penguin Books 2014) 219–23 (hereafter Irwin, *The Alchemists*); Carlo Bastasin, *Saving Europe: Anatomy of a Dream* (Brookings Institution Press 2015) 187–89 (hereafter Bastasin, *Saving Europe*).

[64] According to Bastasin, *Saving Europe* (n 63) 187: 'At 2:42 p.m. New York time (8:42 PM in Lisbon) with the Dow Jones down more than 300 points for the day, the equity markets began to fall rapidly, dropping more than 600 points in five minutes for an almost 1000 point loss by 2:47 p.m. It was the largest intraday loss in the history of Wall Street.'

[65] Bastasin, *Saving Europe* (n 63) 187–88.

[66] ibid 188.

[67] Quoted in Tony Barber, 'Dinner on the edge of the abyss' *Financial Times* (11 October 2010).

[68] Quoted in Peter Ludlow, 'In the Last Resort: The European Council and the Euro Crisis, Spring 2010' (Eurocomment Briefing Note, vol 7, no 7/8) 32 (hereafter Ludlow, 'In the Last Resort').

[69] Quoted in Ludlow, 'In the Last Resort' (n 68) 32.

message resonated with the leaders. In the statement they issued after the meeting, they did not refer to particular ECB measures, instead confining themselves to saying that they supported the institution 'in its action to ensure the stability of the euro area'.[70]

Securing the independence of the ECB only partly explains Trichet's position at the meeting. More important was the need to get euro area leaders to agree on the creation of an assistance fund. Not only because Trichet thereby addressed the issue of 'moral hazard', that is: the risk that the leaders would shift the burden of helping out distressed Member States entirely to the ECB. He also needed their action to enable his own institution to step in. By intervening in government bond markets, after all, the ECB would act on a stability conception fundamentally different from the one that had provided the basis for its original mandate. Only the commitment of the leaders to safeguard financial stability, and confirmation of it in practice, could generate the political backing required for this unparalleled step.

And so it happened. In the early morning of Monday 10 May, euro area finance ministers, who had been put to work by the leaders to hammer out a deal, reached agreement on an assistance fund for the currency union of €500 billion.[71] Shortly thereafter, the ECB announced its decision to purchase government bonds on the basis of the Securities Markets Programme.[72] The programme had been devised in such a way as to make the departure from its original mandate as limited as possible. The ECB could only buy government bonds on the secondary market, not on the primary one, which the prohibition on monetary financing in Article 123 TFEU declares forbidden territory.[73] Moreover, the ECB motivated the programme by the necessity to 'restore an appropriate monetary policy transmission' and thereby secure its ability to safeguard price stability.[74] Finally, any liquidity 'injected' through the bond purchases would be 'sterilised'. This means it would be compensated for by absorbing measures in order to minimize its impact on 'the monetary policy stance' and the inflation target.[75]

[70] European Council, 'Statement of the Heads of State or Government in the euro area' (Brussels, 7 May 2010) <https://www.consilium.europa.eu/media/21430/20100507-statement-of-the-heads-of-state-or-government-of-the-euro-area-en.pdf> accessed 13 July 2021 (hereafter Statement of the Heads of State or Government in the euro area 7 May 2010).

[71] Council of the European Union, 'Decision of the Representatives of the Governments of the Euro Area Member States Meeting Within the Council of the European Union' (Brussels, 10 May 2010, no 9614/10) <https://data.consilium.europa.eu/doc/document/ST%209614%202010%20INIT/EN/pdf> accessed 13 July 2021. For a detailed analysis of the legal nature of this assistance fund, which was partly given shape on the basis of Union law and partly through intergovernmental action, see Borger, *The Currency of Solidarity* (n 4) 229–35.

[72] European Central Bank, 'ECB decides on measures to address severe tensions in financial markets' (ECB Press Release, 10 May 2010) <https://www.ecb.europa.eu/press/pr/date/2010/html/pr100510.en.html> accessed 13 July 2021 (hereafter ECB Press Release 10 May 2010). It is not entirely clear whether the SMP was announced once the finance ministers had decided to establish an assistance fund, or only after they had also announced that decision. Ludlow, 'In the Last Resort' (n 68) 37 takes the former view, whereas the latter is followed by Irwin, *The Alchemists* (n 63) 230 and Bastasin, *Saving Europe* (n 63) 201.

[73] Decision ECB/2010/5 (n 2) Art 1. See also ECB Press Release 10 May 2010 (n 72).

[74] Decision ECB/2010/5 (n 2) recital 3.

[75] ECB Press Release 10 May 2010 (n 72).

B. Outright Monetary Transactions

The Securities Markets Programme brought some temporary relief to the markets, but it did not put a definitive end to the crisis.[76] Yet something else bothered the ECB even more. When it had launched the programme, it had made the use of that instrument conditional on budgetary consolidation by the Member States. Following their meeting on 7 May, political leaders had issued a statement saying that they considered 'the consolidation of public finances' to be a 'priority'.[77] In the preamble to its decision on the programme, the ECB had 'taken note' of that statement,[78] indicating it would stop its bond purchases if Member States would not consolidate their budgets. This strategy put the ECB in an impossible position once it became clear that Member States failed to deliver on their commitment to consolidate their fiscal records. It had to intervene in government bond markets for the sake of financial stability, yet by doing so, it risked rewarding Member States for negligent economic policies.[79] The fix in which the ECB had gotten itself into became painfully apparent in August 2011, when it felt it had to send letters—on a confidential basis—to the governments of Italy and Spain with detailed descriptions of the reform measures it considered important.[80] When they subsequently announced new reforms, the ECB published a statement saying it 'welcomed' the measures and indicated it would 'actively implement its Securities Markets Programme'.[81]

The more uncomfortable the position of the ECB became, however, the more calls for greater government bond market intervention swelled, especially after markets had started to draw a bead on Spain and Italy in the autumn of 2011. When Mario Draghi took over at the helm of the ECB in November that year, he created the impression he was prepared to answer those calls, provided the Member States would act first. In his first visit as ECB President to the European Parliament, he pleaded in favour of a 'fiscal compact', a 'fundamental restatement of the fiscal rules' in the currency union.[82] But when euro area leaders decided at their meeting of 8–9 December 2011 to provide for such a compact by taking the initiative for a balanced budget rule in national constitutions,[83] which would ultimately result in the Treaty on Stability,

[76] The following discussion of the interaction between national political leaders and the ECB in the run-up to the OMT programme is based on the one in Borger, *The Currency of Solidarity* (n 4) 182–87, 268–89.

[77] Statement of the Heads of State or Government in the euro area 7 May 2010 (n 70).

[78] Decision ECB/2010/5 (n 2) recital 4.

[79] Bastasin, *Saving Europe* (n 63) 302.

[80] The letter to the Italian government can be found at <www.corriere.it/economia/11_settembre_29/trichet_draghi_inglese_304a5f1e-ea59-11e0-ae06-4da866778017.shtml> accessed on 13 July 2021. The letter to the Spanish government did not become public. For more information about the letters, see Irwin, *The Alchemists* (n 63) 317–21; Bastasin, *Saving Europe* (n 63) 284–91.

[81] European Central Bank, 'Statement by the President of the ECB' (Frankfurt am Main, 7 August 2011) <https://www.ecb.europa.eu/press/pr/date/2011/html/pr110807.en.html> accessed 13 July 2021. The reforms that were implemented would ultimately fall short of expectations. See Irwin, *The Alchemists* (n 63) 321–22; Bastasin, *Saving Europe* (n 63) 302, 305–07.

[82] Mario Draghi, 'Introductory Statement' (Hearing before the Plenary of the European Parliament on the occasion of the adoption of the Resolution on the ECB's 2010 Annual Report, Brussels, 1 December 2011) <https://www.ecb.europa.eu/press/key/date/2011/html/sp111201.en.html> accessed 13 July 2021.

[83] European Council, 'Statement by the euro area Heads of State or Government' (Brussels, 9 December 2011) <https://www.consilium.europa.eu/uedocs/cms_data/docs/pressdata/en/ec/126658.pdf> accessed 13 July 2021.

Coordination and Governance,[84] ECB action fell short of expectations. It introduced two 'longer-term refinancing operations',[85] which would ultimately allot as much as €1 trillion,[86] yet it did not intensify its government bond purchases. When Draghi, on 19 December 2011, subsequently spoke on the occasion of the quarterly monetary dialogue with the European Parliament, he argued more was needed: 'I think there is a basic fact here that, if you want confidence to return, trust has to return in the euro area ... To achieve that, we have to have in place the proper "compact" which I referred to *at that time* only as far as budgetary matters are concerned ....'[87] At the next dialogue in April 2012, he explained what this restoration of trust required:

> [I]t is not the time to defend the existing situation. It is the time to project what our future design is going to be; it is the time to give a long-term objective to our vision and to say at the same time what conditions have to be implemented in order for this to become reality. It has been done before; it was done at the time of the Maastricht Treaty; it was done at the time of the euro. People established a path ten or fifteen years in advance and then listed the conditions that ought to be satisfied to reach the end of this path. I think we are in a similar situation.[88]

Early in the sovereign debt crisis, political leaders had been working hard to address the immediate consequences of the change in the currency union's stability conception they had set in motion on 11 February 2010. Now, they needed to extend their horizon to the long-term consequences of this change. Draghi himself indicated what he thought this entailed:

> I see financial stability clearly as a common responsibility in a monetary union. During the crisis, we have observed strong negative spill-over effects across euro area countries and between the banking sector and its respective sovereign ... Ensuring a well-functioning European Monetary Union implies strengthening banking supervision and resolution at European level.[89]

Draghi raised an important point. One of the main reasons for the currency union's inability to overcome the crisis concerned the fact that euro area states and banks were

[84] Treaty on Stability, Coordination and Governance in the Economic and Monetary Union, Brussels, 2 March 2012.

[85] Mario Draghi, 'Introductory Statement to the Press Conference (with Q&A)' (ECB Press Conference, Frankfurt am Main, 8 December 2011) <https://www.ecb.europa.eu/press/pressconf/2011/html/is111208.en.html> accessed 13 July 2021.

[86] For an assessment of the (short-term) effects of the refinancing operations on government bond rates, see Christiaan Pattipeilohy and others, 'Unconventional Monetary Policy of the ECB during the Financial Crisis: An Assessment and New Evidence' (2013) DNB Working Paper No 381, 31 <https://papers.ssrn.com/sol3/papers.cfm?abstract_id=2278838> accessed 13 July 2021.

[87] Committee on Economic and Monetary Affairs, 'Text of the Monetary Dialogue with Mario Draghi—President of the ECB' (Brussels, 19 December 2011) 8 (emphasis added).

[88] Committee on Economic and Monetary Affairs, 'Text of the Monetary Dialogue with Mario Draghi—President of the ECB' (Brussels, 25 April 2012) 14 (hereafter 'Text of the Monetary Dialogue with Draghi of 25 April 2012').

[89] ibid 7.

holding each other in a vicious 'embrace'.[90] Banks had heavily invested in government bonds of the Member States in whose jurisdiction they were established, whereas these States were responsible for rescuing such banks.[91] This proved to be a major source for systemic instability. Member States often had no option but to rescue banks that were on the brink of collapse, especially when they were thought to be 'too big to fail'.[92] But such rescue actions had a disastrous effect on their own fiscal records, as private debt shifted into public hands. At the same time, because of their 'sovereign exposure', banks could also be in serious trouble when a Member State came under fire in the markets and interest rates on its government bonds rose.[93]

A month after Draghi had stressed the need for a long-term vision for the currency union, at an informal European Council meeting on 23 May 2012, then President of the European Council, Herman Van Rompuy, was tasked by his colleagues to prepare a report, to be presented to them in June, on how to 'strengthen the economic union to make it commensurate with the monetary union'.[94] The situation in the markets, meanwhile, became untenable. Spain especially found itself on the edge of the abyss. Prior to the crisis, its fiscal record had been in line with the rules of the Stability and Growth Pact, yet due to a property bubble and ailing banking sector it now experienced a steep rise in the interest rates for its government bonds.[95] But the Spanish government was not keen on requesting financial assistance. The currency union's temporary rescue fund, the European Financial Stability Facility, as well as its future replacement, the European Stability Mechanism, could only indirectly assist in the recapitalization of banks: financial support first had to be given to a Member State, which could subsequently transfer it to banks.[96] Such assistance would consequently lead to a deterioration of a State's fiscal position and further stir up marked panic.

This was also precisely what happened when, on 9 June 2012, the Eurogroup finally announced that Spain was considering asking for recapitalization assistance worth €100 billion.[97] In the following days, interest rates for Spanish government bonds reached dangerously high levels.[98] It caused the Spanish Prime Minister Rajoy to plead

[90] Hans Geeroms, Stefaan Ide, and Frank Naert, *The European Union and the Euro: How to Deal with a Currency Built on Dreams* (Intersentia 2014) 172 (hereafter Geeroms, Ide, and Naert, *The European Union and the Euro*).

[91] Jean Pisany-Ferry, 'The Euro Crisis and the New Impossible Trinity' (2012) Bruegel Policy Contribution No 01, 6–7 <https://www.bruegel.org/wp-content/uploads/imported/publications/pc_2012_01_.pdf> accessed 13 July 2021 (hereafter Pisany-Ferry, 'The Euro Crisis and the New Impossible Trinity').

[92] Geeroms, Ide, and Naert, *The European Union and the Euro* (n 90) 173–74.

[93] Pisany-Ferry, 'The Euro Crisis and the New Impossible Trinity' (n 91) 7.

[94] European Council, 'Remarks by President of the European Council Herman Van Rompuy following the informal dinner of the members of the European Council' (Brussels, 24 May 2012) <https://www.consilium.europa.eu/uedocs/cms_Data/docs/pressdata/en/ec/130376.pdf> accessed 13 July 2021.

[95] For an analysis of the crisis in Spain, see Angel Gavilán and others, 'The Crisis in Spain: Origin and Developments' in Miroslav Beblavý, David Cobham, and Ľudovít Ódor (eds), *The Euro Area and the Financial Crisis* (CUP 2011) 81 ff.

[96] Consolidated Version of the EFSF Framework Agreement between the euro area Member States and the EFSF, recital 2 preamble; Treaty establishing the European Stability Mechanism [2012] T/ESM 2012-LT, Art 15 (hereafter ESM Treaty). Note that a revised version of the ESM Treaty was signed on 27 January and 8 February 2021. The contracting parties to the ESM Treaty signed an Agreement Amending the Treaty, which is now awaiting ratification.

[97] Eurogroup, 'Eurogroup statement on Spain' (Brussels, 9 June 2012) <https://www.bde.es/f/webbde/Secciones/SalaPrensa/Relacionados/eurogroup090612e.pdf> accessed 13 July 2021.

[98] Mary Watkins, 'Spanish bond yields rise sharply' *Financial Times* (London, 12 June 2012).

for greater central bank involvement. In a letter to Van Rompuy about the future of the euro, he wrote: 'The only institution which today has the capacity to ensure these conditions of stability and liquidity that we need is the ECB.'[99]

The report that Van Rompuy presented in the run-up to a European Council and Euro Summit meeting on 28 and 29 June, entitled 'Towards a Genuine Economic and Monetary Union', paid significant tribute to Draghi's call for a long-term vision on financial stability. One of its suggested reforms was an 'integrated financial framework', which should rest on three foundations: single banking supervision, a European resolution scheme, and a common deposit and insurance framework.[100] In the report, Van Rompuy stated that he could submit a 'specific and time-bound road map' for the realization of the plans in December 2012,[101] yet political leaders realized that instant action was required. Prior to the meeting, on 22 June, those of Germany, France, Italy, and Spain convened in Rome. There, the contours of a trade-off became visible: Chancellor Merkel made it clear she could support direct recapitalization of Spanish banks on the condition that it was accompanied by structural reform.[102] On 26 June, in Paris, their finance ministers further specified the deal.[103] The German Finance Minister Schäuble suggested that the currency union's permanent assistance fund, the ESM, should have the possibility to directly recapitalize banks, provided they were overseen by a European supervisor.

When the political leaders gathered for their European Council and Euro Summit meeting on 28 June, two contentious issues still had to be hammered out. The first concerned the question when the ESM would be able to engage in direct recapitalization.[104] Spain's Prime Minister Rajoy wished the instrument to be available instantly, whereas Chancellor Merkel insisted that a supervisory mechanism had to be established first. Ultimately, they settled for the compromise that the Council would 'consider' legislative proposals for a supervisory mechanism 'as a matter of urgency by the end of 2012'.[105] The second issue concerned the legal basis for the mechanism.[106] As Van Rompuy had already suggested in his report,[107] the leaders opted for Article 127(6) TFEU.[108] This provision allows the Council to confer upon the ECB specific tasks concerning the supervision of credit institutions.

[99] Quoted in Victor Mallet, 'Rajoy urges battle for euro's survival' *Financial Times* (Madrid, 13 June 2012).

[100] European Council, 'Towards a Genuine Economic and Monetary Union. Report by President of the European Council Herman Van Rompuy' (Brussels, 26 June 2012) 4–5 <https://www.consilium.europa.eu/media/21570/131201.pdf> accessed 13 July 2021 (hereafter 'Towards a Genuine EMU Report June 2012').

[101] ibid 7.

[102] Peter Ludlow, 'Short-Term Help and Long-Term Conditionality: The European Council of 28-29 June 2012' (Eurocomment no 4, 2012) 8 (hereafter Ludlow, 'Short-Term Help'); Pierre de Boissieu and others, *National Leaders and the Making of Europe: Key Episodes in the Life of the European Council* (John Harper Publishing 2015) 266 (hereafter de Boissieu and others, *National Leaders*); Bastasin, *Saving Europe* (n 63) 380.

[103] Ludlow, 'Short-Term Help' (n 102) 9; de Boissieu and others, *National Leaders* (n 102) 266–67; Bastasin, *Saving Europe* (n 63) 380.

[104] Ludlow, 'Short-Term Help' (n 102) 20–21; de Boissieu and others, *National Leaders* (n 102) 271.

[105] European Council, 'Euro Summit statement' (Brussels, 29 June 2012) point 1 <https://www.consilium.europa.eu/media/21400/20120629-euro-area-summit-statement-en.pdf> accessed 13 July 2021 (hereafter Euro Summit statement 29 June 2012).

[106] Ludlow, 'Short-Term Help' (n 102) 21; de Boissieu and others, *National Leaders* (n 102) 271.

[107] Towards a Genuine EMU Report June 2012 (n 100) 4.

[108] Euro Summit statement 29 June 2012 (n 105), point 1.

It was a ground-breaking deal. The leaders had managed to secure the currency union's short-term needs by allowing the ESM to directly recapitalize banks, whilst at the same time initiating much needed structural reform through the establishment of the Single Supervisory Mechanism, the first step towards a Banking Union.[109] After the deal had become public, market sentiment immediately improved as Spanish and Italian bond prices rose significantly.[110] When the next day ECB President Draghi saw Van Rompuy in his office prior to the final deliberations of the meeting, he said to him: 'Herman, do you realise what you all did last night? This is the game-changer we need.'[111] Or in Van Rompuy's words: 'The commitment of political leaders to European banking supervision created the opening *he* [Draghi, ed.] needed for his own institution to step up its role in the crisis.'[112]

A month later, Draghi would act. Speaking at the Global Investment Conference in London on 26 July, he told his audience: 'When people talk about the fragility of the euro … and perhaps the crisis of the euro, very often non-euro area member states or leaders, underestimate the amount of political capital that is being invested in the euro. And so we view this, and I do not think we are unbiased observers, we think the euro is irreversible.'[113] 'But there is another message I want to tell you', he then said:

> Within our mandate, the ECB is ready to do whatever it takes to preserve the euro. And believe me, it will be enough.[114]

In the days after the announcement, interest rates for Spanish and Italian government bonds, which had gone up again after the June meeting of the leaders, declined sharply.[115]

Draghi's 'whatever it takes' pledge had been an act of improvisation: he had put the words into the script of his speech just before he entered the stage.[116] The ECB's Governing Council had consequently been unaware of it. It therefore took some time for the ECB to put flesh on the pledge.[117] But on 6 September 2012, the Governing

[109] The Single Supervisory Mechanism became operational in November 2014. On 8 December 2014 the ESM Board of Governors subsequently decided to add the instrument of direct recapitalization assistance to the ESM's toolbox on the basis of ESM Treaty (n 96) Art 19. See also chapter 7 by Kern Alexander, in this volume.

[110] Hugh Carnegy, Peter Spiegel, and Quentin Peel, 'Markets rebound after Eurozone deal' *Financial Times* (Brussels, 29 June 2012) <https://www.ft.com/content/830ed6a2-c1eb-11e1-b76a-00144feabdc0> accessed 13 July 2021.

[111] Quoted in Van Rompuy, *Europe in the Storm* (n 55) 21.

[112] Van Rompuy, *Europe in the Storm* (n 55) 21. See also de Boissieu and others, *National Leaders* (n 102) 272–73.

[113] Mario Draghi, 'Verbatim of the remarks made by Mario Draghi' (Speech at the Global Investment Conference, London, 26 July 2012) <https://www.ecb.europa.eu/press/key/date/2012/html/sp120726.en.html> accessed 13 July 2021.

[114] ibid.

[115] Dave Shellock, 'ECB pledge to preserve euro fires up markets' *Financial Times* (28 July 2012).

[116] Irwin, *The Alchemists* (n 63) 380.

[117] At the press conference of 2 August 2012, Draghi already indicated that the Eurosystem was considering conducting outright purchases of government bonds so as to get markets out of a 'bad' equilibrium and push down 'exceptionally high risk premia' that were caused by 'fears about the reversibility of the euro' and were negatively affecting the singleness and transmission of its monetary policy. See Mario Draghi and Vítor Constâncio, 'Introductory Statement to the Press Conference (with Q&A)' (ECB Press Conference, Frankfurt am Main, 2 August 2012) <https://www.ecb.europa.eu/press/pressconf/2012/html/is120802.en.html> accessed 13 July 2021.

Council decided on the main elements of its Outright Monetary Transactions and announced them in a press release.[118] Like the Securities Markets Programme, which was stopped immediately, the instrument allowed the Eurosystem to intervene in secondary government bond markets. This time, too, any injected liquidity was 'sterilized'. Compared to its predecessor, however, the OMT programme had undergone some essential changes to boost its effectiveness. First, to fight speculation, there were no 'ex ante quantitative limits' imposed on the amount of purchases.[119] Second, interventions were concentrated on the 'shorter part of the yield curve', that is: on bonds with a maturity between one and three years.[120] Third, to stimulate other investors to keep purchasing government bonds as well, the Eurosystem would rank '*pari passu*'.[121] Fourth, purchases could only take place when the beneficiary Member State had signed up to an ESM 'macroeconomic adjustment programme' or a 'precautionary programme'.[122] This requirement sought to prevent, as had happened under the SMP, that Member States would no longer feel the need to reform their economies once the ECB would purchase their bonds.[123] The moment a Member State no longer abided by ESM conditionality, the purchases would stop. Apart from that, the ECB could cease its purchases, just as it could initiate them, 'in full discretion' with a view to fulfilling its mandate.[124]

The OMT programme has never been activated. What is more, it has not even been incorporated into a legal act. Its proclamation sufficed to calm down markets that for more than two years had been spiralling out of control.[125]

IV. Reconciling the New Stability Conception with the Law

A. The mandate

Before the launch of the programme,[126] right after becoming ECB President in November 2011, President Draghi had stated that he did not think that being a Lender

[118] European Central Bank, 'Technical features of Outright Monetary Transactions' (ECB Press Release, 6 September 2012) <https://www.ecb.europa.eu/press/pr/date/2012/html/pr120906_1.en.html> accessed 13 July 2021 (hereafter ECB Press Release 6 September 2012).

[119] ibid.

[120] ibid.

[121] ibid.

[122] ibid.

[123] See text to n 76.

[124] ECB Press Release 6 September 2012 (n 118).

[125] See also David Quinn, 'The Law and Norms of the European Central Bank as Sovereign Lender of Last Resort: Crystallising Endogenous Authority' (2021) 17 EuConst 78, 103: 'In the eyes of the audience (market actors), the commitment of the Bank to save the euro, along with its technical ability to do so via OMT, removed any doubt about the operational lender of last resort norm; the Bank would act as *de facto* lender of last resort, albeit one only operating on secondary bond markets and subject to certain conditions ....'

[126] The following discussion of how the Court of Justice managed to reconcile the currency union's new stability conception with the mandate of the ECB is based on the one in Borger, *The Currency of Solidarity* (n 4) 162–65, 197–200, 321–37.

of Last Resort for governments was 'within the remit of the ECB'.[127] 'The remit of the ECB', he had argued, 'is maintaining price stability over the medium term'.[128] When he announced the OMT programme in September 2012, he stuck to that reasoning. In line with economists like De Grauwe,[129] he pointed out that the currency union was experiencing a self-fulfilling crisis:

> [T]he assessment of the Governing Council is that we are in a situation now where you have large parts of the euro area in what we call 'a bad equilibrium', namely an equilibrium where you may have self-fulfilling expectations that feed upon themselves and generate very adverse scenarios. So, there is a case for intervening, in a sense, to 'break' these expectations, which, by the way, do not concern only specific countries, but the euro area as a whole.[130]

The ECB maintained, however, that this did not mean that it was acting as a Lender of Last Resort for states. It did target financial stability, as ECB Executive Board Member Yves Mersch has argued, but only because this was justified by its primary goal to maintain price stability.[131] Under normal conditions, the 'signals' stemming from the ECB's policy rates are 'transmitted' to the 'real economy' through various 'channels'.[132] But in the summer of 2012 interest rates for certain government bonds had become very high, to the extent that they no longer reflected the fundamental economic condition of the issuing Member States, as a result of which these channels had become 'dysfunctional'.[133] This made it difficult for the ECB's policy rates to be transmitted evenly across the currency union. To secure their transmission, and in view of the ECB's contributory role in relation to the stability of the financial system in Article 127(5) TFEU, the ECB consequently decided to intervene in government bond markets and restore interest rates to levels reflecting the economic 'fundamentals' of Member States.[134] Yet, it did not seek to harmonize these interest rates across the board, nor guarantee that Member States would always be able to call on the ECB to satisfy their financing needs.

[127] Mario Draghi and Vítor Constâncio, 'Introductory Statement to the Press Conference (with Q&A)' (ECB Press Conference, Frankfurt am Main, 3 November 2011) <https://www.ecb.europa.eu/press/pressconf/2011/html/is111103.en.html> accessed 13 July 2021.

[128] ibid.

[129] See text to n 29.

[130] Mario Draghi and Vítor Constâncio, 'Introductory Statement to the Press Conference (with Q&A)' (ECB Press Conference, Frankfurt am Main, 6 September 2012) <https://www.ecb.europa.eu/press/pressconf/2012/html/is120906.en.html> accessed 13 July 2021.

[131] Mersch refers in this regard to the ESCB's contributory role in relation to the stability of the financial system set out in TFEU (n 21) Art 127(5). On that basis he argues that: '[F]inancial stability is not the ultimate aim of ECB policy but a means to fulfil its basic tasks. In principle, this applies to all the basic tasks of the ECB listed in Article 127(2) of the TFEU, but it is most important for monetary policy. Financial stability, namely the proper functioning of the financial system, is necessary for the transmission of monetary policy.' See Mersch, 'Speech at the ESCB Legal Conference of September 2018' (n 38).

[132] See extensively Philippine Cour-Thimann and Bernhard Winkler, 'The ECB's Non-standard Monetary Policy Measures: The Role of Institutional Factors and Financial Structure' (2012) 28 Oxford Review of Economic Policy 765, 774–75 (hereafter Cour-Thimann and Winkler, 'The ECB's Non-standard Monetary Policy Measures').

[133] ibid 774, 778.

[134] On 'fundamentals', see text to n 32.

But not everyone agreed with this view, not even within the Governing Council of the ECB. That was clearly visible when the OMT programme was challenged before Germany's Constitutional Court, the *Bundesverfassungsgericht*. During the proceedings, *Bundesbank* President Weidmann argued against the programme. He was not the first *Bundesbank* president critical of government bond purchases. His predecessor, Axel Weber, had resigned from office after the launch of the SMP.[135] Weidmann, however, did not leave office but openly voiced his criticism in court. At the oral hearing in Karlsruhe, he confirmed that the crisis had shown the significance of financial stability, but emphasized that the ECB could only pursue it within the constraints of its mandate.[136] Subsequently, he challenged the analysis of the ECB:

> Secondary market purchases in my understanding should, however, not aim at reducing the solvency risk premiums of specific states. For that would risk among other things to knock out the disciplining role of market rates and undermine individual responsibility for financial policy . . . The answer to the question whether investors accurately value the degree or risk associated with the bonds of specific Member States, is to a great extent subjective.[137]

The *Bundesbank* further explained its position in its written submissions. It considered it impossible to establish in how far interest rates for government bonds were in line with the economic fundamentals of the issuing state or driven by self-fulfilling fears among investors.[138] As it could thus be possible that these interest rates were economically sound, their heterogenous impact on monetary policy transmission should not by definition be dismissed as a deficiency.

Considering it highly likely that the OMT programme amounted to an ultra vires act in violation of the German Constitution, the *Bundesverfassungsgericht* referred—for the first time in its history—preliminary questions to the Court of Justice.[139] They concentrated on two central tenets of the ECB's constitutional position: its mandate in Article 127 TFEU and the prohibition on monetary financing in Article 123 TFEU. It is up for debate whether the Court of Justice should have gone into the merits of the case at all, considering that it was not in a position to strike down a government bond programme that had been crucial for the survival not only of the euro, but the Union itself. In fact, there are good reasons to argue that it should have declared the case a political question.[140] But in *Gauweiler* it did go into the merits and in so doing

[135] Daniel Schäfer, 'Weber says his hawkish views drove decision over ECB presidency' *Financial Times* (Frankfurt am Main, 14 February 2011). See also Irwin, *The Alchemists* (n 63) 298–301; Bastasin, *Saving Europe* (n 63) 243–44, 246.

[136] Jens Weidmann, 'Eingangserklärung anlässlich der mündlichen Verhandlung im Hauptsacheverfahren ESM/EZB' (Deutsche Bundesbank Press Release, Karlsruhe, 11 June 2013) <https://www.bundesbank.de/de/presse/stellungnahmen/eingangserklaerung-anlaesslich-der-muendlichen-verhandlung-im-hauptsacheverfahren-esm-ezb-662878> accessed 13 July 2021.

[137] ibid (translation by the author).

[138] Deutsche Bundesbank, 'Stellungnahme Bundesbank' (21 December 2012) <www.bundesbank.de/resource/blob/799684/14bcbdeda81af076aa78e40891f0997a/mL/2012-12-21-omt-data.pdf> accessed 13 July 2021.

[139] BVerfG, Order of the Second Senate of 14 January 2014 2 BvR 2728/13 ECLI:DE:BVerfG:2014:rs20140114.2bvr272813.

[140] Borger, *The Currency of Solidarity* (n 4) 362–71.

faced the challenge of reconciling the OMT programme with a legal set-up that still reflected a stability conception from the past.[141]

This became very apparent when the Court of Justice examined whether the programme fell within the ECB's mandate. Earlier in the crisis, when it had ruled on the legality of the ESM in *Pringle*,[142] it had stated that in order to determine whether a measure constitutes economic or monetary policy, one has to take into account its instruments and connections to other provisions of Union law, but especially its objectives.[143] This had meant that Article 136(3) TFEU, which had been inserted into the TFEU to make clear that Member States have the capacity to establish a mechanism like the ESM,[144] is a measure of economic policy. The Court of Justice had argued that its objective to safeguard the stability of the euro area, which it had equated with financial stability,[145] is 'clearly distinct' from maintaining price stability, the primary objective of monetary policy.[146] It had admitted that the stability of the euro area may have an impact on price stability within that area, yet had argued that 'an economic policy measure cannot be treated as equivalent to a monetary policy measure for the sole reason it may have indirect effects on the stability of the euro'.[147]

In *Gauweiler*, the Court of Justice used the reverse reasoning to conclude that the OMT programme constitutes monetary policy. By securing the singleness and transmission of monetary policy, it argued, the OMT programme supports the ECB in its effort to safeguard price stability and consequently belongs to monetary policy.[148] The fact that the programme may also positively impact on financial stability does not change that finding.[149] 'A monetary policy measure', the Court of Justice reasoned, 'cannot be treated as equivalent to an economic policy measure merely because it may have indirect effects on the stability of the euro area'.[150] Further down in its judgment, the Court of Justice even stated that in as far as it constitutes an objective, of an ultimate nature at least, this stability does not fall 'within monetary policy'.[151] It did concede that the ECB's assessment of the situation in government bond markets had been 'subject to challenge', and so recognized critical voices such as that of the *Bundesbank*, but only when it examined the programme's proportionality, after it had concluded that it belonged to the realm of monetary policy.[152] And the recognition was marginal

[141] Case C-62/14 *Peter Gauweiler and Others v Deutscher Bundestag* [2015] EU:C:2015:400 (hereafter *Gauweiler*).

[142] Case C-370/12 *Thomas Pringle v Government of Ireland and Others* [2012] EU:C:2012:756 (hereafter *Pringle*).

[143] ibid paras 53, 55.

[144] European Council Decision 2011/199/EU of 25 March 2011 amending Article 136 of the Treaty on the Functioning of the European Union with regard to a stability mechanism for Member States whose currency is the euro [2011] OJ L91/1.

[145] See, eg, *Pringle* (n 142) para 65 where the Court states in relation to TFEU (n 21) Art 136(3)—which only speaks about the *stability of the euro area*—that the objective of the mechanism it envisages is to safeguard the *financial stability* of this area. Likewise, in *Gauweiler* (n 141) para 64, it states that the ESM—whose purpose according to ESM Treaty (n 96) Art 3 is to secure the financial stability of the euro area as a whole and of its Member States—aims to safeguard *the stability of the euro area*.

[146] *Pringle* (n 142) para 56.

[147] ibid para 56.

[148] *Gauweiler* (n 141) paras 48–50.

[149] ibid para 51.

[150] ibid para 52.

[151] ibid para 64.

[152] ibid para 75.

as it was immediately followed up by the statement that 'questions of monetary policy are usually of a controversial nature' so that, in view of the ECB's broad discretion, which is only transgressed in case of a 'manifest error', 'nothing more' can be asked of it besides 'that it use its economic expertise ... with all care and accuracy'.[153]

Paradoxically, then, the Court of Justice managed to reconcile the OMT programme with the ECB's original mandate without explicitly recognizing the role that financial stability had come to play in the field of monetary policy. It was consequently even more in denial of the currency union's new stability conception than the ECB itself. Whereas the latter denied it had become a Lender of Last Resort for States, it did acknowledge that it targeted financial stability in view of its importance for the transmission of monetary policy. The Court of Justice followed that reasoning only implicitly by stating that the OMT programme constitutes monetary policy given its purpose to safeguard the transmission mechanism and ultimately price stability.

B. The prohibition on monetary financing

When examining compliance with the prohibition on monetary financing, the Court of Justice again drew inspiration from its judgment in *Pringle*.[154] In that case, it had used a three-pronged reasoning to assess whether the ESM complied with the no-bailout clause in Article 125 TFEU. It had first employed a literal reading of the clause. Given that it only speaks about liability for, or assumption of, financial commitments of a Member State, it does not prohibit any kind of financial assistance.[155] The Court of Justice had supported this finding by referring to the prohibition on monetary financing. Compared to the no-bailout clause, it had considered this prohibition much 'stricter' as it rules out 'overdraft facilities or any other type of credit facility'.[156] The Court of Justice had then adopted a purposive interpretation to discover what kinds of assistance the no-bailout clause does permit. It had argued that the clause seeks to submit Member States 'to the logic of the market when they enter into debt' and had consequently identified budgetary discipline as its aim.[157] Any assistance granted therefore needs to be subject to 'strict conditionality'.[158] But the Court of Justice had not stopped here. Instead, it had resorted to an ultima ratio reading of the clause and had argued that budgetary discipline does not constitute its sole purpose. 'Compliance with such discipline', it had reasoned, 'contributes at Union level to the attainment of a higher objective, namely maintaining the financial stability of the monetary union'.[159] Assistance is therefore only allowed if it is 'indispensable' to safeguard this stability.[160]

[153] ibid paras 74–75.

[154] The following discussion of how the Court of Justice managed to reconcile the currency union's new stability conception with the prohibition on monetary financing is based on the one in Borger, *The Currency of Solidarity* (n 4) 338–43.

[155] *Pringle* (n 142) para 130.

[156] ibid para 132.

[157] ibid para 135.

[158] ibid para 136.

[159] ibid para 135.

[160] ibid para 136.

It had been an explicit recognition of the currency union's widened stability conception and its quest for a Lender of Last Resort for States.

In *Gauweiler*, too, the Court of Justice started its interpretation of the prohibition on monetary financing with a textual reading. It fell back on its observation in *Pringle* that this prohibition is formulated more strictly than the no-bailout clause. By ruling out credit facilities and direct purchases of government bonds, the Court of Justice reasoned, it forbids all kinds of financial assistance by the ECB or National Central Banks to Member States.[161] The text of Article 123 TFEU does not prohibit bond purchases on the secondary market, however. This creates a risk that they are conducted in a way that amounts to direct purchases in disguise. The Court of Justice recognized this risk but noted that the ECB had sought to deal with it under the OMT programme.[162] First, there would be a 'minimum period' between the issuance of a bond on the primary market and its purchase by the ECB on the secondary market in order to enable the formation of a market price. Second, the ECB would not make any prior announcements on its decision to purchase or the volume of its intervention. Together, these conditions were such that the Court of Justice felt confident to conclude that the OMT programme would not 'have an effect equivalent to that of a direct purchase of government bonds'.[163]

Similar to its judgment in *Pringle*, the Court of Justice then resorted to a purposive analysis to further determine the permissibility of secondary market purchases.[164] It noted that, like the no-bailout clause, the prohibition on monetary financing seeks to promote budgetary discipline.[165] Thereafter, it pointed to several characteristics of the OMT programme indicating respect for this purpose. Four of them are especially relevant. First, purchases can only take place in so far as they are required to secure the transmission of monetary policy.[166] Member States can consequently not be certain that the ECB will buy their bonds, nor that interest rates for these bonds will be brought down to levels below those justified by their economic fundamentals. This means that market discipline, at least to some extent, remains in place. Second, by restricting purchases to government bonds with a particular maturity, the ECB has '*de facto*' limited the amount of eligible bonds and the effect their purchase may have on the 'financing conditions' of Member States.[167] Third, given that the ECB decides on the initiation and continuation of bond market interventions 'in full discretion', it has the ability to cease them if it notices that a Member State is trying to 'finance its budget' by excessively issuing bonds eligible for purchase.[168] Fourth, by tying purchases to the condition that beneficiary Member States are subject to an ESM

[161] *Gauweiler* (n 141) paras 94–95.
[162] ibid paras 105–06.
[163] ibid para 107.
[164] In this regard, see also Council Regulation (EC) 3603/93 of 13 December 1993 specifying definitions for the application of the prohibition referred to in Articles 104 and 104(b)(1) of the Treaty [1993] OJ L332/1. The 7th recital of this Regulation makes clear that government bond purchases on the secondary market may not serve 'to circumvent the objective' of TFEU (n 21) Art 123 (ex Art 104 EC).
[165] *Gauweiler* (n 141) paras 99–102.
[166] ibid paras 112–14.
[167] ibid para 116.
[168] ibid para 117.

adjustment programme, the ECB mitigates the risk that they serve as an engine for unsound budgetary policies.[169]

Unlike it had done in *Pringle* in relation to the ESM, however, the Court of Justice did not go on to connect budgetary discipline to the higher calling of financial stability and thereby recognize the OMT programme's character as a Lender of Last Resort instrument. The omission of this third step was a natural consequence of the reasoning it had employed earlier in the judgment to delimit the ECB's mandate. By confining financial stability, at least as an ultimate objective, to the realm of economic policy, with no role to play in monetary policy, the Court of Justice made it impossible to state that government bond purchases are allowed if they are indispensable to safeguard financial stability. On this point too, then, it reconciled the OMT programme with the ECB's original legal set-up without explicitly recognizing the implications of the currency union's widened stability conception.

V. Judicial Review of the New ECB

The decision by the heads of state or government of 11 February 2010 set in motion a fundamental transformation of the currency union, with profound consequences for the ECB. From a central bank with a mandate largely constrained to price stability, it became a guardian of financial stability, which even acts as a Lender of Last Resort for States to secure it. By approving the OMT programme in *Gauweiler*, the Court of Justice reconciled this change with the currency union's original legal set-up and thereby sealed the transformation. In doing so, it also more generally endorsed the ECB's capacity for substantial government bond market intervention. This capacity brings with it a repositioning vis-à-vis other constitutional actors, not least courts.[170] The case of *Weiss*, which equally concerned the purchase of government bonds, illustrates this.[171]

In June 2016, the German Constitutional Court grudgingly accepted the Court of Justice's judgment in *Gauweiler*.[172] It held the OMT programme to be in compliance with the ECB's mandate, yet raised 'serious objections' against the reasoning of the Court of Justice.[173] In particular, the fact that it had accepted the ECB's argument that the programme is within its mandate 'without questioning or at least discussing ... the soundness of the underlying factual assumptions, and without testing

[169] ibid para 120.

[170] The following discussion of the ECB's repositioning vis-à-vis courts is based on those in Borger, *The Currency of Solidarity* (n 4) 343–48; Vestert Borger, 'Central Bank Independence, Discretion and Judicial Review' in Ioana Mendes (ed), *EU Executive Discretion and the Limits of Law* (OUP 2019) (hereafter Borger, 'Central Bank Independence, Discretion and Judicial Review'); Stefaan Van Den Bogaert and Vestert Borger, 'Hoog spel in Karlsruhe: Het Duitse Constitutionele Hof over het Public Sector Purchase Programme van de ECB' (2020) 95 Nederlands juristenblad 2978 (hereafter Van Den Bogaert and Borger, 'Hoog spel in Karlsruhe').

[171] Case C-493/17 *Proceedings brought by Heinrich Weiss and Others* [2018] EU:C:2018:1000 (hereafter *Weiss*).

[172] BVerfG, Judgment of the Second Senate of 21 June 2016 2 BvR 2728/13 ECLI:DE:BVerfG:2016:rs2016 0621.2bvr272813 (hereafter BVerfG *final OMT judgment*).

[173] ibid para 181.

these assumptions against indications that evidently argue against a character of monetary policy' was a thorn in its side.[174] This was all the more so given the independence of the ECB. Two decades earlier, when the German Constitutional Court had ruled on the constitutionality of the Treaty of Maastricht, it had considered this independence a central guarantee for the existence of the currency union as a *Stabilitätsgemeinschaft*, a community based on stability.[175] But now the tone was starkly different. The independence of the ECB severely weakens the 'democratic legitimation of its actions', it argued, and therefore warrants a 'particularly strict judicial review' of its mandate.[176]

These concerns came back with a vengeance a year later, in July 2017, when the German Constitutional Court had to determine whether the ECB acted ultra vires with its 'Public Sector Purchase Programme' (PSPP).[177] The ECB had launched that programme in March 2015 when the currency union had left the worst of the debt crisis behind it. Contrary to the OMT programme, the PSPP was not intended as a last resort instrument but as a means to tackle a different problem: deflation. In the preceding years, the ECB had been lowering its key policy rates, to the extent that they had reached the 'zero lower bound' and risked losing their usefulness as a tool to steer inflation. The ECB had therefore decided to engage in quantitative easing.[178] This means that it purchases securities and thereby expands the amount of money in circulation, which should spur investment and consumption, economic growth, and ultimately inflation.

The PSPP is one of several programmes that the ECB uses to conduct these purchases.[179] Together they constitute the 'Expanded Asset Purchase Programme' (EAPP).[180] After the EAPP had ceased to operate in December 2018, it was reactivated on 1 November 2019.[181] It remains in force as long as is necessary. Monthly net purchases currently stand at €20 billion.[182] The largest share of these purchases takes place in the context of the PSPP, which allows the ECB to buy public securities, including government bonds.[183]

Economically, quantitative easing is closer to the ECB's core task of safeguarding price stability compared to the OMT programme, certainly when judged by the number of central banks that have resorted to it. Over the past decade, central banks

[174] ibid para 182.

[175] BVerfG, Judgment of the Second Senate of 12 October 1993 2 BvR 2134/92, para 80.

[176] BVerfG *final OMT judgment* (n 172) para 187.

[177] BVerfG, Order of the Second Senate of 18 July 2017 2 BvR 859/15 ECLI:DE:BVerfG:2017:rs20170718.2bvr085915 (hereafter BVerfG *PSPP reference decision*).

[178] See further on quantitative easing chapter 3 by Klaus Tuori, in this volume.

[179] The PSPP programme was originally laid down in Decision (EU) 2015/774 of the ECB of 4 March 2015 on a secondary markets public sector asset purchase programme (ECB/2015/10) [2015] OJ L121/20, as last amended by Decision (EU) 2017/100 of the ECB of 11 January 2017 OJ L16/51. That Decision was subsequently replaced by Decision (EU) 2020/188 of the ECB of 3 February 2020 on a secondary markets public sector asset purchase programme (ECB/2020/9) [2020] OJ L39/12.

[180] The other programmes are the 'Third Covered Bond Purchase Programme' (CBPP3), the 'Asset-Backed Securities Purchase Programme' (ABSPP), and the 'Corporate Sector Purchase Programme' (CSPP).

[181] European Central Bank, 'Monetary policy decisions' (ECB Press Release, 12 September 2019) <https://www.ecb.europa.eu/press/pr/date/2019/html/ecb.mp190912~08de50b4d2.en.html> accessed 13 July 2021.

[182] The monthly amount of purchase has varied from €15 billion to €80 billion over time.

[183] A current overview of the cumulative net purchases under the EAPP is available on <www.ecb.europa.eu/mopo/implement/app/html/index.en.html> accessed 13 July 2021.

around the globe, from Japan to the United States and the United Kingdom, have engaged in quantitative easing. Still, the German Constitutional Court referred preliminary questions about the PSPP to the Court of Justice. These questions again concerned the ECB's mandate in Article 127 TFEU and the prohibition on monetary financing in Article 123 TFEU. Of these two, the mandate was the centre of attention. In its judgment in *Weiss*, the Court of Justice resorted to the same reasoning it had used in *Gauweiler* to determine the policy nature of the programme, which meant it attributed central importance to objectives.[184] It noted that the PSPP has as its aim to bring inflation back to levels close to, but below, 2 per cent over the medium term and is therefore in line with the ECB's primary objective to maintain price stability. Together with the fact that Article 18 of the Statute of the ECB specifically allows for outright purchases of government bonds, this shows that the programme constitutes monetary policy.[185]

The reasoning of the Court of Justice did contain an interesting evolution, however. While it still attributed overriding importance to objectives to determine whether the PSPP falls within the mandate of the ECB, it also sought to ease the distinction between economic and monetary policy.[186] 'The authors of the Treaties', it argued, 'did not intend to make an absolute separation between economic and monetary policies'.[187] This made sense from a legal point of view.[188] Article 127(1) TFEU not only refers to price stability but also to objectives of economic policy. It is therefore hardly possible to identify the limits to the mandate of the ECB on the basis of a measure's policy nature, especially not by having regard to its objectives. In combination with the wide discretion granted to the ECB, which led the Court of Justice to again state that 'nothing more' can be asked of it apart from the fact that it use its expertise 'with all care and accuracy',[189] this watering down of the distinction between economic and monetary policy does result in significant freedom of action for the ECB.

The German Constitutional Court, however, doubled down on the distinction between economic and monetary policy. What is more, it even gave a twist to the approach the Court of Justice had used to distinguish the two policies. In its reference decision of 2017, it had argued that economic policy effects can no longer be seen as indirect, without consequences for a measure's classification as monetary policy, if 'they are intended or deliberately accepted, and these effects are at least comparable in weight to the monetary policy objective pursued'.[190] That would be the case for the PSPP, given its impact on the balance sheets of commercial banks and the refinancing conditions of Member States.[191] In its final judgment of May 2020, it lambasted

[184] *Weiss* (n 171) para 53.
[185] ibid paras 69–70.
[186] Borger, *The Currency of Solidarity* (n 4) 336–37, 347–48; Van Den Bogaert and Borger, 'Hoog spel in Karlsruhe' (n 170) 2983.
[187] *Weiss* (n 171) para 60.
[188] Borger, *The Currency of Solidarity* (n 4) 336–37.
[189] *Weiss* (n 171) para 91.
[190] BVerfG *PSPP reference decision* (n 177) para 119.
[191] ibid paras 120–21.

the Court of Justice for not having recognized this concern and again criticized it for 'simply accepting' the ECB's assertion that the PSPP has a monetary policy objective.[192]

And its criticism did not stop here. The German Constitutional Court also argued that, regardless of the question about the policy nature of the PSPP's objectives, its economic policy effects might be of such significance that they are disproportionate when weighted against its official monetary objective, with the result that the programme would fall outside the mandate of the ECB.[193] Yet, the Court of Justice had only conducted a proportionality assessment after it had established that the PSPP constitutes monetary policy.[194] And it had limited this assessment to verifying whether the programme went 'manifestly' beyond what was necessary to achieve its objective.[195] In the eyes of the German Constitutional Court, this rendered its proportionality assessment 'meaningless'.[196] Together with the broad discretion granted to the ECB, it meant the Court of Justice basically allowed 'the ECB ... to expand its competences on its own authority', in defiance of the principle of conferral.[197] The German Constitutional Court therefore saw no option but to conclude that the Court of Justice *itself* had acted ultra vires.[198] It then took matters into its own hands and concluded that also the ECB had acted ultra vires by failing to substantiate the PSPP's proportionality.[199] It required the German government and parliament to 'take steps seeking to ensure that the ECB conducts a proportionality assessment' within three months, on pain of the *Bundesbank* having to cease its participation in the programme.[200]

The reasoning of the German Constitutional Court left much to be desired. It appears unfeasible to determine when a measure's economic policy effects are such that they overshadow its monetary objective.[201] Moreover, by using the principle of proportionality to identify limits to the competence of the ECB, the Constitutional Court seems to confuse it with the principle of conferral.[202] Yet, on a deeper level, its reasoning does reflect a genuine concern about institutional checks on a transformed and empowered ECB. Indeed, it was at pains to stress that its independence 'relates only to the powers conferred upon it in the Treaties and the substantive exercise of such powers but is not applicable with regard to defining the extent and scope of its mandate'.[203] Adherence to the limits of that mandate, on the contrary, 'should be subject to full judicial review'.[204]

192 BVerfG, Judgment of the Second Senate of 5 May 2020 2 BvR 859/15 ECLI:DE:BVerfG:2020:rs20200505.2bvr085915, paras 133, 137, 141 (hereafter BVerfG *final PSPP judgment*).

193 ibid paras 123, 133, 139.

194 *Weiss* (n 171) paras 71–100.

195 ibid paras 81, 86, 93.

196 BVerfG *final PSPP judgment* (n 192) paras 127, 133, 138, 160.

197 ibid paras 156, 158.

198 ibid para 163.

199 ibid paras 164, 177.

200 ibid paras 179, 232–35.

201 Marijn Van der Sluis, 'Similar, Therefore Different: Judicial Review of Another Unconventional Monetary Policy in *Weiss* (C-493/17)' (2019) 49 LIEI 263, 272.

202 Editorial Comments, 'Not Mastering The Treaties: The German Federal Constitutional Court's PSPP Judgment' (2020) 57 CML Rev 965, 970–71; Paul Dermine, 'The Ruling of the Bundesverfassungsgericht in *PSPP*—An Inquiry into its Repercussions on the Economic and Monetary Union' (2020) 16 EuConst 525, 539; Van den Bogaert and Borger, 'Hoog spel in Karlsruhe' (n 170) 2984.

203 BVerfG *final PSPP judgment* (n 192) para 143.

204 ibid para 143.

The problem is that this distinction between the *existence* of a power and its *exercise* is untenable in practice.[205] This becomes apparent from the reasoning of the German Constitutional Court, which can only establish precise limits to the ECB's mandate by engaging in a full-blown review of the PSPP, to the extent that it conducts a far-reaching proportionality assessment. By doing so, it impinges upon the independence of the ECB.[206] This independence, after all, does not only concern its relations with political institutions, secured by Article 130 TFEU; it is also bound up with its mandate. Article 127 TFEU requires that the ECB should primarily aim for price stability, yet leaves it to the institution itself to put flesh on the notion. It is precisely this discretion to define price stability and to devise a policy strategy to achieve it, that bestows on the ECB a significant degree of 'functional independence'.[207] The German Court's intrusive review of the PSPP gives short shrift to that independence, which it once considered essential to secure the currency union's existence as a community of stability.

This is not to say the Court of Justice got it right. By stating that 'nothing more' can be asked of the ECB besides using its expertise 'with all care and accuracy' it imposed no real limits on its exercise of discretion.[208] Does this then mean one is left with a choice between two evils: an intrusive review that sacrifices central bank independence or a hands-off approach with no real checks at all? Some seem to argue as much, taking the view that the government bond buying powers of the ECB place it in a position beyond the control of courts.[209] That is to say: courts can decide, as the German Constitutional Court has done, to put tight constraints on its mandate out of a concern for democratic legitimacy (or the lack thereof) and thereby engage in a full review of its actions for which they are ill-equipped and that affects its independence. Or they can by and large accept its actions—the approach of the Court of Justice. Neither is to be preferred, which shows the need for more political guidance on ECB action.[210]

This view is too absolutist, for two reasons. First, as far as the principle of government bond market intervention is concerned, the ECB has in fact received significant political backing, as this chapter has showed. Second, there is quite a lot the Court of Justice, or any other court for that matter, can do whilst respecting its functional independence. For one thing, the Court of Justice could put more teeth on procedural requirements like the duty of care such that to avoid a manifest error more is required of the ECB then simply making sure it carries out its analysis 'with all care and accuracy'.[211] Indeed, in policy areas like competition law, the Court of Justice does not shy away from demanding not only that the evidence used is 'factually accurate,

[205] Borger, 'Central Bank Independence, Discretion and Judicial Review' (n 170) 123–24.

[206] Van den Bogaert and Borger, 'Hoog spel in Karlsruhe' (n 170) 2985.

[207] For an analysis of various elements of the ECB's independence, see Smits, *The European Central Bank* (n 24) 151–78; Rosa Maria Lastra, 'The Independence of the European System of Central Banks' (1992) 33 Harvard International Law Journal 475, 482–96. On ECB independence, see also chapter 10 by Alexander Thiele, in this volume.

[208] Borger, 'Central Bank Independence, Discretion and Judicial Review' (n 170) 125–26.

[209] Nik de Boer and Jens van 't Klooster, 'The ECB, the Courts and the issue of Democratic Legitimacy after *Weiss*' (2020) 57 CML Rev 1689 (hereafter de Boer and van 't Klooster, 'The ECB, the Courts and the Issue of Democratic Legitimacy').

[210] ibid 1721–24.

[211] Mark Dawson and Ana Bobić, 'Quantitative Easing at the Court of Justice—Doing Whatever it Takes to Save the Euro: *Weiss and Others*' (2019) 56 CML Rev 1005, 1025–26.

reliable and consistent', but also that it is comprehensive enough to thoroughly assess 'a complex situation' and 'is capable of substantiating the conclusions drawn from it'.[212]

The issue of judicial review may seem of theoretical relevance only now that the PSPP controversy has subsided. In June 2020, without mentioning the judgment from Karlsruhe, the Governing Council of the ECB published the notes of its meeting earlier that month in which it extensively reflected on the proportionality of the PSPP.[213] With the help of the *Bundesbank*, it also provided the German government and parliament with unpublished minutes of past meetings where it had discussed the programme. Shortly thereafter, the minister of finance, Olaf Scholz, as well as parliament indicated the ECB had met the demands of the Constitutional Court.[214] Peter Huber, the judge rapporteur in the case, then signalled that even though the *Bundesbank* was bound by its judgment, it had to 'determine on its own responsibility' whether the ECB's sharpened motivation fulfilled the requirements.[215] At the start of August, the *Bundesbank* subsequently announced it would continue its participation in the programme.[216]

But the next case is already in the making. In March 2020, in response to the coronavirus pandemic, the ECB launched the 'Pandemic Emergency Purchase Programme' (PEPP).[217] The programme initially enabled the ECB to purchase an additional €750 billion in securities, including government bonds. Yet, in June of that year its firepower got nearly doubled to €1,350 billion,[218] and it subsequently got further extended to €1,850 billion in December.[219] Several months earlier, in July 2020, one of the parties in parliament, the *Alternative für Deutschland*, announced it would challenge the programme before the Constitutional Court.[220] The question of judicial review of ECB action, that much is clear, is here to stay.

[212] Case C-12/03 *Commission v Tetra Laval BV* [2010] EU:C:2005:87, para 39.

[213] European Central Bank, 'Account of the monetary policy meeting of the Governing Council of the European Central Bank on 3–4 June 2020' (ECB, 25 June 2020) <https://www.ecb.europa.eu/press/accounts/2020/html/ecb.mg200625~fd97330d5f.en.html> accessed 13 July 2021.

[214] Martin Arnold and Guy Chazan, 'Bundesbank to keep buying bonds after court challenge' *Financial Times* (Frankfurt am Main and Berlin, 6 July 2020) <https://www.ft.com/content/9944?f21-46db-465b-8ed0-9a214a898a74> accessed 13 July 2021 (hereafter Arnold and Chazan, 'Bundesbank to keep buying bonds').

[215] See quote in Arnold and Chazan, 'Bundesbank to keep buying bonds' (n 214). See also BVerfG, Order of the Second Senate of 29 April 2021 2 BvR 1651/15 ECLI:DE:BVerfG:2021:rs20210429.2bvr165115, in which the German Constitutional Court dismissed two applications for an order of execution concerning its judgment of 5 May 2020.

[216] 'Bundesbank sieht Forderungen des Verfassungsgerichts als erfüllt an' *Handelsblatt* (Frankfurt am Main, 3 August 2020).

[217] Decision (EU) of the European Central Bank of 24 March 2020 on a temporary pandemic emergency purchase programme (ECB/2020/17) [2020] OJ L91/1.

[218] European Central Bank, 'Monetary policy decisions' (ECB Press Release, 4 June 2020) <https://www.ecb.europa.eu/press/pr/date/2020/html/ecb.mp200604~a307d3429c.en.html> accessed 13 July 2021.

[219] European Central Bank, 'Monetary policy decisions' (ECB Press Release, 10 December 2020) <https://www.ecb.europa.eu/press/pr/date/2020/html/ecb.mp201210~8c2778b843.en.html> accessed 13 July 2021.

[220] David Marsh, 'Fresh German legal battle over ECB easing' (Official Monetary and Financial Institutions Forum, 17 June 2020) <https://www.omfif.org/2020/06/fresh-german-legal-battle-over-ecb-easing/> accessed 13 July 2021.

VI. Conclusion

Government bond purchases provide the clearest evidence that today's ECB differs fundamentally from the one that was put in place by the Treaty of Maastricht back in the 1990s. They show it has not just changed, but transformed. From a central bank almost exclusively focused on price stability, it has become an important guardian of financial stability, which even acts as a Lender of Last Resort for States to secure it. Outright purchases of government bonds, anathema to its old set-up, are now an important part of its toolbox. This transformation of the ECB, evidenced by its SMP and OMT programme, forms part of a broader constitutional overhaul of the currency union during the sovereign debt crisis, one that was initiated by the heads of state and government when they committed to safeguard financial stability on 11 February 2010 and sealed by the Court of Justice in *Gauweiler*.

The ECB's capacity for substantial interventions in government bond markets brings with it an institutional repositioning, not least towards courts. That became very clear when the PSPP, its third bond programme, was challenged. Both the German Constitutional Court and the Court of Justice grappled with the question of how intensely to review the programme in light of the ECB's independence. Just as the purchase of government bonds is here to stay, as the ECB's fourth purchase programme in response to the coronavirus pandemic has shown, so too this question will not disappear.

3

The ECB's Unconventional Quantitative Easing is Turning to Conventional Monetary Policy

Klaus Tuori

I. Introduction

The two decades of the European Central Bank (ECB) monetary policy are not brothers or even cousins. The ECB took over the responsibility of the euro area monetary policy in 1999 with a well-designed monetary policy strategy and an operational framework that had one foot in the central banking theory and the other in the heritage of its constituent central banks, particularly the German Bundesbank. However, from 2008 onwards, this consensus-based conduct of monetary policy was increasingly deemed insufficient to fight the recurring crises that were hitting the euro area.

This chapter will focus on the ECB's quantitative easing (QE) programmes, as the new main form of unconventional monetary policy that is slowly turning into conventional monetary policy with time. Indeed, since 2015, with only minor pauses, large-scale asset purchases have been the main active part of the ECB's monetary policy. It is therefore pertinent to understand to what extent QE can be seen as a continuation of the more traditional monetary policy and what potential differences there might be. Compared with traditional monetary policy, QE could, for example, have a different relationship with the price stability objective assigned to the ECB by EU primary law, it could have other objectives alongside or even as necessary steps towards the primary objective, such as financial stability, and it is foreseen to have a different societal impact. Therefore, the QE programmes might differ from conventional monetary policy in their aims and impact. This assessment keeps the ECB's exceptional institutional and constitutional position as a supranational central bank in mind, but does not engage in an actual legal and constitutional analysis of ECB QE programmes,[1] which may be found elsewhere in this edited volume.[2]

I start by recalling the starting point, that is the ECB's initial model of monetary policy, and then move to describe and analyse the change of heart that corresponds to the moment when the ECB decided to engage in QE. The main QE programmes are discussed in turn. First, the Public Sector Purchase Programme (PSPP) is assessed

[1] See, eg, Klaus Tuori, 'The ECB's Quantitative Easing Programme as a Constitutional Game Changer' (2019) 26 MJ 94.

[2] On this aspect, see chapter 2 by Vestert Borger, in this volume.

Klaus Tuori, *The ECB's Unconventional Quantitative Easing is Turning to Conventional Monetary Policy* In: *The New European Central Bank*. Edited by: Thomas Beukers, Diane Fromage, and Giorgio Monti, Oxford University Press. © Klaus Tuori 2022.
DOI: 10.1093/oso/9780198871231.003.0003

most thoroughly, including its aims, potential efficacy, and also its caveats and societal impact. The ECB's Pandemic Emergency Purchase Programme (PEPP) is then examined mainly from the perspective of the new features it added to those of the pre-existing PSPP. The conclusions will take a slightly broader perspective on QE and even raise the philosophical question, whether QE has become a passage of the ECB from a central bank of institutions and individuals to a central bank of markets, which could point to its deserving to be qualified as a 'new ECB' as suggested in this edited volume.

II. The ECB as a Consensus Model Central Bank—the First Decade

The ECB was established just before the launch of the euro in 1999, and its first formal action included the decision on its monetary policy strategy *A stability-oriented monetary policy strategy for the ESCB* and the basic features of its operation framework. These specified how the ECB was to conduct its monetary policy in order to achieve its primary objective of price stability that was given a numerical value of less than 2 per cent medium-term inflation across the euro area.[3]

The ECB, as any contemporary central bank, derives its power from the monopoly issuance of central bank money, which it uses in various ways to achieve its targets.[4] This relates to the monetary policy transmission mechanism, a process by which monetary policy decisions are assumed to affect the economy and eventually prices. A key feature concerning monetary policy transmission is its vagueness and largely descriptive nature. In the original ECB model, the transmission mechanism started from the current and expected ECB official interest rates that in turn affect other interest rates in the economy, be they bank interest rates or interest rates on government and corporate bonds.

The ECB operational framework specified how the ECB's official interest rates, first and foremost the interest rate on the Main Refinancing Operations (MROs), would seek to affect the interest rates in the economy. In practice, the ECB's Governing Council defines the MRO interest rate in its monthly monetary policy meeting. This rate is the basis for the short-term interest rates on the money the ECB lends to banks through its weekly auctions. The details of these operations have changed somewhat over the years, but the main element until the Global Financial Crisis was that the ECB's minimum reserve requirement[5] created a liquidity shortage among commercial banks that forced them to bid for central bank money. Thereby, in the original operational framework the MRO rate was the benchmark risk-free short-term interest rate

[3] European Central Bank, 'A stability-oriented monetary policy strategy for the ESCB' (ECB Press Release, 13 October 1998) <https://www.ecb.europa.eu/press/pr/date/1998/html/pr981013_1.en.html> accessed 1 July 2021. 'Close to but below' was later added to the 2 per cent-objective to stress the ECB's dislike of deflation.

[4] European Central Bank, 'The Monetary Policy of the ECB' (European Central Bank 2004) 41–43 (hereafter European Central Bank, 'The Monetary Policy of the ECB').

[5] The legal basis for minimum reserves is Protocol No 4 on the Statute of the European System of Central Banks and of the European Central Bank [2016] OJ C202/230, Art 19.1 (hereafter Statute) in accordance with the Consolidated Version of the Treaty on the Functioning of the European Union [2012] OJ C326/47, Art 129 (4) (hereafter TFEU).

for the euro area. The other elements of the operational framework mainly supported this basic function and ensured the smooth operation of inter-bank markets and payment systems.[6]

This conduct of monetary policy was broadly operational until 2011, when the resurfacing euro area crisis triggered a new and more profound round of unconventional monetary policy. The MRO rate was cut to 1 per cent, and most importantly the ECB's provision of short-term central bank money was replaced by two auctions of three-year central bank money in unlimited quantity that totalled more than 1 trillion euros (so-called Longer-Term Refinancing Operations (LTROs)).[7] After that, the MRO rate was gradually cut to zero and provision of short-term liquidity to banks became a demand-driven process, where only the availability of eligible collateral posed limits.

In conclusion, the ECB's era as a 1990s-consensus model central bank lasted more or less until 2011, although the unconventional measures started to appear from May 2010 onwards already with the Securities Market Programme (SMP). The selective bond purchases were conducted alongside the traditional monetary policy. Conventional monetary policy aimed at maintaining price stability, while the unconventional programmes had other aims such as to repair the monetary policy transmission mechanism. The main idea was to affect the pricing and liquidity in selective government bond markets of the troubled Member States, initially Greece, Portugal, and Ireland and later also Italy and Spain. The three-year LTROs had basically the same aim of supporting the government bond markets, as commercial banks in troubled countries were the main bidders for those funds and they used the funds largely to buy local government bonds.

Consequently, at least after the Outright Monetary Transactions (OMT) programme was announced in 2012, the traditional model of central banking was largely part of ECB history. The official short-term interest rates were no longer the main tool of affecting the economy, and the straightforward and transparent monetary policy operations were to some extent replaced by programmes that raised questions concerning their main objectives and motivations. The constitutionally constrained narrow central banking model with a single and clear price stability objective was being challenged. The ECB's actions were arguably equally motivated by price stability concerns as they were by financial stability and the state of Member State public finances.[8]

III. The ECB Turns to QE—the PSPP

Late 2014, more than six years after the Lehmann Brothers collapse, and three years after the ECB launched its three-year LTROs that increased its balance sheet but also

[6] European Central Bank, 'The Monetary Policy of the ECB' (n 4) 44–46.

[7] European Central Bank, 'The Implementation of Monetary Policy in the Euro Area' (European Central Bank 2011).

[8] For a discussion, see also Kaarlo Tuori and Klaus Tuori, *The Eurozone Crisis. A Constitutional Analysis* (CUP 2014). See also chapter 2 by Vestert Borger and chapter 5 by Agnieszka Smoleńska and Thomas Beukers, in this volume.

worsened the link between banks and governments and in the same period when the ECB took over the supervision of euro area banks, the ECB started to hint at large-scale purchases of government bonds.[9] The euro area economic recovery was still behind most developed countries, and declining energy prices were pushing headline consumer price inflation down. Conventional monetary policy was in full use, and banks could get all the liquidity they wanted. The existing unconventional monetary policy measures, particularly the SMP, had evoked constitutional questions, were not unproblematic economically, nor had they provided sustained support for the economy. Nevertheless, the turn to QE was all but easy for the ECB, as sustained purchases of government bonds were problematic for the institutional and constitutional model of euro area central banking, as was also manifested by the prohibition of monetary financing (Article 123 of the Treaty on the Functioning of the European Union (TFEU)) and the overall concern that the EMU could encourage reckless fiscal policy by Member States. Tellingly, President Draghi had rejected QE at the time of his appointment: 'we should not try to circumvent the spirit of the Treaty. No matter what the legal trick is, I think what matters for the people and what matters for the confidence and credibility of the institution is the spirit of this provision of the Treaty.' He continued that 'each central bank has its institutional set-up, within which it operates. The ECB operates within the limits of the Treaty, and I said a moment ago what our primary mandate is, and especially what the Treaty says the ECB cannot do. I think any central bank is constrained by its institutional set-up. In the United States, as you know, the primary mandate of the Federal Reserve is completely different from ours. And the same is true of the Bank of England.'[10]

Nevertheless, the ECB announced its resort to QE in January 2015 in the form of a programme to buy 60 billion euros worth of mainly government bonds monthly.[11] The decisive Governing Council meeting took place after expectations had been building up by speeches and hints of such a programme, and the long internal negotiations and preparations within the Eurosystem had leaked to the press. The PSPP was formally merely an extension of the ECB's Asset Purchase Programme (APP) of October 2014 that included covered bonds[12] and asset-backed securities.[13] However, it was the first QE programme proper in the euro area with government bonds making up the largest bond class, and a specified monthly purchase amount and a minimum running period of one and a half years that was prolonged several times,[14] halted by the end of 2018

[9] Mario Draghi, 'Monetary policy in the euro area' (Speech at the Frankfurt European Banking Congress, Frankfurt am Main, 21 November 2014) <https://www.ecb.europa.eu/press/key/date/2014/html/sp141121.en.html> accessed 1 July 2021.

[10] Mario Draghi and Vítor Constâncio, 'Introductory statement to the press conference (with Q&A)' (ECB Press Conference, Frankfurt am Main, 8 December 2011) <https://www.ecb.europa.eu/press/pressconf/2011/html/is111208.en.html> accessed 1 July 2021.

[11] European Central Bank, 'ECB announces expanded asset purchase programme' (ECB Press Release, 22 January 2015) <https://www.ecb.europa.eu/press/pr/date/2015/html/pr150122_1.en.html> accessed 1 July 2021 (hereafter European Central Bank, 'ECB announces expanded asset purchase programme' 22 January 2015).

[12] Decision (EU) 2014/828 of the European Central Bank of 15 October on the implementation of the third covered bond purchase programme (ECB/2014/40) [2014] OJ L335/22.

[13] Decision (EU) 2015/5 of the European Central Bank of 19 November 2014 on the implementation of the asset-backed securities purchase programme (ECB/2014/45) [2015] OJ L1/4.

[14] Mario Draghi and Vítor Constâncio, 'Introductory statement to the press conference (with Q&A)' (ECB Press Conference, Frankfurt am Main, 10 March 2016) <https://www.ecb.europa.eu/press/pressconf/

and restarted in early 2020.[15] Consequently, the ECB that was (and still is) prohibited from financing governments became the main creditor of the euro area Member States even before the PEPP was launched in 2020.

The PSPP's legal form was an ECB Governing Council decision[16] that referred to the first indent of Article 127(2) TFEU as well as Article 12.1 in conjunction with Articles 3.1 and 18.1 Statute of the ECB and the European System of Central Banks (ESCB Statute) as its legal basis. The PSPP was thus part of conducting monetary policy through buying marketable securities outright.[17] The decision also made a reference to the monetary financing prohibition, declaring it fully compatible without explaining however why.[18]

A. The main features of the PSPP

The PSPP is in many respects a relatively common QE programme, but it has a few features stemming from its peculiar euro area context. The Eurosystem, the ECB, and the euro area National Central Banks (NCBs), committed to buying bonds issued by euro area central governments, certain agencies established in the euro area, as well as a few international or supranational institutions located in the euro area. Instead of focusing only on the most creditworthy bonds in the euro area,[19] the PSPP covered all the euro area government bonds.[20] Bonds issued by regional and local governments located in the euro area were later added to the list. The bonds need to fulfil the ECB guideline on collateral eligibility,[21] although the PSPP can also be used to purchase bonds issued by a country that is under a financial assistance programme, and basically any bonds if it is so decided by the ECB Governing Council.[22]

In addition to controlling for the issuer quality, the PSPP also tries to limit its impact on the market by setting relative limits concerning each bond issuer and each

2016/html/is160310.en.html> accessed 1 July 2021 (hereafter Draghi and Constâncio, 'Introductory statement to the press conference (with Q&A)' 10 March 2016); European Central Bank, 'Monetary policy decisions' (ECB Press Release, 8 December 2016) <https://www.ecb.europa.eu/press/pr/date/2016/html/pr161208.en.html> accessed 1 July 2021.

[15] Decision (EU) 2015/774 of the European Central Bank of 4 March 2015 on a secondary markets public sector asset purchase programme (ECB/2015/10) [2015] OJ L121/20 (hereafter Decision (EU) 2015/774 of the European Central Bank).

[16] ibid.

[17] Statute (n 5) Art 18.1 placed the measures of the PSPP under open market and credit operations. Decision (EU) 2015/774 of the European Central Bank (n 15) recital (1).

[18] Council Regulation (EC) no 3603/93 of 13 December 1993 specifying definitions for the application of the prohibitions referred to in Articles 104 and 104b(1) of the Treaty [1993] OJ L332/1.

[19] At the time the PSPP programme was launched, only Germany had the highest credit rating from all the major rating agencies. Close to the highest rating were also given to Austria, Finland, and the Netherlands. See Trading Economics, 'Euro Area—Credit Rating' (*Trading Economics*, 2021) <http://www.tradingeconomics.com/euro-area/rating> accessed 1 July 2021.

[20] With the exception of Greece.

[21] A first-best credit assessment of at least credit quality step 3 (CQS3); Guideline of the European Central Bank of 20 September 2011 on monetary policy instruments and procedures of the Eurosystem (ECB/2011/14) [2011] OJ L331/1 (hereafter Guideline ECB/2011/14). See also chapter 4 by Jens van 't Klooster, in this volume.

[22] Decision (EU) 2015/774 of the European Central Bank (n 15) Art 3(2)c.

issue. The aim is, in particular, to avoid a Eurosystem blocking minority in a situation of debt restructuring. However, the bond issue limit was soon increased to 33 per cent, which is also the limit for each issuer's outstanding debt. Hence, now the Eurosystem could get so close to the blocking minority that this safety feature has become insignificant.[23] Furthermore, bonds related to financial assistance are exempted from these restrictions, as in practice are those of international organizations and multilateral development banks.[24] The PSPP purchases take place only in the secondary markets, as Article 123 TFEU explicitly prohibits purchases of primary issues. In addition, the ECB has defined, although not published, a so-called 'black-out period' around bond issues during which purchases are not allowed. The idea is to avoid these secondary market purchases being considered as having an effect equivalent to that of a direct purchase of government bonds, for example if the issuer knows with certainty that the ECB would almost immediately buy most of the bonds at issue.[25] The list of eligible counterparties decided for PSPP is very broad in comparison to other central banks.[26]

The most important features of the programme are its monthly size and minimum length. It began with the whole APP totalling 60 billion euros monthly, of which some 50 billion euros were conducted as part of the PSPP. The initial duration was one and a half years, but 'in any case, [was to] be conducted until the Governing Council sees a sustained adjustment in the path of inflation'.[27] It was prolonged several times, first with an increase of the monthly amount and later gradually phasing out purchases towards the end of 2018. It was restarted in March 2020.[28] Initially, the purchases were to reach 1.1 trillion euros, but the extensions pushed the PSPP past 2.4 trillion euros by May 2021 and nearly 3 trillion euros for the whole APP, even excluding the PEPP.

The PSPP does not exclude purchases of bonds with negative yields. Initially, yields were to be above the ECB deposit rate,[29] which at the time of the launch stood at -0.2 per cent and was later cut to -0.5 per cent. However, this was later turned into a guideline rather than a rule, as the lowest-risk rates were pushed even farther into negative territory.

In comparison to earlier monetary policy operations, the PSPP introduced a new feature, namely limited risk-sharing between the NCBs. The full Eurosystem risk-sharing covers only 20 per cent of the purchases, and 80 per cent is at the risk of each NCB purchasing its own government and regional bonds.[30] This unusual setting was

[23] ibid Art 3(3). See also European Central Bank, 'ECB announces expanded asset purchase programme' 22 January 2015 (n 11). To avoid a blocking minority, the 33 per cent threshold includes all the holdings of the ECB (Eurosystem) in an issue. Other holdings resulted from the SMP and investment holdings by the NCBs.

[24] Decision (EU) 2015/774 of the European Central Bank (n 15) recital (6), Arts 5(1) and (2) and Draghi and Constâncio, 'Introductory statement to the press conference (with Q&A)' 10 March 2016 (n 14).

[25] Decision (EU) 2015/774 of the European Central Bank (n 15) Art 4 (1).

[26] ibid Art 7 (a reference to the Guideline ECB/2011/14 (n 21) annex I).

[27] Decision (EU) 2015/774 of the European Central Bank (n 15) recital (7).

[28] European Central Bank, 'Asset purchase programme' <https://www.ecb.europa.eu/mopo/implement/omt/html/index.en.html> accessed 1 July 2021.

[29] Decision (EU) 2015/774 of the European Central Bank (n 15) Art 3(5).

[30] Of the 20 per cent risk-sharing, initially 12 per cent concerned purchase of securities of European institutions allocated to selected NCBs. The ECB was to purchase and hold directly 8 per cent of the bonds. The risk-sharing part was later divided equally between European institutions and ECB purchases: European Central Bank, 'ECB announces expanded asset purchase programme' 22 January 2015 (n 11); Draghi and Constâncio, 'Introductory statement to the press conference (with Q&A)' 10 March 2016 (n 14).

a compromise within the ECB Governing Council, as some members were worried that the PSPP would encourage unwelcome fiscal developments and turn into a fiscal transfer mechanism between the Member States.[31] Indeed, the majority of purchases have been conducted by the NCBs, according to their share in the ECB capital key, which is controlled by the ECB.[32] It could be recalled that the conditionality requirement of the OMT programme was absent from the PSPP whereby an agreement on a European Stability Mechanism (ESM) programme was a pre-condition for the deployment of the OMT programme to purchase the government bonds of a Member State.

B. The stated aims of the PSPP

The PSPP has stated aims and potentially also other effects that were desired or at least accepted by the ECB Governing Council. The main stated aim was to contribute to the achievement of the price stability objective. In contrast to the ECB's earlier selective bond purchase programmes, the PSPP did not aim to repair a perceived malfunctioning of the bond markets or the transmission mechanism of monetary policy in individual Member States. The ECB noted that both actual and expected euro area inflation had declined to historical lows, which risked causing a deflationary development should these expectations become part of the wage- and price-setting behaviour. As conventional monetary policy through official interest rates and bank liquidity was used to the extent deemed possible, a substantial further easing of the monetary policy stance required new measures.[33]

The ECB has explained the economics of the PSPP as follows. The large-scale purchases of government bonds ease monetary conditions, as mainly longer-term bond holdings are replaced by short-term central bank money. This should ensure more affordable financing for companies and households, which would support investment and consumption. Increased investment and consumption is expected to increase overall demand in the economy that should push inflation upwards. The ECB specified three channels through which the PSPP should affect inflation. First, the mere decision increases inflation expectations that then reduce expected real interest rates when nominal rates are close to zero. Second, the PSPP purchases reduce government bond yields that are the benchmark interest rates for all the other financial instruments (bank loans, corporate bonds, and even company shares). Third and most importantly, the PSPP increases financial asset prices through portfolio reallocations to other assets.[34] This portfolio rebalancing effect was seen to be the primary means

[31] European Central Bank, 'ECB announces expanded asset purchase programme' 22 January 2015 (n 11).

[32] The reference to Statute (n 5) Art 12.1 underlined that the Governing Council adopts guidelines as well as takes decisions as a means to formulate monetary policy. These decisions and guidelines form the basis under which the ECB Executive Board operationalizes monetary policy, eg, by giving binding instructions to NCBs, and somewhat strangely, the ECB could now instruct the NCBs to make purchases at their own risk.

[33] European Central Bank, 'ECB announces expanded asset purchase programme' 22 January 2015 (n 11).

[34] This was explained, eg, in a letter from the ECB President to Mr Enrique Calvet Chambon on the extended asset purchase programme (L/MD/15/139, 10 March 2015).

through which the PSPP, as most other QE programmes, was to influence financial conditions, lending, and through them also the real economy and eventually prices. Institutional investors, including pension funds, insurance companies, mutual funds, and in some countries banks, buy other assets and push up their prices.[35] Currencies are also financial assets and their relative price was expected to be affected by the PSPP. However, the euro exchange rate could not be an explicit target for the PSPP as an ECB programme due to competence issues.[36]

The ECB hence classified the PSPP as solely a monetary policy programme without any objectives other than the price stability that at the time was being jeopardized by the risk of deflationary developments. The PSPP functioned mainly through the portfolio rebalancing effect: purchases caused higher asset prices and generally better financial market conditions. This increased lending to households and companies, which increased consumption and investment and eventually increased prices. The PSPP also signalled the ECB's commitment to higher inflation that could increase inflation expectations and push down real longer-term interest rates.

IV. QE and PSPP in Economic Theory and Central Bank Practice

The ECB's decision on the PSPP was a contested and significant change in the euro area monetary policy. How it should be assessed relies mostly on the economics of QE programmes in the peculiar euro area institutional context. While this chapter will not debate whether the PSPP should be considered monetary policy under EU law, it will analyse its nature in comparison to both conventional monetary policy and to QE programmes of other major central banks. The attempt is to understand how the stated aims of the PSPP relate to its content in the light of economic theory and empirical analysis. What is the theoretical link between the PSPP and price stability and how have QE programmes functioned empirically?

A. QE in macroeconomics

The theoretical basis of QE is relatively weak in traditional macroeconomics. In the most basic macroeconomic setting, QE purchases only change the term structure of a state's liabilities from longer term to shorter term, which should not lead to increased demand or inflation.[37] Consequently, QE was not part of the inflation-targeting 'consensus' central banking model of the 1990s. Earlier large-scale purchases of

[35] Matt Clinch and Annette Weisbach, 'Draghi: ECB QE risks are contained' *CNBC* (New Jersey, 11 March 2015) <http://www.cnbc.com/id/102494922> accessed 1 July 2021.

[36] TFEU (n 5) Art 219 (1) gives the Council the power to 'conclude formal agreements on an exchange-rate system for the euro in relation to the currencies of third States', but does not give it exclusive mandate on all subjects related to exchange-rates. See chapter 9 by Florin Coman-Kund, in this volume.

[37] Neil Wallace, 'A Modigliani-Miller Theorem for Open-Market Operations' (1981) 71 American Economic Review 267. The article uses the basic Modigliani-Miller Theorem in government finances and shows that the irrelevance also holds in that environment.

government bonds by central banks had been related to exceptional times (wars) and mostly led to very high inflation.

Arguably, a new perspective on central bank bond purchases, the QE in contemporary understanding, started with the Japanese experience with a stubborn deflation of the 1990s, which brought to light that zero bound interest rates could prevent effective monetary policy easing. In that situation, one theoretical solution was central bank asset purchases, if they could be combined with a credible commitment to higher prices, as the latter would increase inflation expectations.[38] Purchases would push down longer-term nominal interest rates and the commitment to higher inflation would push expected inflation up, resulting in lower real interest rates and equalling monetary policy stimulus to supporting growth.[39] This theoretical model demanded that the central bank would commit 'to being irresponsible',[40] which means that it would commit to allow inflation to rise above its target and thereby reduce expected real interest rates. Also the ECB has used various ways to stress that it would accept higher inflation going forward,[41] although the credibility of this 'commitment' has probably been limited because of its clear price stability mandate.

Another theoretical case for QE incorporates the financial market situation in the model. In particular, a banking crisis or a financial crisis can lead to abnormally low asset prices and even to a negative debt-deflation spiral. This could be remedied by central bank purchases of assets. For example, private banks can face shortages of capital due to losses or a disruption of their normal means of market funding, both of which can lead to insufficient provision of bank lending. In this case, central bank financing through the purchase of financial market assets could prevent a worsening of the situation.[42]

The empirical analysis of QE has gained speed more recently, although the conclusions are not necessarily very firm. The existing research can be divided into those that study the impact on financial markets and those that seek to find a link between QE and real economic variables. The financial market impact should include declines in the yields of bonds that are purchased and their close substitutes. A particularly interesting question is, how far in the area of riskier asset this impact extends. The specific effects that research has aimed to reveal include: the central bank's signalling effect, the portfolio rebalancing effect, and the liquidity effect.[43]

[38] Gauti B Eggertsson and Michael Woodford, 'The Zero Bound on Interest Rates and Optimal Monetary Policy' (2003) Brookings Papers on Economic Activity 139.

[39] Ben S Bernanke and Vincent R Reinhart, 'Conducting Monetary Policy At Very Low Short-Term Interest Rates' (2004) 94 American Economic Review 85 and the discussion on avoiding liquidity traps in Paul R Krugman, 'It's Baaack! Japan's Slump and the return of the Liquidity Trap' (1998) Brookings Papers on Economic Activity 137.

[40] Gauti B Eggertsson, 'The Deflation Bias and Committing to Being Irresponsible' (2006) 38 JMCB 283.

[41] Decision (EU) 2015/774 of the European Central Bank (n 15) recital (7) and Draghi and Constâncio, 'Introductory statement to the press conference (with Q&A)' 10 March 2016 (n 14).

[42] Vasco Cúrdia and Michael Woodford, 'The Central-bank Balance Sheet as an Instrument' (2011) 58 Journal of Monetary Economics 54; Mark Gertler and Peter Karadi, 'A Model of Unconventional Monetary Policy' (2011) 58 Journal of Monetary Economics 17 and Zhiguo He and Arvind Krishnamurthy, 'Intermediary Asset Pricing' (2013) 103 American Economic Review 732.

[43] Diana Hancock and Wayne S Passmore, 'How the Federal Reserve's Large-Scale Asset Purchases (LSAPs) Influence Mortgage-Backed Securities (MBS) Yields and U.S. Mortgage Rates' (2014) FEDS Working Paper No 2014-12 <https://papers.ssrn.com/sol3/papers.cfm?abstract_id=2391966> accessed 1 July 2021.

The first studies concerned Japanese QE programmes from the late 1990s and the US purchases to alleviate the technology bubble crisis at the turn of the millennium. They found evidence that central bank communication affected expectations of future policy and that the asset purchases could have some effect on the targeted bond yields,[44] although the impact on the economy was weaker and very limited on inflation.[45] However, the abundance of the QE programmes and hence empirical material really started with the Great Financial Crisis (GFC). The first US programme from November 2008 hit the peak of the financial crisis and led to substantial declines in yields of government bonds and highly rated corporate bonds, but other corporate bonds were not affected. Some weak evidence was found on increased inflation expectations,[46] but less on longer-term rates.[47] As the financial crisis eased, the evidence from the second US QE programme (late 2010) was less convincing.[48] Similar results were also found for the Bank of England's programmes: clear impact on government bonds, less on other assets,[49] some on economic growth, and some even on inflation.[50]

More broadly, it can be concluded that there is some evidence that QE programmes can affect the prices of purchased assets and their close substitutes. This has become more evident, as the programmes have grown in absolute and relative size. However, the impact on the real economy and on inflation is still less well founded. It perhaps also needs to be acknowledged that many studies have been conducted by central banks themselves, where it is not the most career enhancing conclusion to find that their own programme is a failure.

[44] Ben S Bernanke, Vincent R Reinhart, and Brian P Sack, 'Monetary Policy Alternatives at the Zero Bound: An Empirical Assessment' (2004) FEDS Working Paper No 2004-48 <https://www.federalreserve.gov/pubs/feds/2004/200448/200448pap.pdf> accessed 1 July 2021.

[45] Pelin S Berkmen, 'Bank of Japan's Quantitative and Credit Easing: Are They Now More Effective?' (2012) IMF Working Paper No 12/2 <https://www.imf.org/external/pubs/ft/wp/2012/wp1202.pdf> accessed 1 July 2021.

[46] Arvind Krishnamurthy and Annette Vissing-Jorgensen, 'The Effects of Quantitative Easing on Interest Rates: Channels and Implications for Policy' (2011) NBER Working Paper No 17555 <https://www.nber.org/papers/w17555> accessed 1 July 2021; Arvind Krishnamurthy and Annette Vissing-Jorgensen, 'The Aggregate Demand for Treasury Debt' (2012) 120 Journal of Political Economy 233; Stefania D'Amico and Thomas B King, 'Flow and Stock Effects of Large-Scale Treasury Purchases' (2012) FEDS Working Paper No 2010-52 <https://www.federalreserve.gov/pubs/feds/2010/201052/201052pap.pdf> accessed 1 July 2021; Joseph Gagnon and others, 'Large-Scale Asset Purchases by the Federal Reserve: Did They Work' (2010) FRB of New York Staff Report no 441 <https://www.federalreserve.gov/monetarypolicy/files/fomc20100301memo01.pdf> accessed 1 July 2021; Canlin Li and Min Wei, 'Term Structure Modelling with Supply Factors and the Federal Reserve's Large Scale Asset Purchase Programs' (2012) FEDS Working Paper No 2012-37 <https://www.federalreserve.gov/pubs/feds/2012/201237/201237pap.pdf> accessed 1 July 2021.

[47] Robert Jarrow and Hao Li, 'The Impact of Quantitative Easing on the US Term Structure of Interest Rates' (2014) 17 Review of Derivatives Research 287; James D Hamilton and Jing C Wu, 'The Effectiveness of Alternative Monetary Policy Tools in a Zero Lower Bound Environment' (2012) NBER Working Paper No w16956 <https://www.nber.org/papers/w16956> accessed 1 July 2021.

[48] Brett W Fawley and Christopher J Neely, 'Four Stories of Quantitative Easing' (2013) 95 FRB of St Louis Review 51 (hereafter Fawley and Neely, 'Four Stories of Quantitative Easing').

[49] Michael Joyce and others, 'The Financial Market Impact of Quantitative Easing' (2010) Bank of England Working Paper No 393 <https://www.bankofengland.co.uk/working-paper/2010/the-financial-market-impact-of-quantitative-easing> accessed 1 July 2021.

[50] George Kapetanios and others, 'Assessing the Economy-Wide Effects of Quantitative Easing' (2012) Bank of England Working Paper No 443 <https://www.bankofengland.co.uk/working-paper/2012/assessing-the-economy-wide-effects-of-quantitative-easing> accessed 1 July 2021.

B. QE as a central banking tool

QE programmes can affect the economy in multiple ways, although the actual routes and their relevance are still very uncertain. They can aim to improve the general outlook in output and prices, to facilitate government finances, and to enhance financial stability. It can thus be illuminating to see for what purposes central banks have deemed it appropriate to have recourse to QE. First of all, all the recent QE programmes have been launched at the time when conventional monetary policy had reached its zero bound. This indicates that they are seen as a continuation of monetary policy stimulus with new means. However, many recent programmes were also linked to financial market instability in addition to the overall economic situation such as the ones in the USA, the UK, and also Japan.[51]

By contrast, the ECB has been strict in defining the PSPP purely as a monetary policy instrument and as solely aiming at ensuring price stability. The Governing Council even agreed unanimously that the PSPP is a monetary policy instrument,[52] even if other reservations remained concerning the prohibition of central bank financing and even the democratic legitimatization of a potential redistributive impact of the programme.[53] Furthermore, the classification of QE as monetary policy—by the ECB and accepted by the Court of Justice—is not in itself sufficient to affirm that the ECB's PSPP decision at that time and form had a compelling link with the price stability objective. The specific circumstances and rationalities of a QE programme define whether it was or is an appropriate central bank tool to achieve price stability. At the time when PSPP was designed in late 2014, euro area core inflation was at the low end of its price stability range and headline inflation was temporarily negative due to oil prices. However, the ECB's argumentation for the urgency of the PSPP or its

[51] Federal Open Market Committee, 'Federal Reserve announces it will initiate a program to purchase the direct obligations of housing-related government-sponsored enterprises and mortgage-backed securities backed by Fannie Mae, Freddie Mac, and Ginnie Mac' (FOMC Press Release, 25 November 2008) <https://www.federalreserve.gov/newsevents/pressreleases/monetary20081125b.htm> accessed 1 July 2021; Fawley and Neely, 'Four Stories of Quantitative Easing' (n 48); Bank of England, 'Bank of England reduces Bank Rate by 0.5 Percentage Points to 0.5% and Announces £75 Billion Asset Purchase Programme' (Bank of England Press Release, 5 March 2009) <https://www.bankofengland.co.uk/-/media/boe/files/news/2009/march/mpc-march-2009.pdf?la=en&hash=D1BE3DE42FA1CC9C9887D0B5EC78A4365A9CBCAE> accessed 1 July 2021; and Bank of Japan, 'Statement on Monetary Policy' (Bank of Japan Monetary policy release, 16 November 2011) <https://www.boj.or.jp/en/announcements/release_2011/k111116a.pdf> accessed 1 July 2021, referring to financial stability and, eg, Bank of Japan, 'Statement on Monetary Policy' (Bank of Japan Monetary policy release, 28 October 2010) <https://www.boj.or.jp/en/announcements/release_2010/k101028.pdf> accessed 1 July 2021.

[52] Mario Draghi, 'Introductory statement to the press conference (with Q&A)' (ECB Press Conference, Frankfurt am Main, 22 January 2015) (hereafter Draghi, 'Introductory statement to the press conference (with Q&A)' 22 January 2015).

[53] Jeff Black and Jana Randow, 'ECB's Weidmann Rejects Sovereign QE With No Deflation Seen' *Bloomberg* (New York, 16 December 2014) <https://www.bloomberg.com/news/articles/2014-12-16/weidmann-rejects-sovereign-bond-buying-even-if-deflation-emerges> accessed 1 July 2021. President of the Öesterreichischen Nationalbank, Nowotny echoed these worries: 'to be honest I did not support this decision', he said, adding 'I think of course it has advantages but the risks are not insignificant'; see Michael Shields, 'ECB's Nowotny says QE risk-sharing was resolved well' *Reuters* (Vienna, 23 January 2015) <https://www.reuters.com/article/us-ecb-policy-nowotny/ecbs-nowotny-says-qe-risk-sharing-was-resolved-well-idUSKBN0KW0KY20150123> accessed 1 July 2021.

effectiveness in achieving higher inflation in those circumstances was not particularly solidly anchored in any economic analysis.[54]

The ECB also addressed some economic-constitutional concerns in its communication. The moral hazard considerations, namely the concern that the PSPP would encourage reckless fiscal policy at the Member State level, were raised by some Governing Council members. President Draghi pointed out that monetary policy measures can always have some fiscal consequences and 'these fiscal implications are dealt with easily within a one-country framework, between the central bank and the treasury. But in the euro area ... each national treasury gives an implicit or explicit indemnity to its own central bank, but not the euro system as a whole.'[55]The risk-sharing structure was slightly problematic for the effectiveness and even for the indivisibility of monetary policy. However, it was a compromise or a balancing act between the effectiveness of the programme and its fiscal policy consequences, including moral hazard.

Regardless of the ultimate monetary policy nature of the PSPP, the decision raises some questions concerning possible other aims that could help explain the programme, its size, features, and timing. Such aims could include reducing the euro exchange rate; increasing asset prices to reduce financial instability; and financing of Member States in trouble.[56] Of these, a lower euro exchange rate was an even likelier outcome than higher inflation.[57] It is therefore presumable that the ECB hoped to see a downward pressure on the effective exchange rate of the euro,[58] but did not want to make it explicit as it was outside its mandate. Turning to financial stability considerations, they have remained absent in the ECB's communication on the PSPP that did, however, include the aim to increase asset prices. As mentioned earlier, a QE programme can be an effective tool particularly in a situation of financial instability and

[54] The decision stated that 'these asset purchase programmes are aimed at ... contributing to returning inflation rates to levels closer to 2 percent' by 'enhancing the transmission of monetary policy, facilitating credit provision to the euro area economy, easing borrowing conditions of households and firms'. This was to support consumption and investments: Decision (EU) 2015/774 of the European Central Bank (n 15) recitals (2) and (4). As was also pointed out by the FCC in the *Weiss* case: BVerfG Judgment of the Second Senate of 5 May 2020 2 BvR 859/15 ECLI:DE:BVerfG:2020:rs:20200505.2bvr085915 (hereafter *Weiss* case FCC 2 BvR 859/15).

[55] Draghi stressed that concerning the effectiveness of the PSPP limited risk-sharing had a small negative effect and did not hide that he was against it. Draghi, 'Introductory statement to the press conference (with Q&A)' 22 January 2015 (n 52).

[56] Stefan Wagstyl and Chris Giles, 'Critics Fear ECB Quantitative Easing Will Lead to Crisis' *Financial Times* (Berlin and Davos, 22 January 2015) <https://www.ft.com/content/10a0f880-a25c-11e4-9630-00144feab7de> accessed 1 July 2021; Birgit Jennen, 'Ifo's Sinn Says ECB Using Deflation Risk as Excuse for QE' *Bloomberg* (New York, 12 January 2015) <www.bloomberg.com/news/articles/2015-01-12/ifo-s-sinn-says-ecb-using-deflation-risk-as-excuse-for-qe> accessed 1 July 2021.

[57] Also, in theoretical and empirical considerations, there is evidence of the effect on exchange rates and asset prices: see Udara M Peiris and Herakles Polemarchakis, 'Quantitative easing in an open economy: prices, exchange rates and risk premia' (2015) Warwick Economics Research Paper Series Working Paper No 1094 <http://wrap.warwick.ac.uk/81397/> accessed 1 July 2021 and Michel Dupuy and Sylvie Lacueille, 'The Effects of US and UK Quantitative Easing Policies on Exchange Rates' (2013) 103 International Research Journal of Finance and Economics 61.

[58] Paul de Grauwe, 'The sad consequences of the fear of QE' *The Economist* (London, 21 January 2015) <https://www.economist.com/free-exchange/2015/01/21/the-sad-consequences-of-the-fear-of-qe> accessed 1 July 2021.

then it is also likely to have positive side-effects on financial stability.[59] However, this was not necessarily the case with the ECB's programmes. The PSPP was launched at a time when the prices of most asset classes in most euro area jurisdictions were already elevated, and it has fuelled ever higher asset prices since. It could thus be argued that although the PSPP might have eased some financial stress in some parts of the euro area, its full effect could turn out to be the opposite and increase financial instability going forward through a potential asset price bubble.[60] Finally, the most often claimed motivation for the PSPP is the support for the financing of Member States.[61] Naturally, this never was an official aim of the PSPP due to Article 123 TFEU, but the programme does explicitly aim at lowering the borrowing costs for Member States.

V. The PEPP Adds to the ECB's QE Firepower

The COVID-19 pandemic raised new types of policy questions. The main economic difficulties stemmed from containment measures, making conventional demand and also supply measures ineffective. The broad economic policy line, in the EU and more globally, was to help the economy (and society) through the crisis with as limited permanent output losses as possible. In practice, this meant that companies and households were supported until the containment measures were lifted and recovery could start. Provision of liquidity, bridge financing, and many forms of direct support were initiated.[62] The public finances carried the main burden: various support programmes and public expenditure in health and social policy jumped to a new level. Consequently, fiscal deficits widened dramatically and public debt rose even more, making public sector financing a critical factor.

The ECB took a central role in fighting the economic consequences of the pandemic. Its responses expanded and reactivated earlier measures and initiated new targeted measures. Naturally, the ECB's measures were part of the broader policy response at the national and EU level, including proposals by the Commission.[63] For this chapter, the perspective is that of the changing nature of the ECB's monetary policy and not the pandemic response as such.

[59] As pointed out early on, eg, by Claudio Borio and Philip Lowe, 'Asset Prices, Financial and Monetary Stability: Exploring the Nexus' (2002) BIS Working Paper No 114 <https://www.bis.org/publ/work114.pdf> accessed 1 July 2021.

[60] The potential for an asset price bubble was asked from President Draghi in the European Parliament: Mario Draghi, 'Hearing at the European Parliament's Economic and Monetary Affairs Committee (introductory remarks and Q&A)' (Speech, Brussels, 23 March 2015). Jean Pisani-Ferry, 'The ECB and Its Critics' *Politico* (Arlington County, 7 February 2015) <https://www.politico.eu/article/the-ecb-and-its-critics/> accessed 1 July 2021. Governor of the Bank of England Carney stated: 'in an environment of low interest rates and quantitative easing there can be excessive risk-taking.'

[61] As was pointed out by the Memorandum on the ECB's Monetary Policy by a large group of senior central bankers: see Hervé Hannoun and others, 'Memorandum on the ECB's Monetary Policy' (4 October 2019) <http://www.centerforfinancialstability.org/research/Memorand.pdf> accessed 1 July 2021 and, eg, also noted by the German Constitutional Court in *Weiss* case FCC 2 BvR 859/15 (n 54).

[62] See, eg, International Monetary Fund, 'World Economic Outlook: The Great Lockdown' (International Monetary Fund 2020).

[63] The most fundamental proposals by the Commission were, however, more controversial and took more time to be agreed upon, which in turn placed more emphasis on the ECB. See chapter 14 by Ad van Riet, in this volume.

The first ECB pandemic-induced monetary policy measures were launched in March 2020.[64] The aim was to preserve the flow of credit to households and firms to ensure the transmission of monetary policy to bank lending rates to households and firms across all euro area countries and to guarantee favourable financing conditions for Member States fighting the pandemic. In addition, the ECB's Single Supervisory Mechanism initiated relief measures also on the banking supervision side. Banks were allowed temporary reductions in the minimum level of capital as well as other relaxations.[65]

The first set of measures fought the risk that a financing squeeze would force companies out of business and place households in worse trouble. The ECB offered various forms of additional medium- and longer-term funding to banks at (negative) interest rates of the deposit facility,[66] which incentivized banks to keep lending with a reward negative interest rate.[67] These liquidity measures were accompanied by new pandemic emergency longer-term refinancing operations (PELTROs)[68] that effectively provided money markets with a backstop and a temporary collateral easing. Thus, any euro area bank with some collateral would get liquidity up to the amount of collateral they had available until the latter half of 2021 and with a negative interest rate.

A. PEPP as the pandemic quantitative easing

The most dramatic and far-reaching of the ECB's pandemic measures was the Pandemic Emergency Purchase Programme (PEPP).[69] It was a temporary asset purchase programme for private and public sector securities with an initial amount of €750 billion that is added to the recontinued PSPP.[70] All asset classes of the broad Asset

64 European Central Bank, 'Statement by the President of the ECB' (ECB Press Release, 2 March 2020) <https://www.ecb.europa.eu/press/pr/date/2020/html/ecb.pr200302~f2f6113f52.en.html> accessed 1 July 2021.

65 European Central Bank, 'ECB Banking Supervision provides temporary capital and operational relief in reaction to coronavirus' (ECB Press Release, 12 March 2020) <https://www.ecb.europa.eu/press/pr/date/2020/html/ecb.pr200312~45417d8643.en.html> accessed 1 July 2021.

66 Decision (EU) 2019/1311 of the European Central Bank of 22 July 2019 on a third series of targeted longer-term refinancing operations (ECB/2019/21) [2019] OJ L204/100, and its amendments.

67 European Central Bank, 'Monetary policy decisions' (ECB Press Release, 12 March 2020) <https://www.ecb.europa.eu/press/pr/date/2020/html/ecb.mp200312~8d3aec3ff2.en.html> accessed 1 July 2021; European Central Bank, 'ECB announces easing of conditions for targeted longer-term refinancing operations (TLTRO III)' (ECB Press Release, 12 March 2020) <https://www.ecb.europa.eu/press/pr/date/2020/html/ecb.pr200312_1~39db50b717.en.html> accessed 1 July 2021; and European Central Bank, 'ECB announces measures to support bank liquidity conditions and money market activity' (ECB Press Release, 12 March 2020) <https://www.ecb.europa.eu/press/pr/date/2020/html/ecb.pr200312_2~06c32dabd1.en.html> accessed 1 July 2021.

68 European Central Bank, 'ECB announces new pandemic emergency longer-term refinancing operations' (ECB Press Release, 30 April 2020) <https://www.ecb.europa.eu/press/pr/date/2020/html/ecb.pr200430_1~477f400e39.en.html> accessed 1 July 2021.

69 Decision (EU) 2020/440 of the European Central Bank of 24 March 2020 on a temporary pandemic emergency purchase programme (ECB/2020/17) [2020] OJ L91/1.

70 European Central Bank, 'ECB announces €750 billion Pandemic Emergency Purchase Programme (PEPP)' (ECB Press Release, 18 March 2020) <https://www.ecb.europa.eu/press/pr/date/2020/html/ecb.pr200318_1~3949d6f266.en.html> accessed 1 July 2021 (hereafter European Central Bank, 'ECB announces €750 billion Pandemic Emergency Purchase Programme (PEPP)').

Purchase Programme (APP) were also eligible under the PEPP. The main new feature was flexibility, although the PEPP did, in principle, follow the ECB capital key benchmark allocation for public sector bonds. Now, Greek government bonds were also accepted and the Corporate Sector Purchase Programme (CSPP) was expanded to non-financial commercial paper. The ECB also stressed flexibility concerning the actual implementation of the programme and it was ready to revise any limits when necessary. The purchases were activated quickly in March 2020 with very large amounts. Already by June 2020, the ECB announced an expansion of the PEPP with another 600 billion euros.[71] In December 2020, a second extension raised the total amount of the PEPP to €1,850 billion.[72] The ECB has stated that it will terminate net asset purchases under the PEPP once it judges that the COVID-19 crisis phase is over, but in any case not before the end of March 2022.

The PEPP is a unique pandemic QE programme and the ECB's most forceful overall measure, as its speed, amounts, and flexibility allowed reactions to many unspecified market stress situations and also to problems arising from the COVID-19 containment measures. It was clearly a temporary and exceptional measure that can adjust flexibly to changing situations. It countered the risks to the monetary policy transmission mechanism 'in all jurisdictions of the euro area', which was closely related to the ECB's aim of supporting 'all citizens of the euro area through this extremely challenging time' by ensuring that households, companies, and governments benefit from 'supportive financing conditions'.[73] The PEPP thus aimed to avoid negative spirals in many areas of financial markets, where the early market reactions to the pandemic, in particular with equities and bonds, showed clear signs of elevated stress. At the same time, it was a true bazooka with a focus on power rather than on nuances and detailed economic analysis. The economic and financial market effects of the pandemic were large but very difficult to assess, and the PEPP gave the ECB firepower to react to events as they unfolded.

The ECB's pandemic responses, including the PEPP, were similar to that of other major central banks. Naturally, the actual programmes varied considerably due to differences in the reach of the public sector and particularly social security systems. In the USA, the response was led by the political side, and the Federal Reserve had a supporting role that consisted of rate cuts, an intense period of QE purchases from March to May 2020, and various targeted measures to ensure short-term funding for banks and longer-term credit to households, companies, and state and local governments.[74] The Bank of England's monetary policy also aimed at limiting any lasting damage to the economy by mitigating the tightening in financial conditions. It cut the official rate to 0.1 per cent and launched a funding scheme for small and medium enterprises

[71] European Central Bank, 'Monetary policy decisions' (ECB Press Release, 4 June 2020) <https://www.ecb.europa.eu/press/pr/date/2020/html/ecb.mp200604~a307d3429c.en.html> accessed 1 July 2021 (hereafter European Central Bank, 'Monetary Policy Decisions' 4 June 2020).

[72] European Central Bank, 'Monetary policy decisions' (ECB Press Release, 10 December 2020) <https://www.ecb.europa.eu/press/pr/date/2020/html/ecb.mp201210~8c2778b843.en.html> accessed 1 July 2021.

[73] European Central Bank, 'ECB announces €750 billion Pandemic Emergency Purchase Programme (PEPP)' (n 70).

[74] Jerome H Powell, 'Coronavirus and CARES Act' (Testimony before the Committee on Banking, Housing and Urban Affairs, US Senate, Washington DC, 19 May 2020) <https://www.bis.org/review/r200519a.pdf> accessed 1 July 2021.

(SMEs) and an initial £200 billion QE programme for government and corporate bonds. Similar central bank responses took place across developed countries. The main responsibility lied with the governments, and the central banks assisted when necessary. In particular, as the increase in public expenditure was enormous and led to massive issuance of new public debt, the QE programmes may have mitigated the adverse effects on interest rates and broader financial market conditions. Indeed, central banks have focused on financing conditions and the financial system, while the links between traditional monetary policy objective of price stability and the adopted measures received less attention.

B. Analysing the objectives and effects of PEPP

The pandemic response has rewritten economic policy history and could do the same for economic theory going forward. The economic challenges came from outside the existing framework and with a high level of urgency. This forced new thinking among all the economic policy actors and recourse to untested measures. Many households and companies were deprived of their normal income, which led to social destruction but also risked causing lasting effects on the economic potential. Arguably, the planning horizon of economic policy-makers shortened to an unforeseen extent, which was the case for the ECB as well. Arguably, the problems at hand needed all the attention, and potential longer-term implications and problems were left to be solved in the future.

Compared to other major central banks, the ECB has arguably taken a more prominent role. Where the initial euro area and EU political responses were relatively limited and only gained traction once the initial shock was over, the ECB was the EU institution that could react quickly as explained earlier. In this regard, the ECB was able to calm down fears that government funding costs would start to increase.

In a situation of heightened uncertainty, the ECB, alongside other central banks, was less explicit concerning the impact on the inflation objective in its economic communication. Indeed, the pandemic impact on inflation and inflation process was all but straightforward. The first shock was negative, also driven by lower energy prices. However, while the demand side impact on inflation was negative, the supply side constraints also had the potential of causing price pressures. In this context, the ECB measures mainly targeted overall liquidity and availability of credit for the economy to avoid longer-term damage, not inflation as such.[75]

An even surprisingly clear aim of the ECB as explained by President Lagarde was to maintain favourable funding conditions for the euro area Member States. The ECB ensured that market pressures on some Member States could not lead to higher bond yields at a time of substantial debt issuance.[76] The PEPP purchases were even

[75] European Central Bank, 'Monetary Policy Decisions' 4 June 2020 (n 71) and Christine Lagarde and Luis de Guindos, 'Introductory statement' (ECB Press Conference, Frankfurt am Main, 4 June 2020) <https://www.ecb.europa.eu/press/pressconf/2020/html/ecb.is200604~b479b8cfff.en.html> accessed 1 July 2021 (hereafter Lagarde and de Guindos, 'Introductory statement' 4 June 2020).

[76] Lagarde and de Guindos, 'Introductory statement' 4 June 2020 (n 75).

characterized as a backstop,[77] and at €1,850 billion, they were very large in relative terms. Indeed, the flexibility of the PEPP, which included its explicit backstop function, made it similar to selective bond purchases and particularly the OMT programme. Arguably, as was the case with the OMT announcement in 2012, the key concern related to the risk that government bond yields (in some countries) would edge higher and eventually reach a level where debt servicing costs would make the debt burden unbearable.

Turning to the economic effects of the ECB's measures, the results are only very tentative. The clearest impact was visible in capital markets, where an initial market panic in March 2020 was followed by a broad-based recovery or even a boom in most asset classes.[78] This was not a specific euro area phenomenon, as US equities recovered to their all-time high levels already by July 2020. Indeed, the global response to the pandemic turned the initial decline in asset prices into a sustained trend increase, and even a bubble towards the latter half of 2020 and in 2021. The ECB has provided some early estimates of the effects of the PEPP, which suggest that it brought down euro area government bond yields by some 20 basis points and eased pressures towards euro area fragmentation.[79] However, early indicators of the economic effects of the pandemic did not show any meaningful differentiation between euro area countries, as they mainly reflected the starting point of each country, not their dynamics during and after the pandemic.

A special new feature was central bank activity as bank supervisors on the basis of the needs of the macroeconomic situation. The ECB, the Federal Reserve, and the Bank of England all relaxed some supervisory criteria in order to help banks, for example, through counter-cyclical capital buffers. These relaxations in supervisory criteria could also raise some concerns. If supervisors react to heightened risks by reducing capital requirements and imposing less stringent monitoring, this could become counterproductive for the functioning of the banking sector through diminished trust among banks. On the other side, this macroeconomically rationalized supervisory measure could also be justified by the temporary and external nature of the shock that excludes the moral hazard impact on banks' behaviour going forward. These issues might receive more attention once the situation calms down.

VI. Conclusions: The ECB and New Monetary Policy

Since the GFC, the ECB's monetary policy has relied on 'unconventional' measures to affect the economy and inflation outlook. The conventional monetary policy measures are still intact, but they have been in full use more or less from 2009 onwards. Short-term official interest rates are at zero and short-term provision of liquidity is

[77] ibid.

[78] eg, Scott R Baker and others, 'The Unprecedented Stock Market Reaction to COVID-19' (2020) 10 Review of Asset Pricing Studies 742 or Libo Xu, 'Stock Return and the COVID-19 pandemic: Evidence from Canada and the US' (2021) 38(C) Finance Research Letters 1.

[79] Philip R Lane, 'The market stabilisation role of the pandemic emergency purchase programme' (*The ECB Blog*, 22 June 2020) <https://www.ecb.europa.eu/press/blog/date/2020/html/ecb.blog200622~14c4269b9e.en.htm> accessed 1 July 2021.

constrained only by banks' availability of collateral. Hence, the operations framework designed for the new central bank was deemed sufficient only for a decade, after which the course of events but perhaps also a more general change in central banking have led to substantial changes to the operational mode of the ECB. In fact, it is possible to detect two phases of unconventional monetary policy thus far.

The first phase relied on extending the length of conventional monetary policy and on the introduction of the contested selective government bond purchases. This period of extreme experimentalism in the shadow of existential threats to the whole euro area lasted mainly from 2010 until the initial calming down in 2012. This phase differentiated the ECB from most of the other central banks, and the 'monetary policy transmission' became a critical concept to rationalize the ECB's unconventional measures against the forces of economic, financial, and even political fragmentation.

The second phase of unconventional monetary policy relies mainly on QE programmes, namely large-scale purchases of euro area government bonds and some other public sector debt securities. While QE had been part of the toolbox of most other major central banks since the start of the GFC, the ECB utilized it much later and in somewhat different circumstances. In the euro area context with centralized monetary authority and national fiscal authorities, QE has complicating institutional, economic, and also constitutional implications that prevented the ECB from turning to QE for many years until 2015 and even then the programme contained some peculiarities such as limited risk-sharing among the euro area central banks. What finally changed the ECB's mind was probably a combination of concerns including deflationary fears, worsening of the Greek situation, and financial and fiscal stability concerns. For all of these reasons, the ability to react to adverse financial market situations in addition to a steady increase in bank liquidity were considered necessary. Consequently, more than seven years later, QE has become one of the key features of the ECB's monetary policy, and thereby as conventional a monetary policy tool as it is with other major central banks.

The main programme has been the PSPP, launched in January 2015, that is at the same time a fairly typical QE programme and also a peculiar euro area monetary policy vehicle. It has a very large monthly purchase amount, a long and eagerly extended running-period, and the purchases are mostly directed at low-risk government bonds. The peculiarities relate to limited risk-sharing among the Member States and to the purchase of also less than very highly rated bonds. The pandemic QE programme, the PEPP, is even more peculiar, as it is intended to provide an effective backstop for Member States' government finances. It thus combines some elements of the selective bond purchases with QE as a targeted response to the consequences of the pandemic on the financing conditions of the Member States alongside companies. From this perspective, the PEPP could also be seen as a successor of the OMT programme that provided the ECB 'guarantee' for Member State financing.

This chapter has not engaged in a thorough constitutional assessment of the ECB's new monetary policy and particularly its QE programmes. Still, it can be concluded from the above that they do raise some new issues with regard to the conduct of supranational monetary policy and particularly with regard to the price stability objective and its relationship with other possible objectives. The PSPP and the PEPP have been defined as monetary policy instruments, although particularly the latter was influenced by the exceptional circumstances of the COVID-19 crisis and the urgency it created, which potentially pushed aside some constitutional concerns in relation to the Court of Justice of the EU's earlier case law. Most importantly, the emphasis on the objective of price stability as the main means for defining the monetary policy domain was quite weak in the PEPP that clearly reacted to economic and financial market worries.

Indeed, the main question with regard to QE is its relationship with the potential objectives of monetary policy. First, the link to inflation is not particularly strong nor straightforward. Indeed, central banks turn to QE mostly when other means are no longer effective and the economy is faced with deflationary pressures. The evidence on achieving higher inflation through QE programmes is thus quite weak. And for the future, it is more or less unchartered territory how to control the inflation process that has gained speed, when the central bank holds huge amounts of QE purchases. For example, should the inflation pressures pick up, how quickly and with what consequences could the ECB reduce monetary policy stimuli of its QE programmes?

Apart from the cyclical and also crises-related reasons to turn to QE, another and more structural reason why central banks, including the ECB, have turned to QE is a potential trend decline in the effectiveness of conventional monetary policy. More concretely, many central banks have suggested that there has been a potential trend reduction in the neutral real interest rates of the economy, which forces central banks to look for other means to affect the economy and particularly prices. This simply means that, if the neutral real interest rate is zero, and the central bank has a 2 per cent inflation target, the zero bound of interest rates leaves only two percentage points room for monetary policy stimulus. Consequently, conventional monetary policy could often become insufficient, making the use of unconventional monetary policy tools more frequent and hence conventional. However, it should be kept in mind that it is very early to detect whether the low real rates are a permanent feature or still mainly cycle and crises induced.

Second, with regard to other potential objectives, QE is more complicated particularly in the euro area context due to the specific mandate of the ECB with a primary objective of price stability. QE is theoretically most effective as a monetary policy instrument in a situation of financial instability. However, this increases the likelihood that it is perceived to be used to counteract financial instability instead of maintaining price stability. This can put the ECB in a vulnerable position in light of its specific price stability mandate as well as create complications with the balance of competences within the euro area.

Third, QE can be problematic for financial stability also from another perspective, namely by creating boom and bust cycles. Indeed, if a QE programme pushes asset prices to an unsustainable level this creates vulnerabilities going forward. It can become a source of financial instability in itself that could hardly be corrected by a new set of QE programmes once the bubble bursts. Whether this is already the case in the euro area remains to be seen.

In sum, the ECB has now relied on QE as its main monetary policy tool for more than seven years, which is starting to question the notion that it is still unconventional monetary policy. However, what continues to be unconventional is that the reliance on QE has resulted in a new type of relationship between monetary policy and the rest of the economy and society more generally. It is a heavy machinery monetary policy tool that can have many welcome and unwelcome effects as well as anticipated and unanticipated effects. To this date, the ECB has been clear in its aim to increase economic growth and inflation, and with the PEPP also at supporting short-term financial stability and Member State financing. However, and as pointed out also by the German Constitutional Court, the effects of QE could go well beyond the traditional reach of monetary policy. Without taking a stance on the economic substantive elements of this legal debate, I do find it clear that the ECB's QE has become the most important factor in financial markets and asset prices that contains the possibility of deeply destabilizing developments in the future.

Against this background, a key issue with QE even as a new conventional monetary policy tool relates to its unconventional impact on the economy and particular asset prices. Although conventional monetary policy also affects many areas of the economy and society more generally, QE has brought new features. It affects asset prices directly, and even needs to affect asset prices to become effective. In this regard, the PEPP was most explicit, as the ECB gave it two monetary policy aims: operationalizing the monetary policy stance and ensuring the functioning of monetary policy transmission across asset classes and particularly jurisdictions. The latter, monetary transmission, argument is closely linked to financial stability and Member States' public finances, as it aims at pushing down the interest rates on government bonds amidst market pressures. This follows the ECB's line of argumentation with monetary policy transmission that could be seen as a financial stability objective as well even if it was not made explicit by the ECB. Here, one interesting question is whether the ECB has begun to see the financial market developments as a key indicator of its success, which would be closer to the US monetary policy (and more broadly economic policy) model than the traditional European model that has traditionally focused on institutions and individuals instead of markets. In this case, QE as new conventional monetary policy, could lead to a more philosophical shift in the common monetary policy.

The QE programmes, first the PSPP and particularly the PEPP, have raised most concerns with regard to Member States' fiscal responsibility and the prohibition on central bank financing of governments (Article 123 TFEU).[80] The programmes maintain limited risk-sharing and claim to have sufficient safeguards against providing market participants any certainty that their bonds will be bought.[81] Nevertheless, the bonds are purchased by issuing central bank money, which is a euro area liability. Should a Member State default, this liability would need to be addressed. On the other hand, if the risk-sharing limitation is taken seriously, the NCB of the defaulting Member State would default at the same time with a balance sheet that would have mainly defaulting assets (government bonds and loans to local banks) and mainly intra-Eurosystem liabilities (issuance of central bank money and TARGET2 liabilities). How this would work out, is anybody's guess.

A slightly less dramatic public finances consequence of the QE programmes is that the ECB has arguably become the Lender of Last Resort to the Member States. This

[80] *Weiss* case FCC 2 BvR 859/15 (n 54).

[81] As was explained by the CJEU in Case C-493/17 *Weiss and Others* [2018] ECLI:EU:C:2018:1000.

can be problematic from the perspective of Member States' fiscal responsibility in the Economic and Monetary Union, as the PEPP also lacks the mitigating factor of the OMT, namely conditionality imposed by the link to the ESM assistance programmes. Similarly, the public finance perspective can burden or even constrain the ECB's conduct of monetary policy, for example in a situation in which the inflationary pressures are increasing.

4

The ECB's Collateral Framework from the 1990s until the Pandemic

Jens van 't Klooster

I. Introduction

The implementation of monetary policy involves lending to banks as well as purchases of financial assets. Since banks and issuers can default, these operations unavoidably expose central banks to financial risk. In this chapter, I analyse how the European Central Bank (ECB) has dealt with risk, focusing on its refinancing operations, from its creation in the 1990s to until 2020. I highlight changes to the role of the central bank that cast serious doubt on whether its risk management strategy is still up to date, and propose ways to revise the ECB's current approach to financial risk.[1]

Before the start of the 2010–12 euro area crisis, the ECB's understanding of its role in financial markets was relatively straightforward, which made risk management relatively simple. Although its legal mandate gives the ECB the task to not only implement but also 'define' the euro area's monetary policy, the ECB ascribed to itself a narrow role in pursuing low inflation by setting short-term interest rates.[2] The design of monetary policy operations always involved choices. However, in designing its operations to influence short-term rates, the ECB would mostly follow market practices and focus on protecting itself against risk.

To protect itself against counterparty default, the ECB asks banks to post collateral. Central bank collateral is an asset pledged by a borrower that the central bank acquires if the borrower defaults. By accepting high-quality collateral, the central bank can ensure a very high level of protection against losses. However, although the ECB Statutes require that any credit transactions with financial market participants be 'based on adequate collateral', the interpretation of 'adequate' is left entirely to the ECB.[3] Hence,

[1] ECB, 'The Financial Risk Management of the Eurosystem's Monetary Policy Operations (ECB 2015) <https://www.ecb.europa.eu/pub/pdf/other/financial_risk_management_of_eurosystem_monetary_policy_operations_201507.en.pdf> accessed 13 April 2021 (hereafter ECB, 'The Financial Risk Management of the Eurosystem's Monetary Policy Operations').

[2] Hanspeter Scheller, *The European Central Bank: History, Role and Functions* (2nd edn, European Central Bank 2006) (hereafter Scheller, *The European Central Bank*); Otmar Issing, *The Birth of the Euro* (CUP 2008) (hereafter Issing, *The Birth of the Euro*); Jens van 't Klooster and Clément Fontan, 'The Myth of Market Neutrality: A Comparative Study of the European Central Bank's and the Swiss National Bank's Corporate Security Purchases' (2020) 25 New Political Economy 865 (hereafter van 't Klooster and Fontan, 'The Myth of Market Neutrality'); consolidated version of the Treaty on the Functioning of the European Union [2012] OJ C326/01 (hereafter TFEU), Art 127.

[3] TFEU (n 2) Protocol No 4 On Statute of the European System of Central Banks and the European Central Bank, Art 18.

Jens van 't Klooster, *The ECB's Collateral Framework from the 1990s till the Present* In: *The New European Central Bank.*
Edited by: Thomas Beukers, Diane Fromage, and Giorgio Monti, Oxford University Press. © Jens van 't Klooster 2022.
DOI: 10.1093/oso/9780198871231.003.0004

the choices that the ECB makes in how to deal with risk have an unacknowledged significance within the broader constitution of the EMU.

From the European Monetary Institute (EMI) onwards, which between 1994 and 1998 set out to create the ECB, there have always been lively debates on how to design monetary policy operations. Before the euro area crisis, these debates tended to focus on what assets were sufficiently safe to count as collateral for ECB refinancing operations. Central bankers were also concerned to limit the impact of collateral rules and other choices on market prices. The price of risk, as it was assumed, should be left to market-based price discovery. These assumptions became the basis for the sophisticated Single List of Eligible Collateral in 2006, which replaced a two-tier system that had been in place since 1998. The risk management strategy that informed the Single List ascribes a crucial role to private credit ratings and other risk management practices that became prevalent at the time. Implicit in that strategy was the belief that financial markets would be efficient and that monetary policy should, therefore, focus on the real economy objective of price stability.

Since 2010, however, that complacent view of financial markets has been undermined by repeated failures of European financial markets to adequately price risk. The euro area crisis saw far-reaching and self-enforcing negative spirals between the government finances of the individual Member States and the stability of their domestic banking sector.[4] A crucial role in those crisis dynamics went to private credit rating agencies, whose pivotal role in European financial markets is bolstered by their prominent role in ECB risk management practices.[5] More recently, the ECB has increasingly sought to incorporate environmental and climate-related considerations into its monetary policy operations. Meanwhile, the ECB's official risk management strategy, last updated in 2015, remains informed by the pre-2010 priorities of protecting itself against losses and minimizing its impact on financial markets.

A key question that the ECB faces in the review of its monetary policy strategy is how to deal with risk in these new circumstances. To deal with its new challenges in managing risk, the ECB should clarify under what conditions its objective of minimizing losses is decisive and when risk management should bow to other ECB policy objectives such as financial stability and environmental sustainability. The ECB should also give up on its policy of market neutrality in favour of what I describe as a policy of 'market attentiveness'. To ensure that its policy priorities are duly reflected in its

[4] Paul De Grauwe, 'The European Central Bank: Lender of Last Resort in the Government Bond Markets?' (2011) CESifo Working Paper Series No 3569 <https://papers.ssrn.com/sol3/papers.cfm?abstract_id=1927783> accessed 13 April 2021; Heather D Gibson, Stephen G Hall, and George S Tavlas, 'Self-Fulfilling Dynamics: The Interactions of Sovereign Spreads, Sovereign Ratings and Bank Ratings during the Euro Financial Crisis' (2017) 73 JIMF 371; Nicola Gennaioli, Alberto Martin, and Stefano Rossi, 'Banks, Government Bonds, and Default: What do the Data Say?' (2918) 98 Journal of Monetary Economics 98.

[5] Daniela Gabor and Cornel Ban, 'Banking on Bonds: The New Links between States and Markets' (2016) 54 JCMS 617; Gregory Claeys and Ines Goncalves Raposo, 'Is the ECB Collateral Framework Compromising the Safe-Asset Status of Euro-Area Sovereign Bonds?' (*Bruegel*, 8 June 2018) <http://bruegel.org/2018/06/is-the-ecb-collateral-framework-compromising-the-safe-asset-status-of-euro-area-sovereign-bonds/> accessed 13 April 2021 (hereafter Claeys and Goncalves Raposo, 'Is the ECB Collateral Framework Compromising the Safe-Asset Status of Euro-Area Sovereign Bonds?'); Athanasios Orphanides, 'Monetary Policy and Fiscal Discipline: How the ECB Planted the Seeds of the Euro Area Crisis' (*VoxEU*, 9 March 2018) <https://voxeu.org/article/how-ecb-planted-seeds-euro-area-crisis> accessed 13 April 2021 (hereafter Orphanides, 'Monetary Policy and Fiscal Discipline').

operations and the broader financial markets that they shape, the ECB should expand its own internal credit rating facilities. To calibrate its priorities and clarify the status of its ambiguous mandate, the ECB should enhance coordination with the EU's political institutions.

The chapter is structured as follows. Section II analyses the early history of the ECB collateral framework and the turn to a market-based approach to risk in the mid-2000s. Section III discusses how developments after 2010 forced the ECB to pay more attention to the financial market impact of its risk management strategy; both to the pro-cyclical dynamics in sovereign bond markets and the climate impact of bond issuers. Section IV puts forward four recommendations for how the ECB should deal with these new challenges. Section V concludes.

II. ECB Risk Management before 2010

The monetary operations of the ECB involve transactions with private and public sector counterparties that expose it to financial risk.[6] There is, however, no clear answer in the ECB's mandate to the question of how to manage these risks, which the ECB needs to decide itself. That is not a simple matter and the ECB has only had a harmonized risk management strategy since 2006.

How the central bank manages risk has pervasive impact on financial markets, public finance, and the allocation of capital in the real economy. Because of the central bank's pivotal role in the financial system, an asset that can potentially be pledged as collateral at the central bank is more cash-like; it provides immediate access to the means of payment at the top of the monetary hierarchy.[7] Collateral eligibility makes the asset more attractive to hold for banks and other investors, which are always potentially liquidity constrained. Financial markets, therefore, tend to copy central bank eligibility criteria for transactions between private sector counterparties.[8] Where central banks implement monetary policy through outright purchase, this not only affects long-term rates, but also the financing costs of eligible issuers.[9]

[6] The historical account of the ECB collateral framework builds on Jens van 't Klooster, *The Political Economy of Central Bank Risk Management* (PhD Thesis University of Groningen 2021) and Jens van 't Klooster, 'The Politics of the ECB's Market-Based Approach to Government Debt' (2022) Socio-Economic Review <DOI: https://doi.org/10.1093/ser/mwac014> accessed 13 April 2021. The focus in the following is on financial risk in monetary policy operations. ECB and NCBs, eg, also take on risk through own funds, employee pensions, and through central bank swaplines.

[7] Perry Mehrling, *The New Lombard Street: How the Fed Became the Dealer of Last Resort* (Princeton University Press 2011); Katharina Pistor, 'A Legal Theory of Finance' (2013) 41 Journal of Comparative Economics 315.

[8] BIS, 'Central Bank Collateral Frameworks and Practices' (2013) Markets Committee Paper 6 <https://www.bis.org/publ/mktc06.pdf> accessed 13 April 2021 (hereafter BIS, 'Central Bank Collateral Frameworks and Practices'); Daniela Gabor and Cornel Ban, 'Banking on Bonds: The New Links between States and Markets' (2016) 54 JCMS 617 (hereafter Gabor and Ban, 'Banking on Bonds'); Manmohan Singh, 'Collateral Reuse and Balance Sheet Space' (2017) IMF Working Paper No 17/113 <https://www.imf.org/en/Publications/WP/Issues/2017/05/08/Collateral-Reuse-and-Balance-Sheet-Space-44892> accessed 13 April 2021.

[9] Georgios Georgiadis and Johannes Gräb, 'Global Financial Market Impact of the Announcement of the ECB's Asset Purchase Programme' (2016) 26 Journal of Financial Stability 257; Nordine Abidi and Ixart Miquel-Flores, 'Who Benefits from the Corporate QE? A Regression Discontinuity Design Approach' (2018) ECB Working Paper Series April 2018 <https://econpapers.repec.org/paper/ecbecbwps/20182145.htm> accessed 13 April 2021.

When the European community initiated the process of monetary unification, the task of the central bank was meant to be simple.[10] At the time sometimes referred to as 'Eurofed', it was meant to pursue price stability. In the background of that simple objective were a set of ideas about money and the economy, popularized by Milton Friedman, that deny that monetary policy can make a lasting contribution to the economy's productive capacity. Instead of serving any particular economic policy, the central bank is meant to achieve the well-defined objective of price stability by using one simple tool: setting interest rates.

In the ECB's pre-crisis self-understanding, setting rates was understood as a technical task, which involved the use of one instrument to pursue the clearly defined goal of price stability.[11] The discretion of the central bank was meant to be limited to finding the value of the instrument that allowed it to achieve that objective. The design of the instrument itself, moreover, was also deemed to be relatively straightforward. Although many operational frameworks allow central banks to set interest rates, central bankers argue that the choice of frameworks is primarily a matter of efficiency.[12]

The ECB would set interest rates using credit transaction in which the central bank lends to individual banks—what we today call 'conventional' operations. These transactions allow the central banks to steer interest rates in short-term money markets. The exact operations by which the ECB provides credit to the banking system have evolved considerably over the past decades.[13] Before 2008, a fixed volume of credit was offered to the highest bidder in weekly Main Refinancing Operations (MROs). In October 2008, the financial market panic led the ECB to switch from this so-called variable rate fixed allotment system to a fixed-rate full allotment system, providing an unlimited volume of credit in weekly MROs. In response to the crisis, the ECB also introduced a fixed volume auction of three months or longer credit in its Long-Term and Targeted Longer-Term Refinancing Operations (LTROs and TLTROs), which for the past years have made up by far the largest volume of credit to the banking system.[14]

All these monetary policy operations involve credit to banks, which exposes the ECB to the risk of counterparty default.[15] Although an actual default has happened in

[10] Kathleen McNamara, *The Currency of Ideas: Monetary Politics in the European Union* (Cornell University Press 1998); Harold James, *Making the European Monetary Union* (Harvard University Press 2013).

[11] Scheller, *The European Central Bank* (n 2); Issing, *The Birth of the Euro* (n 2); van 't Klooster and Fontan, 'The Myth of Market Neutrality' (n 2).

[12] Claudio Borio, 'A Hundred Ways to Skin a Cat: Comparing Monetary Policy Operating Procedures in the United States, Japan and the Euro Area' (2001) BIS Working Papers No 9 <https://www.bis.org/publ/bppdf/bispap09a.pdf> accessed 13 April 2021.

[13] Ulrich Bindseil, *Monetary Policy Operations and the Financial System* (OUP 2014) (hereafter Bindseil, *Monetary Policy Operations and the Financial System*); Massimo Rostagno and others, 'A Tale of Two Decades: The ECB's Monetary Policy at 20' (2019) ECB Working Paper Series No 2346 <https://ideas.repec.org/p/ecb/ecbwps/20192346.html> accessed 13 April 2021. See also chapter 2 by Vestert Borger and chapter 3 by Klaus Tuori, respectively, in this volume.

[14] ECB, 'Tender Operations History' (ECB 2020) <https://www.ecb.europa.eu/mopo/implement/omo/html/top_history.en.html> accessed 13 April 2021.

[15] Ulrich Bindseil, Fernando Gonzáles, and Evangelos Tabakis (eds), *Risk Management for Central Banks and Other Public Investors* (CUP 2009); Gareth Rule, 'Collateral Management in Central Bank Balance Policy Operations' (2012) Bank of England Centre for Central Banking Studies, 7 <https://www.bankofengland.co.uk/ccbs/collateral-management-in-central-bank-policy-operations> accessed 13 April 2021; ECB, 'The Financial Risk Management of the Eurosystem's Monetary Policy Operations' (n 1).

its entire history on only five occasions, the largest of which was the €8.5 billion default of Lehman Brother Bankhaus A.G. on the Bundesbank, risk management is an important day-to-day concern to the ECB. Accordingly, the ECB calibrates collateral requirements to protect itself against double default; default of not only the counterparty but also the issuer of the financial asset pledged as collateral.

While protecting itself against risk, however, the ECB also seeks to ensure that banks have sufficient collateral to secure their refinancing transactions.[16] Because a bank that no longer has sufficient collateral defaults, the objective of providing banks with collateral weighs heavier than concerns about losses. Traditionally, central banks are meant to prioritize bank liquidity management over their own risk management concerns.[17] In a financial market panic, central banks accept risky assets as part of the central bank's role as Lender of Last Resort. To stop a panic, as the nineteenth-century financial journalist Walter Bagehot wrote, the central bank should lend 'on every kind of current security, or every sort on which money is ordinarily and usually lent'.[18]

So, how does the ECB decide what assets are eligible as collateral? The ECB mandate does not provide it with much of an answer to that question.[19] This is not the case for every central bank. There is, in fact, considerable variation in the extent to which central bank's mandates address the question of financial market risk management. Before the introduction of the euro, the mandates of European National Central Banks (NCBs) often had detailed provisions governing eligible assets.[20] The Bundesbank, for example, would not have been permitted to pursue a Quantitative Easing programme targeted on private sector assets.[21] To this day, the Federal Reserve Act requires that open market operations rely on Treasuries and agency-bonds.[22]

[16] Ulrich Bindseil and Francesco Papadia, 'Credit Risk Mitigation in Central Bank Operations and Its Effect on Financial Markets: The Case of the Eurosystem' (2006) ECB Occasional Paper Series 49 <http://dx.doi.org/10.1017/CBO9780511575716.009> accessed 13 April 2021; Ulrich Bindseil and others, 'The Eurosystem Collateral Framework Explained' (2017) ECB Occasional Paper Series 189 <https://www.ecb.europa.eu/pub/pdf/scpops/ecb.op189.en.pdf> accessed 13 April 2021 (hereafter Bindseil and others, 'The Eurosystem Collateral Framework Explained').

[17] Michael D Bordo, 'The Lender of Last Resort: Alternative Views and Historical Experience' (1990) 76 FRB Richmond Economic Review 18; Paul Tucker, 'The Lender of Last Resort and Modern Central Banking: Principles and Reconstruction' in Bank for International Settlements (ed), *Re-Thinking the lender of last resort* (79 BIS Papers Chapters 10, BIS 2014).

[18] Walter Bagehot, *Lombard Street: A Description of the Money Market* (John Wiley & Sons 1999) 199.

[19] René Smits, *The European Central Bank, Institutional Aspects* (Kluwer 1997); Christos V Gortsos, *European Central Banking Law: The Role of the European Central Bank and National Central Banks under European Law* (Palgrave Macmillan 2020); Nik de Boer and Jens van 't Klooster, 'The ECB, the Courts and the Issue of Democratic Legitimacy after Weiss' (2020) 57 CML Rev 1689 (hereafter de Boer and van 't Klooster, 'The ECB, the Courts and the Issue of Democratic Legitimacy after Weiss').

[20] EMI, 'Eligible Instruments for Mobilisation and Pledging during Stage 3 of EMU' (Monetary Policy Sub-Committee Task Force on Eligible Debt Instruments for Mobilization and Pledging, European Monetary Institute 1995), 3 (hereafter EMI, 'Eligible Instruments for Mobilisation and Pledging during Stage 3 of EMU').

[21] Deutsche Bundesbank, 'The law concerning the Deutsche Bundesbank' (Deutsche Bundesbank 1957) <https://www.bundesbank.de/en/publications/reports/monthly-reports/monthly-report-august-1957-704612> accessed 13 April 2021, Art 21(1) (hereafter Deutsche Bundesbank, 'The law concerning the Deutsche Bundesbank').

[22] Federal Reserve Act, Art 14(2). Article 13 allows lending to individuals, partnerships, and corporations in 'unusual and exigent circumstances' such as the 2020 pandemic.

Compared to these central banks, the ECB's mandate places only a few constraints on its risk management strategy.[23] The absence of clear operational provisions reflects the fact that the ECB's task is not just to exercise specific powers conferred to it by the mandate, but also to 'define and implement monetary policy'.[24] Article 18 of the ECB and European System of Central Banks (ESCB) Statute permits 'buying and selling outright (spot and forward) or under repurchase agreement and by lending or borrowing claims and marketable instruments, whether in euro or other currencies' as well as trading in precious metals. The ECB and NCBs are also allowed to 'conduct credit operations with credit institutions and other market participants, with lending being based on adequate collateral'. However, what it means for collateral to be adequate is unclear. For example, should adequacy be read to require minimizing losses or does it refer to a broader set of considerations concerning the central bank's market. This is not an arcane question nor is it new. The traditional role of Lender of Last Resort already suggests that the ECB should take into account bank liquidity management in setting its collateral standards. Even if 'adequate' is read to imply minimizing losses, however, lending to private sector counterparties always involves some risk, and the mandate does not say what sort of risk the ECB can permissibly take. Outright purchases do not involve collateral and, hence, the provision does not apply.

Despite the vagueness of its mandate where it concerns risk management and other operational aspects of the ECB, its pre-2008 self-understanding saw its discretion as narrowly circumscribed by the price stability objective:

> Competency for monetary policy is transferred within the limits and the conditions of a mandate which clearly defines the objective of monetary policy and thus limits the amount of legally permitted discretion that the decision-making bodies of the ECB can use in conducting monetary policy.[25]

To this day, ECB officials often confidently assert that principles such as market neutrality or the requirement to minimize losses on monetary policy operations have a firm foundation in the ECB's mandate.[26] However, historically, there was much less agreement about how to deal with risk, and the rules that govern ECB operations result from long internal discussions.

The question what assets to accept as collateral first emerged at the EMI, which between its creation in 1994 and the publication of the first ECB General Documentation in 1998 designed the operational framework of the new central bank.[27] As the EMI

[23] TFEU (n 2) Arts 119, 124, 125, and 126.

[24] Deutsche Bundesbank, 'The law concerning the Deutsche Bundesbank' (n 21) Art 3; TFEU (n 2) Art 127(2).

[25] Scheller, *The European Central Bank* (n 2) 127.

[26] Yves Mersch, 'Central Bank Risk Management in Times of Monetary Policy Normalisation' (International Risk Management Conference, Paris, 8 June 2018) <https://www.ecb.europa.eu/press/key/date/2018/html/ecb.sp180608.en.html> accessed 13 April 2021; Jens Weidmann, 'Climate Change and Central Banks' (Financial Markets Conference, Frankfurt am Main, 29 October 2019) <https://www.bundesbank.de/en/press/speeches/climate-change-and-central-banks-812618> accessed 13 April 2021.

[27] Mats Galvenius and Paul Mercier, 'The Story of the Eurosystem Framework' in Paul Mercier and Francesco Papadia (eds), *The Concrete Euro: Implementing Monetary Policy in the Euro Area* (OUP 2011) 115–214; EMI, 'Eligible Instruments for Mobilisation and Pledging during Stage 3 of EMU' (n 20).

Table 4.1 The two-tiered system of eligible collateral

	Tier-I (ECB list)	Tier-II (NCB lists)
Type of asset	Marketable debt instruments	Marketable and non-marketable debt instruments Equities traded on a regulated market.
Settlement procedures	Instruments must be centrally deposited with NCBs or a central securities depository	Assets must be easily accessible to the National Central Bank which has included them in its Tier-II list.
Credit standard	High credit standards are decided by the ECB but no clear standards are published	High credit standards are decided by the NCB
Risk-sharing	Yes	No

Source: © European Central Bank, Frankfurt am Main, Germany

ECB, 'The Single Monetary Policy in Stage Three: General Documentation on ESCB Monetary Policy Instruments and Procedures' (ECB 1998) 43 <https://www.ecb.europa.eu/press/pr/date/1998/html/pr980918.en.html> accessed 13 April 2021.

legal department at the time already acknowledged, there are 'no explicit rules prescribing or precluding the ECB and NCBs from accepting certain types of collateral'.[28] Deciding what assets to accept as collateral is also difficult because financial market practices and central bank operational frameworks differ immensely between the Member States. The most basic question in the design of the collateral framework is what types of assets to accept as collateral. One option is to accept only government bonds as the Federal Reserve does to this day. An exploratory study conducted at the time estimated that an operational framework for the ECB involving only public debt would have provided banks with sufficient collateral.[29] Despite everything that happened in-between, this remains true today. However, although some favoured this option, the EMI decided that the ECB should also accept debt issued by financial and non-financial issuers. For the ECB, government bonds currently make up less than 18 per cent of assets used to secure conventional monetary policy operations. This set the EMI on a cantankerous journey of finding risk management practices that would be acceptable to all NCBs.

The question of what assets to accept as collateral was not successfully resolved at the EMI and, in fact, it took until 2006 for the ECB to harmonize its collateral requirements.[30] Instead of a harmonized list, the EMI's Monetary Policy Sub Committee adopted a so-called two-tiered system (see Table 4.1). Under the two-tiered system,

[28] EMI, 'Legal Issues Relating to Collateral' (General Secretariat Annex to Report of the Task Force on Eligible Debt Instruments for Mobilisation and Pledging, European Monetary Institute 1995), 7.

[29] EMI, 'Eligible Instruments for Mobilisation and Pledging during Stage 3 of EMU' (n 20) 7.

[30] Guideline of the European Central Bank of 31 August 2006 amending Guideline ECB/2000/7 on monetary policy instruments and procedures of the Eurosystem (ECB/2006/12) [2006] OJ L352/1.

the ECB set its own Tier-I list for eligible assets. It included government debt, but also corporate debt with a sufficiently high credit rating. The Eurosystem NCBs were permitted to create a Tier-II list of assets that were deemed important for their domestic financial markets but are not part of the Tier-I list. In practice, central banks could add almost anything they liked to their Tier-II list so that Tier-II lists quickly came to include a vast range of assets. The Dutch, Spanish, and Portuguese central banks, for example, allowed companies to pledge liquid shares from companies listed on their national stock markets.[31]

Despite the divergent operational practices, risk management standards became harmonized with the creation of a Single List of Eligible Collateral in 2006, which replaced the two-tier system that had been in place since the start of the Economic and Monetary Union.[32] Under this approach, the ECB protects itself against losses through credit quality requirements on eligible assets and the risk controls that are both harmonized using sophisticated risk management techniques. These techniques derive from private sector risk management and accordingly have a narrow focus on minimizing losses. This approach, despite all the changes made to the collateral framework during the crisis, remains broadly in place today.[33]

First, consider credit quality requirements. The Single List evaluates credit quality in terms of annualized probabilities of default. The core of the Single List is the Eurosystem Credit Assessment Facility (ECAF), which sets minimum credit standards for individual assets that banks wish to post (See Table 4.2). The ECAF allows banks to draw on credit assessments from a wide range of sources: private credit rating agencies such as Moody's and S&P, credit ratings issued by Eurosystem NCBs, as well as ratings from the internal risk-models of banks and other third-party rating tools. The ECAF maps ratings from all these sources onto a harmonized scale. Credit quality steps (CQS) 1 to 3 correspond to investment grade ratings, while steps 4 and 5 are junk bond territory. In the process of introducing its Single List and harmonizing eligibility criteria, the ECB announced a minimum credit rating requirement for sovereign debt.[34] This means that from then on only debt issued by Member States with a sufficiently high ECAF rating is eligible as ECB collateral. In practice, the only ratings

[31] Ulrich Bindseil, *Monetary Policy Implementation: Theory--Past--Present* (OUP 2004) 161.

[32] European Central Bank, 'The Single List in the Collateral Framework of the Eurosystem' (2006) ECB Monthly Bulletin May 2006, 75–87 <https://www.ecb.europa.eu/pub/pdf/other/pp75-87_mb200605en.pdf> accessed 13 April 2021; European Central Bank, 'The Implementation of Monetary Policy in the Euro Area—General Documentation on Eurosystem Monetary Policy Instruments and Procedures' (ECB 2006) <https://www.ecb.europa.eu/pub/pdf/other/gendoc2006en.pdf> accessed 13 April 2021 (hereafter European Central Bank, 'The Implementation of Monetary Policy in the Euro Area—General Documentation on Eurosystem Monetary Policy Instruments and Procedures').

[33] European Central Bank, 'The Eurosystem Collateral Framework throughout the Crisis' (2013) ECB Monthly Bulletin July 2013, 72 <https://www.ecb.europa.eu/pub/pdf/other/art1_mb201307en_pp71-86en.pdf> accessed 13 April 2021 (hereafter European Central Bank, 'The Eurosystem Collateral Framework throughout the Crisis'); Bindseil and others, 'The Eurosystem Collateral Framework Explained' (n 16). Guideline (EU) 2015/510 of the ECB of 19 December 2014 on the implementation of the Eurosystem monetary policy framework (ECB/2014/60) [2015], OJ L91/3, last amended by Decision (EU) 2020/506 of the European Central Bank of 7 April 2020 [2020] OJ L109/1.

[34] Jean-Claude Trichet, 'Introductory statement with Q&A' (Press conference, Frankfurt am Main, 7 April 2005) <https://www.ecb.europa.eu/press/pressconf/2005/html/is050407.en.html> accessed 13 April 2021; European Central Bank, 'The Implementation of Monetary Policy in the Euro Area—General Documentation on Eurosystem Monetary Policy Instruments and Procedures' (n 32).

Table 4.2 ECAF credit quality requirements

	Fitch / S&P	Moody's
CQS 1 & 2	AAA to A-	Aaa to A3
CQS 3 (eligible since November 2008	BBB+ / BBB / BBB-	Baa1 / Baa2 / Baa3
CQS 4 (eligible at some NCBs under the 2011 ACC)	BB+	Ba1
CQS 5 (currently eligible for assets CSQ3 before 7 April 2020)	BB	Ba2

Source: © European Central Bank, Frankfurt am Main, Germany

European Central Bank, 'Eurosystem credit assessment framework (ECAF)' (ECB 2020) <https://www.ecb.europa.eu/paym/coll/risk/ecaf/html/index.en.html> accessed 13 April 2021 (hereafter European Central Bank, 'ECAF').

available for sovereign debt are those issued by private credit rating agencies, so that they acquire a crucial role in determining whether government debt is eligible as ECB collateral.

In addition to the ECAF, the Single List manages risk through a Common Eurosystem Pricing Hub (CEPH) and a principled valuation haircut policy. Pricing an asset is important because it determines the value of the collateral posted to secure the loan. The ECB values collateral at its CEPH, which is operated by the Banque de France and the Bundesbank. For assets that are traded on a daily basis, the CEPH relies on market prices. For an estimated 78 per cent of marketable assets there are no sufficiently recent market prices and a theoretical model determines the price.[35] The ECB also accepts assets as collateral that are not traded in regulated markets, which are also priced using a theoretical model or based on the outstanding amount of the bond.[36] Depending on the ECAF credit quality step (and some other criteria such as maturity and coupon structure), the ECB applies a haircut to the collateral.[37] A haircut is a reduction of the value of an asset for the purpose of determining how much can be lent against it. For example, a haircut of 20 per cent means that an asset can be pledged to secure credit up to a value of 80 per cent of the asset. The value of the asset minus the haircut determines how much banks can borrow from the ECB.

The Single List introduced a high degree of harmonization and standardization into the ECB's risk management strategy. Still, there remained differences in the ways that the individual NCBs deal with financial risk and historical specificities. Every central

[35] Kjell G Nyborg, *Collateral Frameworks: The Open Secret of Central Banks* (CUP 2017) ch 7 (hereafter Nyborg, *Collateral Frameworks*).

[36] European Central Bank, 'Valuation' (ECB 2019) <https://www.ecb.europa.eu/paym/coll/risk/valuation/html/index.en.html> accessed 13 April 2021.

[37] Fernando González and Phillipe Molitor, 'Risk Mitigation Measures and Credit Risk Assessment in Central Bank Policy Operations' in Evangelos Tabakis, Fernando González, and Ulrich Bindseil (eds), *Risk Management for Central Banks and Other Public Investors* (CUP 2009) 303–39; Guideline (EU) 2016/65 of the European Central Bank of 18 November 2015 on the valuation haircuts applied in the implementation of the Eurosystem monetary policy framework (ECB/2015/35) [2016] OJ L14/30.

bank has its own operational rulebook. The German Bundesbank, for example, has historically implemented its monetary policy by discounting covered bonds and trade bills.[38] To this day, it has a large credit rating facility for covered bonds and trade bills. Loans posted as collateral can be as small as €25,000. The Banque de France has historically accepted bank loans from non-financial companies. Today, the Banque de France visits 40,000 firms as part of a labour-intensive credit evaluation process. The Dutch central bank has historically had a much leaner system where banks mostly posted securitized mortgages as collateral, and this is still the case today. A minimum size-threshold of €1 million applies to any domestic non-marketable asset posted.[39]

Despite such variation, the Single List sets clear rules for credit evaluation, asset pricing, and valuation haircuts. By following market practices, the ECB achieved a high degree of harmonization across the Eurosystem's wide range of eligible assets.

III. ECB Risk Management since 2010

The past decade, the ECB has made a set of amendments to its collateral framework that is almost impossible to chart, once more giving the NCBs considerable discretion over eligibility criteria for collateral. Through these changes, the ECB sought to ensure that banks had sufficient collateral to access its refinancing operations.[40] The ECB has also introduced a host of unconventional operations which expose it to new (and much greater) risk. Most fundamentally, however, events have increasingly forced the ECB to consider the financial market impact of its risk management strategy.

The ECB's response to the Great Financial Crisis of 2007 and 2008 relies on levers already available within the framework of the Single List.[41] In October 2008, the ECB lowered its ECAF credit quality requirement to accommodate the shock of the Lehman Brothers default.[42] By accepting assets with a CQS3 rating, the ECB greatly expanded the volume of collateral that banks could use to access ECB credit. It is part of the design of the ECAF requirement that could be lowered in response to a crisis, which the ECB collateral framework was accordingly well prepared for.

The euro area crisis, in contrast, forced the ECB to move considerably beyond its earlier risk management strategy in three ways. First, the impact of the euro area crisis was most severe in the Member States at the periphery of its financial system, which necessitated targeted changes to the operational framework. By 2012, 80 per cent of

[38] Deutsche Bundesbank, 'The Bundesbank's Credit Assessment System' (Deutsche Bundesbank 2020) s V.10.5 <https://www.bundesbank.de/en/tasks/monetary-policy/collateral/credit-assessment/the-bundesbank-s-credit-assessment-system-744836> accessed 13 April 2021.

[39] De Nederlandsche Bank, 'Monetary Policy Transactions Conditions' (De Nederlandsche Bank 2021) para 21 <https://www.dnb.nl/media/dynde3wo/monetary-policy-transactions-conditions_edition-january-2021-final.pdf> accessed 13 April 2021. The limit is €500.000 for cross-border use.

[40] Bindseil and others, 'The Eurosystem Collateral Framework Explained' (n 16); Nyborg, *Collateral Frameworks* (n 35).

[41] European Central Bank, 'The Eurosystem Collateral Framework throughout the Crisis' (n 33); European Central Bank, 'Collateral Eligibility and Availability Follow-up to the Report on "Collateral Eligibility Requirements—a Comparative Study across Specific Frameworks"' (ECB 2014) <https://www.ecb.europa.eu/pub/pdf/other/cea201407en.pdf> accessed 13 April 2021.

[42] Guideline of the European Central bank of 23 October 2008 amending Guideline ECB/2000/7 on monetary policy instruments and procedures of the Eurosystem (ECB/2008/13) [2009] OJ L36/31.

ECB credit went to just four Member States: Greece, Ireland, Italy, and Spain.[43] In response to the asymmetric impact of the crisis, the ECB introduced the Additional Credit Claims (ACC) framework in 2011.[44] The ACC allows NCBs to set up country-specific collateral requirements and apply lower credit quality standards.[45] This framework is essentially a return to the earlier two-tiered system.

A second way in which the euro area crisis forced the ECB to move beyond its earlier risk management strategy was that it saw the ECB engage in purchase programmes for a wide range of financial assets. The ECB started purchasing sovereign bonds as part of the Security Markets Programme in May 2010, which peaked at €220 billion in 2012.[46] In 2014, the ECB announced its quantitative easing Asset Purchase Programme (APP). By far the largest share of APP purchases are in the Public Sector Purchase Programme (PSPP), which in September 2020 made up €2.2 trillion out of a total of €2.8 trillion. However, the ECB has also bought corporate bonds (CSPP), covered bonds (CBPP 1, 2, and 3), and (in smaller volumes) asset-backed securities (ABSPP). The €1.85 trillion Pandemic Emergency Purchase Programme (PEPP) saw the ECB delve even deeper into outright purchases. Close to €7 trillion in December 2020, the ECB's balance sheet equals half the euro area's annual GDP.

From a risk management perspective, it is not just the size of the programmes but also the types of risk that come with the ECB's outright purchases that is new. A collateralized loan only results in losses in the event of double default. For an asset purchase this is not the case. Unlike covered bonds and asset-backed securities, some corporate bonds and in particular government bonds, are often not backed by an independent collateral pool. If the issuer defaults, the central bank faces unmediated losses. The ECB only needs to make a loss of 0.3 per cent on its APP programme for losses to be equal to the Lehman Brothers default.

The most important consequence of the euro area crisis, however, is that it increasingly forced the ECB to take the impact of its risk management strategy on financial markets into account. Consider first how the ECB is increasingly acknowledging that its risk management has consequences for financial stability.[47] According to dynamics

[43] Jean Pisani-Ferry and Guntram Wolff, 'Propping up Europe?' (2012) Bruegel Policy Contribution 2012/07 <https://www.bruegel.org/wp-content/uploads/imported/publications/pc_2012_02.pdf> accessed 13 April 2021.

[44] Guideline of the European Central Bank of 20 September 2011 on monetary policy instruments and procedures of the Eurosystem (ECB/2011/14) [2011] OJ L331/1.

[45] Evangelos Tabakis and Kentaro Tamura, 'The Use of Credit Claims as Collateral for Eurosystem Credit Operations' (2013) ECB Occasional Paper Series 148 <https://www.ecb.europa.eu/pub/pdf/scpops/ecbocp148.pdf> accessed 13 April 2021; Bindseil and others, 'The Eurosystem Collateral Framework Explained' (n 16); Jean-Stéphane Mésonnier, Charles O'Donnell, and Olivier Toutain, 'The Interest of Being Eligible' (2017) Banque de France Working Papers No 636 <https://publications.banque-france.fr/en/interest-being-eligible> accessed 13 April 2021.

[46] Paul Wallace, *The Euro Experiment* (CUP 2015) 180.

[47] Bindseil, *Monetary Policy Operations and the Financial System* (n 13); BIS, 'Central Bank Collateral Frameworks and Practices' (n 8); Vítor Constâncio, 'Margins and Haircuts as a Macroprudential Tool' (ESRB international conference on the macroprudential use of margins and haircuts, Frankfurt am Main, 6 June 2016) <https://www.ecb.europa.eu/press/key/date/2016/html/sp160606.en.html> accessed 13 April 2021 (hereafter Constâncio, 'Margins and Haircuts as a Macroprudential Tool'); Gabor and Ban, 'Banking on Bonds' (n 8); Stefano Corradin, Florian Heider, and Marie Hoerova, 'On Collateral: Implications for Financial Stability and Monetary Policy' (2017) ECB Working Papers Series No 2107 <https://papers.ssrn.com/sol3/papers.cfm?abstract_id = 3067254> accessed 13 April 2021 (hereafter Corradin, Heider, and Hoerova, 'On Collateral: Implications for Financial Stability and Monetary Policy').

closely associated with the work of Hyman Minsky and Charles Kindleberger, markets move suddenly from a mania (leading investors to accept immense leverage) to a panic (in which all investors seek to liquidate their positions at the same time).[48] This general dynamic also plays out through pro-cyclical risk management practices: low-quality collateral requirements and haircuts are imposed in the mania, while the panic leads to higher haircuts and more strict collateral requirements.[49]

It has long been understood that central banks can contribute to financial stability by taking on more risk in a crisis. The ECB risk management strategy directly impacts the value of collateral, which in turn affects both its counterparties and the issuers of eligible assets. By lowering its ECAF requirement and other collateral easing measures in October 2008, the ECB effectively counteracted the credit crunch in wholesale markets. While the lowering of the ECAF requirement was counter-cyclical, other design features of the Single List are pro-cyclical and hence can cause financial instability.[50] Since eligibility is conditional on an adequate ECAF rating, ratings downgrades reduce the volume of eligible collateral. Moreover, where possible, the ECB's pricing hub updates the value of collateral based on market prices so that lower prices require counterparties to post more collateral. Because the ECB's eligibility criteria for collateral and haircuts are conditional on ECAF requirements, rating downgrades lead the ECB to restrict the volume of credit available to banks. These mechanisms explain in part why, despite the ECB's efforts to expand eligibility during the euro area crisis, collateral shortage in some Member States still contributed to bank funding stress.[51] In its March and April 2020 responses to the pandemic, the ECB had to take active measures to counteract this pro-cyclical bias of its risk management by broadening eligibility criteria, lowering its haircuts by 20 per cent, and freezing its rating requirement; downgraded assets remained eligible if they had been so before April 2020.[52]

[48] Charles Poor Kindleberger and Robert Z Aliber, *Manias, Panics, and Crashes: A History of Financial Crises* (5th edn, Palgrave Macmillan 2005); Hyman P Minsky, *Stabilizing an Unstable Economy* (McGraw-Hill 2008).

[49] Markus K Brunnermeier, 'Deciphering the Liquidity and Credit Crunch 2007-2008' (2009) 23 Journal of Economic Perspectives 77; Gary Gorton and Andrew Metrick, 'Securitized Banking and the Run on Repo' (2010) Yale ICF Working Paper No 09-14 <https://papers.ssrn.com/sol3/papers.cfm?abstract_id=1440752> accessed 13 April 2021; Gary Gorton, *Slapped by the Invisible Hand. The Panic of 2007* (OUP 2010); BIS, 'The Role of Margin Requirements and Haircuts in Procyclicality' (2010) BIS CGFS 36 <https://www.bis.org/publ/cgfs36.htm> accessed 13 April 2021; BIS, 'Central Bank Operating Frameworks and Collateral Markets' (2015) BIS CGFS Markets Committee Papers 53 <https://www.bis.org/publ/cgfs53.htm> accessed 13 April 2021; Daniela Gabor, 'The (Impossible) Repo Trinity: The Political Economy of Repo Markets' (2016) 23 Review of International Political Economy 967.

[50] Constâncio, 'Margins and Haircuts as a Macroprudential Tool' (n 47); Gabor and Ban, 'Banking on Bonds' (n 8); Corradin, Heider, and Hoerova, 'On Collateral: Implications for Financial Stability and Monetary Policy' (n 47); Vítor Constâncio, 'Completing the Odyssean Journey of the European Monetary Union' (ECB Colloquium on 'The Future of Central Banking', Frankfurt am Main, 16–17 May 2018) <https://www.ecb.europa.eu/press/key/date/2018/html/ecb.sp180517.en.html> accessed 13 April 2021 (hereafter Constâncio, 'Completing the Odyssean Journey of the European Monetary Union').

[51] Jean Barthélemy, Vincent Bignon, and Benoît Nguyen, 'Illiquid Collateral and Bank Lending during the European Sovereign Debt Crisis' (2017) Banque de France Working Paper No 631 <https://papers.ssrn.com/sol3/papers.cfm?abstract_id=2983683> accessed 13 April 2021; Jean Barthélemy, Vincent Bignon, and Benoît Nguyen, 'Monetary Policy and Collateral Constraints since the European Debt Crisis' (2018) Banque de France Working Paper No 669 <https://papers.ssrn.com/sol3/papers.cfm?abstract_id=3144349> accessed 13 April 2021.

[52] Luis de Guindos and Isabel Schnabel, 'Improving Funding Conditions for the Real Economy during the COVID-19 Crisis: The ECB's Collateral Easing Measures' (*The ECB Blog*, 22 April 2020 <https://www.ecb.europa.eu/press/blog/date/2020/html/ecb.blog200422~244d933f86.en.html> accessed 13 April 2021.

The financial stability implications of central bank risk management have been most pronounced for euro area sovereign debt. Without going into depth into the causes of the euro area crisis, which is treated elsewhere,[53] it is clear that the ECAF's minimum credit rating requirement and the haircut policies based on them had an important role in driving the crisis.[54] The possibility that Member State debt loses its status as central bank collateral adds to the financial market panic that strikes individual Member States. Although the ECB issued waivers for the eligibility requirement for Greece in April 2010, Ireland in March 2011, Portugal in July 2011, and Cyprus in July 2013, these waivers were discretionary. The conditions under which the ECB Governing Council provides them are vague. The ECB at the same time also placed specific demands on the crisis-struck Member States, which led to repeated accusations that the ECB used its risk management framework to coerce Member States into pursuing its preferred economic policies.[55]

Moving beyond the topic of financial stability, a more recent challenge for ECB risk management has concerned its relation to the EU's environmental and climate-related objectives. Most major central banks, including the ECB, are involved today in the Network for Greening the Financial System (NGFS). Its members share the view that 'climate-related risks are a source of financial risk. It is therefore within the mandates of central banks and supervisors to ensure the financial system is resilient to these risks.'[56] As members of the NGFS recognize, climate risk is a source of at least two kinds of financial risk. First, physical risks. Without a dramatic change to human consumption and production, continued greenhouse gas emissions will lead to 'severe, pervasive and irreversible impacts for people and ecosystems'.[57] Climate change has already started and will result in more extreme weather events, droughts, fires, floods, and other potentially destructive events, which also impose losses on investors. The changes to economic policy that are needed to mitigate this evolution also give rise to so-called transition risks. Environmental degradation and loss of biodiversity come with an equally disruptive impact on the economy. An important objective of the NGFS is to ensure an adequate pricing of risk, since markets currently fail to adequately price financial risk resulting from climate change and other environmental

[53] See, eg, Jean Pisani-Ferry, *The Euro Crisis and its Aftermath* (OUP 2014).

[54] Claeys and Goncalves Raposo, 'Is the ECB Collateral Framework Compromising the Safe-Asset Status of Euro-Area Sovereign Bonds?' (n 5); Constâncio, 'Completing the Odyssean Journey of the European Monetary Union' (n 50); Orphanides, 'Monetary Policy and Fiscal Discipline' (n 5); Minh Nguyen, 'Collateral Haircuts and Bond Yields in the European Government Bond Markets' (2020) 69 International Review of Financial Analysis 101467.

[55] Thomas Beukers, 'The New ECB and its Relationship with the Eurozone Member States: Between Central Bank Independence and Central Bank Intervention' (2013) 50 CML Rev 1579; Athanasios Orphanides, 'ECB Monetary Policy and Euro Area Governance: Collateral Eligibility Criteria for Sovereign Debt' (2017) MIT Sloan Research Paper 5258-17 <https://papers.ssrn.com/abstract=3076184> accessed 13 April 2021.

[56] NGFS, 'A Call to Action: Climate Change as a Source of Financial Risk' (Network for Greening the Financial System First comprehensive report 2019) <https://www.ngfs.net/en/first-comprehensive-report-call-action> accessed 13 April 2021 (hereafter NGFS, 'A Call to Action: Climate Change as a Source of Financial Risk').

[57] Rajendra K Pachauri and others, 'Climate Change 2014: Synthesis Report. Contribution of Working Groups I, II and III to the Fifth Assessment Report of the Intergovernmental Panel on Climate Change' in Rajendra K Pachauri and Leo Meyer (eds) (IPCC 2014) 8.

dimensions of economic policy.[58] In light of most governments' commitments under the 2015 Paris Agreement, there is also a case for more pro-active central bank efforts to promote a green economic transition.

The ECB has so far refrained from taking the environmental impact of its monetary policy operations into account.[59] Instead, for both its collateral framework and the ECB's Asset Purchase Programme, the eligibility of assets is determined solely by (i) its monetary policy objective of price stability and (ii) the financial risk that operations expose the central bank to. That approach, however, has given the ECB's operations a clear pro-carbon bias. The reason for this is that carbon-intensive firms such as utilities, companies engaged in fossil fuel extraction, and car manufacturers make large upfront investments. Because they need funding for this and the investments can themselves be used to secure bonds, these sectors rely disproportionately on bond financing. Hence, debt issued by such companies takes up a much larger share of the ECB's eligible assets than their relative size within the EU economy. The design of the ECB risk management is effectively a subsidy to large carbon-intensive firms. The ECB's CSPP has benefited car manufacturers such as BMW, Daimler, Renault, and Volkswagen; energy companies such as Eesti Energia (an early investor in US tar sand mines), ENEL, Repsol, and Shell; as well as civil and military aviation companies such as Ryanair and Thales. Its eligibility criteria bring down funding costs for carbon-intensive sectors, thereby encouraging more investment by firms in those sectors. This concern applies both to the ECB CSPP programme, in which it buys corporate bonds, as well as to the ECB collateral framework, which encourages ECB counterparties to hold those corporate bonds for the purposes of accessing its refinancing operations.

The absence of environmental criteria, however, is out of sync with the ECB's own increasingly sophisticated understanding of the environmental impact of financial markets.[60] For one, as part of its banking supervision mandate, the ECB also has a

[58] Jean-Francois Mercure and others, 'Macroeconomic Impact of Stranded Fossil Fuel Assets' (2018) 8 Nature Climate Change 588; Patrick Bolton and others, 'The Green Swan: Central Banking and Financial Stability in the Age of Climate Change' (2020) BIS Other <https://www.bis.org/publ/othp31.htm> accessed 13 April 2021 (hereafter Bolton and others, 'The Green Swan: Central Banking and Financial Stability in the Age of Climate Change').; Hugues Chenet and others, 'Finance, Climate-Change and Radical Uncertainty: Towards a Precautionary Approach to Financial Policy' (2021) Ecological Economics 183.

[59] Sini Matikainen, Emanuele Campiglio, and Dimitri Zenghelis, 'The Climate Impact of Quantitative Easing' (2017) Grantham Research Institute on Climate Change and the Environment Policy Paper May 2017 <https://www.lse.ac.uk/granthaminstitute/publication/the-climate-impact-of-quantitative-easing/> accessed 13 April 2021; Stefano Battiston and Irene Monasterolo, 'How Could the ECB's Monetary Policy Support the Sustainable Finance Transition?' (2019) FINEXUS: Center for Financial Networks and Sustainability 2019 <https://www.finexus.uzh.ch/en/news/cspp_sustainable_finance.html> accessed 13 April 2021; Dirk Schoenmaker, 'Greening Monetary Policy' (2019) Bruegel Working Paper No 02 <http://bruegel.org/2019/02/greening-monetary-policy/> accessed 13 April 2021; van 't Klooster and Fontan, 'The Myth of Market Neutrality' (n 2).

[60] NGFS, 'A Call to Action: Climate Change as a Source of Financial Risk' (n 56); ECB, 'Eurosystem Reply to the European Commission's Public Consultations on the Renewed Sustainable Finance Strategy and the Revision of the Non-Financial Reporting Directive' (ECB 2020) <https://www.ecb.europa.eu/pub/pdf/other/ecb.eurosystemreplyeuropeancommissionpublicconsultations_20200608~cf01a984aa.en.pdf> accessed 13 April 2021 (hereafter ECB, 'Eurosystem Reply to the European Commission's Public Consultations on the Renewed Sustainable Finance Strategy and the Revision of the Non-Financial Reporting Directive'); ECB, 'Guide on Climate-Related and Environmental Risks' (ECB 2020) <https://www.bankingsupervision.europa.eu/ecb/pub/pdf/ssm.202011finalguideonclimate-relatedandenvironmentalrisks~58213f6564.en.pdf> accessed 13 April 2021; Isabel Schnabel, 'When Markets Fail—the Need for Collective Action in Tackling Climate Change' (European Sustainable Finance Summit, Frankfurt am Main, 28 September

task in ensuring that financial institutions adequately price the climate and environmental risks that they are exposed to. Monetary policy that fails to counteract the carbon-intensive bias of existing bank lending patterns enforces that market failure, thereby undermining the ECB's own supervisory efforts. Moreover, environmental and climate-related risks also impact the ECB's ability to achieve price stability. As Isabel Schnabel recently explained, 'the longer the risks of global warming are ignored and policy action delayed, the higher the risks of very large and persistent shocks to output and inflation'.[61] The current review of the ECB's monetary policy strategy is likely to result in climate change being incorporated into the ECB's monetary policy framework. The major open questions today concern what shape its tasks should take.

IV. The Future of ECB Risk Management

Although the euro area crisis has forced the ECB to take the financial market impact of its operations into account, it has not yet incorporated its new lessons into its risk management strategy. In 2015, the ECB published a risk management strategy that summarizes the key principles that govern the design of monetary policy operations.[62] They reflect an approach to risk that is broadly unchanged from that of the 2006 Single List. That is unfortunate because the ECB's risk management strategy is potentially a crucial site for contributing to its new policy priorities of financial stability and environmental sustainability.

In this concluding section, I will analyse the extent to which the ECB's current risk management strategy has withstood the test of time and how it should be revised in the review of the monetary policy strategy conducted by the ECB at the time of writing.[63] I first review the core principles of its risk management strategy and argue that the ECB should (A) revise and clarify the principle of risk-efficiency and (B) do away with risk-equivalence and the closely associated ideal of market neutrality. I then propose two broader institutional conditions for effectively dealing with the financial risk: improved internal credit rating facilities (C) and addressing legitimacy concerns by coordinating with EU political institutions (D).

2020) <https://www.ecb.europa.eu/press/key/date/2020/html/ecb.sp200928_1~268b0b672f.en.html> accessed 13 April 2021 (hereafter Schnabel, 'When Markets Fail—the Need for Collective Action in Tackling Climate Change'); Isabel Schnabel, 'Never Waste a Crisis: COVID-19, Climate Change and Monetary Policy' (Virtual Roundtable on 'Sustainable Crisis Responses in Europe' organized by the INSPIRE research network, 17 July 2020) <https://www.ecb.europa.eu/press/key/date/2020/html/ecb.sp200717~1556b0f988.en.html> accessed 13 April 2021 (hereafter Schnabel, 'Never Waste a Crisis: COVID-19, Climate Change and Monetary Policy'); Alessandro Ferrari and Valerio Nispi Landi, 'Whatever It Takes to Save the Planet? Central Banks and Unconventional Green Policy' (2020) ECB Working Paper Series No 2020/2500 <https://www.ecb.europa.eu/pub/pdf/scpwps/ecb.wp2500~f7a50c6f69.en.pdf> accessed 13 April 2021.

[61] Schnabel, 'Never Waste a Crisis: COVID-19, Climate Change and Monetary Policy' (n 60). See also Schnabel, 'When Markets Fail—the Need for Collective Action in Tackling Climate Change' (n 60); Christine Lagarde, 'Climate Change and the Financial Sector' (Launch of the COP 26 Private Finance Agenda, London, 27 February 2020) <https://www.bis.org/review/r200302c.htm> accessed 13 April 2021 (hereafter Lagarde, 'Climate Change and the Financial Sector').

[62] ECB, 'The Financial Risk Management of the Eurosystem's Monetary Policy Operations' (n 1).

[63] December 2020.

A. Revising the objectives of risk management

A first key principle of the risk management strategy that the ECB should consider revising is risk efficiency. Risk efficiency requires that in pursuing its monetary policy objectives, the ECB minimizes the risk of losses on its operations:

> The Eurosystem aims to achieve its policy objectives with the lowest possible risk. In this sense, risk management means striving to ensure that the Eurosystem uses its risk capacity in the most efficient way in relation to the achievement of policy objectives.[64]

The principle of risk efficiency makes risk management subordinate to the ECB's monetary policy objectives. As a consequence, risk management only takes into account the financial market impact of ECB operations to the extent that it affects an objective of the ECB. Several aspects of the ECB's current formulation of the principle of risk-efficiency should be revised and require further elucidation.

In practice, the ECB seeks to minimize the risk of losses through a minimum credit rating threshold, which ensures that only assets with a high credit rating are eligible as collateral or to be purchased in the APP. For assets pledged as collateral, as we saw, the ECB also imposes risk control measures to be able to recover any losses when selling the asset. Risk efficiency requires that the eligibility of individual assets is solely evaluated from a risk management perspective unless there are explicit policy objectives that justify taking on more risk.

The current formulation of the principle unduly limits the consideration of broader societal repercussions of its operations. Given the ECB's narrow conception of what counts as a monetary policy objective, the risk management strategy is similarly narrow in its ambitions. Beyond price stability, only financial stability has been given any significance in the ECB's strategic choices. The limited interpretation of its objectives is itself not settled by the Treaty, which also assigns to the ECB as a secondary objective to 'support the general economic policies in the Union with a view to contributing to the achievement of the objectives of the Union'.[65]

As we saw in section III, ECB risk management has pervasive impact on sovereign bond markets. In relying on the ECAF's minimum credit rating requirement for determining the eligibility of sovereign debt, the ECB's risk management strategy does not take into account how this requirement affects the ability of governments to fund themselves in financial markets. For those who favour a narrow role for central banks, the fact that the principle of risk efficiency fails to take into account societal impact may also be considered a strength. Where it comes to government finance, the monetary financing prohibition in Article 123 TFEU may be taken to prohibit any explicit consideration. The ECJ, for example, has explicitly pointed to the ECAF requirements on ECB government bond purchases as part of the design feature of the OMT and

[64] ECB, 'The Financial Risk Management of the Eurosystem's Monetary Policy Operations' (n 1) 3.
[65] TFEU (n 2) Art 127(1).

PSPP that prevent illicit monetary financing.[66] However, the ECB has issued waivers for this rule and has not applied it in the design of the 2020 PEPP. Moreover, the ECB has also used its risk management strategy to pursue other objectives. The ECB's loan-level initiative for asset-backed securities imposed the requirement that for ABSs to be eligible, detailed quarterly data needs to be available in a standardized format.[67] The ECB itself explains, with reference to the loan-level initiative, that '[t]hrough its collateral framework, the Eurosystem can help to improve market functioning and the transparency of securitisation structures'.[68]

The ECB should put forward a more principled account of what policy objectives it takes into account in its risk management. Waivers issued by the Governing Council for the minimum credit rating requirement are currently provided ad hoc and without much in the way of justification. The March 2020 changes to the eligibility of Greek government debt illustrate this well: if the journalistic account is correct, the issue was first raised by the Greek governor during a late-night video call.[69] It was decided on the spot to include Greek bonds. Similarly, in 2009 the ECB also tweaked its ECAF rules for sovereign debt by adding a small Canadian rating agency DBRS to the eligible rating providers. In 2015, Portugal would be eligible for the PSPP because the ECB relaxed the rules for its mapping of ratings by DBRS onto the ECAF scale.[70] ECB officials later claimed that the two decisions were unrelated, but that remains difficult to verify.[71] Moreover, would it really be a case of 'favouritism' or 'misconduct' if that allegation were true? The ECB may also on occasion make risk management decisions based on more mundane criteria. For example, the rules for ABSs were loosened in reviews of the risk control framework in 2013 and 2016, which fitted the ECB's stated financial market objectives of reviving euro area securitization markets and building European capital markets.[72]

Given that its risk management has financial stability implications, the ECB should provide a more principled account of how and when these considerations enter into the design of operations. When should risk management be used to achieve the ECB's

[66] See also Case C-62/14 *Gauweiler and Others v Deutscher Bundestag* [2015] EU:C:2015:400, para 125; Case C-493/17 *Weiss and Others* [2018] EU:C:2018:1000, paras 94–95.

[67] ECB, 'ABS Loan-Level Data Initiative' (ECB 2011) <https://www.ecb.europa.eu/paym/coll/loanlevel/shared/files/ABS_loan_level_initiative_letter.pdf?ca73ac293a520c3b8c1b603045cf0e84> accessed 13 April 2021; ECB, 'Loan-Level Initiative' (ECB 2020) <https://www.ecb.europa.eu/paym/coll/loanlevel/html/index.en.html> accessed 13 April 2021 (hereafter ECB, 'Loan-Level Initiative').

[68] ECB, 'Loan-Level Initiative' (n 67).

[69] Jana Randow and Piotr Skolimowski, 'Christine Lagarde's $810 Billion Coronavirus U-Turn Came in Just Four Weeks' (*Bloomberg*, 7 April 2020) <https://www.bloomberg.com/news/features/2020-04-06/coronavirus-lagarde-s-810-billion-u-turn-came-in-just-4-weeks> accessed 13 April 2021.

[70] Nyborg, *Collateral Frameworks* (n 35) 95.

[71] Bindseil and others, 'The Eurosystem Collateral Framework Explained' (n 16) 62.

[72] See the very summary ECB Press Release, 'ECB further reviews its risk control framework allowing for a new treatment of asset-backed securities' (ECB 2013) <https://www.ecb.europa.eu/press/pr/date/2013/html/pr130718.en.html> accessed 13 April 2021; ECB, 'ECB Reviews Its Risk Control Framework for Collateral Assets' (ECB 2016) <https://www.ecb.europa.eu/press/pr/date/2016/html/pr161103_1.en.html> accessed 13 April 2021. See also Benjamin Braun and Marina Hübner, 'Fiscal Fault, Financial Fix? Capital Markets Union and the Quest for Macroeconomic Stabilization in the Euro Area' (2018) 22 Competition & Change 117; Daniela Gabor and Jakob Vestergaard, 'Chasing Unicorns: The European Single Safe Asset Project' (2018) 22 Competition & Change 139.

objectives? Can the ECB also take on more risk to promote market functioning and transparency?

B. Market attentiveness instead of market neutrality

The ECB should do away with its principle of risk-equivalence, since it implies a policy of market neutrality that is incompatible with its financial stability and environmental sustainability roles. Instead, the ECB should adopt a policy of market attentiveness.

Risk equivalence requires that the financial risk that the central bank accepts should be the same for each operation of a given type. It is derived from modern portfolio theory, where ensuring risk-equivalence minimizes the ECB's impact on the process of price discovery and thereby allows investors to achieve the most efficient allocation of resources.[73] In practice, it implies a market neutral approach to risk management. For the design of the collateral framework, this means that:

> [a] collateral framework and its criteria and/or requirements should not lead to the preferential treatment of distinct asset classes, issuers or sectors and should avoid market distortion (implying that e.g. individual issuers or sectors benefit unduly from eligibility requirements).[74]

Applied to the ECB asset purchases it requires that the ECB follows a benchmark that reflects the market value of eligible bonds.[75]

The normative justification for market neutrality is that markets do best in achieving an efficient allocation of resources. This justification, however, is conditional on two assumptions.[76] First, the assumption that markets should be evaluated solely in terms of their efficiency, rather than taking into account a broader range of normative considerations. Second, that the striving for profit by individual firms and investors serves to achieve an efficient allocation of resources. This second assumption is generally justified with reference to the second theorem of welfare economics, which shows that profit-maximization in highly idealized markets indeed tends towards an efficient allocation. There are, however, a range of different ways to explain why market competition may serve to realize the most efficient allocation of resources.[77]

Even if we grant that our evaluative criterion should be efficiency, the second assumption is today no longer tenable without qualification. The reasons that lead central bankers to pursue financial stability and environmental sustainability objectives should make us hesitant to assume that market dynamics will achieve an efficient allocation of resources. Because financial markets are inherently unstable, decentralized

[73] ECB, 'The Financial Risk Management of the Eurosystem's Monetary Policy Operations' (n 1) 3.
[74] Bindseil and others, 'The Eurosystem Collateral Framework Explained' (n 16) 12.
[75] European Central Bank, 'The ECB's Corporate Sector Purchase Programme: Its Implementation and Impact' (2017) 4 ECB Economic Bulletin 40.
[76] Allen Buchanan, *Ethics, Efficiency, and the Market* (Rowman & Littlefield 1985); Hsieh Nien-he and others, 'The Social Purpose of the Corporation' (2018) 6 Journal of the British Academy 49.
[77] See, eg, Joseph A Schumpeter, *Capitalism, Socialism, and Democracy* (Harper & Brothers Publishing 1942); Friedrich August Hayek, 'The Use of Knowledge in Society' (1945) 4 American Economic Review 519.

price discovery does not necessarily result in the most efficient allocation of resources. This is why central banks have turned to macroprudential policies. Similarly, central banks which today participate in the Network for Greening the Financial System do so because they believe that financial markets currently also fail to accurately price climate risk. The cheap price of carbon currently reflected in financial market prices has for good reasons been labelled 'the greatest market failure the world has ever seen'.[78] Following market practices in the implementation of monetary policy, therefore, hinders the ECB from achieving its own objectives. Although it may sometimes be appropriate to reduce the impact of operations on market prices, this should not be the default assumption.

Hence, instead of market neutrality, the ECB should adhere to a policy that may be described as market attentiveness. This attentiveness has two aspects. Facing existing private-sector risk practices, the ECB should ask whether they reflect the ECB's financial stability and environmental sustainability objectives. This would involve actively intervening to end pro-cyclical market practices and pushing for a more vigilant attitude to climate-related risk. In so doing, the ECB should not dogmatically adhere to the objective of risk equivalence. However, market attentiveness does not mean ignoring the ways in which markets price risk. Where appropriate the ECB can use private sector risk management techniques. It should also ensure that operations do not distort risk premia and relative asset prices. In this regard, market attentiveness involves acknowledging the complex interaction between monetary policy and financial markets.

As the euro area's most powerful investor it is only prudent for the ECB to pay attention when markets fail.

C. Developing internal credit rating facilities

What would revising risk efficiency and giving up on risk equivalence mean for the practice of monetary policy implementation? The first concrete proposal I want to make is that the ECB should expand its internal credit rating facilities to better reflect how credit ratings used for its operations impact its objectives.

Improving already existing internal credit risk rating facilities is a modest step forward. Within the Eurosystem, as we saw, the German Bundesbank and the Banque de France retain sizeable internal credit rating facilities, as do seven other NCBs.[79] Developing credit rating facilities also fits even the most conservative understanding of what central banks can be expected to do. As an independent agency, the ECB is hesitant to engage in deliberation on overtly political topics. Credit screening, in contrast, is something that central banks have always done. It involves technical questions of risk assessment, which are in principle clearly demarcated from the broader economic policy objectives of governments.

When it comes to financial risk, there are many different ways to monitor and evaluate risk. Where it comes to sovereign bonds and other assets, the ECB should

[78] Nicholas Stern, *The Economics of Climate Change: The Stern Review* (CUP 2007).
[79] ECB, 'ECAF' (table 4.2).

stop intermittently relying on credit ratings and then side-stepping them in light of specific policy objectives. Instead, it should consider simply integrating relevant policy considerations into its own credit assessments. Although the ECB's new president Christine Lagarde has signalled her dissatisfaction with the ECB's reliance on private credit ratings, the ECB has not yet put forward an alternative approach.[80] The ECB can do this by replacing private credit ratings with internal risk assessment facilities.[81]

Extending internal risk management facilities is an effective way for central banks to contribute to their financial stability objectives and secondary objectives such as environmental sustainability. Because private credit ratings are pro-cyclical, the ECB's ECAF credit rating requirements also are.[82] Instead of suspending the ECAF-rules in a crisis, as the ECB did again in April 2020, its rules should simply be made less dependent on the rating agencies.[83] Similarly, the mispricing of climate risk in financial markets results in part from specific limitations of existing private sector risk management techniques.[84] These techniques are backwards-looking in the sense that they are based on past performance and observations. They also tend to assume a fixed regulatory framework. To avoid stranded assets and other financial market effects of the climate transition the central bank should to some extent anticipate not just physical climate risk (eg extreme weather events) but also transition risks (a high carbon tax etc). Internal central bank rating facilities can do this. The loan-level initiative is a model for how such changes to the ECB's operational framework can in turn improve market functions.

It is currently an open question what shape ECB risk management should take, which is an issue on which central bank research is in its early stages.[85] The ECB's history, however, should make us optimistic. The creation of the Single List was the result of an earlier process of institutional learning in which the ECB developed effective internal procedures in response to the specific challenge of euro area heterogeneity. Finding risk management practices that are effective in promoting financial stability

[80] Christine Lagarde, 'Procyclical Impact of Downgrades of Corporate Bonds on Markets and Entities across the Financial System' (European Systemic Risk Board, Letter ESRB/2020/0089 2020) <https://www.esrb.europa.eu/pub/pdf/other/esrb.letter201001_impact_of_downgrades_of_corporate_bonds~d15087499d.en.pdf?663897b6b8d0af6e4a75657663d4d469> accessed 13 April 2021; Lagarde, 'Climate Change and the Financial Sector' (n 61).

[81] See also the critical report of the Financial Stability Board on central banks' over-reliance on private credit assessment, which is referenced by ECB's 2015 risk management strategy: FSB, 'Principles for Reducing Reliance on CRA Ratings' (Financial Stability Board 2010) <https://www.fsb.org/wp-content/uploads/r_101027.pdf> accessed 13 April 2021; Pierre Monnin, 'Integrating Climate Risks into Credit Risk Assessment—Current Methodologies and the Case of Central Banks Corporate Bond Purchases' (Council on Economic Policies, 2018).

[82] Patrick Bolton, Xavier Freixas, and Joel Shapiro, 'The Credit Ratings Game' (2012) 67 Journal of Finance 85; Heski Bar-Isaac and Joel Shapiro, 'Ratings Quality over the Business Cycle' (2013) 108 Journal of Financial Economics 62.

[83] ECB, 'ECB Takes Steps to Mitigate Impact of Possible Rating Downgrades on Collateral Availability' (ECB 2020) <https://www.ecb.europa.eu/press/pr/date/2020/html/ecb.pr200422_1~95e0f62a2b.en.html> accessed 13 April 2021.

[84] Dirk Schoenmaker and Willem Schramade, *Principles of Sustainable Finance* (OUP 2018); Bolton and others, 'The Green Swan: Central Banking and Financial Stability in the Age of Climate Change' (n 58).

[85] Corradin, Heider, and Hoerova, 'On Collateral: Implications for Financial Stability and Monetary Policy' (n 47); Bolton and others, 'The Green Swan: Central Banking and Financial Stability in the Age of Climate Change' (n 58); Oustry Antoine and others, 'Climate-Related Risks and Central Banks' (2020) Banque de France Working Paper No 790 <https://papers.ssrn.com/sol3/papers.cfm?abstract_id=3771299> accessed 13 April 2021.

and environmental sustainability will also take time, but it can be done. Risk management on monetary policy operations can inform thinking in other policy domains, because it is a domain in which the central bank needs to think like an investor. By reflecting on how to deal with new risks on its monetary policy, central banks build expertise in relation to those risks.

To the extent that the credit ratings remain largely focused on estimating credit risk, central banks can pursue their financial stability and green objectives without wading into too deep political waters.

D. Addressing legitimacy concerns by coordinating with EU political institutions

The past years have seen central banks confronted with increasingly difficult choices, which central banks due to their constitutional status as independent agencies are ill-equipped to deal with.[86] Even when confronted with clear market failures, central bankers remain hesitant to intervene in the allocation of capital.

Although improving its risk management facilities can address some of the challenges that the ECB today faces, it remains the case that the ECB mandate provides almost no guidance on how to deal with financial risk. Issue after issue, its mandate simply does not say what the ECB should do. That is not surprising since it was written decades ago and has remained unchanged since then. The absence of explicit democratic authorization for its policies gives rise to what Nik de Boer and I have described in a recent article as authorization gaps.[87] There are gaps in the ECB's democratic authorization in the sense that the ECB is forced to make choices for which its mandate provides almost no guidance, but which have far-reaching consequences. A key example is the decision whether to accept bonds issued by a Member State as part of the ECB's collateral framework and asset purchase programmes. Similarly, the mandate leaves it to the ECB to decide whether to take into account the environmental impact of its operations, and if so how.

How should the ECB navigate such authorization gaps when it comes to risk management? The ECB can justify changes to its risk management strategy in terms of the price stability objective and its secondary mandate, but almost any change it makes can be justified in this way. This is the fundamental problem with the ECB's authorization gaps; the law has lost much of its role in guiding monetary policy. Authorization

[86] Claudio Borio, 'Central Banking Post-Crisis: What Compass for Uncharted Waters?' in Charles Goodhart and others (ed), *Central Banking at a Crossroads: Europe and Beyond* (Anthem Press 2014) 191–216; Willem Buiter, 'Central Banks: Powerful, Political and Unaccountable?' (2014) 2 Journal of the British Academy 269; Jacqueline Best, 'Rethinking Central Bank Accountability in Uncertain Times' (2016) 30 Ethics & International Affairs 215; Paul Tucker, *Unelected Power: The Quest for Legitimacy in Central Banking and the Regulatory State* (Harvard University Press 2018); Charles Goodhart and Rosa Lastra, 'Populism and Central Bank Independence' (2018) 29 Open Economies Review 49; Jens van 't Klooster, 'Democracy and the European Central Bank's Emergency Powers' (2018) 42 Midwest Studies In Philosophy 270; Jens van 't Klooster, 'The Ethics of Delegating Monetary Policy' (2020) 82 Journal of Politics 587; Leah Downey, 'Delegation in Democracy: A Temporal Analysis' (2020) Journal of Political Philosophy 1.

[87] de Boer and van 't Klooster, 'The ECB, the Courts and the Issue of Democratic Legitimacy after Weiss' (n 19).

gaps make the democratic basis of any actions—activist or not—thin. Acting to green the financial system is arguably less political than doing nothing, but that itself does not legitimize any particular choices. Deciding how to deal with climate risk will unavoidably force the ECB to take a stance not only on how it expects the transition to happen but also shapes how that transition happens.[88] However, it would be a mistake to infer from the absence of legal clarity that the ECB should do nothing. The same was true, as we saw, for the ECB's crisis OMT and PSP programmes. Today, few people think that the ECB should have done nothing instead. Whatever decision the ECB makes has far-reaching consequences.

To resolve the new questions that the ECB faces in managing risk, it should do more to coordinate its decision-making with the EU's political institutions. For one, the EU Council could help the ECB rank the many distinct objectives of EU economic policy listed in Article 3 of the Treaty on European Union (TEU) that is referenced in its secondary mandate. To this end, Article 121(2) TFEU already allows the EU Council to formulate 'the broad guidelines of the economic policies of ... the Union'. The European Parliament could also issue a motion on this issue.[89] Providing democratic guidance on how the ECB should rank its secondary objectives would not undermine the ECB's independence, nor, since they are secondary objectives, its price stability mandate. Similarly, Article 129(3) TFEU allows the Council and the European Parliament to make changes to key articles from the ECB Statutes.[90] This procedure could be used to amend Article 18 to specify eligibility criteria for the ECB's asset purchase programmes and collateral requirements.

The ECB, however, does not need to wait for the EU's political institutions to act. In 2012 the ECB resolved the issue of how to deal with sovereign debt, at least to some extent, by making eligibility for OMT conditional on an ESM programme. Similarly, the European Commission is currently developing a taxonomy of bonds that count as properly green.[91] By relying on taxonomies developed by the political institutions of the EU, the ECB can outsource the decision on what counts as a transition risk. Although still in the early stages of development, better ESG-taxonomies will improve the ability of the ECB to contribute to the EU's economic policy objectives.[92]

[88] Bolton and others, 'The Green Swan: Central Banking and Financial Stability in the Age of Climate Change' (n 58).

[89] See also Grégory Claeys and Marta Domínguez-Jiménez, 'How Can the European Parliament Better Oversee the European Central Bank?' (2020) European Parliament Monetary Dialogue Papers 652.747 <https://www.bruegel.org/wp-content/uploads/2020/09/1_BRUEGEL-final-Mart-and-Gregory.pdf> accessed 13 April 2021.

[90] This includes Art 17 (on ECB deposit facilities), Art 18 (on open market and credit operations), Art 22 (on clearing and payment systems; think Central Bank Digital Currencies), Art 23 (on external operations; think swap lines), and a range of articles at the end of the Statutes on central bank accounting and the distribution of profits.

[91] Regulation (EU) 2020/852 of the European Parliament and of the Council of 18 June 2020 on the establishment of a framework to facilitate sustainable investment, and amending Regulation (EU) 2019/2088 [2020] OJ L198/13.

[92] ECB, 'Eurosystem Reply to the European Commission's Public Consultations on the Renewed Sustainable Finance Strategy and the Revision of the Non-Financial Reporting Directive' (n 60).

V. Conclusion

Since monetary policy is the most important economic competence entirely delegated to the EU-level, it is not surprising that, time and again, the ECB has been expected to act. When its mandate was drafted in the early 90s, the ECB was assigned the narrow task of maintaining price stability. Hence its mandate has little to say about objectives such as financial stability and environmental sustainability. Today, the ECB's official risk management strategy, last updated in 2015, remains informed by ideas from the ECB's pre-crisis self-understanding. Its priorities are simple: the ECB should protect itself against risk and otherwise follow market practices. However, the ECB has in practice already moved far beyond these priorities. Going forward it is neither likely nor desirable that the ECB return to its earlier detached approach to markets. Instead, it should set out principles for how policy priorities such as financial stability and environmental sustainability should inform its approach to risk. Instead of market neutrality, this should involve a policy of market attentiveness; following markets where appropriate but leaning against the wind where necessary. Two key institutional innovations to bring the ECB's risk management practices into the twenty-first century are: improve internal credit rating facilities and enhance political coordination for monetary policy implementation.

PART II
MOVING BEYOND MONETARY POLICY
The ECB, Financial Stability, Economic Integration, and the (Future of the) Banking Union

Part 2 considers the new roles that the ECB has been called upon to play (notably in banking supervision and resolution), the non-strictly monetary policy concerns it has integrated in its decision-making—adding financial stability as an objective in parallel with price stability—and the implications for the ECB of the sectorial tensions between monetary policy, economic policy coordination, and internal market harmonization.

5
The ECB and Financial Stability

*Agnieszka Smoleńska and Thomas Beukers**

I. Introduction

It is often argued that central banks have a natural interest in financial stability, independent of their formal mandate.[1] Several reasons are given for this.[2] A first argument is that only central banks can fulfil the Lender of Last Resort function to institutions or the financial system in case of liquidity shortages.[3] Secondly, financial stability is considered necessary for the smooth functioning of the payment system, which is key to central bank transactions with their counterparties and to public trust in the currency.[4] A third reason regularly given to explain central banks' interest in financial stability is that it is a pre-condition for monetary policy to achieve its price stability objective,[5] since it is through the banking system the transmission of monetary policy takes place.[6]

Considering such a natural interest of central banks in financial stability, one might be surprised to find that financial stability has not been granted a very prominent place in the EU Treaty mandate of the ECB. By contrast, since the Global Financial

* The views expressed by the author are personal and do not necessarily reflect those of the Ministry of Foreign Affairs

1 As the ECB phrases it: 'Central banks have a strong and natural interest in the safeguarding of financial stability.' See European Central Bank, 'Financial Stability Review' (2004) <https://www.ecb.europa.eu/pub/pdf/fsr/financialstabilityreview200412en.pdf> accessed 6 June 2021 (hereafter ECB, 'Financial Stability Review').

2 Goodhart describes how early central banks in Europe were created for financial-stability related purposes rather than for monetary functions, in Charles Goodhart, *The Evolution of Central Banks* (MIT Press 1988) (hereafter Goodhart, *Evolution of Central Banks*).

3 Luis de Guindos, 'The ECB and Financial Stability' (Speech at the joint National Bank of Belgium/Toulouse School of Economics/Solvay Brussels School of Economics and Management/European Central Bank colloquium, Brussels, 5 November 2018) <https://www.ecb.europa.eu/press/key/date/2018/html/ecb.sp181105.en.html> accessed 6 June 2021 (hereafter de Guindos, 'The ECB and Financial Stability'); Padoa-Schioppa argues that 'the role of central banks in financial stability is part of their genetic code': see Tommaso Padoa-Schioppa, *Regulating Finance: Balancing Freedom and Risk* (OUP 2004) 98 (hereafter Padoa-Schioppa, *Regulating Finance*); Gary Schinasi, *Safeguarding Financial Stability: Theory and Practice* (International Monetary Fund 2006) (hereafter Schinasi, *Safeguarding Financial Stability*).

4 Phoebus Athanassiou, 'Payment Systems' in Fabian Amtenbrink and Christoph Herrmann (eds), *The EU Law of Economic and Monetary Union* (OUP 2021) 716–18 (hereafter Athanassiou, 'Payment Systems'); Jakob de Haan, Sander Oosterloo, and Dirk Schoenmaker, *Financial Markets and Institutions. A European Perspective* (CUP 2015) 229 (hereafter de Haan, Oosterloo, and Schoenmaker, *Financial Markets and Institutions*).

5 de Guindos, 'The ECB and Financial Stability' (n 3).

6 Schinasi, *Safeguarding Financial Stability* (n 3); Georgios Psaroudakis, 'The Scope for Financial Stability Considerations in the Fulfilment of the Mandate of the ECB/Eurosystem' (2018) 4 Journal of Financial Regulation 119.

Agnieszka Smoleńska and Thomas Beukers, *The ECB and Financial Stability* In: *The New European Central Bank*. Edited by: Thomas Beukers, Diane Fromage, and Giorgio Monti, Oxford University Press. © Agnieszka Smoleńska and Thomas Beukers 2022. DOI: 10.1093/oso/9780198871231.003.0005

Crisis (GFC) and euro area sovereign debt crises financial stability rose to prominence across a variety of EU policy areas, giving rise to scholarship heralding financial stability as a 'supranational public good'[7] or an 'overriding objective' of European economic policies.[8] It has been argued that financial stability has in practice become a primary concern of central banking.[9] In fact, since the GFC it has been added as an explicit objective to the mandates of some monetary policy authorities such as the Bank of England.[10] As we show in this chapter, notwithstanding the formal narrowness of the European Central Bank's (ECB) mandate,[11] the 'new' ECB's interest in and approach to financial stability has significantly evolved since the twin financial and sovereign debt crises. The way in which this has happened can provide useful insights regarding how the evolution of the ECB takes place in the context of new societal developments and considerations (eg inequality, climate change).

This chapter analyses the extent to which financial stability is, or has since the twin crises become part of, the mandate of the ECB, both in law and in practice. Drawing on economic and institutional discussions (Section II) and legal scholarship on Economic and Monetary Union (EMU) (Section III) concerning financial stability, we point to the lack of clarity as to the precise meaning of this term.[12] We argue that going beyond the content of the Treaty articles and taking a closer look at the operation of the ECB provides a more accurate picture of the role that financial stability plays in the implementation of its mandate. An analysis of various central bank instruments identified by Tomasso Padoa-Schioppa allows us to draw out the ways in which the concept is deployed, and to illustrate how financial stability is relevant in the context of, for example, the monetary policy strategy, crisis coordination or payment system operation (Sections IV–VII). This enables us to illustrate the many different relevant dimensions and aspects of the objective of financial stability in general, and of financial stability instruments in the law and practice of the ECB in particular. Section VIII concludes this chapter.

[7] Gianni Lo Schiavo, *The Role of Financial Stability in EU Law and Policy* (Wolters Kluwer 2017) 3 (hereafter Lo Schiavo, *Role of Financial Stability*).

[8] Kaarlo Tuori and Klaus Tuori, *The Eurozone Crisis. A Constitutional Analysis* (CUP 2014) 183 (hereafter Tuori and Tuori, *The Eurozone Crisis*).

[9] Rosa Maria Lastra, 'Banking Union: An Incomplete Building' in Franklin Allen and others (eds), *Filling the Gaps in Governance: The Case of Europe* (European University Institute 2016) 173 (hereafter Lastra, 'Banking Union: An Incomplete Building').

[10] See UK Financial Services Act 2012, s 2, pt 1.

[11] See, eg, Dirk Schoenmaker, 'Central Banks Role in Financial Stability' in Gerard Caprio (ed), *Handbook of Safeguarding Global Financial Stability: Political, Social, Cultural, and Economic Theories and Models* (Elsevier 2012) 280 (hereafter Schoenmaker, 'Central Banks Role in Financial Stability'); Marco Lamandini, David Ramos, and Javier Solana, 'The European Central Bank (ECB) as a Catalyst for Change in EU Law. Part 1: The ECB's Mandates' (2016) 23 Columbia Journal of European Law 5 (hereafter Lamandini, Ramos, and Solana, 'The ECB's Mandates').

[12] Inherently linked to the question of what financial stability is, is the question of who is best placed to achieve it. It is not the objective of this chapter to take a position in the normative debates about this question. For a discussion, see Matthias Goldmann, 'United in Diversity? The Relationship between Monetary Policy and Prudential Supervision in the Banking Union' (2018) 14 EuConst 283 and Loretta Mester, 'Five Points about Monetary Policy and Financial Stability' (2016) 23 Economic and Financial Review 81.

II. Financial Stability—the Conventional Use of an Economic Concept

In the EU context, the dominant economic definition of 'financial stability', and one endorsed by the ECB itself,[13] has been put forward by Tomasso Padoa-Schioppa. He formulated it as:

> a condition in which the financial system is able to withstand shocks without giving way to cumulative processes that impair the allocation of savings to investment opportunities and the processing of payments in the economy.[14]

There are three essential components to this definition. First, as regards its *scope*, financial stability is linked to the condition of the financial system.[15] This implies that not only traditional banking is of concern, but also other types of financial market actors and infrastructures, both those directly and amply regulated such as insurers, pension funds, or stock exchanges, and those that are less thoroughly regulated that include central counterparties (CCPs) in the derivatives markets or emerging players (especially technology-driven Fintechs).[16]

Second, as regards the *objective* of financial stability, the emphasis is placed on the function that the financial system serves to the real economy, which is non-financial activities such as the manufacturing of goods and provision of services, which account for the dominant part of the economies of most Member States. In general, this refers to the functions of the financial markets with regard to the allocation of capital, management of risks, and operation of the payment system underpinning the real economy. Banking provides critical functions which relate to the safeguarding of finances of citizens (as deposits), smoothing consumption, and investing deposits in firms (loans), in particular the small and medium enterprises (SMEs).[17]

Third, Padoa-Schioppa's definition emphasizes the *resilience* of the financial sector, that is, its ability to withstand shocks as a condition for it to be able to perform its function correctly. This positive dimension relates to the properties of the system and its ability to absorb rather than amplify shocks.[18] Whereas the first two abovementioned elements focus on what the financial system actually *does*, the third focuses on what

[13] ECB's own definition states: 'a condition in which the financial system—which comprises financial intermediaries, markets and market infrastructures—is capable of withstanding shocks and the unravelling of financial imbalances. This mitigates the prospect of disruptions in the financial intermediation process that are severe enough to adversely impact real economic activity.' European Central Bank, 'Financial Stability' (2021) <www.ecb.europa.eu/pub/financial-stability/html/index.en.html> accessed 6 June 2021.

[14] Padoa-Schioppa, *Regulating Finance* (n 3) 111.

[15] See extensively on the definition of a financial system and its functions, de Haan, Oosterloo, and Schoenmaker, *Financial Markets and Institutions* (n 4).

[16] ibid 5.

[17] As is evident in the context of the 'public interest in financial stability' test deployed in the context of EU resolution law: see Single Resolution Board, 'Public Interest Assessment: SRB Approach' (2019) <https://srb.europa.eu/sites/default/files/2019-06-28_draft_pia_paper_v12.pdf> accessed 6 June 2021.

[18] For an overview, see, eg, Hilary Allen, 'What Is "Financial Stability"? The Need for Some Common Language in International Financial Regulation' (2014) 45 Georgetown Journal of International Law 929, 942–43 and Lo Schiavo, *Role of Financial* Stability (n 7) 16–17.

the system is *able to do*,[19] which is not directly observable unless a crisis materialises.[20] In this respect, Padoa-Schioppa's substantive approach contrasts with a negative definition of financial stability (ie absence of instability).[21] We find the focus on the resilience of the financial sector more useful however, as ultimately a degree of uncertainty and instability is inevitable in a system dealing in risk.

A glance at the standard metrics of financial stability helps to understand the conventional operationalization of the concept at both individual institution and systemic levels. First, financial stability can be measured using an individual bank's insolvency risk, that is, how well its performance is matched with the risks taken, or its probability of credit default.[22] Such measures can be aggregated to identify the systemic risks of default of the financial system. Second, central banks and international financial institutions such as the International Monetary Fund (IMF) use indicators such as asset price valuations and corporate yields, default probabilities, bank profitability, and liquidity risks in the non-bank sector to assess financial stability. These measures, in line with Padoa-Schioppa's definition outlined above, look not only at how the financial sector operates, but also at the link between the financial sector (eg asset valuations) and the performance of the economy, hence the rising concern in 2020 and 2021 about the impact of the pandemic-induced economic downturn on financial stability.[23]

III. Financial Stability and the Law of the Economic and Monetary Union

Before the Great Financial Crisis, references to financial stability in EU law were few and far between, which led to claims that the concept was neglected at Maastricht.[24]At the level of the EU Treaties these references remain indirect, for example in the European System of Central Banks' (ESCB) supporting role with regard to the 'smooth conduct of policies pursued by the competent authorities relating to the prudential

[19] cf Schinasi who defines financial stability as: 'a situation in which the financial system is capable of satisfactorily performing its three key functions simultaneously. First, the financial system is efficiently and smoothly facilitating the intertemporal allocation of resources from savers to investors and the allocation of economic resources generally. Second, forward looking financial risks are being assessed and priced reasonably accurately and are being relatively well managed. Third, the financial system is in such condition that it can comfortably if not smoothly absorb financial and real economic surprises and shocks': see Schinasi, *Safeguarding Financial Stability* (n 3) 82.

[20] '… financial stability will not be completely observable because it is not possible to know how an economy would react to every conceivable shock': see William Allen and Geoffrey Wood, 'Defining and Achieving Financial Stability' (2001) 2 Journal of Financial Stability 152, 155 (hereafter Allen and Wood, 'Defining Financial Stability').

[21] Allen and Wood define financial stability as a 'state of affairs in which an episode of financial instability is unlikely to occur', where episodes of financial instability are 'episodes in which a large number of parties, whether they are households, companies, or (individual) governments, experience financial crises which are not warranted by their previous behaviour, and where these crises collectively have seriously adverse macro-economic effects': ibid 159–60.

[22] Luc Laeven and Ross Levine, 'Bank Governance, Regulation and Risk Taking' (2009) 93 Journal of Financial Economics 259.

[23] European Central Bank, 'Financial Stability Review' (2020) <https://www.ecb.europa.eu/pub/pdf/fsr/ecb.fsr202011~b7be9ae1f1.en.pdf> accessed 6 June 2021.

[24] Tuori and Tuori, *The Eurozone Crisis* (n 8) 89, 182; Vestert Borger, *The Transformation of the Euro: Law, Contract, Solidarity* (Meijers Instituut 2018) 188 (hereafter Borger, *The Transformation of the Euro*).

supervision of credit institutions and the stability of the financial system' (Article 127(5) of the Treaty on the Functioning of the European Union (TFEU)).[25] This is the closest it seems to get to a mentioning of financial stability in the Treaties, but the ESCB's role is only auxiliary and no specific tools are mentioned. A fuller picture emerges when we consider policy instruments typically associated with financial stability, such as the promotion of the smooth operation of payment systems (Article 127(2) TFEU) and prudential supervision (Article 127(6) TFEU). Such an observation underpins our approach in this chapter, which rather than focusing merely on formal references studies the law and practice of policy instruments associated with financial stability.

The explanatory merit of such an approach becomes clearer when we look at how pervasive financial stability concerns have become since the twin crises across EU policy areas. First, at the Treaty level, in 2013 an amendment to the TFEU allowed for the European Stability Mechanism to 'safeguard the stability of the euro area as a whole' (Article 136(3) TFEU).[26] Second, with regard to implementation of EU law, financial stability concerns have begun to play a key role in state aid control exercised by the European Commission, with the Member States relying on central banks' assessments to attest that not granting bank bailouts would threaten financial stability.[27] Third, financial stability has become an important consideration in the Court of Justice's jurisprudence, which no longer—as in the pre-crisis case law—refers only to the financial stability *of* a sector, a company, or a financial institution, but also treats financial stability as a standalone principle. For example, in the *Pringle* judgment,[28] the Court identified maintaining the financial stability of the monetary union as the higher objective of Article 125 TFEU.[29] In the *ESMA* case, the objective of financial stability played a role in the Court's reasoning justifying the delegation of powers to a body other than the Commission.[30] Finally, financial stability has increasingly become a point of reference and an objective in EU financial regulation (eg CRD IV,[31] SSM,[32]

[25] Yves Mersch, 'Financial Stability and the ECB' (Speech at the ESCB Legal Conference, Frankfurt am Main, 6 September 2018) <https://www.ecb.europa.eu/press/key/date/2018/html/ecb.sp180906.en.html> accessed 15 June 2021 (hereafter Mersch, 'Financial Stability').

[26] ibid.

[27] This allowed to subsequently confirm that there was a 'serious disturbance to the economy of a Member State' and thus apply the derogation under the Consolidated Version of the Treaty on the Functioning of the European Union [2012] OJ C326/47, Art 107(3)(b) (hereafter TFEU). See Agnieszka Smoleńska, 'Law and governance of EU cross-border bank groups after the Great Financial Crisis' (PhD Thesis, European University Institute 2020), ch 4.

[28] Case C-370/12 *Thomas Pringle v Government of Ireland and Others* [2012] EU:C:2012:756 (hereafter *Pringle*).

[29] ibid para 135.

[30] Case C-270/12 *United Kingdom vs Parliament and Council* [2014] EU:C:2014:18, paras 77–87.

[31] Directive 2013/36/EU of the European Parliament and of the Council of 26 June 2013 on access to the activity of credit institutions and the prudential supervision of credit institutions and investment firms, amending Directive 2002/87/EC and repealing Directives 2006/48/EC and 2006/49/EC [2013] OJ L176/338 (hereafter 'CRD IV').

[32] Regulation (EU) No 468/2014 of the European Central Bank of 16 April 2014 establishing the framework for cooperation within the Single Supervisory Mechanism between the European Central Bank and national competent authorities and with national designated authorities (SSM Framework Regulation) (ECB/2014/17) [2014] OJ L141/1 (hereafter SSM Regulation).

SRM[33]).[34] Last but not least, the language of financial stability has begun to permeate ECB action, as we will illustrate in the sections below. To account for the ubiquity of financial stability, legal scholars have called it a supranational and foundational objective in EU law and policy,[35] or a 'supranational public good' which the EU is striving to provide to its citizens.[36]

In the sections below, we focus on the various instruments that are relevant from a financial stability perspective, using them to illustrate the many different aspects of the concept of financial stability, also in the context of the policy pursued by the ECB. As such, our approach does not solve a number of ongoing debates such as whether the 'stability of the financial system' in Article 127(5) TFEU is to be understood as the conventional meaning of 'financial stability' as per Padoa-Schioppa,[37] or whether the concepts 'stability of the financial system' and 'financial stability of the euro area as a whole' have the same meaning.[38] Rather it helps map and trace what is 'new' about the ECB's approach to financial stability today.

IV. Policy Instruments of Financial Stability

In his seminal work on financial stability and the central bank, Tomasso Padoa-Schioppa identified ten distinct tools which can be used in the pursuit of financial and price stability by central banks endowed with both monetary and supervisory policy roles.[39] These are: (a) monetary policy strategy; (b) short-term interest rates; (c) money market operations; (d) standing facilities; (e) payment systems operation and standards; (f) public and private comments; (g) emergency liquidity support; (h) crisis coordination; (i) prudential regulation and (j) prudential supervision. As he noted himself, the list consists of 'diverse and heterogeneous objects'.[40] Padoa-Schioppa's toolbox largely corresponds to the policy instruments at the disposal of central banks today, even if—as we show in Table 5.1 below—the financialization of the economy and technological progress has somewhat changed the nature of some of them.

[33] Regulation (EU) No 806/2014 of the European Parliament and of the Council of 15 July 2014 establishing uniform rules and a uniform procedure for the resolution of credit institutions and certain investment firms in the framework of a Single Resolution Mechanism and a Single Resolution Fund and amending Regulation (EU) No 1093/2010 [2014] OJ L225/1.

[34] In the past, such prudential rules referred rather to 'stability of the financial system', with the term financial stability being reserved to describe the situation of a particular institution, eg 'financial institutions are subject to specific supervisory rules regarding their financial stability' in Council Directive 92/30/EEC of 6 April 1992 on the supervision of credit institutions on a consolidated basis [1992] OJ L110/52. For a discussion of the objective of financial stability in Banking Union, and of its various functions, see Jonathan Bauerschmidt, 'Financial Stability as the Objective of the Banking Union' (2020) 17 ECFR 155.

[35] Lo Schiavo, *Role of Financial Stability* (n 7) 33.

[36] Joel Trachtman, 'The International Law of Financial Crisis: Spillovers, Subsidiarity, Fragmentation and Cooperation' (2010) 13 JIEL 719, 721.

[37] For discussion, see Lo Schiavo, *Role of Financial Stability* (n 7) 48; Lamandini, Ramos, and Solana, 'The ECB's Mandates' (n 11) 22.

[38] For discussion, see Tuori and Tuori, *The Eurozone Crisis* (n 8) 183–84; Mersch, 'Financial Stability and the ECB' (n 25); see also chapter 2 by Vestert Borger, in this volume.

[39] Padoa-Schioppa, *Regulating Finance* (n 3).

[40] ibid 111.

Table 5.1 Tools for maintaining price and financial stability

	Tool	Price stability	Financial stability System-wide	Financial stability Individual institutions
(a)	Monetary policy strategy	××	×	
(b)	Short-term interest rates	××	×	
(c)	Money market operations	××	×	
(d)	Standing facilities	××	×	×
(e)	Payment systems			×
(f)	Public and private comments	××	⊗	⊗
(g)	Emergency liquidity support		××	××
(h)	Crisis coordination		⊗	⊗⊗
(i)	Prudential regulation		•	••
(j)	Prudential supervision		•	••

Notes: Two symbols (×× or ••) = primary use of the tool; one symbol (× or •) = secondary use of the tool; × = tool of a central bank without supervisory powers; • = tool of an authority other than a central bank; ⊗ = tool available for both

Source: Padoa-Schioppa, *Regulating Finance* (n 3) 111, letters (a)-(j) added by the authors.

Table 5.1 illustrates a number of useful distinctions made by Padoa-Schioppa. A first distinction is that existing between a primary or secondary use of a tool. Padoa-Schioppa suggests that monetary policy tools ((a)–(d) and (f)) are primarily price stability-oriented, while financial stability is of an important, albeit secondary concern in these contexts. By contrast, in his view payment systems (e), emergency liquidity support (g), crisis coordination (h), and prudential regulation and supervision (i)–(j) primarily aim at achieving financial stability. Within the category of tools that are primarily financial stability-oriented, he further distinguishes between tools focusing on the system, on individual institutions, or on both.

In light of the arguments for a natural interest of central banks for financial stability that were recalled in the introduction, it is interesting to note that Padoa-Schioppa considered four of the tools to belong to what he called the 'land in between'. With this he meant that some tools that are not (necessarily) monetary policy tools are available to any central bank, so even one that does not have 'explicit supervisory duties to contribute to financial stability'.[41] These tools are the oversight of the payment system (e), emergency liquidity support (g), crisis coordination (h), and public and private comments (f).

A final distinction made by Padoa-Schioppa is that between tools aimed at crisis prevention and tools aimed at crisis resolution (understood as crisis management).[42] In line with this distinction, we will below distinguish between those primary

[41] Padoa-Schioppa, *Regulating Finance* (n 3) 112.
[42] ibid 122.

instruments which have either a *preventive* effect or a *remedial* (or counteracting or alleviating) effect. Preventive instruments are those which are oriented at instilling the quality of resilience into the financial system through regulation and supervision ((i)–(j)). Remedial financial stability tools are meanwhile those relating to the lender of last resort function (g) or crisis coordination (h).[43]

In the following sections, we will focus on specific instruments of financial stability identified by Padoa-Schioppa to explain their nature and how their use relates to financial stability concerns. We show how these tools fit within the EU legal framework and what role the ECB plays therein. Each section tracks relevant changes in this regard which have occurred since the twin crises by analysing EU legal acts, the ECB's own documents, and any EU Court jurisprudence. We distinguish between *preventive* (prudential regulation and supervision, payment systems) and *remedial* tools (crisis coordination, Emergency Liquidity Assistance (ELA)). First, there are the instruments which have to do with oversight and regulation of the financial markets (banking sector specifically) and the operation of payment and settlement systems. In our typology, these are preventive instruments, related to reinforcing the resilience quality of the financial system (Section V). This is in contrast to the second type, namely crisis management, or remedial instruments, which come into use once the objective of financial stability has been undermined (Section VI). A separate section is devoted to monetary policy strategy, as it can be used both as a preventive and a remedial instrument (see the debate about either leaning or cleaning) (Section VII).

V. Preventive Policy Instruments of Financial Stability

Preventive policy instruments such as *ex ante* regulation and its enforcement through supervision of the financial markets create the underlying conditions for financial stability. Crucial in this regard is the distinction between microprudential (individual institution) and macroprudential (system-wide) oversight over the banking sector. Moreover, central banks have a role in ensuring the smooth operation of payment systems. In these three areas we observe significant change with regard to the ECB's role even as they draw light to different aspects of financial stability.

A. Prudential regulation

Regulation consists in the setting of *ex ante* rules oriented at preventing instability in individual institutions, and—especially since the Great Financial Crisis—into the system as a whole. In the case of banks, such rules establish for example constraints on balance sheets (ie capital requirements) to ensure there is an adequate loss absorption buffer should the bank be faced with adverse conditions. Further, governance obligations ensure that institutions have in place decision-making procedures and processes

[43] cf Allen and Wood, 'Defining Financial Stability' (n 20) who distinguish between preventive measures (laws, official information provision, market conventions, and physical infrastructure) and remedial measures (liquidity and solvency support).

for dealing with risk. Such microprudential measures intend to ensure 'safety and soundness' of individual banks as a condition of financial stability.[44] Prior to the Great Financial Crisis, financial sector regulation was considered a primary responsibility of Member States (even in the euro area). EU competence to legislate in the area of banking regulation emerges meanwhile from the freedom to provide services as well as from its competence to harmonize the internal market and as such has been legislated for under the ordinary legislative procedure by the EU Council and the European Parliament, with further technical standards developed by the European Supervisory Agencies (ESAs).[45] Furthermore, in the context of the EU, financial stability was—and in fact remains—only one of the policy objectives pursued by regulation, alongside more targeted ones related to depositor and investor protection, as well as opening up and integrating the internal market.[46]

In this institutional setting, the ECB does not have the formal power to adopt prudential regulation. It does enjoy, however, an advisory role in the legislative process. The ECB must be consulted (1) on any proposed Union act in its field of competence, and (2) by National (both euro area and others)[47] authorities on any draft legislative provision in its field of competence (Article 127(4) TFEU, Article 25(1) ESCB Statute).

Since 1998, the ECB has issued over 1,500 such opinions, 16 per cent of these concerning proposals for Union acts and 84 per cent draft national legislation.[48] The opinions which explicitly mention financial stability—just 30 per cent of all opinions on EU proposals—illustrate many of the different aspects of the concept identified in Section II as well as its evolution.[49] A 1999 opinion refers to 'financial stability' as a condition *of* a financial institution.[50] Already in 2001 we find references closer to the

[44] SSM Regulation (n 32) recital 16.

[45] Regulation (EU) 2019/2175 of the European Parliament and of the Council of 18 December 2019 amending Regulation (EU) No 1093/2010 establishing a European Supervisory Authority (European Banking Authority); Regulation (EU) No 1094/2010 establishing a European Supervisory Authority (European Insurance and Occupational Pensions Authority); Regulation (EU) No 1095/2010 establishing a European Supervisory Authority (European Securities and Markets Authority); Regulation (EU) No 600/2014 on markets in financial instruments; Regulation (EU) 2016/1011 on indices used as benchmarks in financial instruments and financial contracts or to measure the performance of investment funds; and Regulation (EU) 2015/847 on information accompanying transfers of funds [2019] OJ L334/1. On EU financial regulation, see, eg, David Ramos D Muñoz and Marco Lamandini, *EU Financial Law: An Introduction* (Wolters Kluwer 2016) 52; Sideek Seyad, 'Free Movement of Capital' in Dennis Patterson and Anna Södersten (eds), *A Companion to European Union Law and International Law* (Wiley-Blackwell 2016).

[46] See, eg, CRD IV (n 31) recitals 4 and 47.

[47] See, eg, European Central Bank, 'Opinion on amendments to the financial stability regime in Denmark' (CON/2010/45, 28 May 2010) <https://eur-lex.europa.eu/legal-content/EN/TXT/PDF/?uri=CELEX:52010AB0045&rid=1> accessed 6 June 2021.

[48] As per Eur-lex database dedicated ECB legislative activity statistics <https://eur-lex.europa.eu/browse/institutions/bank/statistics.html> accessed 14 May 2021.

[49] Search conducted using the Eur-lex database search function for ECB opinions made between 1 January 1999 and 14 May 2021 mentioning 'financial stability' yielded sixty-nine opinions in total.

[50] '[S]uch risks may have a material impact on the financial stability of [electronic monetary institutions]': see Opinion of the European Central Bank of 18 January 1999 at the request of the Council of the European Union under Article 105(4) of the Treaty establishing the European Community and Article 4(a) of the Statute of the European System of Central Banks and of the European Central Bank on (1) a Commission proposal for a European Parliament and Council Directive on the taking up, the pursuit and the prudential supervision of the business of electronic money institutions, and (2) a Commission proposal for a European Parliament and Council Directive amending Directive 77/780/EEC on the coordination of laws, regulations and administrative provisions relating to the taking up and pursuit of the business of credit institutions [1999] OJ C189/7, para 21.

conventional meaning, namely the ECB analysing the proposed prudential rules of banks from the perspective of attaining the objective of financial stability as a condition of the financial system in the EU.[51] In fact, the ECB conducts such assessment regardless of whether the piece of legislation itself directly mentions financial stability or not, the latter being the case, for example, with regard to statistical data,[52] credit rating agencies (volatility being a concern),[53] and mortgages (residential prices being a factor relevant for financial stability), showing the broad scope of financial stability concerns.[54] Further, we find evidence of a resilience oriented approach, for example where, in the context of the 2003 Trading Disclosure Directive, the ECB considers the improved market efficiency achieved through the new rules as contributing to financial stability, for example by allowing for more market efficiency and therefore liquidity 'which will allow markets to absorb shocks more effectively'. Such phrasing equally shows the extent to which financial stability pre-crisis was anchored in a specific understanding of market mechanisms.[55] References to financial stability can also be found in opinions on proposed EU acts that deal with topics other than financial regulation, for example a number of euro area economic governance reforms, where the ECB refers to 'financial stability of the euro area' adopting the distinct language of financial stability in the context of macroeconomic concerns.[56] This is in contrast to the ECB opinions on financial regulation proposals, where the geographic scope of financial stability is typically undefined, unless there is a specific cause for concern—for example, the new market infrastructure framework is relevant for 'the financial stability of the Union or for one or more of its Member States' since it specifically concerns granting access to the EU market to entities from the United Kingdom after Brexit.[57]

[51] Opinion of the European Central Bank of 13 September 2001 at the request of the Council of the European Union on a proposal for a Directive of the European Parliament and of the Council on the supplementary supervision of credit institutions, insurance undertakings and investment firms in a financial conglomerate and amending Council Directives 73/239/EEC, 79/267/EEC, 92/49/EEC, 92/96/EEC, 93/6/EEC and 93/22/EEC, and Directives 98/78/EC and 2001/12/EC of the European Parliament and of the Council (COM(2001) 213 final) (CON/2001/25) [2001] OJ C271/10.

[52] 'Sound monetary policy decisions depend on reliable and up-to-date HICP statistics, which support the Eurosystem's tasks in the area of financial stability': Opinion of the European Central Bank of 1 June 2015 on a proposal for a Commission regulation amending Regulation (EC) No 1708/2005 laying down detailed rules for the implementation of Council Regulation (EC) No 2494/95 as regards the common index reference period for the harmonised index of consumer prices (CON/2015/18) [2015] OJ C209/3.

[53] 'In particular, from a financial stability perspective, it is of the utmost importance for the rating process not to lead to excessive volatility of ratings, which could result in a sharp re-pricing of assets and impair market confidence': see Opinion of 21 April 2009 on a proposal for a regulation of the European Parliament and of the Council on credit rating agencies (CON/2009/38) [2009] OJ C115/1, para 3.

[54] From a financial stability perspective, the ECB supports the measures aimed at ensuring responsible borrowing and lending and restoring consumer confidence. See Opinion of 5 July 2011 on a proposal for a directive of the European Parliament and of the Council on credit agreements relating to residential property (CON/2011/58) [2011] OJ C240/37, ε 1.

[55] Opinion of the European Central Bank of 30 September 2003 at the request of the Council of the European Union on a proposal for a directive of the European Parliament and of the Council on the harmonisation of transparency requirements with regard to information about issuers whose securities are admitted to trading on a regulated market and amending Directive 2001/34/EC (COM(2003) 138 final) (CON/2003/21) [2003] OJ C242/6, para 8.

[56] Opinion of the European Central Bank of 7 March 2012 on strengthened economic governance of the euro area (CON/2012/18) [2012] OJ C141/7.

[57] Opinion of the European Central Bank of 4 October 2017 on a proposal for a regulation of the European Parliament and of the Council amending Regulation (EU) No 1095/2010 establishing a European

Although it does not have a general power to adopt prudential regulation, the ECB has drawn on its mandate to contribute to the smooth conduct of 'prudential supervision of credit institutions and the stability of the financial system' to establish a system of collecting data on loans with the 2016 'Ana-Credit' Regulation,[58] and to adopt a 2019 Decision specifying the participation of non-euro area Member States in the system.[59] The former explicitly refers to the 'financial stability tasks' of the ESCB for which data availability is important. A similar approach can be found in a number of other ECB regulations concerning collection of statistical data.[60]

The ECB's influence over prudential rule-making significantly expanded with the proliferation of regulatory reforms introduced after the GFC, and specifically with the conferral on the ECB of certain tasks related to the supervision of euro area banks. There are two facets to this expansion. First, as a supervisor, the ECB took an observer seat on the EBA's Board of Supervisors and as such participates in the drafting of technical standards laying down the detailed provisions of microprudential regulation (the so-called Single Rulebook).[61] Second, in its exercise of supervisory tasks, the ECB provides guidance to individual financial institutions which amounts to administrative rule-making.[62]

B. Prudential supervision

Supervision entails the monitoring of compliance and enforcement of the prudential rulebook vis-à-vis financial institutions. However, in the light of the discretion accorded to supervisors both at the level of individual institutions (microprudential

Supervisory Authority (European Securities and Markets Authority) and amending Regulation (EU) No 648/2012 as regards the procedures and authorities involved for the authorisation of CCPs and requirements for the recognition of third-country CCPs (CON/2017/39) [2017] OJ C385/3.

[58] Regulation (EU) 2016/867 of the European Central Bank of 18 May 2016 on the collection of granular credit and credit risk data (ECB/2016/13) [2016] OJ L144/44, see Federico Ferretti, 'Prudential Supervision and the European Central Bank Credit Data Registry (AnaCredit): Legal Basis and Democratic Accountability' in Stefan Grundmann and Hans-Wolfgang Micklitz (eds), *The European Banking Union and Constitution: Beacon for Advanced Integration or Death-Knell for Democracy?* (Hart Publishing 2019) (hereafter Grundmann and Micklitz, *European Banking Union and Constitution*).

[59] Decision (EU) 2019/1348 of the European Central Bank of 18 July 2019 on the procedure for recognising non-euro area Member States as reporting Member States under Regulation (EU) 2016/867 on the collection of granular credit and credit risk data (ECB/2019/20) [2019] OJ L214/3.

[60] Regulation (EU) No 1011/2012 of the European Central Bank of 17 October 2012 concerning statistics on holdings of securities (ECB/2012/24) [2012] OJ L305/64.

[61] Not having a formal vote in EBA's Board of Supervisors under EBA regulation, the ECB remains an observer, albeit with a strong coordinating role of Banking Union authorities, cf Hans-Wolfgang Micklitz, 'The Internal Market and the Banking Union' in Grundmann and Micklitz, *European Banking Union and Constitution* (n 58) 283.

[62] The sheer scope of instruments available to the ECB with regard to bank supervision effectively amounts to rule-making: see Rinke Bax and Andreas Witte, 'The taxonomy of ECB instruments available for banking supervision' (2019) 6 ECB Economic Bulletin 85 <https://www.ecb.europa.eu/pub/pdf/ecbu/eb201906.en.pdf> accessed 6 June 2021. However, there are scholars who argue that granting ECB administrative rule-making powers would 'require a major overhaul of the Treaty': see, eg, Niamh Moloney, 'Technocratic and Centralised Decision-making in the Banking Union's Single Supervisory Mechanism: Can Single Market and Banking Union Governance Effectively Co-exist in a Post-Brexit World?' in Grundmann and Micklitz, *European Banking Union and Constitution* (n 58) 166.

supervision) and at a systemic level since the GFC (macroprudential oversight) it is much more than a mere mechanic box-ticking exercise. The process of supervision enables the responsible authorities to understand better the business model and the governance of financial institutions, to foresee and pre-empt a crisis or a failure of an individual entity, thereby strengthening the resilience of the financial system and therefore enhancing financial stability. This is why in Padoa-Schioppa's toolbox, financial stability is considered as the primary use of the supervisory tool both at systemic and individual entity level. The supervisory process can be intrusive, which is warranted, *inter alia*, due to financial stability concerns (other reasons include the protection of depositors).

Prior to the GFC, supervision was placed squarely in the hands of euro area national authorities. There was some cooperation at the EU level in the form of structured co-operation between national supervisors within the Committee of European Banking Supervisors (CEBS), which participated in technical rule-making, but had no intervention powers.[63] The absence of centralized supervision for the euro area has been criticized from a financial stability point of view, among others by Padoa-Schioppa.[64] As mentioned, the role of the ECB was auxiliary and limited to contributing to the 'smooth conduct of policies pursued by the competent authorities relating to the prudential supervision of credit institutions and the stability of the financial system' (Article 127(5) TFEU), for example through its advisory role discussed in Section A.

Two important changes took place over the course of the GFC with respect to the role of the ECB in supervision of financial stability, relating to first, macroprudential supervision and second, microprudential supervision.

(1) Macroprudential supervision

The first major reform affecting the role of the ECB in the supervision of financial stability in the EU was the creation of the European Systemic Risk Board (ESRB) and of the macroprudential regime more broadly in 2010.[65] A macroprudential approach, that is, treating the financial system in a holistic way with a view to preventing e.g. the emergence of asset bubbles, is not a completely new invention—in fact, it lies at the very heart of financial stability as conventionally understood. The ECB has further published 'Financial Stability Reviews' since 2004.[66] What is novel however is a dedicated institutional framework at the EU level and a dedicated macroprudential toolbox, which can be drawn on at systemic level.

The ESRB is responsible for the macroprudential oversight of the financial system within the Union. It is tasked essentially with structuring the discussion among national authorities on topics of systemic importance and emerging risks, such reviews not being coupled with ample intervention powers, with the exception of confidential

[63] Despina Chatzimanoli, 'Law and governance in the institutional organisation of EU financial services: The Lamfalussy procedure and the single supervisor revisited' (PhD Thesis, European University Institute 2009).

[64] Padoa-Schioppa, *Regulating Finance* (n 3) 94.

[65] Regulation (EU) No 1092/2010 of the European Parliament and of the Council of 24 November 2010 on European Union macro-prudential oversight of the financial system and establishing a European Systemic Risk Board [2010] OJ L331/1 (hereafter ESRB Regulation).

[66] See ECB, 'Financial Stability Review' (n 1).

and, where appropriate, public warnings. The ECB has been granted a central role in the new framework, where it 'should provide analytical, statistical, administrative and logistical support to the ESRB, also drawing on technical advice from national central banks and supervisors'.[67] The ECB takes a prominent institutional role in the ESRB, with the President and vice-President of the ECB sitting as voting members of the General Board, and the ECB also supporting the ESRB Secretariat due to its expertise in the area of financial stability.[68]

Financial stability concerns were the driving force behind the creation of the ESRB, as recalled in the first recital, which in stating that 'financial stability is a precondition for the real economy to provide jobs, credit and growth'[69] highlights the function that the financial system serves to the real economy. Next to the risk management approach to financial stability emphasized in Article 3 of the ESRB Regulation, we can also find an attempt to anchor the macroprudential approach in concerns for internal market functioning.[70] With regard to sectoral coverage, following the conventional meaning of financial stability, the macroprudential approach is broad: for example, the ESRB publishes regular reports on shadow banking.[71]

Given the breadth of EU macroprudential concerns, it might be somewhat surprising that the framework still reserves most powers to national competent authorities, which can be central banks, specialized committees, or ministries. These include the power to impose special requirements on the financial sector with a view to preventing bubbles building up, such as loan-to-value ratios and income-to-interest ratios restricting access to credit (cf Article 458 CRR).[72] This national focus of macroprudential policy has been highlighted by some as impairing the effectiveness of the framework, given the cross-border spillovers of instability in capital markets.[73] In the context of a currency union which has been prone to sudden stops in capital flows in the past, these macroprudential policy tools left to national authorities can be understood however as a tool to protect local financial stability, which substitutes to a certain extent capital controls. Coordination is then aimed to smooth out any conflicts and the ESRB is seen to play an important role as a 'notification hub'.[74]

The discretion of national authorities is limited by two elements at the EU level. Firstly, macroprudential tools that national competent authorities wish to impose on domestic institutions can be rejected by the Council by qualified majority, so that an

[67] ESRB Regulation (n 65) recital 6.
[68] ibid recital 24.
[69] ibid recital 10.
[70] In line with TFEU (n 27) Art 114 as the legal basis.
[71] eg European Systemic Risk Board, 'EU Shadow Banking Monitor' (no 1, July 2016) <https://www.esrb.europa.eu/pub/pdf/reports/nbfi_monitor/20160727_shadow_banking_report.en.pdf> accessed 6 June 2021.
[72] Regulation (EU) No 575/2013 of the European Parliament and of the Council of 26 June 2013 on prudential requirements for credit institutions and investment firms and amending Regulation (EU) No 648/2012 [2013] OJ L176/1 (hereafter CRR).
[73] For such criticisms, see, eg, Thorsten Beck, Elena Carletti, and Itay Goldstein, 'Financial Regulation in Europe: Foundations and Challenges' in Laszlo Matyas and others (eds), *Economics without Borders: Economic Research for European Policy Challenges* (CUP 2017).
[74] As argued, eg, in Anton Korinek and Damiano Sandri, 'Capital Controls or Macroprudential Regulation?' (2015) IMF Working Paper No 15/218 <https://www.imf.org/external/pubs/ft/wp/2015/wp15218.pdf> accessed 6 June 2021.

overriding EU perspective is maintained.[75] Secondly, and more importantly, to understand the role of the ECB in safeguarding financial stability, the 2013 SSM Regulation provides the ECB with some specific macroprudential instruments, such as the power to impose higher requirements for countercyclical buffers and more stringent measures than those set by the national authorities (Article 5 SSM Regulation).

(2) Microprudential supervision

By contrast to macroprudential policy, in microprudential supervision the ECB was put in the driving seat as the European Banking Union's supervisor under the 2013 SSM Regulation.[76] The new framework grants the ECB direct supervisory powers over the Banking Union's largest banks, with a responsibility for the system as a whole. This happened through the activation of Article 127(6) TFEU, in which the Treaty drafters in Maastricht created a possibility for the Council to confer certain supervisory tasks on the ECB.[77] Unsurprisingly given Padoa-Schioppa's assessment of prudential supervision of individual institutions as a primary tool for pursuing financial stability, in the SSM Regulation we find frequent references to the aims of 'restoring' (recital 2), 'preserving' (recital 5), 'effectively safeguarding' (recital 44), or 'maintaining' (Article 14(6) SSM Regulation) financial stability. Such references fit well with the conventional meaning of financial stability, also where they provide evidence that the goal is not static but one which involves preventive as well as remedial action. However, the SSM is limited in scope to credit institutions (ie not other financial institutions).[78] At the same time, supervision is not only an instrument of financial stability, but—in the EU context—of other policy objectives as well, such as—in the SSM—maintaining and deepening market integration.[79]

C. Payment systems

Payment systems organize the exchange of funds between financial institutions (interbank payment systems), citizens and businesses (retail payment systems), and in the securities markets (clearing and settlement systems).[80] There are several reasons why central banks, including the ECB, are interested in the smooth functioning of payment systems.[81] First, it is an essential condition for maintaining trust in a currency. Second,

[75] See CRR (n 72) Art 458 including grounds for such rejection.

[76] See European Systemic Risk Board, 'Special Feature A: The ESRB as a coordination and notification hub under CRD V and CRR II' in European Systemic Risk Board, 'A Review of Macroprudential Policy in the EU in 2019' (2020) <https://www.esrb.europa.eu/pub/pdf/reports/review_macroprudential_policy/sfa_4~ea618a97e4.en.pdf?afe248b58df0c3ab066204cf5b5c9e36> accessed 6 June 2021.

[77] See chapter 7 by Kern Alexander and chapter 8 by Federico della Negra and Gianno Lo Schiavo, in this volume.

[78] Furthermore, with the creation of the resolution pillar of the Banking Union (the Single Resolution Mechanism), significant responsibility for the resilience aspect of prudential supervision has been placed with the resolution authority. Agnieszka Smoleńska, 'Single Resolution Board: Lost and Found in the Thicket of EU Bank Regulation' in Grundmann and Micklitz, *European Banking Union and Constitution* (n 58).

[79] SSM Regulation (n 32) recital 5.

[80] John Armour and others, *Principles of Financial Regulation* (OUP 2016) 391.

[81] See more extensively, Athanassiou, 'Payment Systems' (n 4) 716–18; de Haan, Oosterloo, and Schoenmaker, 'Financial Markets and Institutions' (n 4) 229.

payment systems play an important role in monetary policy operations and are the vehicle of central bank liquidity providing operations. As such, the transmission of monetary policy depends on the smooth functioning of the payment systems, which enables the financial markets to process a high volume and value of transactions and to fulfil their intermediation function. Financial instability, for example banking panics, can disrupt the payment system.[82] Conversely, sound payment system plumbing can in itself increase financial resilience.

Consequently, ensuring the smooth functioning of payment systems through oversight and running a part of the system is a unique tool in Padoa-Schioppa's toolbox. Though he identifies it as a secondary tool of central banks oriented at individual institutions, it is also one of the instruments directly mentioned in the EU Treaties differently from most of the financial stability tools discussed in this chapter (see Section III).

Within the scope of this basic task, the ECB takes a wide variety of actions. Article 22 ESCB Statute states that the ECB and national central banks may provide facilities, and in fact the Eurosystem owns and operates several payment and securities settlement systems.[83] We will discuss further below the most important real-time gross settlement system (RTGS) owned and operated by the Eurosystem, called TARGET2, and the debate on its relationship to financial stability (Section V.C(1)). Article 22 ESCB Statute also explicitly grants the ECB specific regulatory powers, the scope of which has, however, been interpreted restrictively by the General Court (see Section V.C(2)).[84] So far, this regulatory action has not played a central role in the ECB's promotion of the smooth operation of payment systems.[85] Instead, the ECB resorts to what it calls oversight of financial market infrastructures (a term not referred to in the Treaties),[86] which includes the collection of relevant information, the assessment of this information against its oversight objectives, and inducing changes where necessary.[87]

It should be noted that technological transformation is changing the ECB's approach to payment systems and their relationship to financial stability. One such example is the digital euro, the introduction of which could be conceived of in terms of ECB competence in the area of payment systems. However—as the ECB itself

[82] Gianni Toniolo and Eugene N White, 'The Evolution of the Financial Stability Mandate: From Its Origins to the Present Day' (2015) NBER Working Paper No 20844 <https://www.nber.org/papers/w20844.pdf> accessed 6 June 2021.

[83] The Eurosystem operates three payment systems: TARGET2, which is the real-time gross settlement (RTGS) system; TARGET2-Securities (T2S), which is the securities settlement platform; and TARGET Instant Payment Settlement (TIPS) which is the instant payment settlement service.

[84] TFEU (n 27) Protocol No 4 on the Statute of the European System of Central Banks and of the European Central Bank [2016] OJ C202/230, Art 22 (hereafter ESCB Statute) provides that 'the ECB and national central banks may provide facilities, and the ECB may make regulations, to ensure efficient and sound clearing and payment systems within the Union and with other countries'.

[85] Athanassiou, 'Payment Systems' (n 4) 727.

[86] On this, see also Case T-496/11 *United Kingdom v European Central Bank* [2015] EU:T:2015:133, para 6 (hereafter *Location Policy*).

[87] European Central Bank, 'Eurosystem oversight policy framework' (2016) <https://www.ecb.europa.eu/pub/pdf/other/eurosystemoversightpolicyframework201607.en.pdf> accessed 6 June 2021.

assesses—the digital euro's impact on financial stability is not straightforward and could as well have destabilizing effects.[88]

(1) The operation of euro area payment systems

The ECB established the euro area's Trans-European Automated Real-time Gross Express Transfer System (TARGET2) in 2007,[89] replacing the first-generation TARGET which started operating only a few days after the launch of the euro in 1999. TARGET2 is a wholesale payment system operated by the French, German, and Italian central banks on behalf of the Eurosystem. It allows financial institutions to settle transactions through the use of central bank money.[90] Its balances are therefore 'the net claims and liabilities of national central banks vis-à-vis the ECB that arise through cross-border payments'.[91] By 2019, the system serviced daily 344,120 transactions amounting to 1,731 billion euros which amounts to 89 per cent in terms of value of total large-value payment system traffic.[92] The total balance of TARGET2 rose from around 100 billion in 2007 to over a trillion euros at various times during the sovereign debt crisis in the euro area.[93] This balance reflects the divergences of the claims of the different central banks within the system, in particular between the Northern and Southern European central banks, and demonstrates the increased significance of TARGET2 for euro area financial stability.

This scope for imbalances is seen by some scholars as a secret transfer system within the euro area, hidden within the plumbing of the financial system.[94] This view, which notably gained traction in Germany during the sovereign debt crisis, has been much criticized since.[95] In fact, others perceive it as an important cushion against financial instability of the euro area.[96] Sandbu, for example, argues that although the capital

[88] European Central Bank, 'Report on the digital euro' (2020), 16 <https://www.ecb.europa.eu/pub/pdf/other/Report_on_a_digital_euro~4d7268b458.en.pdf> accessed 6 June 2021.

[89] Decision of the European Central Bank of 24 July 2007 concerning the terms and conditions of TARGET2-ECB (ECB/2007/7) [2007] OJ L237/71.

[90] Our focus on ECB efforts in organizing and overseeing wholesale payment systems is without prejudice to its engagement in EU regulatory efforts with respect to the retail payment system, where it has been the European Commission that has taken the lead and the ECB's involvement is restricted largely to giving detailed opinions on legislative proposals (see Section V). On EU integration in retail payments systems, see further Agnieszka Janczuk-Gorywoda, 'Evolution of EU Retail Payments Law' (2015) 40 EL Rev 858.

[91] Peter Praet, 'Remarks at the BNYM 20th anniversary dinner on the dynamics of TARGET2 balances and monetary policy implementation' (Dinner address at the BNYM 20th anniversary, Brussels, 15 September 2016) (hereafter Praet, TARGET2).

[92] European Central Bank, 'TARGET Annual Report 2019' <https://www.ecb.europa.eu/pub/pdf/targetar/ecb.targetar2019.en.pdf> accessed 6 June 2021.

[93] Praet, TARGET2 (n 91); Ulrich Bindseil, Philippine Cour-Thimann, and Philipp Johann König, 'TARGET and Cross-Border Interbank Payments during the Financial Crisis' (2012) 13 CESifo Forum Special Issue 83.

[94] Hans-Werner Sinn and Timo Wollmershäuser, 'Target Loans, Current Account Balances and Capital Flows: The ECB's Rescue Facility' (2011) 19 International Tax and Public Finance 468.

[95] For this criticism, see, eg, Karl Whelan, 'Professor Sinn misses the target' (*VoxEU*, 9 June 2011) <https://voxeu.org/article/there-hidden-eurozone-bailout> accessed 6 June 2021; Martin Sandbu, *Europe's Orphan. The Future of the Euro and the Politics of Debt* (Princeton University Press 2015) 118–22 (hereafter Sandbu, *Europe's Orphan*).

[96] Lamandini, Ramos, and Solana, 'The ECB's Mandates' (n 11) 21; Matthew Klein, 'Target2 balances reflect euro area's potential to be better than traditional exchange rate peg regime' *Financial Times Alphaville* (15 September 2017) <https://www.ft.com/content/adccc575-4c37-38db-8553-003cc04e59ba> accessed 6 June 2021.

flows that lead to TARGET2 imbalances can be destabilizing,[97] at the same time they show the strength of TARGET2 and the robustness of the euro.[98]

The fact that the financial stability implications of TARGET2 are not explicitly acknowledged in early ECB legal acts should not be a reason to doubt the systemic dimension of TARGET2 in this regard.[99] In these early acts it was rather the systems' diagnostic value,[100] which was relevant from a financial stability perspective, where TARGET2 data are 'necessary in order to perform analyses pertaining to macro-prudential oversight, financial stability, financial integration, market operations, monetary policy functions and the Single Supervisory Mechanism'.[101] A more explicit recognition of the financial stability implications of TARGET2 can be inferred from the establishment of the systemically important payment system regime (SIPS) in the 2014 SIPS Regulation,[102] a notable and exceptional example of the ECB's use of its regulatory powers in this area. With TARGET2 being designated as a systemically important payment system it became bound by specific obligations, including to 'explicitly support financial stability and other relevant public interest considerations, in particular open and efficient financial markets.'[103] The example of TARGET2 shows not only the critical role of the payment system as a resilience-reinforcing element of the financial system, but also the ECB's growing power to regulate the system with stability in mind.

(2) The scope of the ECB's financial market infrastructure oversight

Payment systems are not the only financial market infrastructures (FMIs) relevant from a financial stability perspective. Other FMIs include the CCPs, on which the exchange of securities is centrally cleared. Their smooth operation—from a systemic perspective—is important, for example, due to the existing risks of contagion in a highly integrated market. Furthermore, since the post-crisis growth in central

[97] Similarly, Whelan argues that TARGET balances can be an important indicator of stress in the banking sector: see Karl Whelan, 'Should we be concerned about TARGET balances?' (2017) Directorate General for Internal Polices, Policy Department A: Economic and Scientific Policy PE 607.366, 6 <https://www.europarl.europa.eu/RegData/etudes/IDAN/2017/607366/IPOL_IDA(2017)607366_EN.pdf> accessed 6 June 2021 (hereafter Whelan, 'Should we be concerned about TARGET balances?').

[98] Sandbu, *Europe's Orphan* (n 95) 122.

[99] The more explicit stability focus of these decisions was rather on the stability of the TARGET2 system itself and on the importance of TARGET2 data in performing financial stability analyses. See Decision of the European Central Bank of 24 July 2007 concerning the terms and conditions of TARGET2-ECB (ECB/2007/7) [2007] OJ L237/71, Arts 6(1)(4)(c) and 9(1) and Decision (EU) 2017/2080 of the European Central Bank of 22 September 2017 amending Decision ECB/2010/9 on access to and use of certain TARGET2 data (ECB/2017/29) [2017] OJ L295/86, recital 4 (hereafter ECB, 'Decision on TARGET2 data').

[100] Whelan, eg, argues that TARGET balances are an important indicator of the stress in the euro area financial markets: see Whelan, 'Should we be concerned about TARGET balances?' (n 97).

[101] ECB, 'Decision on TARGET2 data' (n 99) recital 4.

[102] Regulation of the European Central Bank (EU) No 795/2014 of 3 July 2014 on oversight requirements for systemically important payment systems (ECB/2014/28) [2014] OJ L217/16 (hereafter SIPS Regulation).

[103] Following SIPS Regulation (n 102) Art 4(1) specific requirements are imposed on parties in the payment systems, including legal soundness and governance rules. Risk management regulation is covered as well, and differentiated obligations are imposed on the participants where payments take place in central bank money or commercial bank money (Arts 3, 4, 6, and 13–15); Decision of the European Central Bank of 13 August 2014 on the identification of TARGET2 as a systemically important payment system pursuant to Regulation (EU) No 795/2014 on oversight requirements for systemically important payment systems (ECB/2014/35) [2014] OJ L245/5.

clearing, the ECB has become increasingly concerned with this market segment for financial stability reasons, where a large part of the euro market is outside of its formal purview (especially in the UK).[104] The ECB enjoys an oversight function with regard to FMIs such as CCPs, which is not as incisive as its powers in the area of supervision (cf the supervisory powers of the ECB over credit institutions in Section V.A), with most responsibility remaining with the national authorities.[105] However, concerns over financial stability underpinned the ECB's attempt to regulate them via the 'Eurosystem oversight policy', which required all euro-denominated transactions above a set threshold to be conducted by CCPs legally established in the euro area with full managerial and operational control and responsibility exercised from one of its Member States. Since at the time most of these transactions took place on CCPs in the UK, the government in London challenged the ECB's policy before the General Court arguing that the ECB did not have the competence to regulate the activity of institutions such as CCPs.[106] The *Location Policy* case shows the limits of the scope of the ECB's financial stability toolkit.[107]

While the Court recognized the ECB's interest in the smooth operation of clearing markets, it distinguished between oversight and regulation of market activity, where the latter entails imposing uniform requirements, for example with regard to a mandatory location.[108] Further, the Court confirmed that the scope of the 'payment system' under Article 127(2) TFEU covers only the transfer of funds and not the transfer of securities as is the case for CCPs and that therefore the ECB does not have the competence to require euro-denominated derivative transactions to be cleared in the euro area.[109] In so doing, the Court set the limits of the scope of the 'payments' instrument by adopting a restrictive reading of the ECB's competence with regard to regulating payment systems, thereby restricting the scope of this financial stability tool. The judgment has been criticized for failing to address financial stability.[110] For our purposes, the key implication of the judgment is that there are limits to a purposive interpretation of the policy instruments at the disposal of the ECB, in particular when they touch upon regulated areas. In fact, in such contexts, the ECB's 'natural interest' is checked by the Court of Justice and by decisions of the EU legislature; in this case specific market segments are excluded from the scope of the ECB's policy instrument.

The controversy surrounding the legislative reform of the European Market Infrastructure Regulation (EMIR) which followed the *Location policy* judgment, helps to further elucidate this point. Closing the supervisory gap over CCPs—and

[104] For the genesis of the EU's market infrastructure reform after Brexit, see Fabio Bulfone and Agnieszka Smoleńska, 'The Internal and External Centralisation of Capital Markets Union Regulatory Structures: The Case of Central Counterparties' in Adrienne Héritier and Magnus Schoeller (eds), *Governing Finance in Europe* (Edward Elgar Publishing 2020) .

[105] Ibid.

[106] These requirements would also have implications for the access to Target2: see Decision of the Central Bank of 24 July 2007 concerning the terms and conditions of TARGET2-ECB (ECB/2007/7) [2007] OJ L237/71 with subsequent amendments.

[107] *Location Policy* (n 86); for analysis of the financial stability aspects, see Heikki Marjosola, 'Missing Pieces in the Patchwork of EU Financial Stability Regime? The Case of Central Counterparties' (2015) 50 CML Rev 115 (hereafter Marjosola, 'Missing Pieces').

[108] *Location Policy* (n 86)para 102.

[109] ibid paras 97–99.

[110] Marjosola, 'Missing Pieces' (n 107) 1511.

therefore financial instability risks—became all the more pertinent in the aftermath of the Brexit referendum.[111] Initially, the reform proposed by the European Commission foresaw further direct and emergency supervisory powers over the CCPs for central banks and the ECB recommended a Treaty amendment to be able to exercise those powers.[112] However, during the legislative process, fears over concentrating power with the ECB prevailed, and the EU legislature decided to rather transfer supervisory responsibilities to ESMA, with only a residual role for central banks.[113] Such reform outcome was not to the liking of the ECB, which withdrew its recommendation of 22 June 2017 for a Decision of the European Parliament and the Council amending Article 22 of its Statute, emphasizing that to 'protect the stability of the euro', 'the ECB should have the regulatory powers ... to adopt additional requirements for CCPs involved in the clearing of significant amounts of euro-denominated transactions'.[114] The CCP controversy shows the extent to which limits on the financial stability instruments of central banks are set by legislation in areas which lay in Padoa-Schioppa's 'land in-between'. In other words, the role of the ECB in pursuing financial stability is not uncontested even in payment systems. In areas where competences are effectively shared, the ECB's financial stability instruments are constrained by the Treaty and by secondary EU legislation.

VI. Remedial Policy Instruments of Financial Stability

A. ELA: National Central Banks (NCBs) as Lenders of Last Resort (LOLR) to individual institutions

One of the main reasons why central banks are generally considered to have a natural interest in financial stability, is that only they can fulfil the Lender of Last Resort (LOLR) function. This function is traditionally understood as central bank liquidity provision to individual illiquid but solvent banks,[115] although below we will see that the LOLR function is nowadays also more broadly associated with liquidity assistance to the banking system and to an implicit central bank guarantee to sovereign bond holders (on which see Section VII). This has led to distinctions between a credit

[111] As a majority of transactions in euro-denominated securities is centrally cleared at UK-based CCPs.

[112] The ECB recommendation read: 'The ECB and national central banks may provide facilities, and the ECB may make regulations, to ensure efficient and sound clearing and payment systems, and clearing systems for financial instruments, within the Union and with other countries.', European Central Bank, 'ECB recommends amending Article 22 of its Statute' (23 June 2017) <https://www.ecb.europa.eu/press/pr/date/2017/html/ecb.pr170623.en.html> accessed 6 June 2021.

[113] For a discussion of possible explanations of such an outcome, see Agnieszka Smoleńska and Adrienne Héritier 'Political Accountability and effects: Capital Markets Union' in Adrienne Héritier and Johannes Karremans (eds), *Regulating Finance in Europe: Policy Effects and Political Accountability* (Edward Elgar Publishing 2021).

[114] ibid; see also the letter of Mario Draghi to President of the European Parliament Antonio Tajani on the Withdrawal of the Recommendation of the ECB for a Decision of the European Parliament and of the Council amending Article 22 of the Statute of the European System of Central Banks and of the European Central Bank (20 March 2019) <https://eur-lex.europa.eu/legal-content/EN/TXT/PDF/?uri=CELLAR:38f15593-9e6f-11ea-9d2d-01aa75ed71a1&from=EN> accessed 7 June 2021.

[115] The principal architects of the LOLR doctrine were Henry Thornton and Walter Bagehot.

approach and a monetary approach to LOLR, and between micro and macro level liquidity. Micro level liquidity, also referred to as the credit approach to LOLR,[116] in the EU context is referred to as ELA. Like macro-level liquidity support, ELA is traditionally considered a natural task of central banks, independently of whether they have been assigned prudential tasks. In the context of the conventional meaning of financial stability, ELA is typically conceived of as liquidity assistance to banks solely, however its scope could likely in exceptional cases be extended to systemically important market infrastructures, such as the CCPs discussed above.[117]

Temporary liquidity shortages of (financial) institutions, even in the absence of insolvency, can challenge financial stability. ELA can mitigate the risk of contagion and prevent the panic that can lead to a bank run and a possible fall in the confidence in the stability of the financial system.[118] In fact, in the table of Padoa-Schioppa presented in Section IV, this tool is identified as having financial stability as the primary objective. ELA can be understood as a remedial measure as it is provided in case of liquidity problems. It can help preserve (trust in) the ability of the financial system to carry out its function of intermediation, but is not in itself a measure that improves its resilience, understood in the sense of an internal condition of the financial system.[119]

In contrast with liquidity assistance to the banking system, ELA is not provided by the ECB. Whereas the ECB has incorporated the macro-level LOLR function into monetary policy, it has *not* done the same thing with regard to liquidity shortages at micro level/to individual banks, in the form of ELA. ELA is instead provided by Eurosystem NCBs' on the basis of the relevant national legal framework.

In fact, the prevailing interpretation by the ECB of the ESCB Statute has so far been to consider ELA as falling within the purview of NCBs,[120] an interpretation that is not uncontested. Smits has since the very beginning argued that this role could very well be taken up by the ECB itself.[121] More recently, the argument is made more frequently that the ECB should change its position, especially now that it has been given supervisory powers of significant financial institutions.[122] In this context it has again been argued that this would not require Treaty change, as there is already a legal basis for the ECB to provide ELA under Article 18 ESCB Statute.[123]

[116] See chapter 15 by Christy-Ann Petit, in this volume.

[117] Committee on the Global Financial System, 'Designing frameworks for central bank liquidity assistance: addressing new challenges' (2017) CGFS Papers No 58 <https://www.bis.org/publ/cgfs58.pdf> accessed 6 June 2021.

[118] cf de Haan, Oosterloo, and Schoenmaker, 'Financial Markets and Institutions' (n 4) 449.

[119] cf The unconventional monetary policy measures discussed in Section VII.

[120] European Central Bank, 'Agreement on emergency liquidity assistance' (9 November 2020) <https://www.ecb.europa.eu/pub/pdf/other/ecb.agreementemergencyliquidityassistance202012~ba7c45c170.en.pdf> accessed 6 June 2021 (hereafter ECB, '2020 Agreement on ELA').

[121] René Smits, *The European Central Bank. Institutional aspects* (Kluwer Law International 1997) 268–71.

[122] Charles Goodhart and Dirk Schoenmaker, *The ECB as lender of last resort?* (*VoxEU*, 23 October 2014) <https://voxeu.org/article/ecb-lender-last-resort> accessed 6 June 2021; Armin Steinbach, 'The Lender of Last Resort in the Eurozone' (2016) 53 CML Rev 361 (hereafter Steinbach 'Lender of Last Resort Eurozone'); Lastra, 'Banking Union: An Incomplete Building' (n 9) 177; Patrick Honohan, *Currency, Credit and Crisis. Central Banking in Ireland and Europe* (CUP 2019) 310 (hereafter Honohan, *Currency, Credit and Crisis*).

[123] Lastra (n 9) 178; cf Chiara Zilioli, 'Introduction' in European Central Bank, 'ECB Legal Conference 2015: From Monetary Union to Banking Union. On the way to Capital Markets Union New opportunities for European integration' (2015), 52 <https://www.ecb.europa.eu/pub/pdf/other/frommonetaryuniontobankingunion201512.en.pdf> accessed 6 June 2021: 'The ECB has been conferred the exclusive

The fact that ELA is provided by NCBs does not mean that the ECB is not involved in it. On the basis of Article 14.4 of the ESCB Statute, NCBs may perform functions other than those specified in the Statute unless the ECB's Governing Council finds, by a majority of two thirds of the votes cast, that these interfere with the objectives and tasks of the ESCB. This means that NCBs may provide ELA under their respective national frameworks, unless the ECB Governing Council finds that it interferes with ECB monetary policy. Considering the short maturity of ELA, this in practice provides the ECB Governing Council with a veto opportunity every fortnight.[124]

The ECB's involvement in ELA provision by NCBs has brought several challenges with it. These challenges have in particular been highlighted during the Global Financial Crisis and sovereign debt crisis, when the provision of ELA changed notably in scale and duration. In fact, during the crisis the scope of ELA broadened from individual institutions to the entire banking system of some countries.[125] Whereas the relevant rules clearly state that national functions shall be performed on the responsibility and liability of NCBs and that any costs and risks arising from the provision of ELA shall be incurred by the NCB concerned,[126] it has been argued that 'leaving ELA as a national responsibility does not prevent a degree of involuntary risk-sharing across countries'.[127]

Being lenient on ELA provision by NCBs carries a risk for the ECB, as it can lead to a violation of Article 123 TFEU which prohibits monetary financing. In fact, the ECB Agreement on emergency liquidity assistance now provides that ELA provision that exceeds a certain threshold is assessed *ex ante* for compliance with this treaty prohibition.[128] Providing ELA to insolvent institutions is considered as such monetary financing.[129] Making the distinction between illiquid and insolvent institutions during a crisis is however notoriously difficult.[130]

The opposite choice of being strict on ELA provision by NCBs carries financial stability risks, as illustrated by the Global Financial Crisis and sovereign debt crisis, when the entire banking system of some countries in the euro area became dependent on

competence to conduct the monetary policy of the euro area. An implied power of such competence is the power to grant, at the discretion of the central bank, ELA support.'

[124] European Central Bank, 'Agreement on emergency liquidity assistance' (17 May 2017) <https://www.ecb.europa.eu/pub/pdf/other/Agreement_on_emergency_liquidity_assistance_20170517.en.pdf> accessed 15 June 2021. For a discussion of the evolution of ELA during the crisis, see Peter Praet, 'The ECB and its role as Lender of Last Resort during the crisis' (Speech at the Committee on Capital Markets Regulation conference on the lender of Last Resort—an International Perspective, Washington DC, 10 February 2016) <https://www.ecb.europa.eu/press/key/date/2016/html/sp160210.en.html> accessed 15 June 2021 (hereafter Praet, 'ECB as Lender of Last Resort').

[125] See also Honohan, *Currency, Credit and Crisis* (122) 270; cf Praet, 'ECB as Lender of Last Resort' (n 124).

[126] See ESCB Statute (n 84) Art 14.4 and ECB, '2020 Agreement on ELA' (n 120) Art 2.2.

[127] Honohan, *Currency, Credit and Crisis* (n 122) 309.

[128] See ECB, '2020 Agreement on ELA' (n 120) Art 5.2.

[129] ibid Art 5.4.

[130] cf Padoa-Schioppa, *Regulating Finance* (n 3) 102; Schoenmaker, 'Central Banks Role in Financial Stability' (n 11) 278; Joseph Stiglitz, *The Euro: How a Common Currency Threatens the Future of Europe* (WW Norton & Company 2016) 156.

ELA. It has been argued that the development of alternatives to ELA has since made it easier for the ECB to reject ELA provision.[131]

Being strict on ELA moreover carries a risk for the ECB of being accused of acting politically. In fact, a further specific challenge for the ECB concerns its relationship with the democratic process in Member States, and relates to what has elsewhere been called 'central bank intervention' in Member State economic policy making.[132] This concept, and the challenges related to it, are not limited to ELA provision, but the ECB's involvement in ELA provision does illustrate it well. The decision by the ECB Governing Council of 21 March 2013 to reject ELA provision by the Central Bank of Cyprus on 25 March, if no programme would be in place by that date that would ensure solvency of the relevant Cypriot banks,[133] effectively pressured Cyprus into accepting a financial assistance programme.[134] Former Governor of the Central Bank of Ireland Honohan has criticized the Governing Council's authorization to ECB President Trichet to write a letter to the Irish government, because it not only warned Ireland that ELA might be refused if it did not apply for financial assistance, but also made 'no attempt to acknowledge the boundary between (on the one hand) the ECB's need to protect its own balance sheet and adhere to settled policy on emergency liquidity and (on the other hand) the governments sovereign responsibilities'.[135]

B. Crisis coordination

Crisis coordination as a financial stability tool may appear rather underspecified compared to other policy instruments discussed in this chapter. And yet, among the remedial tools in the central bank toolbox, it is of central importance. Padoa-Schioppa conceived this tool essentially in terms of the exchange of information between authorities, with an *ex ante* planning which facilitates the choice of an intermediate policy response once a crisis materializes, allowing for 'the adequate capability of financial institutions to produce relevant information for authorities in a swift manner (contingency plans)'.[136] Though no explicit legal framework for such arrangements is in place, we find such arrangements have indeed existed before the GFC. The Memorandum of Understanding (MoU) on Cross-Border Financial Stability was concluded already in 2003 between banking supervisors and central banks in the EU.[137] In

[131] See Honohan, *Currency, Credit and Crisis* (n 122) 298, who argues that in 2017 ELA could be refused by the ECB to the Spanish *Banco Popular* because of the availability of alternatives (he refers to resolution involving bail-in).

[132] Thomas Beukers, 'The New ECB and its Relationship with the Eurozone Member States: Between Central Bank Intervention and Central Bank Intervention' (2013) 50 CML Rev 1579 (hereafter Beukers, 'The New ECB').

[133] European Central Bank, 'Governing Council decision on Emergency Liquidity Assistance requested by the Central Bank of Cyprus' (ECB Press Release, 21 March 2013) <https://www.ecb.europa.eu/press/pr/date/2013/html/pr130321.nl.html> accessed 15 June 2021.

[134] Beukers, 'The New ECB' (n 132) 1593.

[135] Honohan, *Currency, Credit and Crisis* (n 122) 245.

[136] Padoa-Schioppa, *Regulating Finance* (n 3) 126.

[137] European Central Bank, 'Memorandum of Understanding on high-level principles of co-operation between the banking supervisors and central banks of the European Union in crisis management situations' (ECB Press Release, 10 March 2003) <https://www.ecb.europa.eu/press/pr/date/2003/html/pr030310_3.en.html> accessed 6 June 2021.

2005, Ministers of Finance joined the MoU.[138] The 2008 MoU explains that financial stability is a common concern across the EU due to the integration of financial markets and recognizes that there are various actors tasked with pursuing this objective (recital 2).[139] The MoU's objective is to lay down arrangements for cooperation, which is to be achieved principally through exchange of information (recital 3), in line with Padoa-Schioppa's definition. Specifically, this entails a commitment to policies pursuing financial stability at the lowest collective cost and giving preference to private solutions (as opposed to bailouts). In line with the dominant challenges at the time, the MoU is focused predominantly on managing failures of cross-border banks, and thus has a rather limited financial stability focus. Since the document predates the Banking Union, the role of the ECB is rather limited as well: 'The ECB and the Eurosystem will be involved in accordance with their responsibilities', with the emergency liquidity provision (on which see Section VI.A) to be addressed by the home Member State central bank.[140] The MoU also foresaw a creation of a common and publicly available database on crisis cases. No evidence of such a database is to be found suggesting that this instance of crisis coordination was not effective.

However, accounts of the GFC crisis which have emerged since suggest that, rather than common frameworks, a crisis coordination tool which proved more effective were the swap lines that the ECB established with other non-euro area central banks (in particular the Fed).[141] These arrangements were to smooth out the demand for various currencies in the context of distressed markets and are today understood to have served financial stability more than many other coordination measures, even if they remained obscure at the time. In the context of the financial market instability induced by the COVID-19 pandemic, swap line arrangements and a new Eurosystem repo facility[142] to provide euro liquidity to non-euro area central banks and to also ensure the availability of dollar liquidity to euro area banks, were among the crisis coordination actions taken by the ECB.[143] Such measures help to exemplify the global dimension of this financial stability tool. The ECB is acting here to 'prevent euro liquidity shortages from morphing into financial stability risks',[144] with the specific competence

[138] European Central Bank, 'Memorandum of Understanding on co-operation between the Banking Supervisors, Central Banks and Finance Ministries of the European Union in financial crisis situations' (ECB Press Release, 18 May 2005) <https://www.ecb.europa.eu/press/pr/date/2005/html/pr050518_1.en.html> accessed 6 June 2021.

[139] European Central Bank, 'Memorandum of Understanding on co-operation between the Financial Supervisory Authorities, Central Banks and Finance Ministries of the European Union on cross-border financial stability' (ECB Press Release, 1 June 2008) <https://www.ecb.europa.eu/pub/pdf/other/mou-financialstability2008en.pdf?89dcd39d8b26c43dfc11f70327b78ce2> accessed 6 June 2021. The 2003 and 2005 MoUs have not been made public, which is why they are not included in the analysis here.

[140] ibid point 4.4.

[141] Saleem Bahaj and Ricardo Reis, 'Central bank swap lines' (*VoxEU*, 25 September 2018) <https://voxeu.org/article/central-bank-swap-lines> accessed 6 June 2021. For an account, see Adam Tooze, *Crashed* (Penguin 2018) and Neil Iwrin, *The Alchemists: Three Central Bankers and a World on Fire* (Penguin 2013).

[142] Such arrangements allow central banks to borrow currencies from each other to cover the demand of their domestic banking system.

[143] Fabio Panetta and Isabel Schnabel, 'The provision of euro liquidity through the ECB's swap and repo operations' (*ECB Blog*, 19 August 2020) <https://www.ecb.europa.eu/press/blog/date/2020/html/ecb.blog200819~0d1d04504a.en.html> accessed 6 June 2021.

[144] ibid.

in this area arising from Article 23 Statute dealing with external operations of the ECB.[145] We consider such an arrangement as a 'crisis coordination' measure here to the extent it hinges on joint action between a number of global central banks, and in particular cooperation between the ECB and the US Fed.[146] With the rise in importance of the euro as a global currency, the global financial stability concerns are likely to amplify in the future, further highlighting the geo-economic and macro-financial dimension of this tool of the ECB.

VII. Monetary Policy Tools as Secondary Policy Instrument of Financial Stability

The primary objective of the ECB is to maintain price stability (Article 127(1) TFEU). To this end, Article 127(2) TFEU confers on the ECB the competence 'to define and implement the monetary policy of the Union', while the Statute specifies the details of the specific instruments. The relationship between monetary policy and financial stability has been the subject of much debate by both academics and policy makers. In order to understand the role that financial stability plays in the ECB's monetary policy making, it is useful to look at three broad ways identified by economists in which financial stability can play a role in monetary policy.[147]

In a first approach, financial stability considerations are only taken into account in monetary policy making to the extent that it is necessary to achieve the monetary policy objective.[148] Advocates of this approach often consider macroprudential tools of financial regulation and supervision to be more appropriate for safeguarding financial stability.[149] In a second approach, generally referred to as 'leaning against the wind', monetary policy is used to address financial stability risks.[150] This approach implies that financial stability concerns (eg the prevention of bubbles in asset prices or excessive credit creation) can lead to a different monetary policy decision (eg higher interest rates) than the one justified by achieving the monetary policy objective of price stability. In a third approach, financial stability is considered as an objective of monetary policy. In this view, both objectives are so intertwined that it is impossible to

[145] The ECB itself considers swap lines a standard monetary policy instrument, emphasizing however its crisis origins: European Central Bank, 'What are currency swap lines?' (2021) <https://www.ecb.europa.eu/explainers/tell-me-more/html/currency_swap_lines.en.html> accessed 7 June 2021.

[146] Padoa-Schioppa, *Regulating Finance* (n 3) 126 emphasizing the coordination and international cooperation aspect of crisis management.

[147] For a discussion of these three views, see Frank Smets, 'Financial Stability and Monetary Policy: How Closely Interlinked?' (2014) 10 International Journal of Central Banking 263 (hereafter Smets, 'Financial Stability and Monetary Policy').

[148] This approach has been advocated by, eg, Ben Bernanke, 'Should monetary policy take into account risks to financial stability?' (*Brookings*, 7 April 2015) <https://www.brookings.edu/blog/ben-bernanke/2015/04/07/should-monetary-policy-take-into-account-risks-to-financial-stability/> accessed 15 June 2021. Also Lars Svensson, 'Cost-benefit analysis of leaning against the wind: Are costs larger also with less effective macroprudential policy?' (2016) IMF Working Paper No 16/3 <https://www.imf.org/external/pubs/ft/wp/2016/wp1603.pdf> accessed 6 June 2021.

[149] On these instruments, see Section V.

[150] This approach is associated to, eg, Claudio Borio and Philip Lowe, 'Asset prices, financial and monetary stability: exploring the nexus' (2002) BIS Working Papers No 114 <https://www.bis.org/publ/work114.pdf> accessed 6 June 2021; cf Smets, 'Financial Stability and Monetary Policy' (n 147) 272.

make a distinction, and supporters argue that monetary policy should be used to promote financial stability.[151]

We are not best placed to debate the merits of each approach or their shortcomings. Instead, we intend to use them here to see how the ECB's approach to the relationship between monetary policy and financial stability could be best understood.

First of all, it seems that there is no sign that the ECB has either explicitly adopted, considered, or advocated for the third approach of considering financial stability an objective of monetary policy. Indeed, it seems that the narrow mandate of the ECB (with its primary objective of price stability, and a supporting role for the stability of the financial system—see Article 127 TFEU), would not seem to invite the ECB to adopt this approach, which implies putting both objectives at the same level.

With regard to the second approach of 'leaning against the wind', in a 2005 speech, then President of the ECB Trichet argued that 'it is likely that the circumstances in which a policy-maker will embark with confidence upon an explicit leaning against the wind policy will occur rarely'.[152] In 2011 Drescher identified a slight shift in the ECB's reading of its monetary policy strategy, in which the ECB would acknowledge that the case for a 'leaning against the wind' strategy has strengthened.[153] Smets, an important economist at the ECB, in 2014 advocated that the ECB should be able to lean against the wind if necessary, while maintaining its primary focus on price stability in the medium term.[154] In this volume, both Alexander and Van 't Klooster argue in favour of a 'leaning against the wind' policy.[155]

The fact that several Board Members of the Governing Council have expressed sympathy for the 'leaning against the wind' principle in the past,[156] does not mean, however, that the ECB has embraced it.[157] In fact, Constâncio in 2018 argued that the single monetary policy is not well-suited to deal with financial imbalances at the national level and pointed to the role of the more recent macroprudential tools.[158] And de Guindos has recently argued that monetary policy is too blunt a tool to address specific risks and imbalances, and has pointed at the likely large macroeconomic costs.[159]

[151] This approach has been advocated by Roberto Billi and Anders Vredin, 'Monetary Policy and Financial Stability—A Simple Story' (2014) 2 Sveriges Riksbank Economic Review 7.

[152] Jean-Claude Trichet, 'Asset price bubbles and monetary policy' (Speech, Singapore, 8 June 2005) <https://www.ecb.europa.eu/press/key/date/2005/html/sp050608.en.html> accessed 15 June 2021.

[153] Christian Drescher, 'The Case of the ECB: Better to Lean Against the Wind than to Fight a Hurricane' (2011) 46 Intereconomics. Review of European Economic Policy 197 <https://www.intereconomics.eu/contents/year/2011/number/4/article/the-case-of-the-ecb-better-to-lean-against-the-wind-than-to-fight-a-hurricane.html> accessed 15 June 2021.

[154] Smets, 'Financial Stability and Monetary Policy' (n 147) 292.

[155] See chapter 7 by Kern Alexander and chapter 4 by Jens van 't Klooster, in this volume.

[156] See, for a reference to other members of the Governing Council, Carsten Detken, Dieter Gerdesmeier and Barbara Roffia, 'Interlinkages between Money, Credit and Asset Prices and their Implications for Consumer Price Inflation: Recent Empirical Work' in Lucas D Papademos and Jürgen Stark (eds), *Enhancing Monetary Analysis* (European Central Bank 2010) 321.

[157] It can be argued that the current Treaty framework would allow for such an approach, as long as the primary objective of the ECB as prescribed by TFEU (n 27) Art 127 is not undermined. cf Smets, 'Financial Stability and Monetary Policy' (n 147) 274.

[158] Vítor Constâncio, 'Financial stability risks and macroprudential policy in the euro area' (Speech at the ECB and Its Watchers XIX Conference, Frankfurt am Main, 14 March 2018) <https://www.ecb.europa.eu/press/key/date/2018/html/ecb.sp180314_3.en.html> accessed 15 June 2021.

[159] de Guindos, 'The ECB and Financial Stability' (n 3).

It seems that the ECB itself understands its approach as the first one, namely as taking financial stability considerations into account in monetary policy making to the extent that it is necessary to achieve the monetary policy objective. This is the case for both ECB conventional monetary policy (A) and unconventional monetary policy (B).

A. ECB standard monetary policy

With regard to conventional monetary policy, the use of this approach can be observed by considering the two pillar strategy, in which the ECB assesses risks to price stability with an economic analysis and a monetary analysis, which includes assessments of financial market developments.[160] Recently, Governor of the French Central Bank Villeroy de Galhau has advocated a more integrated approach, in which the current monetary second pillar is broadened into a monetary and financial pillar.[161] Moreover, the principle of proportionality anchored in Article 5(4) TEU is considered to condition the ECB's approach in at least two ways. It means that 'ECB policies regarding financial stability that serve monetary policy need to be appropriate for maintaining price stability and should not go beyond what is necessary to achieve this objective'.[162] At the same time, the principle of proportionality means that, if within the range of monetary policy instruments at the disposal of the ECB, it could choose between different options that can lead to a given result on price stability, it should choose the combination that minimizes the side effects on financial stability.[163]

B. The ECB's unconventional monetary policy measures

The unconventional monetary policy measures taken by the ECB very well illustrate the natural interest of central banks in financial stability identified in our introduction. In fact, several unconventional measures illustrate how the banking system is considered to play an important function as the transmission mechanism through which monetary policy has its effect.[164] Moreover, they illustrate the natural interest in financial stability of central banks because of their Lender of Last Resort function.

[160] See Mersch, 'Financial Stability' (n 25); cf Sabine Lautenschlager, 'Guardians of stability—Central Banks, supervisors and the quest for financial stability' (Speech at the Central Bank of Malta, Valletta, 12 October 2018) <https://www.ecb.europa.eu/press/key/date/2018/html/ecb.sp181012_1.en.html> accessed 15 June 2021.

[161] François Villeroy de Galhau, 'How to revisit central banking and financial stability?' (Speech at the Banque de France, 13 April 2021) <https://www.banque-france.fr/en/intervention/how-revisit-central-banking-and-financial-stability> accessed 15 June 2021 (hereafter de Galhau, 'Central banking and financial stability').

[162] See Mersch, 'Financial Stability' (n 25).

[163] See the Q&A session after Villeroy de Galhau's recent speech (de Galhau, 'Central banking and financial stability' (n 161)) <https://www.youtube.com/watch?v=32-ksk4bj28> accessed 15 June 2021.

[164] Andrew Crockett, 'Andrew Crockett: Monetary policy and financial stability' (Speech given at the Fourth HKMA Distinguished Lecture, Hong Kong, 13 February 2001) <https://www.bis.org/review/r010216b.pdf> accessed 15 June 2021; Mario Draghi, 'The interaction between monetary policy and financial stability in the euro area' (Speech at the First Conference on Financial Stability organized by the Banco de Espana and Centro de Estudios Monetarios y Financieros, Madrid, 24 May 2017) <https://www.ecb.europa.

(1) Enhanced credit support: the ECB as LOLR to the banking system
As a response to the GFC, the ECB since 2008 has decided on enhanced credit support, such as fixed rate tenders with full allotment, long-term refinancing operations (LTROs), a broadened eligible collateral base for refinancing operations, and covered bond purchases.[165] These unconventional monetary policy instruments in the ECB's narrative were warranted by the financial crisis, as the interbank market came to a halt in mid-September 2008 and experienced a credit crunch,[166] impairing the transmission of monetary policy.

This enhanced credit support can be understood as the ECB incorporating a LOLR function to the financial system as a part of its monetary policy.[167] In fact, this macro level liquidity is also called the monetary approach to the LOLR function.[168] Lastra refers to this LOLR as 'market liquidity assistance', arguing the ECB has clear competence which it has exercised widely.[169] Steinbach meanwhile posits that '[i]n instances of a widespread challenge to the liquidity of financial institutions, liquidity supply thus falls within the scope of monetary policy entitling the ECB to take liquidity measures based on Art. 18 of the ECSB Statute'.[170]

(2) Sovereign bond buying: the ECB as LOLR to sovereigns?
Due to severe tensions on the sovereign bond market, the ECB in 2010 expanded its unconventional monetary policy measures with sovereign bond purchases. The measure was aimed at mitigating the impact that the malfunctioning of segments of the sovereign bond market was having on the banking system in vulnerable Member States, hampering the monetary policy transmission mechanism.[171] In the summer of 2012, the effects of fragmentation on the sovereign bond market, a threat to the singleness of monetary policy, and redenomination risks due to what were considered by the ECB as unfounded and unacceptable fears of a break-up of the euro area, caused the ECB to announce its Outright Monetary Transactions Programme (OMT).[172] It has so

eu/press/key/date/2017/html/ecb.sp170524_1.en.html> accessed 15 June 2021; Frank Smets, 'Imbalances in the Euro Area and the ECB's Response' in Franklin Allen, Elena Carletti, and Saverio Simonelli (eds), *Governance for the Eurozone: Integration or Disintegration* (FIC Press 2012) 43 (hereafter Smets, 'Imbalances in the Euro Area').

[165] See also chapter 4 by Jens van 't Klooster, in this volume, who argues that the ECB's collateral policy shows that the ECB can contribute to financial stability by taking on more risk.
[166] See Smets, 'Imbalances in the Euro Area' (n 164) 52.
[167] cf Praet, 'ECB as Lender of Last Resort' (n 124); see also Philippine Cour-Thimann and Bernhard Winkler, 'The ECB's Non-Standard Monetary Policy Measures: The Role of Institutional Factors and Financial Structure' (2013) ECB Working Paper Series No 1528, 41 <https://www.ecb.europa.eu/pub/pdf/scpwps/ecbwp1528.pdf> accessed 6 June 2021.
[168] As opposed to the credit approach to LOLR which consists of ELA—on which see Section VI. For this distinction, see also chapter 15 by Christy-Ann Petit, in this volume.
[169] See Lastra, 'Banking Union: An Incomplete Building' (n 9) 175.
[170] Steinbach, 'Lender of Last Resort Eurozone' (n 122) 367.
[171] See the Decision of the European Central Bank of 14 May 2010 establishing a Securities Markets Programme (ECB/2010/5) [2010] OJ L124/8, 2nd preamble; see also European Central Bank, 'Monetary and Fiscal Policy Interactions in a Monetary Union' (2012) ECB Monthly Bulletin July 59 <https://www.ecb.europa.eu/pub/pdf/mobu/mb201207en.pdf> accessed 6 June 2021.
[172] See European Central Bank, 'Technical features of Outright Monetary Transactions' (ECB Press Release, 12 September 2012) <https://www.ecb.europa.eu/press/pr/date/2012/html/pr120906_1.en.html> accessed 15 June 2021; see also Peter Praet, 'The ECB's monetary policy: past and present' (Speech at the

far not been activated,[173] but its mere announcement is considered by the ECB to have restored financial stability.[174]

Sovereign bond buying technically consists of outright purchases which the Treaty allows the ECB to conduct.[175] They are however controversial because of the prohibition of monetary financing.[176] In fact, these purchases can be linked to the controversial view that a central bank has a LOLR role in the government bond markets by way of an implicit guarantee to bond holders that they will be paid when the bond matures.[177] Some argue that the ECB through its OMT programme has now accepted this role.[178] In fact, Quinn posits that ever since the OMT announcement: 'the Eurozone enjoys a sovereign lender of last resort if not in original intention, then in accomplished fact.'[179] Others, including Borger, point out that this is not the ECB's own reading.[180] Pisani-Ferry considers that saying that Draghi's 'whatever it takes' message amounted to saying that the euro area was a normal country, where the central bank is ready to buy sovereign bonds 'is going a little bit too far'.[181] Arguably, one's conclusion may be different depending on whether one focuses on legal constraints on the one hand or on the perception of market players on the other hand.[182]

C. Unconventional monetary policy and financial stability

How to understand the relationship between the abovementioned unconventional monetary policy measures and financial stability? Both ECB enhanced credit support and the Securities Markets Programme (SMP) and OMT programme were a response to severe tensions in financial markets (interbank money market, sovereign bond market), albeit with different challenges (credit crunch, fragmentation,

Febelfin Connect Event, Brussels/Londerzeel, 16 March 2017) <https://www.ecb.europa.eu/press/key/date/2017/html/sp170316.en.html> accessed 15 June 2021.

[173] The ECB has bought sovereign bonds under the earlier SMP and also under the PSPP and PEPP. For a discussion of PSPP and PEPP, also in light of financial stability, see chapter 3 by Klaus Tuori, in this volume.

[174] cf Praet, 'ECB as Lender of Last Resort' (n 124).

[175] See ESCB Statute (n 84) Art 18.

[176] In Case C-62/14 *Gauweiler and Others v Deutscher Bundestag* [2015] EU:C:2015:400 (hereafter *Gauweiler*), the CJEU has decided that OMT is in conformity with TFEU (n 27) Art 123; see also chapter 2 by Vestert Borger, in this volume.

[177] Paul de Grauwe, *Economics of Monetary Union* (OUP 2012) 120 (hereafter de Grauwe, *Economics of Monetary Union*).

[178] de Grauwe, 'The European Central Bank as Lender of Last Resort in the Government Bond Markets' (2013) 59 CESifo Economic Studies 520, 522. de Grauwe also argues that the hesitation of the ECB to provide LOLR support to sovereigns has forced it to provide it to the banking system, see de Grauwe, *Economics of Monetary Union* (n 177) 203–5.

[179] David Quinn, 'The Law and Norms of the European Central Bank as Sovereign Lender of Last Resort: Crystallising Endogenous Authority' (2021) 17 EuConst 78.

[180] Vestert Borger, 'Outright Monetary Transactions and the stability mandate of the ECB: Gauweiler' (2016) 53 CML Rev 139, 151–52 (hereafter Borger, 'Stability mandate of the ECB: Gauweiler'). See also chapter 2 by Vestert Borger, in this volume.

[181] Jean Pisani-Ferry, *The Euro Crisis and its Aftermath* (OUP 2014) 147.

[182] See Jan Herman Reestman and Thomas Beukers, 'Editorial. On Courts of Last Resort and Lenders of Last Resort' (2015) 11 EuConst 227.

redenomination risk), and both have been related to the LOLR function of central banks.

In both cases, financial stability considerations were taken into account by the ECB to the extent this was considered necessary for its monetary policy objective. In fact, in the ECB's narrative financial stability has not been embraced as the objective of monetary policy. Rather, it has framed financial stability as 'a means to fulfil its basic tasks',[183] and an 'intermediate objective'.[184] According to the ECB, the 'provision of liquidity to prevent a collapse of sound financial institutions during a liquidity crisis is also consistent with the broader ESCB's responsibility to contribute to financial stability'.[185]

Not everybody finds this framing convincing. Tuori and Tuori, for example, argue with regard to OMT that: 'In spite of the pronounced emphasis on monetary policy transmission, it is clear that the central objective of the new programme was to calm down sovereign debt markets and to restore financial stability in the euro area.'[186] Economically, the situation might be somewhat blurred, and it may be difficult to judge whether liquidity provision is to be seen as either monetary policy or a LOLR financial stability measure.[187] In terms of Padoa-Schioppa's table of tools, this seems to translate into a blurring of the distinction between money market operations having system-wide financial stability as secondary objective on the one hand and emergency liquidity support having system-wide financial stability as primary objective on the other hand.

From an EU law perspective, the matter has, however, been concluded with regard to OMT by the Court of Justice, when in the *Gauweiler* case it accepted the monetary policy nature of this programme based on an analysis of both instrument and objective.[188] With regard to enhanced credit support, no final legal decision on the nature or legality of these instruments has been given by the Court of Justice.[189] Steinbach notes that '[t]here is agreement that macro-level liquidity supply falls to the ESCB. What is unclear is the legal basis, due to disagreement about considering liquidity as monetary policy or financial stability measure.'[190] We consider it likely that the Court of Justice would also accept the monetary policy nature of the enhanced liquidity support.

183 In the words of Mersch, 'Financial Stability' (n 25): '*Under such circumstances, financial stability is not the ultimate aim of ECB policy but a means to fulfil its basic tasks*'.

184 Smets, 'Financial Stability and Monetary Policy' (n 147) 292.

185 Vítor Constâncio, 'Challenges to monetary policy in 2012' (Speech at the 26th International Conference on Interest Rates, Frankfurt am Main, 8 December 2011) <www.ecb.europa.eu/press/key/date/2011/html/sp111208.en.html> accessed 15 June 1021.

186 Tuori and Tuori, *The Eurozone Crisis* (n 8) 104. With regard to the ECB's collateral policy, they argue at 164 that: '*The U-turn in collateral policy (..) elevated financial stability to a primary consideration. Consequently, one can argue that increased use of bank-created assets as collateral has questioned the primacy of the ECB's monetary policy tasks in a constitutionally problematic manner*.'.

187 cf Lastra, 'Banking Union: An Incomplete Building' (n 9) 182, who argues that 'what constitutes 'ordinary' liquidity assistance as opposed to 'emergency'/LOLR liquidity assistance becomes blurred during a crisis, since the drying of the inter-bank market gives the central bank a primary role in the provision of liquidity.'.

188 *Gauweiler* (n 176); see also Borger, 'Stability mandate of the ECB: Gauweiler' (n 180) 174.

189 The enhanced credit support measures have not been brought before the CJEU and in fact seem legally less controversial.

190 Steinbach, 'Lender of Last Resort Eurozone' (n 122) 366: '*Article 127(2) TFEU could be considered as a basis if LOLR operations in favour of the entire financial system are assigned to monetary-policy measures—by contrast, Article 127(5) TFEU would be decisive if the macro-level LOLR operations were classified purely as financial stability policy*.'.

D. Monetary policy and the distinction between preventive and remedial instruments

Monetary policy was singled out in this separate section, as in theory it can be used both as a preventive and a remedial financial stability instrument. It was illustrated above that the ECB has so far used it as a remedial instrument. We will end this section with some thoughts about how the concept 'remedial' can be understood.

The concept remedial suggests that the ECB with its unconventional monetary policy has restored financial stability.[191] To understand whether that is actually the case, it is useful to remember two of the main elements in the definition of financial stability identified earlier in this chapter, namely the ability of the financial system to (1) fulfil the function of intermediation, and (2) withstand shocks. With regard to the first, it seems that the effect of the ECB's unconventional monetary policy was indeed (aimed at) providing a condition for banks to lend to the real economy, either by taking up the role of intermediation on the interbank money market (enhanced credit support) or by facilitating the ability of sovereigns to access lending on the sovereign bond markets (sovereign bond purchases).[192]

Should we understand the ECB measures also as making the financial system more resilient to shocks? Different from a preventive 'leaning against the wind' monetary policy or from macroprudential instruments (on which see Section V), the ECB's unconventional monetary policy measures might not be best understood as improving the internal condition of the financial system itself, or its resilience to shocks. Instead, the ECB is stepping in when it becomes clear that the system itself is not resilient enough to withstand a shock. It could be seen as providing a medicine curing or remedying the symptoms, but not the disease. The ECB's LOLR function to the financial system, and the perception of the ECB as providing an implicit guarantee to sovereign bond holders, could be understood as an external element improving the condition of trust in the financial system. Linking it finally to the negative definition of financial stability often given, the (perceived) presence of a LOLR, however, does not mean that there is no systemic risk in the financial system.

There is little doubt though that the ECB with its OMT programme has contributed to what can be considered the most existential meaning of stability of the euro. In the words of Executive Board Member Asmussen before the German Federal Constitutional Court: 'I am firmly convinced that introducing the OMT programme was the right thing to do to ensure price stability in the euro area. After all, a currency can only be stable if its continued existence is not in doubt.'[193]

[191] cf Praet, 'ECB as Lender of Last Resort' (n 124).

[192] See Smets, 'Imbalances in The Euro Area' (n 164) 53.

[193] Jörg Asmussen, 'Introductory statement by the ECB in the proceedings before the Federal Constitutional Court' (Karlsruhe, 11 June 2013) <https://www.ecb.europa.eu/press/key/date/2013/html/sp130611.en.html> accessed 6 June 2021.

VIII. Conclusions

Where history teaches us that the actual creation of several central banks has been driven by financial stability concerns, and that many have a dual role of maintaining price stability and financial stability,[194] the same cannot be said of the ECB. In fact, the specific context in which the ECB was established has led to what has been called a narrow mandate with a primary objective of price stability, and to claims of a neglect of financial stability at Maastricht.[195]

Our analysis of the extent to which several financial stability tools as identified by Padoa-Schioppa are available to the ECB shows that the Maastricht Treaty, with its focus on price stability, nonetheless did contain sufficient seeds for the ECB to develop a significant financial stability toolbox over the first two decades of its existence. Some of these financial stability seeds were explicit, others implicit. The natural interest in financial stability of central banks, including the ECB, combined with the events of especially the Global Financial Crisis and euro area sovereign debt crisis, has made their existence as well as their limits clearly visible.

Among the explicit financial stability tools in the ECB's original toolbox are the clear basic task of the ESCB to promote the smooth functioning of the payments system and a limited advisory role with regard to prudential regulation. But an explicit financial stability seed was also already planted in the Maastricht Treaty with the possibility for a political decision of the Council to give the ECB prudential supervisory powers over credit institutions by unanimity. As a consequence of the negative doom loop between sovereigns and credit institutions illustrated and amplified by the Global Financial Crisis and sovereign debt crisis, an EU Banking Union has been created, which entailed triggering the provision on ECB prudential supervision.

Financial stability tools can also be available without explicit conferral as such though, or only implicitly. This was illustrated with the ECB's monetary policy, in which financial stability concerns have been targeted through monetary policy tools to the extent necessary to attain the monetary policy objective. Thus, the ECB's enhanced credit support, part of its monetary policy, has been interpreted as a LOLR function to the financial system. Many perceive the ECB's OMT bond buying programme—equally part of its monetary policy—as a LOLR role to sovereigns. And thus, without any major treaty reform, financial stability has over time become prominent in the law and practice of the ECB's monetary policy mandate.

At the same time, the responsibility for safeguarding financial stability is shared by the ECB with many other actors, both at EU and at national level. Moreover, in this chapter we have shown some clear limits, either in law or in practice, in the ECB's financial stability toolbox. The ECB has not embraced a 'leaning against the wind' approach in its monetary policy strategy, its regulatory powers with regard to payment systems do not extend to all financial market infrastructures, and the ECB does not provide ELA to individual institutions, leaving the latter role to NCBs instead.

[194] Goodhart, *Evolution of Central Banks* (n 2); Schoenmaker, 'Central Banks Role in Financial Stability' (n 11).

[195] Tuori and Tuori, *The Eurozone Crisis* (n 8) 89, 182; Borger, *The Transformation of the Euro* (n 24) 188.

6
The ECB and Economic Integration

Jonathan Bauerschmidt[*]

I. Introduction

The euro lives on conditions which it cannot guarantee itself. This was already clear to economists such as Milton Friedman when the Economic and Monetary Union was established. He voiced concern regarding the feasibility of a monetary union without a political union: 'It would exacerbate political tensions by converting divergent shocks that could have been readily accommodated by exchange rate changes into divisive political issues. Political unity can pave the way for monetary unity. Monetary unity imposed under unfavourable conditions will prove a barrier to the achievement of political unity.'[1] Thus, Friedman predicted that monetary union would lead to political disunity. His prediction was tested during the Great Financial Crisis which started with the collapse of Lehman Brothers in 2008 and then developed into a sovereign debt crisis in the European Union in 2009.

While Friedman's diagnosis that monetary union creates considerable constraints for politicians is certainly true, he underestimated the existing constitutional framework and the political resolve to use the means within and outside the Treaties to overcome the Great Financial Crisis. This contribution explores the expansive force of monetary policy and how it collides with neighbouring policy areas which apply to all the Member States of the Union, creating tensions for which the Treaties are ill equipped. The European Central Bank (ECB) as the main actor of monetary policy is at the centre of these evolutions. By analysing the ECB's involvement in areas beyond monetary policy, the tensions with neighbouring policies will be uncovered, and it will also allow us to assess whether the ECB's independence and its primary objective of price stability are safeguarded.

To this end, this contribution will briefly recall the asymmetry of Union competences in the areas of monetary policy, economic policy, and internal market harmonization (II). It is not by coincidence that throughout the Great Financial Crisis the Court of Justice had to clarify the delineation of those competences numerous times (III). The exercise of those competences will then be the yardstick to measure

[*] Dr. iur., Member of the Legal Service, Council of the European Union. I wish to thank Alberto de Gregorio Merino, Director at the Council Legal Service, for crucial comments and suggestions as well as Thomas Beukers, Diane Fromage, and Giorgio Monti for their suggestions. The views expressed here are personal and do not engage the institution for which I work.

[1] Milton Friedman, 'The Euro: Monetary Unity to Political Disunity?' (*Project Syndicate*, 28 August 1997) <www.project-syndicate.org/commentary/the-euro--monetary-unity-to-political-disunity> accessed 1 May 2022.

Jonathan Bauerschmidt, *The ECB and Economic Integration* In: *The New European Central Bank*. Edited by: Thomas Beukers, Diane Fromage, and Giorgio Monti, Oxford University Press.
DOI: 10.1093/oso/9780198871231.003.0006

the considerable evolutions of economic integration in the wake of the Great Financial Crisis. Without analysing unconventional monetary policies which are the subject of the first Part of this volume, this chapter will, on the one hand, focus on the measures to promote budgetary stability to enhance economic policy coordination and to establish a permanent mechanism for financial assistance (IV). On the other hand, it will analyse the creation of new forms of supervision for the internal market in order to safeguard financial stability (V). This will reveal how under the Treaties economics and politics are intrinsically connected creating strong incentives to stand together in the face of even severe crises (VI).

II. Asymmetry of Competences and Interdependence of Policy Areas

The Treaties establish a remarkable asymmetry of competences between monetary policy on the one hand and economic policy coordination as well as internal market harmonization on the other hand. A deliberate choice at the inception of the Economic and Monetary Union in the Treaty of Maastricht,[2] this asymmetry is already clear from the types of competences conferred on the Union. Under Article 3(1)(a) Treaty on the Functioning of the European Union (TFEU) the Union has the exclusive competence in the area of monetary policy for the Member States whose currency is the euro. Conversely, economic policies of Member States are coordinated at Union level under Article 5(1) TFEU and the internal market is part of the shared competences of the Union under Article 4(2)(a) TFEU.

This deliberate asymmetry is the result of long debates between 'monetarists' and 'economists'. The former advocated that monetary union should be introduced first and a more comprehensive coordination of economic policies, including national fiscal policies, might then follow. On the contrary, the 'economists' believed that comprehensive coordination of economic policies, including fiscal policies, should happen prior to the introduction of a common currency.[3] Under the Treaty of Maastricht, the 'monetarists' prevailed and the monetary system was given a special role: although it is an integral part of primary law, monetary policy is separated from other economic policy areas in terms of competences, institutional setup, and policy objective. To this end, the exclusive monetary policy is pursued by the European System of Central Banks (ESCB) comprising the ECB and National Central Banks. The ESCB and all its components are supposed to be independent and free from political influence pursuant to Article 130 TFEU. Moreover, the Treaties formulate a clear policy objective

[2] Armin Hatje, 'The Economic Constitution within the Internal Market' in Armin von Bogdandy and Jürgen Bast (eds), *Principles of European Constitutional Law* (2nd edn, Hart Publishing and CH Beck 2009) 615; Alicia Hinarejos, The Euro Area Crisis in Constitutional Perspective (OUP 2015) 5 f; Francis Snyder, 'EMU—Integration and Differentiation' in Paul Craig and Gráinne de Búrca (eds), *The Evolution of EU Law* (2nd edn, OUP 2011) 694–700.

[3] Jean Pisani-Ferry, 'Only One Bed for Two Dreams: A Critical Retrospective on the Debate over the Economic Governance of the Euro Area' (2006) 44 JCMS 823, 831–35. For an excellent reconstruction including the underlying economic philosophies, see also Markus K Brunnermeier, Harold James, and Jean-Pierre Landau, *The Euro and the Battle of Ideas* (Princeton University Press 2016) 58–84 (hereafter Brunnermeier and others, *Euro and the Battle of Ideas*).

with price stability as the primary maxim of monetary union in Articles 127(1) and 282(2) TFEU.

The Treaty framers were not oblivious to possible repercussions of monetary policy on the economic policy of Member States. Rather, the Treaties acknowledge the interdependence between these policy areas and establish strong constitutional safeguards to limit and control interference. To this end, Member States must treat their economic policies as matters of common concern pursuant to Article 121 TFEU, may be subject to excessive deficit procedures under Article 126 TFEU, and need to adhere to the Stability and Growth Pact.[4] This economic policy coordination was complemented by the assumption that Member States remain in control and bear full responsibility for their public debt. In this vein, the no-bailout clause of Article 125 prohibits the Union from assuming public debt of Member States and Article 123 TFEU prohibits the ESCB from engaging in monetary financing.

While the interdependence between monetary policy and the economic policy of Member States was clearly on the mind of the Treaty framers at Maastricht, the repercussions of the single currency on the internal market is less clearly addressed in the Treaties. Only some general, albeit important, provisions can be found that limit and control interference. Pursuant to Article 3(1) of the Treaty on European Union (TEU) the Union shall establish an internal market and shall also work for the sustainable development of Europe based on balanced economic growth and price stability. Moreover, pursuant to Articles 127(1) and 282(2) TFEU and without prejudice to the objective of price stability, the ESCB shall support the general economic policies of the Union in order to contribute to the achievement of its objectives. Finally, under Article 127(5) TFEU the ESCB contributes to the smooth conduct of prudential supervision by competent authorities and the stability of the financial system.

Thus already from the inception of the Economic and Monetary Union in the Treaty of Maastricht it was clear that the exclusive competence for monetary policy is interdependent with and may have repercussions on economic integration more broadly. While this interdependence seems almost like a truism, the fault lines only became apparent in the course of the Great Financial Crisis where the single currency created economic constraints that Member States could not overcome individually. Rather, Member States and the Union had to find common solutions in areas beyond monetary policy in order to ensure sustainable public finances and stabilize the banking sectors. Although these areas lie beyond monetary policy, the ECB is given specific roles where it has no exclusive competence. It is therefore not by coincidence that the delineation of competences between monetary policy and economic policy, which used to be a discussion for specialists, came to the forefront and required adjudication by the Court of Justice for the first time.

[4] Council Regulations (EC) 1466/97 of 7 July 1997 on the strengthening of the surveillance of budgetary positions and the surveillance and coordination of economic policies [1997] OJ L209/1 and 1467/97 of 7 July 1997 on speeding up and clarifying the implementation of the excessive deficit procedure [1997] OJ L209/6. The Stability and Growth Pact was amended by Council Regulations (EC) 1055/2005 of 27 June 2005 [2005] OJ L174/1 and 1056/2005 of 27 June 2005 [2005] OJ L174/5.

III. Delineation of Competences

The Court of Justice had to delineate the Union competences in the area of monetary union and economic policy for the first time at the height of the Great Financial Crisis. Such delineation is important to justify why the ECB can discuss, conceive, and implement its policies in full autonomy without receiving instructions from external bodies. In the past, the Court of Justice only had the opportunity to pronounce itself on the independence of the ECB[5] without having to further define economic and monetary policy. This changed with the *Pringle*, *Gauweiler*, and *Weiss* judgments.[6] Building on well-established case law which emphasizes that the choice of legal basis is of constitutional significance and must assess the aim and the content of the measure in question,[7] these three judgments clarify how to assess the crucial separation between the various areas of economic policy.

In the *Pringle* judgment the Court had to decide whether the new Article 136(3) TFEU and the European Stability Mechanism (ESM) are part of the Union's exclusive competence for monetary policy pursuant to Article 3(1)(c) TFEU. To begin with, the Court observed that the Treaties do not contain an explicit definition of monetary policy but define it by setting as a primary objective the maintenance of price stability.[8] In contrast, the new Article 136(3) TFEU allows a mechanism 'to safeguard the stability of the euro area as a whole' and the ESM pursues 'financial stability of the euro area as a whole' which is the guiding objective in the ESM Treaty.[9] Assessing this new concept of stability, the Court held that: '[e]ven though the stability of the euro area may have repercussions on the stability of the currency used within that area, an economic policy measure cannot be treated as equivalent to a monetary policy measure for the sole reason that it may have indirect effects on the stability of the euro.'[10] The Court therefore clearly states that while stability of the euro area has to be strictly separated from price stability, an individual measure pursuing the former stability may have repercussions or indirect effects on the latter stability. Moreover, by pursuing the objective of safeguarding the stability of the euro area as a whole, the ESM Treaty does not fall under the exclusive competence of the Union but has to be regarded as a measure of economic policy.[11]

While the *Pringle* judgment delineates the boundary between economic and monetary policy for a measure constituting economic policy, the *Gauweiler* judgment deals with the inverse situation. Before the German Constitutional Court, Gauweiler

[5] Case C-11/00 *Commission v ECB* [2003] ECR I-7147, paras 130–45.

[6] On the importance of these judgments, see also chapter 2 by Vestert Borger and chapter 16 by Marijn van der Sluis, in this volume.

[7] *Cartagena Protocol* [2001], Opinion 2/00 ECR I-9713, para 5; *General Agreement on Trade in Services (GATS)* [2009], Opinion 1/08 ECR I-11129, para 110; Case C-370/07 *Commission v Council (CITES)* [2009] ECR I-8917, paras 46–49. See also, more recently, *EU-Canada PNR Agreement* [2017], Opinion 1/15 EU:C:2017:592, para 71; Case C-687/15 *Commission v Council (CMR-15)* [2017] EU:C:2017:803, para 49.

[8] Case C-370/12 *Pringle v Government of Ireland and Others* [2012] EU:C:2012:756, paras 53 f (hereafter *Pringle*).

[9] ESM Treaty, recital (6), Art 3 on the purpose and Arts 12 and 13 on principles for stability support.

[10] *Pringle* (n 8) para 56.

[11] ibid para 97.

and others claimed that Mario Draghi's statement to 'do whatever it takes' and a subsequent press release on Outright Monetary Transactions (OMT)[12] were ultra vires. Pursuant to the Constitutional Court's own case law,[13] Karlsruhe referred the matter to Luxembourg, giving the Court of Justice opportunity to further flesh out the delineation between economic and monetary policy. First, the Court confirms its *Pringle* judgment that a measure contributing to the stability of the euro area is a matter of economic policy.[14] Second, it goes on to examine whether the announced OMT programme constitutes monetary policy because it may have repercussions on the stability of the euro area: 'Indeed, a monetary policy measure cannot be treated as equivalent to an economic policy measure merely because it may have indirect effects on the stability of the euro area.'[15] This finding was again confirmed by the *Weiss* judgment assessing the Public Sector Purchase Programme and other measures of quantitative easing by the ECB.[16]

Taken together, the *Pringle, Gauweiler* and *Weiss* judgments are important clarifications for the delineation of competences. The judgments not only reiterate the ECB's independence when implementing monetary policy, the Court also carefully examines and puts into relation with the other economic policy areas. It emanates from this case law that, in order to assess whether an individual measure falls within the ECB's competence, regard must be had to its objective and its effect. Where a measure pursues price stability and has only indirect effects on the broader economic policy, it is a measure of monetary policy. Where a measure pursues the objectives of budgetary stability or financial stability and has only indirect effects on monetary policy, it is a measure of general economic policy or of internal market harmonization.

This jurisprudence and especially the *Weiss* judgment were severely criticized by the German Federal Constitutional Court because they allegedly disregard the actual effects of ECB measures for the purpose of assessing the measures' proportionality. In the view of the Constitutional Court the manner in which the Court of Justice applies 'the principle of proportionality cannot fulfil its corrective function for the purposes of safeguarding the competences of the Member States'.[17] This criticism, however, fails to see an important distinction enshrined in the two sentences of Article 5(1) TEU which read: 'The *limits* of Union competences are governed by the principle of conferral. The *use* of Union competences is governed by the principles of subsidiarity and

[12] Statement on 26 July 2012, during a conference in London: 'Within our mandate, the ECB is ready to do whatever it takes to preserve the euro. And believe me, it will be enough.' European Central Bank, 'Technical features of Outright Monetary Transactions' (ECB Press Release, 6 September 2012) <https://www.ecb.europa.eu/press/pr/date/2012/html/pr120906_1.en.html> accessed 1 May 2022.

[13] BVerfG 6 July 2010, 2 BvR 2661/06 DE:BVerfG:2010:rs20100706.2bvr266106, para 60 examining the ECJ's judgment in Case C-144/04 *Mangold v Helm* [2005] ECR I-9981. See also the case note by Christoph Mollers, 'Constitutional Review of European Acts Only Under Exceptional Circumstances' (2011) 7 EuConst 161, 165.

[14] Case C-62/14 *Gauweiler and Others v Deutscher Bundestag* [2015] EU:C:2015:400, para 51 (hereafter *Gauweiler*).

[15] ibid para 52. See also the case note by Alicia Hinarejos, '*Gauweiler* and the Outright Monetary Transactions Programme: The Mandate of the European Central Bank and the Changing Nature of Economic and Monetary Union' (2015) 11 EuConst 563, 575 f.

[16] Case C-493/17 *Weiss and Others* [2018] EU:C:2018:1000, para 61 (hereafter *Weiss*).

[17] BVerfG 5 May 2020, 2 BvR 859/15 DE:BVerfG:2020:rs20200505.2bvr085915, paras 121 ff regarding the ECB's Public Sector Purchase Programme (hereafter PSPP).

proportionality.' Whereas the first sentence is about the existence of a Union competence, the second sentence is about the use of such competence. This ties into the distinction made by legal doctrine between the concept of lack of competence and the concept of unlawfulness.[18] Where a Union act violates the principle of proportionality referred to in Article 5(1), second sentence TEU and enshrined in Article 5(4) TEU, the Union has not acted beyond its competence and thus ultra vires, but rather has acted unlawfully but within its competences. The Court of Justice is clearly aware of this distinction bearing in mind that the *Gauweiler* and *Weiss* judgments first establish that the ECB has the competence to act before second examining the proportionality of this act.[19] Therefore, the Constitutional Court's criticism is not very convincing even by its own standards.[20] Moreover, the Constitutional Court's suggestion to apply the principle of proportionality to the division of competences 'would lead to the strange consequence that Member States had to be qualified as competent as far as the EU acted disproportionately. The question of competence would be in constant motion in both directions.'[21]

Against this background, the delineation of competences expressed in the *Pringle*, *Gauweiler*, and *Weiss* judgments is not only more convincing, it also helps central bankers and politicians alike to determine their respective responsibilities[22] when the ECB takes measures under its mandate[23] or when the Union legislator as well as Member States take action to advance economic integration more broadly. In fact, some of the most important evolutions in economic integration were brought about by the Union legislator in areas where the Union possessed competences and by the euro area Member States where the requisite competence was lacking. These evolutions occurred in the area of economic policy to ensure budgetary stability, and in the internal market to safeguard financial stability, and will be examined in turn.

[18] Paul Craig and Gráinne de Búrca, *EU Law: Text, Cases, and Materials* (6th edn, OUP 2015) 96: the Lisbon Treaty 'distinguishes between the existence and the use of competence'; Martin Nettesheim, 'Kompetenzen', in Jürgen Bast and Armin von Bogdandy (eds), *Europäisches Verfassungsrecht* (2nd edn, Springer 2009) 389, 408 ff.

[19] *Gauweiler* (n 14) paras 46–65 on 'The delimitation of monetary policy' and paras 66–92 on 'Proportionality'; *Weiss* (n 15) paras 53–70 on 'Delimitation of the Union's monetary policy' and paras 71–100 on 'Proportionality in relation to the objectives of monetary policy'.

[20] See, eg, Martin Nettesheim, 'Das PSPP-Urteil des BVerfG—ein Angriff auf die EU?' (2020) Neue Juristische Wochenschrift 1631, 1632. This is ultimately the result of a conceptual ambiguity inherent in the term ultra vires, which comes from public international law and encompasses every empowerment and limit of an international organization and, therefore, undermines the distinction between existence of competence and use of competence.

[21] Clearly seen by Mattias Wendel, 'Paradoxes of Ultra-Vires Review: A Critical Review of the PSPP Decision and Its Initial Reception' (2020) 21 Ger Law Journal 979, 987.

[22] On the relation between competence and responsibility, see, eg, Mark Bovens, *The Quest for Responsibility* (CUP 1998) 25–27 with reference to HLA Hart, *Punishment and Responsibility* (2nd edn, OUP 2008) 212–14 on role-responsibility. These are of course variants to Max Weber's famous legal authority from the three types of legitimate rule in *Economy and Society* (University of California Press 1978) 217–20.

[23] On the importance of these judgments for the ECB's mandate, see in particular chapter 2 by Vestert Borger, chapter 3 by Klaus Tuori, and chapter 15 by Christy-Ann Petit, in this volume.

IV. Budgetary Stability: Economic Policy Coordination and Financial Assistance

Budgetary stability requires public authorities to keep public spending at a level that is sustainable by public revenue. The relevant rules for Member States were laid down in the Treaty of Maastricht in what are now Articles 121 and 126 TFEU. These rules were further developed in the Stability and Growth Pact. The Stability and Growth Pact describes budgetary stability as 'the objective of sound government finances as a means of strengthening the conditions for price stability and for strong sustainable growth conducive to employment creation'.[24] Thus, the legal framework fully acknowledges that budgetary stability may have repercussions on price stability and vice-versa. These repercussions were most strongly felt at the height of the Great Financial Crisis when the burden of debt in some Member States threatened the euro area as a whole. The responses to ensure budgetary stability were twofold: strengthening of the Stability and Growth Pact (A) and creating a permanent mechanism for financial assistance (B).

A. Strengthening of the Stability and Growth Pact

The Stability and Growth Pact was strengthened by the Six-Pack.[25] This set of Union legislation enhances budgetary stability and creates an annual cycle of economic policy coordination via the European Semester as well as a procedure for the prevention of macroeconomic imbalances.

The European Semester creates an overall umbrella for economic policy coordination, by amending the Stability and Growth Pact through Regulation 1175/2011.[26] Under the European Semester the policy surveillance and coordination starts with a review where the European Council identifies the main challenges facing the Union. The Semester has a clear timetable, where Member States receive guidance and then submit their policy plans to be assessed at Union level. After an evaluation of these plans, the Commission presents so-called Country Specific Recommendations for each Member State individually, which are discussed in the Council and finally endorsed by the European Council. Member States are expected to take these recommendations into account when they define their budget for the following year and when they take policy decisions. If necessary, they also receive recommendations to correct macroeconomic imbalances.

In addition, Regulation 1176/2011 creates a new procedure to detect, prevent, and correct macroeconomic imbalances. This Macroeconomic Imbalance Procedure allows review of virtually all aspects of economic policy of a Member State by defining imbalance in Article 2(1) as 'any trend giving rise to macroeconomic developments

[24] Respectively recitals (1) and (2) of Council Regulations (EC) 1466/97 and 1467/97 (n 4).

[25] Regulations (EU) 1173/2011 to 1177/2011 of the European Parliament and of the Council of 16 November 2011 [2011] OJ L306/1 and Council Directive 2011/85/EU of 8 November 2011 on requirements for budgetary frameworks of the Member States [2011] OJ L306/41.

[26] Regulation (EU) 1175/2011 (n 25) Art 1(3) introducing Art 2-a in Regulation (EC) 1466/97 (n 4).

which are adversely affecting, or have the potential adversely to affect, the proper functioning of the economy of a Member State or of the economic and monetary union, or of the Union as a whole'. In order to ensure a permanent dialogue with Member States, the Commission carries out enhanced surveillance missions. Where such missions concern euro area Member States or Member States participating in the Exchange Rate Mechanism (ERM II), representatives of the ECB may be invited. However, there is no obligation for the ECB to follow this invitation in order to safeguard its independence. In practice, the ECB seems to accept these invitations and closely follows the application of the Macroeconomic Imbalance Procedure by the Commission. Moreover, the ECB has repeatedly argued that all the tools of this procedure—including its corrective arm—should be fully employed in relation to countries with excessive imbalances. For the ECB the use of such tools is desirable not only in order to increase the economic prospect of the country, but also to help facilitate economic adjustment processes inside the euro area.[27] The Macroeconomic Imbalance Procedure thus opens broad areas of Member State's economic policy to scrutiny, advice, and in case of excessive deficits in euro area Member States also sanctions.

The Six-Pack was criticized for having been adopted 'without regard to the division of European and national competences in the Treaties' because it only lays down rules on procedure without specifying clear rules for the actual exercise of the Commission's powers.[28] However, this does not sufficiently take into account the Treaty competences and the means by which the Six-Pack frames the Commission's powers. Article 121(6) TFEU, which is the legal basis for most of the Six-Pack,[29] confers the competence to adopt detailed rules for the multilateral surveillance procedure. Therefore, it is not surprising that the relevant rules in the Six-Pack are procedural in nature. In addition, as part of the Six-Pack the Macroeconomic Imbalance Procedure tasks the Commission to develop a scoreboard of relevant, practical, simple, measurable, and available macroeconomic and macro-financial indicators. This is followed by in-depth reviews and may trigger the excessive imbalance procedure. Therefore, Article 121(6) TFEU is not only the correct legal basis for most of the Six-Pack, this set of Union legislation also creates the relevant frame for the Commission's exercise of power.

The Six-Pack marks three important evolutions in economic policy coordination. First, in order to enhance budgetary stability, the Six-Pack draws on a wide range of expertise and even allows for representatives of the ECB to participate in surveillance missions. Second, whereas the Stability and Growth Pact sets out numerical rules for government deficits and government debt, the Six-Pack in general and the Macroeconomic Imbalance Procedure in particular strengthen the procedure and thus further institutionalize economic policy surveillance at Union level. Third and although it sets the relevant frame, the Six-Pack leaves a considerable margin of

[27] Beatrice Pierluigi and David Sondermann, 'Macroeconomic Imbalances in the Euro Area: Where Do We Stand?' (2018) ECB Occasional Paper Series No 211, 40 <https://www.ecb.europa.eu/pub/pdf/scpops/ecb.op211.en.pdf> accessed 1 May 2022 including an overview of the ECB's actions.

[28] Fitz Scharpf, 'After the Crash: A Perspective on Multilevel European Democracy' (2015) 21 EL Rev 384, 392 f.

[29] Regulation (EU) 1177/2011 (n 25) and Council Directive 2011/85/EU (n 25) are based on Art 126(14) second and third subparagraph TFEU respectively.

discretion to the Commission.[30] The Commission has used this discretion in turn by finding flexibilities within the Stability and Growth Pact;[31] a development strongly defended by former Commission President Jean-Claude Juncker.[32] Instead of depoliticizing economic policy coordination in the Council by strengthening the role of the Commission, it seems the Six-Pack has led to a considerable politicization of the Commission. The lesson to be learned is that it is difficult to reduce economic policy coordination to the mere application of predefined rules and that such coordination will always entail exercising political discretion.

B. The European Stability Mechanism and the ECB

In addition to strengthening the Stability and Growth Pact, budgetary stability was also enhanced by creating a permanent mechanism for financial assistance. The European Stability Mechanism (ESM) was created by an intergovernmental treaty of the euro area Member States as Article 122(2) TFEU could not be used to establish such a mechanism on a permanent basis.[33] Although Member States did not make use of Union competences and created a satellite, they stayed within the orbit of Union law.[34] This is not only relevant for the no-bailout clause, the Treaties also have to be respected when Union institutions are given additional tasks by way of public international law.

In the *Pringle* judgment the Court also had to assess whether the European Stability Mechanism and the assistance programmes violate the no-bailout clause enshrined in Article 125 TFEU. Examining the *travaux préparatoires* of the Maastricht Treaty, the Court found that the prohibition laid down in this Article ensures that Member States remain subject to the logic of the market when they enter into debt, prompting them to maintain budgetary discipline. According to the Court, 'compliance with such discipline contributes at Union level to the attainment of a higher objective, namely maintaining the financial stability of the monetary union'.[35] In this light, Article 125 TFEU does not prohibit granting financial assistance to a Member State in distress if this is indispensable for safeguarding the stability of the euro area as a whole, subject to strict conditions and aimed at encouraging that Member State to implement a sound budgetary policy.[36]

[30] Päivi Leino and Tuomas Saarenheimo, 'Sovereignty and Subordination: On the Limits of EU Economic Policy Co-ordination' (2017) 42 EL Rev 166, 174 f.

[31] Commission, 'Making the best use of the flexibility within the existing rules of the SGP' (Communication) COM(2015) 12 final.

[32] See, eg, his statement that fiscal rules should not be applied blindly: Francesco Guarascio, 'EU Gives Budget Leeway to France 'Because it is France'—Junker' *Reuters* (London, 31 May 2016). <http://www.reuters.com/article/uk-eu-deficit-france-idUKKCN0YM1N0> accessed 1 May 2022.

[33] *Pringle* (n 8) para 65.

[34] See, in general, Bruno de Witte, '"Old Flexibility": International Agreements Between Member States of the EU' in Gráinne de Búrca and Joanne Scott (eds), *Constitutional Change in the EU* (Hart Publishing 2000) 31 and regarding the ESM Alberto de Gregorio Merino, 'Legal Developments in the Economic and Monetary Union during the Debt Crisis: The Mechanisms of Financial Assistance' (2012) 49 CML Rev 1613, 1635–40 and Jonathan Bauerschmidt, *Die Rechtsperson der Europäischen Union im Wandel* (Mohr Siebeck 2019) 222–39, 263–73 (hereafter Bauerschmidt, *Die Rechtsperson der EU im Wandel*).

[35] *Pringle* (n 8) para 135.

[36] ibid paras 136 f.

The ECB received three different tasks within the ESM Treaty. These tasks include the responsibility to assess the urgency of the request for stability support and to liaise with the Commission when it assesses the request for stability support, negotiate the Memorandum of Understanding, and monitor the conditionality attached to the financial assistance.[37] In practice, the ECB assumes a limited role when its participation is mostly focused on financial and banking aspects as well as fiscal aspects of the assistance programmes. Moreover, it uses data which it has already available. Conversely, the ECB does not appear to play a significant role in the actual computation of the financing needs of a country which is mostly done by the European Commission and the International Monetary Fund. Nevertheless, there may be also conflicts of interests for the ECB. On the one hand, in relation to fiscal policy the ECB might be tempted to deviate from its price stability objective in order to help improve budgetary stability in a programme country or it might advise fiscal consolidation because of its focus on price stability. On the other hand, by buying government bonds in the framework of the various programmes aimed at quantitative easing, the ECB becomes a creditor of the countries receiving financial assistance. This may influence its position in the negotiations on fiscal consolidation and private sector involvement in debt restructuring.[38] It is therefore of the utmost importance that the legal situation of the ECB is clarified when it takes on additional tasks.

When carrying out additional tasks within the ESM Treaty, the ECB finds itself in a situation of *dédoublement fonctionnel* or role splitting. Pursuant to George Scelle's famous theory (national) organs when applying international law act in a dual role: on the one hand, they remain organizationally embedded in their state of origin. On the other hand, they act as international agents because they are giving effect to rules originating in the international legal order.[39] In the same vein, where Union institutions decide to carry out tasks under international law, they give effect to this legal order, while remaining firmly embedded in the EU legal order and pursuing the Union's objectives.

Scelle's theory of role splitting uncovers the organizational link between the EU legal order and the international legal order when Union institutions carry out tasks under the ESM Treaty.[40] In a series of important, yet little known judgments, the Court of Justice has shown some openness towards this form of role splitting provided the accompanying tasks fall outside the exclusive competence of the Union.[41] Moreover,

[37] ESM Treaty, Arts 4(4), 13(1), (3), and (7).

[38] Thomas Beukers, 'The New ECB and its Relationship with the Eurozone Member States: Between Central Bank Independence and Central Bank Intervention' (2013) 50 CML Rev 1579, 1588–91; Jean Pisani-Ferry, André Sapir, and Guntram Wolf, *EU-IMF Assistance to Euro-Area Countries* (Bruegel Blueprint 2013) 21–26 and 109–113.

[39] On Scelle's theory of dédoublement fonctionnel, see in particular his *Précis de droit des gens* (vol 1, Sirey 1932) 43, 47, 54–57; (vol 2, Sirey 1934) 10 f, 20 f, 438–43, 450–55; 'Règles générales du droit de la paix', 46 Recueil des cours de l'Academie de La Haye (1933) 356; 'Le phénomène juridique du dédoublement fonctionnel' in Walter Schätzel and Hans-Jürgen Schlochauer (eds), *Rechtsfragen der Internationalen Organisation—Festschrift für Hans Wehberg* (Vittorio Klostermann 1956) 324. For an overview, see Antonio Cassese, 'Remarks on Scelle's Theory of "Role Splitting" (dédoublement fonctionnel) in International Law' (1990) 1 EJIL 210.

[40] See in detail Bauerschmidt, *Die Rechtsperson der EU im Wandel* (n 34) 309–21, 363–67.

[41] Joined Cases C-181/91 and C-248/91 *European Parliament v Council and Commission* [1993] ECR I-3685, paras 16, 20, and 22; Case C-316/91 *European Parliament v Council* [1994] ECR I-625, paras 26, 34, and 41.

when carrying out additional tasks two further conditions have to be met. First, these tasks have to be separated from the tasks under Union law and 'do not entail any power to make decisions of their own'.[42] Therefore, the additional tasks under international law cannot make use of the competences under Union law and do not have the power to derogate from Union law. Rather, the activities pursued by the ECB under the ESM Treaty solely commit the ESM. Second, the tasks conferred on the ECB are prohibited from altering the essential character of the powers conferred on the ECB under the Treaties.[43] Thus, in order to safeguard the institutional balance, the additional tasks must fit within the existing powers of this Union institution under the Treaties.[44]

Applying these conditions, the Court found that the additional tasks conferred on the ECB can be separated and do not alter the essential character of this Union institution. In particular, these tasks fit into the powers of the ECB which supports the general economic policies in the Union pursuant to Article 282(2) TFEU and may establish relations with international monetary institutions pursuant to Articles 6.2 and 23 of the ESCB Statute.[45] That the ECB needs to remain committed to its primary objective of price stability was again underlined by the Court in its *Gauweiler* judgment.[46] Moreover, even when carrying out tasks conferred under international law and acting outside the EU legal framework, Union institutions remain bound by the Charter of Fundamental Rights.[47] Thus, the ECB is not 'borrowed' by Member States with the effect that it becomes subject to national law or is released into some sort of legal vacuum.[48] Rather, in line with Scelle's theory of role splitting the ECB remains firmly embedded in the EU legal order even when carrying out additional tasks.[49] This does not exclude that pursuant to well-established case law direct actions by individuals against the ECB are usually inadmissible because these tasks do not entail any decision-making power and solely commit the ESM.[50]

In the wake of the Great Financial Crisis budgetary stability was enhanced by a number of measures within and outside the Treaties. In this area of economic policy the ECB assumes some additional tasks which are fully compatible with its role under the Treaties. Even if these tasks are conferred by a treaty of public international law, this Union institution remains fully embedded in the EU legal order. Thus, the ECB's

[42] *Pringle* (n 8) paras 158 and 161.

[43] ibid paras 158 and 162 with reference to *European Economic Area 2* [1992] ECR I-2821, Opinion 1/92, paras 32 and 41; *European Common Aviation Area* [2002] ECR I-3493, Opinion 1/00, para 20; *European and Community Patents Court* [2011] ECR I-1137, Opinion 1/09, para 75.

[44] Alberto de Gregorio Merino, 'Institutional Aspects of Variable Geometry' (2013) 66 Studia Diplomatica 101, 111. See also in detail Bauerschmidt, *Die Rechtsperson der EU im Wandel* (n 34) 318–21, 342–45.

[45] *Pringle* (n 8) para 165.

[46] *Gauweiler* (n 14) paras 64 f.

[47] Joined Cases C-8/15 P to C-10/15 P *Ledra Advertising Ltd and Others v Commission and ECB* [2016] EU:C:2016:701, para 67.

[48] On the unclear concept of 'borrowing of institutions', see Andreas Fischer-Lescano and Lukas Oberndorfer, 'Fiskalvertrag und Unionsrecht—Unionsrechtliche Grenzen völkervertraglicher Fiskalregulierung und Organleihe' (2013) Neue Juristische Wochenschrift 9; Steve Peers, 'Towards a New Form of EU Law? The Use of EU Institutions outside the EU Legal Framework' (2013) 9 EuConst 37, 70–72.

[49] Bauerschmidt, *Die Rechtsperson der EU im Wandel* (n 34) 363–67.

[50] Case T-327/13 *Mallis and Malli v Commission and ECB* [2014] EU:T:2014:909, paras 48–50; Joined Cases C-105/15 P to C-109/15 P *Mallis and Others v Commission and ECB* [2016] EU:C:2016:702, paras 53–57.

independence and its commitment to price stability must be observed even when participating in measures advancing budgetary stability.

V. Financial Stability: New Forms of Supervision for the Internal Market

Besides uncovering the need to strengthen budgetary stability, the Great Financial Crisis also revealed that most sources of financial instability were overlooked in the Maastricht Treaty.[51] Underlying this neglect was the misguided belief that, as long as the ECB can guarantee price stability, existing microprudential supervision would be sufficient to ensure the stability of the financial system.[52] This form of supervision was not only blind for macrofinancial developments, where even the collapse of smaller institutions may have domino effects in a highly interconnected banking sector and pose a risk to financial stability, it also underestimated how systemically important institutions due to their size, (international) interconnectedness and complexity of operations may severely affect the stability of the financial system.[53]

These two types of risk thus needed to be matched by appropriate forms of supervision: while the risks associated with contagion and domino effects for the entire financial system are to be detected and mitigated by macroprudential supervision, the systemically important institutions are monitored by the actor-centred microprudential supervision. At the same time, macro and microprudential supervision should by no means be played off against each other. Rather, both perspectives need to be complementary. Thus, the Union legislator created a new form of macroprudential supervision in the European Systemic Risk Board (A) and strengthened microprudential supervision in the Single Supervisory Mechanism (B).

A. Macroprudential supervision in the European Systemic Risk Board

Macroprudential supervision was established in the form of the European Systemic Risk Board (ESRB) in the course of the financial crisis.[54] The task of the ESRB is to monitor developments in the financial system and to avert and contain systemic risks to financial stability in the Union.[55] To accomplish this task, the Systemic Risk Board has a noteworthy organizational structure and acts in the form of soft law.

[51] On financial stability, see also chapter 3 by Vestert Borger, and chapter 5 by Agnieszka Smoleńska and Thomas Beukers, in this volume.

[52] Brunnermeier and others, *Euro and the Battle of Ideas* (n 3) 160.

[53] The following builds on Jonathan Bauerschmidt, 'Financial Stability as the Objective of the Banking Union' (2020) 17 ECFR 155; also published in German (2019) 183 Zeitschrift für das gesamte Handelsrecht und Wirtschaftsrecht 467.

[54] Regulation (EU) 1092/2010 of the European Parliament and of the Council of 24 November 2010 on European Union macro-prudential oversight of the financial system and establishing a European Systemic Risk Board [2010] OJ L331/1.

[55] ibid Art 3(1) 1st sentence and recitals (10) and (11).

The ESRB is based on Article 114 TFEU.[56] But unlike three newly established European Supervisory Authorities (ESAs), the ESRB has no legal personality and no enforcement powers vis-à-vis third parties. The central body is the Governing Board, which comprises national central bankers and representatives of the supervisory authorities, the President and Vice-President of the ECB, a member of the Commission, and the chairpersons of the ESAs.[57] The Board is assisted and controlled by the Steering Committee and advised by a scientific committee and a technical committee.[58] The ESRB is chaired by the President of the ECB, which also ensures close proximity with the monetary policy analyses and decisions of the Eurosystem. In addition, the ECB provides the secretariat, for which additional tasks to support financial stability in the internal market have been transferred to the ECB through a specific authorization under Article 127(6) TFEU.[59]

The ESRB may take actions in the form of warnings and recommendations pursuant to Article 16 of the ESRB Regulation if it finds significant risks to the stability of the financial system. Thus, the ESRB acts through soft law, which can be understood as rules of conduct that are laid down in instruments which have not been attributed legally binding force as such, but nevertheless may have certain (indirect) legal effects in Union law.[60]

Warnings and recommendations shall, at the discretion of the ESRB, be addressed to the Union as a whole, to one or more Member States, to the ESAs, or to national supervisors and may be more general or specific. While both are strictly confidential, they can be published in accordance with Article 18 of the ESRB Regulation by a decision of the Board of Directors acting with a two-thirds majority.[61] Whereas warnings are non-binding knowledge statements of the ESRB, Article 17 of the ESRB Regulation provides for a noteworthy 'act or explain' mechanism for recommendations: the addressee of the recommendation must inform the ESRB (and the Council) of the implementation measures or justify its inaction. As the 'act of explain' mechanism does not require certain kinds of reasons, any legal and factual obstacle may in principle justify inaction. In fact, even a deviating risk assessment by the addressee may be suitable to justify inaction, but will then require a significantly increased justification.[62] Thus, neither warnings nor recommendations are legally binding, but are intended to be

[56] On the legal basis, see Eilís Ferran and Kern Alexander, 'Can Soft Law Bodies be Effective? The Special Case of the European Systemic Risk Board' (2010) 35 EL Rev 751, 768 ff (hereafter Ferran and Alexander, 'Can Soft Law Bodies be Effective?').

[57] Regulation (EU) 1092/2010 (n 54) Art 6 distinguishes between members with and without voting rights and foresees the participation of the chairs of the Advisory Scientific Committee, the Advisory Technical Committee, as well as the Economic and Financial Committee (EFC).

[58] ibid Arts 4–13.

[59] Council Regulation (EU) 1096/2010 of 17 November 2010 conferring specific tasks upon the European Central Bank concerning the functioning of the European Systemic Risk Board [2010] OJ L331/162.

[60] Linda Senden, *Soft Law in European Community Law* (Hart Publishing 2004) 112; Karel Wellens and Glenn Borchardt, 'Soft Law in European Community Law' (1989) 14 EL Rev 267, 285.

[61] Regulation (EU) 1092/2010 (n 54) Art 10(3). Similarly, recommendations have to be adopted with a two-thirds majority whereas unpublished warnings can be adopted by simple majority.

[62] Ferran and Alexander, 'Can Soft Law Bodies be Effective?' (n 56) 774 f; Ann-Katrin Kaufhold, 'Der Europäische Ausschuss für Systemrisiken im Finanzsystem als Ausprägung einer neuen Aufsichtsform' (2013) 46 Die Verwaltung 21, 45 ff; Christoph Ohler, 'Finanzmarktregulierung und -aufsicht' in Matthias Ruffert (ed), *Enzyklopädie Europarecht Vol. 5* (2nd edn, Nomos 2020)para 134.

actually taken note of and if necessary obeyed. Therefore, warnings and recommendations fall into the wide range of soft law instruments in the field of financial market regulation, which, although not legally binding, have proved to be quite effective. Not least the result of the political and constitutional limits to establish broad hard law obligations for macrofinancial supervision at Union level, the new arrangements in the ESRB rely heavily on influence and reputation, that is to say on the exercise of soft power. The ESRB thus creates a strong compliance pull for all participants.[63]

The ESRB's inclusive governance structure and the issuance of soft law measures was again strengthened when a review was concluded in 2019 in three important aspects.[64] First, the President of the ECB, who has chaired the ESRB for the first five years and thereafter assumed this task only on an interim basis, was made permanent Chair. Conversely, the first Vice-Chair now needs to be elected from 'national members' of the ESRB's General Board and creates something of a national counter balance to the ECB President. Second, the Chair of the ECB's Supervisory Board and the Chair of the Single Resolution Board were made non-voting members of the ESRB's General Board to tap into their expertise on banking supervision and resolution. Third, in order to strengthen democratic control, the European Parliament now also receives warnings and recommendations with the obligations to ensure confidentiality if those are non-public. This creates an even stronger incentive for any addressee to follow those soft law measures in the realm of macrofinancial supervision.

B. Microprudential supervision in the Single Supervisory Mechanism

A further contribution to financial stability by way of microprudential supervision is the establishment of the Single Supervisory Mechanism (SSM).[65] The SSM Regulation (EU) 1024/2013[66] confers on the European Central Bank the task of supervising systemically important banks. The aim is to contribute to the safety and soundness of credit institutions and the stability of the financial system in the Union in accordance with Article 1 of the SSM Regulation. Financial stability is key in justifying recourse to Article 127(6) TFEU as a legal basis and it helps delineate supervisory from monetary tasks of the ECB.

The suitability of Article 127(6) TFEU as legal basis for the SSM Regulation is contested especially in German language contributions. It is argued that this provision only allows a narrow transfer of 'special tasks' or 'besondere Aufgaben' related to banking supervision. Therefore, the full transfer of banking supervision is not possible

[63] See in more detail Ferran and Alexander, 'Can Soft Law Bodies be Effective?' (n 56) 760 f.

[64] Regulation (EU) 2019/2176 of the European Parliament and of the Council of 18 December 2019 amending Regulation (EU) 1092/2010 of 24 November 2010 on European Union macro-prudential oversight of the financial system and establishing a European Systemic Risk Board [2019] OJ L334/146.

[65] On the role of the ECB in the Banking Union, see also chapter 7 by Kern Alexander and chapter 8 by Federico della Negra and Gianni Lo Schiavo, in this volume.

[66] Council Regulation (EU) 1024/2013 of 15 October 2013 conferring specific tasks on the European Central Bank concerning policies relating to the prudential supervision of credit institutions [2013] OJ L287/63.

and the ECB may only have a supporting role according to this view.[67] The same argument was also advanced before the German Constitutional Court in the case on the Banking Union.[68] While the German version suggests a narrower reading, the provision has to be interpreted in the light of all official languages and by reference to the purpose and general scheme of the rules of which it forms part.[69] In this vein, the French text uses 'missions spécifiques', Italian 'compiti specifici', Spanish 'tareas específicas', and Polish 'szczególne zadania' and, therefore, seem to require delimited tasks rather than only subordinated or purely supportive tasks.

Against this background, the SSM Regulation confers limited tasks *ratione personae* to supervise in principle only the largest and systemically most relevant banks. Moreover, *ratione materiae* not all supervisory powers are transferred as questions of consumer protection, the fight against money laundering and the supervision of third-country credit institutions remain at national level. Also the extent of supervision *ratione loci* is limited by virtue of involving the ECB because only those banks established in euro area Member States and in Member States which have established an agreement on close cooperation come within the ECB's supervision. Finally, a comparison of Article 127(5) and 127(6) TFEU supports the possibility of conferring specific supervisory powers to the ECB. Whereas the former provision allows the ESCB to contribute to supervisory policy and support (national) supervisors without any further legislation, the latter provision requires a special legislative procedure. This forms part of a compromise during the negotiations of the Treaty of Maastricht which left the question of prudential supervision at European level open to political deliberations subject to a unanimous decision of the Council. Therefore, the Union legislator rightfully empowered the ECB to assume supervisory tasks through the SSM Regulation based on Article 127(6) TFEU.[70] This conclusion does not prevent an eventual amendment of Article 127(6) TFEU to clarify the scope of the competence as envisaged in a declaration by finance ministers before the adoption of the SSM Regulation.[71]

This immediately raises the subsequent question of how monetary policy should be conducted separately from the new tasks of banking supervision within the ECB. This separation is of fundamental importance and by no means a purely theoretical problem. Rather, the ECB may be tempted to lower its interest rates or loosen the

[67] Matthias Herdegen, 'Europäische Bankenunion' (2012) Wertpapiermitteilungen 1889, 1891 f; Ann-Katrin Kaufhold, *Systemaufsicht* (Mohr Siebeck 2016) 285 ff; Benedikt Wolfers and Thomas Voland, 'Europäische Zentralbank und Bankenaufsicht' (2014) Zeitschrift für Bank- und Kapitalmarktrecht 177, 178 f.

[68] BVerfG 30 July 2019, 2 BvR 1685/14 and 2 BvR 2631/14 DE:BVerfG:2019:rs20190730.2bvr168514, paras 44–49, rejected in paras 171–95.

[69] Case 29/69 *Stauder v City of Ulm—Sozialamt* [1969] ECR 419, para 3; Case C-488/11 *Asbeek Brusse and de Man Garabito v Jahani BV* [2013] EU:C:2013:341, para 26.

[70] That the SSM Regulation can be adopted on the basis of Art 126(7) TFEU is also shown by Kern Alexander, 'European Banking Union: A Legal and Institutional Analysis of the SSM and the SRM' (2015) 40 EL Rev 154, 168; Alberto de Gregorio Merino, 'Institutional Report' in Gyula Bándi and others (eds), *FIDE Report on European Banking Union* (Kluwer 2016) 168 ff; Klaus Lackhoff, *Single Supervisory Mechanism* (CH Beck 2017) 16 f; Gianni Lo Schiavo, *The Role of Financial Stability in EU Law and Policy* (Kluwer 2017) 207 ff; Martin Selmayr, 'Artikel 127 AEUV' in Hans von der Groeben, Jürgen Schwarze, and Armin Hatje (eds), *Europäisches Unionsrecht* (7th edn, CH Beck 2015)paras 51 ff.

[71] See the Declaration made by Member States at the informal Economic and Financial Affairs Council (ECOFIN) in Dublin on 12 April 2013 contained in the Annex of Council document ST 8417/1/13 REV 1 of 17 April 2013. Also partly reflected in recital (85) of the SSM Regulation.

conditions for its purchases in order to facilitate access to liquidity for banks, thereby undermining banking supervision through monetary policy. Conversely, the ECB relies on a functioning banking system that serves as a transfer mechanism for its monetary policy. Banking supervision may thus spill over into monetary policy.[72]

An adequate separation of monetary and supervisory functions is based on the distinction between price and financial stability. Under Articles 127(1) and 282(2) TFEU, the primary objective of monetary policy is to ensure price stability. By contrast, the SSM Regulation, based on Article 127(6) TFEU, pursues the objective of financial stability. This is accompanied by an important distinction in the separation of competences: While monetary policy in the euro area pursuant to Article 3(1)(c) TFEU constitutes an exclusive competence, supervisory policy is part of the shared competence. Thus, not only the substantive rules for banking supervision as set out in the Capital Requirements Regulation (EU) 575/2013[73] and in the Capital Requirements Directive 2013/36/EU[74] are part of the shared competence for the internal market under Article 4(2)(a) TFEU, the SSM Regulation itself also falls into the area of shared competence[75] as it goes beyond monetary policy, and the supervisory tasks envisaged under Article 127(6) TFEU do not belong to the exclusive competence of the Union.[76]

The different objectives of stability have a direct impact on the separation of functions. Thus, the SSM Regulation requires a strict separation of supervisory and monetary functions: According to Article 25(1), when exercising supervisory tasks, the ECB may only pursue the objective of the SSM Regulation and, in particular, the objective of financial stability. In addition, supervisory tasks must be exercised separately from monetary policy according to Article 25(2).

[72] On this tension between monetary and supervisory policy, see Cornelia Manger-Nestler and Robert Böttner, 'Ménage à trois?—Zur gewandelten Rolle der EZB im Spannungsfeld zwischen Geldpolitik, Finanzaufsicht und Fiskalpolitik' (2014) Europarecht 621, 630 ff and Kern Alexander, 'The European Central Bank and Banking Supervision' (2016) 13 ECFR 467, 488 f. The separation model is questioned by Matthias Goldmann, 'United in Diversity? The Relationship between Monetary Policy and Prudential Supervision in the Banking Union' (2018) 14 EuConst 283, 292–305 who draws from the interplay between monetary and supervisory policy that both should be pursued by the ECB under a holistic approach. Although the overall aim is to strengthen the democratic legitimacy of the ECB, this holistic approach focuses too much on the ECB and underestimates the democratic legitimacy generated by the Union legislator which takes into account broader policy objectives. Based on these considerations the Union legislator establishes the supervisory policy (mainly in the Capital Requirements Regulation and Directive) and subsequently the ECB has to implement this supervisory policy.

[73] Regulation (EU) 575/2013 of the European Parliament and of the Council of 26 June 2013 on prudential requirements for credit institutions and investment firms [2013] OJ L176/1. Last amended by Regulation (EU) 2020/873 of the European Parliament and of the Council of 24 June 2020 as regards certain adjustments in response to the COVID-19 pandemic [2020] OJ L204/4.

[74] Directive 2013/36/EU of the European Parliament and of the Council of 26 June 2013 on access to the activity of credit institutions and the prudential supervision of credit institutions and investment firms [2013] OJ L176/338. Last amended by Directive (EU) 2019/2034 of the European Parliament and of the Council of 27 November 2019 on the prudential supervision of investment firms [2019] OJ L314/64.

[75] See Martin Nettesheim, 'Artikel 4 AEUV' in Eberhard Grabitz, Meinard Hilf, and Martin Nettesheim (eds), *Das Recht der EU* (70th Ergänzung, CH Beck 2020), para 6 on shared competence as 'catch-all' category for those instances where the category of competence is not explicitly laid down in the Treaties.

[76] This is not called into question by the findings in Case T-122/15 *Landeskreditbank Baden-Württemberg v ECB* [2017] EU:T:2017:337, paras 54, 63, and 72 (confirmed on appeal Case C-450/17 P [2019] EU:C:2019:372, para 49) that Art 4(1) of the SSM Regulation confers an 'exclusive competence' on the ECB as the exclusivity relates to the tasks enumerated in this provision and applies to the banks under direct ECB supervision but not to the entire field of prudential supervision.

In order to categorize a specific measure in an individual case, regard must be had to the objective and the effect of that measure. First, it must be determined whether the measure pursues the objective of financial stability or price stability.[77] For this, the content and justification of the measure must be evaluated. Secondly, a supervisory measure must be assessed as to whether it interferes with or is determined by monetary policy. Whether there is an interference with monetary policy can be assessed by means of the case law of the Court of Justice. In *Pringle*, the Court held that an indirect effect on price stability was not sufficient to classify a measure as monetary policy.[78] However, this also means that direct effects on price stability affect monetary policy and that such supervisory measures are prohibited.

Whether a supervisory measure is determined by monetary policy can be examined by having recourse to the *Gauweiler* and *Weiss* cases. According to the Court, indirect effects on the stability of the euro area are not sufficient to treat as equivalent a monetary policy measure with an economic policy measure.[79] However, it can also be deduced that monetary policy measures with a direct effect on financial stability go beyond the monetary mandate and improperly determine supervisory measures.

The separation between monetary and supervisory functions is supported by institutional arrangements. Pursuant to Article 26 of the SSM Regulation the Supervisory Board is an internal body of the ECB which plans and executes supervision.[80] Binding decisions, however, can only be taken by the Governing Council. Thus, the Supervisory Board proposes complete draft decisions, which are deemed adopted unless the Governing Council objects within a period of not more than ten working days. The Governing Council may object to the draft decision and invoke for example monetary policy concerns. Should there be disagreements regarding the separation of functions, Article 25(5) of the SSM Regulation foresees a mediation panel which ensures that each function is exercised in accordance with the applicable objectives.

In addition to these normative and institutional arrangements, Articles 20 and 21 of the SSM Regulation create a noteworthy system of accountability. The ECB is not only responsible to the European Parliament and the Council for the implementation of the SSM Regulation, which is a significant difference compared to the ECB's monetary independence, the ECB must also respond to the comments and questions of the national parliaments, which may invite the chairperson or a member of the supervisory board to participate in an exchange of views on the prudential supervision of credit institutions.[81]

It is therefore not surprising that the independence of the ECB regarding monetary policy goes much further than its independence regarding banking supervision.[82]

[77] On the scope of review, see *Pringle* (n 8) paras 53 and 55; *Gauweiler* (n 14) para 46; *Weiss* (n 16) para 53.

[78] *Pringle* (n 8) para 56.

[79] *Gauweiler* (n 14) para 52; *Weiss* (n 16) para 61.

[80] Lackhoff, *Single Supervisory Mechanism* (n 70) 60 ff. See also chapter 13 by Diane Fromage, in this volume.

[81] Lackhoff, *Single Supervisory Mechanism* (n 70) 18–20. On ECB accountability, see also chapter 11 by Fabian Amtenbrink and Menelaos Markakis, in this volume.

[82] On the difference in independence and accountability in monetary and supervisory policy, see Chiara Zilioli, 'The Independence of the ECB and Its New Banking Supervisory Competences' in Dominique Ritleng (ed), *Independence and Legitimacy in the Institutional System of the EU* (OUP 2016) 125, 165 ff; On ECB independence, see also chapter 10 by Alexander Thiele, in this volume.

This new system of accountability is well aligned with the executive role of the ECB in supervision: in contrast to monetary policy, which the ECB (together with National Central Banks) conceives and implements on its own to achieve price stability, the rules for supervisory policy with the objective of financial stability are set by the Union legislature (with some options and discretions left to national authorities) and the ECB has to implement this supervisory policy.

Financial stability was thus advanced significantly by new forms of macro and microprudential supervision. At the intersection between monetary policy and internal market harmonization, the ECB assumes crucial supervisory tasks to ensure the stability of the financial system. Especially in the Single Supervisory Mechanism, the ECB has become an executor of Union policy not unlike the Commission or Member States when implementing Union law under Article 291(1) and (2) TFEU. This new executive role is particularly clear from the considerable number of court cases against the ECB where the it is confronted with alleged violations against the right to good administration and the details of prudential supervision. Despite this new role, supervisory and monetary policy are sufficiently separated and normative as well as institutional safeguards protect against spillovers from one policy area to the other.

VI. The Cunning of European Integration

After the storm of the Great Financial Crisis had settled and reflecting on *Europe's Functional Constitution*, Turkuler Isiksel in 2016 made the following remark about economic integration:

> The cunning of attempt to deploy economic integration as an instrumental means of political integration has itself fallen victim to the cunning of economics. Today, EU member states find themselves ruled by the logic of economic necessity that was set in train by their own deliberate decisions to create an internal market and an economic and monetary union.[83]

The feeling that politics has fallen victim to economics is also shared by some economists who lament the inability of democratically elected governments to curb the power of capital[84] and the deplorable state of democracy in the European Union.[85]

The feeling that politics has fallen victim to the cunning of economics echoes a much older observation by the German philosopher Friedrich Hegel on the cunning of reason. Exactly 200 years ago Hegel introduced the cunning of reason or *die List der Vernunft* to express the idea that human beings, following their passions, actually serve some higher world-historical purpose of which they are unaware. In his *Philosophy of*

[83] Turkuler Isiksel, *Europe's Functional Constitution—A Theory of Constitutionalism Beyond the State* (OUP 2016) 17.

[84] Thomas Piketty, *Capital in the Twenty-First Century* (Harvard University Press 2014) ch 13.

[85] Wolfgang Streeck, *Buying Time—The Delayed Crisis of Democratic Capitalism* (2nd edn, Verso 2017) ch 3.

History Hegel transformed Kant's comments on the 'the hidden plan of nature'[86] into his doctrine: 'This is to be called the cunning of reason, that it lets the passions do its works.'[87] The historical agent, by acting out of his own will, inadvertently acts as an instrument of reason; his passions, ambitions, jealousy, greed, and the like are thus viewed as the handmaids of reason working in history. In Isiksel's account, however, the cunning of reason is replaced by the cunning of economy to signify that the EU Member States with their political decisions to create an internal market and monetary union have fallen victim to economic necessity and the forces of the market to the detriment of political self-determination.

This narrative of the cunning of economics, however, underestimates that by creating an internal market and a monetary union, the framers of the Treaties not only set in motion a project of economic integration but also of political integration. This can be called the cunning of European integration and means that by establishing the Treaties, the framers not only acknowledged the interdependence of politics and economics in modern societies, they also established a frame to treat economic policy as a matter of common concern and conferred on the Union competences to regulate economic activity and coordinate economic policy. Thus, instead of being subjected to the mercy of the markets, politicians in Europe have at their disposal a range of powerful tools to tackle the challenges posed by economic crisis. The constitutional framework established by the Treaties has proven to be strong and resilient enough to weather the storm. In hindsight and looking at the various measures which were taken, the Treaties provided the necessary competences to strengthen economic policy coordination and establish a Banking Union where the ECB assumes crucial tasks in macro and microprudential supervision. Moreover, the Treaties even provide the frame for satellite agreements by some Member States and the involvement of Union institutions and, thus, create the gravitational force for such agreements to remain within the orbit of the European Union.

The cunning of European integration does not mean that there is an automaticity for ever more integration. Rather, all the measures were taken after intense political deliberations weighing alternatives and different approaches. Admittedly, the existence of a monetary union ruled out the possibility of overcoming the crisis by unilaterally altering exchange rates. Thus, monetary union limits political choices and leads to a convergence of political interests as individual devaluation under the common currency is simply not an option. At the same time monetary union creates a sense of belonging together in a common political endeavour beyond monetary policy. This common interest was the basis for creating a permanent mechanism of financial assistance and advancing financial supervision. In the political debates leading up to the adoption of the relevant acts one could observe a remarkable Europeanization of national politics which, despite all the struggles, actually reinforced and strengthened the unity in Europe.

[86] Immanuel Kant, 'Idee zu einer allgemeinen Geschichte in weltbürgerlicher Absicht' in *Werke Bd. 6* (Insel Verlag 1784 (1964)) 32, 45.

[87] Georg Wilhelm Friedrich Hegel, *Vorlesungen über die Philosophie der Geschichte—Werke Bd. 7* (Suhrkamp 1821 (1986)) 49.

The expansive force of monetary policy to neighbouring policy areas in economic coordination and the internal market has caused a centripetal effect: monetary policy has unravelled a mutualization of risks whose effective management requires a mutualization of instruments for the control of such risks. This amounts to policing sovereigns and ultimately to a sort of federalization. In Hegel's terms, this integration process is less the result of a preconceived plan than an evolution for which the drafters of the Maastricht Treaty merely planted a seed. The ECB is not surprisingly at the centre of this evolution. While the Treaties establish the ECB with the clear mandate to pursue price stability, monetary policy may have repercussions on areas such as economic policy coordination and the internal market. The delineation of competences in these fields has been clarified by the Court of Justice with important effects for unconventional monetary policy. Beyond monetary policy and without prejudice to price stability, the ECB also provides expert knowledge to facilitate budgetary stability as part of the economic policy coordination and within the assistance programmes by the European Stability Mechanism. Moreover, to strengthen financial stability the ECB not only has a central role in the European Systemic Risk Board ensuring macroprudential supervision, but has also become a fully fledged microprudential supervisor in the Single Supervisory Mechanism. Compared to the initial vision of a central bank which would mainly pursue financial stability, the new ECB now also contributes to the attainment of other forms of stability within the limits of the Treaties.

Milton Friedman did not live to see the Great Financial Crisis and could not re-evaluate his prediction that monetary union in Europe would lead to political disunity. But it seems safe to say that the European Union came out of the Financial Crisis stronger and, despite all the difficult debates, more unified than before. Of course, the European Union is far away from the United States of Europe and may never exhibit the level of political and economic integration that the United States of America does. Nevertheless, the ability and resolve to overcome the Great Financial Crisis bode well for the new challenges posed by the COVID-19 pandemic. At the same time, there are also important differences. Whereas the Financial Crisis was about ensuring stability in its many facets ranging from price stability to budgetary stability and financial stability, the response to COVID-19 will be about generating growth which is fairly distributed within the European Union. To this end, political leaders have decided to create a programme called the Next Generation EU which contains a Recovery and Resilience Facility and is supported and financed by the financial markets. It is too early to predict whether this will amount to a Hamiltonian moment. However, these developments will certainly also have an impact on the ECB and monetary policy which may be the subject of an investigation when this remarkable institution turns thirty.

7

The ECB's Role in the European Banking Union

Kern Alexander

I. Introduction

The European Banking Union (EBU) is the most significant step in promoting European integration since the Treaty of Maastricht's creation of the euro. The Banking Union was designed to restore the financial health and stability of the European banking system and to sever the link between weak euro area banking systems and fragile sovereign debt finances.[1] The Banking Union consists of three pillars: the Single Supervisory Mechanism (SSM), Single Resolution Mechanism (SRM), and the European Deposit Insurance System (EDIS).[2] Under the SSM—that became operational in November 2014, the European Central Bank (ECB) has assumed extensive and wide-ranging powers to supervise banks, banking groups, and mixed financial holding companies, and to be responsible for ensuring banking sector and financial stability in participating Member States of the BU.

The second pillar of the Banking Union is the Single Resolution Mechanism (SRM).[3] It took effect in 2016 and operates through the Single Resolution Board (SRB) that oversees the application of the Bank Recovery and Resolution Directive in the Banking Union jurisdictions.[4] The SRB has authority to take a bank or a systemically important investment firm into resolution and to utilize resolution tools to restructure or recapitalize the institution, if necessary, to prevent a crisis and to avoid a taxpayer funded bailout. The SRB can draw on a Single Resolution Fund,[5] which can be tapped to help wind down a systemically important institution.[6]

[1] Council Regulation (EU) 1024/2013 of 15 October 2013 conferring specific tasks on the European Central Bank concerning policies relating to the prudential supervision of credit institutions [2013] OJ L287/63 (hereafter SSM Regulation); Regulation (EU) 806/2014 of the European Parliament and of the Council of 15 July 2014 establishing uniform rules and a uniform procedure for the resolution of credit institutions and certain investment firms in the framework of a Single Resolution Mechanism and a Single Resolution Fund and amending Regulation (EU) 1093/2010 [2014] OJ L225/1 (hereafter SRM Regulation).

[2] Kern Alexander, 'European Banking Union: Effectiveness, Impact and Future Challenges' in Danny Bush and Guido Ferrarini (eds), *European Banking Union* (2nd edn, OUP 2020) (hereafter Alexander, 'European Banking Union').

[3] SRM Regulation (n 1).

[4] Directive 2014/59/EU of the European Parliament and of the Council of 15 May 2014 establishing a framework for the recovery and resolution of credit institutions and investment firms and amending Council Directive 82/891/EEC, and Directives 2001/24/EC, 2002/47/EC, 2004/25/EC, 2005/56/EC, 2007/36/EC, 2011/35/EU, 2012/30/EU and 2013/36/EU, and Regulations (EU) 1093/2010 and (EU) 648/2012 of the European Parliament and of the Council [2014] OJ L173/190 (hereafter BRRD).

[5] European Council, 'Agreement on the transfer and mutualisation of contributions to the Single Resolution Fund' (8457/14, EF 121, ECOFIN 342, 14 May 2014), Art 3 <http://register.consilium.europa.eu/doc/srv?l=EN&f=ST%208457%202014%20INIT> accessed 29 May 2021.

[6] SRM Regulation (n 1) ch 2 'Single Resolution Fund', Arts 67–79.

Kern Alexander, *The ECB's Role in the European Banking Union* In: *The New European Central Bank.* Edited by: Thomas Beukers, Diane Fromage, and Giorgio Monti, Oxford University Press. © Kern Alexander 2022.
DOI: 10.1093/oso/9780198871231.003.0007

The third pillar is the European Deposit Insurance System (known as 'EDIS'), which represents a common scheme to insure bank deposits across the Banking Union, but is still under negotiation and faces strong political opposition in Germany and other countries primarily because its future implementation will likely involve some form of cross-border pooling of resources to provide deposit guarantees for banks located in Banking Union jurisdictions.[7]

This chapter analyses the institutional and legal framework governing the ECB's responsibility in monetary policy, banking supervision, and resolution. The discussion raises issues concerning the primacy of monetary policy and the price stability mandate of Article 127(1) of the Treaty on the Functioning of the EU (TFEU) and how this can be reconciled with the ECB's support for the Union's general economic policies (so-called secondary objectives) and for the discharge of its other responsibilities, including banking supervision, within the BU. Part II considers the institutional context of the ECB's role in the Banking Union by analysing its price stability mandate and the importance of its secondary objectives in informing its role as a bank supervisor. Section III discusses how the ECB carries out its supervisory functions and the need for coordination with national competent authorities (NCAs). Section IV discusses the SRM, particularly the role of the SRB in ensuring that banks can be resolved in a centralized and coordinated manner and the role of the ECB in coordinating with the SRB. In this context, the legal and policy issues raised by the ECB's role will be discussed along with the questions it raises concerning the SRB's effectiveness. Section V concludes with future challenges facing the Banking Union including the need for further integration in banking markets and the need for the ECB as a supervisor to address emerging risks such as environmental sustainability risks.

II. The Banking Union's Context—the ECB's Mandate

A. Price stability

Price stability is the all-encompassing objective that shapes and informs the ECB's fulfilment of its various functions. Generally, price stability emerged as the primary objective for most central banks in the late 1980s following the dramatic inflation and stagflation experienced by most advanced developed countries in the 1970s and 1980s. Based on this experience, a consensus view developed amongst central bankers that the only effective way to control inflation was for central banks to use mainly

[7] See European Commission, 'Proposal for a Regulation of the European Parliament and of the Council amending Regulation (EU) 806/2014 in order to establish in the medium term a European Deposit Insurance Fund' COM (2015) 586 final. Then German Finance Minister Olaf Scholz outlined proposals in November 2019 aimed to complete the stalled negotiations over the third pillar of the Banking Union to provide 'a form of common European deposit insurance' for Banking Union member countries. The German coalition government, however, has not accepted Scholz's proposal primarily because of the political concerns associated with using German taxpayer money to provide customer deposit guarantees of up to €100,000 for banks based in other Banking Union countries that are unable to meet their obligations to repay depositors. See Jim Brunsden, Sam Fleming, and Mehreen Khan, 'Scholz's Gamble' *Financial Times* (London, 6 November 2019) <www.ft.com/content/968f43ba-004f-11ea-b7bc-f3fa4e77dd47> accessed 29 May 2021.

interest rates to achieve an inflation target that was defined by either the government or the central bank. Moreover, it was considered necessary that central banks have independence from political influence in deciding which tools they could use to achieve their price stability objective. The European Union (EU) Maastricht Treaty of 1992 adopted a model based on independence for the newly created ECB, Article 105(1) of the European Community Treaty providing that the ECB's primary objective was to be price stability. This mandate is now set forth in clear terms in Article 127(1) TFEU):

> The primary objective of the European System of Central Banks (hereinafter referred to as 'ESCB') shall be to maintain price stability. Without prejudice to the objective of price stability, the ESCB shall support the general economic policies in the Union with a view to contributing to the achievement of the objectives of the Union as laid down in Article 3 of the Treaty on European Union.

Whilst Article 127(1) TFEU establishes the primacy of the price stability mandate, it does not give a precise definition of what is meant by price stability. The ECB Executive Board has therefore defined price stability to be a quantitative target that is 'defined as a year-on-year increase in the Harmonised Index of Consumer Prices (HICP) for the euro area of below 2%' and clarified that, in the pursuit of price stability, it aims to maintain inflation rates 'below, but close to, 2% over the medium term'.[8]

The typical way the ECB works to achieve its price stability objective is by utilizing a number of monetary policy tools, which include setting interest rates on inter-bank loans and creating credit for the banking system by electronically printing money, which can be used to purchase assets, such as bonds issued by banks, corporates, and governments with the effect of stimulating the economy to achieve the 2 per cent price stability objective.

Until now and historically, the ECB has been focused on its primary objective of price stability that is defined as a 2 per cent consumer price inflation target. This narrow definition of price stability was adopted based on macroeconomic models that assume markets are efficient and that an open-market economy with free competition results in an efficient allocation of resources, but as mainstream economists have pointed out this ignores standard economic theory and empirical evidence that markets are prone to failure and that government regulation is necessary to reduce moral hazard and to curb externalities.[9] During the early years of the euro, the ECB was generally inconsistent in achieving its inflation target between 2001 and 2008 while between 2008 and 2012 not only did it fail to achieve its inflation target it presided over record fluctuations in output and employment, which were caused by the financial crisis of 2007–08.[10] The crisis underscored the ECB's disproportionate attention to price stability at

[8] European Central Bank, 'The definition of price stability' (2020), <www.ecb.europa.eu/mopo/strategy/pricestab/html/index.en.html> accessed 29 May 2021. In Case C-493/17 *Weiss and Others* [2018] ECLI:EU:C:2018:1000, the European Court of Justice (ECJ) agreed that the 2 per cent interpretation was proportionate, saying it is for the ECB to decide and that 2 per cent does not appear manifestly erroneous (para 56).

[9] See Joseph Stiglitz, *The Euro: And its Threat to the Future of Europe* (Penguin and Random House UK 2016) 146–49 (hereafter Stiglitz, *The Euro*). See discussion in Kern Alexander, *Principles of Banking Regulation* (CUP 2019) 37–42 (hereafter Alexander, *Principles of Banking Regulation*).

[10] ibid. See Organisation for Economic Cooperation and Development (OECD) (Database, 2020).

the expense of growth, employment, and financial stability. Inadequate regulation resulted in weak banking systems, which led to Member State bailouts of banks and in turn to the European sovereign debt crisis of 2012. Between 2012 and 2020, inflation was below target more often than not and in some cases below 0 per cent, which is deflation.[11] Beginning in 2021, the economic crisis caused by COVID-19 created the spectre of deflation.[12] These developments brought the secondary objectives of the ECB to the forefront, such as the objective of supporting the general economic policies of the EU, including 'sustainable development', 'full employment and social progress', and 'a high level of protection and improvement of the quality of the environment'.

The ECB's overall failure since 2001 to achieve its primary objective of price stability and to achieve adequate growth targets in comparison with other advanced developed economies raises questions regarding its accountability and independence.[13] The ECB is vested with a high degree of independence, which is closely linked to its objective of maintaining price stability.[14] The primacy of price stability is based on the idea of monetary dominance which came to the fore in the 1980s and 1990s. Monetary dominance postulates apolitical, technical monetary policies targeting low inflation and can be seen as reaction to the experiences of the 1970s where central banks were pushed by governments for monetary stimuli for the economy. The idea behind monetary dominance was based on the notion that governments would be forced to abandon expansive monetary policies to stimulate demand and instead push economic growth by improving the supply side of the economy by incentivizing investment and the training of the workforce through fiscal and other economic policies. The appeal of this idea that monetary policy should merely be concerned with technical issues in managing the value of the currency which is unrelated to economic policy was underpinned by the economic success of Germany and its independent *Bundesbank*.[15] Accordingly, in the Maastricht Treaty monetary and economic policy were separated.[16] Further, the Maastricht Treaty ensured strong independence for the ECB to protect its decision-making from political influence.[17]

[11] European Central Bank, 'Economic Bulletin 8' (2020) 30 <https://www.ecb.europa.eu/pub/pdf/ecbu/eb202008.en.pdf> accessed 29 May 2021; Eurostat, 'Inflation in the euro area' (2021) <https://ec.europa.eu/eurostat/statistics-explained/index.php/Inflation_in_the_euro_area#Euro_area_annual_inflation_rate_and_its_main_components> accessed 29 May 2021; Michael Heise, 'The ECB has consistently missed the mark on inflation—here's how it can change that' (*World Economic Forum*, 8 July 2019) <https://www.weforum.org/agenda/2019/07/the-ecb-needs-new-inflation-rules/> accessed 29 May 2021. See also Stiglitz, *The Euro* (n 9) 63–71.

[12] See Martin Arnold, 'Eurozone slide into deflation for the first time in four years' *Financial Times* (London, 1 September 2020).

[13] On ECB independence, see chapter 10 by Alexander Thiele; on ECB accountability, see chapter 11 by Fabian Amtenbrink and Menelaos Markakis, in this volume.

[14] Michael Ioannidis, 'The European Central Bank' in Fabian Amtenbrink and Christoph Herrmann (eds), *The EU Law of Economic and Monetary Union* (OUP 2020) 14.51 (hereafter Ioannidis, 'The European Central Bank').

[15] Darius Adamski, 'Objectives of the EMU' in Fabian Amtenbrink and Christoph Herrmann (eds), *The EU Law of Economic and Monetary Union* (OUP 2020) 9.15–9.18 (hereafter Adamski, 'Objectives of the EMU'); for an overview of the critique on price stability as primary monetary objective, see Tommaso Padoa-Schioppa, *Regulating Finance: Balancing Freedom and Risk* (OUP 2008) 112.

[16] See Adamski, 'Objectives of the EMU' (n 15) 9.16–19.18. See also chapter 6 by Jonathan Bauerschmidt, in this volume.

[17] Ioannidis, 'The European Central Bank' (n 14) 14.51–14.52.

The separation of monetary from economic policy, however, created asymmetries between the monetary and the economic union which have led to a divergence of monetary and economic integration causing systematic vulnerabilities.[18] There is a growing body of research challenging the distinction between monetary and economic policy as not reflecting economic reality. It is argued that monetary policy focusing on price stability has distributional consequences. Hence, it cannot be separated from economic policy and also cannot be deemed apolitical.[19] Consequently, rethinking the balance between the ECB's independence and accountability and the asymmetric architecture of the monetary union appears necessary.

B. The ECB's secondary objectives

The ECB's secondary objectives are referred to in Article 127(1) TFEU which makes clear reference to Article 3 (paragraph 3) of the Treaty on European Union (TEU) that defines broadly the secondary objective of the European System of Central Banks (ESCB) to support the economic policies of the Union as follows:

> The Union shall establish an internal market. It shall work for the sustainable development of Europe based on balanced economic growth and price stability, a highly competitive social market economy, aiming at full employment and social progress, and a high level of protection and improvement of the quality of the environment. It shall promote scientific and technological advance.
>
> It shall combat social exclusion and discrimination, and shall promote social justice and protection, equality between women and men, solidarity between generations and protection of the rights of the child.
>
> It shall promote economic, social and territorial cohesion, and solidarity among Member States.
>
> It shall respect its rich cultural and linguistic diversity, and shall ensure that Europe's cultural heritage is safeguarded and enhanced.

The Treaty provisions are less clear in defining the ECB's role in supporting the general economic policies of the Union. It can be maintained, however, that the starting point for analysing the ECB/ESCB's support for these policies forms both an implicit part of the ECB's primary price stability objective and an explicit part of its secondary objectives. For instance, regarding the ECB's pursuit of its secondary objective in Article 3(3) TEU to support 'a high level of protection and improvement of the quality of the environment', the objectives of price stability and environmental sustainability are

[18] Cornelia Manger-Nestler, 'The Architecture of EMU' in Fabian Amtenbrink and Christoph Herrmann (eds), *The EU Law of Economic and Monetary Union* (OUP 2020) 8.8–8.15; Christian Joerges, 'Pereat iustitia, fiat mundus, What is left of the European Economic Constitution after the Gauweiler Litigation' (2016) 23 MJ 99, 108.

[19] Fabian Amtenbrink and René Repasi, 'The German Federal Constitutional Court's Decision in Weiss: A Contextual Analysis' (2020) EL Rev 757, 759–63; Kathleen McNamara, 'Rational Fictions: Central Bank Independence and the Social Logic of Delegation' (2002) West European Politics 47, 54; Joseph Stiglitz, 'Central Banking in a Democratic Society' (1998) 146 *The Economist* 199, 210–12.

interlinked. Price stability is a precondition for environmental protection policies to succeed. Stable nominal prices are key to enabling the market to interpret correctly relative price signals. Simultaneously, timely and forceful environmental mitigation policies will diminish the effects on inflation and growth of environmental degradation. Hence, from a medium to longer-term perspective, one may surmise that price stability and environmental sustainability are mutually reinforcing policy objectives.

Similarly, another secondary objective to support financial stability can be interpreted in Article 127(5) TFEU that states: 'The ESCB shall contribute to the smooth conduct of policies pursued by the competent authorities relating to prudential supervision of credit institutions and the stability of the financial system.' While the Global Financial Crisis (GFC) of 2007–08 demonstrated the importance of financial stability for central banks, financial stability was not considered at the time the Maastricht Treaty was signed in 1992 as relevant to the 'primary' goal of price stability.[20] Indeed, while the wording of the Treaty is clear: 'The primary objective of the European System of Central Banks shall be to maintain price stability', the language of Article 127(5) TFEU is much less forceful and suggests that the Treaty language adopted in 1992 simply reflected the division of responsibilities at that time.

The 'basic' task conferred by the Maastricht Treaty onto the ECB was monetary policy (one goal: price stability, one instrument: monetary policy) while prudential supervision remained decentralized at the level of the Member States. However, there is now a consensus that the neglect of financial stability considerations in the early 2000s and inadequate supervision by Member State national competent authorities contributed to the 2007–08 GFC. So consideration of the ECB's role in financial stability (recognized in Articles 127(5) TFEU and 3.3 of the ESCB Statute), including any role it may exercise as a bank supervisor, should be assessed in terms of how it supports the ECB's principal objective of price stability. In other words, the ECB's role in financial stability is secondary to its primary mandate of price stability. Indeed, as discussed below, even with the Banking Union, the ECB's secondary objective of financial stability is shared with other Member State authorities and European institutions and bodies, which have a more primary and direct responsibility for financial stability, including Member State authorities having explicit competences for financial stability, including the use of macroprudential supervisory tools. In the EU, the pursuit of financial stability[21] transcends geographic boundaries and institutional mandates. It is a fundamental public good for the euro area and also for the single market in financial services.

The other condition mentioned in Article 127(1) TFEU, namely to act in accordance with the principle of an open market economy with free competition and favouring an efficient allocation of resources, and in compliance with the principles set out in Article 119 TFEU is a general statement of respect for market economics in the workings of the ESCB.[22] The potential limitations imposed by the Treaty principle of an

[20] See Rosa M Lastra, *International Financial and Monetary Law* (2nd edn, OUP 2015) 1265.

[21] On the ECB and financial stability, see chapter 5 by Agnieszka Smoleńska and Thomas Beukers, in this volume.

[22] As it is for the Union and the Member States under the Consolidated Version of the Treaty on the Functioning of the European Union [2012] OJ C326/47, Arts 119 and 120 (hereafter TFEU).

open market economy—also referred to as market neutrality—should be considered in the context of the secondary objective of providing 'a high level of protection and improvement of the quality of the environment'. In light of the climate change debate, in which environmental sustainability risks continue to be mispriced because of multiple market failures in the European financial system, it is questionable whether the market neutrality principle applies at all.[23] The legal rationale of the principle of an open market economy, namely, that it favours 'an efficient allocation of resources', no longer holds true in the face of dysfunctional markets, which arise from the physical and transition risks of environmentally unsustainable economic activity. Moreover, the absence of market neutrality is demonstrated most clearly by the distortions that the ECB itself directly creates in the financial system through its extensive asset purchase programmes and related quantitative easing measures that have substantially disrupted the market price of financial assets. But even if this vague principle were applied, monetary measures to counteract existing market failures and other distortions may still be necessary and proportionate in that their benefits for price stability may outweigh the costs or obstacles posed to an open market economy.

In the euro area, the different jurisdictional domains of the EU and the Member States (of the euro area) make it difficult for the ECB to reconcile the pursuit of the primary and the secondary objectives, as well as for the ECB to coordinate its pursuit of its secondary objectives in a decentralized manner with Member State economic policies. As we have already noted, whilst price stability in the euro area is a Union objective pursued by a single centralized monetary policy, the pursuit of the secondary objectives, including environmental protection and financial stability, relies upon decentralized fiscal policies and financial stability measures (subject to coordination). During the COVID-19 crisis, Member State fiscal mechanisms and funding have been challenged, but the adoption of the EU Recovery Plan consisting of the Multiannual Financial Framework (€1,074 billion ordinary budget) and the Next Generation EU (€750 billion extraordinary budget) demonstrates improved Member State fiscal coordination in comparison with the post-crisis response to the GFC.[24] In contrast, in countries such as the United Kingdom, where the jurisdictional domain of monetary, financial, and fiscal policy is coordinated, the support of the economic policy of Her Majesty's Government, including its objectives for growth and employment, is aligned more directly with the Bank of England's use of monetary policy tools to support its price stability mandate or its use of macroprudential tools to promote financial stability.[25] In this regard, the Banking Union has created new challenges for the ECB in coordinating and reconciling its pursuit of the price stability objective with its tasks to ensure the stability of banking institutions in the Banking Union. As discussed below, these challenges seem to be of a substantive and institutional nature. Substantively,

[23] For an argument for 'market attentiveness', see chapter 4 by Jens van 't Klooster, in this volume.

[24] See Eirini Chrysolora, Interview with Fabio Panetta, Member of the Executive Board of the ECB (17 October 2020), stating that '[m]onetary policy and fiscal policy reacted rapidly to the shock and have mutually reinforced each other. Together, monetary policy and fiscal policy have increased confidence'. See chapter 14 by Ad van Riet, in this volume.

[25] See Silvana Teneyro, 'Covid-19 and the economy: what are the lessons so far?' (Speech at a London School of Economics webinar, 15 July 2020) 5 <www.bankofengland.co.uk/speech/2020/silvana-tenreyro-speech-as-part-of-the-lse-covid-19-policy-response-webinar-series> accessed 29 May 2021.

the ECB's pursuit of its prudential supervisory tasks for banking institutions can only be assessed within the constraints created by its pursuit of its principal objective of price stability. Its institutional challenge is to ensure that within the ECB its Banking Union tasks (ie prudential supervision) are carried out effectively—and quite possibly pursued independently—from its other principal task (ie monetary policy). The next section will analyse these challenges and examine the implications for the ECB in the future.

III. The Banking Union and the Single Supervisory Mechanism

The SSM was designed to enhance supervision of the European banking sector and to promote European banking stability and financial integration following the euro area sovereign debt crisis of 2010–12 and the associated banking sector collapses particularly in Spain (2011–12), Ireland (2008–09), and Cyprus (2012–13). Under the SSM, the ECB carries out prudential supervision of credit institutions and financial holding companies established in participating Member States and allocates supervisory responsibilities to the national competent authorities of participating Member States to supervise less significant institutions.[26] The SSM raises important legal and institutional issues regarding the extent and scope of the ECB's competence to supervise credit institutions and banking groups, especially on a cross-border basis, and whether or not its powers and capabilities are adequate to achieve prudential regulatory objectives.

A. The legal basis of ECB supervision

Under the Treaty (TFEU), the ECB initially did not have conferred powers to exercise supervision over credit and other financial institutions unless it was authorized by unanimous consent of all Member States voting in the Council.[27] The so-called enabling clause of Article 127(6) TFEU requires the Council to approve unanimously the triggering of the ECB's competence to act as a supervisor for credit and other financial institutions.[28] According to the language of Article 127(6), however, the ECB can only

[26] See SSM Regulation (n 1) Art 6(4), providing that the ECB has exclusive competence for all credit institutions in the euro area for the tasks listed in Art 4(1)(a) and (c) (ie authorization and withdrawal thereof and assessment of qualifying holdings) but in case of less significant institutions the tasks are carried out by national competence authorities. See discussion in Alexander, 'European Banking Union' (n 2) 28–31 and also chapter 8 by Federico Della Negra and Gianni Lo Schiavo, in this volume.

[27] The rationale for prohibiting central banks from conducting prudential supervision and for the separation of bank supervisory tasks to a separate regulator was the concern of many economists in the 1990s that moral hazard could lead central banks to pursue a more accommodating monetary policy (less stringent in pursuit of the inflation target) in order to support ailing banks or other financial institutions during periods of market distress. See Charles Goodhart and others, *Financial Regulation: Why, How, and Where Now?* (Routledge 1998).

[28] TFEU (n 22) Art 127(6) provides that the Council may confer specific tasks upon the ECB concerning policies relating to the prudential supervision of credit institutions (banks) and other financial institutions with the exception of insurance undertakings.

have supervisory powers conferred on it 'concerning policies relating to the prudential supervision of credit institutions and other financial institutions with the exception of insurance undertakings'.[29] This means it can only have supervisory powers conferred on it for individual credit and financial institutions, not wider powers involving bank resolution, nor oversight of financial conglomerates or investment firms not defined under EU law as 'credit or other financial institutions'. This would also exclude the supervision of other financial firms or areas of the financial markets, such as clearing and settlement and the so-called shadow banking market.[30] The restrictive language of Article 127(6) TFEU is presumably why the SSM Regulation was designed to apply only to individual 'credit institutions' as defined under EU law and to the larger banking groups in which they are owned or controlled.

As discussed below, the enumerated microprudential supervisory tasks set forth in Article 4(1)(a) and (c) of the SSM Regulation suggests a rather limited scope of competence for the ECB in its supervisory oversight of the financial system, excluding, among other things, the shadow banking industry, the wholesale structured securities markets and the over-the-counter derivatives markets and derivatives clearing houses, and bank resolution, probably because of the rather limited constitutional basis for such authority in Article 127(6) TFEU that does not authorize the ECB to carry out broader supervisory powers over the financial system beyond that of credit and financial institutions and the groups in which they operate. This should be considered within the broader context of the scope of the ECB's price stability mandate and the extent to which it must coordinate with Member States in a decentralized system of oversight in respect of the general economic policies of the Union including ensuring the stability of the financial system.

B. ECB competences and tasks as a bank supervisor

The SSM's overriding objectives are to ensure safety and soundness of the European banking system and to ensure the unity and integrity of the EU internal market. The ECB's supervisory tasks are enumerated in Articles 4 and 5 of the SSM Regulation. Before discussing these powers, it is important to bear in mind that, generally, banking regulation consists of developing and adopting principles, standards, and rules that govern, among other things, minimum capital levels, disclosure requirements, and conduct standards for bankers, including senior management and board members. Whereas, banking supervision involves monitoring and surveillance of compliance

[29] TFEU (n 22) Art 13(2) provides that EU institutions operate under the doctrine of conferred powers, which holds that public institutions are constrained by law, in this case the EU Treaty, because they are creatures of law. See Case C-133/06 *Parliament v Council* [2008] ECLI:EU:C:2008:257, paras 44 and 54, holding, inter alia, 'each institution is to act within the powers conferred upon it by the Treaty', and 'it has already been held that the rules regarding the manner in which the Community institutions arrive at their decisions are laid down in the Treaty and are not at the disposal of the Member States of the institutions themselves'.

[30] See Financial Stability Board, 'Shadow Banking: Strengthening Oversight and Regulation—Recommendations of the Financial Stability Board' (October 2011) 2 <www.fsb.org/wp-content/uploads/r_111027a.pdf> accessed 29 May 2021. The Financial Stability Board defines shadow banking as 'a system of credit intermediation that involves entities and activities outside the regular banking system'.

by both institutions and individuals and is concerned with investigations and enforcement against institutions or individuals allegedly in violation of regulations.[31]

Based on the enabling provision of Article 127(6) TFEU the ECB's competence to pursue 'policies relating to the prudential supervision of credit institutions and other financial institutions with the exception of insurance undertakings' was triggered by unanimous Council agreement in 2012 thus providing the political basis for the European Commission to propose, in September 2012, the draft SSM Regulation.[32] The ECB's prudential regulatory authority and supervisory powers are enumerated in the SSM Regulation of 2013 and the allocation of home–host state competencies for the supervision of cross-border institutions are set forth in the SSM Framework Regulation of 2014.[33] The substantive content of ECB and Member State supervisory powers in the form of prudential regulations are set forth in the Capital Requirements Regulation (CRR) and Capital Requirements Directive (CRD).[34] The CRR defines the capital and liquidity adequacy requirements for credit institutions, while the CRD defines requirements for sound corporate governance, including remuneration limits on risk-takers, design of stress tests, and counter-cyclical capital buffers and effective and dissuasive administrative sanctions, including penalties.

EU legislation does not define as prudential regulation the regulatory standards and rules that are designed mainly to protect investors, customers, and to ensure the integrity of financial markets. These latter regulatory standards fall under the category of conduct of business rules, which tend to be more investor and consumer focused, for example, addressing the mis-selling of financial products, market abuse, and anti-money laundering controls. In some European Member States, regulatory law allocates regulatory and supervisory responsibilities to two different institutional authorities: a prudential regulator and a conduct of business regulator. This so-called Twin Peaks approach is followed in several EU Member States and in principle is partly respected by the ECB to the extent that its competence and authority derive from Article 127(6) TFEU and apply only regarding the 'policies relating to the prudential supervision of credit institutions and other financial institutions', the latter of which are defined under EU secondary law.

The SSM Regulation specifies, in Article 4(1), that the ECB shall have competence and the powers to supervise credit institutions and banking groups by applying and enforcing the relevant provisions of EU banking law, such as the CRR and CRD.[35]

[31] See Alexander, *Principles of Banking Regulation* (n 9) 41–44.

[32] Based on the doctrine of conferred powers, the ECB derives its competence from the Treaty and by secondary legislation that elaborates on the meaning of the language in the Treaty that confers powers in respect of prudential supervision.

[33] See Regulation (EU) no 468/2014 of the European Central Bank of 16 April 2014 establishing the framework for cooperation within the Single Supervisory Mechanism between the European Central Bank and national competent authorities and with national designated authorities (SSM Framework Regulation) (ECB/2014/17) [2014] OJ L141.

[34] Directive 2013/36/EU of the European Parliament and of the Council of 26 June 2013 on access to the activity of credit institutions and the prudential supervision of credit institutions and investment firms, amending Directive 2002/87/EC and repealing Directives 2006/48/EC and 2006/49/EC [2013] OJ L176/338 (hereafter CRD IV). Regulation (EU) no 575/2013 of the European Parliament and of the Council of 26 June 2013 on prudential requirements for credit institutions and investment firms [2013] OJ L176 (hereafter CRR).

[35] See CRD IV (n 34); see CRR (n 34). In addition, the Directive (EU) 2019/878 of the European Parliament and of the Council of 20 May 2019 amending Directive 2013/36/EU as regards exempted entities, financial

The subject matter or area of competence for the ECB is enumerated in Article 4 of the SSM Regulation that empowers the ECB to monitor capital adequacy, liquidity buffers, and leverage limits[36] and approve bank recovery plans and asset transfers between affiliates within banking groups or mixed financial conglomerates.[37] The broad scope and extent of the ECB's supervisory powers is probably most robustly expressed in Article 4(3), first subparagraph, which specifies that:

> the ECB shall apply all relevant Union law, and where this Union law is composed of Directives, the national legislation transposing those Directives. Where the relevant Union law is composed of Regulations and where currently those Regulation explicitly grant options for Member States, the ECB shall apply also the national legislation exercising those options.[38]

This so-called 'cornerstone' provision, in conjunction with Article 9(1) of the Regulation combined with recitals 34 and 35, sets forth the legal basis establishing the ECB's 'direct' supervisory powers in respect of significant entities and the exercise of options and discretions granted to Member States under EU prudential supervisory law.[39] These provisions have dramatically restructured the traditional decentralized system of Member State competences in the area of banking supervision under EU law by vesting centralized authority with the ECB to exercise not only exclusive competence in approving the authorization of institutions and their acquisition of qualifying holdings in other credit institutions along with the enumerated competences in Article 4(1)–(3), but also the prudential bank requirements found in EU Regulations, such as the CRR, including their discretions and options, and also the supervisory powers set forth in Member State domestic law that derive from EU prudential banking law, such as the CRD. In carrying out these prudential supervisory powers, the SSM allocates day-to-day supervisory duties to the national competent authorities of participating Member States for less significant institutions to be discharged under the oversight and direction of the ECB.[40]

holding companies, mixed financial holding companies, remuneration, supervisory measures and powers and capital conservation measures [2019] OJ L150/253 (hereafter CRD V) and the Regulation (EU) 2019/876 of the European Parliament and of the Council of 20 May 2019 amending Regulation (EU) no 575/2013 as regards the leverage ratio, the net stable funding ratio, requirements for own funds and eligible liabilities, counterparty credit risk, market risk, exposures to central counterparties, exposures to collective investment undertakings, large exposures, reporting and disclosure requirements, and Regulation (EU) no 648/2012 [2019] OJ L150/1 (hereafter CRR II), whereby CRR II will apply from 28 June 2021 (CRR II Art 3). Member States must adopt the necessary measures to comply with CRD V by 28 December 2020 (CRD V Art 2). However, due to the recent COVID-19 crisis, Regulation (EU) 2020/873 of the European Parliament and of the Council of 24 June 2020 amending Regulations (EU) no 575/2013 and (EU) 2019/876 as regards certain adjustments in response to the COVID-19 pandemic [2020] OJ L204/4, already applies from 27 June 2020 to give institutions a better possibility to cope with the COVID-19 crisis.

[36] SSM Regulation (n 1) Art 4(1)–(3), especially Art 4(1)(d) and (e).

[37] ibid Art 4(1)(g) and (h) mention 'mixed financial holding companies' and 'financial conglomerate', respectively, over which the ECB has certain supervisory powers.

[38] ibid Art 4(3)(1).

[39] See discussion in Giovanni Bassani, 'The Centralisation of Prudential Supervision in the Euro Area: The Emergence of a New "Conventional Wisdom" and the Establishment of the SSM' (2020) 31 EBLR 1001, 1007–09.

[40] SSM Regulation (n 1) Art 1.

Under the SSM Regulation, the ECB is a bank supervisor responsible for oversight and surveillance of individual credit institutions but does not promulgate the regulatory and technical implementing standards, which are adopted by the European Banking Authority and approved by the European Commission.[41] This division of responsibilities exists in order to ensure the integrity of the EU internal market through the harmonized implementation of EU law by all Member States, including the ECB acting as the bank supervisor for Banking Union Member States, based on the EBA's adoption of regulatory implementing and technical standards. Nevertheless, the CJEU recognized in the *Förderbank* case[42] the 'important prerogatives' retained by the ECB, including that it may issue regulations, guidelines, and general instructions to national competent authorities regarding their supervisory practices, and may also in its discretion assume the powers of national authorities with regard to one or more credit institutions.[43]

C. The Supervisory Board

The ECB acts through an executive board—the Supervisory Board[44]—which is responsible for supervising directly and licensing the euro area's largest cross-border banks and the top three banks by size in each participating Member State. The Supervisory Board is also responsible for overseeing the supervisory actions of participating national competent authorities who directly supervise small and medium-sized credit institutions in the SSM regime.[45] The Supervisory Board takes final supervisory decisions (with ultimate approval by the ECB Governing Council) against larger, systemically important institutions regarding compliance with and enforcement of prudential regulatory requirements set forth by EU secondary law, including capital adequacy requirements, liquidity buffers, leverage limits, oversight of bank governance, and stress testing.[46] The institutional design of the Supervisory Board, whose decisions are subject to ultimate review by the Governing Council, reflects both the primacy of the price stability mandate as set forth in Article 127(1) TFEU and the institutional challenge of separating the ECB's monetary policy tasks from other tasks conferred on the ECB through EU legislation, including its new tasks in the Banking Union.

The Supervisory Board is responsible for overseeing supervision of 'significant' banks (ie large cross-border euro area banks), which constitute over 80 per cent of

[41] See Nikoletta Kleftouri, *Deposit Protection and Bank Resolution* (OUP 2015) 83–88 (discussing European Banking Authority and its powers to adopt technical and regulatory implementing standards).

[42] Case T-122/15 *Landeskreditbank Baden-Wurtemberg-Forderbank v European Central Bank* [2017] ECLI:EU:T:2017:337, para 59.

[43] SSM Regulation (n 1) Art 6(5)(a) and (b).

[44] ibid Art 26 ('planning and execution of the tasks conferred on the ECB shall be fully undertaken by an internal body composed of its Chair and Vice Chair').

[45] ibid Art 6(7)(a)–(c). See also Art 25(8) (the Supervisory Board shall adopt 'draft decisions' 'to be transmitted to the national competent authorities of the Member States concerned'). See chapter 8 by Federico Della Negra and Gianni Lo Schiavo, in this volume.

[46] ibid Art 4(1)(b), (d)–(i) and Art 6(4)–(6) e contrario.

banking assets in the euro area.[47] The criteria used to define a bank as significant are: total value of assets; whether it is one of the top three largest banks in its home Member State; its importance to the economy of its home state or the EU as a whole; and whether it has requested or received direct public financial assistance from the European Stability Mechanism (ESM) or the European Financial Stability Facility (ESFS).[48]

The Supervisory Board utilizes joint supervisory teams (JSTs) to oversee the operations of the significant banks. The ECB has built on the EBA's practice of establishing colleges of supervisors consisting of home and host state supervisors in the Member States where banks operate by creating JSTs that conduct day-to-day supervision of ECB supervised credit institutions.[49] The JSTs consist of supervisory representatives from many of the colleges and technical expert groups. The JSTs have been praised as achieving much progress in enhancing the robustness of supervision since the creation of the SSM, including improved collaboration between different supervisory tasks and establishing trust between JST members from different NCAs. Some supervisors, however, have noted challenges to their effectiveness, including geographical distance, language barriers, multi-dimensional reporting lines, and different supervisory cultures, all of which together have undermined effective communication and transparency of decision-making.[50] To address these weaknesses, the former President of the Banque de France and some NCAs have stated that the Supervisory Board should work with NCAs to develop common review processes that would be followed by all JSTs which would deal with these concerns.[51]

Under the SSM, the ECB acting through the Supervisory Board is also indirectly responsible for overseeing the supervisory actions of national competent authorities responsible for supervising small and medium-sized (less systemically important) banks in participating Member States.[52] The ECB has ultimate discretionary authority to decide whether to intervene and to take supervisory decisions that could supersede the decisions of national competent authorities with respect to smaller credit institutions which the ECB does not directly supervise. Essentially, the ECB's competence (based on Article 127(6) TFEU and as defined more precisely in the SSM Regulation) is to ensure that its tasks (as enumerated in Article 4 SSM regulation) are fulfilled by supervision of 'significant' credit institutions and the financial groups in which they operate and to be indirectly responsible for—and to have discretionary authority—ensuring that the supervisory tasks set forth in Article 4 SSM Regulation are fulfilled, which

[47] As of January 2021, the ECB directly supervises 115 credit institutions in the Banking Union. See European Central Bank, Banking Supervision webpage <https://www.bankingsupervision.europa.eu/banking/list/html/index.en.html> accessed 29 May 2021.

[48] SSM Regulation (n 1) Art 6(4)(i)–(iii).

[49] See Kern Alexander, 'European Banking Union: Effectiveness, Impact and Future Challenges' in Danny Busch and Guido Ferrarini (eds), *European Banking Union* (2nd edn, OUP 2020) 27–91, 64–65.

[50] See Stefan Iwankowski and Miguel Guthausen, 'Two years of the SSM: a lot done, a lot more to do' (2016) BaFin Division for SSM/SB Coordination <https://www.bafin.de/SharedDocs/Veroeffentlichungen/EN/Fachartikel/2016/fa_bj_1610_EinheitlicherAufsichtsmechanismus_en.html> accessed 29 May 2021.

[51] Frederic Visnovsky, 'Le Mecanisme de Supervision Unique Deux Ans Apres' (Seminaire de Recherché Sciences-Po/Banque de France, 23 November 2016).

[52] SSM Regulation (n 1) Art 4(1).

may entail taking direct oversight of small and medium-sized institutions that are ordinarily subject to direct supervisory control by national competent authorities.[53]

Among other tasks, the Supervisory Board is empowered to approve bank recovery plans[54] or make use of supervisory measures that aim to address systemic risks at the level of individual banks.[55] For banks not significant enough to fall under the direct supervision of the ECB, these tasks will be exercised by national authorities, nonetheless following the regulations, guidelines, and general instructions issued by the ECB to that effect.[56]

The SSM regulatory system is complex because of its federal structure, which aims to incentivize information sharing among national regulators and the central coordinating regulator (as well as the interaction with the countries outside the euro area). The shift towards ECB supervision represents a toughening of enforcement, since national supervisors had incentives to be more lenient with their national banks under the pre-SSM regime.[57]

Even with the creation of the European Banking Authority at the EU level to promote a more harmonized system of supervision across Member States and to oversee the implementation and application of harmonized technical and regulatory standards (the so-called single rulebook) for banking supervision, the challenge of coordination among decentralized regulators and supervisors within the EU remains acute. Indeed, a supervisor based in another EU state is less likely to consider the consequences (systemic or not) for domestic residents of failure, or restructuring of a local branch or subsidiary, but only the consequences in terms of systemic stability at home. For example, a consequence of the 2007–08 financial crisis was that some host Member State supervisors have limited or even forbidden the local subsidiaries of EU/EEA-based banks from transferring liquidity across jurisdictions.[58] This is why the creation of the Banking Union and in particular the SSM with the ECB taking full responsibility for supervising the largest euro area banks and for overseeing the supervision of smaller banks by the national competent authorities has been an important innovation in the development of EU banking supervision.

All euro area Member States are automatically SSM members, while non-euro area members can decide to participate in the SSM through a procedure involving

[53] ibid Art 6(5)(b), 'when necessary to ensure consistent application of high supervisory standards, the ECB may at any time, or on its own initiative after consulting with national competent authorities or upon request by a national competent authority, decide to exercise directly itself all the relevant powers for one or more credit institutions'.

[54] ibid Art 4(1)(i).

[55] CRD IV (n 34) Art 97(1)(b), discussing the review of systemic risks affecting the Member State's financial system, and Arts 104–105, and the subsequent imposition of specific capital, liquidity, operational, or governance requirements addressing those risks.

[56] SSM Regulation (n 1) Art 6(4)–(6).

[57] See Silvia Allegrezza, 'The Single Supervisory Mechanism: Institutional Design, Punitive Powers and the Interplay with Criminal Law' in Silvia Allegrezza, *The Enforcement Dimension of the Single Supervisory Mechanism* (Kluwer 2020) 4–5. See also Andrea Enria, 'Oral Evidence before the House of Lords and House of Commons Joint Select Committee on the draft Financial Services Bill' (Session 2010–12, 13 September 2011).

[58] See Sharlene Goff and Elaine Moore, 'Bank of Cyprus seeks FSA cover for UK savers' *Financial Times* (London, 6 June 2012) <www.ft.com/content/b1121e20-afd9-11e1-b737-00144feabdc0> accessed 29 May 2021. See also Sharlene Goff, 'Santander seeks cover from pain in Spain' *Financial Times* (London, 29 October 2010) <www.ft.com/content/3eedbc74-e388-11df-8ad3-00144feabdc0> accessed 29 May 2021.

the national competent authority entering into a 'close cooperation' with the ECB.[59] In 2020, for example, Bulgaria and Croatia—two non-euro area Member States—joined the Banking Union and the SSM as participating Member States. For the other Member States that are non-participating in the BU, the ECB has adopted a memorandum of understanding (MoU) with the relevant national competent authority that explains how the ECB will cooperate with the NCA in performing their respective supervisory tasks.[60] The ECB also has concluded memoranda of understanding with each competent authority of EU states outside the Banking Union where systemically important financial institutions with operations in the Banking Union are based.[61]

As mentioned above, a significant limitation of the SSM is that the ECB only has jurisdiction to apply and enforce EU prudential banking law and regulatory requirements against 'credit institutions' defined as such under EU law.[62] For instance, financial institutions that do not accept retail deposits are not defined as 'credit institutions' under EU law and therefore are not subject to SSM jurisdiction.[63] Similarly, a 'credit institution' subject to SSM jurisdiction for carrying on activities governed by EU prudential banking law is not subject to SSM jurisdiction for activities not subject to EU prudential banking law, such as brokering and dealing securities or the marketing and sale of retail financial products. For such non-prudential activities, the bank would be subject to other EU banking and financial law requirements, such as conduct of business rules, which are the sole responsibility of national competent authorities to monitor and enforce (not the ECB).

D. ECB, banking regulation, and sustainability

The European Commission adopted a Sustainable Finance Action Plan in 2018,[64] which proposed amendments to the CRD V that delegate authority to the EBA to undertake assessments of the materiality of sustainability risks and to recommend how they should be included in prudential regulatory requirements (such as exposure limits) and for the EBA to report back to the Commission regarding several categories

[59] SSM Regulation (n 1) Art 7(1), (2)(a)—(c) providing the legal requirements for ECB cooperation with national competent authorities that enter 'close cooperation' with the SSM, including rules that apply directly to banks established in participating countries. On 1 October 2020, Croatia and Bulgaria joined the Banking Union as part of the legal mechanism of 'close cooperation' of participating Member States. See ECB website: <https://www.bankingsupervision.europa.eu/press/pr/date/2020/html/ssm.pr200710~ae2abe1f23.en.html> accessed 29 May 2021.

[60] SSM Regulation (n 1) Art 8.

[61] ibid Art 6(7)(b).

[62] 'Credit institution' is defined as a firm which accepts deposits from the public that are insured by the EU Deposit Guarantee Scheme Directive. See CRD IV (n 34), entered into force 1 January 2014.

[63] See CRR (n 34) Art 4.1(1).

[64] European Commission, 'Action Plan: Financing Sustainable Growth' (Communication) COM (2018) 97 final. See also, Kern Alexander and Paul Fisher, 'Central Banking and Climate Change' (2019) Research Network for Sustainable Finance Working Paper No. 17-19 <https://www.ius.uzh.ch/dam/jcr:41b9c485-4653-48c9-9eb1-25c58d3e6619/Fisher%20and%20Alexander%20first%20revision.pdf> accessed 29 May 2021, arguing that the EU prudential rulebook should remain risk based if and when it includes sustainability risk measures to calculate regulatory capital.

of risks between 2021 and 2025.[65] This could potentially lead to amendments to the EU bank regulatory rulebook that the ECB is required to apply as bank supervisor.

These developments at the EU level will have implications for how the ECB carries out its supervisory responsibilities under the SSM, particularly how it plans to carry out changes to incorporate climate and other sustainability risks into its supervisory review enhancement programme and what its input is likely to be in the forthcoming EBA Reports that will assess the materiality of these risks. Indeed, the ECB's expectations for banks regarding how they manage the financial risks associated with sustainability are evolving.[66] The ECB is a member of the Network for Greening the Financial System (NGFS) and its contribution to that forum should be monitored by the European Parliament in order to gauge how it might fulfil its supervisory responsibilities in this area and to assess the scope of its mandate as a European institution bound to provisions such as Article 11 TFEU and to its very own secondary objective which refers to Article 3 TEU. In this regard, the chairman of the NGFS, Frank Elderson, stated in the NGFS Annual Report 2019 that:

> Currently, the Coronavirus and its consequences seem to overshadow everything else and, no doubt, they require coordinated action. However, even in this crisis, we should not lose sight of the fact that climate change stays an urgent and vital issue. Hence, the NGFS members' strong response to continue their collective contribution to the greening of the financial system is key. The greener the recovery from the current crisis is, the better.[67]

In addition, the ECB will have to comply with the amendments to the CRR that became effective in 2020 and relate to the incorporation of sustainability metrics and other criteria into EU prudential financial regulation.[68] These changes to EU banking regulation will place the ECB into the forefront of ensuring that credit institutions and connected financial groups are identifying and managing environmental and social risks. For instance, the ECB can help banks build stress tests based on forward-looking scenarios that will help the industry judge what its capital and liquidity requirements should be in the face of physical risks caused by intensifying environmental or social phenomena caused by climate change, loss of biodiversity, and related pandemics, and increasing social risks associated with growing inequality, inadequate health care, and intensifying migration patterns. The ECB will also be concerned with the

[65] The CRD V instructs the EBA to report—by 28 June 2021 on inclusion of Environmental, Social and Governance (ESG) risks in the Supervisory Review and Evaluation Process (SREP) (CRD V (n 35) Art 98(8)) (and)—by 28 June 2025 'whether a dedicated prudential treatment of exposures related to assets or activities associated substantially with environmental and/or social objectives would be justified', 'if appropriate' followed by a legislative proposal from the Commission (CRR II (n 35) Art 501c). The CRR 2124 provides for—disclosure of ESG risks, as defined by the EBA report, by large institutions as of 28 June 2022 'on an annual basis for the first year and biannually thereafter' (CRR II (n 35) Art 449a).

[66] See chapter 4 by Jens van 't Klooster, in this volume.

[67] Network for Greening the Financial System, 'NGFS Annual Report 2019' (NGFS 2020) 2 <www.ngfs.net/sites/default/files/medias/documents/ngfs_annual_report_2019.pdf> accessed 29 May 2021.

[68] CRR II (n 35) Art 501c, providing a green supporting factor measuring sustainability risks and own funds. EBA must assess whether a dedicated prudential treatment of exposures related to assets or activities associated substantially with environmental and/or social objectives would be justified. The European Banking Authority shall submit a report on its findings by 28 June 2025.

sustainability challenges associated with the volatility in asset prices and sudden reallocation of capital away from unsustainable high carbon economic sectors to lower carbon sustainable sectors.

E. ECB primary task of price stability and new supervisory role

The ECB's role as a bank supervisor may have implications for (and possibly bring it into conflict with) its pursuit of its Treaty objective of price stability.[69] According to this view, the ECB might be tempted to lower interest rates or to loosen conditions for bank access to liquidity in order to stabilize the banking sector, but this might lead to easier terms of credit thereby increasing inflation and potentially undermining price stability.[70] This is why supervisory mandates for central banks tend to be controversial. In general, the price stability mandate of central banks is obstructed by short-term goals, for example avoiding high interest rates and unemployment due to electoral and political pressures—hence the need for central banks to be independent so that they are immune from these pressures.[71]

Accordingly, a central bank receiving explicit or implicit employment or economic growth mandates will face the same conflict. A supervisory mandate thus potentially results in lenient monetary policies to prevent bank illiquidity and insolvency; central banks also enjoy easier 'bureaucratic entrenchment' than a supervision-only agency would, making them less accountable for the moral hazard they create. The optimal governance architecture needed for such a double mandate is unclear: law-makers struggle to combine an efficient relationship between the monetary and supervisory sides whilst yet ensuring adequate accountability.[72] Other governance issues are both external (especially towards national competent authorities) and internal, such as the transparency of central bank policies: while excessive transparency may potentially damage the credibility of central banks, for example when responding to temporary market disturbance, empirical evidence shows that higher transparency in forecasts is associated with lower average inflation, and to some extent less inflation persistence as well as reduced inflation volatility.[73]

The SSM Regulation attempts to address the potential conflict in dual central bank mandates by requiring that bank supervision decisions and monetary policy be strictly separated by creating a Supervisory Board, which has separate staff to work solely on

[69] TFEU (n 22) Art 127(6) provides that 'price stability' is the primary objective of the European System of Central Banks. In relation to the ECB's primary objective of 'price stability', a 'financial stability' objective is mentioned incidentally in TFEU Art 127(5) as follows: 'The ESCB shall contribute to the smooth conduct of policies pursued by the competent authorities relating to the prudential supervision of credit institutions and the stability of the financial system'. See chapter 5 by Agnieszka Smoleńska and Thomas Beukers, in this volume.

[70] This is why Principle 2 of the Basel Core Principles for Effective Banking Supervision recommends that the functions of the bank supervisor and monetary policy-maker be independent from one another. See Bank for International Settlements, 'Core Principles for Effective Banking Supervision' (Basel Committee on Banking Supervision, 14 September 2012), Principle 2 <https://www.bis.org/publ/bcbs230.htm> accessed 29 May 2021.

[71] See chapter 10 by Alexander Thiele, in this volume.

[72] See chapter 11 by Fabian Amtenbrink and Menelaos Markakis, in this volume.

[73] ibid.

banking supervision matters while not having links with staff involved with monetary policy.[74] It is an important policy objective, therefore, for the ECB that supervision and monetary policy are 'rigorously separated', and the Supervisory Board governance structure allows national supervisors to play a significant role in any supervisory plan for participating states.

The SSM Regulation attempts to address this institutional challenge with Article 25 that governs the Supervisory Board's organizational structure and which requires that the Supervisory Board's operational functions are separate from the ECB's monetary policy operations and related functions.[75] For instance, the SSM tasks are further prohibited from interfering with or being determined by the ECB's other mandates, whether in relation to the European Systemic Risk Board or to the solvency monitoring of monetary policy counterparties.[76] Indeed, the separation between monetary policy and supervisory tasks within the ECB is reinforced by a requirement to ensure the organizational separation of both the staff involved and their reporting lines.[77] Beyond the separation of the staff involved on both sides of these firewalls, the Regulation requires the ECB to ensure an operational separation for the Governing Council itself as regards monetary and supervisory functions, for example through separated meetings and agendas. Moreover, the procedure for appointing the Chair and Vice Chair of the Supervisory Board also reflects this separation: rather than having the ECB Governing Council elect a member of the Supervisory Board, the Chair and Vice Chair are now appointed by the ECOFIN and cannot be a member of the ECB Governing Council.[78]

The Supervisory Board's oversight of the SSM, however, is ultimately accountable to, and dependent for approval from, the ECB's Governing Council, whose strong form of independence is guaranteed by the Treaty and whose overriding mandate is to maintain price stability, which under the Treaty arguably takes precedence over the ECB's banking supervision mandate. However, the Governing Council's dual oversight of monetary policy and banking supervision will be subject to separate agendas that rely on separate groups of staff and reporting channels respectively to maintain a semblance of independence for the Council whilst making decisions on monetary policy and banking supervision.

[74] Germany insisted on separation of the ECB's supervisory functions from its monetary policy functions in order to protect ECB monetary policy from being influenced by the pursuit of banking supervision mandates. See Peter Mulbert, 'Presentation at European Company and Financial Law conference' (Bundestag, Berlin, 7 November 2014) (on file with author).

[75] SSM Regulation (n 1) Art 25 ('Separation from monetary policy function'). Art 25(2) states '[t]he ECB shall carry out the tasks conferred on it by this Regulation without prejudice to and separately from its tasks relating to monetary policy and any other tasks'.

[76] ibid Art 25(2).

[77] ibid.

[78] ibid Art 26(3). But the Supervisory Board's oversight of the SSM is ultimately accountable to the ECB's Governing Council, whose strong form of independence is guaranteed by the Treaty and whose overriding mandate is to maintain price stability, which under the Treaty arguably takes precedence over the ECB's banking supervision mandate. However, the Governing Council's dual oversight of monetary policy and banking supervision will be subject to separate agendas that rely on separate groups of staff and reporting channels respectively to maintain a semblance of independence for the Council whilst making decisions on monetary policy and banking supervision. However the Council's oversight of these dual areas is subject to the 'separation' requirement in Art 25, which mandates that Council decision-making is based on separate agendas that rely on separate staff and reporting channels.

Despite these provisions to ensure the independence of the ECB in carrying out its monetary policy and banking supervision functions, it is submitted that the ECB, in order to fulfil its price stability and banking supervision mandates, should have regard for broader macroprudential financial stability risks, which will necessitate a more comprehensive approach to macroprudential policy and the use of a wide-range of macroprudential tools. This will require some degree of coordination between monetary policy and banking supervision. Indeed, much of the literature justifying the separation of monetary policy from banking supervision arose in a period when monetary policy was seen to be independent from banking supervision and that the use of monetary policy instruments to increase bank lending in certain sectors of the economy (ie small and medium size businesses) were considered not to be within a central bank's mandate. However, since the GFC, central banks have adopted extraordinary measures of monetary policy (ie the ECB's Long-Term Refinancing Operations and the Pandemic Emergency Purchase Programmes (PEPPs)) that necessarily involve central banks in assessing the healthiness and viability of bank balance sheets in order to have a better understanding of whether they can lend to the broader economy in an effort to support their monetary policy objectives. This has particularly been the case with the ECB in the creation of its various asset purchase programmes and quantitative easing schemes, designed to stimulate bank lending with an overall view of increasing inflation to 2 per cent and promoting equivalent funding conditions for euro area sovereigns in order to ensure an effective monetary policy transmission mechanism.

The ECB should address whether the use of such expansionary measures requires it to have more information and a view as to the healthiness and ability of individual banks or groups of banks in order to support more lending to the broader economy. In financial systems where central bank use of monetary policy measures have grown to play such an important role in affecting bank lending and banking regulatory policy, it calls into question the utility of the strict separation between monetary policy and the supervision of individual banking institutions, thus questioning the strong degree of separation as mandated in Article 25 of the SSM Regulation between the ECB's monetary policy and its banking supervision functions. Further, the ECB's new mandates in banking supervision and the potentially more flexible interpretation of its secondary objectives to support the broad policies of the Union raises the important question whether the ECB should retain its primary mandate of price stability as set forth in Article 127(1) TFEU or should the Treaty be amended to have several mandates, such as price stability, financial stability, and stable economic growth (as the US Federal Reserve does).[79] Alternatively, if amending the Treaty is too fraught with political obstacles perhaps the ECB could reconceptualize its price stability mandate to place more emphasis on a more flexible pursuit of the secondary objectives as set forth in Article 3(3) TEU in order to contribute to and support its overall price stability objective.

In considering the latter option, the main legal principles that are relevant in this context are the inter-connected principles of proportionality and of an open market economy. For instance, the ECB should consider how a well-explained proportionality

[79] See chapter 15 by Christy-Ann Petit, in this volume.

assessment can include the release of analysis and supporting data that demonstrate the necessity of certain monetary policy measures, including a balancing of the measure's benefits, costs and unintended effects, all in the context of pursuing the price stability objective.

IV. Banking Union and the Single Resolution Mechanism

The second pillar of the Banking Union is the Single Resolution Mechanism (SRM). The SRM took effect in 2016 and operates through the Single Resolution Board (SRB), which has authority to take a bank or systemically important investment firm into resolution and to utilize resolution tools to restructure or recapitalize the institution, if necessary, to prevent a crisis and to avoid a taxpayer funded bailout. The SRB can draw on a Single Resolution Fund, which can provide temporary financing to a systemically important financial institution that may need to be wound down gradually to avoid a systemic crisis or bailout.

The rationale for bank resolution regimes is that an effective banking supervisory regime requires a coordinated process involving supervisory assessments of individual institutions with the monitoring of risks across the financial system along with crisis management measures, including the use of resolution tools to stabilize individual institutions that pose a threat to financial stability.[80] This allows unviable banks to be restructured or wound-up in a manner that does not precipitate or exacerbate a financial crisis. Prior to the GFC, most EU states did not have resolution regimes for banks and other systemically important firms. The European Union's Bank Recovery and Resolution Directive (BRRD),[81] which took effect on 1 January 2016, provides minimum legal standards requiring, among other things, that Member States adopt resolution laws and related regulations that include the creation of national resolution authorities (NRAs). NRAs are authorized to utilize resolution tools, namely, the sale of the business tool, the bridge institution tool, the asset separation tool, and the bail-in tool. Resolution authorities may execute the resolution tools individually or in any combination.[82]

For the ECB to carry out its functions effectively, it is submitted that it should play a meaningful role in supporting the competent authorities at the EU and national levels to take the necessary measures to take prompt corrective action in cases involving the possible resolution of a distressed bank that is systemically important.

[80] See SSM Regulation (n 1) recital 85; and European Commission, 'A Roadmap towards a Banking Union' COM (2012) 510 final, para 9; and European Council, 'Conclusions, EUCO 205/12' (CONCL 5, Brussels, 13–14 December 2012) <www.consilium.europa.eu/uedocs/cms_data/docs/pressdata/en/ec/134353.pdf> accessed 29 May 2021. See para 11, stating 'where bank supervision is effectively moved to a single supervisory mechanism, a single resolution mechanism will be required, with the necessary powers to ensure that any bank in participating Member States can be resolved with the appropriate tools'.

[81] BRRD (n 4) 190–348.

[82] ibid Art 37(3) enumerates the resolution tools as sale of business tool, bridge institution tool, asset separation tool, and the bail-in tool. Article 37(4) provides that resolution authorities have discretion whether or not to use the resolution tools, or in what combination to use them, including use of the bail-in tool to impose losses on bank liabilities, such as bondholders, when an institution is experiencing financial difficulties.

It is suggested in this section that although the ECB/SSM plays a role already in approving bank recovery plans and in recommending whether or not a bank should be taken into resolution, the ECB should play a more proactive role in the area of bank resolution. This would build on post-GFC international regulatory reforms that encourage national authorities to establish MoUs and other coordination mechanisms between supervisory and resolution authorities to create a seamless process between the microprudential supervision of individual institutions and the use of resolution tools to restructure a bank's liabilities during periods of market distress while enabling the institution to operate as a going concern.

A. The Single Resolution Mechanism

The SRM aims to create a more uniform and harmonized resolution process and substantive rules across the Banking Union that can more effectively place banks and certain investment firms experiencing solvency problems into resolution with minimal costs to taxpayers.[83] The SRM applies the substantive rules of the BRRD to banks that are supervised by the ECB/SSM, but also has more extensive jurisdiction over systemically important investment firms. Unlike the SSM, the SRM's SRB has direct oversight of resolution matters for over 6,000 credit institutions and investment firms based in the euro area, regardless of their size and cross-border operations.[84] Whereas the ECB is responsible for direct supervision of the largest and systemically important banking institutions—about 130 banking groups—NCAs exercise delegated supervision for about 3,500 banking groups in the Banking Union.

Given that the SRM Regulation was agreed in 2014 and became effective in 2016, the SRB is not explicitly mentioned in the SSM Regulation that was agreed in 2013 and took effect in 2014, but the SSM Regulation contains a general reference to the role of a resolution authority. An important difference arises between the ECB's scope of direct supervision and the remit of national resolution authorities falling under the competence of the SRB. Compared to the SSM, the SRB has wider jurisdiction, covering credit institutions and non-bank financial institutions and large systemically important non-bank financial institutions not directly supervised by the ECB. These institutional and jurisdictional overlaps and gaps reflect a certain lack of symmetry in the design of the BU's supervision and resolution frameworks. For instance, the ECB only has direct authority to make determinations of whether a bank should be taken into resolution under the SRM regime for about 130 banking groups and only indirect authority to make such a determination through the relevant NCAs for the other 3,500 small and medium-sized credit institutions. In contrast, the SRB must consult with the relevant NCAs—either central banks, standalone bank supervisors, or securities regulators—in order to trigger the resolutions of covered investment firms and certain financial groups not subject to SSM supervision.

The BRRD and SRM regulations provide a badly needed resolution regime for the EU and Banking Union, respectively, which did not previously exist, and can only

[83] SRM Regulation (n 1) recital 12.
[84] ibid Arts 2 and 6(1)–(7).

supplement and enhance the EU regulatory and supervisory framework for banking institutions, particularly in the Banking Union where the ECB has taken on important new supervisory functions. For instance, under the BRRD, banks and covered investment firms are required to hold minimum required eligible liabilities (MREL) as loss-absorbent capital.[85] Under the BRRD and SRM Regulation, MREL capital was a new type of capital requirement (also referred to as 'bail-in-able-debt') that could take the form of debt (or equity) or a hybrid instrument (both debt and equity) so long as it was loss absorbent and could result in losses imposed on the holders of these instruments when the institution was no longer viable or close to unviable. Whereas regulatory capital serves as a buffer and consists of Tier 1 equity capital that could be dipped into when an institution is experiencing distress—either endogenous or exogenous stresses—while continuing to operate outside resolution. MREL liabilities require an institution to issue or hold more loss absorbent capital, as part of the bail-in tool, which can consist of bonds and certain other unsecured debt instruments whose maturity is required to be longer than one year and are subject to mandatory write-downs if the institution or financial group's capital levels fall sharply below 5.12 per cent of risk-based assets.[86] At this point, so-called resolution capital, that is, Alternative Tier 1 capital (hybrid bonds that can be converted to equity) and Tier 2 capital (usually subordinated bonds or convertible bonds with higher trigger points) will only absorb losses based on the bail-in tool when the institution is at the point of non-viability.

Although the ECB takes the lead in assessing the adequacy of Tier 1 and Tier 2 regulatory capital for credit institutions it supervises, it plays no role in assessing how much MREL loss-absorbent capital a credit institution should hold, as this is the responsibility of the SRB acting in conjunction with the relevant national resolution authority. In such a scenario, the ECB's expertise in assessing and monitoring regulatory capital would be useful for resolution authorities whose responsibility in the Banking Union is to monitor and measure MREL capital. The lack of meaningful coordination and ongoing dialogue between the ECB and the SRB and the relevant resolution authorities in this regard is a vulnerability in the Banking Union supervisory and resolution regime. The ECB and SRB should enhance their coordination and oversight in this area in order to monitor the safety and soundness of institutions more effectively.

Moreover, the ECB is responsible for overseeing and approving bank recovery plans[87] whilst resolution authorities are required to write resolution plans (also known as 'living wills') to plan for how the bank would deal with disorderly markets and even its own failure in the event that it became unviable.[88] The stricter requirements that banks issue debt capital that can bail-in bondholders and other creditors along with

[85] Minimum Requirement for own Funds and Eligible Liabilities (MREL) in the BRRD and total loss absorbing capacity (TLAC) from Basel III. See European Banking Authority, 'Regulatory Technical Standards on minimum requirement for own funds and eligible liabilities (MREL)' (EBA/RTS/2015/05, 3 July 2015) <https://www.eba.europa.eu/sites/default/documents/files/documents/10180/1132900/a0fc8387-e98e-4c3f-ae9d-11fb75511662/EBA-RTS-2015-05%20RTS%20on%20MREL%20Criteria.pdf?retry=1> accessed 29 May 2021. See also Basel Committee on Banking Supervision, 'Standard: TLAC holdings: Amendments to the Basel III standard on the definition of capital' (Bank for International Settlements, October 2016) <https://www.bis.org/bcbs/publ/d387.pdf> accessed 29 May 2021.

[86] SRM Regulation (n 1) Art 27 ('Bail-in tool').

[87] ibid Art 4 (h)(1).

[88] ibid ch 1 'Resolution Planning', Art 8 ('Resolution plans drawn up by the Board').

the requirements for recovery and resolution planning means that the resolution framework not only intends to reduce taxpayer exposure to a bank bailout, but also serves the regulatory objective of reducing excessive risk-taking by banks and covered investment firms.[89]

In practice, when a bank is experiencing financial difficulties, the SRM Regulation envisions a necessary sequence of events that should occur when a bank is determined to be unsound and should be taken into resolution. First, the ECB identifies when a bank is in serious financial difficulties and should be resolved. Second, the SRB—consisting of representatives from the Commission, the ECB, and national authorities of Member States where the bank operates—makes a recommendation on resolution to the Commission. Third, the Commission decides whether to approve the Board's recommendation for resolution and approve a resolution plan and refers its decision to the Council for final review and approval. Fourth, national resolution authorities of the jurisdictions where the bank operates implement the approved resolution plan under the supervision of the SRB.[90]

The effectiveness of this process was tested in 2017 in the case involving the Spanish bank Banco Popular. In this case, the SSM's Supervisory Board made a determination that Banco Popular had lost access to the wholesale funding markets and would soon collapse without adequate funding. After the ECB Governing Council's approval of the Supervisory Board determination that Banco Popular was likely to fail, the SRB decided to put the institution into resolution after approval from the Spanish authorities, the Commission, and Council. The SRB then conducted a valuation of Banco Popular's assets and liabilities and decided to transfer the bank's viable assets to Santander for a nominal payment and to use the bail-in tool to recapitalize the bank and impose losses on most of the bank's bondholders. Although the SRB's valuation of the bank's assets and liabilities attracted much criticism and led to many lawsuits in Spanish and European courts, the restructuring of Banco Popular can be considered to be a successful exercise in coordination between the ECB/SSM and the SRB that demonstrated the effectiveness of the SSM–SRM framework and how it can be used successfully to restructure an ailing institution without causing a systemic crisis.

Nevertheless, the ECB and SRB coordination in the Banco Popular case has been heavily criticized by former bondholders and shareholders of Banco Popular who suffered substantial losses because of the SRB's decision to use the bail-in tool against certain bondholders and shareholders and not others on the grounds that the ECB Governing Council had failed to approve (through the Central Bank of Spain) adequate liquidity support for Banco Popular that would have arguably enabled it to continue operations while it was attempting to restructure its operations.[91] Moreover, the SRB had ordered bail-in on some foreign institutional bondholders and shareholders

[89] ibid recital 55.

[90] ibid Art 18(7).

[91] Case 1:18-mc-00085-ER *Notice of Arbitration pursuant to Rules of Arbitration of UNCITRAL between Antonio Del Valle Ruiz et al v Kingdom of Spain*, paras 58–83 and para 121; Case T-497/17 *Sánchez del Valle and Calatrava Real State 2015 v Commission and SRB* [2017]; Gareth Gore, 'Rushed Popular resolution casts long shadow over Europe's banks (*International Financing Review*, 7 June 2019) <https://www.ifre.com/story/1586009/rushed-popular-resolution-casts-long-shadow-over-europes-banks-53fvxp7lqv> accessed 29 May 2021.

while favouring local institutional and retail bondholders and shareholders. This discrimination between different groups of investors has been alleged as lacking proportionality and to have been unnecessary for an adequate restructuring of the bank.[92] The ECB was also criticized on the grounds that it ordered, through the Central Bank of Spain, that the bank undertake draconian recovery measures to restructure itself and reduce its reliance on certain sources of wholesale funding that had the effect of worsening the bank's plight at a time when the bank required continued access to wholesale markets. The ongoing litigation continuing in Member State courts, European courts, and before international arbitration tribunals suggests that what has been praised as the SRB's first effective bank resolution may not have been undertaken with adequate regard to the rights of investors in the bank and could have been managed more effectively.

B. ECB/SSM coordination with the SRB

As discussed above, the ECB/SSM has established other channels of close cooperation with the SRB. The SSM and SRB agreed a MoU that allows for the exchange of information necessary for the SRB to prepare and take resolution actions.[93] However, there appears to be some overlap between the early intervention powers in the BRRD[94] and similar early intervention powers listed in the SSM Regulation, each backed by different procedures. The ECB can opt for the BRRD early intervention powers in respect to ordering the bank to take recovery measures, such as recapitalizing itself or modifying its business practices, during market stresses (but before the bank is taken into resolution) that are transposed into national legislation, or can choose the same or equivalent powers set forth in the SSM Regulation. The ECB may decide to circumvent the more complex domestic legal and procedural requirements attached to the use of early intervention powers under the BRRD, and instead rely on the more familiar early intervention powers of the SSM Regulation. In deciding what legal instruments to apply (eg Member State law or SSM Regulation) in ordering a bank to undertake recovery measures, its actions should nevertheless be coordinated with the SRB and the relevant NRAs, but ECB coordination is not required by the SSM Regulation in this regard and any further decision to coordinate directly with the SRB in deciding, for instance, whether to use a resolution measure such as the bail-in tool to impose losses on MREL liabilities would be questioned on the grounds of its legal competence. A truly effective Banking Union should have the ECB—as the bank supervisor—meaningfully involved in the decision to use both recovery and resolution tools that may have the effect of imposing losses on the holders of bail-in-able bonds.

[92] Also, the auditors Deloitte who were engaged by the SRB to perform a valuation of Banco Popular's balance sheet substantially under-valued the bank's assets while not disclosing that Deloitte was also advising Santander—the bank which ultimately purchased the viable branch operations of Banco Popular for a nominal sum.

[93] European Commission, 'Report to the European Parliament and the Council on the Single Supervisory Mechanism established pursuant to Regulation (EU) 1024/2013' COM (2017) 591 final, 53–54.

[94] BRRD (n 4) title III.

The institutional and legal complexities of coordinating early intervention powers between bank supervisors and resolution authorities are discussed in a White Paper published in 2017 by the Banco Central do Portugal that analyses some of the main legal and regulatory issues involved in the allocation of powers between central banks, supervisory authorities, and resolution authorities in the Banking Union. The report critically analyses the institutional gaps and legal uncertainties that limit the effectiveness of the SRM in part due to the limited role of the SSM in the resolution process. The necessity of having the ECB involved in the resolution process was emphasized.[95]

Further complexities regarding early intervention powers and supervisory powers arise in the context of the SRB's (and other Member State authorities') powers to require banks and covered financial groups and conglomerates to change their organizational structure if the SRB determines that the bank or banking group's organizational structure is a substantial impediment to a feasible and credible resolution of the bank or group.[96] If the SRB, acting in consultation with national resolution authorities, determines that there are substantial impediments to the implementation of the resolution plan, it may order the institution to remove the impediments, including changing its organizational structure or business activities.[97] Indeed, this could involve changes to the legal, operational and financial structure of institutions or the group itself and their business activities.[98]

To this end, the SRM Regulation requires the SRB to draw up resolution plans after consultation with the national competent authorities (including the ECB) and national resolution authorities, including the group resolution authority. Article 10(11) SRM Regulation requires the SRB, when drafting and revising the resolution plan, to identify any material impediments to resolvability and, based on the EU legal principles of necessity and proportionality, to instruct the relevant national resolution authority to take the necessary measures to address those impediments.[99] The SRB can also require the relevant national resolution authority to take specific measures to require the institution to remove the impediments, if the institution subject to resolution powers can potentially draw on funds from the Single Resolution Fund.[100]

The SRM Regulation provides that if the firm's or financial group's measures are considered inadequate, the resolution authority will have the power to take specific

[95] See Banco de Portugal, 'White Paper on the regulation and supervision of the financial system' (2016) Banco de Portugal White Paper, part VI <https://www.bportugal.pt/sites/default/files/anexos/pdf-boletim/livro_branco_web_en.pdf> accessed 29 May 2021.

[96] BRRD (n 4) Art 17(5). Under BRRD (n 4) Art 17(5) the resolution authority is empowered to conduct a resolvability assessment to identify whether or not there are substantial impediments to the implementation of a credible and feasible resolution plan.

[97] In considering whether to order a bank to remove such organizational impediments, BRRD Arts 15 and 16 and SRM Regulation provide that the resolution authority must consult the competent supervisory authority regarding the resolution authority's determination of whether or not there are substantial impediments to the resolvability of a firm.

[98] The European Banking Authority has developed a Guideline on 'Conditions for Measures to Overcome Obstacles to Resolvability' (EBA/GL/2014/11 Appendix 1, 22 December 2014) for resolution authorities to rely on in considering whether to take measures under Art 17(5).

[99] SRM Regulation (n 1) Art 10(11).

[100] ibid ('Where applicable, the national resolution authorities shall directly take the measures referred to in points (a) to (j) of the first subparagraph').

actions that address or remove the impediments to resolvability.[101] In selecting the appropriate measure to remove the impediments, the ECB has worked with resolution authorities to choose a measure based on the nature of the impediment. These measures can be classified in three categories—structural, financial and information-related, or data management. The use of these measures involves a large degree of technical analysis of bank balance sheets and corporate group structures, but nevertheless also involves a substantial amount of discretionary decision-making based on criteria that fall within a large range and are not prioritized in any meaningful way. These assessments of the nature of organizational impediments to effective resolution planning should necessarily involve the ECB in close cooperation with the SRB and Member State resolution authorities regarding the extent of organizational impediments and how they should be addressed in the context of resolution and recovery planning.

V. Summing Up and Future Challenges

The Banking Union was designed to give the ECB an important role in restoring the financial health and stability of the European banking system and to sever the link between weak banking systems and fragile sovereign debt finances.[102] Regarding banking supervision, since becoming operational in November 2014, the Single Supervisory Mechanism has been credited with helping the European banking system address some of its most pressing challenges. For example, some euro area Member State regulators have developed the view that the SSM has proven itself to be an effective supervisory network that has functioned smoothly and has supported the stability and resilience of the European banking system.[103] For instance, the German Federal Financial Supervisory Authority (the 'BaFin') has observed that '[i]t now plays an important role in safeguarding long-term financial stability and advancing financial market integration'.[104] Another view, however, asserts that the SSM has limited the flexibility that national competent authorities previously had to address risks in local banking markets and has increased the operational costs for NCAs with a view to ensuring that they comply with the SSM regime. Furthermore, it is claimed that increased compliance costs for banks have hindered their capacity to support the euro area's post-crisis economic recovery.[105]

Moreover, the economic risks arising from environmental and social sustainability pose major challenges to the ECB as a bank supervisor. The ECB will have to consider

[101] BRRD (n 4) Art 17(5), which provides a non-exhaustive range of powers for authorities to remove firm impediments to resolvability in advance of failure that may be used if measures proposed by firms are insufficient to ensure resolvability.

[102] SSM Regulation (n 1); SRM Regulation (n 1).

[103] German Federal Ministry of Finance, 'The Single Supervisory Mechanism: Lessons learned after the first three years' (German Federal Ministry of Finance's Monthly Report, January 2018) <www.bundesfinanzministerium.de/Content/EN/Downloads/2018-01-26-SSM.pdf> accessed 29 May 2021.

[104] ibid.

[105] See Frank Mehlhorn, 'Bankgeschafte in Europa: Wie einheitlich ist die Regulierung und Aufsichtwirklich?' (*Bankenverband*, 1 March 2018).

the risks posed to financial stability by the growing number of financial institutions that are invested in assets whose values will drop substantially in the medium term as the effects of climate change are incorporated into the value of bank and other financial institution balance sheets and transferred into the balance sheets of other financial institutions and their investors. It has been predicted that many of these assets will be 'stranded' and potentially a source of substantial losses and possibly systemic risk for the financial system.

Although banking mergers and consolidation have increased significantly since the early 1990s, the euro area and EU cannot expect further integration of retail banking or the emergence of EU cross-border wholesale banking, and consolidation of wholesale banking integration, without the completion of the Banking Union with a common deposit insurance fund and an effective resolution framework. However, the SSM's regulation of credit institutions does not cover the growing number of non-bank financial intermediaries and structured entities that are not defined as 'credit institutions' under EU law. These non-bank financial intermediaries or 'shadow banks' are playing an increasingly important role in the maturity transformation process—borrowing short and lending long—outside the formal banking sector in the European economy and without being subject to prudential regulatory controls.

Regarding monetary stability, the ECB has pursued its primary objective of price stability by seeking to achieve a low and stable retail price inflation rate of about 2 per cent. As discussed above, this rather narrow pursuit of price stability has hindered the ECB's ability to support its secondary objectives as set forth in Article 3 TEU, such as the general economic policies of the Union and having regard to competitiveness, and environmental sustainability. This disproportionate focus on a low rate of retail price inflation has contributed to the ECB failing to achieve sustainable economic growth since the 2008 crisis by substantially under-shooting its inflation and growth targets in recent years.[106]

Moreover, the GFC highlighted the merits of a monetary policy that 'leans against the wind' to safeguard financial stability in the short-to-medium term, whilst achieving price stability over the medium to longer-term. This experience could be instructive in considering a future role for the ECB in which it interprets its secondary objectives to support the general economic policies of the Union in respect of protecting the environment by considering that price stability and environmental sustainability need not be mutually exclusive objectives, and in fact can be pursued in a complementary way. With the help of natural scientists and economists, it will be important to gain a better understanding of the potential trade-offs between the two objectives. This might require a certain inter-temporal flexibility in pursuing the price stability objective that might allow monetary policy to help facilitate the transition to an environmentally sustainable economy without losing sight of price stability over the longer-term.[107]

[106] See Stiglitz, *The Euro* (n 9) 63–99.

[107] For a similar view, see Isabel Schnabel, 'Never waste a crisis: COVID-19, climate change and monetary policy' (Speech at a virtual roundtable on 'Sustainable crisis responses in Europe' organized by the INSPIRE research network, 17 July 2020).

Despite SSM reforms to banking supervision, there is more room to improve regulation so that it can achieve financial stability objectives. This potentially involves enhanced coordination between the SSM and ECB monetary policy, which is currently not permitted under the SSM Regulation. Moreover, under Article 5 SSM Regulation, the ECB has limited competence to use macroprudential tools to address systemic risks in the banking sector and across the financial system.

Nevertheless, the ECB's conduct of banking supervision through the SSM (along with monetary policy) has stabilized the euro area banking sector in the face of the euro area sovereign debt crisis and oversaw implementation of post-crisis regulatory reforms, such as Basel III's capital and liquidity requirements and bank governance standards. Despite having an overall positive effect on banking sector performance, the Banking Union faces serious challenges in stabilizing the euro area banking sector and overseeing its return to a sustainable financial position. The ECB should consider how to manage the risks that arise from the legal limitations on its competences, while EU policy-makers and Member States should consider whether revision of the EU Treaty is necessary to grant the ECB adequate competence to manage financial risks outside the banking sector and to address the need for more effective coordination and intervention in the area of bank resolution.

8

The Relationship between the ECB and the National Competent Authorities in the Single Supervisory Mechanism

Problems and Perspectives

*Federico Della Negra and Gianni Lo Schiavo**

I. Introduction

The Single Supervisory Mechanism (SSM) is one of the three pillars of the European Banking Union, together with the Single Resolution Mechanism (SRM) and a (still to be) European Deposit Insurance Scheme. The SSM was set up by Council Regulation (EU) No 1024/2013 ('SSM Regulation')[1] which confers on the European Central Bank (ECB) specific tasks for the prudential supervision of credit institutions.

The SSM is one of the clearest examples of multi-layered, composite administration created in the European Union (EU). The multi-layered (EU and national) nature of EU administration is not a novelty in EU law. The administration on the EU level has been traditionally described as primarily engaged with the making of policies rather than with their implementation which is generally left to national authorities.[2] Only in limited fields are EU institutions directly responsible for the implementation or execution of law (ie direct administration).[3] The distinctive feature of the SSM is that within this multi-layered administration, an EU institution, the ECB, has been granted a wide range of direct administrative powers vis-à-vis credit institutions.[4]

* The opinions expressed in this article are personal and do not necessarily reflect those of the ECB. While this chapter is the result of joint research, Federico Della Negra drafted Sections II and V and Gianni Lo Schiavo drafted Sections III and IV.

[1] Council Regulation (EU) 1024/2013 of 15 October 2013 conferring specific tasks on the European Central Bank concerning policies relating to the prudential supervision of credit institutions [2013] OJ L287/63 (hereafter SSM Regulation).

[2] See in particular Loïc Azoulai, 'The Judge and the Community's Administrative Governance' in Christian Joerges and Renaud Dehousse (eds), *Good Governance in Europe's Integrated Market* (OUP 2002) 110.

[3] See Herwig CH Hofmann, Gerard C Rowe, and Alexander H Türk, *Administrative Law and Policy of the European Union* (OUP 2011) 13.

[4] To show the magnitude of administrative competences of the ECB, suffices here to mention that in 2020 the ECB supervised directly 115 banking groups and issued 2,643 supervisory decisions addressed to specific supervised entities. See European Central Bank, 'ECB Annual Report on supervisory activities 2020' (ECB, 23 March 2021) <https://www.bankingsupervision.europa.eu/press/publications/annual-report/html/ssm.ar2020~1a59f5757c.en.html> accessed 27 May 2022 (hereafter European Central Bank, 'ECB Annual Report on supervisory activities 2020'). For an account of the rise of EU administrative,

Federico Della Negra and Gianni Lo Schiavo, *The Relationship between the ECB and the National Competent Authorities in the Single Supervisory Mechanism* In: *The New European Central Bank*. Edited by: Thomas Beukers, Diane Fromage, and Giorgio Monti, Oxford University Press.
DOI: 10.1093/oso/9780198871231.003.0008

However, the adoption of an administrative decision represents in most cases only the final step of a long and complex decision-making process that may involve several different stages both at the Union and national level and different forms of cooperation between these two layers.

The complexity of the system derives from the presence of a plurality of actors both at the EU and the national level. The SSM comprises a Union level, formed by the ECB, and a national level, formed by National competent authorities (NCAs).[5] Like the European System of Financial Supervision (ESFS) and the SRM, the SSM does not have legal personality and therefore the acts adopted within this framework need to be legally attributed to the ECB or to the NCAs.

Thus far, the SSM has delivered important results in terms of non-performing loans supervision, transparency in decision-making, and operational efficiency. However, the allocation of tasks, powers, and responsibilities between the Union and national level is complex because it reflects a difficult balancing exercise between fostering centralization to ensure a supranational oversight of the banking system and address financial stability risks, whilst exercising a need for proximity of supervisory action. Union courts have contributed to clarify the division of competences between ECB and NCAs, setting out clearer boundaries between the mandates of these institutions, but some issues on the practical implementation of responsibilities remain.

Against this background, this chapter focuses on the relationship between the ECB and the NCAs in the SSM, showing, in particular, the current problems and perspectives in this relationship and how the case law of Union courts contributes to the (clearer) definition of the ECB and NCAs respective tasks, powers, and responsibilities. The aim of this analysis is to understand whether and to what extent the conferral of prudential supervisory tasks and powers to the ECB within a multi-layered framework composed by ECB and NCAs alters or affect the ECB's role and standing.

This chapter is organized as follows. Section II outlines the role of the ECB and the NCAs within the SSM as designed by the SSM Regulation and SSM Framework Regulation.[6] Section III looks at the role of cooperation between the ECB and the NCAs in day-to-day supervision. Section IV examines their cooperation in the context of authorization procedures. Section V looks at the oversight function of the ECB in the SSM. Section VI concludes.

executive powers after the 2008 Global Financial Crisis, see, in particular, Renaud Dehousse, 'Why Has EU Macroeconomic Governance become More Supranational?' (2016) 38 Journal of European Integration 617.

[5] Alberto de Gregorio Merino, 'Banking Union in EU Law: An EU Institutional Law Perspective' in Gianni Lo Schiavo (ed), *The European Banking Union and the Role of Law* (Edward Elgar Publishing 2019) 189. NCAs may be National Central Banks or administrative agencies (a list is kept by the European Banking Authority; see EBA, 'Competent Authorities' (EBA, --) <https://www.eba.europa.eu/supervisory-convergence/supervisory-disclosure/competent-authorities> accessed 27 May 2022).

[6] Regulation (EU) 468/2014 of the European Central Bank of 16 April 2014 establishing the framework for cooperation within the Single Supervisory Mechanism between the European Central Bank and national competent authorities and with national designated authorities (hereafter SSM Framework Regulation) (ECB/2014/17) [2014] OJ L141/1.

II. The Role of the ECB and the NCAs within the SSM: An Overview

A. The SSM: rationale and organization

The SSM is one of the most important examples of centralization of administrative powers made by the EU.[7] The creation of the SSM was strictly interlinked to the financial and economic developments of the euro area crisis.[8] It is important to remember that for a long time, EU legal scholarship and policy-makers followed the 'conventional wisdom' that monetary policy could be kept separate from prudential supervision, one at the EU level, the other one at the national level. This was based on the conviction that monetary policy centralization did not significantly affect the conduct of prudential supervision and could therefore be kept distinct, separate from monetary policy.[9] The financial crisis however showed that it would be difficult to achieve simultaneously a single financial market and financial stability while preserving a high degree of national prudential supervision.[10] From a wider historical perspective, the SSM, and the Banking Union should be seen and understood as a 'predictable outcome' of an incremental process of supranational legal integration which culminated in the conferral of administrative, executive powers at the EU level.[11]

The idea of supranational prudential supervision and the conferral of prudential supervisory tasks on the ECB was expressly contemplated in the Maastricht Treaty.[12]

[7] See Koen Lenaerts, 'EMU and the European Union's Constitutional Framework' (2014) 39 EL Rev 753; Hans W Micklitz, 'The Internal Market and the Banking Union' in Stefan Grundmann and Hans-W Micklitz (eds), *The European Banking Union and Constitution: Beacon for Advanced Integration or Death-Knell for Democracy* (Hart Publishing 2019) 281; Chiara Zilioli and Karl-Philipp Wojcik, 'European Banking Union: A Giant Step Towards European Integration and a Challenge for Judicial Review' in Chiara Zilioli and Karl-Philipp Wojcik (eds), *Judicial Review in the European Banking Union* (Edward Elgar Publishing 2021) 7 (hereafter Zilioli and Wojcik, 'European Banking Union: A Giant Step Towards European Integration and a Challenge for Judicial Review').

[8] For an overview of the reforms undertaken by the EU in the wake of the euro area crisis, see, in particular, Edoardo Chiti and Pedro Gustavo Teixeira, 'The Constitutional Implications of the European Responses to the Financial and Public Debt Crisis' (2013) 50 CML Rev 683; Thomas Beukers, 'Legal Writing(s) on the Eurozone Crisis' (2015) EUI LAW Working Paper No 2015/11 <https://cadmus.eui.eu/handle/1814/35418> accessed 27 May 2022.

[9] See Giovanni Bassani, 'The Centralisation of Prudential Supervision in the Euroarea: The Emergence of a New 'Conventional Wisdom' and the Establishment of the SSM' (2020) 31 EBLR 1001 (hereafter Bassani, 'The Centralisation of Prudential Supervision').

[10] See Tommaso Padoa-Schioppa, 'Lecture by Tommaso Padoa-Schioppa Member of the Executive Board of the European Central Bank at the London School of Economics' (Financial Markets Group, London, 24 February 1999) <https://www.ecb.europa.eu/press/key/date/1999/html/sp990224.en.html> accessed 27 May 2022; Rosa Maria Lastra, *International Financial and Monetary Law* (OUP 2015) 299 and generally Dirk Schoenmaker, *Governance of International Banking: The Financial Trilemma* (OUP 2013).

[11] See Pedro Gustavo Teixeira, *The Legal History of the European Banking Union. How European Law Led to the Supranational Integration of the Single Financial Market* (Hart Publishing 2020) 280 and 299 (hereafter Teixeira, *The Legal History of the European Banking Union*).

[12] See Commission of the European Communities, 'Draft Treaty amending the Treaty establishing the European Economic Community with a view to achieving economic and monetary union' (Bulletin of the European Communities, Supplement 2/91 1991). On the discussions that preceded this inclusion, see René Smits, *The European Central Bank. Institutional Aspects* (Kluwer 1997) 327 ff (hereafter Smits, *The European Central Bank*).

However, the 'enabling clause' of Article 126(7) TFEU was activated only after the out break of the euro area crisis.[13] As it is well known, the first response to the fiscal and budgetary difficulties of some euro area Member States was the creation of budgetary coordination measures put in place between 2011 and 2012 (ie European Semester). However, in the midst of this crisis, it became clear that, due to the prevalent bank-based nature of the euro area financial system, sovereign debt and banks' stability are two sides of the same coin and can create a 'vicious circle' for both sovereigns and banks. The stability of the euro area is closely linked to the safety of its credit institutions and, conversely, the safety of credit institutions may be affected by the market value of sovereign debt (government bonds) they hold on their balance sheets and therefore, ultimately, by the sustainability of public debt.[14] Therefore, the centralization of prudential supervisory tasks and powers at the Union level was seen as an *ex ante* institutional response to avoid *ex post* burdensome interventions of public funds to prevent banks' failures and to restore financial stability.[15]

The second connected rationale was to achieve a higher level of supervisory convergence and integration in the internal market.[16] The underlying premise is that co-ordination between national supervisors is not enough, in particular in the context of a single currency, in order to reduce the risk of different interpretations and contradictory decisions on the individual entity level, particularly in case of banking groups. The presence of a duality of rationales, one rooted in the EMU, the other in the internal market-building logic, led to the SSM being described as 'a two-sided construction, with a foot in the internal market and another one in the EMU'.[17] To avoid the risk of a disconnection between the SSM and the internal market, the EU legislators require the ECB to have 'full regard and duty of care for the unity and integrity of the internal market based on equal treatment of credit institutions with a view to preventing regulatory arbitrage'.[18]

These two rationales, and especially the first one, led to the creation of a supranational model for prudential supervision that is profoundly different from the European System of Financial Supervision (ESFS), which was created in 2010. The ESFS, which was built on the recommendations of the de Larosière group advocated more coordination between the institutional actors involved in financial supervision

[13] For an overview of the phases of the financial crisis, started from the 2008 US sub-prime crisis, see Erkki Liikanen, 'High-level Expert Group on reforming the structure of the EU banking sector' (Final report, Brussels, 2 October 2012) <https://ec.europa.eu/info/sites/info/files/liikanen-report-02102012_en.pdf> accessed 27 May 2022. For a detailed analysis of the Union post-crisis reforms, see House of Lords, 'The post-crisis EU financial regulatory framework: do the pieces fit?' (European Union Committee, 5th Report of Session 2014–15, 2 February 2015).

[14] See also chapter 2 by Vestert Borger, chapter 5 by Agnieszka Smoleńska and Thomas Beukers, and chapter 7 by Kern Alexander, in this volume.

[15] SSM Regulation (n 1) recital 6. See also Gavin Garret, 'The Relationship between the Banking Union and the EMU' in Gianni Lo Schiavo (ed), *The European Banking Union and the Role of Law* (Edward Elgar Publishing 2019) 13.

[16] SSM Regulation (n 1) recital 5.

[17] Alberto de Gregorio Merino, 'Banking Union in EU law: An EU Institutional Law Perspective' in Gianni Lo Schiavo (ed), *The European Banking Union and the Role of Law* (Edward Elgar Publishing 2019) 31.

[18] SSM Regulation (n 1) Art 1.

and oversight but within a largely decentralized structure.[19] Reflecting this idea, the ESFS envisages an 'intervention-based supervisory model',[20] where the European Supervisory Authorities (ESAs) act as 'supervisors of supervisors'[21] and can take direct measures against supervised entities only exceptionally, while direct supervision remains in the remit of the NCAs. This intervention-based supervisory model aimed to ensure compliance with the limitations set out by Union courts to the delegation of administrative powers to bodies based only on secondary law.[22]

By contrast, the SSM is part of a set of measures aimed to address the threat to financial stability posed by the sovereign debt crisis and could be established on the basis of the 'enabling clause' of Article 127(6) TFEU which empowers the Council, acting by unanimity, to confer specific tasks on the ECB on policies relating to the prudential supervision of credit institutions and other financial institutions with the exception of insurance undertakings.[23] In the middle of the euro area crisis, this enabling clause was seen as the most suitable legal basis to contribute to banks' and financial system stability in the euro area, also in light of the extensive expertise gained by the ECB as the euro area central bank and its contributing role in macroeconomic and financial stability issues.[24] The use of Article 127(6) TFEU as legal basis restricted the SSM jurisdiction to the euro area. However, the Member States outside the euro area can join the SSM only voluntarily, in the regime of close cooperation.[25] The SSM has thus given shape to an 'integration through differentiation' where an inner core of deep integration and an outer core of looser integration with differentiated membership co-exist.[26]

Within the SSM, both the ECB and the NCAs have tasks, powers, and responsibilities. To understand the role of the NCAs within the SSM it is necessary to highlight that since Article 127(6) TFEU enables the Council to confer prudential tasks only

[19] Niamh Moloney, 'European Banking Union: Assessing its Risks and Resilience' (2014) 51 CML Rev 1621.

[20] See Pierre Schammo, 'EU Day-to-Day Supervision or Intervention-based Supervision: Which Way Forward for the European System of Financial Supervision?' (2012) 32 OJLS 771; Mads Andenas and Gudula Deipenbrock, *Regulating and Supervising European Financial Markets. More Risks than Achievements* (Springer 2016).

[21] Niamh Moloney, *EU Securities and Financial Markets Regulation* (OUP 2014) 973.

[22] See in particular Case 9/56 *Meroni v High Authority* [1958] EU:C:1958:7. In Case C-270/12 *United Kingdom v European Parliament and Council* [2014] EU:C:2014:18 it was held that Art 28 of Regulation (EU) 236/2012 of the European Parliament and of the Council of 14 March 2012 on short selling and certain aspects of credit default swap [2012] OJ L86/1 improves the conditions for the establishment and functioning of the internal market in the financial field and therefore Art 114 of the Consolidated Version of the Treaty on the Functioning of the European Union [2012] OJ C326/47 (hereafter TFEU) is an appropriate legal basis for the adoption of Art 28 of Regulation 236/2012.

[23] For a detailed historical account of TFEU (n 22) Art 127(6), see Smits, *The European Central Bank* (n 12) 334–38 and Teixeira, *The Legal History of the European Banking Union* (n 11) 223–25. For an overview of the different interpretations of this provision, see Giorgio Monti and Christy Ann Petit, 'The Single Supervisory Mechanism: Legal Fragilities and Possible Solutions' (2016) ADEMU Working Paper Series No 2016/016, 2 <https://repositori.upf.edu/bitstream/handle/10230/27288/Ademu-WP-016-2016%20The%20single%20supervisory.pdf?sequence=1> accessed 27 May 2022 (hereafter Monti and Petit, 'The Single Supervisory Mechanism: Legal Fragilities and Possible Solutions'). See also chapter 7 by Kern Alexander, in this volume.

[24] SSM Regulation (n 1) recital 13.

[25] As of October 2020, after concluding the relevant comprehensive assessments, the ECB started directly supervising five banks in Bulgaria and eight banks in Croatia. See ECB, 'ECB Annual Report on supervisory activities 2020' (n 4) 7.

[26] See in more detail Teixeira, *The Legal History of the European Banking Union* (n 11) 270–71.

on the ECB,[27] no tasks could be attributed to the NCAs on the basis of this provision.[28] However, the need to ensure the effective functioning of the SSM, taking into account also the NCA's expertise and experience, led to the creation of a complex institutional model where NCAs assist the ECB in the supervision of significant institutions (SIs), carry out the direct day-to-day supervision of less significant institutions (LSIs), smaller credit institutions in the SSM, have specific responsibilities in relation to common procedures and are represented, like the ECB appointed members, in the Supervisory Board.[29]

In legal terms, the degree of involvement of the NCAs in the SSM is determined by the concepts of 'task' and 'power'.[30] In short, a task indicates a more practical, factual dimension of an assignment conferred by law and aims to further specify the limits of the mandate bestowed on an EU institution or body.[31] To carry out a task, the authority may exercise different powers. A power indicates the faculty to unilaterally change the legal position of a third party.[32] Tasks and powers need to be exercised—on the basis of a specific legislative competence (ie Article 127(6) TFEU)—to achieve a legislative objective (ie the safety and soundness of individual credit institutions).[33]

The ECB, in the light of the abovementioned formulation of Article 127(6) TFEU, has been granted the exclusive competence to carry out the microprudential supervisory tasks with regard to both SIs and LSIs, with NCAs having certain powers, leading to a decentralized implementation of the SSM.

B. The ECB tasks, powers, and responsibilities

The ECB's microprudential tasks are listed in Article 4 SSM Regulation.[34] It has been debated whether the ECB may exercise these tasks with regard to the SIs only or with

[27] By contrast, TFEU (n 22) Art 127(1) grants tasks to the ESCB, which comprises both the ECB and the National Central Banks (NCBs).

[28] See Agnese Pizzolla, 'The Role of the European Central Bank in the Single Supervisory Mechanism: A New Paradigm for EU Governance' (2018) 43 EL Rev 17 (hereafter Pizzolla, 'The Role of the European Central Bank in the Single Supervisory Mechanism'. This marks an important difference in comparison to EU competition law where TFEU Art 103 empowers the Council to adopt regulations to implement TFEU (n 22) Arts 101 and 102 without restricting this conferral of power to the European Commission only.

[29] See Section II.A.

[30] For an overview of the different interpretations of tasks and powers, see Raffaele D'Ambrosio, 'The SSM: Allocation of Tasks and Powers between the ECB and the NCAs and Organisational Issue' in Raffaele D'Ambrosio (ed), 'Law and Practice of the Banking Union and of its governing Institutions (Cases and Materials)' (2020) Quaderni di Ricerca Giuridica della Consulenza Legale della Banca d'Italia No 88, 28 <https://www.bancaditalia.it/pubblicazioni/quaderni-giuridici/2020-0088/index.html> accessed 27 May 2022 (hereafter D'Ambrosio, 'The SSM: Allocation of Tasks and Powers between the ECB and the NCAs and Organisational issue').

[31] The concept of task is also mentioned by the TFEU in relation to the ESCB (TFEU (n 22) Art 127(2) and (7)). In this regard, the concept of 'task' seems to be narrower than that of 'field of action' that is used by TFEU (n 22) Art 85 to define the mandate of Eurojust.

[32] Pizzolla, 'The Role of the European Central Bank in the Single Supervisory Mechanism' (n 28) 15.

[33] The competence concerns both the basis for the authority to carry out a task or use a specific power which is set out in the SSM Regulation (n 1), for the ECB, or national law, for the NCA, and the substantive basis governing the subject matter, which is set out in CRR or national law transposing CRD.

[34] SSM Regulation (n 1) Art 5 sets out the ECB's macroprudential tasks. This chapter focuses only on ECB microprudential tasks.

regard to LSIs too. The initial part of this Article provides that these tasks shall be exercised within the framework of Article 6 (which introduces the differentiation between SIs and LSIs). However, Article 4 later specifies that the ECB is 'exclusively competent' to carry out these tasks in relation to all credit institutions (thus both SIs and LSIs). According to one view, the ECB is exclusively competent to carry them out only towards SIs because these tasks can be exercised only within the framework of Article 6 SSM Regulation.[35] According to a different and most predominant view, these tasks can be exclusively exercised with regard to all credit institutions, including LSIs.[36]

The Court of Justice of the EU (CJEU) provided clarity on this controversial issue in the *L-Bank* case where the General Court and the Court of Justice dismissed a challenge brought by a credit institution for the annulment of an ECB supervisory decision classifying the bank as a SI.[37] One of the applicants' arguments in support of the claim for annulment was that the SSM Regulation did not transfer to the ECB all the tasks referred to in Article 4(1) and in respect of all entities, but only did so with respect to 'significant' entities, with the direct prudential supervision of 'less significant' entities remaining within the competence of the national authorities. In response to this view, the Court of Justice, reiterating in substance the point made by the General Court and by the ECB and the European Commission in the proceedings, made three important points: (i) under Article 4(1) the ECB is exclusively competent to carry out the tasks stated in that provision in relation to both SIs and LSI;[38] (ii) under Article 6(1) SSM Regulation, the ECB shall carry out its tasks within an SSM composed of the ECB and NCAs;[39] and (iii) the NCAs assist the ECB in carrying out these tasks 'by a decentralised implementation of some of those tasks in relation to less significant credit institutions'.[40]

The CJEU's reasoning points to the conclusion that the ECB's exclusive competence regarding LSIs is not restricted to the definition of 'special circumstances' under Article 6(4), paragraph 4, subsection 2 of the SSM Regulation, but includes the exercise of all the tasks listed in Article 4 SSM Regulation. This conclusion is coherent with the SSM Regulation's rationale[41] that smaller banks can also pose a threat to financial stability and that the ECB is ultimately responsible and accountable for the effective

[35] D'Ambrosio, 'The SSM: Allocation of Tasks and Powers between the ECB and the NCAs and Organisational issue' (n 30) 41.

[36] Klaus Lackhoff, *The Single Supervisory Mechanism. A Practitioner's Guide* (Beck & Hart Publishing 2017) para 844.

[37] It should also be stressed that the new CRR/CRD revision has brought some credit institutions, including the one challenging the ECB in the case at issue, outside the scope of prudential supervision in the SSM.

[38] Case C-450/17 P *Landeskreditbank Baden-Württemberg—Förderbank v ECB* [2019] EU:C:2019:372, para 38.

[39] ibid para 39.

[40] ibid para 41.

[41] SSM Regulation (n 1) recital 16. See, however, the judgment of the German Federal Constitutional Court (Bundesverfassungsgericht, BVerfG) of 30 July 2019 (2 BvR 1685/14, 2 BvR 2631/14) where the BVerfG held that the SSM Regulation has to be interpreted strictly and therefore a full transfer of supervisory competences to the ECB would not be compatible with Article 127(6) TFEU (see in particular paras 166–170 of the judgment). The BVerfG decided not to refer a question for a preliminary ruling to the CJEU because it considered that the interpretation of the SSMR was to be considered ('acte clair') and that the deliberations of the CJEU on LSI supervision were only an 'obiter dictum' (see in particular para 317 of the judgment).

functioning of the entire system.[42] More broadly, the CJEU supports the reading of the SSM as a Mechanism where the ECB's exclusive tasks need to be operationally implemented, under the oversight of the ECB at the national level, 'rather than having a distribution of competences between the ECB and the national authorities in the performance of the tasks referred to in Article 4(1) of that regulation'.[43]

The ECB can exercise its tasks through several different powers. Whereas the conferral of tasks needs to be based on Union law (Article 127(6) TFEU), the specific powers to fulfil these tasks can derive also from national law and therefore can predate the SSM. More specifically, the ECB can apply directly applicable Union law (eg Article 16 SSM Regulation or powers based on the Capital Requirements Regulation (CRR)) or national law transposing EU directives, in accordance with Article 4(3) SSM Regulation.[44] It can also apply supervisory powers granted under national law that are not explicitly provided for in EU law as long as such powers fall within the ECB's tasks under Article 4 SSM Regulation and underpin a supervisory function (so called 'national powers').[45] The application of national law by an Union institution is a novelty in Union law which responds to the need for ensuring supervisory consistency on the basis of a (still) fragmented prudential regulatory framework. Prudential regulation is largely based on EU directives (*in primis*, the Capital Requirements Directive (CRD)[46]) which set out, in general, minimum standards of harmonization.[47]

For the present purposes, it is important to distinguish between the ECB's powers vis-à-vis credit institutions and vis-à-vis NCAs. With regard to SIs, the ECB may adopt supervisory decisions, which are legally binding acts adopted by the Governing

[42] For more detail on the aspects of decentralization within the SSM, see Michael Ioannidis, 'The European Central Bank' in Christoph Hermann and Fabian Amtenbrink (eds), *The Law of the EMU* (OUP 2020) 360.

[43] *Landeskreditbank Baden-Württemberg—Förderbank v ECB* (n 38) para 54.

[44] Joined Cases T-133/16 to T-136/16 *Caisse régionale de crédit agricole mutuel Alpes Provence and Others v ECB* [2018] EU:T:2018:219, para 92, which states that, when applying national law, the ECB shall also take into account the relevant national case law.

[45] For this notion, see the Decision (EU) 2019/322 of the European Central Bank of 31 January 2019 on delegation of the power to adopt decisions regarding supervisory powers granted under national law (ECB/2019/4) [2019] OJ L55/1, recital 3. See European Central Bank, 'Additional clarification regarding the ECB's competence to exercise supervisory powers granted under national law' (SSM/2017/0140, 31 March 2017) <https://www.bankingsupervision.europa.eu/press/letterstobanks/shared/pdf/2017/Letter_to_SI_Entry_point_information_letter.pdf?cb0801df81ba2db9d450ce4fb53065c8> accessed 27 May 2022 (hereafter 'European Central Bank clarification letter'). In more detail, see Gianni Lo Schiavo, 'The ECB and its Application of National Law in the SSM' in Gianni Lo Schiavo (ed), *The European Banking Union and the Role of Law* (Edward Elgar Publishing 2019) 189.

[46] Directive 2013/36/EU of the European Parliament and of the Council of 26 June 2013 on access to the activity of credit institutions and the prudential supervision of credit institutions and investment firms, amending Directive 2002/87/EC and repealing Directives 2006/48/EC and 2006/49/EC [2013] OJ L176/338 (hereafter CRD). This Directive sets out, in particular, the requirements for access to the activity of credit institutions (licensing of new credit institutions and acquisitions of qualifying holdings in credit institutions), the requirements on internal governance, suitability of management bodies, and remuneration as well as the supervisory review and evaluation process.

[47] For an overview of the problems, see Andreas Witte, 'The Application of National Banking Supervision Law by the ECB: Three Parallel Modes of Executing EU Law?' (2014) 21 MJ 105 (hereafter Witte, 'The Application of National Banking Supervision Law by the ECB: Three Parallel Modes of Executing EU Law?'); Lena Boucon and Daniela Jaros, 'The Application of National Law by the European Central Bank within the EU Banking Union's Single Supervisory Mechanism: A New Mode of European Integration?' (2018) 10 European Journal of Legal Studies 155 ff; Filippo Annunziata and Raffaele D'Ambrosio, 'L'applicazione del diritto degli Stati membri da parte della Banca Centrale Europea' (2019) 4 Giurisprudenza commerciale 707.

Council,[48] upon a proposal made by the Supervisory Board, as well as guidelines and recommendations.[49] It can also adopt operational acts, request information, and conduct on-site inspections. With regard to LSIs, the ECB can make use of its investigatory powers, including the power to conduct on-site inspections,[50] can adopt supervisory decisions in the context of common procedures,[51] and can decide, when necessary, to ensure consistent application of high supervisory standards, to exercise directly itself the supervision of a LSIs.[52] The ECB, however, cannot issue individual instructions to NCAs regarding a specific LSI because the SSM Regulation did not grant to the ECB general day-to-day or direct supervisory powers regarding LSIs. The range of powers conferred on the ECB with regard to LSIs reflects a model of 'intervention-based' supervision in which direct action of the ECB vis-à-vis LSIs is envisaged only in the specific cases mentioned above in order to balance centralization with proximity of supervisory action. Therefore, within the SSM the NCAs do not retain their pre-existing prudential competences in respect of LSIs (which would be in contrast with the exclusive nature of the prudential supervisory tasks granted on the ECB by Article 4 SSM Regulation). Rather, the ECB can exercise its tasks of Article 4 SSM Regulation in respect to LSIs.

The ECB may adopt regulations, guidelines, or general instructions to NCAs under Article 6(5)(a) SSM Regulation[53] and can request information from the NCAs on the performance of their tasks under Article 6(5)(e) SSM Regulation. Moreover, the ECB can address individual instructions to the NCAs with regard to SIs (but never with regard to LSIs), in accordance with Article 9(1), third paragraph, of the same regulation, in order to require NCAs to make use of their powers, under and in accordance with the conditions set out in national law, but only where this Regulation does not confer such powers on the ECB. When the ECB acts by means of instructions, supervisory action is implemented through a two-step process which concludes with a national legal act.[54] For example, for credit institutions established in Member States in close cooperation, which is the arrangement envisaged in the SSM Regulation for non-euro area Member States to join the European Banking Union, the ECB shall perform its tasks by addressing instructions to the NCA concerned, in accordance with Article 7(4) SSM Regulation.[55] It is useful to remember that the European Commission's original proposal on the SSM Regulation did not envisage the conferral of direct supervisory

[48] Supervisory decisions may also be adopted via delegation, that is, by ECB heads of work units, without involvement of the Supervisory Board and Governing Council. See in more detail Christy Ann Petit, 'The SSM and the ECB Decision-Making Governance' in Gianni Lo Schiavo (ed), *The European Banking Union and the Role of Law* (Edward Elgar Publishing 2019) 117.

[49] SSM Regulation (n 1) Art 4(3) second para.

[50] ibid Art 6(5)(d).

[51] ibid Arts 14 and 15.

[52] ibid Art 6(5)(b).

[53] ibid Art 6(5)(a) (the provision uses the word 'shall', but the ECB has a discretion to decide whether to issue this type of act).

[54] See in more detail Witte, 'The Application of National Banking Supervision Law by the ECB: Three Parallel Modes of Executing EU Law?' (n 47) 99.

[55] For the legal issues arising in the context of close cooperation, see Rosa Maria Lastra, 'Close cooperation in the SSM' in ECB, 'Building bridges: central banking law in an interconnected world' (2019) ECB Legal Conference 2019, 283 <https://www.ecb.europa.eu/pub/pdf/other/ecb.ecblegalconferenceproceedings201912~9325c45957.en.pdf?258d648ffcf1be39f9d927e5c13f393f> accessed 27 May 2022.

powers on the ECB when the ECB had to apply national law implementing EU law. The ECB would have acted only by means of instructions addressed to NCAs, without having direct powers vis-à-vis credit institutions, until EU law would not have granted such powers.[56] The final version of the SSM Regulation has limited the power to issue instructions to NCAs to those instances where the ECB has a supervisory task but no related power to act vis-à-vis credit institutions.[57]

To conclude, the SSM Regulation makes sure that the ECB has the necessary powers to carry out its tasks but does not establish a perfect correspondence between tasks and powers. In particular, some powers can be exercised by the ECB only on the basis of EU law, others can be exercised by the ECB but on the basis of national law transposing EU law, and others have to be exercised by the NCAs on the basis of an ECB's instruction. From the ECB's perspective, this means that prudential supervisory powers have been designed with a 'variable geometry'[58] because their scope and intensity changes in the light of the type of task (micro or macroprudential), the nature of the credit institution (SI or LSI), and its location (euro area or close cooperation). This means that in these three scenarios, NCAs cannot autonomously exercise powers for the purpose of carrying out a prudential task which has been attributed to the ECB but can act only if instructed by the ECB.[59]

C. The NCA tasks, powers, and responsibilities

As noted above, the conferral of prudential supervisory tasks to the ECB was seen as a necessity driven by the wording of Article 127(6) TFEU. However, replacing the NCAs with the ECB, and entrusting it with the responsibility for the supervision of over 6,000 banks (SIs are stand-alone SIs and Sis' groups, which include the mother company and all the group banking subsidiaries established in the SSM) would have clearly been challenging. To ensure that the NCAs' expertise, experience, and proximity with the supervised entities is functional to the ECB performance of its prudential tasks, the SSM Regulation designed a complex framework which includes different models of 'institutional' or multi-level vertical differentiation, such as the decentralization of operational tasks, the preservation of certain tasks with the NCAs, and the separation of tasks between ECB and NCAs.[60]

In legislative terms, the 'fusion of competences'[61] between ECB and NCAs was achieved, first of all, as mentioned, by granting on the ECB the exclusive competence

[56] Recital 45 of Commission Proposal on SSM Regulation, COM/2012/0511 final. See further Bassani, 'The Centralisation of Prudential Supervision' (n 9) 1008–09.

[57] The ECB always has a power to adopt decisions, but the power to instruct is only provided in SSM Regulation (n 1) Art 6 para 3 and Art 9 para 1, third indent.

[58] Bassani, 'The Centralisation of Prudential Supervision' (n 9) 1014.

[59] See similarly Pizzolla, 'The Role of the European Central Bank in the Single Supervisory Mechanism' (n 28) 22.

[60] See in more detail Teixeira, *The Legal History of the European Banking Union* (n 11) 230–31 (noting that decentralization of operational tasks resembles the ESCB institutional framework, the preservation of previous NCAs tasks resembles a model of delegation of decision-making from the ECB to the NCAs, and the separation of tasks resembles the US dual banking model).

[61] ibid 230.

to exercise the tasks listed in Article 4(1) SSM Regulation and by requiring the NCAs to assist the ECB in the performance of these tasks. Outside this boundary, NCAs remain competent to carry out the tasks that have not been expressly granted on the ECB as specified by recital 28 of the SSM Regulation (eg market supervision, the prevention of the use of the financial system for the purpose of money laundering and terrorist financing, and consumer protection). Moreover, the NCAs remain competent to conduct supervision on entities not qualifying as credit institutions, financial holdings, or mixed financial holdings in Union law.

Second, NCAs carry out the prudential supervisory tasks in relation to the LSIs. As mentioned, these are not equal to the NCAs' pre-SSM tasks but have been 're-shaped' by the conferral of prudential tasks on the ECB. In fact, not only can the ECB exercise some specific powers also with regard to LSIs, but it is also responsible for licensing, qualifying holdings, and withdrawal of licence procedures (common procedures) with regard to LSIs.[62] The reason is that common procedures determine the entry and exit of credit institutions, as well as their shareholders, in the market and therefore the ECB, as supranational authority, should have the final decision-making power with regard to these crucial procedures with regard to the euro area.[63] In relation to these procedures, the NCAs carry out one step of the process that leads to the adoption of an ECB supervisory decision.[64]

Third, in order to enable the ECB to exercise oversight over the functioning of the system, the SSM Framework Regulation[65] details a set of information and reporting duties for the NCAs to the ECB. In particular, NCAs shall inform the ECB in case of financial deterioration of a LSI, when material NCA supervisory procedures are planned to be adopted, and shall send to the ECB draft supervisory decisions which relate to the removal of members of the management board and the appointment of special managers or have a significant impact on the LSIs.[66]

Fourth, NCAs maintain some powers also with regard to SIs. In particular, Article 6(6) SSM Regulation empowers NCAs to obtain information from SIs and to perform on-site inspections on SIs. When these activities are performed, NCAs shall then report to the ECB. Moreover, NCAs have the power to address binding supervisory decisions based on ECB instructions, to supervised entities in close cooperation.[67] Lastly, it is for the NCAs to apply penalties also to SIs, in the cases specified by Article 18(5) SSM Regulation.

Finally, NCAs have a general duty to assist the ECB in the performance of its tasks, including with regard to the SIs. The rationale of this duty (literally phrased as a responsibility for the NCAs) is to ensure that NCAs, which have important and long-established expertise in the supervision of credit institutions within their territory and their economic, organizational and cultural specificities,[68] can effectively support the

[62] SSM Regulation (n 1) Arts 14 and 15 and SSM Framework Regulation (n 6) part V.

[63] By virtue of the principle of a single passport, embraced by the CRD, once authorized to carry out banking activity in one Member State of the Union, the credit institution can provide services and open branches across the Union.

[64] See Section IV.

[65] SSM Framework Regulation (n 6).

[66] ibid Arts 96–98.

[67] SSM Regulation (n 1) Art 9(1) third subpara and Art 7(4).

[68] SSM Framework Regulation (n 6) recital 37.

ECB in the exercise of its tasks. In turn, the NCAs' role in assisting the ECB enables the ECB to take into account 'the diversity of credit institutions and their size and business models, as well as the systemic benefits of diversity in the banking industry of the Union'.[69] As shown later on, this duty can manifest itself in different forms depending on the specific tasks and circumstances of the case.

In conclusion, the NCA's powers vary greatly because they reflect different institutional models of cooperation, coordination between the 'centre' and the 'periphery' in banking supervision. They concern in particular the adoption of binding supervisory decisions with regard to LSIs in the cases mentioned above, the exercise of inspections and request for information powers towards SIs and LSIs, and the adoption of other types of preparatory acts in relation to an ECB supervisory decision (ie acts taken in the context of common procedures or fit and proper assessments).

III. The Role of the ECB and the NCAs in Day-to-Day SSM Banking Supervision of Significant Institutions

The ECB's tasks and powers in the SSM should be assessed in light of the day-to-day supervision of supervised entities to show how the relationship between ECB and NCAs works in practice. An analysis of the role of the ECB in the SSM should take into account the application of the rules and requires an examination of the three forms of day-to-day supervision: the functioning of the joint supervisory teams (JSTs), the Supervisory Examination Programme (SEP) and the Supervisory Review and Evaluation Programme (SREP).

A. The JSTs

The SSM Framework Regulation establishes the main modalities to achieve cooperation in supervising SIs and creates an instrument of direct cooperation between the ECB and the NCAs in the SSM, the 'joint supervisory teams' (JST).[70] These teams are composed of ECB and NCA officials with an ECB JST coordinator and an NCA sub-coordinator in charge of the day-to-day supervision of SIs.[71]

The day-to-day work of the JSTs consists in supervising on a daily basis the bank, in particular by requesting orally the adoption of a certain conduct or by adopting operational acts. It can also be by requesting the initiation of an inspection or requiring information from an individual entity or by authorizing operations. These tools are used in day-to-day banking supervision and are conducted in a cooperative way: the ECB staff in the person of the JST coordinator is in the lead and the NCA staff provides assistance.

The JSTs are a key and effective component of the SSM, in particular because the JSTs act closely and review day-to-day the status, activities, and risks of individual

[69] SSM Regulation (n 1) recitals 17 and 37.
[70] See SSM Framework Regulation (n 6) Art 3.
[71] ibid Art 6.

credit institutions. The JST structure aims to ensure that there is an adequate level of staffing and centralization while relying on national expertise and resources. It allows the ECB to have adequate supervisory staff and resources with ultimate decision-making power while drawing on national experts and NCA staff for established and national supervisory knowledge and practices. While the formal and informal decision-making rests within the ECB or the ECB staff in the JSTs, the preparation of documentation and the level of responsibilities in the SSM is usually semi-parallel in the JSTs with the division of work between ECB and NCA staff and only an overall coordinating role for the ECB JST coordinator. In most cases, the ECB staff supervises directly the mother entity of a significant group, while the NCA staff conducts supervision over the subsidiaries of the significant group and assists the ECB staff in the supervision of the mother entity. The JSTs are thus a specific feature of the supervision of significant institutions.

B. The SEP: off-site and on-site supervision

The Supervisory Examination Programme (SEP) is a general tool prepared by the ECB horizontal functions and the JSTs.[72] It sets out the main strategies and supervisory priorities for the calendar year and distributes the tasks between the ECB and the NCA staff. This tool is basically a dashboard of the main off-site and on-site activities conducted in the day-to-day supervision and helps to focus the JST's attention on the main aspects of ongoing supervision on a yearly basis. As part of the off-site activities, the SEP sets out deep dives, closer examinations, and studies on the supervised entities, while the on-site part provides for a general overview of the on-site inspections and internal model investigations planned for the following year.

The off-site activities are usually conducted by the JSTs with the assistance of the ECB horizontal functions in charge of cross-sectorial or common topics or risks, and the responsible NCA.

The on-site supervision is a set of tools used to analyse more specifically certain aspects that are subject to supervisory scrutiny for a specific reason by the prudential supervisor. The two instruments used for these purposes are on-site inspections and internal model investigations. The first is the typical instrument used to assess more in detail and directly in the premises of the supervised entity a specific area that is relevant for prudential supervision. For example, the ECB can decide to launch an inspection on the governance framework of a supervised entity (eg inspection on the remuneration framework or the compliance function of a bank). The latter is a specific investigation on the internal models used by a supervised entity to comply with prudential requirements with close scrutiny on the model design, implementation, and processes. For example, the ECB can launch an inspection on credit risk modelling of a supervised entity.

[72] See European Central Bank, 'SSM Supervisory Manual. European banking supervision: functioning of the SSM and supervisory approach' (ECB, March 2018), 61 <https://www.bankingsupervision.europa.eu/ecb/pub/pdf/ssm.supervisorymanual201803.en.pdf> accessed 27 May 2022.

On-site inspections are one of the most intrusive supervisory powers of the ECB and NCAs in the SSM.[73] The inspections are usually managed by a Head of Mission, who acts as the main counterpart for the supervised entity and is responsible to direct the on-site inspection. The staff of the ECB and the NCAs are then involved in the specific on-site inspection activities with day-to-day on-site supervision in the context of the specific mission. The result of the on-site inspection is a report that is then shared with the credit institution and that contains a series of recommendations addressed to the credit institution to improve specific aspects identified in the inspection over a specific amount of time.[74] The remediation of the findings of the on-site inspection report are then monitored by the JST in ongoing supervision.

One key aspect of on-site inspection is the joint participation of ECB and NCA staff. Given the high number of on-site inspections carried out each year, the ECB staff are insufficient to attend and participate in all on-site inspections for SIs. Assistance of and coordination with NCAs' staff for on-site inspections are therefore essential in the SSM. While the ECB is the competent authority to supervise SIs, on-site inspections are usually conducted by NCA staff with limited participation by ECB staff due to lack of resources and staff. In order to detach the national dimension from on-site inspection, the ECB and NCAs have agreed on having a *de facto* rotation of NCA staff for inspections in a cross-country manner or to have an ECB Head of Mission for important on-site missions. This means that a tool to detach the national bias in on-site inspections is to confer the ad hoc Head of Mission position to an ECB staff member or an NCA of a different Member State.

Overall, the level of cooperation between the ECB and the NCAs in the SEP planning and execution is strong and important for the collection of findings and deficiencies in supervised groups.

C. The SREP

The SREP is a supervisory review exercise that the ECB conducts usually on an annual basis on the 'significant' supervised entities. This review takes the form of an ECB decision that assesses some aspects of a bank at a point in time. In other words, the SREP is an annual health check of the supervised entity.[75] The ECB SREP decision contains a detailed assessment of a credit institution or a banking group based on four axes: the business model, internal governance and risk management, capital adequacy, and liquidity adequacy. The assessment is grounded on the evaluation of the supervisory

[73] See SSM Regulation (n 1) Art 12.

[74] See, eg, European Central Bank, 'ECB Annual Report on supervisory activities 2019' (ECB, 19 March 2020), 43 ff <https://www.bankingsupervision.europa.eu/press/publications/annual-report/html/ssm.ar2019~4851adc406.en.html#toc13> accessed 27 May 2022; European Central Bank, 'Guide to onsite inspections and internal model investigations' (ECB, September 2018) <https://www.bankingsupervision.europa.eu/ecb/pub/pdf/ssm.osi_guide201809.en.pdf> accessed 27 May 2022.

[75] See European Central Bank, 'What is the SREP?' (*ECB*, 16 June 2016 updated 13 November 2017) <https://www.bankingsupervision.europa.eu/about/ssmexplained/html/srep.en.html> accessed 27 May 2022.

activities conducted in previous years and takes into account the results of off-site activities and on-site inspection reports.

In general terms, the ECB has the task and power to adopt supervisory decisions imposing significant institutions to hold own funds beyond the so-called Pillar 1 regulatory requirements, which are the requirements set out in the CRR.[76] Moreover, it can also impose additional qualitative measures in order to remediate specific deficiencies or findings identified in its assessment. Therefore, the SREP is considered an essential supervisory review, which imposes Pillar 2 requirements on top of the Pillar 1 requirements and is exercised directly by the prudential supervisor. In other words, the ECB makes an overall assessment of the supervised entity and may impose prudential quantitative and qualitative requirements that are additional to the minimum requirements set out in the CRR.[77] This power allows the ECB to impose capital requirements and other additional quantitative and qualitative measures on supervised entities.[78].

Overall, SREP is the most important power conferred to the ECB pursuant to Article 16 SSM Regulation. It is exercised directly by the ECB with the use of a horizontal standardized SREP methodology,[79] an ongoing supervisory dialogue between the JST and the supervised entity, and the preparation and notification of an ECB SREP decision.

IV. The Role of the ECB and the NCAs in SSM Authorizations

This section looks at the general powers of authorization that the ECB has in the SSM and its relationship with the NCAs. Together with the day-to-day supervision, there is also a wide array of authorization powers that the ECB exercises directly on significant institutions. The authorization powers and the rules on the procedure are both provided in directly applicable EU law and national law implementing EU law. A general categorization, based on the SSM Framework Regulation, is the following: common procedures, 'fit and proper' authorization procedures, and other authorization procedures.

[76] SSM Regulation (n 1) Art 16. See European Commission, 'Commission Staff Working Document Accompanying the document Report from the Commission to the European Parliament and the Council on the Single Supervisory Mechanism established pursuant to Regulation (EU) No 1024/2013' SWD(2017) 336 final, 42 ff.

[77] The legal basis for the adoption of a SREP decision is SSM Regulation (n 1) Art 16, which contains, in para 1, the requirements for the adoption of a supervisory decision and, in para 2, a list of powers that can be exercised also as part of the SREP assessment with quantitative or qualitative requirements.

[78] SSM Regulation (n 1) Art 16 para 2 in conjunction with CRD (n 46) Art 97.

[79] See European Central Bank, 'Supervisory methodology' (ECB, 20 January 2020) <https://www.bankingsupervision.europa.eu/banking/srep/2019/html/methodology.en.html#toc1> accessed 27 May 2022.

A. SSM common procedures (banking licences and qualifying holding authorizations)

Common procedures are those applying to all credit institutions, both SIs and LSIs, established in the SSM and are the licensing, withdrawal of licence, and qualifying holding authorization. Common procedures are the only composite formal administrative procedures in the SSM. They comprise first a national phase at NCA level and then a supranational phase at ECB level.[80] While there are two phases in these procedures, the NCA and the ECB phase, the ECB has the decisive and final power to adopt these authorizations, with one exception that is assessed below. The licensing and qualifying holding powers have been identified by the EU legislators as the most important ones for unity and cohesion in the SSM and therefore have been attributed to the ECB both for SIs and LSIs. At the same time, the structure of these procedures also faces some challenges, especially for the LSIs, as there is a mismatch between the day-to-day supervision and the one-off authorization adopted by the ECB.

As to the licensing power, the ECB has the exclusive task and power to confer and withdraw banking licences in the SSM.[81] Article 14 of the SSM Regulation establishes a bottom-up administrative procedure where the NCAs analyse the application for an authorization on the part of the credit institution.[82] The NCA will issue a draft decision for the ECB to assess. According to the SSM Framework Regulation, once the draft decision of the NCA is submitted to the ECB, the ECB has only ten working days to adopt a decision. However, in practice there is a pre-application stage between the applicant, the ECB, and the NCA that can also last several months where all the terms of the authorization are discussed in detail. Only when the draft decision does not comply with the conditions for authorization, will the ECB object to the authorization.[83] In case the ECB does not object to the draft decision, the decision is deemed to be adopted as a positively silent ECB decision.[84] One exception to the exclusive ECB decision-making power is the case in which the NCA decides to reject the application for a licence due to reasons of national law. In this case, the ECB is in principle not involved in the procedure and the NCA as the entry point can decide on the application.

The licence application is assessed on the basis of the criteria contained in the CRD[85] and national law. Nevertheless, the ECB remains the main decision maker for licensing applications and can also overturn the positive assessment made by the NCA in the procedure.

Withdrawals of licences are subject to a similar procedure, with the notable difference that the ECB shall adopt an explicit decision withdrawing the licence without the possibility of having a silent decision. The ECB assesses the withdrawal of a licence in light of the criteria established in the CRD and in national law.[86] The ECB remains

[80] See, among others, Filipe Brito Bastos, 'Derivative Illegality in European Composite Administrative Procedures' (2018) 55 CML Rev 101.

[81] SSM Regulation (n 1) Art 4 para 1 subpara (a) in conjunction with Art 6 para 4 4.

[82] SSM Regulation (n 1) Art 14.

[83] ibid Art 14 para 2.

[84] SSM Regulation (n 1) Art 14 paras 5–6.

[85] CRD (n 46) Arts 8–16.

[86] ibid Art 18.

the ultimate decision-maker for the withdrawal of a licence, again based on a draft NCA decision. This decision can be difficult and burdensome in practice, in particular when the credit institution has its licence withdrawn against its intention as it is not complying with prudential requirements or other requirements set out in EU law and national law as set out in the CRD and implementing national law. The withdrawal of the licence can also interfere with other procedures, such as the ECB's 'failing or likely to fail' assessment or liquidation procedures in national law.[87] Therefore, cooperation between the ECB and the NCAs is key for this procedure. However, there may be cases in which the different tasks assigned to NCAs, such as the conduct of liquidation procedures or the appointments of special functions in the bank, may impact the ECB intention to withdraw the licence. Furthermore, the withdrawal of a licence gives grounds to judicial challenges, especially from shareholders or creditors that may be affected. There is now some CJEU case law in the field, which shows that some aspects related to admissibility, the grounds for judicial protection, and the substance of the assessment remain contested. In particular, the *Trasta* case[88] sheds some light on the relationship between the ECB as exclusive decision-making authority to withdraw the banking licences and national competences related to the liquidation of entities.[89] The Court of Justice takes into account the complexities of ensuring judicial protection arising from the withdrawal of a licence and the consequent appointment of a liquidator under national law. In the judgment, the Court held that some restrictions on judicial protection due to the liquidator's appointment on the bank shareholders after the withdrawal of a licence have taken place. It also refers to the contributing role of the NCA in starting the withdrawal procedure and the subsequent role of the NCA in the liquidation procedure.[90] This judgment shows the challenges of the withdrawal of licence procedure, such as the level of judicial protection and the different assessments made in each case, especially in cases where the NCA also acts as a competent authority in the liquidation procedures. It calls into question further coordination and attention on this procedure, especially in cases of withdrawal of a licence of LSIs taken to address deficiencies or issues, where the ECB does not conduct day-to-day supervision.

The qualifying holding procedure, that is, the acquisition of a holding giving to a shareholder control or significant influence on an SSM credit institution, is the third common procedure in the SSM. The ECB has the exclusive task and power to authorize qualifying holdings in credit institutions established in the SSM.[91] The procedure is based on the assessment criteria contained in the CRD[92] and follows a

[87] ibid Art 18 letter (d) in combination with Directive 2014/59/EU of the European Parliament and of the Council of 15 May 2014 establishing a framework for the recovery and resolution of credit institutions and investment firms and amending Council Directive 82/891/EEC, and Directives 2001/24/EC, 2002/47/EC, 2004/25/EC, 2005/56/EC, 2007/36/EC, 2011/35/EU, 2012/30/EU and 2013/36/EU, and Regulations (EU) No 1093/2010 and (EU) No 648/2012, of the European Parliament and of the Council (BRRD), Art 32.

[88] C-663/17 P *ECB v Trasta Komercbanka and Others* [2019] EU:C:2019:923 (hereafter *ECB v Trasta Komercbanka and Others*). See in literature Andreas Witte, 'Avoiding lacunae for Judicial Review in the Interplay between National and Union law in the Banking Union—Notes on the Judgment of the Court of Justice in Joined Cases C-663/17 P, C-665/17 P and C-669/17 P Trasta Komercbanka' (2020) 45 EL Rev 569.

[89] *ECB v Trasta Komercbanka and Others* (n 88) para 71.

[90] ibid para 74.

[91] SSM Regulation (n 1) Art 4(c) in conjunction with Art 6 para 4. See also SSM Regulation (n 1) Art 15.

[92] CRD (n 46) Art 23.

bottom-up administrative procedure where the NCA is the entry point for the authorization and issues a draft decision for the ECB that ultimately adopts a decision within the timeframe provided in the CRD.[93] Differently from the licensing procedures, the qualifying holding procedure is a composite administrative procedure where the ECB remains in any case the ultimate decision maker with no exception for the NCAs. The exclusive role of the ECB in this procedure has been confirmed in the *Berlusconi* case,[94] where the CJEU held that the ECB is exclusively competent to adopt the qualifying holding decision, with a supporting role for the NCAs. The case dealt with a negative qualifying holding authorization initiated *ex officio* by the NCA against Berlusconi and Fininvest as shareholders in a less significant institution. Berlusconi and Fininvest challenged the negative assessment made by the Banca d'Italia (the Italian NCA) in the qualifying holding procedure before the national courts. As the question related to the ECB competence in qualifying holdings for banks in the SSM, the Court of Justice was called in a preliminary ruling to assess the ECB competence and the nature of the qualifying holding procedure. The Court of Justice held that the ECB is exclusively competent to assess qualifying holdings in the SSM and the procedure is an administrative procedure where the ECB as the competent EU institution is exclusively competent to authorize such authorizations. This judgment is to be welcomed as it clarifies the nature of the qualifying holding procedure, the ECB's task in approving qualifying holdings, and the CJEU's scrutiny on SSM common procedures. The CJEU considers the ECB as the exclusive decision maker at the centre of the SSM authorizations for qualifying holding procedures.[95] The NCAs only have a supporting or assisting role in the process.[96]

A relevant issue of the qualifying holding procedures concerns the relationship between the ECB and the NCAs for the authorizations on LSIs. The qualifying holding procedure assesses a structural operation of a bank at a point in time. However, there is no strong link between the ECB's authorization and the NCA's day-to-day supervision of the LSIs. The NCA exercises the day-to-day supervision of the LSIs, while the ECB is only responsible to authorize a qualifying holding. This means that the ECB's authorization is not sufficient to address deficiencies and findings related to a shareholder of an 'LSI' that materialize after the authorization is granted or that are of a more general nature. While the first phase of the procedure is with the NCA, it leaves it to the NCAs to follow up in ongoing supervision and arguably has a limited influence on the life of the supervised entity.

[93] ibid Art 22.

[94] Case C-219/17 *Silvio Berlusconi and Finanziaria d'investimento Fininvest SpA (Fininvest) v Banca d'Italia and Istituto per la Vigilanza Sulle Assicurazioni (IVASS)* [2018] EU:C:2018:1023 (hereafter *Silvio Berlusconi*). In literature see the commentary of Paul Dermine and Mariolina Eliantonio, 'Case Note: CJEU (Grand Chamber), Judgment of 19 December 2018, C-219/17, Silvio Berlusconi and Finanziaria d'investimento Fininvest SpA (Fininvest) v Banca d'Italia and Istituto per la Vigilanza Sulle Assicurazioni (IVASS)' (2019) 12 European Review of Administrative Law 244.

[95] *Silvio Berlusconi* (n 94) paras 43–44 and 55.

[96] ibid.

B. Fit and proper authorizations

Fit and proper authorizations are the administrative approvals of managers at board or senior level in supervised entities. These are specific procedures in the SSM compared to the other ECB procedures and the common procedures. They are provided in the SSM Framework Regulation as a 'quasi' common procedure, as the entry point of notification of the intention to appoint or the bank decision to appoint a member of the management body is made at the NCA level and not directly to the JST.[97] The ECB has the exclusive power to adopt a fit and proper decision for members of SIs, while the NCAs exercise fit and proper powers for LSIs. The ECB is the final decision maker for managers of SIs and adopts the final decisions in accordance with national law procedural rules. Fit and proper procedures entail a complex interaction between EU law and national law as regards the substantive requirements and procedural rules. In particular, pursuant to Article 93 of the SSM Framework Regulation the rules on timeline for adoption, suspension, or interruption are set out in national law. Furthermore, differently from the qualifying holding procedure, the assessment criteria are not subject to maximum harmonization, but to national law implementing the CRD. This means that there are divergences in national laws relating to the fit and proper assessment in the SSM, which impact the ECB in adopting these authorizations.

C. Other SSM authorizations for SIs

Other authorization procedures are those that apply with a direct notification to the ECB for SIs and which follow Article 95 SSM Framework Regulation. This article simply states that a significant institution shall submit all the requests, applications, and notifications under substantive EU and national law to the ECB. The ECB shall keep the NCAs informed and may ask the NCAs to prepare a draft decision to be submitted to it. However, this article does not provide further clarity on the types of authorizations that the ECB can adopt in the SSM. In general terms, the ECB is empowered to adopt all authorizations that are provided in directly applicable EU law related to prudential supervision and national law implementing EU law on prudential supervision.

Authorizations under directly applicable EU law are usually provided in the CRR, delegated and implementing EU Regulations, or Decisions and any other directly applicable EU rule that sets out an authorizing power for the competent authority in prudential supervision. The role of the ECB in this case is exclusive for SIs and there is only an assisting role for the NCAs, usually in the JSTs preparing and supporting the ECB and its staff in adopting these decisions. Cooperation between the ECB and NCAs takes place in the JSTs, with the support of other ECB or NCA horizontal functions if needed. The scope of these authorizations refers to provisions on own funds requirements, internal models, prudential waivers, and other authorizations that are usually provided in directly applicable EU law.

[97] SSM Framework Regulation (n 6) Art 93.

Mention should be made of the passporting procedure, which applies when a credit institution established in the SSM intends to open a branch in the SSM or outside the SSM but in the EU/EEA, or a non-SSM EU credit institution intends to open a branch in the SSM.[98] In these cases, the SSM Framework Regulation does not require the adoption of an ECB decision, but simply sets out a two-month period to object to the passporting application, which is submitted to the home NCA as an entry point. The general good grounds for objections to the passporting application would require the adoption of a negative ECB decision.

Authorizations under national law implementing EU law are generally provided in the national law implementing EU directives.[99] National law usually provides for specific authorizations that are only present in some jurisdictions and are related to specific operations of credit institutions.[100] These are requests, authorizations, or notifications concerning mergers, acquisitions in non-banks, outsourcing, key function holders, statute amendments, and operations with related parties.

The scope for the ECB's application of national law through these authorizations has been clarified by the ECB in 2017 with the publication of a letter on 'national powers'.[101] This letter sets out the main rules on the application of authorizing powers for the ECB in national law implementing EU law and includes a non-exhaustive list of provisions where such authorizations are provided.

These national powers are various and usually respect the substantive and procedural rules of the jurisdictions of the requesting supervised entity. This means that the ECB applies the substantive criteria provided for in these national laws and the procedural requirements related to these procedures such as the timeline for adoption, unless there are EU administrative rules in the field (ie right to be heard, access to the file).[102] The role of the NCAs in these procedures is to support the ECB in looking at the application or notification, contributing to making a draft assessment that will be made available to the ECB, and providing clarity on national practices and specificities whenever needed. The NCAs are subject to the duty of cooperation in good faith with the ECB in receiving, assessing, and processing these authorizations in the SSM.

The 2017 letter clarifies that these authorizations are adopted by the ECB when they concern 'SIs', relate to one of the ECB tasks under Article 4 SSM Regulation, and underpin a supervisory function under EU prudential law, in particular for rules provided in the CRD.

There is yet no specific CJEU case law on these authorizations. It is, however, worth mentioning the *VTB Bank* preliminary ruling.[103] The case concerned penalties imposed under national law by the Austrian NCA regarding prudential findings and deficiencies in the VTB bank. The preliminary question was whether this penalty provided in Austrian law is covered by EU law or not. The CJEU considered that the contested penalty under national law is not in line with the relevant CRR provision, as an automatic levy is raised without taking into account the criteria provided in the CRR

[98] ibid Arts 11–17.
[99] See Section II.A.
[100] See generally Lo Schiavo, 'The ECB and its application of National Law' (n 45) 177.
[101] 'European Central Bank clarification letter' (n 45) 1.
[102] SSM Framework Regulation (n 6) Arts 31, 32, and 33.
[103] Case C-52/17 *VTB Bank (Austria) v Finanzmarktaufsichtsbehörde* [2018] EU:C:2018:648.

as the matter comes within the scope of EU law. This judgment suggests that national provisions going against directly applicable EU law or EU maximum harmonization rules cannot be considered in line with EU law. Therefore, national measures adopted by national legislators or authorities creating new authorizations or administrative measures could infringe EU prudential rules and, generally, national legislators and authorities should respect the principle of primacy of EU law.

At the same time, challenges for the ECB relating to its application of national law for these authorizations consist of the fact that the ECB has no power to amend the national law in question and is subject to the interpretation and the approach taken by the NCA in the field, especially when the relevant national law is adopted directly by the NCA by way of orders, circulars, or decree having a general scope.[104] In perspective, it is hoped that these national authorizations are replaced by directly applicable EU law or that NCAs or national legislators repeal such authorizations, especially when considered not material in the overall SSM framework.[105]

To conclude, the level of cooperation between ECB and NCAs in authorizations is clear in general terms, but less clear when it comes to apply the rules in practice, as there are different levels of interpretation and application of the rules especially when the ECB applies national law.

V. The Role of the ECB in the Oversight of the Functioning of the SSM

A. The ECB's responsibility for oversight

Article 6(1) SSM Regulation allocates to the ECB the responsibility for the effective and consistent functioning of the SSM and imposes on both the ECB and NCAs a duty of cooperation in good faith and an obligation to exchange information. The duties laid down in this article should be seen in strict connection with the overriding objectives of the SSM (banks' and financial system stability). In the more and more integrated and globalized financial markets, the coordination between the 'centre' and the 'periphery' is crucial to monitor individual as well as systemic risks but also to ensure that swift actions are taken when necessary.[106] The emergence of multi-layered and composite EU and national administrative structures after the 2008 Global Financial Crisis (ESFS, SSM, and SRM) has undoubtedly increased the need to foster centralization, to tackle risks that are not purely national and require a supranational

[104] See, eg, Jörg Deslandes, Cristina Dias, and Marcel Magnus, 'Banking Union: Completing the Single Rule Book' (2019) European Parliament Briefing PE 634.375 <https://www.europarl.europa.eu/RegData/etudes/BRIE/2019/634375/IPOL_BRI(2019)634375_EN.pdf> accessed 27 May 2022.

[105] See Lo Schiavo, 'The ECB and its Application of National Law' (n 45) 177; Andrea Biondi and Alessandro Spano, 'The ECB and the Application of National Law in the SSM: New Yet Old ... ' (2020) 31 EBL Rev 1023; Florin Coman-Kund and Fabian Amtenbrink, 'On the Scope and Limits of the Application of National Law by the European Central Bank within the Single Supervisory Mechanism' (2018) 33 Banking & Finance Law Review 133.

[106] Katharina Pistor, 'A Legal Theory of Finance' (2013) 41 Journal of Comparative Economics 319.

coordinated response, while ensuring a strong connection with the supervised entities that are embedded in their national economies, cultures, and traditions.

Conceptually, several different theoretical constructions have been proposed to qualify the ECB–NCAs relationships.[107] Some legal scholars described the relationship between the ECB and the NCAs in a vertical fashion, using the category of a principal–agent relationship, where the ECB acts as a principal and the NCA acts as an agent.[108] Others relied on horizontal theoretical constructions, where powers are shared on the same level between the national and the EU level.[109] In the complex legal construction of the SSM, both vertical and horizontal elements of governance can be found. It also seems clear that traditional categories of national administrative law, like administrative hierarchy, do not fit this model because the ECB and the NCAs are not part of the same administration.[110] In fact, the ECB cannot overrule a decision taken by the NCA on an LSI and cannot issue individual instructions to an NCA regarding a specific LSI. Similarly, the NCA cannot overrule a decision of the ECB for SIs or an ECB decision under SSM common procedures.

At the same time, the theoretical constructions that qualify the SSM as a network or forum between different bodies, including the ECB, with equal tasks and powers, do not reflect the economic rationale and the legal design of the SSM. As mentioned earlier, the SSM was created to reduce risks posed by the banking sector to the stability of the euro area and, more generally, the entire EU. The provisions of the SSM Regulation should be read in light of this statutory objective which required a multi-layered (national and EU) organizational structure to make sure that the ECB has the necessary support, in terms of resources, experience, and expertise, from the NCAs to carry out its tasks. In legal terms, this objective was reflected in the exclusive conferral of the prudential supervisory tasks listed in Article 4 SSM Regulation to the ECB and the allocation to the ECB of the responsibility for the functioning of the SSM. This is also reflected in a range of mechanisms established to ensure the ECB's accountability before EU and national institutions[111] and in the ECB's power to take over, in specific cases, the supervision of LSIs.[112] The allocation of tasks and powers between the ECB and NCAs is instrumental to ensure the effective functioning of the SSM, which supervises thousands of credit institutions (SIs and LSIs) located in the euro area as well as in participating Member States whose currency is not the euro (currently, Bulgaria and Croatia).

[107] Filippo Annunziata, 'Fostering Centralization of EU Banking Supervision Through Case-Law. The European Court of Justice and the Role of the European Central Bank' (2019) Bocconi Legal Studies Research Paper 3372346 <https://papers.ssrn.com/sol3/papers.cfm?abstract_id=3372346> accessed 27 May 2022.

[108] Monti and Petit, 'The Single Supervisory Mechanism: Legal Fragilities and Possible Solutions' (n 23) 5 (raising doubts about the incentives for the NCAs to act in line with ECB interests).

[109] See Marcello Clarich, 'I poteri di vigilanza della Banca Centrale Europea' (2013) Diritto pubblico 986.

[110] See, however, Case T-122/15 *Landeskreditbank Baden-Württemberg—Förderbank v ECB* [2017] EU:T:2017:337, paras 59 and 61 (the Court expressly speaks of a relationship of 'subordination' between the NCAs and the ECB).

[111] SSM Regulation (n 1) Arts 20 and 21.

[112] The procedure for 'taking over' the supervision of a LSI is regulated in detail by SSM Framework Regulation (n 6) Arts 67, 68, and 69. See, eg, European Central Bank, 'ECB takes over direct supervision of AS PNB Banka in Latvia' (ECB Press Release, 11 March 2019) <https://www.bankingsupervision.europa.eu/press/pr/date/2019/html/ssm.pr190311~24201e56e0.en.html> accessed 27 May 2022.

There are two 'bridges' to connect the EU and national levels: the ECB and NCAs duty to cooperation and exchange of information; and the NCA's duty to assist the ECB. The duty of cooperation in good faith reflects the general duty of sincere cooperation between the Union and Member States[113] and is also set out in the ESFS and in the SRM.[114]

The duty to exchange information is the most important corollary of the duty to cooperate in good faith. Ensuring an appropriate and reliable flow of information between the ECB and the NCAs applies at every level of governance, from the JST to the Supervisory Board. This requires both the ECB and the NCA to exchange information relating to significant supervised entities where there is a serious indication that those entities can no longer be relied on to fulfil their obligations towards their creditors and, in particular, can no longer provide security for the assets entrusted to them by their depositors, or where there is a serious indication of circumstances that could lead to a determination that the credit institution concerned is unable to repay the deposits.[115]

B. The NCA's duty of assistance

The NCA's duty to assist the ECB in the performance of its tasks aims to ensure that the ECB can operate taking into account geographical proximity, operational effectiveness, and local knowledge which are ensured by the NCAs.[116] As held earlier, the EU courts framed the NCAs' duty of assistance in terms of decentralized implementation of ECB tasks. In legal terms, this conceptualization aimed to clarify, as shown in the *L-Bank* case, that the NCAs do not keep their pre-SSM tasks and powers with regard to LSIs and that the SSM Regulation did not intend to create a system of parallel tasks and powers, one EU and one national, but rather to centralize specific, enumerated microprudential tasks at the EU level. The duty of assistance, defined by Advocate

[113] Consolidated Version of the Treaty on European Union [2012] OJ C326/1, Art 4.

[114] See Regulation (EU) 1093/2010 of the European Parliament and of the Council of 24 November 2010 establishing a European Supervisory Authority (European Banking Authority), amending Decision No 716/2009/EC and repealing Commission Decision 2009/78/EC [2010] OJ L331/12, Regulation (EU) 1095/2010 of the European Parliament and of the Council of 24 November 2010 establishing a European Supervisory Authority (European Securities and Markets Authority), amending Decision No 716/2009/EC and repealing Commission Decision 2009/77/EC [2010] OJ L331/84 and Regulation (EU) No 1094/2010 of the European Parliament and of the Council of 24 November 2010 establishing a European Supervisory Authority (European Insurance and Occupational Pensions Authority), amending Decision No 716/2009/EC and repealing Commission Decision 2009/79/EC [2010] OJ L331/48 (ESAs Regulations), Art 2(4); Regulation (EU) 1092/2010 of the European Parliament and of the Council of 24 November 2010 on European Union macro-prudential oversight of the financial system and establishing a European Systemic Risk Board [2010] OJ L331/1 (ESRB Regulation), Art 1(4); Regulation (EU) 806/2014 of the European Parliament and of the Council of 15 July 2014 establishing uniform rules and a uniform procedure for the resolution of credit institutions and certain investment firms in the framework of a Single Resolution Mechanism and a Single Resolution Fund and amending Regulation (EU) 1093/2010 [2010] OJ L225/1 (SRM Regulation), Art 31.

[115] SSM Framework Regulation (n 6) Art 92.

[116] Niamh Moloney, 'Banking Union and the Implications for Financial Markets Governance in the EU. Convergence or Divergence?' in Danny Busch and Guido Ferrarini (eds), *European Banking Union* (OUP 2015) 537.

General Hogan as ancillary to the ECB tasks,[117] is of crucial importance for the good functioning of the entire system in that it enables the ECB to carry out effectively and efficiently the supervision over credit institutions of participating Member States.

The NCAs assist the ECB in a variety of forms. As mentioned earlier, the most important form of assistance and mutual cooperation takes place within the JST structure, which brings together local and supranational supervisory experience. The NCA's assistance is also envisaged through more formalized tools like the common procedures, the submission of draft decisions to the ECB in accordance with Article 91 SSM Framework Regulation, the preparation and implementation of any acts related to the ECB tasks, the enforcement of ECB decisions using, when necessary, the powers referred to in the third subparagraph of Article 9(1) and Article 11(2) of the SSM Regulation.[118] Importantly, Article 6(3) of the SSM Regulation specifies that when assisting the ECB the NCA shall follow the ECB's instructions in relation to significant supervised entities.[119]

VI. Conclusion

The SSM Regulation has designed a complex system where the Union and national levels of supervision need to cooperate to achieve the objective of achieving a stable banking and financial system. In the *L-Bank* judgments, the CJEU has clarified that in this multi-layered institutional setting micro-prudential supervisory tasks have been conferred only on the ECB, whereas NCAs should cooperate with the ECB for the implementation of these tasks at the national level.

Notwithstanding the complexities of the SSM, this institutional reform has provided new grounds for supervisory convergence, consistency, and transparency in banking supervision that did not exist before 2014. The ECB has surely been empowered as a direct administrative authority of new tasks that are essential for the good functioning of financial markets and the economy in the EU. Centralization of supervisory tasks and powers at the supranational level is important to ensure a consistent supervisory approach particularly in respect of banking groups operating cross-border and becomes essential in times of crisis and economic shocks having systemic effects, like the COVID-19 pandemic.[120] The most remarkable feature of the SSM is that it entrusts the ECB with direct administrative powers that entail day-to-day supervision and decision-making on the conduct of banks' business that can also adversely affect the rights of individual supervised entities. This form of EU direct administration is

[117] Case C-450/17 P *Landeskreditbank Baden-Württemberg—Förderbank v ECB* [2018] EU:C:2018:982, Opinion of AG Hogan, para 53 ('given the sheer breadth of the competences conferred on the ECB in respect of less significant entities and the clearly secondary or ancillary role played by the national competent authorities in that regard'). See also Eddy Wymeersch, 'The Single Supervisory Mechanism or "SSM", Challenging the Prudential Supervisor: liability Part One of the Banking Union' (2014) Ghent University Financial Law Institute Working Paper No 2014-01, 31 <https://papers.ssrn.com/sol3/papers.cfm?abstract_id=2403859> accessed 27 May 2022.

[118] SSM Regulation (n 1) Art 90(1).

[119] SSM Framework Regulation (n 6) Art 90(2).

[120] On the measures taken by the ECB Banking Supervision to tackle the risks of the COVID-19 pandemic, see Klaus Lackhoff (ed), *Banking Supervision and COVID-19* (CH Beck 2020).

necessary to preserve the integration of the financial market against the materialization of financial and systemic risks which have supranational effects.[121]

Finally, while the SSM could be described as a successful experiment of EU integration through direct administration, the persisting divergences across national laws on prudential supervisory powers, the existence of multiple options and discretions which Member States can exercise, the minimum harmonization of relevant regulatory areas cannot be levelled only with the integrated SSM supervisory approach.[122] In perspective and going forward, the level of administrative integration achieved with the SSM would require a stronger, more harmonized and consistent EU regulatory framework.

[121] See in particular Teixeira, *The Legal History of the European Banking Union* (n 11) 280 and 295 (arguing that going forward Treaty-based arrangements to enable risk-sharing and democratic legitimacy are crucial for the sustainability of the Banking Union).

[122] On the problem of regulatory fragmentation within the 'single rule-book', see in particular Zilioli and Wojcik, 'European Banking Union: A Giant Step Towards European Integration and a Challenge for Judicial Review' (n 7) 10 and Stefan Grundmann, 'The European Banking Union and Integration' in Grundmann and Micklitz (eds), *The European Banking Union and Constitution: Beacon for Advanced Integration or Death-Knell for Democracy* (Hart Publishing 2019) 103.

9

The Role of the ECB in the International Arena and the External Dimension of EMU

A 'New' ECB within a Crippled Legal Framework?

Florin Coman-Kund

I. Introduction

Since its creation back in 1998, the European Central Bank (ECB) has gradually evolved both in its role as a core manager of the single currency and by acquiring new roles and tasks. The latter entails most obviously the ECB's supervisory tasks within the Single Supervisory Mechanism (SSM), as well as its various unconventional measures aimed at saving the euro and pushing for economic policy reforms in the context of the financial and euro area sovereign debt crisis. These developments prompted Beukers already in 2013 to signal that fundamental changes in the institutional role and functioning of the ECB were taking place, and that in fact a 'new' ECB had come into existence.[1]

One dimension of the ECB's activities that has also increased over time concerns its international cooperation. The ECB established progressively close cooperation with central banks and financial institutions worldwide, joined relevant international organizations, in particular the Bank for International Settlements (BIS) and the International Monetary Fund (IMF), and participates in various informal international fora and networks, such as the Group of Twenty (G20), the Group of Seven (G7), the Financial Stability Board (FSB), and the Basel Committee on Banking Supervision (BCBS) to name just a few.[2] Moreover, there is an intriguing intra-EU international dimension[3] of the ECB consisting of its participation in the complex intergovernmental framework established under the European Financial Stability Facility (EFSF)[4] and later under the European Stability Mechanism

[1] See Thomas Beukers, 'The New ECB and its Relationship with the Eurozone Member States: Between Central Bank Independence and Central Bank Intervention' (2013) 50 CML Rev 1579 (hereafter Beukers, 'The New ECB'). On the SSM, see chapter 7 by Kern Alexander and chapter 8 by Federico Della Negra and Gianni Lo Schiavo, in this volume. On the ECB's unconventional measures, see chapter 2 by Vestert Borger and Chapter 3 by Klaus Tuori, in this volume.

[2] See European Central Bank, 'International affairs' <https://www.ecb.europa.eu/ecb/tasks/international/html/index.en.html> accessed 27 June 2021 (hereafter European Central Bank, 'International affairs').

[3] This formula conveys the fact that the ECB's actions are confined to the euro area Member States, but they take place nevertheless within a legal framework established by international instruments adopted by the Member States outside the Founding Treaties of the European Union (EU).

[4] Consolidated Version of the EFSF Framework Agreement [2010], signed on 10 June 2010, and amended in 2011.

Florin Coman-Kund, *The Role of the ECB in the International Arena and the External Dimension of EMU* In: *The New European Central Bank*. Edited by: Thomas Beukers, Diane Fromage, and Giorgio Monti, Oxford University Press. © Florin Coman-Kund 2022. DOI: 10.1093/oso/9780198871231.003.0009

(ESM).[5] In this very specific context, entailing the mobilization of significant emergency funds to remedy the sovereign debt crisis in the euro area, the ECB was entrusted with tasks concerning the negotiation of financial assistance and the monitoring of the implementation of conditionality measures by euro area Member States in difficulty; as such, it became part of the infamous 'Troika' together with the European Commission and the IMF.[6] As a side note, the ECB may also contribute, within its area of competence and in close cooperation with the European Commission, to broader EU external policies, such as enlargement, for instance by supporting the adoption of the relevant *acquis* and the consolidation process of the central banks in candidate countries to EU accession.[7]

In line with the central query of the volume, this chapter examines the evolution of the ECB's international dimension with a view to assessing its transformative effects and side effects on the ECB of today. For this purpose, a close look is taken at the legal framework governing the ECB's international cooperation to understand the potential and limits shaping its international dimension, and its legal status as a global actor. The ECB's international cooperation practice is also reviewed to assess the dynamics of its international dimension over time. The integrated analysis of the legal framework and practice prompts a number of conclusions, critical observations, and forward-looking reflections regarding the ECB's current international dimension. It is argued that, in a way, there is a 'new' ECB becoming much more active on the international plane, partly because of its established and extensive international practice in its traditional monetary policy field, and partly because of the external projection of its expanding 'internal' powers over time. Yet, at the same time, the ECB's international dimension is also constrained by the Founding Treaties establishing a specific institutional balance in the field of Economic and Monetary Union (EMU) external relations that has not changed much over time. What is more, the ECB's potential as an international actor is arguably restricted by various international legal frameworks (eg IMF membership requirements) that do not allow the Union's central bank to fully exploit on the global level its role and powers under EU law. Finally, but yet importantly, some legally problematic aspects of the ECB's international dimension might require adjustments in the current legal framework to reflect the realities of today's ECB.

The chapter begins with an analysis of the ECB's legal framework for international cooperation combining general EU external relations with EMU specific external relations law (Section II). Next, the ECB's thorny legal status as an international actor is discussed (Section III), followed by an overview of the ECB's evolving international cooperation practice (Section IV). Then a critical appraisal is offered of the ECB's current international dimension, providing a diagnosis of the status quo and highlighting a number of problematic issues as well as suggesting some proposals for reform (Section V), before concluding (Section VI).

[5] Treaty Establishing the European Stability Mechanism [2012] T/ESM 2012-LT, signed on 2 February 2012 (hereafter ESM Treaty).

[6] See Beukers, 'The New ECB' (n 1) 1581 and 1588–89.

[7] See, for instance, European Central Bank, 'Annual Report 2019' (Section 10.2 'International relations', 2020) <https://www.ecb.europa.eu/pub/annual/html/ar2019~c199d3633e.en.html#toc77> accessed 27 June 2021 (hereafter European Central Bank, 'Annual Report 2019').

II. The Legal Framework of the ECB's International Dimension

While monetary policy related to the euro area is an exclusive EU competence, the exercise of this competence, including its external relations, is subject to the distribution of powers among the EU institutions according to the Treaties. Hence, assessing the ECB's international dimension requires looking at the role and powers entrusted to it by primary law, at the specific provisions governing EMU external relations, as well as at the general system of EU external relations.

To begin with, the Treaties establish a specific institutional balance in the field of EU external relations, whereby the European Council identifies the strategic interests and objectives of the Union's external action,[8] the Council is in charge of policy-making in EU external relations,[9] and the Commission ensures the overall external representation of the Union.[10] By virtue of this role, the Commission is entrusted with the task of establishing cooperative relations between the EU and various international organizations.[11] Regarding one of the most important forms of EU external action—that is, the conclusion of international agreements with third countries and international organizations—Article 218 TFEU lays down a complex procedure involving the Commission (initiating the process and carrying out the negotiation process), the Council (opening negotiations, overseeing the negotiation process, signing and concluding the agreement), and the European Parliament (EP) (expressing its consent or, in some cases, opinion before the agreement is concluded by the Council).[12] In view of the scattered EU external relations landscape across various external policies and internal policies with an external dimension, coherence and consistency represent both a daunting challenge and an existential need for the Union as a global actor.[13] Article 21(3) of the Treaty on European Union (TEU) entrusts this task jointly to the Council and the Commission, required to work closely together to ensure consistency both between the various areas of EU external action and between the Union's external action

[8] See the Consolidated Version of the Treaty on the Functioning of the European Union [2012] OJ C326/47, art 22 (1) (hereafter TFEU).

[9] ibid Art 16(1) and (6).

[10] ibid Art 17(1). Some clarity regarding the delineation between the Commission's external representation role and the Council's policy making in external relations has been brought by the Court of Justice (CJEU) in its judgment in Case C-660/13 *Council v Commission* [2016] ECLI:EU:C:2016:616 (hereafter Case C-660/13 *Council v Commission*).

[11] TFEU (n 8) Art 220(1).

[12] For a detailed overview of the procedure, see Bart van Vooren and Ramses Wessel, *EU External Relations Law. Text, Cases and Materials* (CUP 2014) 45–51. According to CJEU, Art 218 enshrines a single EU treaty-making procedure generally applicable to the negotiation and conclusion of Union's international agreements, except for those instances where special procedures are laid down in the Treaties: see Case C-658/11 *European Parliament v Council (Pirate Transfer Agreement with Mauritius)* [2014] ECLI:EU:C:2014:2025 para 52 (hereafter Case C-658/11 *European Parliament v Council*) and Case C-263/14 *European Parliament v Council (EU–Tanzania Transfer Agreement)* [2016] ECLI:EU:C:2016:435 para 68 (hereafter Case C-263/14 *European Parliament v Council*).

[13] For terminological clarifications regarding the concepts of 'coherence' and 'consistency', see Marise Cremona, 'Coherence in European Union Foreign Policy' in Panos Koutrakos (ed), *European Foreign Policy: Legal and Political Perspectives* (Edward Elgar Publishing 2011) 55–92.

and its internal policies.[14] One important aspect related to the exercise of external powers by EU institutions, which is particularly relevant for the ECB's international dimension, concerns the interplay between the issue of parallelism or complementarity between the internal–external powers[15] of EU institutions, originating in the *ERTA* case law concerning the Union's external implied powers,[16] and the principle of institutional balance enshrined in Article 13(2) TFEU.[17] In this regard, whereas EU institutions could in principle carry out external tasks to the extent necessary to fulfil their internal powers,[18] such tasks and activities may not affect the allocation and balance of powers in external relations explicitly enshrined in the Treaties.[19]

In the field of monetary policy, the ECB's primary mission is to maintain price stability. For this purpose, the ECB is in charge, in tandem with the National Central Banks of the euro area, of the Union's monetary policy,[20] and it is entrusted with core tasks regarding the definition and implementation of the Union's monetary policy,

[14] According to Hillion, 'consistency' in EU external actions not only entails '... the assurance that the different policies do not legally contradict each other ...', but also '... a quest for synergy and added value in the different components of EU policies': Christophe Hillion, 'Tous pour un, un pour tous! Coherence in the External Relations of the European Union' in Marise Cremona (ed), *Developments in EU External Relations Law* (OUP 2008) 17.

[15] On the doctrine of parallelism or the principle of complementarity in the context of Union's external competences, see Alan Dashwood and Joni Heliskoski, 'The Classic Authorities Revisited' in Alan Dashwood and Christophe Hillion (eds), *The General Law of E.C. External Relations* (Sweet & Maxwell 2000) 12–13; Andrea Ott and Ramses A Wessel, 'The EU's External Relations Regime: Multilevel Complexity in an Expanding Union' in Steven Blockmans and Adam Lazowski (eds), *The European Union and Its Neighbours* (TMC Asser Instituut 2006) 24; Jan Wouters, Dominic Coppens, and Bart de Meester, 'The European Union's External Relations after the Lisbon Treaty' in Stefan Griller and Jacques Ziller (eds), *The Lisbon Treaty. EU Constitutionalism without a Constitutional Treaty* (Springer 2008) 168, 174, and 178.

[16] Case 22/70 *Commission v Council. European Agreement on Road Transport (ERTA)* [1971] ECLI:EU:C:1971:32, and further Opinion 1/76 *Draft Agreement establishing a European laying-up fund for inland waterway vessels* [1977] ECLI:EU:C:1977:63; Opinion 1/94 *Competence of the Community to conclude international agreements concerning services and the protection of intellectual property (WTO)* [1994] ECLI:EU:C:1994:384. The *ERTA* case law on Union's external implied powers has been codified in TFEU (n 8) Arts 3(2) and 216(1).

[17] The latter entails that EU institutions must act within the limits of the powers and according to the procedures and conditions provided by the Founding Treaties; institutional balance thus entails a system of checks and balances aimed at preserving the positions and powers of the EU institutions as agreed upon in the Founding Treaties, see on the principle of institutional balance: Koen Lenaerts, 'Regulating the Regulatory Process: "Delegation of Powers" in the European Community' (1993) 18 EL Rev 23; Sacha Prechal, 'Institutional Balance: A Fragile Principle with Uncertain Contents' in Ton Heukel, Niels Blokker, and Marcel Brus (eds), *The European Union after Amsterdam. A Legal Analysis* (Kluwer Law International 1998) 273–94; Giandomenico Majone, 'Delegation of Regulatory Powers in a Mixed Polity' (2002) 8 ELJ 319; Jean-Paul Jacqué, 'The Principle of Institutional Balance' (2004) 41 CML Rev 383.

[18] For an illustration of how external powers may be implied from powers entrusted by relevant EU internal rules in the case of the ECB, see Marise Cremona and Päivi Leino-Sandberg, 'International Agreements of the EU in the Field of EMU' in Fabian Amtenbrink and Christoph Hermann (eds), *The EU Law of the Economic and Monetary Union* (OUP 2020) 176 (hereafter Cremona and Leino-Sandberg, 'International Agreements of the EU'); for a more nuanced view on the application of the ERTA-based parallelism or complementarity to the internal-external powers of EU institutions, see Andrea Ott, 'EU Regulatory Agencies in EU External Relations: Trapped in a Legal Minefield between European and International Law' (2008) 13 EFAR 515, 521 (hereafter Ott, 'EU Regulatory Agencies').

[19] See Case C-327/91 *France v Commission* [1994] ECLI:EU:C:1994:305, paras 36 and 41 (hereafter Case C-327/91 *France v Commission*) and Case C-233/02 *France v Commission* [2004] ECLI:EU:C:2004:173, para 40; see also Florin Coman-Kund, *European Union Agencies as Global Actors. A Legal Study of the European Aviation Safety Agency, Frontex and Europol* (Routledge 2018) 73–75 (hereafter Coman-Kund, *European Union Agencies*).

[20] TFEU (n 8) Art 282(1).

the conduct of foreign-exchange operations, and the promotion of the smooth operation of payment systems.[21] In addition to its traditional role, the ECB has been assigned, based on Article 127(6) TFEU, a significant role within the Single Supervisory Mechanism (SSM), one of the main pillars of the European Banking Union (EBU).[22] In line with this role aimed at ensuring the soundness of the banking sector and the stability of the financial system,[23] 'not only does the ECB bear the responsibility for direct supervision of most "significant institutions" (SIs) primarily within the euro area, but it also exercises system oversight by performing specific responsibilities and facilitating cooperation vis-à-vis competent national supervisors'.[24]

The architecture of the ECB's international dimension is carved through primary law provisions pertaining specifically to the ECB, and to EMU external relations more broadly, as well as via secondary legislation regarding the ECB's tasks within the SSM.

The ECB Statute[25] reflects to a large extent the idea of parallelism or complementarity between internal–external powers as regards the ECB's international dimension. Article 6 ECB Statute establishes that the ECB is in charge of the external representation pertaining to the monetary tasks entrusted to the European System of Central Banks (ESCB), including the possibility to participate in international monetary institutions.[26] Additionally, Article 23 ECB Statute enables the ECB (but also National Central Banks) to establish cooperation with third country central banks and financial institutions, as well as with relevant international organizations, and to perform '... all types of banking transactions in relations with third countries and international organisations, including borrowing and lending operations'. Other external aspects of the ECB's central banking tasks cover operations with foreign exchange assets,[27] holding and managing the IMF reserve positions and Special Drawings Rights (SDRs),[28] as well as approving operations in foreign reserve assets by National Central Banks '... to ensure consistency with the exchange rate and monetary policy of the Union'.[29] This overview suggests that the ECB is entrusted with a large range of autonomous external tasks and powers pertaining to the EU's single monetary policy.

However, the ECB's monetary functions do not appear to be fully matched by its external powers, as the Treaties design a special institutional balance in the field of EMU external relations.[30] First, according to Article 219

[21] ibid Art 127(2).

[22] Council Regulation (EU) 1024/2013 of 15 October 2013 conferring specific tasks on the European Central Bank concerning policies relating to the prudential supervision of credit institutions [2013] OJ L287/63 (hereafter SSM Regulation). See also chapter 7 by Kern Alexander and chapter 8 by Federico Della Negra and Gianni Lo Schiavo, in this volume.

[23] SSM Regulation (n 22) recital 65.

[24] Florin Coman-Kund and Fabian Amtenbrink, 'On the Scope and Limits of the Application of National Law by the European Central Bank within the Single Supervisory Mechanism' (2018) 33 Banking & Finance Law Review 133, 135 (hereafter Coman-Kund and Amtenbrink, 'On the Scope and Limits').

[25] Protocol No 4 on the Statute of the European System of Central Banks and of the European Central Bank [2016] OJ C 202/230 (hereafter ECB Statute).

[26] According to ECB Statute (n 25) Art 6(2), National Central Banks may also participate in international monetary institutions, but only with the approval of the ECB.

[27] ibid Art 23.

[28] ibid Art 30(5).

[29] ibid Art 31(2).

[30] See in this respect, Der-Chin Horng, 'The ECB's Membership in the IMF: Legal Approaches to Constitutional Challenges' (2005) 11 ELJ 802, 804–05.

TFEU,[31] formal international agreements on an exchange-rate system for the euro in relation to the currencies of third countries, as well as agreements concerning monetary or foreign-exchange regime matters are concluded by the Council with the participation of the Commission (recommendation and participation in negotiations) and the ECB (independent recommendation, or consultation when the Council acts on a recommendation from the Commission).[32] Similarly, it is the Council (not the ECB) that formulates 'general orientations for exchange-rate policies' in relation to third country currencies, in the absence of a formal exchange-rate system.[33] As a result, the ECB's foreign-exchange operations should be conducted in accordance with the Council's agreements and general orientations adopted under Article 219 TFEU.[34] Second, the same institutional trio is involved in a very similar fashion in the international representation of the euro area. Thus, common positions and measures to ensure unified representation on EMU matters within international financial institutions and fora are adopted by the Council on the basis of a Commission proposal and after ECB consultation.[35] In this respect, the ECB's role and actions regarding the international representation of the ESCB may not affect the institutional balance established under Article 138 TFEU.[36]

The resulting picture thus displays a rather complex external representation of the Union's single monetary policy, which does not seem to fully match the ECB's exclusive competences related to the Eurosystem. The reason for this is that EU external action follows a logic according to which important decisions in foreign affairs require the intervention of relevant external relations actors with a view to ensuring consistency, coherence, coordination, and effectiveness. In other words, when taking decisions/adopting instruments with wider policy/political implications, the ECB cannot act alone as a technocratic body specialized in monetary matters, but the intervention

[31] This provision represents a *lex specialis* by reference to the EU's ordinary treaty-making procedure laid down in TFEU (n 8) Art 218.

[32] TFEU (n 8) Art 219(1) and (3); whereas formal international agreements on an exchange-rate system for the euro are based on Art 219(1) junto (3), the agreements concerning overall monetary or foreign-exchange regime matters are based on Art 219(3) only: see Alexander Thiele, 'Foreign-Exchange Operations of the ECB and Exchange Rate Policy' in Fabian Amtenbrink and Christoph Hermann (eds), *The EU Law of the Economic and Monetary Union* (OUP 2020) 706–10 (hereafter Thiele, 'Foreign-Exchange Operations'). According to one view, the derogatory procedure under TFEU (n 8) Art 219(3) allows the Council to involve the ECB as a participant in negotiations or even to put ECB in charge of conducting the negotiation process for such agreements, see Chiara Zilioli and Martin Selmayr, 'The External Relations of the Euro Area: Legal Aspects' (1999) 36 CML Rev 273, 302–03 (hereafter Zilioli and Selmayr, 'The External Relations').

[33] TFEU (n 8) Art 219(2). Again, the Council acts on a recommendation from the ECB, or from the Commission after consulting the ECB. ECB independence in conducting the single monetary policy is protected as the Council's general orientations may not affect the primary objective of price stability; more drastically, some authors suggest that the 'general orientations' are not binding on the ECB, as otherwise ECB independence enshrined in TFEU (n 8) Art 130 would be affected: see Zilioli and Selmayr, 'The External Relations' (n 32) 308–09.

[34] TFEU (n 8) Art 127(2) provides that the foreign-exchange operations conducted by the ECB must be *consistent* (emphasis added) with Art 219; see also Christoph Herrmann, 'Monetary Sovereignty over the Euro and the External Relations of the Euro Area: Competences, Procedures and Practice' (2002) 7 EFAR 1, 10–13. This author suggests that in the absence of legal instruments adopted under TFEU (n 8) Art 219, the ECB has a large degree of freedom to intervene on foreign exchange markets, without, however, being able to conclude international binding agreements (13).

[35] TFEU (n 8) Art 138(1)–(2).

[36] According to ECB Statute (n 25) Art 6(3), ECB's international cooperation '... shall be without prejudice to Article 138 of the Treaty on the Functioning of the European Union'.

of the most important political actors in charge of EU external relations is required. Hence, the euro area external dimension reflects a specific division and balance between the ECB's exclusive external competence on operational issues related to the Eurosystem and the competence of the Council and the Commission regarding political decision-making and management of the Union's external action.[37] This balance, which has remained fundamentally unchanged since the Presidency conclusions of the Luxembourg European Council back in 1997,[38] puts the Economic and Financial Affairs (ECOFIN) Council in the driver's seat as regards binding international agreements and decisions on the unified international representation of the euro area, assisted by a 'co-pilot' (the Commission as the actor in charge of the management of the Union's overall external representation), and finally supported by a 'technical specialist' (the ECB as the expert technocratic body specialized in monetary policy). From Articles 138 and 219 TFEU, Article 6 ECB Statute as well as from the general duty of interinstitutional loyal cooperation enshrined in Article 13(2) TEU, one may infer that these actors must work closely together and coordinate their actions to ensure coherence and effectiveness in EMU external relations. To add more complexity, Member States remain important actors in EMU external relations, as conveyed by Article 219(4) TFEU, in particular as regards participation in international financial institutions, which in turn requires close cooperation with the EU institutions in the spirit of the principle of sincere cooperation.[39]

A somewhat similar parallelism/complementarity logic is visible as regards the ECB's international cooperation pertaining to its role within the SSM. Article 8 SSM Regulation enables the ECB to establish cooperation with international organizations and supervisory authorities of third countries within the realm of its supervisory tasks. However, more prominently than in the field of monetary policy, this provision reflects utmost care for the principles of conferral and institutional balance. One reason for this could be the rather light wording in Article 127(6) TFEU referring to the conferral on the ECB of 'specific tasks ... concerning policies' relating to prudential supervision. Another closely related reason pertains to the rather complicated internal distribution of tasks in the field of banking supervision entailing crucial tasks for the Commission and the European Banking Authority (EBA) on regulatory matters,[40] as well as a shared SSM governance structure whereby national supervisory authorities also play a significant role, alongside the ECB, within the system of EU banking supervision.[41] First, the ECB's international dimension pertaining to banking supervision

[37] See Der-Chin Horng, 'The European Central's Bank External Relations with Third Countries and the IMF' (2004) 9 EFAR 323, 337 (hereafter Horng, 'The European Central's Bank External Relations').

[38] European Council, 'Presidency Conclusions' (Luxembourg, 12–13 December 1997), para 46 <https://www.europarl.europa.eu/summits/lux1_en.htm> accessed 27 June 2021. In this respect, Piris observes that the Lisbon Treaty did not bring much change to the international representation of the euro: Jean-Claude Piris, *The Lisbon Treaty. A Legal and Political Analysis* (CUP 2010) 305.

[39] Consolidated Version of the Treaty on European Union [2012] OJ C326/01, Art 4(3) (hereafter TEU). For a detailed analysis of the relationship between EU institutions and the Member States in the context of EMU external relations, see Marise Cremona and Päivi Leino-Sandberg, 'External Relations of the EU and Euro Area in the Field of EMU' in Fabian Amtenbrink and Christoph Hermann (eds), *The EU Law of the Economic and Monetary Union* (OUP 2020) 134–73 (hereafter Cremona and Leino-Sandberg, 'External Relations of the EU').

[40] See SSM Regulation (n 22) Art 4(3) subpara 2.

[41] See Coman-Kund and Amtenbrink, 'On the Scope and Limits' (n 24) 139–44.

must not affect the competences of the Member States and of the EU institutions and bodies, in particular those of the EBA.[42] Second, the ECB's international cooperation is further circumscribed to mere contacts and administrative arrangements, to be established in coordination with the EBA, that cannot bind the EU and its Member States.[43] The downgrading of the ECB's international dimension to 'administrative arrangements' is also intended to leave unaffected the distribution of powers regarding the adoption of Union international agreements laid down in Article 218 TFEU.

The analysis of the relevant legal framework reveals quite a significant role for the ECB externally, but also that its external role does not fully match its internal one. There are variations, in that the ECB has a far more important role and leeway as regards the external relations of the single monetary policy as compared to the Single Supervisory Mechanism. At the same time, the ECB's autonomous international cooperation tasks and powers must respect the institutional balance established by the Treaties and the role of other EU actors and the Member States in EMU and banking supervision. This formal legal analysis does not represent, however, the whole story, since, as will be seen in Section IV, legal and practical developments concerning the EMU external relations and the ECB's international cooperation offer a completer and more nuanced picture of its international dimension. But before that, it is relevant to discuss the issue of the legal status of the ECB to clarify one core question, namely: what kind of actor is the ECB on the international plane?

III. The Tricky International Legal Status of the ECB

One topic amply debated by legal scholars concerns the legal status of the ECB on the international plane. After the establishment of the ECB, a heated discussion started among scholars, with some views supporting without reservations the ECB's international legal personality in combination with a large measure of international capacity on monetary matters,[44] others firmly rejecting the international legal personality of the ECB,[45] and, finally, others taking a middle ground position—that is, conditional

[42] The special emphasis on the EBA can be explained by the intermingling and likely overlap between the roles and tasks of the two authorities relating to prudential supervision of credit institutions.

[43] Arguably, the explicit provision that the ECB's administrative arrangements with international organizations and third country authorities cannot bind the EU and its Member States, does not inherently entail that such international cooperation instruments are always non-binding, but could also imply that their potential legal effects are incumbent on the ECB only.

[44] Zilioli and Selmayr, 'The External Relations' (n 32); Chiara Zilioli and Martin Selmayr, 'The European Central Bank: An Independent Specialized Organization of Community Law' (2000) 37 CML Rev 591 (hereafter Zilioli and Selmayr, 'The European Central Bank'); Chiara Zilioli and Martin Selmayr, 'Recent Developments in the Law of the ECB' in Piet Eeckhout and Takis Tridimas (eds), *Yearbook of European Law 25/2006* (OUP 2007) 77–87 (hereafter Zilioli and Selmayr, 'Recent Developments in the Law of the ECB'); Horng, 'The European Central's Bank External Relations' (n 37) 325–46. Zilioli and Selmayr went as far as calling the ECB a specialized supranational organization within the EU framework, 'independent from, albeit associated to, the existing three Communities': Zilioli and Selmayr, 'The European Central Bank' (n 44) 621–22.

[45] Ramon Torrent, 'Whom is the European Central Bank the Central Bank of? Reaction to Zilioli and Selmayr' (1999) 36 CML Rev 1229.

acceptance of the ECB's status as an international legal person with a limited international capacity.[46]

The verdict on the ECB's international legal status very much depends on the understanding of the concept of international personality one has,[47] and on whether, based on its legal framework and practice, the ECB meets the parameters for becoming a legal person under international law.

While there is general agreement that international legal personality indicates that an entity can act as a distinct subject on the international plane and is capable of having rights and duties,[48] the international personality of various organizations and entities is subject to intensive debates.[49] According to what seems to be the prevailing view, reflected in the International Court of Justice's famous 'Reparations for Injuries' Advisory Opinion,[50] international legal personality is derived from explicit conferment by the creators of the organization, but it can also be implied from the competence or powers of the relevant entity as laid down in its constitutive act.[51] Put simply, for an entity to have international legal personality it must meet three basic criteria: (1) organizational distinctiveness; (2) a large degree of autonomy entailing that the entity acts in detachment from its creators; and (3) international capacity or, in other words, powers that can be exercised on the international plane (possessing treaty-making powers is an important indicator in this respect though not a mandatory requirement since the extent of rights and obligations may vary among subjects of international law).[52] In this respect, besides the design of the entity as provided in its relevant legal framework, the international cooperation practice developed and the recognition by other subjects of international law are important factors to consider when assessing the existence of international legal personality.[53]

Regarding the issue of '(in)divisibility of international legal personality'[54] or 'multiple legal personalities'[55] entailing the possibility for organs or agencies of

[46] Christoph Herrmann, 'Monetary Sovereignty over the Euro and the External Relations of the Euro Area: Competences, Procedures and Practice' (2002) 7 EFAR 1 (hereafter Herrmann, 'Monetary Sovereignty'); Henry G Schermers and Niels M Blokker, *International Institutional Law. Unity within Diversity* (5th edn, Martinus Nijhoff Publishers 2011) 994 (hereafter Schermers and Blokker, *International Institutional Law*), Piet Eeckhout, *EU External Relations Law* (OUP 2011) 207–08 (hereafter Eeckhout, *EU External Relations Law*); Matthias Ruffert, 'Personality under EU Law: A Conceptual Answer towards the Pluralisation of the EU' (2014) 20 ELJ 346, 356–59 (hereafter Ruffert, 'Personality under EU Law').

[47] For a more detailed analysis on the international legal personality of organs or agencies of international organisations (including the EU), see Coman-Kund, *European Union Agencies* (n 19) 105–09.

[48] See Nigel D White, *The Law of International Organisations* (Manchester University Press 2005) 30–32 (hereafter White, *The Law of International Organisations*); Schermers and Blokker, *International Institutional Law* (n 46) 993.

[49] See White, *The Law of International Organisations* (n 48) 32 and 35–40.

[50] Reparation for injuries suffered in the service of the Unite Nations (Advisory Opinion) [1949] ICJ Rep 174.

[51] See Schermers and Blokker, *International Institutional Law* (n 46) 989 and White, *The Law of International Organisations* (n 48) 39.

[52] See Coman-Kund, *European Union Agencies* (n 19) 105–7.

[53] See, eg, Rachel Frid, *The Relations Between the EC and International Organizations: Legal Theory and Practice* (Kluwer Law International 1995) 16–19 and 23; Schermers and Blokker, *International Institutional Law* (n 46) 992–93.

[54] Schermers and Blokker, *International Institutional Law* (n 46) 994.

[55] See Andrea Ott, Ellen Vos, and Florin Coman-Kund, 'EU Agencies on the Global Scene: EU and International Law Perspectives' in Michelle Everson, Cosimo Monda, and Ellen Vos (eds), *European Agencies in-between Institutions and Member States* (Kluwer Law International 2014) 94.

international organizations to acquire their own legal status on the international plane, things remain theoretically fuzzy.[56] Yet some scholars cautiously recognize various entities of states and international organizations as subjects of international law with a limited legal capacity.[57] Such 'anomalies' are often justified by practical and pragmatic reasons,[58] and result from a complex assessment of the legal status, powers, and independence of the respective entity according to the legal framework, international cooperation practice, and the recognition of that entity by other subjects of international law.[59]

A look at its legal framework reveals that the ECB, similarly to the EU itself, is provided with legal personality via EU primary law.[60] Interestingly, the ECB is the only EU institution listed in Article 13(1) TEU entrusted with its own legal personality; the European Investment Bank (EIB) benefits from the same treatment in Article 308 TFEU, but it is not formally listed as an EU institution. The distinctive legal status of the ECB becomes obvious also from other Treaty provisions. For instance, Article 340 TFEU refers in two separate paragraphs to the non-contractual liability of the Union, on the one hand, and the non-contractual liability of the ECB, on the other hand. Similarly, Article 343 TFEU first provides for the privileges and immunities of the Union, and then extends this legal regime to the ECB and the EIB too. Moreover, Articles 130 and 282(3) TFEU equip the ECB with a large degree of independence both from the EU institutional framework and from the Member States.[61] As shown previously, both the TFEU and in particular the ECB Statute, confer on the ECB quite significant international cooperation tasks and powers.[62] The ECB's international dimension has also materialized in a rich international practice over time, as discussed in more detail in the next section. For now, suffice it to say that the ECB is a full member of the BIS, has an observer status in the IMF, participates in various other international organizations and bodies, and has entered into numerous cooperative arrangements and agreements with central banks and financial authorities of third countries, as well as with international organizations.[63]

[56] Coman-Kund, *European Union Agencies* (n 19) 106.

[57] See Ian Brownlie, *Principles of Public International Law* (7th edn, OUP 2008) 61 and 67; Schermers and Blokker, *International Institutional Law* (n 46) 994; Gregor Schusterschitz, 'European Agencies as Subjects of International Law' (2004) 1 International Organizations Law Review 163; Ruffert, 'Personality under EU Law' (n 46).

[58] See Ruffert, 'Personality under EU Law' (n 46) 357.

[59] See Coman-Kund, *European Union Agencies* (n 19) 106.

[60] TFEU (n 8) Art 282(3) junto ECB Statute (n 25) Art 9(1); compare with TEU (n 39) Art 47 entrusting the EU with legal personality.

[61] According to some, the ECB can be regarded as one of the most independent central banks in the world, see Nergiz Dincer and Barry Eichengreen, 'Central Bank Transparency and Independence: Updates and New Measures' (2014) 10 International Journal of Central Banking 189 and Sebastian Heidebrecht, 'Technocratic Governance at the Centre of the European Economic and Monetary Union. Exploring the Accountability of Expert-based Decision-making in the European Central Bank' in Alessandra Arcuri and Florin Coman-Kund (eds), *Technocracy and the Law: Accountability, Governance and Expertise* (Routledge 2021) 110–12 (hereafter Heidebrecht, 'Technocratic Governance at the Centre of the European Economic and Monetary Union').

[62] Though not the power to conclude binding international agreements regarding monetary and foreign exchange regimes, nor the exclusive power to ensure the international representation of the euro; according to Ott, the ECB acquired international legal personality through the international cooperation tasks assigned to it via ECB Statute (n 25) Arts 6 and 23, Ott, 'EU Regulatory Agencies' (n 18) 527.

[63] See European Central Bank, 'International affairs' (n 2).

Based on all these factors, one may carefully conclude that the ECB is perhaps the only EU institution listed in Article 13(1) TEU that meets squarely the criteria for international legal personality.[64] This conclusion was arguably more straightforward before the Lisbon Treaty when the ECB was not formally an EU institution, entailing that it was not officially subsumed to the institutional framework representing the Community/Union having its own international legal personality.[65] The European Court of Justice (CJEU) acknowledged the ECB's very special legal status (encompassing own legal personality, privileges and immunities and a large degree of independence),[66] but at the same time it emphasized that such a special legal status does not have the consequence of separating the ECB 'entirely from the European Community and exempting it from every rule of Community law'.[67] Arguably, as a follow-up reaction to this judgment, the Lisbon Treaty explicitly included the ECB within the EU's institutional framework, which would imply a comparable legal treatment to that accorded to the other EU institutions as far as the issue of international legal personality is concerned.[68]

However, besides formally turning the ECB into an EU institution, the Lisbon Treaty left unchanged all the other elements of the ECB's special legal status from the previous legal framework (separate provisions on legal personality, privileges, and immunities, non-contractual liability, etc). The current constitutional framework continues thus to reflect in very much the same way, the unique legal standing of the ECB within the EU, by virtue of its exclusive competence and powers, its special way of functioning, and its large degree of independence. This still offers arguments for supporting a derivative and functionally limited international legal personality for the ECB.[69] Eeckhout acknowledges that, post-Lisbon, the ECB is 'part of the EU's institutional framework in much the same way as any of the other institutions', but at the same time, he agrees with Hermann that 'in the small world of banking operations ... the ECB is recognized as an international legal person with certain powers stemming from the merely operational tasks it is entrusted with'.[70] In an article published before the Lisbon Treaty, Zilioli and Selmayr already emphasized the growing recognition of the ECB's international personality by third countries, their central banks, as well

[64] See Schermers and Blokker, *International Institutional Law* (n 46) 994.

[65] The main point here is that the organs that are formally part of the EU institutional framework only act on behalf of the EU to enable it to exercise its own international legal personality, and, as a result, they cannot claim in principle a separate international legal status from that of the Union; see in this respect, Case C-327/91 *France v Commission* (n 19) paras 24–25 and Coman-Kund, *European Union Agencies* (n 19) 74. From this perspective, the fact that the ECB was not formally part of the EU institutional framework, but rather a somewhat separate body with a special legal status, offered better prospects for the ECB to claim its own legal status on the international plane.

[66] Case C-11/00 *Commission v European Central Bank (ECB)* [2003] ECLI:EU:C:2003:395, paras 130–32.

[67] ibid, para 135. However, in that case the Court was not concerned with the ECB's international legal status, but with the question whether the EU legislator could adopt measures applicable to the ECB.

[68] In other words, it is the EU having international legal personality based on TEU (n 39) Art 47 (not its institutions, including the ECB).

[69] Coman-Kund, *European Union Agencies* (n 19) 108.

[70] Eeckhout, *EU External Relations Law* (n 46) 207–08 and Herrmann, 'Monetary Sovereignty' (n 46) 9; the ECB does not seem to be a singular case, as according to Zilioli and Selmayr, (some) National Central Banks also enjoy, by virtue of their special functions and independence, a derived and limited international legal personality: see Zilioli and Selmayr, 'The External Relations' (n 32) 277–79 and Zilioli and Selmayr, 'The European Central Bank' (n 44) 625.

as by various international organizations and financial institutions establishing relationships with the ECB in its own right.[71] The rather paradoxical situation of an EU institution showing off as a rather distinct subject on the international plane could be explained by the idea of relative and divisible EU international personality reflecting the complex organizational plurality of the Union.[72]

IV. The Evolution of the ECB's International Dimension: The ECB as a Growing Global Player?

A more comprehensive assessment of the ECB's international dimension requires, next to the analysis of the formal legal framework in Section II, looking at the application of this legal framework and at the ECB's international cooperation practice developed over time. A bird's eye view of 'the reality on the ground' reveals interesting dynamics and developments shedding a more complex and nuanced perspective on the ECB's actual role as a global actor.

A. 'Article 219 TFEU' practice

To begin with, Article 219 TFEU remained almost a dead letter in practice because of the alleged political sensitivity surrounding foreign-exchange matters and the risk of impinging on the ECB's monetary mandate.[73] Reportedly, formal agreements on exchange-rate systems based on Article 219(1) have never been adopted so far.[74] The same goes for the general orientations for exchange-rate policy in relation to third country currencies.[75] In fact, only Article 219(3) TFEU has been activated to conclude a few minor monetary agreements regarding the use of the euro by some overseas territories and a few small non-EU states.[76] The ECB was involved in the procedure leading to the adoption of these instruments in its consultative capacity based on Article 219 (3) TFEU, but in practice the Council entrusted the ECB with quite a prominent role in the negotiation process; thus, the Council decisions on negotiation arrangements provided that the ECB had to be fully associated with the negotiations of the monetary agreements and moreover that the ECB's agreement was needed on matters pertaining to its own competence.[77] Additionally, the ECB participates in the monitoring

[71] Zilioli and Selmayr, 'Recent Developments in the Law of the ECB' (n 44) 78–79.

[72] See Ruffert, 'Personality under EU Law' (n 46) 357–58.

[73] See Thiele, 'Foreign-Exchange Operations' (n 32) 706–09.

[74] ibid 706.

[75] ibid.

[76] ibid. For an extensive overview of these agreements, see Cremona and Leino-Sandberg, 'International Agreements of the EU' (n 18) 182–86. Monetary agreements have been concluded by the EU with the following European states: Vatican (2009); Andorra (2011); Monaco (2011), and San Marino (2012).

[77] See, for instance, Council Decision 2009/904/EC of 26 November 2009 on the position to be taken by the European Community regarding the renegotiation of the Monetary Agreement with the Republic of San Marino [2009] OJ L322/12, Art 3 and Council Decision of 26 November 2009 on the position to be taken by the European Community regarding the renegotiation of the Monetary Agreement with the Vatican City State [2009] OJ L321/36, Art 3; see also Cremona and Leino-Sandberg, 'External Relations of the EU' (n 39) 182.

of the implementation process as part of the joint committee established under each monetary agreement.[78] The ensuing consequence of the lack of formal agreements and general orientations on foreign-exchange operations consists of a large room for manoeuvring in this field by the ECB based on Article 23 ECB Statute; the ECB remains thus free to conduct virtually 'any form of foreign-exchange operations it deems necessary to fulfil its mandate'.[79] Hence, after more than twenty years, the apparent mismatch between the ECB's monetary mandate and its external powers enshrined in Article 219 TFEU is not fully reflected yet in the current institutional practice.

B. Relationship with international organizations and fora

Regarding participation in relevant international financial and monetary institutions and organizations, Article 6 ECB Statute gives the ECB a large measure of discretion as to the external representation of the ECSB tasks concerning the single monetary policy.[80] One important limit, however, is Article 138 TFEU on EMU external representation in international financial organizations, but until now no Council decisions have been adopted under this Article[81] in spite of several initiatives and proposals in this respect.[82] Among the main factors precluding the use of Article 138 TFEU in practice are: (1) the complex intertwinement between the competences of the EU and the Member States on EMU matters, (2) the difficulties created in terms of international representation by the distinction between the euro area and the EU as a whole, (3) the intricate distribution of competences on EMU external representation between the EU institutions, (4) the state-based design model of most international financial organizations ensuring a more prominent position for the Member States rather than the EU, and (5) the failure to reconcile the different interests and positions of the EU actors involved in international financial organizations.[83] This still leaves the EU representation in international financial and monetary organizations and fora subject to various formal and informal coordination mechanisms and arrangements among the relevant EU actors (including the ECB) and the EU Member States, guided by the principle of sincere cooperation as well as the allocation of internal and external powers among the relevant EU institutions.[84] Things are by no means simple in

[78] See, for instance, the Monetary Agreement between the European Union and the Principality of Andorra [2011] OJ C369/1, Art 11.

[79] Thiele, 'Foreign-Exchange Operations' (n 32) 710.

[80] See European Central Bank, 'The External Representation of the EU and EMU' (ECB Monthly Bulletin, May 2011) 89 <https://www.ecb.europa.eu/pub/pdf/other/art2_mb201105en_pp87-97en.pdf> accessed 27 June 2021 (hereafter European Central Bank, 'The External Representation of the EU and EMU').

[81] Cremona and Leino-Sandberg, 'External Relations of the EU' (n 39) 165–66.

[82] See, eg, European Commission, 'A blueprint for a deep and genuine economic and monetary union: Launching a European Debate' (Communication) COM (2012) 777 final; European Commission, 'A roadmap for moving towards a more consistent external representation of the euro area in international fora' COM (2015) 602; European Commission, 'Proposal for a Council Decision laying down measures in view of progressively establishing unified representation of the euro area in the International Monetary Fund' COM (2015) 603 final (hereafter European Commission, COM (2015) 603 final).

[83] See European Central Bank, 'The External Representation of the EU and EMU' (n 80) 90–91 and Cremona and Leino-Sandberg, 'External Relations of the EU' (n 39) 171–73.

[84] Cremona and Leino-Sandberg, 'External Relations of the EU' (n 39) 162–71.

practice, as pragmatism leads to interesting dynamics whereby informal actors, such as the Eurogroup,[85] play an influential role,[86] whereas sub-optimal cooperation and coordination might result in 'turf wars' among EU actors keen to extend or wary to defend their 'territory'.[87] The limited coherence and effectiveness of EMU's intricate international representation has been highlighted repeatedly and it remains an area in which improvements are badly needed.[88] In this context, the ECB continues to exercise important discretionary powers on the external representation of the 'monetary leg' of EMU based on Articles 6(3) and 23 ECB Statute.[89]

Another limitation of the ECB's potential for international representation resides in the membership requirements of various international financial and monetary organizations and fora. Since only states can be full members of important international organizations competent in monetary matters, such as IMF or G20, the ECB needs to rely on pragmatic arrangements (eg participation as an observer) as well as on the cooperation of the participant EU Member States to ensure the external representation of the single monetary policy.[90]

At the other end of the spectrum, the ECB (not the EU) is a full member and shareholder of the BIS, the main specialized international organization promoting cooperation on monetary policy among central banks or 'the bank of central banks',[91] the president of the ECB being a member of the BIS board of directors.[92] Similarly to the EIB's separate membership to the European Bank for Reconstruction and Development (EBRD),[93] the ECB's membership to the BIS[94] has been invoked as a compelling argument in favour of the ECB's derivative functional international legal personality.[95]

In contrast, in the IMF, one of the most significant international financial organizations, only EU Member States are full members, their participation being based

[85] The CJEU clarified that the Eurogroup has no legal status as an EU institution or body, Joined Cases C-105/15 P to C-109/15 *P Konstantinos Mallis and Others v European Commission and European Central Bank (ECB)* [2016] ECLI:EU:C:2016:702, para 61.

[86] For instance, on exchange-rate matters, a competence formally shared between the ECB and the Council according to TFEU (n 8) Art 219 junto Art 127(2), the President of the Eurogroup regularly attends meetings on exchange-rate issues: European Central Bank, 'The External Representation of the EU and EMU' (n 80) 89; also 'the various topics on the agenda of international meetings at the level of finance ministers—such as international economic, policy cooperation, financial regulation and reform of the international monetary system—are discussed and prepared at euro area/EU level by the Eurogroup and the ECOFIN Council': European Central Bank, 'The External Representation of the EU and EMU' (n 80) 91.

[87] In this respect, the discussions revolving around the question 'Who should be Mr. Euro?' are a telling example: see Zilioli and Selmayr, 'Recent Developments in the Law of the ECB' (n 44) 82–87.

[88] See, for instance, Cremona and Leino-Sandberg, 'External Relations of the EU' (n 39) 162–73.

[89] European Central Bank, 'The External Representation of the EU and EMU' (n 80) 89.

[90] ibid 89–94.

[91] ibid 93.

[92] Bank for International Settlements, 'Board of Directors' <https://www.bis.org/about/board.htm> accessed 27 June 2021.

[93] See Schermers and Blokker, *International Institutional Law* (n 46) 994.

[94] According to some, the international legal personality of BIS is undisputed nowadays: see Zilioli and Selmayr 'The European Central Bank' (n 44) 600.

[95] By analogy, this argument could be used to support the idea of a derived and functionally limited international personality of National Central Banks participating in the BIS. On the thesis regarding the international legal personality of National Central Banks, see Zilioli and Selmayr 'The European Central Bank' (n 44) 625.

on a complex system of quota subscriptions and constituencies between IMF members.[96] The role of the ECB in the IMF is limited to that of an observer, with no voting rights. As such, the ECB may participate in the meetings of the IMF Executive Board meetings and express views on issues within its competence.[97] Additionally, the ECB, represented by its president, attends the meetings of the International Monetary and Financial Committee (IMFC), together with the European Commissioner in charge of the Union's economic and monetary affairs.[98] The ECB also brings its contribution to the consultations with the IMF within the context of the euro area surveillance under Article IV of the IMF Articles of Agreement.[99] Here coordination takes place between the EU Member States, the Commission, and the ECB with a view to express a common position;[100] in this context, the ECB is involved in exchanges with the IMF on monetary policy and other issues within its competence, and prepares the monetary policy section of the euro area report.[101] Proposals for a unified representation of the euro area within the IMF better reflecting the role of the EU and of its institutions, including the ECB, have been put forward,[102] but the success of this quest very much depends on the willingness of the EU Member States to move in this direction as well as on reforming the IMF legal framework. With quite a rigid quota subscription-based voting power distribution among the members of the Executive Board and of the Board of Governors,[103] the ECB is left with few possibilities to formally influence IMF decision-making. Yet, the ECB could arguably make full use of its observer role within the Executive Board and IMFC to shape discussions on monetary policy and financial supervision issues by relying on the cooperation and support of the EU Member States holding IMF full membership.[104]

96 See International Monetary Fund, 'Articles of Agreement' (Adopted on 22 July 1944, amended on 26 January 2016, Bretton Woods) <https://www.imf.org/external/pubs/ft/aa/pdf/aa.pdf> accessed 27 June 2021, Arts III and XII (hereafter International Monetary Fund, 'Articles of Agreement'); see also European Central Bank, 'The External Representation of the EU and EMU' (n 80) 91.

97 Arguably the extension of the ECB's internal competence to prudential supervision of credit institutions, its expansive and controversial unconventional monetary policy measures like the Outright Monetary Transactions Programme (OMT) and the Public Sector Purchase Programme (PSPP), as well as its new tasks on economic policy conditionality conferred under ESM are reflected accordingly on the extent of issues on which the ECB may address the IMF Executive Board.

98 European Central Bank, 'The External Representation of the EU and EMU' (n 80) 91.

99 ibid 92.

100 The main IMF coordination mechanisms in place are the Sub-Committee on IMF-Related issues (SCIMF), under the Economic and Financial Committee (EFC) of the ECOFIN, composed of (two) representatives of the Commission, the ECB and each Member State, and the EU Representatives to the IMF (EURIMF) in Washington, in which the ECB and the Commission participate as observers: European Central Bank, 'The External Representation of the EU and EMU' (n 80) 92; see also Cremona and Leino-Sandberg, 'External Relations of the EU' (n 39) 162–63.

101 European Central Bank, 'The External Representation of the EU and EMU' (n 80) 92; see also Cremona and Leino-Sandberg, 'External Relations of the EU' (n 39) 151.

102 European Commission, COM (2015) 603 final (n 82); Opinion of the European Central Bank of 6 April 2016 on a proposal for a Council Decision laying down measures in view of progressively establishing unified representation of the euro area in the International Monetary Fund (CON/2016/22) [2016] OJ C216/1; see also Cremona and Leino-Sandberg, 'External Relations of the EU' (n 39) 160–62.

103 See International Monetary Fund, 'Articles of Agreement' (n 96), Art XII, s 5, and further International Monetary Fund, 'IMF Executive Directors and Voting Power' <https://www.imf.org/external/np/sec/memdir/eds.aspx> accessed 27 June 2021; International Monetary Fund, 'IMF Members' Quotas and Voting Power, and IMF Board of Governors' <https://www.imf.org/external/np/sec/memdir/members.aspx> accessed 27 June 2021.

104 Assessing the ECB's informal influence in this respect requires more empirical evidence.

As is the case with the IMF, membership to the OECD is restricted to states, entailing that the EU may participate in certain meetings and committees as an observer, but has not voting rights.[105] However, unlike the situation with the IMF, the Commission is in charge of representing the EU at the OECD, the ECB having no formal status except for the possibility to participate in some relevant OECD meetings.[106] The ECB also participates in more informal, though arguably highly influential, international bodies that are part of the current global financial framework.[107] Thus, the President of the ECB contributes, together with the President of the Eurogroup and the European Commissioner in charge of economic and monetary affairs, to the representation of the EU in the G7 meetings of the finance ministers and central bank governors.[108] Similarly, the ECB, the rotating EU Council Presidency, and the European Commission ensure the EU representation at the G20 forum of finance ministers and central bank governors.[109] Furthermore, the ECB has a strong presence in the Financial Stability Board (FSB), the overarching regulatory body concerned with the stability of the global financial system and the coordination of relevant international standard-setting bodies.[110] Last but not least, the ECB is a full member (with two seats) of the Basel Committee on Banking Supervision (BCBS), while the Commission and the European Banking Authority participate only as observers.[111] This suggests a rather significant role for the ECB within the global financial architecture, while the cases of the FSB and BCSB are good illustrations of how the extension of the ECB's internal powers relating to banking supervision entailed a consolidation of its presence in relevant international bodies.[112] However, relatively little is known about the practice of ECB's participation in international organizations and bodies, which makes it rather difficult to assess with precision this aspect of its international dimension.

C. The ECB's international cooperation instruments

One important aspect of the ECB's international dimension consists of the cooperation instruments used in relation to third countries and international organizations,

105 See Cremona and Leino-Sandberg, 'External Relations of the EU' (n 39) 156.

106 European Central Bank, 'The External Representation of the EU and EMU' (n 80) 92.

107 For a comprehensive analysis of the global financial stability architecture, see Shawn Donnelly and Ramses Wessel, 'The International Dimension of EMU. The Interplay Between the Global Financial Stability Architecture and the European Union' in Fabian Amtenbrink and Christoph Hermann (eds), *The EU Law of the Economic and Monetary Union* (OUP 2020) 99–133 (hereafter Donnelly and Wessel, 'The International Dimension of EMU').

108 See European Central Bank, 'The External Representation of the EU and EMU' (n 80) 93.

109 ibid.

110 The ECB has two seats (the Commission has only one seat) in the board—as monetary authority and as banking supervisor—and further participates in various committees: see also Donnelly and Wessel, 'The International Dimension of EMU' (n 107) 108–09.

111 Bank for International Settlements, 'Basel Committee Membership' <https://www.bis.org/bcbs/membership.htm> accessed 27 June 2021.

112 The reason for obtaining an additional seat, in its supervisory role (as the ECB-SSM), within the FSB and the BCSB is that the ECB (not the SSM) is equipped with legal personality, the main body actually in charge of the supervisory tasks under SSM (the Supervisory Board) being an internal structure of the ECB devoid of an independent legal status (SSM Regulation (n 22) Art 26): see Diane Fromage, 'The (Multilevel) Articulation of the European Participation in International Financial Fora: The Example of the Basel Accords' Journal of Banking Regulation (forthcoming).

as these are some of the most visible manifestations of its external powers from a legal perspective. Interestingly, in spite of their legal relevance, very little attention is paid in the ECB's legal framework to such instruments; in fact, only Article 8 SSM Regulation explicitly mentions the possibility for the ECB to conclude 'administrative arrangements' with third country authorities and international organizations as a way to fulfil the external dimension of its supervisory tasks. However, the scarcity of the legal framework in this respect did not preclude the ECB from developing a rich international cooperation practice, abundant with agreements,[113] memoranda of understanding (MoU),[114] and various administrative arrangements with competent authorities of third countries and international organizations. These cooperation instruments, covering the spectrum of the ECB's monetary and supervisory tasks, raise interesting legal questions as to their legal nature and effects. One recurrent issue concerns the relationship between the ECB's cooperation instruments, in particular if they prove to be legally binding agreements, and the institutional balance in EU external relations law. As illustrated in Section II above, both Article 218 TFEU, for EU treaties in general, and Article 219 TFEU, for the special case of monetary and foreign exchange-rate agreements, enshrine a well-defined institutional balance as regards EU treaty-making, entailing that the Council is in charge of concluding binding international agreements on behalf of the Union.

As a result, to the extent that one would conclude that the ECB's cooperation instruments with third countries and international organizations amount to legally binding agreements, they could arguably breach the division of powers regarding EU treaty-making.[115] As the label of the agreement is not decisive for the legal nature of the instrument, a case-by-case analysis of the wording, substance, and context of the agreement is required to clarify its status.[116] Such detailed assessments of the ECB's agreements and MoUs with third countries and international organizations reveal that at least some of them[117] can indeed be qualified as legally binding agreements[118]

[113] See, eg, Cooperation Agreement between the European Central Bank—ECB—and the International Criminal Police Organisation—INTERPOL [2004] OJ C134/6; swap agreements between the ECB and third-country central banks, European Central Bank, 'What are currency swap lines?' (27 September 2016) <https://www.ecb.europa.eu/explainers/tell-me-more/html/currency_swap_lines.en.html> accessed 27 June 2021; see also Zilioli and Selmayr 'Recent Developments in the Law of the ECB' (n 12) 79.

[114] ECB has concluded MoUs with central banks all over the world with a view to establishing cooperation, exchanges, and a dialogue on monetary matters—see European Central Bank, 'Annual Report 2019' (n 7); additionally, based on SSM Regulation (n 22) Art 8 the ECB, has concluded or is negotiating an increasing number of MoUs for supervisory cooperation with third country competent authorities—see European Central Bank, 'ECB Annual Report on Supervisory Activities 2019' (19 March 2020) <https://www.bankingsupervision.europa.eu/press/publications/annual-report/html/ssm.ar2019~4851adc406.en.html#toc81> accessed 27 June 2021.

[115] Especially in light of the 'single EU treaty-making procedure' approach embraced by the CJEU in Case C-658/11 *European Parliament v Council* (n 12) and Case C-263/14 *European Parliament v Council* (n 12); moreover, in Case C-327/91 *France v Commission* (n 19) the CJEU famously said that the particular institutional balance established by the Founding Treaties regarding EU treaty-making cannot be affected by the internal powers or practice of EU institutions.

[116] See Coman-Kund, *European Union Agencies* (n 19) 89–91.

[117] MoUs and other arrangements pertaining to voluntary routine administrative cooperation (eg exchange of best practices, trainings, technical assistance) concluded by the ECB with third country counterparts do not qualify in principle as legally binding instruments.

[118] For instance, the Cooperation Agreement between the ECB and INTERPOL of 2004 looks like a binding international agreement, entailing reciprocal obligations between the ECB and INTERPOL with

or at least they entail legal effects.[119] What is more, the Court established recently that even non-binding MoUs may affect the institutional balance in EU external relations.[120] While the ECB's power to conclude formal international cooperation instruments may admittedly be implied from its internal competence and a rather generic international cooperation legal framework,[121] it is essential for the validity of such instruments that they cover issues within the realm of ECB competence, are consistent with Union's international agreements and legislation, and do not affect the powers of other EU institutions and bodies.[122] As such, ECB cooperation instruments could be compatible with the Treaties if they qualify as a specific category of (binding or non-binding) operational or technical-administrative agreements concluded outside the scope of the 'politically significant' agreements under Articles 218–219 TFEU.[123] This in turn would require sufficient oversight and coordination in particular with the Council and the Commission by virtue of their roles under Articles 16–17, 21 TEU and Articles 218–219 TFEU, as well as with the Member States to preserve the balance of powers in EU external relations and the distribution of competences enshrined in the Treaties.[124]

A potential reform of the ECB's international cooperation legal framework could enhance clarity, consistency, and legal certainty by formalizing some of the elements of the ECB's international cooperation practice and by addressing the concerns posed by the ECB's cooperation agreements. It could, for instance, enshrine the categories of international cooperation instruments the ECB is using in practice and include

regard to exchanging and handling information for the purpose of the prevention and detection of the counterfeiting of euro banknotes. Also, the swap and repurchase agreements concluded by the ECB with non-euro central banks for the purpose of providing euros to another central bank in exchange for foreign currency or euro-denominated assets seem to amount to legally binding agreements: see European Central Bank, 'Central Bank Liquidity Lines' <https://www.ecb.europa.eu/mopo/implement/liquidity_lines/html/index.en.html> accessed 27 June 2021.

119 See, eg, the MoUs concluded by the ECB with third countries supervisory authorities on the exchange of confidential information on market participants; such confidentiality clauses are said to make these MoUs '"more" binding': Roberto Ugena, 'Confidentiality Clauses in MoUs: The Implications of the Absence of a Definition for Confidential Information' in European Central Bank, 'Building Bridges: Central Banking Law in an Interconnected World' (ECB Legal Conference 2019) 249 (hereafter European Central Bank, 'Building Bridges'). Arguably such MoUs may raise compatibility problems with SSM Regulation (n 22) Art 8 stipulating that the ECB's administrative arrangements 'shall not create legal obligations in respect of the Union and its Member States'; these problems could be alleviated if the ECB has its own international legal personality entailing that the obligations flowing from such agreements are incumbent on the ECB itself (not the EU). On the legal nature, effects, and review of MoUs in the EMU area generally, see Dariusz Adamski, 'Judicial Review of Economic and Financial Governance MoUs—between Legal Impeccability and Economic Flaws' in European Central Bank, 'Building Bridges' (n 119) 263–75.

120 Case C-660/13 *Council v Commission* (n 10).

121 As noted, this is actually the case in practice as regards the ECB's international cooperation instruments pertaining to its monetary functions featuring 'agreements' and 'memoranda of understanding' without these categories being explicitly enshrined in the ECB Statute; see also Coman-Kund, *European Union Agencies* (n 19) 102–03.

122 See Coman-Kund, *European Union Agencies* (n 19) 83–84.

123 In this way, it is also possible to alleviate the 'single EU treaty-making procedure' objection based on Art 218; on the conceptualization of the category of 'technical-administrative agreements' within the EU legal framework and the relationship between these agreements and the Union's 'politically significant agreements', see Coman-Kund, *European Union Agencies* (n 19) 98–104.

124 ibid 84.

provisions on their scope and legal effects, essential procedural aspects, as well as safeguards ensuring observance of the institutional balance in EU external relations.[125] In this respect, explicit obligations could be enshrined for the ECB to inform at an early stage the Council and the Commission about its intention to conclude a formal international cooperation instrument and to coordinate throughout the negotiation process with these institutions in line with their competences. While, for the sake of clarity, these issues could be best addressed in a renewed legal framework of the ECB, they could also be pursued pragmatically by way of improving the practice of cooperation and coordination between the ECB and the Council/Commission, without a formal amendment of the legal framework.

D. 'Borrowing' of the ECB outside the EU Treaty framework

An intriguing aspect of the ECB's (intra-EU) international dimension consists of the possibility to grant this institution new tasks outside the EU Treaty framework. This arose in the context of the financial support mechanisms (ie EFSF and ESM) established to safeguard the stability of the euro area during the sovereign debt crisis. The ECB has been given an unprecedented role in establishing, negotiating, and monitoring economic policy conditionality accompanying the financial assistance granted to euro area Member States in difficulty, and, as such, it became part of the twilight 'Troika' (the informal coordination tool of rescue operations). Most famously, the ECB was 'borrowed' by the euro area Member States for the purpose of implementing the ESM Treaty,[126] and was granted quite far-reaching tasks relating to economic policy conditionality[127] and financial stability.[128]

Arguably such tasks, carried out within the framework of an intergovernmental organization like the ESM, require quite a creative interpretation of the ECB's mandate to render them fit for purpose.[129] As shown by the *Pringle* case,[130] one core objection to granting extra tasks to the ECB via an international agreement is Article 13(2) TEU according to which EU institutions may only act within the powers and according to the conditions, procedures, and objectives laid down in the Founding Treaties.[131] However, by drawing analogy with somewhat similar external relations case law,[132] the Court generously endorsed the possibility to confer new

[125] This is already largely the case with respect to the international cooperation instruments concluded by the ECB in its supervisory role under SSM Regulation (n 22) Art 8.

[126] See Bruno de Witte and Thomas Beukers, 'The Court of Justice Approves the Creation of the European Stability Mechanism outside the EU Legal Order: Pringle' (2013) 50 CML Rev 805, 843–47 (hereafter de Witte and Beukers, 'The Court of Justice') as well as chapter 2 by Vestert Borger, in this volume, generally on this judgment.

[127] ESM Treaty (n 5) Art 13.

[128] See, eg, ibid Arts 4 and 18.

[129] See Beukers, 'The New ECB' (n 1) 1590–91.

[130] Case C-370/12 *Thomas Pringle v Government of Ireland and Others* [2012] ECLI:EU:C:2012:756 (hereafter Case C-370/12 *Pringle*).

[131] See de Witte and Beukers, 'The Court of Justice' (n 126) 844.

[132] Opinion 1/92 *Draft agreement between the Community, on the one hand, and the countries of the European Free Trade Association, on the other, relating to the creation of the European Economic Area* [1992] ECLI:EU:1992:189; Opinion 1/00 *Proposed agreement between the European Community and non-Member*

tasks[133] on the Commission and the ECB via the ESM Treaty, on the condition that such tasks 'do not alter the essential character of the powers conferred on those institutions' by the Treaties.[134] While this condition remains rather vague and controversial regarding the meaning of the 'essential character of the powers' and whether powers deemed as 'non-essential' could be altered by new tasks outside the Treaties, on a closer analysis, the Court indulgently found that the ECB's tasks under the ESM pass the test. The fact that the ECB's ESM-related tasks do not entail the possibility to take formal decisions, and that the performance of these tasks only commits the ESM (not the EU or the ECB)[135] seem to have been crucial factors leading to this conclusion.[136] Additionally, the Court[137] relied on a remarkably concise and loose interpretation of the ECB's supportive role of general economic policies under Article 282(2) TFEU and of its international cooperation framework relating in particular to establishing contacts with international organizations.[138]

Doubts have been raised as to whether the ECB's ESM-related tasks belong to its supportive role of general economic policies,[139] while some subsumed *Pringle* to a broader CJEU approach entailing a 'very formal and minimalist understanding of the ECB's involvement in financial assistance.[140] The CJEU's assessment of the ECB's minor role is also relativized by recent empirical insights into the Troika practice under the ESM, suggesting that the ECB has a much more influential role in practice than it has on paper.[141] Last but not least, one may wonder if the Court's approach in *Pringle* is fully consistent with its own case law on the relevance of non-binding international cooperation instruments under EU law,[142] and, more specifically, as regards the duties of the EU institutions to comply with EU law also when they perform tasks that 'do not entail any power to make decisions of their own' outside EU law.[143] All in all, a

States on the establishment of a European Common Aviation Area [2002] ECLI:EU:2002:231 and Opinion 1/09 *Draft Agreement—Creation of a Unified Patent Litigation System—European and Community Patents Court* [2011] ECLI:EU:2011:123; see also de Witte and Beukers, 'The Court of Justice' (n 126) 845–46.

[133] de Witte and Beukers note that, in its reasoning, the CJEU draws a distinction between 'powers' (laid down in the EU Treaties) and 'tasks' (not specifically articulated in the EU Treaties but 'gradually defined as EU law develops') of the EU institutions: de Witte and Beukers, 'The Court of Justice' (n 126) 846.

[134] Case C-370/12 *Pringle* (n 130) para 158.

[135] In the initial ESM Treaty, the conditionality MoUs based on Art 13 were signed by the European Commission on behalf of the ESM; according to the 2019 revised version of the ESM Treaty, Art 13 MoUs are signed on behalf of the ESM both by the Commission and the ESM Managing Director.

[136] Case C-370/12 *Pringle* (n 130) para 162.

[137] ibid para 165.

[138] ECB Statute (n 25) Arts 6(2) and 23.

[139] Paul Dermine, 'Out of the Comfort Zone? The ECB, Financial Assistance, Independence and Accountability' (2019) 26 MJ 108, 110–11.

[140] ibid 114.

[141] ibid 115. This alludes that, on the ground, the ECB's position might amount to more than mere support for general economic policies, thereby bringing into question the observance of the 'non-alteration of the essential character of ECB's powers under the Treaties' condition.

[142] See, eg, the signing by the Commission of a non-binding agreement (addendum to an MoU) covering essential EU policy aspects was found in breach of the institutional balance in EU external relations: Case C-660/13 *Council v Commission* (n 10). This judgment pertained to an MoU concluded by the EU with a third country, and it is not entirely sure whether the CJEU's reasoning would apply *mutatis mutandis* to MoUs concluded under the ESM Treaty.

[143] See Joined Cases C-8/15 to C-10/15 *Ledra Advertising and Others v European Commission and European Central Bank* [2016] ECLI:EU:C:2016:701, in particular paras 53, 57–60 and 67.

'Pandora's box' seems to have been opened by the Court in *Pringle*, whereby a reckless use of the possibility to grant EU institutions, such as the ECB, tasks and powers outside the Treaties could easily erode the Union's constitutional framework.[144]

V. A Critical Appraisal of the ECB's International Dimension: A 'New' ECB within a Crippled Legal Framework?

The above analysis of the ECB's international dimension reveals a constitutional framework almost unchanged in the past twenty years within which nevertheless important and sometimes problematic international cooperation dynamics have developed over time. This raises salient questions as to whether the ECB's current international practice is fully in line with the relevant EU legal framework, and whether there is a need for legal reforms considering the ECB's present-day international dimension. The limited space here does not allow answering these questions extensively, but in what follows, a succinct diagnosis of the current status quo is provided, highlighting a number of problematic issues and suggesting some remedies to 'cure the disease'.

First, the complex and fragmented international representation of the EMU reveals that a technocratic ECB cannot be fully in charge of the international dimension of the single monetary policy. International relations very often entail a political dimension requiring the intervention of the Council and the Commission as the main EU external action actors, as well as the involvement of the Member States. Arguably, the ECB could gain more extensive powers regarding the external representation of EMU provided that it would become a more political institution; developments in this direction are signalled by the ECB's unconventional monetary policies aimed at saving the euro, as well as by its participation in the 'Troika' entailing increased involvement in the coordination of the economic policies of the Member States. This would nonetheless engender a fundamental transformation of the ECB's current status, and would require a major reform of the EU constitutional framework.[145]

However, the fact that Articles 138 and 219 TFEU remained almost a dead letter in practice arguably offered the ECB quite some leeway to act externally based on Articles 6 and 23 ECB Statute, which might be problematic in light of the inherent political aspects related to the international representation of the euro. Under the Statute, the ECB's actions can be quite far-reaching, for instance, in the conduct of discretionary foreign exchange interventions and the conclusion of swap agreements. As for the participation in international organizations and bodies, uncoordinated actions between the ECB and other EU actors may render the EU's position ineffective, and result in damaging consequences.[146] In all the abovementioned instances it is, therefore, all the

[144] This risk is considerably higher if the CJEU only conducts a marginal review of its Pringle conditions regarding the 'borrowing' of EU institutions.

[145] For the time being, such a far-reaching reform does not seem politically feasible nor normatively desirable in view of the predominant economic thinking on the role of central banks: see Heidebrecht, 'Technocratic Governance at the Centre of the European Economic and Monetary Union' (n 61) 111–12.

[146] For instance, there seem to be insufficient coordination between the ECB, the Commission, and the EU Member States within the FSB, which leads sometimes to different views and opinions being expressed by these actors: see Cremona and Leino-Sandberg, 'External Relations of the EU' (n 39) 165.

more important that the ECB informs and cooperates with the Council (including the Eurogroup) and the Commission in charge of the external dimension of EMU and of the overall consistency of EU external action; in this way an extra safeguard is provided ensuring that the ECB's international actions do not affect the principle of institutional balance and the Union's external relations. The ECB's duty to cooperate on these matters can be inferred from the general obligation of EU institutions to 'practice mutual sincere cooperation' enshrined in Article 13(2) TEU, and, in practice, such information exchanges and cooperation already happen to some degree. Yet, perhaps it would still be useful to build on existing practice and further specify the application of the general sincere cooperation obligation in this context, by including an explicit duty of information and cooperation in Articles 6 and 23 ECB Statute, and perhaps also in Articles 138 and 219 TFEU. This could represent an acceptable middle ground between the need for the ECB to act externally in the single monetary policy and in the absence of common positions, decisions, and agreements based on Articles 138 and 219 TFEU,[147] and the institutional balance in external relations, without necessarily affecting the ECB's independence.

Second, the mismatch between the ECB's internal powers and its halfway international capacity linked to the restricted membership of important international organizations like the IMF, the OECD, or the G20 cannot be solved by an EU constitutional reform alone. Up to the moment that such international organizations will permit granting full membership status also to subjects of international law other than states, the current pragmatic arrangements, entailing limited participation of the ECB and cooperation with EU Member States enjoying full membership, will be applicable. Once more, close coordination and interaction in the spirit of the principle of loyal cooperation[148] will remain crucial to ensure the full effectiveness of ECB actions.

Third, the extension of the ECB's powers over time is also reflected in its evolving international dimension, as illustrated, for instance, by its enhanced position in the FSB and BCBS, as well as by the increasing number of MoUs concluded with third country supervisory authorities, after having been granted a central role within the SSM. This development corresponds to the functionalist logic behind the complementarity between internal and external powers, but it is also circumscribed by the principle of institutional balance and by the distribution of powers between the EU and its Member States. The external projection of the ECB's extended powers may easily affect the roles and competences of other EU institutions and of the Member States. It may create ambiguity and tensions externally, because of potential overlaps and an unclear

[147] The lack of political agreement between the EU institutions and the Member States that lies at the heart of the problematic (non) use of TFEU (n 8) Arts 138 and 219 is likely to persist in the future; therefore, including more detailed information and cooperation duties for the ECB when acting within the scope of TFEU (n 8) Arts 138 and 219 could enhance clarity regarding its responsibilities under such a scenario.

[148] In instances where the EU is not a member of an international organization, the principle of loyal cooperation entails that, (1) its Member States may not act as members of that international organization in such a way as to endanger the attainment of the Union's objectives and (2) the Union's external competence will be exercised through the Member States participating in that international organization acting jointly in the Union's interest: see Case C-45/07 *Commission v Greece* [2009] ECLI:EU:C:2009:81, paras 30–31 and Case C-399/12 *Germany v Council (International Organisation of Vine and Wine (OIV))* [2014] ECLI:EU:C:2014:2258, para 52.

division of tasks between the ECB and other relevant actors involved, for instance, as far as participation in international organizations is concerned. These concerns, so visible as regards the international dimension of the ECB's supervisory tasks under the SSM,[149] are also present in the case of the ECB's more controversial unconventional monetary measures and its new tasks conferred under the ESM.[150] Such tasks and measures, stretching to the maximum the ECB's monetary policy mandate or being situated arguably in the grey area between monetary and economic/fiscal policy,[151] are likely to entail further complications and tensions as regards the international representation of EMU.[152]

Fourth, the rather problematic 'borrowing' of the ECB outside the EU Treaties, endorsed by the Court in *Pringle*, should be enshrined in the Treaties[153] and made subject to more adequate safeguards. Precisely because of the high risk of departing from the EU constitutional framework, the possibility to entrust the ECB with tasks via international agreements and instruments should remain exceptional and strictly circumscribed. In this respect, it is suggested to drop the 'essential character of powers' criterion in *Pringle*, and to simply specify that such potential new tasks may only be entrusted to the ECB exceptionally, and they may not alter its powers conferred by the Treaties as well as the institutional balance. Moreover, expanding on the *Pringle* and *Ledra* line of case law, a separate paragraph of Article 127 TFEU or Article 282 TFEU concerning the 'borrowing' of the ECB could stipulate that the ECB is under a duty to fully comply with EU law in the exercise of its 'outside EU Treaties' tasks, and that such compliance is subject to legal review by the CJEU. Such constitutional guarantees would enhance the level of protection currently ensured by the CJEU against the alienation of elements of Union's own institutional framework, and they would protect more specifically the ECB's independence and legal status by preventing it from being 'highjacked' and used for purposes incompatible with its role under the Treaties.[154]

Fifth, ECB binding and non-binding agreements and MoUs are in principle compatible with EU law as long as they remain international cooperation instruments of a technical-administrative nature, covering issues within the ECB's mandate, and

[149] SSM Regulation (n 22) recital 80 of the preamble and Art 8.

[150] For instance, in the case of the PSPP, debt issued by international organizations is also eligible for purchase under the PSPP, subject to certain criteria, whereas the purchase of debt issued/guaranteed by Member States under financial assistance programmes requires a positive outcome review decision by the ESM and IMF—Decision (EU) 2020/188 of the European Central Bank of 3 February 2020 on a secondary markets public sector asset purchase programme (ECB/2020/9) [2020] OJ L39/12, Arts 2–4.

[151] For a recent analysis of the ECB's unconventional monetary policy programmes, with a special focus on the PSPP and the related judicial controversy between the CJEU and the German Constitutional Court, see Paul Dermine, 'The Ruling of the Bundesverfassungsgericht in PSPP—An Inquiry into its Repercussions on the Economic and Monetary Union. Bundesverfassungsgericht 5 May 2020, 2 BvR 859/15 and others, PSPP' (2020) 16 EuConst 525–51. See chapter 3 by Klaus Tuori, in this volume.

[152] For instance, within the IMF and other international fora, the ECB might gradually express views on economic policy matters pertaining to the EU Member States subjected to economic conditionality under ESM or on the economic/fiscal side-effects of its unconventional monetary policy tools, thereby creeping into the competences of the Council, Commission, and the Member States on economic and financial matters.

[153] For instance, by amending TFEU (n 8) Art 127 or 282, and/or the ECB Statute (n 25).

[154] Also, a horizontal clause concerning the limits and conditions for the 'borrowing' of EU institutions in general could be enshrined in TEU (n 39) Art 13.

as long as they comply with international agreements of the Union under Articles 218–219 TFEU and with EU secondary legislation. Thus, even when they entail legally binding effects, ECB international cooperation instruments do not automatically breach the institutional balance in EU external relations, provided that they pertain exclusively to cooperation between administrations.[155] However, this requires adequate safeguards built in the legal framework, ensuring that ECB international cooperation instruments remain within these parameters. In this respect, we recommend including in the ECB Statute more detailed provisions regarding its formal cooperation instruments. Such provisions could reflect the types of agreements used in the ECB's current cooperation practice; formalize important aspects pertaining to the negotiation, conclusion, and the effects of such instruments; but also lay down in more detail the ECB's duty to consult and coordinate with the main EU external relation actors and other relevant actors. Moreover, in order to enhance scrutiny and review of ECB international cooperation instruments, it is recommended to overcome the current scarcity of information regarding the ECB's international dimension,[156] by enshrining clearer information duties. For instance, the ECB could be compelled to publish its international cooperation strategy and planning, as well as its agreements, MoUs, and other international formal cooperation instruments.[157] This can only facilitate understanding and assessing the ECB's international cooperation instruments and its current rather nebulous international practice.

Sixth, a recurring issue concerns the ECB's derived international legal personality and the (in)divisibility of the Union's international legal personality. If the Lisbon Treaty reform, aimed at transforming the EU in a more unitary global actor speaking with one voice on the international plane, is to be continued, should then the legal status of the ECB be further aligned to that of the other EU institutions, which do not have their own international legal personality but only act externally to enable the Union to exercise its capacity as an international legal person? A positive answer to this question entails considering removing from the Treaties the elements conferring the ECB a special legal status and which fuel the idea of the ECB's own international legal personality.[158] If, on the contrary, the pragmatic reasons enabling the ECB to claim its own functionally derived international legal personality remain valid at this stage of the ECB's development, then its special legal status enshrined in the Treaties could be maintained, potentially fuelling the visibility of the ECB as an actor in the international arena.

[155] See Coman-Kund, *European Union Agencies* (n 19) 276–77.

[156] The main sources of public information about the ECB's international cooperation are its webpage section on international affairs, annual activity reports, and some ECB press releases and papers; none of these sources however, provide direct access to ECB's agreements and MoUs with third countries and international organizations.

[157] This obligation could also encompass other 'twilight' aspects of the ECB's international dimension, such as the ECB's participation in the IMF, the FSB, and the BSCB.

[158] ie the separate provisions on the ECB's legal personality, privileges and immunities, and liability for damages.

VI. Conclusion

Since its establishment, more than twenty years ago, the ECB has grown into an increasingly important global actor featuring a rich international cooperation practice and, arguably, a derived and functionally limited international legal personality. Besides assuming a core role with regard to the external dimension of the single monetary policy and foreign-exchange operations, the ECB has also seen its international dimension amplified as a result of its extended powers over time, through unconventional monetary measures and new 'outside EU Treaties' tasks during the euro area crisis, as well as through its new role in banking supervision. While these dynamics confer arguably more weight to the ECB on the international plane, they also raise significant challenges and problems. Thus, in spite of its large degree of independence and autonomy in pursuing international cooperation, one recurrent concern is to ensure that the ECB's actions comply with the principle of institutional balance and the distribution of competences between the EU and its Member States. Another challenge is to improve the effectiveness of the ECB's international dimension along with the consistency of the Union's external action on matters pertaining to EMU external representation. Addressing these challenges requires closer cooperation and coordination between the ECB and the EU external actors, as well as the Member States. Also, more clarity and safeguards are welcome regarding certain aspects of the ECB's international dimension, in particular the problematic 'borrowing' outside the EU framework and the international cooperation instruments concluded with non-EU partners. Therefore, we suggest it is time to seriously consider revisiting the ECB's international cooperation legal framework to reflect the needs and constraints of its present-day international dimension.

PART III
INSTITUTIONAL SETTING
The ECB'S 'Institutional Logic' and Its Relationship with Governments, Courts, and Parliaments

Part 3 revisits the significance of various transformations to inter- and intra-institutional relations concerning the ECB, including the vexed question of the balance between independence and accountability of the ECB. It asks what new inter- and intra-institutional balance has been struck by considering the issue of the ECB's independence and accountability as mentioned, but also its relationship to the Court of Justice, its standing within the EU's institutional structure and its relationship to sovereigns.

10
The Independence of the ECB
Justification, Challenges, and Possible Threats

Alexander Thiele

I. Independence in Times of Crisis

'It shall be independent in the exercise of its powers and in the management of its finances.'[1] This fundamental rule concerning the status of the European Central Bank (ECB) is by now probably known to any regular newspaper reader—it was cited regularly during the various crises the EU had to face in the last years (Great Financial Crisis (GFC) and euro area crisis) and still has to cope with today (climate crisis and COVID-19 pandemic). From a normative perspective recent developments that 'pushed the European Central Bank (ECB) in another dimension',[2] however, have once again raised the question of justification and precise content of central bank independence.[3] How does this institutional setting, for instance, influence the lawfulness of the various bond purchases the ECB has undertaken since 2010 (and has extended under its fourth President *Christine Lagarde*)?[4] Could such programmes create a questionable dependency of the ECB on the fiscal policy of the respective Member States? And vice versa: Could the ECB's independent status impose normative boundaries on the fiscal and economic policy of a Member State? In the last years, several decisions of the German Constitutional Court[5] also brought up the question of judicial control: is

[1] TFEU, Art 282(3).

[2] Diane Fromage and others, 'ECB Independence and Accountability Today: Towards a (Necessary) Redefinition?' (2019) 26 MJ 3, 4 (hereafter Fromage and others, 'ECB Independence'); see also Anna-Lena Högenauer and David Howarth, 'The Democratic Deficit and European Central Bank Crisis Monetary Policies' (2019) 26 MJ 81 (hereafter Högenauer and Howarth, 'The Democratic Deficit').

[3] See also Fabian Amtenbrink, 'The European Central Bank's Intricate Independence Versus Accountability Conundrum in the Post-Crisis Governance Framework' (2019) 26 MJ 165, 166 (hereafter Amtenbrink, 'The European Central Bank's intricate independence').

[4] As Amtenbrink, 'The European Central Bank's intricate independence' (n 3) 167 rightly states these purchase programmes 'have taken centre stage in the debates on the scope of the competence of the ECB and the legality of its crisis-related measures'.

[5] BVerfG 14 January 2014, 2 BvR 2728/13 DE:BVerfG:2014:rs20140114.2bvr272813 (hereafter BVerfG 14 January 2014, 2 BvR 2728/13) (request for preliminary ruling) and BVerfG 21 June 2016, 2 BvR 2728/13 DE:BVerfG:2016:rs20160621.2bvr272813 (hereafter BVerfG 21 June 2016, 2 BvR 2728/13) (final decision). In 2017 the German Constitutional Court initiated a second preliminary ruling, see BVerfG 18 July 2017, 2 BvR 859/15 DE:BVerfG:2017:rs20170718.2bvr085915 and others (hereafter BVerfG 18 July 2017, 2 BvR 859/15). The ECJ decided on this preliminary ruling on 11 December 2018 in Case C-493/17 *Weiss and Others* [2018] EU:C:2018:1000 (hereafter *Weiss*). In its final decision the German Constitutional Court declared the PSPP to be unconstitutional if the ECB was not able to prove the proportionality of the programme within a period of three months: see BVerfG 5 May 2020, 2 BvR 859/15 DE:BVerfG:2020:rs20200505.2bvr085915 and others (hereafter BVerfG 5 May 2020, 2 BvR 859/15).

Alexander Thiele, *The Independence of the ECB* In: *The New European Central Bank*. Edited by: Thomas Beukers, Diane Fromage, and Giorgio Monti, Oxford University Press. © Alexander Thiele 2022. DOI: 10.1093/oso/9780198871231.003.0010

such control compatible with the ECB's independent status, or do we need to consider certain restrictions (for instance as regards the review-intensity)?[6] These—among others—are the questions this chapter seeks to answer.

To do so, I will first take a brief look at the general economic and judicial justification for the independent status of central banks (II). I will thereby also illustrate the different manifestations of independence we need to distinguish (III)—though the ECB, the Bank of England, as well as the American Federal Reserve all enjoy some sort of independence, its degree and design differ significantly. Recent developments will then form the initial point for a detailed analysis of the normative content of the ECB's independence (IV). Simple criticism of the ECB's actions brought forward by the media, scholars, or politicians will be unproblematic from a normative perspective. The same is true concerning certain duties of the ECB to report to, or to cooperate with other institutions. It remains nonetheless the case that the Member States' fiscal and wage policy, bond purchases by the ECB, as well as a too extensive judicial control might—at least under certain circumstances—pose a threat to the independent status of the ECB. Yet, this chapter will end with a hopeful conclusion: until today, the ECB's independent status has not been severely impaired by any of the analysed measures and events. Possible threats, however, continue to exist. Safeguarding the independent status of the ECB remains an important challenge (also) for legal scholars. However, due to its somewhat new (more political) role the ECB has played in recent years, discussions will most certainly come up asking the question whether this special status remains to be justified or should be (partially) amended (V).

II. The Justification of Central Bank Independence

A. Economic background

Though this might come as a surprise to the general public, the independent status of a central bank is no matter of course. As central banks perform duties of public administration with potentially major impacts on people's (economic) lives, integrating these institutions into the hierarchical organization of administration—with the politically accountable government at the top—appears far more self-evident. We would surely not consider granting the Ministry of Finance such a status, for instance. In fact, central banks did also not enjoy such independence from governmental interference for quite a long time:[7] 'Until recently, central bank independence was more an exception than a rule.'[8] Not least the Bank of England (as the oldest central bank) was in fact founded in 1694 explicitly to help Great Britain's government out of its financial misery that had occurred due to several (and not always successful) war

[6] See Mark Dawson and Ana Bobic, 'Quantitative Easing at the Court of Justice—Doing Whatever it Takes to Save the Euro: *Weiss and Others*' (2019) 56 CML Rev 1005 (hereafter Dawson and Bobic, 'Quantitative Easing').

[7] For the development of central banks, see Alexander Thiele, *Finanzaufsicht* (Mohr Siebeck 2014) 188 ff (hereafter Thiele, *Finanzaufsicht*).

[8] Fromage and others, 'ECB Independence' (n 2) 9.

affairs: 'Finally, and almost as a last resource, they founded the Bank of England.'[9] Quite similarly, Alexander Hamilton hoped for significant assistance, 'in obtaining pecuniary aids, especially in sudden emergencies'[10] when founding the first Bank of the United States in 1791—evidently quite the opposite of independence. Serving as 'Banks of the State' being independent *from* the state did obviously not appear to be a very convincing idea.

This changed as the central banks progressively expanded their role during the nineteenth and twentieth centuries. In this period, central banks gradually changed from being 'Banks of the State' to being 'Banks of the Banks'[11]—a process that was accelerated when the central banks were granted the money monopoly. Central Banks were now responsible for the money supply and started to act as Lender of Last Resort. Since then, the main objective of central banks (with diverging focal points) became safeguarding price stability.[12] This new responsibility soon provoked a debate concerning the appropriate status of central banks. The question was: can a central bank perform this specific task effectively as long as it is integrated into and thus dependent on (or even controlled by) the government? Two aspects might hinder an effective performance of such a dependent central bank:[13] First of all, several inflation favouring conflicts of interest could arise that might lead to a trade-off between price stability and the government's fiscal, wage, and employment policy.[14] And second of all, politicians might be apt to consider a price-enhancing expansion of money supply in order to profit from expected short-term economy-boosting effects,[15] while neglecting the long-term inflationary impact of such measures—especially during election campaigns.[16] Anticipated governmental actions by the market participants could have the potential to create an inflationary environment—even if the government promised

[9] Albert Edgar Feavearyear, *The Pound Stearling* (OUP 1963) 125. See also Forest Capie and others, 'The Development of Central Banking' in Forest Capie and others (ed), *The Future of Central Banking* (CUP 1994) 4 ff (hereafter Capie, 'The Development of Central Banking').

[10] Alexander Hamilton, 'Report on a National Bank' in Herman E Kroos (ed), *Documentary History of Banking and Currency in the United States* (Chelsea Publishing House 1985) 231 ff.

[11] For the changing relationship of central banks and the government, see Capie, 'The Development of Central Banking' (n 9) 48 ff.

[12] ibid 81 for government. See also Harold James, *Making the European Monetary Union* (Harvard University Press 2012) 15 (hereafter James, *Making the European Monetary Union*). According to Charles AE Goodhart, *The Regulatory Response to the Financial Crisis* (Edward Elgar Publishing 2010) 34 ff (hereafter Goodhart, *The Regulatory Response to the Financial Crisis*) the financial crisis has shown that central banks also have a responsibility for maintaining financial stability and should see this as their second core purpose. Unsurprisingly, this specific task therefore also stands at the centre of the ECB's mandate according to TFEU Art 127(1).

[13] See also Fromage and others, 'ECB Independence' (n 2) 9.

[14] See Jan Endler, *Europäische Zentralbank und Preisstabilität* (Boorberg 1998) 185 ff (hereafter Endler, *Europäische Zentralbank und Preisstabilität*).

[15] See, for instance, Robert J Barro and David B Gordon, 'Rules, Discretion, and Reputation in a Positive Model of Monetary Policy' (1983) 12 Journal of Monetary Economics 101 (hereafter Barro and Gordon, 'Rules, Discretion, and Reputation in a Positive Model of Monetary Policy'): 'The benefits from this surprise inflation may include expansions of economic activity and reductions in the real value of the government's national liabilities.'

[16] See Hans-Joachim Jarchow, *Grundriss der Geldpolitik* (12th edn, Lucius & Lucius 2010) 3 as well as Helmut Siekmann in Helmut Siekmann (ed), *EWU-Kommentar zur Europäischen Währungsunion* (Mohr Siebeck 2013) TFEU Art 130 paras 26 ff (hereafter Siekmann in Siekmann (ed), *EWU*). See also Michael Ioannidis, 'The European Central Bank' in Fabian Amtenbrink and Christoph Herrmann (eds), *The EU Law of Economic and Monetary Union* (OUP 2020) para 14.51.

to refrain from taking such measures.[17] Respective promises would lack the necessary credibility[18]—a phenomenon also known as 'time inconsistency' or 'dynamic inconsistence'.[19]

An article published by *Milton Friedman* in 1962[20] illustrates that the answer to this fundamental question of independence was nonetheless discussed more or less openly for a long period of time. In the middle of the 1980s, however, the pendulum gradually began to swing towards the supporters of independence. Trend-setting was a paper by Kenneth Rogoff, who proposed—in order to avoid inflationary incentives of the 'policy-maker'[21] analysed game-theoretically by Robert Barro and David Gordon[22]—to lay monetary policy in the hands of a conservative (and independent) agent. This independent agent should be known to place a greater weight on inflation stabilization relative to unemployment stabilization.[23] In other words: he should be '(somewhat) more inflation-conscious than average'.[24] Rogoff realized that such an institutional setting might impair the economy-stabilizing function of monetary policy[25]—a function visible during the last GFC, the following euro- and the current coronavirus crisis. He nonetheless believed that such an effect could be reduced by choosing a conservative (that is 'hawkish'), but not too conservative agent.[26] During the 1990s, central bank independence—supported by several empirical studies[27]—finally became[28] a central, if not the central, pillar of modern central bank theory,[29]

[17] See Barro and Gordon, 'Rules, Discretion, and Reputation in a Positive Model of Monetary Policy' (n 15), who point out that governmental assurance in this area is simply not credible.

[18] See Endler, *Europäische Zentralbank und Preisstabilität* (n 14) 190 ff.

[19] See Finn E Kydland and Edward C Prescott, 'Rules Rather than Discretion: The Inconsistency of Optimal Plans' (1977) 85 Journal of Political Economy 473; Fromage and others, 'ECB Independence' (n 2) 9.

[20] Milton Friedman, 'Should There Be an Independent Monetary Authority?' in Leland B Yeager (ed), *In Search of a Monetary Constitution* (Harvard University Press 1962) 219 ff (hereafter Friedman, 'Should There Be an Independent Monetary Authority?'). Friedman spoke out against an independent central bank: 'Money is too important to be left to the central bankers.' See also Werner Heun, 'Die Zentralbank in den USA—das Federal Reserve System' (1998) 9 Staatswissenschaften und Staatspraxis 241, 262 (hereafter Heun, 'Die Zentralbank in den USA—das Federal Reserve System').

[21] Meaning a government that is also responsible for monetary policy.

[22] Robert J Barro and David B Gordon, 'A Positive Theory of Monetary Policy in a Natural Rate Model' (1983) 91 Journal of Political Economy 588; Barro and Gordon, 'Rules, Discretion, and Reputation in a Positive Model of Monetary Policy' (n 15).

[23] Kenneth Rogoff, 'The Optimal Degree of Commitment to an Immediate Monetary Target' (1985) 100 Quarterly Journal of Economics 1169, 1177 (hereafter Rogoff, 'The Optimal Degree of Commitment to an Immediate Monetary Target').

[24] ibid 1180.

[25] For instance, as regards the unemployment rate.

[26] Rogoff, 'The Optimal Degree of Commitment to an Immediate Monetary Target' (n 23) 1177: '... it is never optimal to choose an individual who is known to care "too little" about unemployment [...]'.

[27] See especially the detailed study by Alex Cukierman, *Central Bank Strategy, Credibility, and Independence: Theory and Evidence* (MIT Press 1992). See also Endler, *Europäische Zentralbank und Preisstabilität* (n 14) 215 ff.

[28] See James, *Making the European Monetary Union* (n 12) 270. However, the studies revealed significant differences between developed and non-developed countries: see Carl E Walsh, *Central Bank Independence* (New Palgrave Dictionary for Economics 2005) 6 ff (hereafter Walsh, *Central Bank Independence*).

[29] Bernd Hayo and Carsten Hefeker, 'Reconsidering Central Bank Independence' (2002) 18 European Journal of Political Economy 653 (hereafter Hayo and Hefeker, 'Reconsidering Central Bank Independence'). See also James, *Making the European Monetary Union* (n 12) 265: 'The 1990s saw the emergence of a new philosophy of central banking, in which the independence of central banks from the political process became a core component of the culture of monetary stability.'

finding its temporary endpoint in the creation of the possibly 'most independent central bank of all':[30] the ECB.[31]

This 'intellectual revolution',[32] or 'intellectual shift towards central bank independence',[33] did not remain undisputed, and has since been challenged several times within the (academic) economic field. The last years have actually seen an increasing number of scholars arguing that central bank independence is not necessary. Some believe it might even hinder the central bank from achieving its central goal—and the experience of the several recent and ongoing crises has added volume to these critical voices.[34] Not least John B Taylor, referring to the abovementioned article by the monetarist[35] Milton Friedman, has consistently argued in favour of focusing more on the rules determining a central bank's monetary policy and less on its institutional setting.[36] According to Taylor, who proved his point with several empirical studies, a central bank's success depended decisively on the amount of discretion it had when applying these underlying rules: less discretion would result in more success—and vice versa. From a normative perspective, however, Taylor's arguments hardly make a convincing point against central bank independence for two reasons. First of all, rules need to be interpreted.[37] Although Taylor's rules might include clear legal consequences depending on certain economic circumstances, it will be impossible to conclude whether such circumstances are given without some sort of discretion—especially in the field of monetary policy. Different interpretations of economic settings remain possible—otherwise monetary policy might as well be left to electronic devices, a conclusion even Taylor would probably not agree to. These remaining discretionary considerations, however, should remain in the hands of an independent central bank (or should at least not be put into those of the government). And second of all (and probably more importantly): nobody has yet been able to formulate monetary rules that fit any economic development without any exception.[38] Taylor himself did not believe his 'Taylor-Rule' (to which several central banks have reverted to in the past) should be followed under all circumstances—exceptions were to remain

[30] Hayo and Hefeker, 'Reconsidering Central Bank Independence' (n 29) 654. For the difficulties when trying to measure the individual degree of independence, see James, *Making the European Monetary Union* (n 12) 271 ff.

[31] See also Fromage and others, 'ECB Independence' (n 2) 10.

[32] James, *Making the European Monetary Union* (n 12) 15.

[33] ibid.

[34] See James, *Making the European Monetary Union* (n 12) 15, who believes that this effect is at least partly rooted in the experiences of the financial crisis.

[35] See Heun, 'Die Zentralbank in den USA—das Federal Reserve System' (n 20) 262.

[36] John B Taylor, 'Discretion versus Monetary Policy Rules in Practice' (1993) 39 Carnegie Rochester Conference Series on Public Policy 195; John B Taylor, 'Monetary Policy Rules Work and Discretion Doesn't: A Tale of Two Eras' (2012) 44 JMCB 1017 (hereafter Taylor, 'Monetary Policy Rules Work and Discretion Doesn't: A Tale of Two Eras'); John B Taylor, 'The Effectiveness of Central Bank Independence Versus Policy Rules' (2013) 48 Business Economics 155 (hereafter Taylor, 'The Effectiveness of Central Bank Independence Versus Policy Rules').

[37] See Horst Dreier, *Hierarchische Verwaltung im demokratischen Staat* (Mohr Siebeck 1991) 169: 'Selbst der handlungsfreudigste, optimal informierte, seiner selbst gewisse Gesetzgeber kann heute auf Dauer nicht verbindliche Normen mit einem Konkretisierungsgrad und einer Detailgenauigkeit produzieren, die den Handlungsspielraum der zur Normexekution befugten Instanzen auf das sprachphilosophisch und methodologisch begründbare unvermeidliche Mindestmaß beschränken.'

[38] Heun, 'Die Zentralbank in den USA—das Federal Reserve System' (n 20) 262 ff.

possible. Designing monetary policy without any discretion for the relevant actors appears to be impossible (at least as of today), even if we should have clear-cut rules for everyday monetary policy.[39] In other words: normatively, we will not be able to evade discretion completely. American central bankers have always emphasized that monetary policy is 'a matter of judgement'[40] and thus 'an art rather than a science'.[41] Taylor's findings therefore might give reason to demand a detailed explanation by the central bank when it deviates from a well-formulated monetary rule. His statement 'Monetary Policy Rules Work and Discretion doesn't',[42] however, appears too simplistic (and was probably intended to appear so). Putting the remaining discretionary decisions in the hands of independent central bankers (and not the government) is not something that Taylor's rules concept would be opposed to. Taylor nonetheless makes a valid point when he underlines the importance of the internal independence of central bankers referring to their (mental) willingness and ability to act independently.[43] And indeed: formal independence alone will not suffice where central bankers are either influenced by the respective government or generally biased towards their preferred political party—a behaviour Roland Vaubel was able to prove for many central bankers, including some members of the German Bundesbank: 'The members of the Bundesbank council, like most ordinary citizens, seem to derive utility from the election of their preferred party. If they are independent . . . , they use their power to improve the electoral chances of their preferred party.'[44] However, formal independence from any governmental influence still remains a necessary (though therefore not sufficient) condition[45] where one wants to uphold at least the chance of internal independence (how big or small it may be).[46]

The criticism formulated by Bernd Hayo and Carsten Hefeker focuses on a different aspect of the independence dogma. They point out that the negative correlation between independence and inflation was merely a statistical correlation and was not to be confused with causality.[47] Several empirical studies also pointed to the conclusion that reaching price stability depended less on the institutional setting than on the inflation culture of a society.[48] In countries where preventing inflation was regarded as a necessary requirement for the prosperity of a society even a state-controlled central

[39] See Capie, 'The Development of Central Banking' (n 9) 85: 'Given the continuing rapid pace of the evolution of such structures, central banks will rightly aim to retain their discretionary flexibility.'

[40] Board of Governors of the Federal Reserve System, *Tenth Annual Report* (1923) 32.

[41] William McChesney Martin, 'Statement before the Subcommittee on a National Security and International Operations of the Senate Committee on Government Operations' (1965) 51 Federal Reserve Board 1237, 1238. See also Heun, 'Die Zentralbank in den USA—das Federal Reserve System' (n 20) 263.

[42] Taylor, 'Monetary Policy Rules Work and Discretion Doesn't: A Tale of Two Eras' (n 36) 1017 ff.

[43] Taylor, 'The Effectiveness of Central Bank Independence Versus Policy Rules' (n 36) 14. See also Hayo and Hefeker, 'Reconsidering Central Bank Independence' (n 29) 657 ff.

[44] Roland Vaubel, 'The Bureaucratic and Partisan Behavior of Independent Central Banks: German and International Evidence' (1997) 13 European Journal of Political Economy 201, 222—incidentally, a problem known and debated regarding the independent judicial branch too.

[45] See also Ute Reumann, *Die Europäische Zentralbank* (Centaurus Verlag & Media 2001) 26.

[46] See Heun, 'Die Zentralbank in den USA—das Federal Reserve System' (n 20) 263.

[47] Hayo and Hefeker, 'Reconsidering Central Bank Independence' (n 29) 654: 'In other words, this correlation does not indicate causality.'

[48] ibid 663ff for the different inflation cultures. According to them an independent central bank is mainly installed in countries where preventing inflation is deemed highly significant. See also Endler, *Europäische Zentralbank und Preisstabilität* (n 14) 219 ff.

bank would be able to safeguard price stability.[49] No independent central bank would indeed stand a chance against a 'culture of inflation'—especially as the independent status would usually not be founded in the constitution but in ordinary (and thus easily amendable) regular statutes.[50] Yet again, these findings do not include a decisive argument against independence as such: in the worst case, independence would be useless but not harmful. Hayo and Hefeker, however, doubt such a 'useless but not harmful' conclusion due to the fact that there is no proven negative correlation between independence and inflation. Under such circumstances, Hayo and Hefeker point out, it appeared hardly justifiable to put monetary policy in the hands of an independent and conservative agent whose decisions were not foreseeable, yet once taken, impossible to amend for the accountable politicians in charge[51]—especially due to the lobbying structures that might influence the decisions taken by such an agent.[52] Nevertheless, Hayo and Hefeker do not oppose an independent central bank under all circumstances. According to their findings, there might be rational reasons for a society to stick to such a model where it was compatible with the general political and legal system as well as the organization of the labour market. What they wanted to point out was the fact that independence was neither generally the best status nor for itself sufficient for safeguarding price stability. It appears fair to say, therefore, that economically quite a few questions remain open.

As a legal scholar, one will not be able to solve this ongoing economic dispute (and as we will see later, judges should also refrain from trying to do so). However, it makes clear that a society deciding in favour of an independent central bank is probably not completely off track as regards its economic rationality.[53] Yet, from a legal perspective such a decision still needs to comply with the relevant constitutional requirements, especially the democratic principle (and the necessity for democratic accountability)—an aspect not least the German literature has dealt with in abundance (originally regarding the Bundesbank and now the ECB).

B. (German) democratic theory

Compliance with the democratic principle, first of all, does not follow automatically from the abovementioned (possible) economic rationality behind the independent status of a central bank.[54] To quote the German legal scholar Christoph Möllers: 'Good

[49] See also James, *Making the European Monetary Union* (n 12) 272.

[50] Especially regarding this aspect, see Hayo and Hefeker, 'Reconsidering Central Bank Independence' (n 29) 659 ff. Respective threats to remove the independent status occurred in Germany, for instance, in 1956 when *Konrad Adenauer* was unhappy with the monetary policy of the Bundesbank. However, to change the independent status of the ECB the European Treaties would have to be amended, including a ratification of such an amendment in all the Member States (TEU Art 48).

[51] Hayo and Hefeker, 'Reconsidering Central Bank Independence' (n 29) 659.

[52] ibid 665 ff.

[53] cf Siekmann in Siekmann (ed), *EWU* (n 16) para 34 and Ulrich Häde in Christian Calliess and Matthias Ruffert (eds), *EUV/AEUV* (4th edn, CH Beck 2011) TFEU art 130 para 9 (hereafter Häde in Calliess and Ruffert (eds), *EUV/AEUV*): '… deutliche Hinweise auf einen Zusammenhang zwischen Unabhängigkeit und Preisstabilität.' Whether the ECB should receive such an independent status, however, was highly disputed when constructing the EMU: see James, *Making the European Monetary Union* (n 12) 278 ff.

[54] See Häde in Calliess and Ruffert (eds), *EUV/AEUV* (n 53) paras 37 ff.

reasons (alone) do not create democratic legitimation.'[55] If one considers the dual democratic concept of Ernst Wolfgang Böckenförde—a two-pillar concept especially the German Constitutional Court relies on in its case law[56]—an independent central bank, though formally legitimized by the constitution and the relevant legal order (first pillar), lacks the necessary material legitimation or 'content-legitimation' (second pillar).[57] Due to the unavoidable discretion of any central bank as regards its monetary policy—unavoidable even for a rules based 'taylorized' central bank—this deficit of legitimacy can be compensated only partly (if at all) by binding the central bank to a more detailed statutory framework.[58] The question especially for German legal scholars therefore is whether this unavoidable deficit of (material) democratic legitimacy can be justified or not. The literature to this question appears endless,[59] yet the answer given is more or less undisputed today: due to the at least defensible relationship between an independent central bank and price stability, the overwhelming majority of German scholars negate a violation of the democratic principle.[60] We thus find a 'justification by task'[61] with the following argument: if there is indeed a relationship between the two (independence and price stability), it seems impossible to transfer the task of safeguarding price stability onto a central bank while denying it the mandatory status needed to perform successfully. Such a 'justification by task', however, is only possible for the area of monetary policy, as it is only here that the independent status is perceived necessary to fulfil the transferred task.[62] Most scholars indeed agree that there is no problem of legitimacy as long as the actions of the ECB 'are framed by a clear and narrow mandate'[63]—that is, a mandate to safeguard price stability. In other cases, independence might be helpful for fulfilling the respective task according to some economic voices, yet not absolutely necessary. According to the

[55] Christoph Möllers, *Demokratie—Zumutungen und Versprechungen* (Bundeszentrale für politische Bildung 2008)para 54 (hereafter Möllers, *Demokratie—Zumutungen und Versprechungen*).

[56] See Horst Dreier in Horst Dreier (ed), *Grundgesetz Band II* (Mohr Siebeck 2015) Art 20 paras 113 ff.

[57] For a detailed analysis, see Karl-Peter Sommermann in Hermann von Mangoldt, Friedrich Klein, and Christian Starck (eds), *Grundgesetz Band II* (6th edn, Vahlen 2010) Art 20 abs 2 para 168.

[58] Which, incidentally, marks a significant difference to the judiciary.

[59] Among many, see Frauke Brosius-Gersdorf, *Deutsche Bundesbank und Demokratieprinzip* (Duncker und Humblot 1997) 127 ff.

[60] See, for instance, Bernhard Kempen in Rudolf Streinz (ed), *EUV/AEUV* (2nd edn, CH Beck 2010) TFEU Art 130 para 5; Endler, *Europäische Zentralbank und Preisstabilität* (n 14) 272 ff. See also the remarks of the German Constitutional Court in its Maastricht-Decision: BVerfG 12 October 1993, 2 BvR 2134/92 2 BvR 2159/92, para 208: 'Die Verselbständigung der meisten Aufgaben der Währungspolitik bei einer unabhängigen Zentralbank löst staatliche Hoheitsgewalt aus unmittelbarer staatlicher oder supranationaler parlamentarischer Verantwortlichkeit, um das Währungswesen dem Zugriff von Interessengruppen und der an einer Wiederwahl interessierten politischen Mandatsträger zu entziehen … Diese Einschränkung der von den Wählern in den Mitgliedstaaten ausgehenden demokratischen Legitimation berührt das Demokratieprinzip, ist jedoch als eine in Art. 88 Satz 2 GG vorgesehene Modifikation dieses Prinzips mit Art. 79 Abs. 3 GG vereinbar.' See also Helge Sodan, 'Die funktionelle Unabhängigkeit der Zentralbanken' (1999) Neue Juristische Wochenschrift 1521, 1521 ff.

[61] Marcus Höreth, *Die Europäische Union im Legitimationstrilemma* (Nomos 1999) 230.

[62] Siekmann in Siekmann (ed), *EWU* (n 16) paras 69 ff; Endler, *Europäische Zentralbank und Preisstabilität* (n 14) 272 ff, 566 ff; Enrico Peuker, 'Die Anwendung nationaler Rechtsvorschriften durch Unionsorgane—ein Konstruktionsfehler der europäischen Bankenaufsicht' (2014) JuristenZeitung 764, 768.

[63] See Högenauer and Howarth, 'The Democratic Deficit' (n 2) 84; see also Amtenbrink 'The European Central Banks intricate independence' (n 3) 172: 'Yet, it is this perception of the (limited) role of the ECB that has arguably been the foundation of the acceptance of its scope of independence within the EU constitutional order.'

German doctrine, an independent status therefore will not be justified in such cases.[64] From a German perspective—and this perspective plays a vital role in the European discourse not only because the ECB was organized with the German Bundesbank as reference model[65]— an independent central bank officially equipped with economic competences will therefore always be looked at sceptically. The fact that Article 127(1) of the TFEU (Treaty on the functioning of the European Union) states that 'the ESCB shall support the general economic policies in the Union' appears acceptable to German scholars (and the Constitutional Court) only as long as this part of its mandate is interpreted in a very narrow sense respecting the clear subordination under the ECB's primary task of safeguarding price stability. This 'German sensibility' forms the background of the dispute that arose between the German Constitutional Court and the ECB during the euro area crisis and found its climax in the Court's decision of 5 May 2020 (*Weiss* decision) according to which the Public Sector Purchase Programme (PSPP) was unconstitutional as it manifestly disregarded the principle of proportionality considering its massive economic policy effects.[66] In other words: the Court was unhappy with an independent institution interfering into matters outside its ordinary monetary mandate. Concerning the economic part of the ECB mandate, the German Constitutional Court had in fact already positioned itself in its request for preliminary ruling regarding the ECB's OMT programme,[67] and thereby made clear that it was not willing to accept any extensive interpretation that might lead to a substantial influence on economic policy or even independent economic assessments: 'This inevitably requires independent economic assessments which must not merely retrace the decisions of the Commission, the so-called Troika or other institutions, and which, for this reason alone, extends beyond a mere "support" of the economic policy in the Union.'[68] How any form of economic support should actually be possible without an independent assessment performed by the ECB, however, remains a mystery to everyone outside the Court.

With the ECB currently reviewing the role it might be able to play in the general (political) efforts to fight climate change, it will nonetheless have to keep this specific 'German scepticism' as regards a 'political' central bank in view if it wants to prevent further and possibly more hurtful interventions by the German Constitutional Court: The more the ECB finds its possible 'green' monetary actions in this specific economic part of its mandate, the more probable it will be that it will have to face further court challenges in Karlsruhe.[69] In order to prevent such challenges it therefore

[64] See, for instance, BVerfG 18 July 2017, 2 BvR 859/15 and others (n 5) para 103: 'The endorsement under constitutional law of the ECB's independence hinges on the requirement that its mandate be interpreted restrictively. The ECB mandate is primarily limited to matters of monetary policy serving the aim of stability; it cannot be extended to other areas of policy.'

[65] See Fromage and others, 'ECB Independence' (n 2) 6 and Simon Mee, *Central Bank Independence and the Legacy of the German Past* (Cambridge 2019).

[66] BVerfG 5 May 2020, 2 BvR 859/15 and others (n 5) para 165.

[67] See chapter 2 by Vestert Borger, in this volume, and on the programme itself, see chapter 3 by Klaus Tuori, in this volume.

[68] BVerfG 14 January 2014, 2 BvR 2728/13 and others (n 5) para 82.

[69] The support competence has so far played no vital role in the ECB's monetary strategy. In order to prevent a conflict with the German Constitutional Court it thereby might be helpful for the ECB to commit itself to a restrictive interpretation of this part of its mandate by making clear that it does not intend to support all the aims of the EU mentioned in TEU Art 3. The all-inclusive cross-reference in TFEU Art 127

might be wise for the ECB to actively propose new accountability procedures, granting the European Parliament a bigger say in this respect (for instance a stricter accountability procedure concerning those measures formally based on the economic part of the ECB's mandate). To simply ignore the possible conflict between the independent status and a more politically involved ECB would be unwise in any case.

It also seems noteworthy that the independent status of the central bank cannot be justified with the special expertise or competence of the relevant central bankers, automatically leading to 'better' monetary decisions. There is of course no doubt concerning the monetary expertise of the current central bankers at the ECB (explicitly including President Christine Lagarde, despite the fact that she is not an economist); the treaties indeed explicitly and rightly demand such an expertise.[70] However, it is not their expertise that justifies their independent status but the specific task they are obliged to fulfil. A justification 'by expertise' would not be acceptable to the German Basic Law as it would undermine (at least in the long run) the general requirement of dual legitimation:[71] Why not revert to such a 'rule of authorised experts'[72] in all political areas if experts are more competent to find 'right' or at least 'better' answers than 'normal' politicians? Such a concept—recently proposed by Jason Brennan[73]—would lead to a self-abolishment of democracy, and indeed, Brennan prefers a 'moderate epistocracy'. However, this idea not only neglects the fundamental democratic promise of free political equality of each individual citizen but also (and more importantly) misses the fact that it is impossible to conclude which decision would actually have been 'right' or 'better' in political affairs. Even experts (or epistocrats) might be mistaken and with more than one expert involved, we will usually find more than one opinion on how to proceed. Winston Churchill put it as follows: 'If you put two economists in a room, you get two opinions, unless one of them is Lord Keynes, in which case you get three opinions.' So, which one of these expert opinions is 'right' or 'better'? The ongoing debate since the euro area crisis concerning the monetary policy of the ECB in general and especially its quantitative easing programmes makes this problem evident: German experts are criticizing ECB experts with each side believing to have the better arguments. But why should a society have to live with the opinion of the more or less randomly chosen expert leading the independent agency and not be free to choose whichever expert (or rather: which policy) to follow? In the case of monetary policy, we might be able to justify such a situation, but otherwise: 'auctoritas, non

would thus be restricted to politically more or less undisputed aims strongly linked to the economic and financial stability within the euro area. See also Nik de Boer and Jens van 't Klooster, 'The ECB, the Courts and the Issue of Democratic Legitimacy after *Weiss*' (2020) 57 CMLR 1689, 1704 for existing gaps in the mandate of the ECB.

[70] See also Högenauer and Howarth, 'The Democratic Deficit' (n 2) 93. 'ECB policy making requires, without a doubt, high levels of expertise'.

[71] See also Jan Henrik Klement, 'Der Euro und seine Demokratie' (2014) ZG 169, 191; Alexander Thiele, *Verlustdemokratie* (2nd edn, Mohr Siebeck 2018) 244 ff; Thiele, *Finanzaufsicht* (n 7) 429 ff. See also Laura Münkler, *Expertokratie* (Mohr Siebeck 2020).

[72] For that term, see Hans Peter Bull, 'Die "völlig unabhängige" Aufsichtsbehörde. Zum Urteil des EuGH vom 9.3.2010 in Sachen Datenschutzaufsicht' (2010) EuZW 488, 492 (hereafter Bull, 'Die "völlig unabhängige" Aufsichtsbehörde').

[73] Jason Brennan, *Against Democracy* (Princeton University Press 2017) (hereafter Brennan, *Against Democracy*).

veritas facit legem.'[74] These relations between independence and democracy should be kept in mind as the voices demanding more independent agencies are getting louder—not only at the European level.[75] It does not appear to be a very democratic demand.

III. Manifestations of Independence

Independence can manifest itself in various forms.[76] When speaking of independence, it is thus vital to define what is actually meant. There is no such thing as 'the' independence that either prevails or not; it is rather a question of degree. In the following, I want to give a short summary of the three probably most relevant manifestations of independence[77] before taking a closer look at possible limitations and threats.[78]

The first type of independence is 'Goal-independence'. It grants the central bank the authority to define its monetary objective autonomously without interference by third parties, especially the government. This form of independence is not to be misinterpreted as giving the central bank complete freedom about which monetary policy goal(s) to pursue. The general monetary policy goals are, in fact, assigned to the central bank normatively by statute (with safeguarding price stability regularly standing in the centre). Goal-independence allows a central bank not to choose but to autonomously interpret these goals and formulate its understanding of price stability, which then forms the foundation of the monetary measures taken. The concrete understanding of price stability is economically less clear than one might think, but obviously has tremendous consequences for the monetary policy of a central bank. Although practically all central banks therefore are assigned with the task of safeguarding price stability, the internal inflation target can differ and also might change over time—the Bank of Japan, for instance, doubled its internal inflation target from 1 per cent to 2 per cent in January 2013 (with the general goal of price stability remaining unaltered). Next to the Fed (that in August 2020 presented its new understanding of price stability)[79] the ECB also enjoys such goal-independence; from a normative perspective, the ECB therefore not only has the possibility but the duty to autonomously set its internal inflation target[80] and, according to Art 130 TFEU, is thereby

[74] See Jörg Schmidt, *Die demokratische Legitimationsfunktion der parlamentarischen Kontrolle* (Duncker & Humblot 2007) 321 (hereafter Schmidt, *Die demokratische Legitimationsfunktion der parlamentarischen Kontrolle*). And another quote by Möllers, *Demokratie—Zumutungen und Versprechungen* (n 55) para 57: 'Der Einwand von Experten, dass in Demokratien ohne Kompetenz entschieden würde, zeigt die demokratische Inkompetenz der Experten.'

[75] Bull, 'Die "völlig unabhängige" Aufsichtsbehörde' (n 72) 488 ff. See also Paul Tucker, *Unelected Power: The Quest for Legitimacy in Central Banking and the Regulatory State* (Princeton University Press 2018) (hereafter Tucker, *Unelected Power*).

[76] Siekmann in Siekmann (ed), *EWU* (n 16) para 41. See also Julian Langner, 'ESCB/Eurosystem/National Central Banks' in Fabian Amtenbrink and Christoph Herrmann (eds), *The EU Law of Economic and Monetary Union* (OUP 2020)paras 15.46 ff.

[77] Walsh, *Central Bank Independence* (n 28) 3 ff, who especially highlights the 'goal independence' and the 'instrumental independence'.

[78] For further manifestations, see Siekmann in Siekmann (ed), *EWU* (n 16) paras 42 ff.

[79] Board of Governors of the Federal Reserve System, *Statement on Longer-Run Goals and Monetary Policy Strategy* (2020).

[80] Walsh, *Central Bank Independence* (n 28) 3 ff.

not allowed to 'seek or take instructions' (neither from other Union institutions nor from the Member States). The term 'price stability' in Art 127(1) TFEU is a so-called 'undefined legal term' that has to be 'filled with life' primarily by the ECB itself—a conclusion that (as we will see later) necessarily has consequences as regards the intensity of judicial control in this core area of monetary policy. Currently, the ECB has set its inflation target at 'under, but close to 2%'.[81] Compatible with its mandate, however, would not only be a slightly lower but also a slightly higher inflation target of up to 3 per cent or even 4 per cent.[82] Due to the low inflation-rate within the euro area in the last years, its President, Christine Lagarde, has indeed announced to reconsider the internal definition during her term of office. The Bank of England—not only the oldest but clearly one of the most important central banks worldwide—enjoys no such goal-independence, as the concrete inflation target is decided upon by the government on a yearly basis;[83] its degree of independence thus differs significantly when compared to the ECB's. In practice this might not appear to make a major difference—the British inflation target hardly ever deviates from the ECB's definition of price stability. Without such goal-independence ordinary and monetary policy nonetheless become intertwined and by raising or reducing the inflation target the political sphere would gain the formal possibility to influence monetary actions in favour of their political ambitions, risking undermining the general trust in the political independence of the central bank. Goal-independence should thus remain a central pillar within the European monetary union.

Goal-choice-independence as the second type of independence allows a central bank to choose autonomously from a certain catalogue of assigned goals and to decide which of these goals to pursue with priority among them depending on the economic environment. It thus reaches further than mere goal-independence. We find this form of functional independence in the United States with Section 2A of the Federal Reserve Act defining the general monetary goals by stating that the Fed 'shall maintain long run growth of the monetary and credit aggregates commensurate with the economy's long run potential to increase production, so as to promote effectively the goals of maximum employment, stable prices, and moderate long-term interest rates'. Section 2A, however, does not mention a possible hierarchy of these individual goals, a question which is thus left for the Fed to decide. In contrast, the ECB has to pursue its core purpose—price stability—with priority and is only allowed to support the economic policy in the Union as long as this core purpose is not inflicted (see Art 127 TFEU). The same is true for the Bank of England according to Art 11 of the Bank of England Act 1998. From a German perspective, such a normative priority appears mandatory due to the abovementioned assumptions regarding the democratic principle—any form of functional independence similar to the Fed's would not be acceptable.

[81] See ECB, *Die Geldpolitik der EZB* (2011) 71. For the economic background, see Alexander Thiele, *Das Mandat der EZB und die Krise des Euro* (Mohr Siebeck 2013) 27 ff (hereafter Thiele, *Das Mandat der EZB und die Krise des Euro*); Alexander Thiele, *Die Europäische Zentralbank* (Mohr Siebeck 2019) 69 ff (hereafter Thiele, *Die Europäische Zentralbank*). Now, see also BVerfG 18 July 2017, 2 BvR 859/15 and others (n 5) para 117: 'Das Ziel des PSPP, die Inflationsrate auf knapp 2% steigern zu wollen, stellt nach Auffassung des Senats eine grundsätzlich zulässige Konkretisierung der Aufgabe dar, die Preisstabilität zu sichern.'

[82] See also Thiele, *Das Mandat der EZB und die Krise des Euro* (n 81) 31.

[83] See Art 12 of the Bank of England Act 1998. See also Walsh, *Central Bank Independence* (n 28) 3.

Finally, instrumental independence (that necessarily includes financial independence) enables a central bank to autonomously decide on the instruments it deems most fitting to reach the general monetary policy goals. Once again, a central bank will usually not be completely free, but bound to a certain instrumental mix laid down in the relevant statutes. But this instrumental mix will mostly be broad and not exclusive, thus allowing the central bank to react to the countless possible economic surroundings that might occur.[84] Specific restrictions will usually be introduced by a catalogue of generally forbidden instruments. Article 127(1) TFEU for instance states that the ECB shall act in accordance with the principle of an open market economy with free competition,[85] binding the ECB to a wide range of market-compliant instruments (and possibly some sort of market neutrality), while explicitly prohibiting the direct (not the indirect) purchase of state bonds in Art 123 TFEU.[86] The statute also lists typical monetary policy instruments, and then even introduces an 'instrument-invention-right' in Art 20 according to which the ECB Governing Council 'may, by a majority of two thirds of the votes cast, decide upon the use of such other operational methods of monetary control as it sees fit, respecting Article 2'.[87] This instrumental-independence also includes the right of a central bank to decide autonomously on the methods it uses to measure the inflation rate and the general economic situation of the respective monetary area and to decide on the monetary strategy. Again, we find no broadly accepted economic methods central banks would have to revert to in this field—and the existing models vary significantly in the results they produce. An example is the possible implementation of asset prices when measuring inflation: it is highly disputed whether their development should be (and if so: how it should be) considered when evaluating the inflation rate—a question obviously of great relevance for the final outcome.[88] The ECB has up to now refused to consider the asset prices directly, but uses the respective data when implementing the two-pillar strategy, especially when considering possible threats to economic stability caused by asset price bubbles for instance. From a normative perspective, this is a decision clearly covered by its wide instrumental independence.[89] As regards the monetary strategy—that is, the decision how to react to certain economic surroundings and inflationary developments—we also find no universal model all central banks have to revert to. When and how to interfere will usually be highly disputed not only outside but sometimes also within the respective central bank. Monetary interventions (especially in times of crisis) are thus sure to be criticized; yet the competence to take this decision forms a key part of the central bank's instrumental independence.

[84] See also Thiele, *Das Mandat der EZB und die Krise des Euro* (n 81) 41 ff.

[85] For details, see Ute Reumann, *Die Europäische Zentralbank* (Centaurus Verlag & Media 2001) 91 ff (hereafter Reumann, *Die Europäische Zentralbank*).

[86] In detail, see Thiele, *Das Mandat der EZB und die Krise des Euro* (n 81) 63 ff.

[87] See Endler, Europäische Zentralbank und Preisstabilität (n 14) 477 ff and Reumann, *Die Europäische Zentralbank* (n 85) 96 ff.

[88] In its recent Report on the European Central Bank Annual Report 2020 the European Parliament explicitly welcomed the fact that the ECB was discussing the adaption of inflation measurements and encouraged the ECB to also take into account the asset price inflation caused, *inter alia*, by low interest rates.

[89] See Thiele, *Das Mandat der EZB und die Krise des Euro* (n 81) 32 ff.

IV. Challenges and Threats

What are the challenges these three forms of independence face, and what actions might even pose a normative threat to the independent status of the ECB (and might thus be normatively prohibited)?

A. Challenges to independence

Challenges here refer to (external or internal) actions that might challenge the independent status without normatively violating it (despite some parts of the public believing otherwise). These actions are thus permissible from a normative perspective though they might infringe on other social behavioural customs or on the idea of 'approved political etiquette'. As it is obviously not possible to discuss all actions challenging yet complying with the independent status, I would like to focus on the following three: public criticism by the media and political or economic actors (1); specific duties to report to other European institutions (2); and finally duties to cooperate with other institutions that have arisen since the ECB was transformed into a formal institution listed in Art 13 TEU (3).

(1) Public criticism

The fact that monetary policy will hardly ever remain undisputed in public was proven during the GFC and the following euro area crisis. The ECB faced criticism not only but especially from German scholars, media, and politicians[90]—and these disputes continued during the COVID-19 crisis and are sure to intensify with the ECB trying to find its role in fighting climate change. In most cases, the criticism tends to focus on concrete measures taken by the ECB, touching its instrumental independence. The ECB's definition of price stability—as part of its goal-independence—has hardly ever been part of such a broad public debate and in actual fact seemed mostly accepted[91] (with just a few German scholars making an exception).[92] This appears to have changed in the last months due to very low inflation rates and due to the ECB searching for its new role in changing economic surroundings, its possible contribution to fighting climate change ('Green Monetary Policy'), as well as the coronavirus pandemic (see especially the Pandemic Emergency Purchase Programme). Open criticism in this field thus might increase in the coming years and Christine Lagarde has already announced that the understanding of price stability will be part of the internal revision process concerning the ECB's monetary strategy. The relevant question here, however, is: when does open and sometimes quite harsh critique of the ECB appear problematic as regards its independence? Is it compatible with the independent status, for instance,

[90] See Amtenbrink, 'The European Central Bank's intricate independence' (n 3) 170 ff; Högenauer and Howarth, 'The Democratic Deficit' (n 2) 90.

[91] This question, however, was highly disputed when constructing the EMU.

[92] The German Constitutional Court has now explicitly accepted the ECB's definition: see BVerfG 18 July 2017, 2 BvR 859/15 and others (n 5) para 117: 'It is the view of the Federal Court that objective of the PSPP to increase the inflation rate to close but below 2% is, in principle, a permissible measure lending effect to the mandate of maintaining price stability.'

if a former German finance minister (Wolfgang Schäuble) publicly finds the policy of the ECB to have contributed to the success of the AfD (a German right-wing populist party)?[93] Or if Alexander Dobrindt, a Member of the German Parliament, accuses then ECB-President Mario Draghi of being an adulterator ('Falschmünzer')? In other words: does the independent status somewhat exempt the ECB from public debate and openly articulated criticism? To answer this question, it is necessary to draw the following distinctions.

First of all, critique, possibly even harsh critique, expressed by the interested public (either by academic scholars or the relevant media) will generally not infringe the ECB's instrumental independence. The conduct of monetary policy of an independent central bank does not take place in a discourse-free area, and it may and has to be expected that any central bank (respectively its governor) is able to withstand such open critique. At least in a democratic system, no institution can claim to act without being criticized and this is mirrored in Art 282 TFEU that explicitly only obliges the EU institutions and the governments of the Member States and not the general public to respect the ECB's independent status. In fact, in a highly disputed policy area such as monetary policy, public criticism might even positively influence the performance of a central bank as it constantly forces it to reflect on its own decisions and to diligently examine the proposed alternatives. And this is true even if the critique were in the end not to be mirrored in an adjustment of its monetary actions. External input of this sort can rationalize the internal decision-making process and lead to a 'better' central bank. Any central bank is therefore well-advised not to neglect such critique but to include it into the public explanation of its policy measures and to clarify why it might have decided to take different steps. It would also not be condemnable if a central bank were to react to such critique by modifying or reversing its decisions. Commentaries such as 'the central bank capitulated to the critique' are simply mistaken. It would obviously not be helpful if a central bank were to stick to decisions only in order to prevent the impression that it might have reacted to publically expressed and well-founded external critique. Independence does not manifest itself in a general resistance to criticism, even though it would be just as senseless if a central bank were to generally guide its actions according to public opinion. Its own conclusion as regards the 'correct' economic decision must always remain the benchmark for its monetary policy, no matter who formulated it in the first place—something that requires a certain amount of internal independence of the central bankers, especially in times of crisis.

Criticism by politicians might have to be interpreted differently.[94] Even though such criticism does not constitute a formal instruction in the sense of Art 130 TFEU, depending on how and by whom it is formulated and on the respective content of the critique (fundamental opposition vs very specific critique concerning individual actions), it might come very close. Although independent central bankers should again generally not let themselves be influenced by such critique,[95] their internal independence might be on for a tough test, depending on who expresses such

[93] See Högenauer and Howarth, 'The Democratic Deficit' (n 2) 90.
[94] See also Endler, *Europäische Zentralbank und Preisstabilität* (n 14) 413.
[95] See also Häde in Calliess and Ruffert (eds), *EUV/AEUV* (n 53) para 15.

critique (a back-bencher, an acting minister, a head of government). To avoid giving the impression of being influenced, central bankers might decide to act 'too independently' and decide to generally ignore such political critique in order to prove their independence—even in cases where they might agree with the presented arguments and would consider an amendment of their policy. This danger prevails especially where the independent status of a central bank is not easily amendable by the respective government,[96] as is the case for the ECB.[97] Well-intentioned critique by high positioned politicians thus might lead to worse central bank decisions—a result no one would want (not even politicians), yet an outcome we might indeed have witnessed in the United States in 2019 due to very harsh critique regarding the Fed's policy by President Donald Trump.[98]

Such possible negative effects of political critique, however, should not lead to the conclusion that politicians should have to refrain from making any comments regarding the ECB's monetary policy. Again: independence does not uncouple the central bank from the political discourse—as Milton Friedman rightly pointed out, 'Money is too important to be left to the central bankers'.[99] Or, in other words: elected politicians have to be able to talk about monetary policy. Well-intentioned advice—that is advice presented in a factual, cooperative, and respectful manner—is thus perfectly acceptable.[100] One must expect a certain amount of coolness on the side of the central bankers in this respect. Practical experience confirms this result. Being appointed as a central banker will usually lead to an appropriate amount of independence-awareness on the side of the appointee[101]—a phenomenon commonly known as the Beckett-Effect.[102] Political statements, however, become problematic and thus a challenge for the independence when they are formulated in a prescriptive manner and are more or less openly connected with the expectation that the central bank should react in the demanded manner—especially if such statements are formulated by leading politicians and members of government. Yet, in most cases and as long as these statements are not linked to the threat of concrete consequences or sanctions,[103] such behaviour will be less a normative question than a question of

96 Because the central bank then does not have to fear such an amendment and can thus present its independence more or less risk free. See also Endler, *Europäische Zentralbank und Preisstabilität* (n 14) 248.

97 As the independence of the ECB is laid down in the treaties, any modification would require a treaty amendment according to TEU Art 48 including a ratification in all Member States. By contrast, the independence of the German Bundesbank was only guaranteed by a simple statute (and not the constitution).

98 Spencer Kimball, 'Trump says he never threatened to denote Federal Reserve Chairman Jerome Powell, but has the right to do so' *CNBC* (23 June 2019) <https://www.cnbc.com/2019/06/23/trump-says-he-never-threatened-to-demote-federal-reserve-chairman-jerome-powell.html> accessed 23 April 2021.

99 Friedman, 'Should There Be an Independent Monetary Authority?' (n 20) 219. Friedman, however, spoke out against the independent status generally.

100 Endler, *Europäische Zentralbank und Preisstabilität* (n 14) 413.

101 True also for other independent positions; see, for instance, the actions taken by Christine Lagarde, the Executive Director of the IMF and former French finance minister.

102 Thomas Beckett was Lord Chancellor and Adviser to King Henry II and became Archbishop of Canterbury in 1162. In this new position he vividly fought for the interests of the church (and not those of the King) so that he was finally murdered by the King's cronies. See Endler, *Europäische Zentralbank und Preisstabilität* (n 14) 249 ff.

103 Such threats might raise inflation expectations of the market participants no matter whether they were successful or not; see Endler, *Europäische Zentralbank und Preisstabilität* (n 14) 413 ff.

decent political style[104]—the abovementioned critique by the American President quite clearly violated these decency rules and the same is probably true for the remarks made by the member of the German Parliament Alexander Dobrindt (Mario Draghi as 'adulterator'). There is, however, no clear line between acceptable political statements on the one hand and unacceptable influencing on the other,[105] and it would obviously be utopian to link the independent status with the end of any form of political pressure packed into publically expressed (harsh) critique.[106] Monetary policy is too important from a political perspective and the persistence of political pressure thus expectable. The granting of independence in this sense is the necessary (though not sufficient) requirement for the central bankers to face up to such political pressure. One should thereby also consider that it might be more threatening for the democratic process if politicians were to generally refrain from any critical statement than if they were to go a little too far with their critique in individual cases—especially as neither the public nor the media would probably appreciate such 'over-the-line-criticism'. As a general rule, therefore, critical statements formulated by politicians—and we will most surely witness such comments in the coming years concerning the ECB's role in the fight against climate change—might challenge the internal independence of the central bankers but will not violate the instrumental independence of the ECB from a normative perspective.

(2) Duties to report to European institutions

Compatible with the independent status and necessary in a democratic system are duties to report to other institutions (as well as the public). Such duties are thus foreseen in practically all modern central bank systems. For the ECB, we find such rules in Art 15 of its statute and Art 284(3) TFEU.[107] Additionally, the ECB is monitored by the Court of Auditors and integrated into the European Anti-Fraud System (OLAF).[108] Such duties to report to the European Parliament, the Council, and the Commission secure the minimum standard of accountability[109] necessary for any authority in a democracy[110] and thus contribute 'to the emergence of a new kind of democratic legitimation for highly technocratic, independent bodies'.[111] By reporting and explaining its actions, the central bank takes the necessary responsibility, and ensures that no other institution (for instance the government) is held responsible in public instead. Above that, reporting and openly discussing its policies has at least partly the same

[104] For a different opinion, see Siekmann in Siekmann (ed), *EWU* (n 16) para 19.

[105] See also Häde in Calliess and Ruffert (eds), *EUV/AEUV* (n 53) para 15.

[106] Not convincing therefore the statement of the ECJ (Case C-11/00 *Commission v European Central Bank* [2003] ECR I-7147, para 134 (hereafter *Commission v ECB*) according to which the independent status 'seeks, in essence, to shield the ECB from all political pressure in order to enable it effectively to pursue the objectives attributed to its tasks, through the independent exercise of the specific powers conferred on it for that purpose by the EC Treaty and the ESCB Statute'.

[107] See also Reumann, *Die Europäische Zentralbank* (n 85) 184 ff. For the American central bank, see Werner Heun, 'Die Zentralbank in den USA—das Federal Reserve System' (n 20) 260.

[108] As regards the relationship between the ECB and OLAF concerning its independent status, see *Commission v ECB* (n 106) para 135. See also Siekmann in Siekmann (ed), *EWU* (n 16) paras 136 ff.

[109] See Larisa Dragomir, 'The ECB's Accountability: Adjusting Accountability Arrangements to the ECB's Evolving Roles' (2019) 26 MJ 35, 37 ff (hereafter Dragomir, 'The ECB's Accountability').

[110] Walsh, *Central Bank Independence* (n 28) 9.

[111] Fromage and others, 'ECB Independence' (n 2) 12.

effect as public criticism: the ECB is forced to publically explain and thereby reflect on its actions and might find better solutions how to react in the future. In the long run, a central bank will only succeed if it is able to explain why it acted in a certain way (and not in another) in a comprehensible manner, making arbitrary actions more or less impossible.[112] Independent activity is no secret occupation, the ECB is no 'Black-Box', which is the reason why Christine Lagarde has already indicated to reform the way the ECB presents its actions and communicates with the public.[113] To ensure sufficient accountability, the ECB's actions need to be critically followed and discussed not only by the public but especially by the European institutions such as Parliament, Commission, and Council.[114] Within this process, critical statements are not only possible but welcomed. Central bankers do not have to be handled as if they were 'raw eggs'.

(3) Duties to cooperate

The ECB was assigned formal institutional status by being included in the list of institutions in Art. 13 TEU with the Treaty of Lisbon in December 2009.[115] Its independent status was not formally affected by this amendment. Yet, the ECB nonetheless articulated concerns that the 'mutual sincere cooperation' with other institutions it is now obliged to practice according to Art 13(2) TEU might interfere with its independent status.[116] These concerns, however, were unfounded. First of all, such an obligation to cooperate with other institutions might not have been laid down explicitly in the Treaty of Nice, but it nonetheless existed. The ECB never acted completely outside the EU's formal institutional system[117] and was in fact smoothly embedded in this complex structure, a point made quite clear by the European Court of Justice (ECJ) in its OLAF judgment.[118] And second of all, the degree of this imperative to cooperate is limited by the concrete institutional mandate and status of the respective institution as created by the treaties. A duty to cooperate therefore only comes into consideration as far as the mandate of the ECB and its independent status is not threatened or infringed. It is only within this framework that the ECB is obliged to consider the

[112] This is also the reason why the publication of the minutes of the ECB Council meetings is to be welcomed.

[113] See Christine Lagarde's remarks on the monetary policy strategy review: Christine Lagarde, 'The monetary policy strategy review: some preliminary considerations' (ECB, 20 September 2020) <https://www.ecb.europa.eu/press/key/date/2020/html/ecb.sp200930~169abb1202.en.html> accessed 23 April 2021: 'There is one issue, however, on which I can be decisive today: we must explain much better to the general public what we are doing and why, and we must talk to people that we do not normally reach. This imperative has to cascade through all the elements of our review: our inflation aim, our inflation measure, our tools and their effectiveness, and how we take into account new challenges that people care about, like climate change or inequality.'

[114] See Reumann, *Die Europäische Zentralbank* (n 85) 184 ff.

[115] For the institutional settings according to the Lisbon Treaty, see Alexander Thiele, *Europarecht* (17th edn, Niederle Media 2020) 64 (hereafter Thiele, *Europarecht*).

[116] See Häde in Calliess, and Ruffert (eds), *EUV/AEUV* (n 53) TFEU Art 282 para 49.

[117] A view that had before been claimed by, for instance, Chiara Zilioli and Martin Selmayr, *The Law of the European Central Bank* (Hart Publishing 2001) 9.

[118] *Commission v ECB* (n 106) paras 92, 135 ff; see also Menelaos Markakis, *Accountability in the Economic and Monetary Union. Foundations, Policy, and Governance* (OUP 2020) 286 ff (hereafter Markakis, *Accountability*) and Dawson and Bobic, 'Quantitative Easing' (n 6) 1028 ff.

interests of the other institutions and commence a cooperative dialogue;[119] an obligation, however, that never turns into an unconditional duty to coordinate in advance—a conclusion confirmed when looking at the other independent institutions (ECJ and Court of Auditors).[120] Such a dialogue between the relevant institutions is more than sensible, especially when it comes to the overlapping areas of monetary and fiscal and economic policy. It can thus not be seen as a threat to its independence but rather as a requirement for a coherent policy strategy for the whole euro area.[121]

B. Threats to independent monetary policy

As possible threats to independent monetary policy making, I would like to discuss certain scenarios in which the ECB might still be acting independently from a formal perspective, while its actual scope of action appears significantly reduced due to specific (external) influences. In such cases, the central bank might be forced to take actions it would not have taken otherwise, a scenario discussed here regarding the fiscal and wage policy of the Member States (1) and the ECB's partly already carried out bond purchase programmes (2). Finally, a certain external monetary philosophy might be imposed on the 'independent' central bank where a too extensive judicial review makes certain monetary actions impossible the ECB deems necessary to safeguard price stability (3).

(1) Fiscal and wage policy of the Member States

The fiscal and wage policies of the euro area Member States have a significant influence on monetary policy, a fact which is neither surprising nor specifically problematic. These policies might formally pursue different objectives, yet do not stand completely separately next to each other.[122] A central bank reacting to fiscal or wage policy decisions by amending its monetary policy is nothing objectionable—just as monetary policy decisions might have consequences for the fiscal policy of a Member State. Regular consultations between the ECB and euro area Member States therefore appear sensible in order to avoid unexpected decisions for the other side. As regards independence, it is essential, however, that the ECB decides on its monetary policy autonomously based solely on its monetary mandate. Within this decision-making process, it is not objectionable if the central bank should finally vote for a measure that interferes least with (or even supports) fiscal policy. Well-founded and independent monetary policy is not necessarily linked to hurting fiscal or other policies of the Member States. For the ECB this already follows from the obligation to support the general economic policies within the European Union according to Art 127(1) TFEU. Actions of a central bank in general and of the ECB in particular need only then have negative consequences for the Member States as far as this is unavoidable from a monetary policy

[119] See Christian Calliess in Christian Calliess and Matthias Ruffert (eds), *EUV/AEUV* (4th edn, CH Beck 2011) TEU Art 13 para 28.

[120] In this sense, see also Siekmann in Siekmann (ed), *EWU* (n 16) para 160.

[121] More on this relationship below.

[122] See also Egon Görgens, Karlheinz Ruckriegel, and Franz Seitz, *Europäische Geldpolitik* (6th edn, UTB GmbH 2013) 370 ff (hereafter Görgens, Ruckriegel, and Seitz, *Europäische Geldpolitik*).

perspective. Then, however, the central bank has no other choice than to interfere and take such 'hurtful' actions. But if and as far as the ECB can support the general economic policies, it must support.

Independence, especially the instrumental independence, is threatened, however, if fiscal and wage policy should provoke economic consequences that make it more or less impossible for the central bank to fulfil its mandate. As regards fiscal policy, this may be the case in times of excessive public debt. Due to the reduced political scope of action in such times, states have an interest to (at least partly) reduce their debt burden by monetizing their debt with the help of an unanticipated inflationary monetary policy and additional seigniorage earnings—and might look to their central bank for respective actions.[123] In 'normal' times an independent central bank should be able to resist such political pressure. In fact, this kind of pressure was the reason for introducing independent central banks in the first place. But as soon as the public debt ratio reaches a level that raises doubt on the medium- and long-term sustainability of public debt, things might get out of control. If the real interest rate should already be above the economic growth rate (r bigger g)—and this is no particularly unrealistic scenario—the debt ratio will rise further even in the case of a balanced primary budget (so called 'dept trap').[124] If one excludes a national bankruptcy that can only be the last resort from a political perspective, we find only two ways to reduce the debt ratio under such circumstances: either the state manages to produce significant primary surpluses (an option that will not only be stressful due to the necessary austerity policies but hardly possible overnight), or monetary policy becomes more expansive. The rising pressure on a central bank to do the latter is easily imaginable and might for itself create inflationary tendencies no matter whether the central bank finally gives in or not. Normative instruments such as the fiscal compact[125] and others trying to keep public debt at a sustainable level therefore also serve as a protection shield of central bank independence.[126] However, to avoid dramatic economic downfalls it needs to be ensured that debt-reducing measures founded on these instruments are not taken by all Member States simultaneously—an aspect in my view currently not sufficiently respected[127]—especially as the debt ratios are by no means critical in all Member States of the euro area. In particular, the German public debate completely negates the positive consequences of a modest public indebtedness. In actual fact, too much public saving might have a similarly harmful effect on monetary policy—especially in an economic setting with low interest rates. As we can currently

[123] Endler, *Europäische Zentralbank und Preisstabilität* (n 14) 252.

[124] See Görgens, Ruckriegel, and Seitz, *Europäische Geldpolitik* (n 122) 384 ff.

[125] For details on the fiscal compact, see Christian Calliess and Christopher Schoenfleisch, 'Auf dem Weg in die europäische "Fiskalunion"?' (2012) JuristenZeitung 477 (hereafter Calliess and Schoenfleisch, 'Auf dem Weg in die europäische Fiskalunion'); Frank Schorkopf, 'Europas politische Verfasstheit im Lichte des Fiskalvertrages' (2012) 10 Zeitschrift für Staats- und Europawissenschaften 1 (hereafter Schorkopf, 'Europas politische Verfasstheit') as well as Alexander Thiele, 'The "German Way" of Curbing Public Debt: The Constitutional Debt Brake and the Fiscal Compact—Why Germany has to Work on its Language Skills' (2015) 11 EuConst 30 (hereafter Thiele, 'The 'German Way' of Curbing Public Debt'). For further instruments trying to ensure budgetary discipline, see Christian Calliess, 'Finanzkrisen als Herausforderung der internationalen, europäischen und nationalen Rechtsetzung' (2012) 71 Veröffentlichungen der Vereinigung der Deutschen Staatsrechtslehrer 113, 166 ff (hereafter Calliess, 'Finanzkrisen als Herausforderung').

[126] See also Endler, *Europäische Zentralbank und Preisstabilität* (n 14) 254 ff, 259 ff.

[127] See Thiele, 'The "German Way" of Curbing Public Debt' (n 125) 30 ff.

see, without sufficient public spending and investment central banks will have problems reaching their inflation target, which is the actual reason for the various asset and bond purchase programmes performed by the ECB in the last years. Though not a problem for the independence as such, the lack of public investments thus remains a challenge for central banks worldwide and confirms that monetary and fiscal policies cannot be regarded as completely independent from each other.

The consequences for monetary policy of a failed national wage policy also became visible during the euro area crisis. As the alternative remedy of a currency depreciation is impossible, it is essential that wage rises do not exceed the rise in productivity in order to prevent a reduction of competitiveness. If this requirement is not respected, trade deficits as well as rising unemployment rates might follow creating an additional burden on the national finances that will again augment the pressure on the central bank. Within the European Monetary Union, and due also to different wage calculation regimes,[128] several Member States, especially Greece, did not stick to this necessity. The reforms initiated in the respective Member States in the last years therefore point in the right direction. Yet, all these measures should not lead to an 'austerity policy at all costs'—granting sufficient time for the reforms is vital for their success in the long run.[129]

(2) Bond purchases

During the euro area crisis, the ECB purchased a significant amount of bonds of so called 'crisis states' following its 'Securities Market Programme' (SMP).[130] The SMP was finally replaced by the 'Outright Monetary Transactions' (OMT) programme,[131] that, however, has not yet led to a single bond purchase (and most probably will not in the future). Some media reports thereby insinuated that the ECB might have initiated these programmes not entirely for monetary policy reasons but at least partly due to political pressure formulated especially by then French President Nicolas Sarkozy. It is obviously difficult to verify these accusations. But even if they were true, this might have an effect on the legality of the measures taken[132] but would not have infringed the ECB's independent status. As said before, political pressure—especially in times of crisis is to be expected and from the perspective of independence it is only necessary that the final decision is taken autonomously by the ECB. And this was the case

[128] See Martin Höpner and Mark Lutter, 'One Currency and Many Modes of Wage Formation' (2014) MPIfG Discussion Paper No 14/14 <https://papers.ssrn.com/sol3/papers.cfm?abstract_id=2553185> accessed 23 April 2021 (hereafter Höpner and Lutter, 'One Currency and Many Modes of Wage Formation') regarding the different wage calculation regimes in the Member States.

[129] For a detailed critique as regards the austerity policy of the Member States, see Mark Blyth, *Austerity. The History of a Dangerous Idea* (OUP 2013) (hereafter Blyth, *Austerity*). This, by the way, now also seems to be the official position of the IMF: see Susanne Lütz, 'Vom Washington Consensus zum Flexiblen Keynesianismus—der internationale Währungsfonds nach der Finanzkrise' (2014) 55 Politische Vieteljahresschrift 427, 436 ff (hereafter Lütz, 'Vom Washington Consensus zum Flexiblen Keynesianismus').

[130] See also Fromage and others, 'ECB Independence' (n 2) 7. See further chapter 2 by Vestert Borger and chapter 3 by Klaus Tuori, in this volume.

[131] On redistributive effects of these measures see Högenauer and Howarth, 'The Democratic Deficit' (n 2) 86 ff.

[132] The purchase programmes might be regarded as void due to a misuse of powers according to TFEU Art 263.

not only for these programmes but also for the several following quantitative easing programmes, with which the ECB has since then tried to raise the too low inflation rate, by again purchasing bonds worth billions of Euros. Taking the official reasoning for all these measures into account (and not a possibly hidden political motive), they were all covered by the ECB's monetary policy mandate. The doubts concerning the OMT programme raised by the German Constitutional Court in 2014[133] were convincingly rejected by the Court of Justice in 2015.[134] The same is true as regards the quantitative easing programme (PSPP) that was again brought before the European Court by the German Constitutional Court—that once more rejected the concerns.[135] In its final decision, the German Constitutional Court nonetheless found the PSPP to be lacking a significant analysis of proportionality: 'For this lack of balancing and lack of stating the reasons informing such balancing, the ECB decisions at issue violate Art. 5(1) second sentence and Art. 5(4) TEU and, in consequence, exceed the monetary policy mandate of the ECB deriving from Art. 127(1) first sentence TFEU.'[136] It therefore demanded the ECB to conduct a proportionality assessment within three months and threatened to otherwise declare the whole programme ultra vires. As a result of this (not very convincing) German judgment, the ECB disclosed its internal discussion process through the Bundesbank and was able to show that proportionality had played a significant role in the decision-making process, and how it had done so. The German government as well as the German parliament found this sufficient to meet the requirements formulated by the Court. Whether this view is shared by the German Constitutional Court—the court case has formally not ended—is yet to be seen but appears highly probable. However, during the hearings concerning these programmes, the German Bundesbank brought forward that bond purchases might also raise questions as regards their compatibility with the independent status of the ECB. Though possibly justified to ensure the monetary transitional process respectively to raise the inflation rate, the Bundesbank pointed to the fact that the purchase programmes would nonetheless open the ECB to blackmail (especially by the Member States' governments) due to its own growing interest to prevent any form of state bankruptcy with a significant amount of bonds failing (leading to respective losses on the side of the ECB).[137] This raises an interesting question: is it possible for the ECB to infringe upon its own independent status when reverting to certain monetary measures by creating a situation where (some time in the future) it might refrain from necessary monetary actions and risk missing its own inflation target in order to prevent possible and in the end self-inflicted losses?

[133] Werner Heun, 'Eine verfassungswidrige Verfassungsgerichtsentscheidung' (2014) JuristenZeitung 331 (hereafter Heun, 'Eine verfassungswidrige Verfassungsgerichtsentscheidung'); Alexander Thiele, 'Friendly or Unfriendly Act?' (2014) 15 German Law Journal 241 (hereafter Thiele, 'Friendly or Unfriendly Act'). In detail, see Thiele, *Das Mandat der EZB und die Krise des Euro* (n 81) 57 ff.

[134] Case C-62/14 *Gauweiler and Others v Deutscher Bundestag* [2015] EU:C:2015:400.

[135] See BVerfG 18 July 2017, 2 BvR 859/15 and others (n 5). The ECJ decided on this preliminary ruling on 11 December 2018: *Weiss* (n 5).

[136] BVerfG 5 May 2020, 2 BvR 859/15 and others (n 5) para 177.

[137] See also Otmar Issing, 'A New Paradigm for Monetary Policy?' (2013) 16 International Finance 273, 275 (hereafter Issing, 'A New Paradigm for Monetary Policy?'): 'And huge stocks of government bond expose the central bank to economic risks and political pressure.'

To answer this question, it is important to recall that loss risks occur any time a central bank purchases security papers outright. Such risks are no special feature of state bonds. However, potential losses will usually be higher in these cases than with other security papers and it is only with state bonds that central banks have a significant indirect influence on their default risk by setting the relevant interest rates. The dilemma a central bank finds itself in can thus hardly be denied. To be distinguished from this possible dilemma, however, is the question whether it can be used to formulate clear normative limitations for state bond purchases by a central bank. If one does not want to generally forbid such purchases—a step hardly convincing due to the fact that bond purchases form a classical monetary instrument all important central banks worldwide make use of—one will have to set certain quantitative restrictions. But where? The relatively small amount of equity of the ECB (currently about 11 billion euro) is obviously too low. So how much instead? Ten times the amount? Twenty times? And how to value each bond purchase while respecting the differing insolvency risks of the Member States within the euro area?[138] These problems show that any quantitative limitation would be arbitrary and speak out for a formalistic interpretation. From a normative perspective (as regards the independent status) it is therefore again only relevant whether the ECB took its final decisions uninfluenced and autonomously from other European or national institutions. The fact that the ECB thereby might limit its future scope of action is nothing its independency seeks to prevent. The central bank therefore is responsible for assessing possible risks when purchasing bonds and thereby also has to consider possible political pressure that might occur in times of crisis. In the end it once again all depends on the central bankers themselves: 'As long as there is no absolute (and absolute convincing) strict rule, the people and personalities in charge will matter.'[139]

(3) Intensity of judicial control

Let me finally take a look at the relationship between independence and judicial control.[140] While this had been more of an academic question in the past—hardly any central bank's monetary actions worldwide were ever taken to court[141]—the problem became practical in the aftermath of the euro area crisis with the German Constitutional Court putting the ECB's OMT programme to a normative test by initiating a preliminary procedure before the Court of Justice in 2014.[142] In July 2017, it initiated a second preliminary ruling regarding the ECB's general bond purchase program (PSPP). From a rule of law-perspective the general possibility of judicial review thereby seems virtually mandatory, as Menelaos Markakis rightly points out: 'Judicial review is a core rule of law requirement.'[143] It would not be acceptable if an institution dealing with administrative affairs were exempted from any judicial

[138] In detail, Thiele, *Das Mandat der EZB und die Krise des Euro* (n 81) 78 ff.

[139] Issing, 'A New Paradigm for Monetary Policy?' (n 137) 283.

[140] See also Dawson and Bobic, 'Quantitative Easing' (n 6) 1028 ff. See chapter 16 by Marijn van der Sluis, in this volume.

[141] Not even the Bundesbank ever had to face such a court procedure regarding its monetary policy measures.

[142] BVerfG 14 January 2014, 2 BvR 2728/13 (n 5).

[143] Markakis, *Accountability* (n 118) 287.

control simply because of its independent status[144]—and Art. 35 Statute of the ESCB and the ECB normatively confirms this general assessment.[145] Additionally, such judicial control is able to at least partly reduce the justified yet still unsatisfying legitimacy deficit of the ECB and to contribute to an acceptable level of accountability.[146] And finally, even from the perspective of the central bank, judicial review appears acceptable as judicial proceedings offer 'an essential forum for the ECB to illustrate and justify the challenged measures'[147] and are not intended to direct its monetary policy in detail but simply seeks to monitor the compliance with the general normative requirements. However, this last point marks the potential area of conflict: if a central bank wants to pursue its monetary goals effectively, it needs sufficient room for manoeuvre—especially in such a complex and inhomogeneous monetary area as the Economic and Monetary Union. As mentioned above, it will usually be impossible to determine a single monetary measure that clearly strikes out all possible others—in this respect monetary policy indeed resembles probably any other economic policy: 'It involves forward-looking estimates about economic growth and risks and makes use of complex empirical methods in order to measure actual growth or risks, or at least to reduce uncertainty about it.'[148] Under such circumstances, the independent status itself only makes sense as far as it enables the central bank to generally choose autonomously when to act and how to act. Where such a choice is taken either by the normative frame itself or the interpreting court, hardly any room remains for autonomous decisions of the ECB. As regards the independence of a central bank, it is thus not judicial review as such[149] but the intensity of such review that can be problematic and pose a threat to its independent status.[150] Judicial control therefore—and this is true whether it is conducted by the ECJ or any national (constitutional) court—has to step back where the respective court is functionally overstrained due to the economic complexity of the respective matter as it would otherwise not only threaten the independent status of the central bank but also risk worse monetary decisions. The central bank therefore needs to be equipped with a sufficient margin of appreciation concerning the substance of its decision that is extracted from judicial control.[151] The

[144] Reumann, *Die Europäische Zentralbank* (n 85) 216; see also Dawson and Bobic, 'Quantitative Easing' (n 6) 1028: 'Independence is granted not to allow central banks to escape constitutional supervision per se, but rather to allow them to develop credible long-term policies without political manipulation.'

[145] See also Paul Craig, 'EMU, the European Central Bank, and Judicial Review' in Paul Beaumont and Neil Walker (eds), *Legal Framework of the Single European Currency* (Hart Publishing 1999) 102: 'The general principle underlying this Article is that the ECB will be subject to the general rules on judicial review and the like laid down in the treaty.' See also Amtenbrink, 'The European Central Bank's intricate independence' (n 3) 177.

[146] See also Siekmann in Siekmann (ed), *EWU* (n 16) para 91 ('Korrelat zur Autonomie').

[147] Dragomir, 'The ECB's Accountability' (n 109) 39.

[148] Matthias Goldmann, 'Adjudicating Economics? Central Bank Independence and the Appropriate Standard of Judicial Review' (2014) German Law Journal 265, 268 (hereafter Goldmann, 'Adjudicating Economics?').

[149] The fact that Art 35 of its statute explicitly allows such a judicial control is thus no threat to its independent status per se.

[150] This is not seen by Helmut Siekmann in Siekmann (ed), *EWU* (n 16) para 81, who does not mention the problem of the control intensity.

[151] cf also Endler, *Europäische Zentralbank und Preisstabilität* (n 14) 239, 518 ff and Reumann, *Die Europäische Zentralbank* (n 85) 61; Thiele, *Die Europäische Zentralbank* (n 81) 109 ff; Goldmann, 'Adjudicating Economics?' (n 148) 265 ff; Markakis, *Accountability* (n 118) 286 ff.

general content of undefined legal terms (such as 'price stability') as part of the 'goal-independence' is thus to be determined not by the respective court but by the ECB itself.[152] And the same is true for the evaluation of the current and future economic surroundings of the whole monetary area and the decision on the necessary monetary actions that follow from this complex analysis. The German Constitutional Court, however, takes a somewhat different approach when it holds that: 'the independence granted to the European Central Bank (Art 130 TFEU) leads to a noticeable reduction in the level of democratic legitimation of its actions and should thus lead to a restrictive interpretation, as well as to a particular strict judicial review, of the mandate of the Central Bank.'[153] Though this is a feasible assertion, such strict control does not necessarily contradict a sufficient margin of appreciation of the ECB when it comes to the substance of its monetary decisions. Instead, the reviewing courts should focus on the procedural requirements monetary decisions have to meet. Within its judicial control the Court is thus limited to verifying the general tenability (the rationality) of the central bank's conclusions and the reasonableness of its argumentation and reasoning, while linking the requested intensity of control and the requirements the reasoning has to meet to the respective measure taken by the ECB. Strict review thus refers to a strict procedural but not substantive review. The Court could, for instance, thereby differentiate between traditional measures (setting the interest rate) and more unconventional measures (bond purchases, quantitative easing). Under such a procedural approach[154] it would, however, not be compatible with the ECB's independent status if a court were to replace such tenable conclusions with its own—even if these might be regarded as equally tenable.[155] Such a 'control' would simply result in a transfer of the monetary decision from one counter-majoritarian institution (the ECB) to another (the Court)—with the latter obviously lacking the necessary competence in monetary matters. Only such a limited judicial review as an example of judicial self-restraint[156] thus guarantees a review that fully respects the involved institutions' competences and thereby ensures the best possible decision as regards monetary policy.

In its first request for preliminary ruling, however, the German Constitutional Court did not respect these boundaries to judicial review: in effect, it simply resumed the opposing position of the German Bundesbank, without spending a word regarding the tenability of the opinion and the reasoning of the ECB.[157] Why, however, should the opinion of the Bundesbank be of any higher normative value than the one of the ECB, especially if one considers that the Bundesbank is a dependent part of the European System of Central Banks (ESCB) with the ECB at the top and the ongoing disputes amongst central bank economists concerning the right way to proceed in economically difficult times?[158] As Matthias Goldmann rightly

[152] Dragomir, 'The ECB's Accountability' (n 109) 42.

[153] BVerfG 21 June 2016, 2 BvR 2728/13 (n 5) paras 187 ff.

[154] See Dawson and Bobic, 'Quantitative Easing' (n 6) 1031 ff. The authors are, however, sceptical towards such an approach when it comes to the judicial review of bond purchase programmes.

[155] Reumann, *Die Europäische Zentralbank* (n 85) 223.

[156] See Amtenbrink, 'The European Central Bank's intricate independence' (n 3) 169.

[157] Likewise, Goldmann, 'Adjudicating Economics?' (n 148) 279: 'Nevertheless, the FCC opted for an inadvertently non-deferential full review, replacing the ECB's policy choices with its own.'

[158] In actual fact it was more than debatable whether it was acceptable that the German Constitutional Court heard the president of the German Bundesbank, Jens Weidmann, as an authorized expert during its

underlines: 'However, judges usually do not possess the qualification or legitimacy to adjudicate economics. A court that gets engaged in economic debates might compromise its legitimacy when its views are contested by those with more expertise on the issue.'[159] In its second request for preliminary ruling initiated in July 2017, the Constitutional Court therefore (rightly) explicitly pointed out that 'the acceptance of the goals as defined by the relevant European institutions combined with the appreciation of a wide margin of discretion of these institutions and a limitation of judicial control is eligible to enable these institutions an independent disposition as regards the range of the competences transferred upon them.'[160] It then nonetheless rejected such an interpretation as not sufficiently respecting the principle of conferral and the necessity to interpret the ECB's mandate in a restrictive manner. Yet, instead of showing a theoretical and practical way to smoothly combine these somewhat conflicting assumptions—for instance by focusing judicial review more on procedural requirements of decision finding and reasoning—the Constitutional Court simply pointed out why it believed that the ECB's bond purchase programme in its own view neither respected Art 123 TFEU (the prohibition of monetary financing) nor Art 127 TFEU (the policy mandate of the ECB) and thereby once again reverted solely to a particular economic opinion without taking opposing statements[161] into account that might have proven the tenability of the ECB's actions or the reasonableness of its arguments. The Constitutional Court's final decision on PSPP unfortunately was no less problematic in this respect when it held that the ECB needed to take possible consequences for the Member States economic policy into account when deciding on the necessary monetary measures:

> A programme adopted by the ESCB for the purchase of government bonds, such as the PSPP, that has significant economic policy effects must satisfy the principle of proportionality … The PSPP's monetary policy objective is in principle not (yet) objectionable. However, by pursuing that objective unconditionally while ignoring the economic policy effects resulting from the programme, the ECB manifestly disregards the principle of proportionality enshrined in Art. 5(1) second sentence and Art. 5(4) TEU. This violation of the principle of proportionality is structurally significant so that the actions of the ECB constitute an ultra vires act.

Such an obligation could first of all have the effect of undermining the primary mandate of the ECB as it could result in the ECB refraining from necessary monetary measures due to possible consequences for the economic policies of the Member States—though the independent status and the tight policy mandate of the ECB were explicitly granted in order to ensure that price stability was ensured 'no matter what'.

proceedings as the Bundesbank is a dependent part of the ESCB lead by the ECB and represented only by its president Mario Draghi.

[159] Goldmann, 'Adjudicating Economics?' (n 148) 271 ff.

[160] BVerfG 18 July 2017, 2 BvR 859/15 and others (n 5) para 119.

[161] The only exception being Julian Langner in Helmut Siekmann (ed), *EWU—Kommentar zur Europäischen Währungsunion* (Mohr Siebeck 2013)ESZB-Satzung Art 32 para 41 in para 132 of the ruling.

However, second of all and more relevant in the context of this article: it is obvious that Member States now have the chance to claim possible infringements of their economic policies when the ECB takes disputed monetary policy decisions. Until now, the ECB was able to repel such claims by simply pointing to its independence. That is no longer feasible if it were true that it was normatively obliged to take such political aspects into account when deciding on its monetary actions. The independence of the ECB therefore once again might be on for a tough test and the irony is: this situation was caused by a judgment of the German Constitutional Court and thus by 'those that wished to safeguard it'.[162]

V. Conclusion and Outlook

The independent status of a central bank remains economically disputed yet can be normatively justified and continues to be the 'normative reality' for the ECB. This status might be challenged, yet usually not normatively violated, by harsh critique or by duties to report or to cooperate with other institutions that, in fact, might even have a positive effect on the performance of the ECB. However, a mistaken finance and wage policy of the Member States might have problematic consequences. It is therefore sensible that Member States try to ensure a sustainable level of debt—without implying that the level of Member State debt should already be regarded as problematic. Generally, the positive effects of public indebtedness should not be neglected in this context[163] and this remains true even though the debt level has indeed risen significantly due to the coronavirus pandemic. In actual fact, too little public debt might actually make it harder for the ECB to reach its inflation target due to lacking public investments—a situation to be witnessed in several Member States of the European Union. The biggest threat for independence nonetheless appears to be a too intensive judicial review not granting the ECB the necessary margin of appreciation it needs to successfully pursue its monetary goals. Finding the right balance between necessary review and independence of a central bank will thus remain an important task not only for legal scholars—even more so as the German Constitutional Court is apparently struggling to accept any limits to judicial review at all. This is especially true as the ECB is currently not only reviewing its monetary policy strategy in general but in this context is also trying to formulate a possible role it might play in the overall efforts to fight climate change—a question indeed all relevant central banks worldwide are currently trying to find answers to. This somewhat new idea of central banking has already led to critical (and sometimes enraged) comments not only in Germany, pointing out that central banks should refrain from trying to get involved in such highly political matters, as these need to be left to democratically accountable politicians. Concerning its independent status, we therefore might not find a new situation

162 Goldmann, 'Adjudicating Economics?' (n 148) 280.

163 On the relationship between public debt and democracy generally, see Alexander Thiele, 'Staatsverschuldung und Demokratie' (2018) Leviathan 337.

from a formal perspective, no 'new ECB'. It has enjoyed this status since its founding in 1999. However, in the light of a more active—some might say a more political—ECB, involved for instance in selective (not 'market neutral') and thus highly disputed bond purchases as well as other measures not thought of when designing the Monetary Union, this special institutional status will most certainly be looked upon very closely in the next years. In other words: new cases from 'Karlsruhe' are sure to come.

11

The Legitimacy and Accountability of the ECB at the Age of Twenty

Fabian Amtenbrink and Menelaos Markakis

I. Introduction

This edited volume on the European Central Bank (ECB) comes at an opportune time, not only and perhaps not even primarily because the ECB recently celebrated its 20th birthday –an age which, compared to some other central banks, still puts it in the category of 'early childhood'–, but because of the greater scrutiny under which this European Union (EU) institution has found itself since the beginning of the European sovereign debt crisis and as a consequence of its new role in banking supervision. The proliferation of the ECB's tasks has raised questions concerning the economic and legal feasibility of the current framework. It has also flared up concerns regarding the democratic legitimacy of its actions. Accordingly, and in keeping with the general theme of this edited volume, this chapter analyses the ECB's accountability and transparency framework and related practice over its more than twenty years of existence. In doing so, it combines a chronological with a contextual analysis of the relevant legal and institutional arrangements, from which conclusions can be drawn with regard to the nature and extent of the ECB's democratic legitimacy.[1] We will draw on the concepts of input, throughput, and output legitimacy where appropriate.[2] Moreover, the principal-agent model is used as a basic reference point in considering the past and present arrangements at the ECB.[3]

With regard to the rationale for democratic accountability, it suffices to observe that, in the case of independent central banks, an agency situated outside the trias politica is exercising public power (the conduct of monetary policy) on behalf of the executive. As such, the rationale for the accountability of the ECB is not different from other cases of delegation of executive tasks to agencies that operate at arm's length from the Union institutions. What distinguishes the ECB and other independent central banks

[1] The ECB's independence and the judicial review of its actions are discussed in chapter 2 by Vestert Borger, chapter 6 by Jonathan Bauerschmidt, chapter 10 by Alexander Thiele, chapter 12 by Takis Tridimas, and chapter 16 by Marijn van der Sluis, in this volume.

[2] On these concepts, see Vivien Schmidt, 'Democracy and Legitimacy in the European Union Revisited: Input, Output *and* "Throughput"' (2013) 61 Political Studies 2, 4 ff, with further references (hereafter Schmidt, 'Democracy and Legitimacy in the European Union Revisited'). See also Vivien Schmidt and Matthew Wood, 'Conceptualizing Throughput Legitimacy: Procedural Mechanisms of Accountability, Transparency, Inclusiveness and Openness in EU Governance' (2019) 97 Public Administration 727.

[3] See, eg, Robert Elgie, 'The Politics of the European Central Bank: Principal-Agent Theory and the Democratic Deficit' (2002) 9 JEPP 186, with further references.

Fabian Amtenbrink and Menelaos Markakis, *The Legitimacy and Accountability of the ECB at the Age of Twenty* In: *The New European Central Bank*. Edited by: Thomas Beukers, Diane Fromage, and Giorgio Monti, Oxford University Press. © Fabian Amtenbrink and Menelaos Markakis 2022. DOI: 10.1093/oso/9780198871231.003.0011

for that matter from many other examples of delegation is the degree of legal insulation from the political institutions and the magnitude of the socio-economic consequences that the exercise of monetary policy can entail. What is more, due to its supranational nature, the ECB is situated at a greater distance from democratically legitimized institutions than is often the case in the national context, while at the same time also not benefitting from the same level of trust and support that has historically grown in the case of many major central banks. Following Gailmard's approach to public accountability as 'a function of the capabilities of principals to judge the performance of their agents',[4] this calls for governance structures that ensure that the central bank in charge of monetary policy is democratically accountable to its principal for the exercise of this power, thereby ensuring its continuous democratic legitimation.[5] This then has to translate into concrete legal and practical arrangements, which would ensure not only that the agent is required to explain its conduct and to provide relevant information to enable the principal to make an informed judgment, but also that the principal is provided with instruments allowing it to intervene where it is concluded that the agent is not discharging its tasks as was agreed upon initially. This approach to the function and main characteristics of accountability paints a symbiotic relationship between accountability and transparency, in which the latter arguably constitutes a prerequisite, a *conditio sine qua non*, for purposeful accountability arrangements.[6] At the same time, it is acknowledged that the importance of observing transparency arrangements is not limited to the principal-agent relationship between a central bank and the executive, as public access to information can also enhance accountability to other stakeholders, such as the civil society or financial markets. Moreover, in the case of the supranational ECB, democratic legitimacy may emanate through supranational and national (constitutional) channels.

This contribution examines the ECB's legal and institutional framework informing its degree of democratic legitimacy at the time of its inception, a framework that—as will become clear in the course of this contribution—in many regards continues to form the backbone of the ECB's existence today. Particular attention is paid to the way in which the accountability arrangements in the Treaties were advanced in practice in the initial years of the ECB's operation, thereby highlighting their dynamic character. Thereafter, the contribution turns to the evolution of the ECB's tasks over the course of the last twenty years, which has resulted in changes to the demands for arrangements securing its democratic legitimacy. The main question is whether the accountability arrangements laid down in primary and secondary Union law match these

[4] Sean Gailmard, 'Accountability and Principal–Agent Theory' in Mark Bovens, Robert E Goodin, and Thomas Schillemans (eds), *The Oxford Handbook of Public Accountability* (OUP 2014) 91.

[5] Tonny Lybek, 'Central Bank Autonomy, Accountability, and Governance: Conceptual Framework' in International Monetary Fund, 'Current Developments in Monetary and Financial Law' (vol 4, 6 November 2008) 147; Fabian Amtenbrink, 'The Three Pillars of Central Bank Governance: Towards a Model Central Bank Law or a Code of Good Governance?' in International Monetary Fund, 'Current Developments in Monetary and Financial Law' (vol 4, 6 November 2008) 103–04.

[6] Fabian Amtenbrink, *The Democratic Accountability of Central Banks: A Comparative Study of the European Central Bank* (Hart Publishing 1999) 339 ff (hereafter Amtenbrink, *The Democratic Accountability of Central Banks*); Peter Dyrberg, 'Accountability and Legitimacy: What is the Contribution of Transparency?' in Anthony Arnull and Daniel Wincott (eds), *Accountability and Legitimacy in the European Union* (OUP 2002) 83.

developments. The chapter identifies the (remaining) gaps across its main fields of activity (monetary policy, financial assistance programmes, and banking supervision), also in light of the ECB's role during the COVID-19 pandemic. It concludes by looking ahead, namely by asking whether the forthcoming push towards the 'greening' of monetary policy could enhance the ECB's legitimacy and what it would demand of its accountability framework.

The main argument in this contribution is that the accountability framework applicable to the ECB has not evolved sufficiently to match its expanded powers, thereby rendering this EU institution vulnerable to accusations regarding the degree of democratic legitimacy of its action. Whether these shortcomings can (still) be considered 'childhood diseases' of the ECB is questionable. A strategic reorientation of the ECB, thereby using monetary policy to help address broader societal challenges, such as climate change, may increase its output legitimacy. However, it should not be considered a substitute for robust accountability arrangements.

II. The ECB's Inception

Unlike various major central banks that have developed more or less organically over many decades or even centuries, such as the Sveriges Riksbank (1668),[7] the Bank of England (1694), or the Banque de France (1800), or could at least build on a tradition of central banking, such as the post-war Deutsche Bundesbank (1957), the ECB is a rather new institution. It is situated at the centre of the European System of Central Banks (ESCB) and the Eurosystem. Established on 1 July 1998, its creation marked in many regards a milestone in the unprecedented project of supranational economic, legal, and—albeit to a lesser extent—political integration that has led to the pooling of competences for monetary policy and the replacing of the national currencies of the Member States participating in the single currency area. It is the latter that necessitated the establishment of a transnational monetary policy authority.

Created from scratch by the drafters of the Treaty on European Union[8] against the backdrop of the rather broad sketch provided by the Delors Report,[9] the creation of the ECB was, as has been observed by Scheller, 'the embodiment of modern central banking'.[10] This is first and foremost so because, at the time of drafting the basic legal framework of the ECB, its key institutional characteristics reflected the emerging new consensus that monetary policy should be conducted at a safe distance from elected

[7] Originally founded under the name Riksens Ständers Bank.

[8] Namely through the introduction of Arts 3a, 4a, the provisions of Title VI on economic and monetary policy into the Treaty establishing the European Community [1992] OJ C224/1 (hereafter EC Treaty), as well as the Protocol on the Statute of the European System of Central Banks and of the European Central Bank, annexed to the EC Treaty. Currently Protocol No 4 on the Statute of the European System of Central Banks and of the European Central Bank [2016] OJ C202/230 (hereafter ESCB and ECB Statute).

[9] Committee for the Study of Economic and Monetary Union, 'Report on the Economic and Monetary Union in the European Communities' (17 April 1989) <https://ec.europa.eu/economy_finance/publications/pages/publication6161_en.pdf> accessed 17 March 2021 (hereafter Delors Report).

[10] Hanspeter Scheller, *The European Central Bank: History, Role and Functions* (European Central Bank 2004) 12.

officials and that the best direct contribution that monetary policy could make to the economic development of a country was to combat inflation.[11]

The discussion on the requisite institutional characteristics of a central bank to ensure the effectiveness of its policies very much focused on its relationship with the political institutions, notably the negative impact that the mingling of (democratically elected) politicians, who are more often than not driven by competing interests, can have on monetary policy outcomes. Having regard to the so-called inflationary biases, which are linked to the political business cycle, and the time-inconsistency problem associated with the conduct of monetary policy,[12] a strong case emerged for the delegation of monetary policy to an independent and conservative central bank(er).[13] A conservative central bank(er) 'is more inflation averse than the social planner',[14] or—put differently—'is someone who still sets policy in a discretionary fashion but is more concerned with reducing inflation than is the rest of society'.[15] Theoretical and empirical evidence emerged, supporting the view that the delegation of monetary policy onto an independent central bank was positively correlated to economic performance and in particular inflation.[16] The vesting of a single, overriding objective has also been considered to strengthen the independent position of a central bank 'against the unavoidable political pressure to pursue short run expansionary policies, particularly in times of economic distress'.[17]

The basic characteristics of the legal framework of the ECB thus were in line with what may be described as a shift in dogma away from monetary policy authorities being considered 'departments of ministries of finance … expected, by law, custom, or both, to utilize their policy instruments to achieve a myriad of objectives like high levels of growth and employment, provision of funds to government for the financing of public expenditures, and to address balance of payments problems',[18] and were linked to a global trend towards central bank independence and price stability as the main or primary objective of monetary policy. In fact, at least in the case of one EU Member State, Germany, the presence of these two basic characteristics was even

[11] See, eg, Mario Bleijer, 'Central Banks and Price Stability: Is a Single Objective Enough?' (1998) 1 Journal of Applied Economics 105, 105–06; José de Gregorio, 'Price and Financial Stability in Modern Central Banking' (2012) 13 Economía 1, 2.

[12] For more details, see Jakob de Haan and Sylvester Eijffinger, 'The Politics of Central Bank Independence' (2016) CentER Discussion Paper No 2016-047 <https://pure.uvt.nl/ws/portalfiles/portal/13825254/2016_047.pdf> accessed 17 March 2021, with further references to the relevant literature.

[13] Robert Barro and David Gordon, 'Rules, Discretion and Reputation in a Model of Monetary Policy' (1983) 12 Journal of Monetary Economics 101; Kenneth Rogoff, 'The Optimal Degree of Commitment to an Intermediate Target' (1985) 100 Quarterly Journal of Economics 1169.

[14] Peter Tillmann, 'The Conservative Central Banker Revisited: Too Conservative Is More Costly Than Too Liberal' (2008) 24 European Journal of Political Economy 737, 737.

[15] Christopher Waller, 'The Choice of a Conservative Central Banker in a Multisector Economy' (1992) 82 American Economic Review 1006, 1006.

[16] For an overview of the relevant literature, see Alex Cukierman, 'Central Bank Independence and Monetary Policymaking Institutions—Past, Present and Future' (2008) 24 European Journal of Political Economy 722 (hereafter Cukierman, 'Central Bank Independence and Monetary Policymaking Institutions'); Jakob de Haan, Donato Masciandaro, and Marc Quintyn, 'Does Central Bank Independence Still Matter?' (2008) 24 European Journal of Political Economy 717, 718 ff.

[17] Alberto Alesina and Vittorio Grilli, 'The European Central Bank: Reshaping Monetary Politics in Europe' (1991) NBER Working Paper No 3860, 14 <https://papers.ssrn.com/sol3/papers.cfm?abstract_id=453813> accessed 17 March 2021 (hereafter Alesina and Grilli, 'The European Central Bank').

[18] Cukierman, 'Central Bank Independence and Monetary Policymaking Institutions' (n 16) 722, 726 ff.

made a constitutional requirement for the transfer of responsibilities and powers of the National Central Bank to the supranational monetary policy authority in the run-up to the establishment of the ECB.[19] With Article 107 of the Treaty establishing the European Community (EC Treaty) [Article 130 of the Treaty on the Functioning of the European Union (TFEU)] on the independence of the ECB and Article 105(1) EC Treaty [Article 127(1) TFEU] on the overriding objective of price stability, this global trend in central banking was embedded, quite prominently, in the primary Union law provisions on the ECB.[20]

The unequivocal wording of Article 130 TFEU and the prioritization of price stability over any other, potentially conflicting economic objectives, differently to what can for example be observed for the US Federal Reserve System,[21] can also be interpreted as an attempt by the drafters of the Treaty on European Union to send out a clear signal in support of the new currency and the new supranational agency that would be managing it. In contrast to long-standing central bank systems that could rely on their credibility, meaning the 'commitment to follow well-articulated and transparent rules and policy goals' that is built by actual behaviour over time (track record),[22] in the case of the ECB this credibility could initially only emanate from its 'state-of-the-art' legal and institutional arrangements,[23] and its institutional similarities with the highly respected Deutsche Bundesbank.[24]

Cukierman has observed in a 2008 contribution that accountability and transparency are 'two buzz words of modern monetary institutions [that] were hardly heard twenty years ago or earlier'.[25] The author's explanation for this is that: 'In the absence of independence accountability was unnecessary and, as political entities, governments and ministries of finance had no incentives to raise questions about their own transparency in the conduct of monetary policy'.[26] Yet, in the case of the ECB it cannot be concluded that, when the Treaty on European Union was originally drafted, the mechanisms securing the accountability of the new institution received as much attention

[19] According to the second sentence of Art 88 of the German Basic Law, the ECB has to be independent and committed to the overriding goal of assuring price stability. This sentence was only added in December 1992, namely less than a year before the coming into force of the Treaty on European Union [1992] OJ C191/1 (Maastricht Treaty). See further Matthias Herdegen, 'GG Art. 88' in Roman Herzog and others (eds), *Maunz/Düring, Grundgesetz-Kommentar* (CH Beck 2020).

[20] Consolidated Version of the Treaty on the Functioning of the European Union [2012] OJ C326/47; ESCB and ECB Statute (n 8), Arts 7 and 2 respectively. See also Consolidated Version of the Treaty on European Union [2012] OJ C202/1, Art 3(3) (hereafter TEU), which refers to price stability as one of the objectives of the Union.

[21] See Federal Reserve Act 1913, Art 2A, 12 USC para 225a, as added by the Federal Reserve Reform Act 1977 (91 Stat. 1387) and amended by acts of 27 October 1978 (92 Stat. 1897), 23 August 1988 (102 Stat 1375), and 27 December 2000 (114 Stat 3028), which refers to 'the goals of maximum employment, stable prices, and moderate long-term interest rates'. On this, see further chapter 15 by Christy-Ann Petit, in this volume.

[22] Michael Bordo and Pierre Siklos, 'Central Bank Credibility: An Historical and Quantitative Exploration' (2015) NBER Working Paper No w20824 <https://papers.ssrn.com/sol3/papers.cfm?abstract_id=2548344> accessed 17 March 2021.

[23] But note Alesina and Grilli, 'The European Central Bank' (n 17) 14, who have observed that credibility is not reached 'by simply writing general objectives in the Central Bank statutes'.

[24] Karl Kaltenthaler, 'The Bundesbank and the Formation of the ECB's Monetary Policy Strategy' (2005) 14 German Politics 297.

[25] Cukierman, 'Central Bank Independence and Monetary Policymaking Institutions' (n 16) 732.

[26] ibid 723.

as its insulation from political influence, that is, its independence. In fact, while accountability and transparency issues have gained more prominence on the agenda of policy-makers and central bankers, but also in the academic discourse over the last three decades, there is little evidence to be found in the legal and institutional framework of the ECB that the drafters of the Treaty on European Union paid the same level of attention to this issue.

The Delors Report, which is sometimes referred to as a blueprint for the Economic and Monetary Union (EMU), stated that the institutional framework necessary for the 'management' of EMU 'would have to promote efficient economic management, properly embedded in the democratic process', whereby this 'would require the creation of a new monetary institution, placed in the constellation of Community institutions'.[27] In reality, with the aim of guarding against any suspicions of political proximity to national or European political institutions, the ECB has by and large been placed outside the democratic process. Its legal basis has provided for a degree of legal insulation that even surpassed that of the Deutsche Bundesbank, thereby making the ECB at the time of its establishment one of the most independent central banks in the world.[28] However, as regards the ECB's accountability framework, it could hardly be considered 'best practice' when compared to other modern central bank systems already in the mid-1990s.[29]

These weaknesses of the legal and institutional arrangements in the (original) legal provisions on the ECB (in the Treaties and Statute) have been examined extensively elsewhere.[30] They relate, first of all, to the conditions under which accountability can be effectively exercised, namely the absence of a quantified monetary policy objective in the ECB's legal basis, of an obligation to publish minutes of the policy meetings of the ECB's Governing Council, and of clear legal arrangements providing for a meaningful relationship with the European Parliament. Moreover, save for the option of amending primary Union law pursuant to the highly cumbersome procedure laid down in Article 48 TEU, the Treaty provisions on the ECB have not foreseen any concrete instruments that would allow for a consequential intervention of those in charge of holding the ECB to account, such as through performance-based dismissals of central bank officials, an override mechanism allowing for the (temporary) suspension of monetary policy decisions, or control over the ECB's budget.[31] Overall, this diagnosis of an accountability deficit regarding the ECB posed a challenge for its legitimacy from the outset. For the reasons discussed in the next section, this problem has become more pressing as a result of the evolution of the ECB's role.

While the law in the books thus had relatively little to offer in terms of providing channels for legitimizing the ECB's exercise of public power, beyond the ratification

[27] Delors Report (n 9) 21.

[28] For a comparative legal analysis of the accountability arrangements at the Bundesbank prior to the establishment of the ECB, see Amtenbrink, *The Democratic Accountability of Central Banks* (n 6) 334 ff.

[29] Jakob de Haan, Fabian Amtenbrink, and Sylvester Eijffinger, 'Accountability of Central Banks: Aspects and Quantifications' (1999) 52 BNL Quarterly Review 169.

[30] Amtenbrink, *The Democratic Accountability of Central Banks* (n 6).

[31] ibid 359–63; Menelaos Markakis, *Accountability in the Economic and Monetary Union: Foundations, Policy, and Governance* (OUP 2020) 15–17 (hereafter Markakis, *Accountability in the Economic and Monetary Union*).

of its legal basis by all Member States, the law in action following the ECB's inception has provided for a somewhat more nuanced picture from the start. Two main factors contributed to this: the increased focus on transparency and, more importantly, the way in which the ECB's relationship with the European Parliament has developed.[32]

As regards reporting requirements, the Treaty provisions on the ECB refer in rather broad terms to a publicly accessible annual report on the activities of the ESCB, quarterly activity reports, and weekly consolidated financial statements.[33] One important, albeit foreseeable, development was that the ECB started to hold regular press conferences after every meeting of the Governing Council for which monetary policy decisions were scheduled, to explain its decisions. Moreover, the ECB immediately started publishing monthly, rather than the statutorily foreseen quarterly, reports, which until the end of 2014 were known as Monthly Bulletins and are now referred to as Economic Bulletins. These have not only explained the ECB's monetary policy decisions but also included a broader outlook on the economic developments in the euro area, as well as a timeline of the monetary policy decisions.[34] In doing so, rather than ensuring the openness of its decision-making processes,[35] the ECB has principally focused on the publicity of its decisions, thereby using transparency as a policy tool. Furthermore, early evidence suggests that it could not be concluded from the ECB's pro-active approach to transparency that financial market participants necessarily considered the ECB to be transparent, which may be explained by the quality or scope of information that was provided.[36]

What is more, similarly to what has been observed for its transparency, and leaving aside Article 130 TFEU for a moment, the provisions on the ECB originally included in the Treaties and those in force today provide little detail on its relationship with the EU political institutions, notably the European Parliament. Pursuant to Article 284(1)–(2) TFEU (ex Article 113(1)–(2) EC Treaty) the President of the Council and a Member of the Commission may participate, without having the right to vote, in meetings of the ECB's Governing Council. Moreover, the President of the Council may submit a motion for deliberation to the Governing Council. On the other hand, the ECB President must be invited to participate in Council meetings when it is discussing matters relating to the objectives and tasks of the ESCB.[37] The European Parliament is not mentioned in these provisions. Instead, pursuant to Article 284(3) TFEU (ex Article 113(3) EC Treaty) the ECB President presents the annual report not only to the Council, but also to the European Parliament, which can hold a debate on that basis.

[32] See Fabian Amtenbrink, 'On the Legitimacy and Democratic Accountability of the European Central Bank: Legal Arrangements and Practical Experience' in Anthony Arnull and Daniel Wincott (eds), *Accountability and Legitimacy in the European Union* (OUP 2002).

[33] ESCB and ECB Statute (n 8) Art 15.

[34] Introduced in 2015, the monthly Economic Bulletins provide, *inter alia*, an update on economic and monetary developments and include in-depth articles on more specific issues related to the ECB's operation.

[35] For a long time, ESCB and ECB Statute (n 8) Art 10.4 has been interpreted so as to basically exclude the disclosure of any details of the meetings of the ECB's Governing Council.

[36] Jakob de Haan and Fabian Amtenbrink, 'A Non-Transparent European Central Bank? Who Is to Blame?' (2003) <https://papers.ssrn.com/sol3/papers.cfm?abstract_id=1138224> accessed 17 March 2021.

[37] See also ESCB and ECB Statute (n 8) Art 45.2, according to which the President of the Council and a Member of the Commission can participate, without having the right to vote, in meetings of the ECB's General Council.

More importantly, Article 284(3) TFEU states in rather general and noncommittal language that the ECB President and other Executive Board members *may*, at the request of the European Parliament or on their own initiative, be heard by the competent committees of the European Parliament. While this wording can hardly be construed to establish a legal obligation under primary Union law on the ECB to appear before the European Parliament or any of its committees, the European Parliament took at the time of the inception of the ECB a proactive stance in shaping its relationship with the latter, pointing out that '... the independence of the future ECB will only meet with public acceptance if the ECB enjoys a high degree of legitimacy; whereas the only way to ensure this is full accountability of the ECB for its actions ... ' and '... as the future ESCB and the ECB will conduct a single monetary policy for all the Member States taking part in European monetary union, democratic accountability must similarly be exercised at the European level ... as the only directly elected institution at this level, the European Parliament is a particularly appropriate institution to hold the ECB to account'.[38] Correspondingly, the European Parliament called '... for the organization of a dialogue between the European Parliament and the future ECB on monetary and economic affairs, the framework for which dialogue should be confirmed through a mutual agreement'.[39]

With the agreement of the ECB, this has resulted in a practice of quarterly exchanges between the ECB President and also other members of the Executive Board and the Committee on Economic and Monetary Affairs (ECON) of the European Parliament, better known as *monetary dialogue*.[40] These arrangements certainly constitute a major improvement over what could have been expected on the basis of the relevant legal requirements, and the ECB has been praised for being 'highly responsive to the ECON'.[41] At the same time, their usefulness as a mechanism to ensure the democratic accountability of the ECB has been questioned, by and large due to the absence of instruments at the disposal of the European Parliament to actually impose any sanctions if it concludes that the ECB is not performing adequately.[42] This means that the monetary dialogue can be mainly seen as a forum in which the democratically elected representatives of the EU citizens can ask the ECB to explain its strategy and actions and they can express their support or rejection thereof. Moreover, as Collignon has rightly observed, it can be considered as 'one of the few bridges to link monetary policy with

[38] Resolution of the European Parliament on democratic accountability in the third phase of EMU [1998] OJ C138/177, under C and F.5.

[39] ibid under F.7.

[40] Nowadays, see Rules of Procedure of the European Parliament (9th parliamentary term—September 2021), Rule 135(3).

[41] Sylvester Eijffinger and Edin Mujagic, 'An Assessment of the Effectiveness of the Monetary Dialogue on the ECB's Accountability and Transparency: A Qualitative Approach' (2004) 39 Intereconomics 190. For various reflections on the workings of the monetary dialogue and proposals for improvements, see Gregory Claeys and others, 'Monetary Dialogue 2009-2014: Looking Backward, Looking Forward' (2014) Directorate General for Internal Policies, Policy Department A: Economic and Scientific Policy PE 518.753 <https://www.europarl.europa.eu/RegData/etudes/IDAN/2014/518753/IPOL_IDA(2014)518753_EN.pdf> accessed 17 March 2021 (hereafter Claeys and others, 'Monetary Dialogue 2009-2014').

[42] Fabian Amtenbrink and Kees van Duin, 'The European Central Bank before the European Parliament: Theory and Practice After Ten Years of Monetary Dialogue' (2009) 34 EL Rev 561 (hereafter Amtenbrink and van Duin, 'The European Central Bank before the European Parliament').

other policy considerations'.[43] Yet, the monetary dialogue has not only functioned as a tool for MEPs (and the broader public) to gain information on the conduct of monetary policy relevant for the evaluation of the ECB's performance, but also as a communication channel for the ECB itself to explain and defend its monetary policy stance, such as with regard to its reluctance in the past to actively pursue the secondary objective laid down in Article 127(1) TFEU to support the Union's general economic policies with a view to contributing to the achievement of the objectives stated in Article 3(3) TEU. Measuring the effectiveness of the monetary dialogue as an accountability tool is difficult, in particular when considering that, due to the abovementioned lack of effective instruments, the influence of the European Parliament has been informal and through the power of persuasion.[44] One notable change at the ECB that may be attributed to the relentless insistence on this point by MEPs has been the practice from 2015 onwards of publishing the accounts of the monetary policy meetings of the ECB's Governing Council.[45] Previously, the ECB had taken the view that the publication of minutes from the meetings of the Governing Council would run contrary to the confidentiality provision of the Statute of the ESCB and ECB, and hamper the internal deliberations between the National Central Bank governors.[46] As a result, it had categorically ruled out the publication of any details of these meetings. As has been observed elsewhere, while the accounts do not identify proponents and opponents of a specific monetary policy stance or measures, they still provide useful insights into the main considerations that influenced the decision-making process.[47]

III. The Evolution of the ECB's Democratic Legitimacy and Accountability

With the abovementioned approach to accountability and transparency, the position of the ECB in the pursuit of its statutory objectives remained relatively unchallenged during the first ten years of its existence. However, in the last decade the ECB has undergone a major transformation, reigniting and intensifying the debate about the democratic legitimacy of its position and powers in the European legal order. Two major developments have triggered this: the ECB's role as crisis manager, namely during the European sovereign debt crisis, and its new tasks in the European Banking Union. These will be discussed hereafter in turn.

[43] Stefan Collignon, 'Central Bank Accountability in Times of Crisis. The Monetary Dialogue: 2009-2014' in Claeys and others, 'Monetary Dialogue 2009-2014' (n 41) 68.

[44] For a qualitative analysis, see Amtenbrink and van Duin, 'The European Central Bank before the European Parliament' (n 42); Stefan Collignon and Sebastian Diessner, 'The ECB's Monetary Dialogue with the European Parliament: Efficiency and Accountability During the Euro Crisis?' (2016) 54 JCMS 1296 (hereafter Collignon and Diessner, 'The ECB's Monetary Dialogue with the European Parliament').

[45] European Central Bank, 'ECB to Publish Accounts of Monetary Policy Discussions from January' (18 December 2014) <https://www.ecb.europa.eu/press/pr/date/2014/html/pr141218.en.html> accessed 17 March 2021.

[46] See ESCB and ECB Statute (n 8) Art 10.4, according to which the proceedings of the meetings are confidential, but the Governing Council may decide to make the outcome of its deliberations public. See also Fabian Amtenbrink, 'Economic and Monetary Union' in Pieter Jan Kuijper and others (eds), *The Law of the European Union* (5th edn, Kluwer Law International 2018) 939.

[47] ibid 939–40.

A. The ECB's role as crisis manager

Much has been written about the role of the ECB as crisis manager during the sovereign debt crisis that need not be repeated here. The two main areas of contestation were the ECB's approach to monetary policy and its involvement in the financial assistance programmes for euro area Member States.

In the face of tensions in the financial system that negatively impacted the transmission of monetary policy to the real economy, and with the declared aim of ensuring the effectiveness of its monetary policy toolbox and 'the singleness of monetary policy', that is, the effectiveness of its policies in the whole euro area,[48] the ECB engaged in non-standard or unconventional monetary policy measures. Initially, these included, *inter alia*, the unprecedented lowering of its key interest rates, the widening of the range of eligible collateral, and targeted longer-term refinancing operations.[49] Yet, the most controversial measures taken by the ECB were the numerous asset purchase programmes, covering both private and public securities, including three covered bond purchase programmes (2009–10, 2011–12, and from 2014 onwards), an asset-backed securities purchase programme (2014–18, and from 2019 onwards), a corporate sector purchase programme (2016–18, and from 2019 onwards), and a public sector purchase programme (2015–18, and from 2019 onwards). Moreover, in August 2012 the ECB's Governing Council announced the use of outright monetary transactions (OMT) on the secondary markets for sovereign bonds.[50] While this programme was never put into operation, its announcement alone is believed to have produced effects.[51] By February 2021 the ECB's net purchases under its asset purchase programmes had accumulated to €3,086 billion.[52]

Ever since the first financial assistance programme for Greece was agreed in 2010, the ECB has also been involved in the negotiations for the economic adjustment programmes that have been consistently attached to the financial assistance granted to euro area Member States, including in the context of the temporary European Financial Stabilisation Mechanism (EFSM) and European Financial Stability Facility (EFSF), as well as the permanent European Stability Mechanism (ESM). Through a

[48] Jörg Bibow, 'The Euro's Savior? Assessing the ECB's Crisis Management Performance and Potential for Crisis Resolution' (2015) IMK Study No 42, 8 <http://gesd.free.fr/imk4215.pdf> accessed 17 March 2021 refers to a policy that 'translates into broadly uniform financial conditions across the currency union'.

[49] For an overview of these early measures, see Philippine Cour-Thimann and Bernhard Winkler, 'The ECB's Non-Standard Monetary Policy Measures: The Role of Institutional Factors and Financial Structure' (2013) ECB Working Paper No 1528 <https://www.ecb.europa.eu/pub/pdf/scpwps/ecbwp1528.pdf> accessed 17 March 2021; Klaus Tuori, 'Monetary Policy (Objectives and Instruments)' in Fabian Amtenbrink and Christoph Herrmann (eds), *The EU Law of Economic and Monetary Union* (OUP 2020).

[50] European Central Bank, 'Technical Features of Outright Monetary Transactions' (6 September 2012) <https://www.ecb.europa.eu/press/pr/date/2012/html/pr120906_1.en.html> accessed 17 March 2021 (hereafter European Central Bank, 'Technical Features of Outright Monetary Transactions').

[51] See Carlo Altavilla, Domenico Giannone, and Michele Lenza, 'The Financial and Macroeconomic Effects of the OMT Announcements' (2014) ECB Working Paper No 1707 <https://www.ecb.europa.eu/pub/pdf/scpwps/ecbwp1707.pdf> accessed 17 March 2021, who observe effects on the bond yields of some euro area Member States.

[52] See European Central Bank, 'Asset Purchase Programmes' <https://www.ecb.europa.eu/mopo/implement/app/html/index.en.html#abspp> accessed 15 March 2021.

series of memoranda of understanding (MoUs), Member States receiving financial assistance commit themselves to specific economic (reform) plans, often entailing significant austerity measures.[53] These MoUs effectively function as a benchmark for assessing the country's compliance with the economic adjustment programme and for the decision on the pay-out of tranches from the loan.[54]

In the case of the EFSM/EFSF and the ESM, the ECB's involvement has been written into their respective legal instruments. The ESM Treaty, as is currently in force, states that the European Commission in liaison with the ECB is entrusted with assessing the financing needs of the Member State in need of financial assistance; negotiating the general economic policy conditions attached to the ESM financial assistance; and monitoring, in regular intervals, compliance with these conditions.[55] In fact, the ECB itself has linked its unconventional monetary policy measures to financial assistance programmes, as in certain cases it constitutes an eligibility criterion for the purchasing of marketable debt securities of euro area Member States.[56]

The involvement of the ECB in the management of the European financial and sovereign debt crisis has been met with considerable criticism. The legality of its actions has been questioned, and doubts were raised about the legitimacy of its powers and its involvement in the economic adjustment programmes. With regard to the former, the scope of the monetary policy mandate of the ECB and whether it covers the announced and implemented asset purchase programmes has become the subject of fierce legal debate and eventually of the well-documented legal challenges brought against the OMT and the public sector purchase programme before the German Federal Constitutional Court (*Bundesverfassungsgericht* or BVerfG) and the Court of Justice of the European Union (ECJ).[57] Interestingly, in its preliminary reference in *Weiss*, the BVerfG flagged the issue of the democratic legitimacy of the ECB's action. It ruled that, 'The independence enjoyed by the ECB and the national central banks in the exercise of the powers conferred to them … is in conflict with requirements

[53] Usually referred to in the past as the Memorandum on Economic and Financial Policies, the Memorandum of Understanding on Specific Economic Policy Conditionality, and the Technical Memorandum of Understanding.

[54] See further Roderic O'Gorman, 'Adjustment Programmes, the European Central Bank and Conditionality' in Federico Fabbrini and Marco Ventoruzzo (eds), *Research Handbook on EU Economic Law* (Edward Elgar Publishing 2019); Markakis, *Accountability in the Economic and Monetary Union* (n 31) ch 3, esp 85–102.

[55] Treaty Establishing the European Stability Mechanism [2012] T/ESM 2012-LT, Art 13 (hereafter ESM Treaty).

[56] See Decision (EU) 2020/188 of the European Central Bank of 3 February 2020 on a secondary markets public sector asset purchase programme (ECB/2020/9) [2020] OJ L39/12, Arts 3 and 4, as amended. See also European Central Bank, 'Technical Features of Outright Monetary Transactions' (n 50).

[57] On judicial review of ECB monetary policy measures, see further Stefania Baroncelli, 'Monetary Policy and Judicial Review' in Federico Fabbrini and Marco Ventoruzzo (eds), *Research Handbook on EU Economic Law* (Edward Elgar Publishing 2019); Alicia Hinarejos, 'The Legality of Responses to the Crisis' in Fabian Amtenbrink and Christoph Herrmann (eds), *The EU Law of Economic and Monetary Union* (OUP 2020); Markakis, *Accountability in the Economic and Monetary Union* (n 31) ch 8; Annelieke Mooij and Stefania Baroncelli, 'What Kind of Judicial Review for the European Central Bank?' (2020) BRIDGE Network Working Paper No 9 <https://papers.ssrn.com/sol3/papers.cfm?abstract_id=3745244> accessed 18 March 2021; Nik de Boer and Jens van't Klooster, 'The ECB, the Courts and the Issue of Democratic Legitimacy after *Weiss*' (2020) 57 CMLR 1689. For a discussion of judicial review of monetary policy measures, see also chapter 2 by Vestert Borger, chapter 6 by Jonathan Bauerschmidt, chapter 10 by Alexander Thiele, chapter 12 by Takis Tridimas, and chapter 16 by Marijn van der Sluis, in this volume.

pertaining to the democratic legitimation of political decisions', but that it did not run contrary to democratic principles 'on the grounds that it takes into account the proven and scientifically supported particularity of monetary policy'.[58] Yet, in the view of the BVerfG, this conclusion 'hinges on the requirement that its mandate be interpreted restrictively', thereby being limited to its price stability objective.[59] From the perspective of the BVerfG and its interpretation of German constitutional law, acts by Union institutions that exceed the competences assigned to the EU lack the democratic legitimation that derives from the transfer of sovereign powers by the Member States by means of a democratic process onto the supranational level and that justifies 'the decrease in the level of democratic legitimation of the public authority exercised by the European Union'.[60] In its decision in *Weiss*, the ECJ does not engage with the question whether, in light of Article 10 TEU on the principle of democracy, the reduced democratic legitimation of public power resulting from assigning monetary policy onto an independent Union institution calls for a narrow definition of the ECB's monetary policy mandate.

This debate on the democratic legitimacy of the powers exercised by the ECB during the crisis and, in the case of the public sector purchase programme, until this very day, has been further fuelled by the controversy on the effectiveness of the unconventional monetary policy measures and, even more so, their unintended economic side effects. These side effects do not only relate to possible constraints for future monetary policy operations and a reduced appetite of Member States for economic reforms and budgetary discipline, but also to the effects of the unconventional measures on the distribution of wealth and income.[61] As has been pointed out elsewhere, it is these (potential) side effects that have put the spotlight on the independence and democratic legitimacy of central banks.[62] Moreover, this has resulted in demands for the ECB, but also for the ECJ, to take such consequences more explicitly into account in considering the proportionality of monetary policy measures.[63]

[58] BVerfG Order of the Second Senate of 18 July 2017 2 BvR 859/15 ECLI:DE:BVerfG:2017:rs20170718.2bvr085915, para 103 (hereafter BVerfG 18 July 2017 2 BvR 859/15).

[59] ibid.

[60] BVerfG Judgment of the Second Senate of 5 May 2020 2 BvR 859/15 ECLI:DE:BVerfG:2020:rs:20200505.2bvr085915, paras 143 and 158.

[61] For an overview, see Joscha Beckmann and others, 'The ECB's Asset Purchase Programmes: Effectiveness, Risks, Alternatives' (2020) Directorate General for Internal Policies, Policy Department for Economic, Scientific and Quality of Life Policies PE 652.741, 18 ff <https://www.europarl.europa.eu/cmsdata/211391/2_KIEL%20final.pdf> accessed 17 March 2021; Gregory Claeys and others, 'ECB Quantitative Easing (QE): What Are the Side Effects?' (2015) Directorate General for Internal Policies, Policy Department A: Economic and Scientific Policy PE 587.287 <http://www.europarl.europa.eu/RegData/etudes/IDAN/2015/587287/IPOL_IDA(2015)587287_EN.pdf> accessed 17 March 2021.

[62] Boris Vujčić, 'The Role of Central Banks and How to Insure Their Independence' (Speech at the Symposium on 'Central Banking in Central and Eastern Europe: Policy Making, Investment and Low Yields', Prague, 10 June 2016) <https://www.bis.org/review/r1607012b.htm> accessed 17 March 2021. See also Nicolò Fraccaroli, Alessandro Giovannini, and Jean-François Jamet, 'The Evolution of the ECB's Accountability Practices During the Crisis', ECB Economic Bulletin Issue 5/2018 <https://www.ecb.europa.eu/pub/economic-bulletin/articles/2018/html/ecb.ebart201805_01.en.html> accessed 17 March 2021, who provide evidence for increased media attention and public awareness (hereafter Fraccaroli, Giovannini, and Jamet, 'The Evolution of the ECB's Accountability Practices During the Crisis').

[63] BVerfG 18 July 2017 2 BvR 859/15 (n 58) para 139, referring to the effects of a government bond purchasing programme on, *inter alia*, personal savings, pension and retirement schemes, and real estate prices.

The increased scrutiny of the ECB's role in the negotiation and monitoring of the financial assistance programmes can be explained by the socio-economic impact that the implementation of these programmes has had in the respective countries. It can be observed that the actual decision-making process in the ESM does not grant the ECB a (formal) role in the adoption of sensitive measures.[64] The recipient Member State itself actively participates in the conclusion of the programme, and the application of what has been agreed is subject to national implementing measures adopted by means of the domestic democratic decision-making process. Yet, next to the European Commission, the ECB has been perceived as the main author (or co-author) of economic policy conditionality, to the point of triggering (unsuccessful) challenges against the ECB before the EU courts for its involvement.[65] The ECB is perceived, as has been observed elsewhere, 'as entering the arena typically reserved for political decision making; an arena where competing (public) interests are balanced and decisions with direct distributional effects are taken'.[66]

The evolution of the ECB's role, both objectively and certainly in the perception of many observers, begs the question as to what extent the mechanisms ensuring the legitimacy of its monetary policy function have sufficiently evolved in parallel to these developments. First, it can be noted that these developments have formally taken place within the scope of the existing monetary policy mandate of the ECB or resulted from developments outside the direct control of the ECB, such as the establishment of the ESM. This means that the Treaty provisions on the ECB have remained unchanged. A formal recognition of the transformed role of the ECB as monetary policy authority by the masters of the Treaties is thus missing. In the absence of an amendment of the primary Union law provisions on the ECB, the existing accountability mechanisms have remained unchanged, thereby also limiting any possible evolution of the legal framework governing its accountability. In this connection, it should be further noted that the reformed ESM Treaty would clarify the respective roles of the institutions involved in financial assistance programmes, including the ECB for that matter. However, the developments on the accountability front would be minimal.[67]

The most significant development from a legal perspective has been the engagement of national and EU courts with the ECB's role as crisis manager. First and foremost, while this could hardly be questioned before the sovereign debt crisis, it has become clear that the independent ECB is subject to the rule of law and thus to judicial review by the EU courts.[68] At the same time, the *Gauweiler* and *Weiss* cases have highlighted the complexity involved in the judicial review of monetary policy decisions.

[64] For the tasks conferred on the ECB in the ESM, see notably ESM Treaty (n 55) Arts 4(4), 13(1), (3) and (7), 14(6) and 18(2).

[65] Francesco Costamagna, 'The EMU and the European Social Dimension' in Fabian Amtenbrink and Christoph Herrmann (eds), *The EU Law of Economic and Monetary Union* (OUP 2020). On the evolving role of the ECB, see also Alexander Thiele, *Das Mandat der EZB und die Krise des Euro* (Mohr Siebeck 2013).

[66] Fabian Amtenbrink, 'The European Central Bank's Intricate Independence versus Accountability Conundrum in the Post-Crisis Governance Framework' (2019) 26 MJ 165, 178.

[67] See further Menelaos Markakis, 'The Reform of the European Stability Mechanism: Process, Substance, and the Pandemic' (2020) 47 LIEI 359.

[68] On the position of the ECB within the Union legal order, see Case C-11/00 *Commission of the European Communities v European Central Bank* [2003] ECLI:EU:C:2003:395.

Following legal challenges to the ECB's unconventional monetary policy measures in the domestic legal order, the ECJ found itself in the rather unique position of having to enforce the primary Union law 'legal fiction' of a clear delineation of monetary policy from economic policy in the face of a different economic reality.[69] Moreover, it had to legally review the decisions of an independent expert body that were based on complex economic considerations. The ECJ's approach in *Gauweiler* and *Weiss* may be summarized as the exercise of judicial restraint rather than activism. This is the case for the ECJ's approach to determining the monetary policy character of an ECB measure, as this is 'principally' determined with reference to the objectives of that measure, which the author of the measure itself determines. This is also the case for the ECJ's approach to proportionality review, which essentially amounts to 'an arbitrariness test, which only reviews whether the ECB ... has not exceeded the outer limits of its discretion',[70] and hence which does not entail a detailed balancing act of the potentially conflicting objectives, interests, and effects that a concrete monetary policy measure may entail. The ECJ's approach to judicial review has been met with considerable resistance by the German Federal Constitutional Court, which effectively considers full judicial review as an instrument of checks and balances for the independent ECB and accuses the ECJ of falling short of fulfilling this function adequately. Yet, judicial review cannot function as a replacement or sufficiently compensate for instruments of democratic accountability. As has been observed elsewhere:

> If judges act as counterbalances to expert bodies, they effectively substitute their judgment for that of experts. Or, to put it more bluntly, one non-majoritarian body (a court) replaces the decision by another non-majoritarian body (a central bank). The issue of the fragile democratic legitimation of decisions with potentially far reaching implications is hardly solved by such a switching of actors.[71]

Beyond judicial review, it has been observed that the monetary dialogue between the ECB and the European Parliament has evolved during the crisis, as 'the ECB and the European Parliament have increased the frequency of their interactions, innovated on format and increased the focus of exchanges in response to the demand for greater scrutiny of the ECB's actions'.[72] Yet, the conclusion that 'this has resulted in an enhanced use by the European Parliament of the accountability instruments at its disposal'[73] is based on a narrow conception of accountability, according to which the agent has to explain and justify its action but is not subject to any concrete instruments by means of which the principal can assign consequences to its assessment of the agent's performance. Put somewhat more bluntly, neither the directly

[69] Fabian Amtenbrink and René Repasi, 'The German Federal Constitutional Court's Decision in Weiss: A Contextual Analysis' (2020) 45 EL Rev 757, 759 ff.

[70] ibid 775.

[71] ibid 776.

[72] Fraccaroli, Giovannini, and Jamet, 'The Evolution of the ECB's Accountability Practices During the Crisis' (n 62), s 5 (Conclusions); Collignon and Diessner, 'The ECB's Monetary Dialogue with the European Parliament' (n 44).

[73] Fraccaroli, Giovannini, and Jamet, 'The Evolution of the ECB's Accountability Practices During the Crisis' (n 62), s 5 (Conclusions).

democratically legitimized European Parliament nor the indirectly democratically legitimized Council of the EU have any effective instruments at their disposal to convince the ECB to make different policy choices, thereby signalling their preferences for fewer (or differently weighted) economic side effects. At first sight, such a possibility could be considered undesirable from the standpoint of safeguarding the ECB's independence. Yet, this comes at the expense of the democratic legitimacy (namely in the shape of throughput legitimacy) of the ECB, which in turn results in open (political) challenges of its independent position.

Finally, while an argument can certainly be made that in its role in managing the crisis the ECB has served the general or public interest, it cannot be readily concluded that the ECB's legitimacy in this regard derives from its policies. Indeed, as has been observed: 'Output legitimacy requires policies to work effectively while resonating with citizens' values, and identity.'[74] The scepticism with which the ECB's crisis management has been met by the citizens in different countries and for different reasons suggests that the latter is anything but certain.

B. The ECB's role in the European Banking Union

In formal legal terms, the most important evolution of the ECB's accountability framework can be attributed to the development of the European Banking Union.[75] With the establishment of the Single Supervisory Mechanism (SSM)[76] and the Single Resolution Mechanism (SRM),[77] specific accountability arrangements were set out in secondary Union law for the scrutiny of the tasks that the ECB carries out in the Banking Union. These arrangements reflect not only an updated thinking among the EU institutions on the importance of explicitly providing for accountability mechanisms in the applicable legal framework, but perhaps also the difference in the role played by the ECB as a bank supervisor in comparison to monetary policy.[78]

The SSM Regulation, which was adopted on the basis of Article 127(6) TFEU, has conferred specific supervisory tasks on the ECB.[79] The SSM comprises the ECB and the national competent authorities, and the ECB is responsible for its effective and consistent functioning.[80] The ECB directly supervises 111 'significant' banks or cross-border groups that are established in Member States participating in the Banking

[74] Schmidt, 'Democracy and Legitimacy in the European Union Revisited' (n 2) 7.
[75] See chapter 7 by Kern Alexander, in this volume.
[76] Council Regulation (EU) 1024/2013 of 15 October 2013 conferring specific tasks on the European Central Bank concerning policies relating to the prudential supervision of credit institutions [2013] OJ L287/63 (hereafter SSM Regulation).
[77] Regulation (EU) 806/2014 of the European Parliament and of the Council establishing uniform rules and a uniform procedure for the resolution of credit institutions and certain investment firms in the framework of a Single Resolution Mechanism and a Single Resolution Fund and amending Regulation (EU) No 1093/2010 [2014] OJ L225/1.
[78] In this connection, Paul Tucker argues that the central banks' 'newly fortified powers to oversee and set the terms of trade for banking and other parts of finance unambiguously make them part of the "regulatory state"': Paul Tucker, *Unelected Power: The Quest for Legitimacy in Central Banking and the Regulatory State* (Princeton University Press 2018) 8.
[79] SSM Regulation (n 76) Art 1.
[80] ibid Art 6(1). See chapter 8 by Federico Della Negra and Gianni Lo Schiavo, in this volume.

Union.[81] The ECB's supervisory function is organizationally separate from its monetary policy function.[82] Its supervisory tasks are carried out by the Supervisory Board, which is an internal body of the ECB.[83] Nevertheless, the ECB's Governing Council formally remains the main decision-making body in the SSM, as required by EU primary law.[84] More specifically, the Supervisory Board approves draft supervisory decisions, which shall be deemed to be adopted unless the Governing Council objects to them.[85]

The framework for the accountability of the ECB in the SSM is partly dependent on existing arrangements and partly dependent on new provisions, following the inclusion of specific rules in the SSM Regulation, notably in Articles 20–21.[86] The relevant provisions of the SSM Regulation are complemented by the Interinstitutional Agreement (IIA) between the European Parliament and the ECB;[87] and the Memorandum of Understanding (MoU) between the Council of the EU and the ECB.[88] Overall, it can be observed that this accountability framework is more elaborate than the one for its monetary policy function.

Article 20(1) SSM Regulation provides that the ECB shall be accountable to the European Parliament and to the Council of the EU for the implementation of this Regulation and thus for ensuring that the SSM's aims are achieved. Article 1 SSM Regulation sets out the objectives pursued by the SSM. It has been observed that, in contrast to the ECB's monetary policy objectives, the SSM Regulation 'includes multiple, vague objectives, without establishing a clear hierarchal order between them'.[89] To the extent that 'the safety and soundness of credit institutions' and 'the stability of the financial system within the Union and each Member State' may be qualified as the core objectives to be pursued by the ECB in the SSM, it has been argued that 'they hardly amount to a quantifiable yardstick based on which the performance of the ECB can be objectively evaluated'.[90] What is more, it might be difficult to monitor whether these objectives are achieved in practice, as a clear benchmark is absent.[91] In its 2016

[81] European Central Bank, 'List of Supervised Banks' (1 April 2022) <https://www.bankingsupervision.europa.eu/banking/list/html/index.en.html> accessed 24 May 2022.

[82] SSM Regulation (n 76) Art 25.

[83] ibid Art 26(1).

[84] See Arts 129(1) and 282(2) TFEU; ESCB and ECB Statute (n 8) Art 12.

[85] SSM Regulation (n 76) Art 26(8).

[86] See generally, Fabian Amtenbrink, 'Art. 20 SSMR Accountability and Reporting' and 'Art. 21 SSMR National Parliaments' in Jens-Hinrich Binder, Christos V. Gortsos, Klaus Lackhoff, and Christoph Ohler (eds), *Brussels Commentary. European Banking Union* (Beck, Hart, Nomos 2022).

[87] Interinstitutional Agreement between the European Parliament and the European Central Bank on the practical modalities of the exercise of democratic accountability and oversight over the exercise of the tasks conferred on the ECB within the framework of the Single Supervisory Mechanism (2013/694/EU) [2013] OJ L320/1 (hereafter IIA between the European Parliament and the ECB).

[88] Memorandum of Understanding between the Council of the European Union and the European Central Bank on the cooperation on procedures related to the Single Supervisory Mechanism (SSM) [2013] <https://www.ecb.europa.eu/ecb/legal/pdf/mou_between_eucouncil_ecb.pdf> accessed 9 February 2021 (hereafter MoU between the Council and the ECB).

[89] Fabian Amtenbrink and Menelaos Markakis, 'Towards a Meaningful Prudential Supervision Dialogue in the Euro Area? A Study of the Interaction between the European Parliament and the European Central Bank in the Single Supervisory Mechanism' (2019) 44 EL Rev 3, 11–12 (hereafter Amtenbrink and Markakis, 'Towards a Meaningful Prudential Supervision Dialogue in the Euro Area?').

[90] ibid 11. On the ECB and financial stability, see chapter 5 by Agnieszka Smoleńska and Thomas Beukers, in this volume.

[91] ibid 12. See also the analysis by Phedon Nicolaides, 'Accountability of the ECB's Supervisory Activities (SSM): Evolving and Responsive' (2019) 26 MJ 136.

report on the SSM, the European Court of Auditors notes that 'the ECB has not yet developed a formal performance framework for the SSM'.[92] The SSM Supervisory Dashboard Pilot, which allows the ECB to track and assess the most important aspects of its supervisory activities and to monitor the effectiveness with which supervisory priorities are translated into practice, is only available to the Supervisory Board and to senior management.[93] Accordingly, Transparency International EU recommended that the ECB create a public version of this tool, which would allow the public to assess whether the ECB is achieving its objectives.[94]

The SSM Regulation, read together with the IIA between the European Parliament and the ECB and the MoU with the Council, introduces a relatively detailed framework on the provision of information to and institutional contacts with the EU institutions. The ECB must submit a report on the execution of its tasks to the European Parliament, the Council, the Commission, and the Eurogroup.[95] Yet, instead of the ECB President, it is the Chair of the Supervisory Board, who is not a member of the Governing Council (that is, the formal decision-making body in the SSM), that presents that report in public to the European Parliament, and to the Eurogroup in the presence of representatives from participating Member States whose currency is not the euro[96]—a structure which has been described in the literature as 'the Eurogroup+'.[97] The IIA sets out in detail the contents of this report and requires that it be made available to the European Parliament in advance of the hearing.[98]

The Chair of the Supervisory Board may, at the request of the Eurogroup, be heard on the execution of the ECB's supervisory tasks.[99] The information exchanged during such hearings and exchanges of views shall be confidential.[100] Furthermore, at the request of the European Parliament, the Chair of the Supervisory Board must participate in a hearing on the execution of the ECB's supervisory tasks by the competent committee of the European Parliament (namely, the ECON Committee).[101] The ECB shall reply orally or in writing to questions put to it by the European Parliament or the Eurogroup.[102] Upon request, the Chair of the Supervisory Board shall hold confidential oral discussions behind closed doors with the Chair and Vice-Chairs of Parliament's competent committee concerning its supervisory tasks when such

[92] European Court of Auditors, 'Single Supervisory Mechanism—Good Start but Further Improvements Needed' (2016) Special Report No 29/2016, 46 <https://www.eca.europa.eu/Lists/ECADocuments/SR16_29/SR_SSM_EN.pdf> accessed 17 March 2021.

[93] ibid.

[94] Benjamin Braun, 'Two Sides of the Same Coin? Independence and Accountability of the European Central Bank' (Transparency International EU, 2017) 7, 48 <https://transparency.eu/wp-content/uploads/2017/03/TI-EU_ECB_Report_DIGITAL.pdf> accessed 9 February 2021.

[95] SSM Regulation (n 76) Art 20(2).

[96] ibid Art 20(3).

[97] Jean-Victor Louis, 'Democracy and the European Central Bank. Some Comments on Independence and Accountability' in Gregorio Garzón Clariana (ed), *Democracy in the New Economic Governance of the European Union* (Marcial Pons 2015) 142–43.

[98] IIA between the European Parliament and the ECB (n 87) s I.1.

[99] SSM Regulation (n 76) Art 20(4).

[100] MoU between the Council and the ECB (n 88) s I.2.(3).

[101] SSM Regulation (n 76) Art 20(5). See further the IIA between the European Parliament and the ECB (n 87) s I.2.

[102] SSM Regulation (n 76) Art 20(6). See further the IIA between the European Parliament and the ECB (n 87) s I.3.

discussions are required for the exercise of Parliament's powers under the TFEU.[103] The hearings, exchanges of views, and confidential meetings with the European Parliament and the 'Eurogroup+' shall cover all aspects of the activity and functioning of the SSM.[104] No minutes or any other recording of the confidential meetings shall be taken.[105] Furthermore, the ECB shall cooperate sincerely with any investigations by the European Parliament, subject to the TFEU.[106] The IIA complements the SSM Regulation by granting additional information and consultation rights to the European Parliament concerning the records of the proceedings of the Supervisory Board, the principles and kinds of indicators or information used in developing acts and policy recommendations, informal exchanges of views on draft acts, and so on.[107]

A first assessment of the banking supervision dialogue between the European Parliament and the ECB has indicated that 'overall the MEPs raise informed questions that show an understanding of the relevant issues'.[108] At the same time, the queries are not necessarily geared towards evaluating the performance of the ECB as a banking supervisor, as it has been further observed that 'the MEPs do not (explicitly) ask questions on the achievement of the SSM's objectives, but rather focus on the overall performance of the banking sector or the financial health of individual banks'.[109] Moreover, it should be noted that in the past MEPs asked plenty of questions that concerned issues that clearly fall outside the remit of the SSM, questions that touch upon cross-cutting issues that do not exclusively fall within the remit of one institution, agency, or body (eg concerning both the SSM and the SRM), or questions that concern the exercise of the duties of authorities located at different levels of this system of governance (eg the Supervisory Board and the national competent authorities).[110] This can be partly explained by the complex division of tasks between and across the EU and national authorities acting in this area. Yet, as has been noted elsewhere, the appropriate forum for discussing such cross-cutting issues is unclear.[111]

Interestingly, in comparison to the monetary policy function of the ECB, somewhat more potent accountability instruments seem to be available to its principals to hold the ECB to account for the execution of its SSM-related tasks. This conclusion can first and foremost be drawn with reference to the nature of the enabling statute of the SSM, which constitutes secondary Union law and thus does not require a Treaty

[103] SSM Regulation (n 76) Art 20(8).

[104] IIA between the European Parliament and the ECB (n 87) s I.2; MoU between the Council and the ECB (n 88) s I.2.(4).

[105] IIA between the European Parliament and the ECB (n 87) s I.2.

[106] SSM Regulation (n 76) Art 20(9). See further the IIA between the European Parliament and the ECB (n 87) s III.

[107] See further Markakis, *Accountability in the Economic and Monetary Union* (n 31) 158.

[108] Amtenbrink and Markakis, 'Towards a Meaningful Prudential Supervision Dialogue in the Euro Area?' (n 88) 20. On these interactions, see also the study by Adina Maricut-Akbik, 'Contesting the European Central Bank in Banking Supervision: Accountability in Practice at the European Parliament' (2020) 58 JCMS 1199.

[109] Amtenbrink and Markakis, 'Towards a Meaningful Prudential Supervision Dialogue in the Euro Area?' (n 88) 21.

[110] ibid 18–19.

[111] ibid 19, where it is also argued that 'interparliamentary committee meetings taking place at the EP ... may provide a forum for discussion of such cross-cutting issues'.

revision in order to be amended.[112] If the Council is displeased with the functioning of the SSM or the role of the ECB therein, it may amend, replace, or even repeal the SSM Regulation, pursuant to Article 127(6) TFEU, acting by means of Regulations in accordance with a special legislative procedure and after consulting the European Parliament and the ECB. It may use this power to impose additional obligations on the ECB and/or to amend the accountability framework applicable to its activities in the SSM. Yet, the Member States must be unanimous in the Council, including the Member States which are not (yet) participating in the Banking Union for that matter. Moreover, by providing the European Parliament merely with the right to be consulted in the legislative procedure, Article 127(6) TFEU is a relic from the dark ages of European parliamentarianism, when the consultation procedure was the main *modus operandi* in supranational law-making.[113] It has been observed elsewhere that it is possible, in the absence of opposition by national parliaments, for the European Council to decide to switch to an ordinary legislative procedure, an option that should be seriously considered.[114]

The role of the European Parliament in the appointment and dismissal of the Chair and Vice-Chair of the Supervisory Board is considerably greater than its role in the appointment of the members of the ECB's Executive Board. The European Parliament's approval is required prior to the appointment of the Chair and the Vice-Chair of the Supervisory Board by the Council by means of an implementing decision.[115] The IIA between the European Parliament and the ECB lays down in detail the procedure to be followed for their appointment.[116] By contrast, the European Parliament is merely consulted on the appointment of the ECB Executive Board members. These are appointed by the European Council, on a recommendation from the Council, after it has consulted the European Parliament and the Governing Council of the ECB.[117]

The European Parliament's approval is further required for the removal of the Chair and Vice-Chair of the Supervisory Board from office.[118] If the Chair of the Supervisory Board no longer fulfils the conditions required for the performance of her/his duties or has been guilty of serious misconduct, the Council may, following a proposal by the ECB, which has been approved by the European Parliament, adopt an implementing decision to remove her/him from office.[119] The same procedure is followed to remove the Vice-Chair from office (who is chosen from among the Executive Board members), following her/his compulsory retirement as a member of the Executive Board.[120] The involvement of the European Parliament in the procedure for removing the Chair or Vice-Chair of the Supervisory Board from office is important from an

[112] This is of course with the exception of those provisions from the ECSB and ECB Statute which can be amended without a Treaty revision.

[113] Amtenbrink and Markakis, 'Towards a Meaningful Prudential Supervision Dialogue in the Euro Area?' (n 88) 22. On the development of the legislative role of the European Parliament, see Fabian Amtenbrink and Hans Vedder, *European Union Law: A Textbook* (Eleven Publishing 2021) 590 ff.

[114] Markakis, *Accountability in the Economic and Monetary Union* (n 31) 327.

[115] SSM Regulation (n 76) Art 26(3).

[116] IIA between the European Parliament and the ECB (n 87) s II.

[117] Art 283(2) second subpara TFEU.

[118] SSM Regulation (n 76) Art 26(4).

[119] ibid first subpara.

[120] ibid second subpara.

accountability standpoint. The fact that the dismissal procedure relies on a proposal from the ECB does not devalue it as an accountability mechanism. In this context, it is crucial that the European Parliament or the Council may inform the ECB that it considers the conditions for the removal of the Chair or Vice-Chair from office to be fulfilled, to which the ECB shall respond in writing.[121] By comparison, if a member of the Executive Board no longer fulfils the conditions required for the performance of her/his duties or if s/he has been guilty of serious misconduct, the Court of Justice may, on application by the Governing Council or the Executive Board, compulsorily retire her/him.[122] It should be stressed that the procedure followed for the appointment or removal from office of the Executive Board members is also important for the governance of the SSM, as they are also members of the Governing Council,[123] which formally adopts (or objects to) the draft decisions prepared by the Supervisory Board.[124] This perforce limits the extent to which the European Parliament and Council could influence the composition of the SSM's decision-making bodies.[125] In this connection, the European Parliament has asked that its role in the appointment of the Executive Board members be enhanced, by requiring that it consents to the recommendations of the Council.[126]

A further novelty in the SSM Regulation is that Article 21 lays down a framework for scrutiny by national parliaments. Their involvement is justified on grounds of the potential impact that supervisory measures may have on public finances, credit institutions, their customers and employees, and the markets in the participating Member States.[127] More specifically, it is provided that the ECB is obliged to simultaneously forward its annual report directly to the national parliaments of the participating Member States. These may address to the ECB their reasoned observations on that report.[128] They may further submit observations or questions to the ECB in respect of its tasks under the SSM Regulation.[129] Moreover, they may invite the Chair or a member of the Supervisory Board to participate in an exchange of views in relation to the supervision of credit institutions in that Member State together with a representative of the national competent authority.[130] It is rightly observed that there is no

[121] ibid third subpara; IIA between the European Parliament and the ECB (n 87) s II; MoU between the Council and the ECB (n 88) s II.(6).

[122] ECSB and ECB Statute (n 8) Art 11.4.

[123] Art 283(1) TFEU.

[124] SSM Regulation (n 76) Art 26(8).

[125] Markakis, *Accountability in the Economic and Monetary Union* (n 31) 166–67.

[126] Committee on Constitutional Affairs, 'Report on Constitutional Problems of a Multitier Governance in the European Union' (2012/2078(INI)), 15 November 2013, para 75 <https://www.europarl.europa.eu/doceo/document/A-7-2013-0372_EN.html> accessed 10 February 2021.

[127] SSM Regulation (n 76) preamble recital 56.

[128] ibid Art 21(1).

[129] ibid Art 21(2).

[130] ibid Art 21(3). See Diane Fromage and Renato Ibrido, 'Accountability and Democratic Oversight in the European Banking Union' in Gianni Lo Schiavo (ed), *The European Banking Union and the Role of Law* (Edward Elgar Publishing 2019) 81, who note that: 'More transparency and publicity on this dialogue between national parliaments and the ECB would in any case be desirable as they are, at present, barely mentioned in the annual reports.' The most recent annual reports underscore this observation: European Central Bank, 'ECB Annual Report on Supervisory Activities 2019' (19 March 2020) <https://www.bankingsupervision.europa.eu/press/publications/annual-report/html/ssm.ar2019~4851adc406.en.html>

legal framework for scrutiny by national parliaments in the area of monetary policy.[131] In fact, as the EU has the exclusive competence for monetary policy for euro area countries, the directly democratically legitimized European Parliament should be the prime forum for the scrutiny of the ECB's monetary policy. Nevertheless, in practice, the ECB President has visited from time to time a number of national parliaments in order to explain the ECB's monetary policy.[132] Until now, these practical arrangements are not formalized in the Treaties and certainly do not pose an obligation for the ECB.

C. The ECB and the COVID-19 pandemic

Next to the European financial and sovereign debt crisis and the emergence of two main pillars of the Banking Union, the ECB has most recently also played an important role in addressing the economic consequences of the COVID-19 pandemic.[133] The ECB has mainly acted in its capacity as monetary policy authority, whilst in the field of banking supervision it has used the flexibility that is provided within the existing rules.[134] The ECB's role as crisis manager was broadened, thereby putting additional strain on the already precarious accountability and transparency framework. In fact, the latter has remained (by and large) unaltered.

In response to the COVID-19 crisis, the ECB has scaled up its use of unconventional monetary policy instruments, by expanding existing asset purchase programmes or adopting new ones. It has further used other monetary policy tools, such as conducting additional longer-term refinancing operations (LTROs) and applying more favourable terms to targeted longer-term refinancing operations (TLTROs).[135]

accessed 13 February 2021; European Central Bank, 'ECB Annual Report on Supervisory Activities 2020' (23 March 2021) <https://www.bankingsupervision.europa.eu/press/publications/annual-report/html/ssm.ar2020~1a59f5757c.en.html> accessed 24 May 2022; European Central Bank, 'ECB Annual Report on Supervisory Activities 2021' (31 March 2022) <https://www.bankingsupervision.europa.eu/press/publications/annual-report/html/ssm.ar2021~52a7d32451.en.html> accessed 24 May 2022.

[131] Deirdre Curtin, 'Democratic Accountability of EU Executive Power: A Reform Agenda for Parliaments' in Federico Fabbrini, Ernst Hirsch Ballin, and Han Somsen (eds), *What Form of Government for the European Union and the Eurozone?* (Hart Publishing 2015) 185. See also Diane Fromage, 'Guaranteeing the ECB's Democratic Accountability in the Post-Banking Union Era: An Ever More Difficult Task?' (2019) 26 MJ 48, 50, 61, who argues that national parliaments should have a role in the field of monetary policy, too, in light of the consequences of the ECB's actions for financial stability in the Member States, in order to increase its democratic legitimacy.

[132] See further Davor Jančić, 'Accountability of the European Central Bank in a Deepening Economic and Monetary Union' in Davor Jančić (ed), *National Parliaments after the Lisbon Treaty and the Euro Crisis: Resilience or Resignation?* (OUP 2017) 150–54; Tobias Tesche, 'Instrumentalizing EMU's Democratic Deficit: The ECB's Unconventional Accountability Measures During the Eurozone Crisis' (2018) 41 Journal of European Integration 447, 454–58.

[133] See generally Paul Dermine and Menelaos Markakis, 'EU Economic Governance and the COVID-19 Crisis: Between Path-Dependency and Paradigmatic Shift' (2020) 6 International Journal of Public Law and Policy 326 (hereafter Dermine and Markakis, 'EU Economic Governance and the COVID-19 Crisis').

[134] It should be noted that there have further been targeted changes to the prudential regulatory framework. See Regulation (EU) 2020/873 of the European Parliament and of the Council of 24 June 2020 amending Regulations (EU) No 575/2013 and (EU) 2019/876 as regards certain adjustments in response to the COVID-19 pandemic [2020] OJ L204/4.

[135] European Central Bank, 'Monetary Policy Decisions' (12 March 2020) <https://www.ecb.europa.eu/press/pr/date/2020/html/ecb.mp200312~8d3aec3ff2.en.html> accessed 17 June 2020.

More specifically, the ECB has expanded its asset purchases, ensuring a strong contribution from the private sector purchase programmes, by adding a temporary envelope of additional net asset purchases of €120 billion, in order to create favourable financing conditions for the real economy.[136] The ECB also announced a new temporary asset purchase programme of private and public sector securities to counter the serious risks to the monetary policy transmission mechanism and the outlook for the euro area.[137] The Pandemic Emergency Purchase Programme (PEPP) had an initial overall envelope of €750 billion.[138] Purchases would be conducted until the end of 2020 and would include all the asset categories eligible under the existing Asset Purchase Programme (APP). The PEPP differs from the APP in various important respects.[139] Moreover, purchases under the PEPP are envisaged to be conducted in a flexible manner.[140] The ECB has already increased the envelope for the PEPP twice, first to a total of €1.35 trillion[141] and thereafter to €1.85 trillion.[142] It has also extended the horizon for net purchases to end of March 2022. Moreover, the maturing principal payments from securities purchased under the PEPP will be reinvested until at least the end of 2024 and, in any case, the future roll-off of the PEPP portfolio will be managed to avoid interference with the appropriate monetary policy stance.

The ECB further adopted a package of temporary collateral easing measures to facilitate the availability of eligible collateral for Eurosystem counterparties to participate in liquidity providing operations.[143] The package is complementary to other ECB measures such as LTROs and the PEPP. They collectively support the provision of bank lending especially by easing the conditions at which credit claims are accepted as collateral. Furthermore, the ECB announced additional LTROs, called pandemic emergency longer-term refinancing operations (PELTROs).[144] These operations are

[136] ibid.

[137] European Central Bank, 'ECB Announces €750 Billion Pandemic Emergency Purchase Programme (PEPP)' (18 March 2020) <https://www.ecb.europa.eu/press/pr/date/2020/html/ecb.pr200318_1~3949d6f266.en.html> accessed 17 June 2020 (hereafter European Central Bank, 'ECB Announces €750 Billion Pandemic Emergency Purchase Programme (PEPP)').

[138] See further chapter 3 by Klaus Tuori, in this volume.

[139] See extensively Dermine and Markakis, 'EU Economic Governance and the COVID-19 Crisis' (n 133) 328–29.

[140] European Central Bank, 'ECB Announces €750 Billion Pandemic Emergency Purchase Programme (PEPP)' (n 137). See further Decision (EU) 2020/440 of the European Central Bank of 24 March 2020 on a temporary pandemic emergency purchase programme (ECB/2020/17) [2020] OJ L91/1.

[141] European Central Bank, 'Monetary Policy Decisions' (4 June 2020) <https://www.ecb.europa.eu/press/pr/date/2020/html/ecb.mp200604~a307d3429c.en.html> accessed 8 January 2021.

[142] European Central Bank, 'Monetary Policy Decisions' (10 December 2020) <https://www.ecb.europa.eu/press/pr/date/2020/html/ecb.mp201210~8c2778b843.en.html> accessed 8 January 2021.

[143] European Central Bank, 'ECB Announces Package of Temporary Collateral Easing Measures' (7 April 2020) <https://www.ecb.europa.eu/press/pr/date/2020/html/ecb.pr200407~2472a8ccda.en.html> accessed 8 January 2021. See also chapter 4 by Jens van 't Klooster, in this volume. The ECB has decided to gradually phase out this package of pandemic collateral easing measures: European Central Bank, 'ECB Announces Timeline to Gradually Phase Out Temporary Pandemic Collateral Easing Measures' (24 March 2022) <https://www.ecb.europa.eu/press/pr/date/2022/html/ecb.pr220324~8b7f2ff5ea.en.html> accessed 24 May 2022.

[144] European Central Bank, 'ECB Announces New Pandemic Emergency Longer-Term Refinancing Operations' (30 April 2020) <https://www.ecb.europa.eu/press/pr/date/2020/html/ecb.pr200430_1~477f400e39.en.html> accessed 8 January 2021.

aimed at supporting liquidity conditions in the euro area financial system and contribute to preserving the smooth functioning of money markets by providing an effective liquidity backstop.[145]

What follows from this summary of the main monetary policy measures aimed at dealing with the economic externalities of the pandemic is that, similarly to what has been observed for the European financial and sovereign debt crisis, the ECB again takes on a very active role in crisis management. However, the accountability framework applicable to its monetary policy activities has remained the same, as it is by-and-large hardwired into the EU Treaties. Some recent small improvements can be noted on the transparency front, albeit these are not necessarily linked to the pandemic. The ECB has published its key findings from the ECB Listens Portal, which was launched as part of the framework for its strategy review, encouraging the general public to express their views on a range of issues.[146] It has further announced that it will begin publishing aggregate results of the Survey of Monetary Analysts, which collects information on market participants' expectations about the future evolution of key monetary policy parameters, financial market variables, and the economy.[147] These are by no means cosmetic changes, but it is argued here that they do not (yet) match the very important powers of the ECB, as these were outlined above.

IV. The ECB's Accountability at Twenty and Beyond

What becomes clear from the reflections in this contribution is that the legal and institutional framework of the ECB has evolved considerably. This is not so much the result of amendments to the relevant Treaty provisions. The legal framework of the ECB is, due to its quasi-constitutional embedding, relatively static in nature. Instead, this evolution is owed to the need to respond to the evolving economic landscape. It is largely the result of the ECB's own understanding of its role and duties, notably during the European financial and sovereign debt crisis, as well as of its new tasks in the SSM.

This contribution argues that the legal and practical arrangements securing the democratic accountability of the ECB have been only partially adjusted to this new reality. The most notable changes concern the accountability and transparency arrangements for the supervisory tasks of the ECB in the SSM. Regarding its monetary policy function, the ECB finds itself, as a consequence of its role as crisis manager, in a rather precarious position when it comes to the public acceptance of its independent position in the Union legal order. It is further exposed to criticism regarding the democratic legitimacy of the powers it exercises. Indeed, considering the significant (re) distributive consequences of its actions, the existing legal and practical arrangements

145 ibid. See also European Central Bank, 'ECB Extends Pandemic Emergency Longer-Term Refinancing Operations' (10 December 2020) <https://www.ecb.europa.eu/press/pr/date/2020/html/ecb.pr201210~8acfa5026f.en.html> accessed 24 May 2022.

146 European Central Bank, 'Key Findings' <https://www.ecb.europa.eu/home/search/review/html/ecb.strategyreview002.en.html> accessed 16 February 2021.

147 European Central Bank, 'ECB to Publish Results of the Survey of Monetary Analysts' (8 February 2021) <https://www.ecb.europa.eu/press/pr/date/2021/html/ecb.pr210208~076431b103.en.html> accessed 16 February 2021.

pertaining to its monetary policy tasks offer little in terms of throughput legitimacy deriving from the accountability and transparency arrangements in its governance structures. At the same time, the (input) legitimacy that the ECB derives from its legal basis cannot cover the continued exercise of (an increased amount of) public power by this Union institution.

Venues thus need to be explored to strengthen all three dimensions of the legitimacy of the ECB, namely input, throughput, and output legitimacy. To be sure, increasing the democratic legitimacy of the ECB whilst not exposing monetary policy to undesirable political influence calls for a careful balancing exercise. Yet, this does not necessarily have to amount to a zero-sum game, as measures strengthening the democratic accountability of a central bank can under certain conditions also reinforce its independence. This is notably the case for any arrangements aimed at strengthening input legitimacy, that is 'the participatory quality of the process leading to laws and rules as ensured by the "majoritarian" institutions of electoral representation'.[148] Leaving aside the valid questions pertaining to the democratic quality of the Union's political institutions, an option that could be explored, in our opinion, is to give the directly or indirectly democratically legitimized Union political institutions a greater involvement in the determination of the monetary policy objectives of the ECB and in particular, albeit not limited to, the quantification of its primary objective, that is, price stability. This idea takes its inspiration from what can be observed for several central banking systems around the world, which provide for the participation of the government in the establishment of the (inflation-)targeting framework of the central bank either on a legal or on a voluntary basis.[149] One such well-known example is the Reserve Bank of New Zealand Act 1989, which effectively requires the New Zealand Minister of Finance and the Governor of the Reserve Bank of New Zealand to agree on monetary policy targets, setting out 'the operational objectives for carrying out the function of formulating monetary policy' and thus quantifying the Bank's statutory policy objective to achieve and maintain price stability over the medium term and to support maximum sustainable employment.[150] Another example is the Bank of Canada, whose framework features since the early 1990s a so-called inflation-control target that is jointly agreed between the Canadian government and the Bank of Canada for a five-year period.[151]

It is readily admitted that applying such an approach to the supranational ECB would be anything but straightforward given the current ECB legal framework provided by primary Union law, the asymmetric integration of monetary and fiscal policy

[148] Schmidt, 'Democracy and Legitimacy in the European Union Revisited' (n 2) 4, with reference to a definition provided by Fritz Scharpf, *Governing in Europe: Effective and Democratic?* (OUP 1999).

[149] See Amber Wadsworth, 'An International Comparison of Inflation-Targeting Frameworks' (2017) 80(8) Reserve Bank of New Zealand Bulletin 3 ff.

[150] Reserve Bank of New Zealand Act 1989, part 1, s 1A and part 2 s 8. See nowadays Reserve Bank of New Zealand (Replacement of Remit for Monetary Policy Committee) Order 2021 (2021/29). For details on the Remit and its predecessor, the Policy Targets Agreement, see Reserve Bank of New Zealand, 'Monetary Policy Framework' <https://www.rbnz.govt.nz/monetary-policy/about-monetary-policy/monetary-policy-framework> accessed 17 March 2021.

[151] See Bank of Canada, 'Joint Statement of the Government of Canada and the Bank of Canada on the Renewal of the Inflation-Control Target' (24 October 2016) <https://www.bankofcanada.ca/2016/10/renewal-of-the-inflation-control-target-2016/> accessed 17 March 2021.

in EMU, as well as the obvious absence of the European equivalent to a Minister of Finance representing the European executive government and an exclusive or at least shared competence for economic policy at the supranational level. In the light of the latter observation, it can be argued that such an agreement should be concluded between the European Parliament, the Council (in the composition of the governments of the euro area Member States), and the Governing Council of the ECB.[152] The involvement of the European Parliament is justified given its prominent role in the current accountability arrangements (namely the monetary dialogue) and the direct democratic legitimation it enjoys as a Union institution. The involvement of the Council would contribute to the democratic legitimation of the ECB, while at the same time also committing national governments to the monetary policy objective of the ECB, thereby recognizing that price developments and inflation are not only in the hands of the central banks.[153]

It is further readily admitted that the introduction of a formal framework into the primary Union law provisions on the ECB laying down a legal obligation to establish such an agreement could lead to substantial difficulties in practice. While the simplified Treaty revision procedure pursuant to Article 48(6) TEU could be utilized, the necessary amendments would still require unanimity in the European Council and the approval by all Member States in accordance with their constitutional requirements.[154] Whether the introduction of such a framework on a voluntary basis by means of an Interinstitutional Agreement between the European Parliament, the Council, and the ECB provides a viable alternative route depends on whether such an agreement would effectively be considered to compromise Article 127(2) TFEU, according to which one of the basic tasks to be carried out by the ESCB is to define and implement the monetary policy of the Union, and, moreover, Article 130 TFEU which prohibits the ECB from seeking or taking instructions from Union institutions when exercising the powers and carrying out the tasks and duties conferred upon it by the Treaties and the Statute.[155]

To be sure, it is not suggested that such an agreement would also cover details on when or how the ECB utilizes the monetary policy instruments at its disposal, *inter alia*, through open market and credit operations, such as in the context of an asset

[152] See already Amtenbrink, *The Democratic Accountability of Central Banks* (n 6) 365, where it is argued that the Council should be in the lead. Yet, given the central role that the European Parliament has acquired in the accountability of the ECB over the years, it should be included in this process on an equal footing.

[153] For an interesting proposal regarding the secondary objectives of the ECB, see most recently Stanislas Jourdan, 'The ECB Needs Political Guidance on Secondary Objectives' (*Positive Money Europe*, 26 April 2021) <https://www.positivemoney.eu/2021/04/ecb-guidance-secondary-objectives/> accessed 15 May 2021.

[154] This proposal is predicated on the assumption that such an amendment would only concern provisions in part 3 TFEU (n 20) relating to the internal policies and action of the Union, and that it would not increase the competences conferred on the Union in the Treaties.

[155] Article 295 TFEU, which allows for the conclusion of legally binding interinstitutional agreements between the European Parliament, the Council, and the Commission, could not be relied upon as a legal basis for such an agreement, as this provision does not refer to the ECB. On the legal status of interinstitutional agreements that do not have an explicit legal basis in primary Union law, see generally Jörg Monar, 'Interinstitutional Agreements: The Phenomenon and its New Dynamics after Maastricht' (1994) 31 CMLR 693. See also Deirdre Curtin, *Executive Power of the European Union: Law, Practices, and the Living Constitution* (OUP 2009) 233.

purchase programme. Put differently, the existence of such an agreement would not have increased the legitimacy of the ECB's unconventional monetary policy measures. More is thus needed to enhance the throughput legitimacy of the ECB, since, beyond the realm of expressing its disapproval (eg through a resolution on the ECB's annual report), the European Parliament is currently lacking any instruments to hold the ECB to account for its action. This could include, as argued above, an enhanced role for the European Parliament in the appointment of Executive Board members pursuant to Article 283(2) TFEU. Furthermore, in the field of the Banking Union, it could entail, as was explained above, a greater role for the European Parliament in adopting or amending legislation on the basis of Article 127(6) TFEU, by switching from a special to an ordinary legislative procedure.

Finally, while certainly not constituting a substitute for adequate input and throughput legitimacy, the ECB's output could also contribute to its legitimacy, and some would argue that this is already currently the case. In fact, in the eyes of some groups of citizens the significant role that the ECB has played as a crisis manager in the past decade, as well as in the ongoing COVID-19 pandemic, has produced positive results in terms of the stability of the euro area as a whole and of its Member States, justifying the ECB's policy stance. Yet, the very measures that have warranted these results and in particular the unconventional monetary policy of the ECB but also its involvement in the negotiation and monitoring of painful austerity measures in certain Member States,[156] have alienated other groups of citizens that consider the ECB's interventions as lying beyond its policy mandate and perhaps illegitimate. As such, it can be noted that output legitimacy certainly lies in the eye of the beholder.[157]

For the future, one venue to increase the output legitimacy of the ECB in the eyes of the citizens in a less abstract and more tangible way could be to put more emphasis on the role that the ECB can play in tackling major societal challenges, such as by contributing to environmental and social sustainability. With regard to the former, it has been argued that, in light of both its primary and secondary objectives, the ECB is under a legal obligation to partake in the fight against climate change, and that Article 11 TFEU requires that environmental protection requirements be integrated into the definition and implementation of the ECB's actions.[158] Various ways in which the ECB can contribute to the fight against climate change have been highlighted.[159] It was

[156] See also chapter 9 by Florin Coman-Kund, in this volume.

[157] This is something that has, more generally, already been observed by Carol Harlow, 'The Limping Legitimacy of EU Lawmaking: A Barrier to Integration' (2016) 1 European Papers 29, 54.

[158] Frank Elderson, 'Greening Monetary Policy' (*The ECB Blog*, 13 February 2021) <https://www.ecb.europa.eu/press/blog/date/2021/html/ecb.blog210213~7c26af0606.en.html> accessed 6 March 2021. On Art 11 TFEU, see also Javier Solana, 'The Power of the Eurosystem to Promote Environmental Protection' (2019) 30 EBLR 547.

[159] See, eg, Dirk Schoenmaker, 'Greening Monetary Policy' (2019) Bruegel Working Paper Issue No 2 <https://www.bruegel.org/wp-content/uploads/2019/02/Greening-monetary-policy.pdf> accessed 6 March 2021; Christine Lagarde, 'Climate Change and Central Banking' (Speech at the ILF conference on Green Banking and Green Central Banking, Frankfurt am Main, 25 January 2021) <https://www.ecb.europa.eu/press/key/date/2021/html/ecb.sp210125~f87e826ca5.en.html> accessed 19 March 2021; Nathan de Arriba-Sellier, 'Turning Gold into Green: Green Finance in the Mandate of European Financial Supervision' (2021) 58 CMLR 1097.

thus no coincidence that both the 2020 ESCB Legal Conference[160] and the 2021 ECB Strategy Review Legal Roundtable[161] (which was part of its monetary policy strategy review) focused on the ECB's mandate and climate change, and it did not come as a surprise that when the ECB in early 2021 finally announced its new monetary policy strategy it included a 'Detailed roadmap of climate change-related actions'.[162] Whilst not denying the fact that the ECB could (and indeed *should*) make an indispensable contribution to tackling climate change, this could not compensate for existing shortcomings of the accountability framework observed throughout this contribution. In fact, it would broaden the areas of activities for which the accountability and transparency of the ECB must be ensured.

[160] See Iñigo Arruga Oleaga, 'Introduction to the Panel on the EU Taxonomy and Action Plan on Sustainable Finance: What Uses for the ESCB?' in European Central Bank, 'ESCB Legal Conference 2020' (2021) (hereafter European Central Bank, 'ESCB Legal Conference 2020'); Willem Bovenschen and René Lieshout, 'EU Taxonomy, Action Plan & Supervisory Developments on Sustainable Finance: What Uses May These Have for the E(S)CB?' in European Central Bank, 'ESCB Legal Conference 2020' (n 160); György Várhelyi, 'EU Taxonomy and the Monetary Policy Prism' in European Central Bank, 'ESCB Legal Conference 2020' (n 160).

[161] Held on 23 February 2021.

[162] See European Central Bank, 'ECB's Governing Council Approves its New Monetary Policy Strategy' (8 June 2021) <https://www.ecb.europa.eu/press/pr/date/2021/html/ecb.pr210708~dc78cc4b0d.en.html> accessed 28 July 2021; European Central Bank, 'ECB Presents Action Plan to Include Climate Change Considerations in Its Monetary Policy Strategy' (8 June 2021) <https://www.ecb.europa.eu/press/pr/date/2021/html/ecb.pr210708_1~f104919225.en.html> accessed 28 July 2021.

12

The ECB and the Court of Justice

Old Toolbox, New Problems

Takis Tridimas

I. Introduction

In recent years, litigation involving the European Central Bank (ECB) has increased exponentially. This is the result of two factors: the leading role that the ECB has taken in combating the euro area crisis, not least through the use of non-standard monetary policy measures,[1] and the establishment of the Banking Union which has elevated it to the principal supervisor of euro area credit institutions.[2] There is no doubt that, as a result of the euro area crisis, the powers, remit, and importance of the ECB have been considerably strengthened. This is in part owing to the ECB's institutional posture. It showed leadership and took decisive action at critical times which, in turn, increased its influence and, ultimately, promoted the output legitimacy of the Union. More generally, the close relation between economic and monetary policy and the shift of emphasis necessitated by the euro area crisis from price stability to the stability of the financial system expanded the ECB's influence on matters of economic policy.[3]

So far, the issues raised before the Court of Justice of the European Union (CJEU) fall within the realm of constitutional and administrative law and pertain to the distinction between monetary policy and economic policy, prudential supervision, the ECB's independence, and, to a lesser extent, its involvement in conditionality programmes.[4] In the disputes that have arisen, one finds the usual fault lines that characterize litigation before the CJEU, namely the division of powers between the EU and the Member States, the scope of institutional powers, and the rights of individuals. There are also novel issues arising from composite decision-making processes and greater engagement of the ECB with national law, both being features of Banking Union. This chapter examines selectively aspects of the judicial accountability of the ECB by focusing on the areas of conflict that have reached the CJEU in the last ten years and the wider tension points of judicial intervention pertaining to the scope and mechanisms of review. It starts by considering an issue of principle, namely, whether

[1] On this, see chapter 2 by Vestert Borger and chapter 3 by Klaus Tuori, in this volume.

[2] See generally on the ECB's role in the Banking Union: chapter 7 by Kern Alexander, in this volume.

[3] On financial stability and the ECB, see chapter 5 by Agnieszka Smoleńska and Thomas Beukers, in this volume.

[4] See Joined Cases C-597/18 P, C-598/18 P, C-603/18 P, and C-604/18 P *Council v Chrysostomides and Others* [2020] EU:C:2020:1028 (hereafter *Chrysostomides*).

Takis Tridimas, *The ECB and the Court of Justice* In: *The New European Central Bank*. Edited by: Thomas Beukers, Diane Fromage, and Giorgio Monti, Oxford University Press. © Takis Tridimas 2022. DOI: 10.1093/oso/9780198871231.003.0012

the ECB as a central bank should be subject to judicial control.[5] It then focuses on the distinction between economic and monetary policy and the role of proportionality. It continues by exploring the standard of review and the application of process requirements by the CJEU. It then looks at the new litigation landscape of prudential supervision focusing on composite procedures, the application of national law by the ECB, and litigation on the imposition of fines. The assessment of these developments is germane to the central theme of this volume. Some twenty years after its establishment, both the normative context within which the ECB operates and the functions it is called upon to perform in practice have changed substantially. Has the judicial accountability of the ECB kept pace with these developments? How has the CJEU reacted to the new ECB? Also, to what extent can it be said that the CJEU has itself contributed to the transformation of ECB's role? After all, the Court has an established track record as the initiator of constitutional change. The study of the case law reveals a dialectic interaction where the judiciary both generates, and reacts to, constitutional reform.

The judicial accountability of the ECB has to be seen in the wider context of the colonization of economic governance and financial regulation by EU law, a tectonic shift that has increased the involvement of the CJEU in those areas. An innovation of EU law, particularly prominent in post-crisis developments, is that it has elevated matters of economic policy to higher ranking legal doctrines adding a new dimension to constitution law which has traditionally stayed away from such matters.[6] National constitutions, as developed in western democracies in the nineteenth and the twentieth centuries, asserted parliamentary supremacy over public expenditure and acknowledged the interaction between the state and the economy but did not commit to rules of fiscal discipline. Although the EMU model introduced by the Maastricht Treaty firmly signalled a change of direction, it was the euro area crisis, and the normative reforms promoted thereby, that truly brought home the constraining effect of EU economic governance.[7] The judicialization of economic policy and financial regulation have to be seen in the light of these developments. Even where litigation does not directly target the ECB, court rulings may reflectively impact on its powers or affect the regulatory framework within which it operates. This is the case, for example, when the Court is called upon to determine the powers of national authorities in banking supervision,[8] the definition of the single currency,[9] or the European Banking

[5] For a discussion of the relationship between central bank independence and judicial control, see chapter 10 by Alexander Thiele, in this volume.

[6] See the analysis of George Gerapetritis, *New Economic Constitutionalism in Europe* (Hart Publishing 2019).

[7] See Thomas Beukers and Marijn van der Sluis, 'The variable geometry of the Euro-crisis: a look at the non-euro area member states' (2015) EUI Law Working Paper No 2015/33 <https://papers.ssrn.com/sol3/papers.cfm?abstract_id=2616717> accessed 1 December 2021 and chapter 16 by Marijn van der Sluis, in this volume.

[8] See Case C-52/17 *VTB Bank (Austria) AG v Finanzmarktaufsichtsbehörde* [2018] EU:C:2018:648 (hereafter *VTB Bank*).

[9] See Joined Cases C-422/19 and C-423/19 *Dietrich and Häring v Hessischer Rundfunk* [2021] EU:C:2021:63 (hereafter *Dietrich*).

Authority (EBA)'s power to issue recommendations or guidelines and their legal effects.[10]

Unsurprisingly, in the overwhelming majority of cases, the ECB is a defendant. Under Article 263(3) of the Treaty on the Functioning of the European Union (TFEU), the ECB is a prerogatives-based applicant in actions for annulment but, so far, it has not availed itself of that provision. It is however interesting to see how the ECB perceives its position as a contributor to the legal landscape by considering its behaviour as an intervener. Notably, in the field of economic governance, some Member States appear to take an active interest and intervene in cases where it is not apparent that they are affected more than other Member States.[11] The ECB has followed a measured intervention policy. Although, as expected, it has submitted observations in preliminary references pertaining to the validity of its acts or directly affecting its areas of responsibility,[12] it has been conspicuously absent in key cases concerning financial governance, wisely seeking to stay out of the broader political game.[13] There is another notable aspect of interventions. In the cases where judicial review against acts of the ECB was successful, the Commission had not intervened in favour of the ECB.[14] This is perhaps a sign that the Commission did not share the Bank's interpretation of the law.

The CJEU takes the independence of the ECB seriously. In *Rimšēvičs*[15] it held that, although the decision to dismiss a Governor of a euro area central bank from office is a national act, Article 14.2 of the European System of Central Banks (ESCB) Statute vests the CJEU with jurisdiction to annul it. The novelty of *Rimšēvičs* lies in that the Court of Justice annulled a national measure. This challenges the established model of judicial protection which allocates jurisdiction between the CJEU and the national courts on the basis of the EU or national authorship of a measure. The effectiveness-driven rationale of the judgment contrasts with the orthodoxy of the Advocate General's approach. *Rimšēvičs* is bold. Although its export value may be limited, it is indicative of a trajectory of increasing hybridity where traditional boundaries between EU and national action as separate expressions of *pouvoir public* break down. Although a detailed analysis of *Rimšēvičs* is beyond the scope of this chapter,[16] some examples of hybridity and their unsettling effects will be discussed below.

[10] See Case C-501/18 *BT v Balgarska Narodna Banka* [2021] EU:C:2021:249 (hereafter *Balgarska Narodna Banka*); Case C-911/19 *Fédération bancaire française (FBF) v Autorité de contrôle prudentiel et de résolution (ACPR)* [2021] EU:C:2021:599.

[11] This applies to Finland, which intervened on issues of principle in *Chrysostomides* (n 4), and Case T-758/16 *Credit Agricole SA v ECB* [2018] EU:T:2018:472 (hereafter *Credit Agricole SA*).

[12] See, eg, Case C-219/17 *Berlusconi and Finanziaria d'investimento Fininvest SpA v Banca d'Italia and Istituto per la Vigilanza Sulle Assicurazioni (IVASS)* [2018] EU:C:2018:1023 (hereafter *Berlusconi and Fininvest*); *Dietrich* (n 9); *VTB Bank* (n 8).

[13] Thus, the ECB did not intervene in the excessive deficit case: see Case C-27/04 *Commission v Council* [2004] EU:C:2004:436 or Case C-370/12 *Pringle v Ireland and Others* [2012] EU:C:2012:756 (hereafter *Pringle*). Also, it did not intervene in *Balgarska Narodna Banka* (n 10) (pertaining to depositor rights).

[14] See Case T-496/11 *UK v European Central Bank* [2015] EU:T:2015:133 (*location policy framework case*) (hereafter *UK v ECB (location policy framework case)*); *Credit Agricole SA* (n 11).

[15] Joined Cases C-202/18 and C-238/18 *Rimšēvičs and European Central Bank v Latvia* [2019] EU:C:2019:139 (hereafter *Rimšēvičs*).

[16] See Takis Tridimas and Luigi Lonardo, 'When Can a National Measure Be Annulled by the ECJ?' (2020) 45 EL Rev 732 (hereafter Tridimas and Lonardo, 'When Can a National Measure Be Annulled by the ECJ?').

II. Is there a Role for the CJEU?

Economic and monetary policy have traditionally been outside the realm of the judiciary. They are *par excellence* closely related to the business of government where accountability is pursued through parliamentary control. In relation to monetary policy, in particular, there are several reasons which countenance against a strong involvement of courts. Its macro character as a policy that affects public finances and the economy as a whole, the multiplicity of interests involved, the specialist and technical nature of the area, and the quest for central bank independence caution against close judicial control. Nonetheless, none of those reasons dictates immunity. They may convincingly inform the limits of judicial review but do not deny its existence. The fundamental underpinnings of judicial review, namely the need to correct errors, ensure that decision-makers stick to their mandate, and that public power is legitimate, also apply in relation to central banks. There is no guarantee that, in a specific time, a central bank may not be dominated by a strong purist economic ideology[17] or undue rigidity in its evaluations, or an over-jealous understanding of its own independence. Judicial review is an attribute of the rule of law and the risks of under-enforcement, that is, granting a central bank immunity or exercising too much deference to its decisions by exempting it, for example, from the requirement to give reasons, are as high, if not higher, than those of over-enforcement. There are also specific reasons which make judicial accountability necessary in the field of EU law.[18] The EU is an organization of limited competence and it is therefore necessary to ensure that 'federal' institutions, including the ECB, do not encroach on the powers of the Member States. Also, other forms of accountability, such as parliamentary control either at the national or the EU level, remain subdued. The EU integration project is law bound and rights defined. It would be an aberration if a pivotal institution were exempted from the accountability equation. As a matter of positive law, the founding Treaties do not immunize the ECB from judicial control. It is subject to the principle of conferred powers,[19] the Charter

[17] Jon Elster, 'Constitutional Courts and Central Banks: Suicide Prevention or Suicide Pact?' (1994) 3 East European Constitutional Review 66, 69.

[18] For the judicial accountability of the ECB, see among others, Chiara Zilioli and Karl-Philipp Wojcik (eds), *Judicial Review in the European Banking Union* (Edward Elgar Publishing 2021) (hereafter Zilioli and Wojcik, *Judicial Review in the European Banking Union*); Menelaos Markakis, *Accountability in the Economic and Monetary Union. Foundations, Policy and Governance* (OUP 2020) (hereafter Markakis, *Accountability*); Manuel López Escudero, 'Le contrôle juridictionnel de la Cour de justice dans la domaine de l'union bancaire' (2020) 56 Cahiers De droit Européen 549. See further Claire Kilpatrick, 'On the Rule of Law and Economic Emergency: The Degradation of Basic Legal Values in Europe's Bailouts' (2015) 35 OJLS 325; Annamaria Viterbo, 'Legal and Accountability Issues Arising from the ECB's Conditionality' (2016) 1 European Papers 501; Christian Joerges and Maria Weimer, 'A Crisis of Executive Managerialism in the EU: No Alternatives?' (2012) Maastricht Faculty of Law Working Paper No 2012-7, 20 <https://papers.ssrn.com/sol3/papers.cfm?abstract_id=2190362 > accessed 1 December 2021; Michael Ioannidis, 'Europe's New Transformations: How the EU Economic Constitution Changed During the Eurozone Crisis' (2016) 53 CML Rev 1237, 1245–46; Federico Fabbrini, 'The Euro-Crisis and the Courts: Judicial Review and the Political Process in Comparative Perspective' (2014) 32 Berkeley Journal of International Law 64; Alicia Hinarejos, 'A Missed Opportunity: The Fundamental Rights Agency and the Euro Area Crisis' (2016) 22 ELJ 61 (hereafter Hinarejos, 'A Missed Opportunity').

[19] Consolidated Version of the Treaty on European Union [2012] OJ C326/01 (hereafter TEU), Art 13(2).

of Fundamental Rights, and the general remedies.[20] All in all, there is no compelling reason why the ECB should be exempted from the normal forms of judicial control as expressly recognized by Article 35 of the ESCB Statute.[21]

Within this context, three points may be made. First, unless the CJEU is prepared to exercise meaningful control of ECB action, national courts will sooner or later fill the gap, questioning the primacy and the integrity of EU law. Secondly, although judicial review is an integral part of the accountability toolbox, there are inherent limits as to what the CJEU can do. Judicial accountability is no substitute for political accountability within the bounds of legitimate independence. Thirdly, in contrast to the view that has sometimes been expressed,[22] there is no need for a specialist chamber within the CJEU to pronounce on controversies pertaining to EMU matters. Distinct as they may be, they are part and parcel of constitutional adjudication. First, the role of courts that operate as constitutional or quasi-constitutional tribunals is to resolve issues pertaining to the limits of lawful authority irrespective of the area where the government acts. They must thus exercise, by definition, general jurisdiction. The underlying themes within which judicial balancing occurs are common irrespective of subject-matter: the rights of the individual, the division of competences between the EU and the Member States, and the relative allocation of powers among the EU institutions. Secondly, given the central role of EMU in the integration model of the Treaties, an appreciation of the way it interacts with other areas of law is necessary. Such appreciation is better achieved through a generalist court. Finally, there are many areas of law, such as competition, tax, or social security, that require the assessment of economic evidence or involve the application of complex technical rules. It would thus be difficult to defend EMU exceptionalism.

III. Objectives Versus Effects and the Elusive Quest for the Boundaries of Monetary Policy

The most important issue that the Court has had to face in relation to ECB powers is the distinction between economic and monetary policy. The two policies are closely intertwined but their distinction is constitutionally material as authority for the two belongs to different actors. For the euro area Member States, monetary policy is an exclusive EU competence to be carried out by the ECB, whilst economic policy rests with the Member States, the EU having only a coordinating role.[23] According to the test used by the CJEU, to determine whether a measure falls within monetary or economic policy, reference must be made principally to the objectives of the measure, the

[20] These are provided in Consolidated version of the Treaty on the Functioning of the European Union [2012] OJ C326/47 (hereafter TFEU), Arts 263, 265, 267, and 277. TFEU (n 20) Art 340(3), by separating the ECB from the general rule of liability of TFEU (n 20) Art 340(2), recognizes that the principles which govern the liability of central banks may be different from those that govern the liability of other public authorities.

[21] See Markakis, *Accountability* (n 18) 289.

[22] See Charles Goodhart and Rosa Lastra, 'Central Bank Accountability and Judicial Review' (2018) SUERF Policy Note No 32 <https://www.suerf.org/docx/f_36e729ec173b94133d8fa552e4029f8b_2585_suerf.pdf> accessed 1 December 2021.

[23] See TFEU (n 20) Arts 3(1)(c), 5(1), 119, 120, and 127.

instruments which are employed also being relevant.[24] The above criteria were first used in *Pringle*[25] where, the CJEU drew a distinction between maintaining price stability, which is the primary objective of the Union's monetary policy, and the broader objective of the European Stability Mechanism (ESM), which was to safeguard the stability of the euro area as a whole. The grant of financial assistance to a Member State served the second objective and did not fall within monetary policy.[26] The CJEU held that even if the activities of the ESM might influence the rate of inflation, such an influence would constitute only the indirect consequence of the economic policy measures adopted.[27] Also, even though the stability of the euro area may have repercussions on the stability of the currency, an economic policy measure cannot be treated as equivalent to a monetary policy one for the sole reason that it may have indirect effects on the stability of the euro.[28]

The objectives-based reasoning of *Pringle* is not in line with the approach of the CJEU in other areas where, in deciding the dividing line between EU and Member State competence or in deciding whether national action is compatible with EU law, it focuses on the effects rather than the objectives of state action.[29] Nonetheless, the treaty framework in relation to EMU is different and reliance on objectives, at least as a starting point, appears appropriate. As the Court pointed out, the TFEU does not provide a definition of monetary policy but it is clear on its objectives,[30] and identifies its instruments.[31] Also, *Pringle* was different from earlier cases where the Court was called upon to determine the compatibility with EU law of national action, such as measures affecting free movement. There, the focus on effects rather that objectives serves to uphold primacy and the integration model of market access. What matters is not the goals that a national policy seeks to achieve but its adverse effect on inter-state trade. In *Pringle*, by contrast, State action sought to rescue the euro area and make up for Treaty ambiguity. The Court's approach can be characterized as one of constitutional containment. It sought to facilitate collective action by the Member States through parallel arrangements set up outside of EU law whilst safeguarding the

[24] See *Pringle* (n 13) paras 53 and 55; Case C-62/14 *Gauweiler and Others v Deutscher Bundestag* [2015] EU:C:2015:400, para 46 (hereafter *Gauweiler*); Case C-493/17 *Proceedings brought by Heinrich Weiss and Others* [2018] EU:C:2018:1000, para 53 (hereafter *Weiss*).

[25] See *Pringle* (n 13).

[26] ibid paras 56–57.

[27] ibid para 97.

[28] ibid para 56.

[29] This is the case, for example, in determining the compatibility of national law with the free movement provisions of the Treaties. It is also the case in determining the pre-emptive effect of EU law on the external competence of the Member States. For example, in the context of Bilateral Investment Treaties (BIT) concluded by Member States, the CJEU has gone as far as to endorse a far-reaching doctrine of potential obstacle pre-emption: see Case C-205/06 *Commission v Republic of Austria* [2009] EU:C:2009:118 and Case C-249/06 *Commission v Republic of Sweden* [2009] EU:C:2009:119; Case C-118/07 *Commission v Republic of Finland* [2009] EU:C:2009:715. Similarly, in applying the pre-Lisbon version of the inter-pillar clause, the CJEU used the full force of an integrative rationale to procure an expansive, some might say imperialist, view of the first pillar. Anything that may potentially be done under the first pillar could not be done under the third or even the second: see Case C-176/03 *Commission v Council* [2005] EU:C:2005:542; Case C-440/05 *Commission v Council* [2007] EU:C:2007:625; Case C-91/05 *Commission v Council (ECOWAS case)* [2008] EU:C:2008:288.

[30] See *Pringle* (n 13) para 53.

[31] See TFEU (n 20) Art 127(2).

integrity of the EU legal system. *Pringle* also elevated conditionality to a constitutional virtue providing normative justification to the austerity model by taking a narrow interpretation of the no-bailout clause.

Following *Pringle*, the objectives test became the subject of a tense and gradually more hostile conversation between the German Federal Constitutional Court (FCC) and the CJEU. In *Gauweiler*,[32] in response to the first ever preliminary reference made by the *Bundesverfassungsgericht*, the CJEU gave the green light to the Outright Monetary Transaction Programme by which the ECB declared its readiness to purchase selectively euro area government bonds in secondary markets without setting any quantitative limits.[33] Whilst the CJEU sets some limits to the ECB's authority relying on the golden standard of proportionality, *Gauweiler* is a judgment of institutional empowerment.[34]

The *Bundesverfassungsgericht* raised, among others, the objection that the OMT Programme exceeded the ECB's mandate by straying into the realm of economic policy. Applying the objectives test, the CJEU noted that the OMT decision aims at safeguarding both 'an appropriate monetary policy transmission and the singleness of the monetary policy'.[35] Both aims fell within the objectives of monetary policy: safeguarding the singleness of monetary policy contributed to achieving its objectives, since, under Article 119(2) TFEU, monetary policy must be single;[36] safeguarding an appropriate transmission was likely both to preserve the singleness of monetary policy and to contribute to maintaining price stability.[37] The CJEU endorsed the ECB's submission that the effectiveness of the single monetary policy and its ability to influence price developments depends on whether it can transmit 'impulses' across the money market to the economy.[38] If the monetary policy transmission mechanism is disrupted, the ESCB's ability to guarantee price stability will be undermined.[39] Such disruption would be likely to render the ESCB's decisions ineffective in a part of the euro area thereby undermining the singleness of monetary policy. Also, since disruption of the transmission mechanism undermines the effectiveness of ESCB measures, that would necessarily affect the ESCB's ability to guarantee price stability.[40] Accordingly, the introduction of measures that are intended to preserve the monetary transmission mechanism may be regarded as pertaining to the primary objective of maintaining

[32] See *Gauweiler* (n 24).

[33] On this, see further chapter 2 by Vestert Borger, in this volume.

[34] See Takis Tridimas and Napoleon Xanthoulis, 'A Legal Analysis of the Gauweiler Case: Between Monetary Policy and Constitutional Conflict' in Federico Fabbrini (ed), 'The European Court of Justice, the European Central Bank and the Supremacy of EU Law' (2016) 23 MJ 17.

[35] The term 'monetary policy transmission' refers to the process through which monetary policy decisions affect economic variables, such as output and prices. The individual links between monetary policy decisions and economic variables are referred to as 'transmission channels', for example interest-rate or credit-rate channels. See Antonio Luca Riso, 'An analysis of the OMT case from an EU law perspective' in Helmut Siekmann, Vikrant Vig, and Volker Wieland (eds), 'The ECB's Outright Monetary Transactions in the Courts' (2015) IMFS Interdisciplinary Studies in Monetary and Financial Stability 1/2015, 19–20 <https://www.imfs-frankfurt.de/fileadmin/user_upload/Interdisc_Studies/IMFS_Interdisc_Studies_2015_1_OMT_webversion.pdf> accessed 1 December 2021.

[36] See *Gauweiler* (n 24) para 48.

[37] ibid para 49.

[38] ibid para 50.

[39] ibid.

[40] ibid.

price stability.[41] Focusing on objectives rather than effects allows the same action to be considered either as part of economic or as part of monetary policy depending on the entity that undertakes it and its objectives. This results in the fusion of the two policies and, as *Pringle* and *Gauweiler* indicate, grants immense discretion to the entity that undertakes the action. Also, the interdependence between economic and monetary policy works mostly to the advantage of the ECB whose broad powers to pursue monetary policy objectives may have substantial and widespread spillover effects in economic policy. Essentially, the tensions and instability arising from the separation of competences in monetary and economic policy gravitate to the advantage of the Union and the ECB.

By contrast to the CJEU, in its preliminary reference in *Gauweiler*, the *Bundesverfassungsgericht* favoured an approach less oriented to the objectives of the OMT decision and interpreted those objectives as falling within the field of economic policy. It thus appeared to disagree both on the test to be applied and the way it should be applied.[42] Nonetheless, upon the return of the case to it following the judgment of the CJEU, the *Bundesverfassungsgericht* grudgingly towed the line finding that the OMT decision does not manifestly exceed the powers that can be given to the ECB under the Basic Law and pulling back from a head-on confrontation.[43]

The CJEU came to revisit the distinction between economic and monetary policy in *Weiss*.[44] The origins of the litigation lie in the ECB's Public Sector Asset Purchase Programme (PSPP) under which the Eurosystem central banks purchased debt securities issued by the central governments of euro area Member States. On a reference from the FCC, the CJEU held that Decision 2015/774[45] by which the ECB introduced the Programme did not violate the EU Treaties. It found, *inter alia*, that the PSPP fell within the sphere of monetary policy and was suitable and necessary to achieve its objectives. Upon the return of the case to the FCC, the latter held that Decision 2015/774 was a qualified ultra vires act, openly contradicting the CJEU.[46] The FCC found,

[41] ibid.

[42] See BVerfG, Order of the Second Senate of 14 January 2014 2 BvR 2728/13 ECLI:DE:BVerfG:2014:rs20140114.2bvr272813 (hereafter BVerfG, 'Order of 14 January 2014'). Starting from the principle that budgetary responsibility lies with the Bundestag and that that principle is an integral part of the constitutional identity of Germany, the *Bundesverfassungsgericht* favoured a narrow understanding of the ECB's mandate. It held that the constitutional justification of ECB independence is limited only to measures which are primarily stability-oriented (para 59 of the order). It held that to determine whether a measure directly pursues economic policy objectives, account must be taken of its objectives, the instruments it uses and their objectives and effects, and the way the measure relates to other provisions: see BVerfG, 'Order of 14 January 2014' (n 42) paras 64–66. The OMT decision appeared to be predominantly an economic policy act owing to its immediate objectives, its selectivity, its connection with financial assistance programmes, and the risk of undermining their objectives and requirements.

[43] See BVerfG, Judgement of the Second Senate of 21 June 2016 2 BvR 2728/13 ECLI:DE:BVerfG:2016:rs20160621.2bvr272813.

[44] See *Weiss* (n 24). See, among others, Mark Dawson and Ana Bobić, 'Quantitative Easing at the Court of Justice—Doing Whatever it Takes to Save the Euro: Weiss and Others' (2019) 56 CML Rev 1005; Marijn van der Sluis, 'Similar, Therefore Different: Judicial Review of Another Unconventional Monetary Policy in Weiss (C- 493/ 17)' (2019) 46 LIEI 263.

[45] Decision (EU) 2015/774 of the European Central Bank of 4 March 2015 on a secondary markets public sector asset purchase programme (ECB2015/10) OJ L121/20, as amended by Decision (EU) 2017/100 of the European Central Bank of 11 January 2017 amending Decision (EU) 2015/774 on a secondary markets public sector asset purchase programme (ECB/2017/1) OJ L16/51.

[46] See BVerfG, Judgement of the Second Senate of 5 May 2020 2 BvR 859/15 ECLI:DE:BVerfG:2020:rs20200505085915 (hereafter BVerfG, 'Judgement of 5 May 2020').

in particular, that the PSPP did not satisfy the principle of proportionality. The latter requires the monetary objectives of the Programme and its economic policy effects to be identified, weighted, and balanced against each other. The failure of the ECB and the CJEU to do so amounted to a manifest and structurally significant excess of the competences that could permissibly be transferred to the EU pursuant to the principle of conferral under the German Constitution. The judgment of the FCC has not been received well by commentators who have expressed critique or even outcry, viewing it as an attack on the EU,[47] a failure of German constitutionalism through a departure from the FCC's earlier case law,[48] and even 'self-righteous' and 'rogue'.[49]

A key point of difference between the CJEU and the *Bundesverfassungsgericht* is the criterion to be deployed to decide on the distinction between economic and monetary policy. Following the objectives test, the CJEU held that the PSPP fell within the scope of monetary policy despite the fact that it has considerable effects on the balance sheets of commercial banks and the refinancing terms of the euro area Member States.[50] According to the avowed objectives of Decision 2015/774, its purpose was to contribute to a return of inflation rates to levels below, but close to, 2 per cent over the medium term. This objective fell squarely within the objective of price stability. According to the CJEU, the fact that the PSPP was capable of having an impact on the balance sheets of commercial banks and the financing of the Member States and that such effects could be sought through economic policy measures did not make the PSPP a measure of economic policy. A monetary policy measure cannot be treated as equivalent to an economic policy one for the sole reason that it may have indirect effects that can also be sought in the context of economic policy.[51] Also, the conduct of monetary policy will always entail an impact on interest rates and bank refinancing conditions, which necessarily has consequences for the financing conditions of the public deficit of the Member States.[52]

In *Weiss*, essentially, the CJEU invoked two arguments to justify the objectives-based test. First, the inter-connectedness of monetary and economic policy, and secondly, the premise that the authors of the Treaties did not intend to make an absolute separation between economic and monetary policies. This was evidenced by Article 127(1) TFEU, under which, without prejudice to its primary objective of maintaining price stability, the ESCB is to support the general economic policies in the Union.[53]

[47] See Peter Meier-Beck 'Ultra Vires? Peter Meier-Beck on the judgment of the German Constitutional Court' (*D'Kart Antitrust Blog*, 11 May 2020) <https://www.d-kart.de/en/blog/2020/05/11/ultra-vires/?fbclid=IwAR1072Y74rDHPkiGhr2TG2ElequDoUm6mdoi0U--kLjGMvWK-SiWYror0B0> accessed 1 December 2020.

[48] Pavlos Elftheriadis, 'The German Constitutional Court's Weiss judgment is a Failure of German Constitutionalism' (2020) ELIAMEP Policy Brief No 116 <https://www.eliamep.gr/en/publication/η-απόφαση-weiss-ως-αποτυχια-του-γερμανικού/> accessed 1 December 2021, and Pavlos Elftheriadis, 'Germany's Failing Court' (*Verfassungsblog*, 18 May 2020) <https://verfassungsblog.de/germanys-failing-court/ > accessed 1 December 2021.

[49] Katharina Pistor, 'Germany's Constitutional Court Goes Rogue' *Project Syndicate* (Washington, 8 May 2020) <https://www.project-syndicate.org/commentary/german-constitutional-court-ecb-ruling-may-threaten-euro-by-katharina-pistor-2020-05> accessed 1 December 2021.

[50] See *Weiss* (n 24) para 58.

[51] ibid para 61.

[52] ibid para 64.

[53] ibid para 60.

The FCC took issue with three aspects of the CJEU's reasoning: the use of objectives as the main criterion for defining the remit of monetary policy; the manifest error standard of review followed by the CJEU; and the application of the third test of proportionality, so called *stricto sensu* proportionality, which in its view entailed a balancing exercise that the CJEU failed to perform.

The judgment of the *Bundesverfassungsgericht* highlights some real concerns. Too much deference to the ECB's decision-making risks the uncontrollable expansion of its powers. If the ECB is allowed a free hand to decide what the objectives of monetary policy might be or what action might be necessary to achieve those objectives, the system of checks and balances provided for in the Treaties is overturned. Classifying a measure as one of economic or monetary policy primarily on the basis of the objectives pursued places the decision-maker firmly in control. Nonetheless, the alternative effects-based test favoured by the FCC is problematic. The FCC appears to suggest that (a) where an ECB measure has direct and foreseeable consequences on matters of economic policy, (b) these effects are intended or knowingly accepted, and (c) are at least comparable in weight to the monetary policy objectives of a measure, that measure may be classified as one of economic rather than monetary policy and thus beyond the ECB's remit. There are several objections to this. First, from the perspective of policy-making, the test is incorrect. If the ECB is charged with pursuing monetary policy, why should it abstain from doing what it considers best for the attainment of the objectives of that policy because its decision might impact on economic policy? The justification would appear to be that the Treaty draws a distinction between economic and monetary policy and grants competence in relation to each of them to different constitutional actors. But such separation of competences cannot require the ECB to follow a course of suboptimal intervention in the monetary field. From the economic viewpoint, it is doubtful whether the FCC test is workable. It may make it impossible for a central bank to carry out a meaningful monetary policy. It is liable to lead to stagnation and demand stasis where progress is needed. To put it bluntly, depending on how one applies the test of the FCC, which is not fully articulated, it may be viewed as asking a lifeguard to stay still while the swimmers drown.

In legal terms, the test proposed by the FCC is by no means closer to the letter or the intentions of the authors of the Treaties than the test used by the CJEU. The Treaties do not define with precision the bounds of either policy. It is however clear that, under Article 18.1 of the ESCB Statute, to achieve its objectives, the ECB and the central banks of the Member States may operate in the financial markets by buying and selling outright marketable instruments denominated in euros. The PSPP therefore does fall, in principle, within the policy instruments that the ECB may deploy. Furthermore, the FCC test is not clear. What does it mean that the enquiry must focus on whether the effects of the measure on economic policy are comparable in weight to its monetary policy objectives? What is a court supposed to do? How can it carry out that balancing? The test appears to require some kind of assessment of the magnitude of probability of the effects of the measure on economic policy which cannot be expressed in arithmetical terms and would be very difficult to ascertain in advance. It would also turn proportionality in a wide-ranging inquiry on the likely macro-economic redistributive effects of ECB intervention which would be impossible to carry out.

The FCC test subjects ECB intervention to a *stricto sensu* proportionality assessment under which the ECB cannot validly take certain action even if that would be appropriate to achieve its objectives and there were no less restrictive alternatives, where such action has predictable substantial effects on economic policy. This assumes an organic separation between economic and monetary policy which simply does not exist. It cannot be the intention of the Treaty authors to charge the ECB with following an ineffective monetary policy. The model of separation that the FCC envisages may make sense from a strict national constitutional perspective but does not appear to be in line with the EMU model envisaged in the Treaties. It risks sacrificing the effective exercise of monetary policy on the altar of constitutional orthodoxy of a single Member State.

IV. The Role of Proportionality

A distinct feature of the CJEU's reasoning in both *Gauweiler* and *Weiss* is that it decoupled the competence enquiry from the proportionality enquiry. It first established whether the contested ECB action fell within the scope of monetary or economic policy and then proceeded to examine whether it complied with proportionality. This is consistent with Article 5 TEU but bears important constitutional implications. By excluding the degree of interference of monetary on economic policy from being a definitional criterion, the door opens for a wider understanding of monetary policy. By contrast, in *Weiss*, the FCC applied proportionality at the definitional stage.[54] The FCC endorsed a distinctly German conception of proportionality which is not in line with the CJEU case law. It is incorrect to state, as the FCC does, that the standard applied by the CJEU in *Weiss* 'contradicts the methodological approach by the CJEU in virtually all other areas of EU law.'[55] Proportionality is a standard, not a hard and fast rule that can be applied mechanically. Its bite depends on the standard of judicial scrutiny which accompanies its application and which depends on a range of factors. The high standard of scrutiny applied to assess national restrictions on free movement or interferences with civil liberties is not appropriate in the context of high-level policy measures in the monetary or economic sphere. Furthermore, it is not correct to claim that the CJEU's interpretation disregards the general principles common to the laws of the Member States.[56] There is simply no common tradition in Europe (or to the knowledge of this author anywhere else in the world) of strict judicial scrutiny over monetary and economic policy decisions. Whether one agrees or disagrees with the approach of the CJEU in determining the bounds of EU competence (and there are many things to disagree with), it is difficult to characterize the way it applied proportionality in *Weiss* as manifestly wrong or arbitrary.[57]

[54] See Hinarejos, 'A Missed Opportunity' (n 18).
[55] See BVerfG, 'Judgement of 5 May 2020' (n 46) para 133.
[56] ibid paras 112 and 156.
[57] See Theodore Konstantinides, 'The German Constitutional Court's decision on PSPP: Between mental gymnastics and common sense' (*UK Constitutional Law Association*, 14 May 2020) <https://ukconstitutionallaw.org/2020/05/14/theodore-konstadinides-the-german-constitutional-courts-decision-on-pspp-between-mental-gymnastics-and-common-sense/> accessed 1 December 2021.

Both in *Gauweiler* and *Weiss*, the analysis of the CJEU appears more persuasive than that of the FCC. Yet the FCC highlights some real concerns of accountability. A distinct feature of these judgments is that the CJEU attached importance not only on the primary but also on the secondary objective of the ESCB, namely to support the economic policies of the Member States. As Hinarejos argues, the CJEU's approach reflects the evolution from the original, rule-based conception of the Economic and Monetary Union (EMU) to a 'more policy-oriented EMU that rose out of the crisis'.[58] Nonetheless, the greater emphasis on the secondary aims of the ESCB and the infusion of the ECB's mandate with objectives which lie outside price stability pose challenges. First, these objectives are very wide-ranging in nature. The more the ECB relies on secondary objectives, the more blurred the boundaries between monetary and economic policy become. This tests ECB independence. It also gives rise to a paradox. On the one hand, expanding the ECB's mandate places more decisions beyond the mechanisms of democratic control and makes it more difficult to justify judicial deference. On the other hand, as an evolution in this direction expands the multitude of interests that the ECB must balance, it also increases its discretion and gives more space to the manifest error test. The bottom line is that the greater the range of interests the ECB is permitted to embrace, the greater the need for accountability and transparency in ECB decision-making.[59]

V. Judicial Scrutiny and Standard of Review

A. Principles of judicial review

The principles which govern judicial review of ECB action are the same as those which apply to all EU institutions. The ECB must act within the limits of its powers and, in exercising its discretion, comply with the applicable rules and the general principles of EU law. It is also subject to the Charter of Fundamental Rights which applies not only where the ECB acts *qua* EU institution but also where it is validly mandated to act by the Member States or an international organization such as the ESM.[60]

There is a pivotal distinction between error of law and error of assessment. The first occurs where the ECB misinterprets the applicable rules. The EU institutions do not have any discretion in the interpretation of the law:[61] technically, 'error of law'

[58] Alicia Hinarejos, *The Euro Area Crisis in Constitutional Perspective* (OUP 2015) 143.

[59] For the accountability of the ECB, see, among others, Markakis, *Accountability* (n 18), Édouard Fernandez-Bollo, 'Democratic Accountability within the Framework of the SSM and the SRM as a Competent to Judicial Review' in Zilioli and Wojcik, *Judicial Review in the European Banking Union* (n 18) 17–27; Diane Fromage, Paul Dermine, and Phedon Nicolaides, 'ECB Independence and Accountability Today: Towards a (Necessary) Redefinition?' (2019) 26 MJ 3; Larisa Dragomir, 'The ECB's Accountability: Adjusting Accountability Arrangements to the ECB's Evolving Roles' (2019) 26 MJ 35. See also chapter 11 by Fabian Amtenbrink and Menelaos Markakis, in this volume.

[60] Joined Cases C-8/15 P to C-10/15 P *Ledra Advertising and Others v Commission and European Central Bank* [2016] EU:C:2016:701, para 67; Case T-680/13 *Chrysostomides and Others v Council and Others* [2018] EU:T:2018:486, para 203.

[61] See, eg, Case T-712/15 *Crédit mutuel Arkéa v European Central Bank* [2017] EU:T:2017:900, para 75; Case T-576/18 *Crédit agricole SA v European Central Bank* [2020] EU:T:2020:304, para 62 (hereafter *Crédit agricole SA*).

is a singular concept. EU law does not recognize the US *Chevron* doctrine.[62] Error of assessment occurs where, in exercising its powers, an EU authority oversteps its discretion. This, in turn, requires an analysis of the applicable rules with a view to determining the degree of discretion granted to the decision-maker, and an examination of the way the latter has exercised its powers.

Where it comes to the interpretation of the law, the picture is mixed. Whilst the CJEU has understood the concept of monetary policy relatively broadly and granted the ECB ample discretion to determine its content, outside that field it has been more sceptical of ECB initiatives. In the *OLAF* case,[63] the Court rejected an over-reaching understanding of independence by annulling an ECB decision establishing its own anti-fraud regime and placing it beyond the scope of the powers of OLAF. The Court essentially held that the institutional independence of the Bank must correspond, and cannot go beyond, its functional independence. Subsequently, in the *Location policy* case,[64] the General Court annulled the Eurosystem Oversight Policy Framework by which the ECB required central counterparties (CCPs) providing clearing services for euro-denominated securities to be located in the euro area. Both cases can be seen as efforts by the Bank to flex its muscles, the first, at an early stage of the euro area era, the second at a time when the gravitational force of EMU on policy making began to rival that of the internal market. In the *Location policy* case, it was held that the task of promoting the smooth operation of payment systems, which the ESCB can regulate under Article 127(2) TFEU, does not include securities clearing systems. The General Court took a somewhat narrow view of implied powers. Two reasons may account for that. First, the ECB does not enjoy the law-making prerogative of the legislature; secondly, the Court was mindful of the balance of power between euro area and non-euro area Member States. All in all, the freedom of action accorded to the ECB in the exercise of its core function, that is, monetary policy, does appear to be replicated in other areas.[65]

B. Standard of scrutiny

In reviewing the actions of EU institutions, the CJEU will review both substance and process. However, according to the standard formula used by the Court, judicial review of merits does not vest the Court with the power to substitute its own assessment for that of the institution whose action it is called to review but instead focuses on whether the contested decision is based on materially incorrect facts, or is vitiated by an error of law, a manifest error of assessment or misuse of powers.[66]

The level of judicial scrutiny exercised will depend on a number of factors, the most important being the degree of discretion that the ECB enjoys under the applicable

[62] See *Chevron USA Inc v Natural Resources Defense Council Inc* 468 US 837 (1984). See in this respect, Markakis, *Accountability* (n 18) 291–92.

[63] See Case C-11/00 *Commission v European Central Bank* [2003] EU:C:2003:395.

[64] See *UK v ECB (location policy framework case)* (n 14). For a discussion of this case, see also chapter 5 by Agnieszka Smoleńska and Thomas Beukers, in this volume.

[65] For judicial review in the field of Banking Union, see section VI.

[66] This is the standard formula used. See, eg, *Credit Agricole SA* (n 11) para 30; Case T-342/11 *CEEES and Asociación de Gestores de Estaciones de Servicio v Commission* [2014] EU:T:2014:60, para 70.

rules. Other factors include whether the act under review is a policy measure or an individual decision and the degree to which the act interferes with a fundamental right, for example the right to property. Discretion is a key consideration.[67] The greater the scope of discretion left to the ECB, the more difficult for the Court to intervene. Thus, where the ECB enjoys wide power of assessment or has to make a value judgement balancing many factors or has to make choices of a technical nature and undertake forecasts and complex assessments, it will be allowed a larger margin of manoeuvring.[68] This is because judicial review is review of legality. As stated above, it does not vest the court with power to substitute the ECB's assessment with its own.[69] The nature of the act, that is, whether it is a policy measure or an individual decision, is also material. The reason why the Court can have a more active role in reviewing micro decisions (eg relating to a specific bank) is not because the analysis is less technical but because they tend to concern the application of specific rules to concrete facts, the inquiry is less open ended, and they pertain less to the governance of the polis and more to the treatment of a specific entity by the public authorities. This is not to say that administrative law litigation may not engage constitutional themes. But the contours of the inquiry tend to suffer less from uncertainty. The case law so far shows that, in matters of prudential supervision, the level of scrutiny is stricter.[70]

Perhaps the key points may be summarized as follows. First, in matters of monetary policy, the primary perspective from which process and substance review is carried out is the perspective of supranational functionalism and not the perspective of sovereignty. This is the fundamental difference that accounts for the disagreement between the CJEU and the FCC in *Weiss*. Secondly, although judicial language juxtaposes substance and process review, the two are closely intertwined. The requirement of reasoning, although in form purely procedural, if applied strictly, may unravel the decision-making process in a way that expresses substantive preferences. After all, the requirement of reasoning entails an obligation to give good reasons as opposed to irrelevant ones.[71] The close connection between substance and process is evident in *Gauweiler*, where as part of the proportionality inquiry the CJEU examined closely the ECB's statement of reasons.[72] Proportionality review merged with process review. Thirdly, the concept of 'manifest error' goes only some way towards explaining judicial attitude. Caution should be exercised in attributing too much importance to that label. The term 'manifest error' is susceptible to different interpretations and may hide varying degrees of scrutiny. The precise threshold remains elusive not least because a court would rarely, if ever, admit that the decision-maker has committed an error but that error was not manifest.

[67] See Markakis, *Accountability* (n 18) 299.

[68] See, eg, *Gauweiler* (n 24) para 68; Case C-343/09 *Afton Chemical v Secretary of State for Transport* [2010] EU:C:2010:419, para 28 (hereafter *Afton Chemical*); Case C-203/12 *Billerud Karlsborg and Billerud Skärblacka v Naturvårdsverket* [2013] EU:C:2013:664, para 35.

[69] *Credit Agricole SA* (n 11) para 30.

[70] See the cases discussed below, and Michael Ioannidis, 'The Judicial Review of Discretion in the Banking Union: From Soft to Hard(er) Look?' in Zilioli and Wojcik, *Judicial Review in the European Banking Union* (n 18) 130ff.

[71] See Martin Shapiro, 'The Giving Reasons Requirement' (1992) The University of Chicago Legal Forum 179, 192.

[72] See *Gauweiler* (n 24) paras 66ff.

Fourthly, overall, the standard of scrutiny applied by the CJEU on ECB decisions is fairly strict. Although it varies depending on the degree of discretion, even in matters of monetary policy the Court demands more than an unsearching standard of rationality.[73] In the field of monetary policy, the ECB is accorded wide discretion. This is justified by a number of considerations. The ECB has a specific mandate to take decisions in that field. In line with the principle of separation of powers and the principle of institutional balance, it is not for the judiciary to substitute its own views for those of the ECB. Also, decision-making in that field requires expertise and the exercise of value judgement balancing many different inputs and considerations. Further, it requires the ECB to make choices of a technical nature and to undertake forecasts and complex assessments.[74] By contrast, the fact that monetary policy is a matter of exclusive competence does not in itself justify granting wide discretion to the ECB. The leeway permitted is not determined by the nature of competence but the attributes of the subject-matter over which it is allocated. If anything, the principle of enumerated competences has a sovereignty bias which would suggest that EU exclusivity should be interpreted strictly. Also, the CJEU has not linked the deferential standard of review specifically to the Bank's independence even though this is a relevant consideration.[75]

C. Process requirements

Where the ECB enjoys ample discretion, process requirements assume 'even more fundamental significance'.[76] The manifest error test does not apply to them and the standard of scrutiny, although not uniform, tends to be higher. Process requirements include the obligation for the ECB to examine carefully and impartially all the relevant elements of the situation in question and to give an adequate statement of reasons.[77] The cases decided so far suggest that the level of scrutiny applied to administrative decisions taken by the ECB has been close and that it has been consistent with that applied to the other EU institutions.[78]

The duty to examine carefully and impartially all the relevant aspects of the individual case emanates from the duty of sound administration.[79] It requires that where the applicable regulations grant it discretion, the ECB must exercise it genuinely. Thus, where prudential rules enable the ECB to grant a derogation from a rule, it must not deny a request for a derogation without balancing the interests involved and assessing which option serves best the objectives pursued by the derogation. In *Crédit agricole SA v ECB*,[80] the General Court held that in refusing Crédit Agricole the benefit of

[73] The standard applied by the CJEU in relation to crisis-related measures has been characterized as 'fairly consistent'. See Matthias Goldmann, 'Constitutional Pluralism as Mutually Assured Discretion' (2016) 23 MJ 119, 125.

[74] See *Gauweiler* (n 24) para 68; *Afton Chemical* (n 68) para 28.

[75] See Markakis, *Accountability* (n 18) 295.

[76] See *Crédit agricole SA* (n 61) para 31

[77] See *Gauweiler* (n 24) para 69; *Crédit agricole SA* (n 61) para 31.

[78] See eg *Credit Agricole SA* (n 11); *Crédit agricole SA* (n 61).

[79] See *Crédit agricole SA* (n 61) para 31.

[80] See *Credit Agricole SA* (n 11). The case is part of a group of similar cases: see, to the same effect, Case T-733/16 *La Banque postale v European Central Bank* [2018] EU:T:2018:477; Case T-745/16 *BPCE v European Central Bank* [2018] EU:T:2018:476; Case T-757/16 *Société générale v European Central Bank* [2018]

the exception provided by Article 429(14) of Regulation No 575/2013 on prudential requirements which enables the ECB to exclude from the calculation of leverage ratio certain exposures of a credit institution to public entities, the ECB had acted wrongly. The legislature's intention was to provide the possibility that exposures to public-sector entities which, because of a State guarantee, have the same level of risk as exposures to the State itself could be excluded in the calculation of the leverage ratio. The ECB therefore had to consider if the granting of the exclusion was justified. A refusal given on the theoretical ground that a State may be in a payment default situation, without considering the likelihood of such a possibility in the case of the State concerned, would amount to rendering the possibility envisaged by Article 429(14) virtually inapplicable in practice.[81]

Litigation tends to focus on the requirement of reasoning. In assessing whether the requirement of reasons is satisfied in relation to policy measures, the CJEU exercises a fairly strict level of scrutiny. According to the general principles laid down in the case law, although the statement of reasons must show clearly and unequivocally the reasoning of the decision-maker, so as to enable the persons concerned to ascertain the reasons for the measure and to enable the Court to exercise its power of review, it is not required to go into every relevant point of fact and law.[82] In the case of measures of general application, a specific statement of reasons for each of the technical choices made by the institutions is not necessary.[83] The question whether the duty to state reasons has been satisfied must, moreover, be assessed by reference not only to the wording of the measure but also to its context and to the whole body of legal rules governing the matter in question.[84] In determining whether the requirement to state reasons is satisfied, the Court will also consider sources external to the act in question which are in the public domain provided that they are sufficiently specific. In *Weiss*, it pointed out that the reasoning of the PSPP decision was clarified by press releases, introductory statements of the President of the ECB at press conferences, accompanied by answers to the questions raised by the press, and by the accounts of the ECB Governing Council's monetary policy meetings, which outline the discussions within that body.[85]

The requirement of reasoning has been applied particularly strongly in relation to fines given their punitive character and their negative financial consequences.[86]

EU:T:2018:473; Case T-751/16 *Confédération nationale du Crédit mutuel v European Central Bank* [2018] EU:T:2018:475; Case T-768/16 *BNP Paribas v European Central Bank* [2018] EU:T:2018:471.

[81] See *Credit Agricole SA* (n 11) para 61.
[82] See *Gauweiler* (n 24) para 70; *Weiss* (n 24) para 31.
[83] See *Weiss* (n 24) para 32; Case C-304/16 *American Express v The Lords Commissioners of Her Majesty's Treasury* [2018] EU:C:2018:66, para 76.
[84] See Case C-63/12 *Commission v Council* [2013] EU:C:2013:752, para 99; *Weiss* (n 24) para 33.
[85] See *Weiss* (n 24) paras 37 and 39; see also *Gauweiler* (n 24) para 71.
[86] See *Crédit agricole SA* (n 61) para 134; see section VIII.

VI. Prudential Supervision: A New Litigation Landscape

A significant body of case law has begun to develop in the field of prudential supervision. Litigation pertains to diverse areas including the classification of a bank as significant,[87] consolidated supervision,[88] the calculation of leverage ratios,[89] the corporate governance of credit institutions,[90] ECB penalties,[91] and access to ECB documents.[92] Although some cases raise issues of wider constitutional significance, most pertain to statutory interpretation and the exercise of executive powers. More often than not, they entail close analysis of technical rules. In some cases, the CJEU had the opportunity to visit the application of general issues, for example *locus standi* under Article 263(4) TFEU or the meaning of a reviewable act, in the field of banking regulation.[93] The growth of case law was to be expected. The Banking Union is a novel structure that provides for a fundamental overhauling of the supervisory system. It gives rise to many ambiguities and involves the application of a plethora of detailed and often highly technical measures. Such a systemic change challenges well-engrained regulatory patterns and paths of dependency. It is not accidental that some of the first litigants have been institutions of special status, that is, German banks involving Länder participation and French credit cooperatives, which resisted ECB powers.[94]

So far, the CJEU has had the opportunity to adjudicate on a few cases involving the Single Supervisory Mechanism. *Landeskreditbank* stands out. *Crédit mutuel Arkéa* is also noteworthy.

Landeskreditbank[95] raised some interesting questions pertaining to the distinction between significant and less significant banks. Under Article 6(4) SSM Regulation,[96]

[87] See Case T-122/15 *Landeskreditbank Baden-Württemberg—Förderbank v European Central Bank* [2017] EU:T:2017:337 (hereafter *Landeskreditbank Baden-Württemberg (2017)*), confirming on appeal Case C-450/17 P *Landeskreditbank Baden-Württemberg—Förderbank v European Central Bank* [2019] EU:C:2019:372 (hereafter *Landeskreditbank Baden-Württemberg (2019)*).

[88] Joined Cases C-152/18 P and C-153/18 P *Crédit Mutuel Arkéa v European Central Bank* [2019] EU:C:2019:810 (hereafter *Crédit Mutuel Arkéa*).

[89] *Credit Agricole SA* (n 11).

[90] Joined Cases T-133/16 to T-136/16 *Caisse régionale de crédit agricole mutuel Alpes Provence and Others v European Central Bank* [2018] EU:T:2018:219 (hereafter *Caisse régionale de crédit agricole mutuel Alpes Provence*).

[91] Case T-203/18 *VQ v European Central Bank* [2020] EU:T:2020:313 (hereafter *VQ*); *Crédit agricole SA* (n 61); Case T-577/18 *Crédit agricole Corporate and Investment Bank v European Central Bank* [2020] EU:T:2020:305 (hereafter *Crédit agricole Corporate and Investment Bank*); Case T-578/18 *CA Consumer Finance v European Central Bank* [2020] EU:T:2020:306 (hereafter *CA Consumer Finance*).

[92] See, eg, Case T-730/16 *Espírito Santo Financial Group v European Central Bank* [2019] EU:T:2019:161.

[93] See respectively Case T-247/16 RENV *Trasta Komercbanka v European Central Bank* [2017] EU:T:2017:623 (hereafter *Trasta Komercbanka*) and Joined Cases C-551/19 P and C-552/19 P *ABLV Bank and Others v European Central Bank* [2021] EU:C:2021:369 (hereafter *ABLV Bank and Others*). In *Trasta Komercbanka*, the General Court held that the shareholders of a bank have direct and individual concern to bring proceedings for the annulment of the ECB decision withdrawing its authorization since such withdrawal directly affects their legal position *qua* shareholders and differentiates them from all other persons.

[94] See *Landeskreditbank Baden-Württemberg (2017)* (n 87); *Crédit Mutuel Arkéa* (n 88); *Caisse régionale de crédit agricole mutuel Alpes Provence* (n 90).

[95] See *Landeskreditbank Baden-Württemberg (2017)* (n 87), confirming on appeal *Landeskreditbank Baden-Württemberg (2019)* (n 87).

[96] Council Regulation (EU) No 1024/2013 of 15 October 2013 conferring specific tasks on the European Central Bank concerning policies relating to the prudential supervision of credit institutions [2013] OJ L287/63 (hereafter 'SSM Regulation').

the ECB is exclusively responsible for the supervision of significant banks whilst the supervision of less significant ones falls within the joint purview of the ECB and the national supervisory authorities.[97] Although the distinction is based on objective criteria, it remains porous as it combines legislative guidance with executive discretion granting a central role to the ECB, and it is relativized by the fact that, under Article 6, both the ECB and the NCAs have a role to play in the supervision of both categories.[98] Article 6(4) provides that, where certain conditions are met, a credit institution is not to be considered less significant, unless justified by particular circumstances. Under Article 70(1) SSM Framework Regulation,[99] which contains more specific provisions, particular circumstances are defined as specific and factual circumstances that make the classification of a supervised entity as significant inappropriate, taking into account the objectives and principles of the SSM Regulation, in particular the need to ensure the consistent application of high supervisory standards.

In *Landeskreditbank*, a regional credit bank governed by public law had been classified as significant since it fulfilled the criterion of size under the SSM regulation. It argued that, given its particularly weak risk profile, the prudential supervision conducted by the national authorities was sufficient and therefore it should be classified as less significant. Its argument was essentially that the SSM Regulation did not effect a transfer of prudential competence to the ECB with respect to all banks but only with respect to significant ones. Both the General Court and, on appeal, the CJEU rejected that interpretation. They held that, in adopting the SSM Regulation, the Council did not seek to distribute autonomous powers to the ECB and the NCAs but to confer exclusive powers to the ECB whilst, in certain cases, facilitating their decentralized exercise. Under the SSM, the national authorities acted within the scope of decentralized implementation of an exclusive competence of the Union, not the exercise of a national competence.[100] That interpretation is supported by the letter of both the SSM Regulation and the SSM Framework Regulation. Notably, however, in its judgment of 30 July 2019, the FCC took a different view.[101] It held that the SSM Regulation did not exceed the competences of the EU because it did not provide for a full delegation of powers to the ECB in the field of prudential supervision. It recognized rather than conferred supervisory powers to the NCAs. The FCC provided only qualified and reversible support to Banking Union holding that the SSM and the SRM are compatible with the German constitutional identity clause on condition that the legal framework that they establish is interpreted strictly.[102]

[97] On this, see further chapter 7 by Kern Alexander, and chapter 8 by Federico Della Negra and Gianni Lo Schiavo, in this volume.

[98] See, in particular, the criteria and dispositions provided in SSM Regulation (n 96), Art 6(4) and Art 6(5)(b).

[99] See SSM Regulation (n 96).

[100] See *Landeskreditbank Baden-Württemberg (2017)* (n 87) paras 37–41.

[101] BVerfG, Judgement of the Second Senate of 30 July 2019 no 2 BvR 1685/14 ECLI:DE:BVerfG:2019:rs20190730.2bvr168514.

[102] For a critique, see Raffaele D'Ambrosio, 'The Strict Interpretation of the SSM and SRM Regulations and the Accountability Requirements of the ECB and the SRB in the BVerfG's View' in Raffaele D'Ambrosio and Donato Messineo (eds), *The German Federal Constitutional Court and the Banking Union* (Banca d'Italia, Quaderni di Ricerca Giuridica della Consulenza Legale, No 91, 2021) <https://www.bancaditalia.it/pubblicazioni/quaderni-giuridici/2021-0091/qrg-91.pdf?language_id=1> accessed 1 December 2021.

Crédit mutuel Arkéa v ECB[103] brought to the fore the scope of ECB powers to organize the supervision of credit institutions on a consolidated basis. It was held that the SSM Framework Regulation and Regulation No 575/2013 on prudential requirements[104] allow the ECB to provide for the consolidated prudential supervision of institutions affiliated to a central body even where that body does not have credit institution status. Prudential supervision on a consolidated basis has two aims: to enable the ECB to identify the risks likely to affect a credit institution which derive not from itself but from the group of which it forms part, and to ensure that supervision of the constituent entities is not fragmented.[105] The ECB must therefore be able to exercise prudential supervision on a consolidated basis over a group irrespective of the legal form of the central body to which the entities forming part of that group are affiliated. Otherwise, a group could evade prudential supervision on a consolidated basis by reason of the legal form of its central part and thus undermine the effective exercise of ECB tasks.[106]

A. Composite procedures and hybridity

A distinct feature of the Banking Union is the use of composite administrative procedures under which the adoption of a decision involves several steps, some of which take place at national level and others at EU level. Challenges arise because decision-making becomes more integrated but judicial recourse is based on jurisdictional rules firmly embedded in the EU—State dichotomy.[107] *Fininvest*[108] concerned the jurisdiction of national courts to review national acts which formed preparatory steps in the adoption of an ECB decision.

EU law requires that holders of qualifying holdings in a credit institution must pass an integrity threshold.[109] Under the SSM, the final decision to allow the acquisition of a qualifying holding rests with the ECB but it is for the national competent authority (NCA) to collect all the information, interact with the notifier, and make to the ECB a proposal for a decision to oppose or not the acquisition.[110] In *Fininvest* the CJEU held

[103] See *Crédit Mutuel Arkéa* (n 88).

[104] Regulation (EU) No 575/2013 of the European Parliament and of the Council of 26 June 2013 on prudential requirements for credit institutions and investment firms and amending Regulation (EU) No 648/2012 [2013] OJ L176/1 (hereafter 'Regulation on prudential requirements for credit institutions and investment firms').

[105] See *Crédit Mutuel Arkéa* (n 88) para 63.

[106] ibid para 66.

[107] See Zilioli and Wojcik, *Judicial Review in the European Banking Union* (n 18).

[108] See *Berlusconi and Fininvest* (n 12). See also Case C-414/18 *Iccrea Banca SpA Istituto Centrale del Credito Cooperativo v Banca d'Italia* [2019] EU:C:2019:1036 (hereafter *Iccrea Banca SpA*). For a discussion of this case, see also chapter 8 by Federico Della Negra and Gianni Lo Schiavo, in this volume.

[109] See Directive 2013/36/EU of the European Parliament and of the Council of 26 June 2013 on access to the activity of credit institutions and the prudential supervision of credit institutions and investment firms, amending Directive 2002/87/EC and repealing Directives 2006/48/EC and 2006/49/EC [2013] OJ L176/338, Art 23(1)(b) (hereafter 'CRD IV'). A qualifying holding is one that would result in a person reaching or exceeding 20 per cent, 30 per cent, or 50 per cent of voting rights: see CRD IV (n 109) Art 22(1).

[110] See SSM Regulation (n 96) Art 15 and Regulation (EU) No 468/2014 of the European Central Bank of 16 April 2014 establishing the framework for cooperation within the Single Supervisory Mechanism between the European Central Bank and national competent authorities and with national designated

that only the final decision of the ECB can be challenged before the CJEU. National courts, by contrast, do not have jurisdiction to annul the proposal made by the NCA to the ECB even if that proposal is a final decision under national administrative law. The exclusivity of the CJEU's jurisdiction is founded on the duty of cooperation provided by Article 4(3) TEU and the effectiveness of the decision-making process.[111] Any defects from which the national acts suffered and which vitiated the final EU act could be reviewed by the CJEU when it exercised judicial review over the latter. This approach is logical[112] and avoids problems that would ensue if double jurisdictional redress were allowed.[113] It does however displace national administrative law doctrines and places on the ECB the burden of ensuring that all steps of the process, including those taking place at national level comply with the law. Essentially, in composite procedures, acts of national authorities fall under the jurisdiction of national courts only where EU law attributes decision-making power to those authorities.[114] The key criterion is whether EU law vests an EU authority with exclusive decision-making power in the sense that it is for that authority to take the decision without being bound by the proposal made by the national authority.[115] The principle of single judicial review applies to all composite procedures where the final decision is taken by an EU authority.[116]

Thus, where the final decision is taken by the ECB, the CJEU must determine if any defects vitiating the preparatory acts exist and if those defects are such as to affect the validity of the final ECB act. The first question may well require an assessment of whether national law was complied with. The CJEU would inevitably be drawn on issues such as whether a provision of national law is applicable and how it should be interpreted. The difficulty is that the national agency may not be party to the proceedings before the CJEU especially if the validity of the ECB action is contested by way of direct action as it may have to be under the *TWD* rule.[117] The CJEU may also have to

authorities (SSM Framework Regulation) (ECB/2014/17) [2014] OJ L141/1 (hereafter 'SSM Framework Regulation'), Arts 85–86.

[111] See *Berlusconi and Fininvest* (n 12) paras 47 and 49.

[112] See Paul Dermine and Mariolina Eliantonio, 'Case Note: CJEU (Grand Chamber), Judgment of 19 December 2018, C-219/17, Silvio Berlusconi and Finanziaria d'Investimento Fininvest SpA (Fininvest) v Banca d'Italia and Istituto per la Vigilanza Sulle Assicurazioni (IVASS)' (2019) 12 European Review of Administrative Law 237, 244 (hereafter Eliantonio and Dermine, 'Case Note: Berlusconi and Fininvest').

[113] In such a case, for example, there could be divergent assessments or a situation where a national court annulled the national act which, albeit not binding, is a necessary part for the adoption of a final ECB decision after the CJEU had ruled on the validity of the latter thus opening up again the procedure and jeopardizing finality and efficiency.

[114] See *Iccrea Banca SpA* (n 108) para 50.

[115] See *Berlusconi and Fininvest* (n 12) para 44; by contrast, where the national act is binding on the EU institution, it is the national courts that have jurisdiction: see Case C-97/91 *Oleificio Borelli SpA v Commission* [1992] EU:C:1992:491, paras 9 and 10 and *Berlusconi and Fininvest* (n 12) para 45.

[116] As noted by Eliantonio and Dermine, 'Case Note: Berlusconi and Fininvest' (n 112) at 252, the *Fininvest* principle applies also to the granting and the withdrawal of banking authorizations under SSM Regulation (n 96) Art 4(1)(a). Note also that in *Iccrea Banca SpA* (n 108), the CJEU held that the determination of the amount of the individual *ex ante* contribution to the Single Resolution Fund of a credit institution is for the SRB to make. The role of the national resolution authorities is confined to providing operational support to the Board. Consequently, the EU Courts alone have jurisdiction to determine, when reviewing the legality of a decision of the Board, whether a preparatory act adopted by a national resolution authority is vitiated by defects capable of affecting that decision of the Board.

[117] See Case C-188/92 *TWD Textilwerke Deggendorf GmbH v Bundesrepublik Deutschland* [1994] EU:C:1994:90.

assess factual evidence. Whether the CJEU procedure lends itself to this kind of enquiry is an open question.

The review however must be EU-law driven. All national preparatory acts must comply with the general principles of EU law since they fall within its scope. Thus, the national part of the procedure is subject to the EU procedural standards and principles although there may well be scope for national law to apply. It is submitted that not only irregularities under EU law but also potentially irregularities under national law fall within the jurisdiction of the CJEU as a consequence of the *Fininvest* ruling. Otherwise, such irregularities would not be subject to control in any judicial forum.[118]

In *ABLV Bank*,[119] the CJEU had the opportunity to consider a different type of hybrid procedure, this time involving the participation of the ECB and the Single Resolution Board (SRB). It held that the ECB's assessment under Article 18(1) SRM Regulation[120] that a bank is likely to fail is not a reviewable act under Article 263 TFEU but only a step in the adoption of a resolution scheme by the SRB. The Court held that the SRB is not bound in law to follow the ECB's assessment.[121] This is not the only reading of Article 18(1). In fact, a strictly literal interpretation would lead to the opposite conclusion. Article 18(1) uses peremptory language contrasting authority for assessing whether an entity is failing or likely to fail, an assessment which 'shall be made by the ECB', with authority to assess if there is no reasonable prospect of any alternative private sector measures, an assessment which 'shall be made by the Board'.[122] Also, Article 18(1) does not state that the SRB is not bound to follow the ECB's assessment on whether the entity in question is failing or likely to fail. The Court's judgment seeks essentially to keep all things under one roof. It suggests that the only act that can be challenged is the adoption of a resolution scheme by the SRB and not its assessments as to whether the individual conditions that must be fulfilled for such a scheme to be adopted are met.[123] There is, however, little doubt that a self-standing assessment by the ECB to the effect that a credit institution fails or is likely to fail causes harm to the institution concerned and also may well affect its legal position, for example by activating contractual default clauses.

[118] See Eliantonio and Dermine, 'Case Note: Berlusconi and Fininvest' (n 112).

[119] See *ABLV Bank and Others* (n 93).

[120] See Regulation (EU) No 806/2014 of the European Parliament and of the Council of 15 July 2014 establishing uniform rules and a uniform procedure for the resolution of credit institutions and certain investment firms in the framework of a Single Resolution Mechanism and a Single Resolution Fund and amending Regulation (EU) No 1093/2010 [2014] OJ L225/1 (hereafter 'SRM Regulation').

[121] See *ABLV Bank and Others* (n 93) paras 68–70. An issue that was left open by the judgment is redress in the event that the ECB comes to the conclusion that a bank is not failing or likely to fail. In such a case, under the terms of Art 18(1), no assessment is sent to the SRB and the resolution procedure is not initiated. It is not clear if, in such a case, a party that might have interest could challenge the ECB assessment or the SRB failure to procure such an assessment by an action for failure to act under TFEU (n 20) Art 265. It would appear that, since the assessment of the ECB is not binding, it could not be challenged under TFEU (n 20) Art 265, the only course of redress being an action against the SRB, although its chances of success would be very limited. The latter appears more in line with Art 18 and the rationale of the judgment in *ABLV Bank and Others* (n 93).

[122] See SRM Regulation (n 120) Art 18(1), second and fourth subparas respectively.

[123] Under SRM Regulation (n 120) Art 18(1), these conditions are the following: (a) the entity is failing or is likely to fail; (b) there is no reasonable prospect that any alternative private sector measures would prevent its failure within a reasonable timeframe, and (c) a resolution action is necessary in the public interest.

Composite procedures may place administrative action outside traditional hierarchical paths.[124] The complex forms of decision-making outlined above highlight the need for judicial vigilance and the need to avoid purely formal criteria. The greater the number of agencies involved in taking a decision, the greater the risk of obfuscation, the more difficult to co-relate legal and economic harm, and the more difficult it is to impute legal responsibility to the disadvantage of judicial protection and accountability.

VII. Application of National Law by the ECB

An innovation of the Banking Union is that it entrusts the ECB with the task of applying national law. Under Article 4(3) SSM Regulation, for the purpose of carrying out its supervisory tasks, the ECB is to apply all relevant Union law. This includes national legislation transposing directives and national choices permitted by EU regulations.[125] This novel arrangement raises some interesting issues.[126] The ECB will have to interpret national law in order to apply it. Is it bound by an interpretation provided by a national court? EU institutions cannot claim to have the final say over the interpretation of national law which remains within the national judicial province. What, however, if the ECB considers that the national measures fall short of the requirements of a regulation or, more generally, EU law? An obligation on the ECB to apply national law as it finds it, even if it infringes EU law, would strain the principle of legality although regard must be paid here to the principle of legal certainty. Suffice it to say that the limitations which apply to national authorities in relation to directives also apply to the ECB. It cannot rely on an unimplemented directive against a private entity since, in principle, that would run counter to the principle of legal certainty.[127] By contrast, the ECB could rely, within the somewhat uncertain contours of the *Marleasing* case law, on the principle of *interprétation conforme*.[128] It is likely that the SSM structure will give rise to some delicate issues pertaining to the joint liability of EU and national agencies on which the case law remains unclear. It is also likely that it will lead to the

[124] Herwig CH Hofman, Gerard C Rowe, and Alexander H Türk, *Administrative Law and Policy of the European Union* (OUP 2011) 408. This is further illustrated by *Rimšēvičs* (n 15). See Tridimas and Lonardo, 'When Can a National Measure be Annulled by the ECJ?' (n 16); for a detailed analysis, see Filipe Brito Bastos, 'An Administrative Crack in the EU's Rule of Law: Composite Decision-making and Nonjusticiable National Law' (2020) 16 EuConst 63; Eliantonio and Dermine, 'Case Note: Berlusconi and Fininvest' (n 112) 244.

[125] See SSM Regulation (n 96) Art 4(3) subpara 1.

[126] See Karen Banks, 'Incorrect implementation of EU directives: what effects for the ECB and the CJEU, and what mechanisms for rectification?' in European Central Bank, 'Building bridges: central banking law in an interconnected world' (ECB Legal Conference 2019) 119ff <https://www.ecb.europa.eu/pub/pdf/other/ecb.ecblegalconferenceproceedings201912~9325c45957.en.pdf> accessed 1 December 2021 (hereafter Banks, 'Incorrect implementation of EU directives').

[127] But see the discussion in Banks, 'Incorrect implementation of EU directives' (n 126), and Vittorio Di Bucci, 'Quelques questions concernant le contrôle juridictionnel sur le mécanisme de surveillance unique' in Roberto Adam et al (eds), *Liber Amicorum Antonio Tizzano* (Giappichelli Editore 2018).

[128] See Case C-106/89 *Marleasing SA v La Comercial Internacional de Alimentacion SA* [1990] EU:C:1990:395; Case C-168/95 *Criminal Proceedings against Luciano Arcaro* [1996] EU:C:1996:363.

CJEU having to interpret national law. In the labyrinthine structures of the SSM, legal uncertainty reigns.

An example of the application of Article 4(3) is provided by *Caisse régionale de crédit agricole mutuel Alpes Provence.*[129] The ECB had refused to allow the same person to be appointed both chair of the board of directors and effective director of a significant French bank. The General Court held that, pursuant to Article 4(3), it had to assess the legality of the contested decision in the light of both Article 13(1) of Directive 2013/36 and the provision of French law transposing it. It came to the conclusion that the ECB had not erred. Both Article 13(1) of Directive 2013/36 and the second paragraph of Article L. 511–13 of the *Code Monétaire et Financier* pointed to the same conclusion. In construing the latter, it took into account the case law of the *Conseil d'Etat*. It pointed out that the scope of national provisions must be assessed in the light of the interpretation given to them by national courts.[130] This however begs a number of questions: what would happen if there was no national case law or if the national judgments were contradictory? Should the CJEU interpret national law in the light of the methods of interpretation prevailing in the national legal system or those used by the CJEU itself? What if EU and national law contradicted each other? In such a case, it would be necessary to establish whether national law could be interpreted in line with the directive under the *Marleasing* principle. If so, the directive would prevail. If not, the limits of the principle of legality would be tested but, as stated above, absent transposition, a directive may not impose obligations on individuals. It would be otherwise if the provision was contained in a regulation or a decision. In banking regulation, EU law is interwoven with national law and the CJEU may increasingly find itself in a situation where it has to interpret national law. The General Court has also had recourse to national case law in other cases concerning the legality of ECB action.[131]

VIII. Fines

Under the SSM, the ECB acquires the fining powers granted by EU measures to the competent prudential supervisor.[132] The fines are substantial and can reach up to 10 per cent of the consolidated annual turnover of the group to which the recalcitrant entity belongs.[133] The penalties applied must be effective, proportionate, and dissuasive.[134] When an institution is allocated new powers, the way they are first exercised bears an important signalling factor. In some respects, the financial sector lends itself to a strict penalty policy. Financial institutions are affluent and, in diffuse societal discourse, the emphasis tends to be not so much on their contribution to wealth generation as on their excesses. Furthermore, the euro area crisis brought to the fore the need for both

[129] See *Caisse régionale de crédit agricole mutuel Alpes Provence* (n 90).

[130] ibid para 48.

[131] See *Crédit Mutuel Arkéa* (n 88) (pertaining to the obligation to transfer capital and liquid assets within a banking group to ensure that the condition laid down in Regulation on prudential requirements for credit institutions and investment firms (n 104), Art 10(1)(a) was fulfilled).

[132] See SSM Regulation (n 96) Art 18(1).

[133] ibid Art 18(2).

[134] ibid Art 18(3).

tougher regulation and stricter compliance. All this establishes a climate conducive to a robust penalties regime. Nonetheless, this does not give the whole picture. European commercial law is, perhaps, over-criminalized. Penalties policy must be robust but prioritize incentivization and effective compliance rather than punishment. Sight must also not be lost of the need to adhere to strict process. Already, a lively case law has begun to develop in relation to the ECB's fining powers. Notably, the General Court has been equivocal as to whether it has the power to exercise unlimited jurisdiction in relation to the size of the fine pursuant to Article 261 TFEU.[135] This would be a matter of interpretation of the EU measure under which the fine is imposed.

Given that proportionality is a general principle of EU law, in imposing penalties under Article 18(1) of the SSM Regulation, the ECB must observe it not only when determining the amount of the penalty but also when deciding whether the breach committed justifies the imposition of a penalty.[136] In *VQ v ECB*[137] the ECB fined a bank with a sum amounting to 0.03 per cent of its annual turnover for breaching the obligation to obtain prior permission before repurchasing its own shares.[138] In deciding that the penalty was proportionate, the General Court took into account that the provision violated was clear and the applicant had continued its breach after having been informed of the scope of its obligations.

The few cases decided so far suggest that the requirement of reasoning applies particularly strictly in relation to the imposition of penalties. This is justified given the ample discretion that the ECB has and the high level that fines may reach. In *Crédit agricole SA*[139] the General Court annulled a fine of €4,300,000 amounting to 0.0015 per cent of the consolidated annual turnover imposed on the ground that the applicant had classified certain instruments as Common Equity Tier 1 capital without the ECB's prior permission. The ECB explained that it followed a two-stage approach in calculating the fine. In the first stage, it determined the basic sum based on the seriousness of the violation, its effects on the bank's position, and the bank's conduct. It then also took into account the bank's total assets. In the second stage, the basic sum was adjusted taking on board mitigating or aggravating factors. The General Court held that the ECB must indicate not only which factors it takes into account and why they are relevant but also the methodology of applying them: how it assesses each of them and what is the effect of each in the level of the fine. The threshold is high. Even though the methodology can be explained on a case-by-case basis, essentially the judgment requires the ECB to have a policy which must be known in advance. The ECB has now

[135] The issue was expressly left open in *Crédit agricole SA* (n 61).

[136] See *VQ* (n 91) para 62.

[137] ibid.

[138] See Regulation on prudential requirements for credit institutions and investment firms (n 104), Art 77(a). Commission Delegated Regulation (EU) No 241/2014 of 7 January 2014 supplementing Regulation (EU) No 575/2013 of the European Parliament and of the Council with regard to regulatory technical standards for Own Funds requirements for institutions [2014] OJ L74/8, Art 77a read in conjunction with Art 29(1) and Art 31(1) requires that a credit institution wishing to repurchase Common Equity Tier 1 instruments has to obtain prior permission from the competent authority.

[139] See *Crédit agricole SA* (n 61). To the same effect, see *Crédit agricole Corporate and Investment Bank* (n 91); *CA Consumer Finance* (n 91); *VQ* (n 91). The judgments were appealed unsuccessfully on other grounds: Joined Cases C-456/20 P to C-458/20 P *Crédit agricole SA and Others v European Central Bank* [2021] EU:C:2021:502.

published guidelines for the calculation of fines.[140] The General Court also reiterated that the statement of reasons must, in principle, be notified to the person concerned at the same time as the decision adversely affecting him. The absence of reasoning cannot be legitimized by an *ex post* explanation provided during the procedure before the CJEU.

A view more favourable to the ECB was taken in *VQ v ECB*.[141] According to Article 18(6) SSM Regulation, the ECB must publish any penalty imposed, whether it has been appealed or not. Article 132(1)(b) SSM Framework Regulation provides that, by way of exception, where eponymous publication causes disproportionate damage to the institution concerned, a penalty decision is to be published on an anonymized basis. In *VQ v ECB*, the General Court held that, in deciding whether eponymous publication causes disproportionate harm, the gravity of the breach is not a relevant factor. Article 132(1)(b) does not entail a balancing of the gravity of the conduct in question against the effects of publication. Even a penalty for a minor breach must be published. The decision must be made solely on the basis of an assessment of the consequences of such a lack of anonymization for the situation of that entity.[142] Although the opposite view is by no means inconceivable,[143] the General Court encourages the use of publicity as an enforcement device.

IX. Conclusion

There is no doubt that the role of the ECB since its inception has evolved considerably in several respects. There are signs that judicial control has kept pace with this functional transformation although the greatest challenges are perhaps still to come. It would be unwise to lay down hard and fast rules concerning the optimum level of judicial scrutiny of ECB decisions. A lot will depend on context, the key consideration being discretion. The broader the discretion that the ECB enjoys, the more difficult for the CJEU to intervene. *Gauweiler* and *Weiss* suggest that the CJEU shows deference by applying a rationality standard, albeit not necessarily a soft one. Review is firmly conducted from the perspective of a functional integration model, not from the perspective of a federal necessity one. This has earned the CJEU no friends in Karlsruhe but, in the view of this author, the rationale of the CJEU appears more persuasive than that of the FCC. Nonetheless, the ECB takes decisions which have important distributional repercussions, and from a democratic perspective, it is a salutary that it is subject to scrutiny not only by the CJEU but also national, and indeed EU, institutional forces. From this perspective, it is ironic that the FCC's petulant response in *Weiss* encourages

[140] See European Central Bank, 'Guide to the method of setting administrative pecuniary penalties pursuant to Article 18(1) and (7) of Council Regulation (EU) No 1024/2013' (European Central Bank 2021) <https://www.bankingsupervision.europa.eu/ecb/pub/pdf/ssm.guidetothemethodofsettingadministrativepecuniarypenalties_202103~400cbafa55.en.pdf> accessed 1 December 2021.

[141] See *VQ* (n 91).

[142] ibid para 87.

[143] The ECB must assess in the light of proportionality not only the level of the penalty but also whether the imposition of a penalty is necessary. To the extent that the publication of the fine is in itself a penalty, it must also be subject to proportionality.

better decision-making. The close nexus between economic and monetary policy and the greater emphasis placed on the secondary objective of monetary policy call for more discerning judicial vigilance. Still, judicial control is no panacea. Its effectiveness is limited especially in relation to macro decisions of monetary policy which do not have an immediate impact on concrete rights but where the individual is affected in an indirect albeit significant way as a member of the collectivity.

Outside the field of monetary policy, the judicial inquiry is a lot more searching. It is right that it should be. The case law suggests that the ECB will have a much rougher ride as a supervisor than as a policy-maker. A key area here is the interaction between EU and national law outside established hierarchical patterns. The effects of hybrid forms of governance as manifested in composite processes and the application of national law by the ECB will pose new challenges.

More generally, the ECB is part of a governance framework that suffers from an undue level of uncertainty. There are too many cases where it is difficult to determine the true source of authority[144] and legal and economic harm become completely detached from each other. There is no denying that the Court has sought to empower rather than constrain the EU institutions and has understood EU competence broadly in three separate but interrelated areas which are conflated in the field of EMU: internal market harmonization, agency power, and financial crisis management. For the optimist, the EU's response to the financial crisis was, to borrow from Professor Jeffrey Garten, 'the best that imperfect men could achieve operating in a caldron of political and economic change'.[145] But as the dust of the crisis settles, there is a lot more to do to honour good governance.

[144] This applies, for example, to the measures accompanying conditionality for which see *Chrysostomides* (n 4); for a more general discussion, see Takis Tridimas, 'Indeterminacy and Legal Uncertainty in EU Law' in Joana Mendes (ed), *EU Executive Discretion and the Limits of Law* (OUP 2019) 40–63.

[145] Jeffrey E Garten, *Three Days at Camp David: How a Secret Meeting in 1971 Transformed the Global Economy* (HarperCollins 2021); see review in Justin Fox, 'How Richard Nixon Changed America's Place in the World' *The New York Times* (New York, 16 July 2021) <https://www.nytimes.com/2021/07/16/books/review/jeffrey-e-garten-three-days-at-camp-david.html?action=click&module=Features&pgtype=Homepage> accessed 1 December 2021.

13

Assessing and (Re-)situating Today's ECB in the EU's Institutional Landscape

*Diane Fromage**

I. Introduction

The European Central Bank (ECB) is different from the other European Union (EU) institutions: it presents unique features, on several accounts. Furthermore, its institutional structures have suffered important changes since it was first created two decades ago, such that the balance between, on the one hand, its supranational nature and, on the other, national component within its governance structures has evolved over time.

The ECB became an EU institution with the entry into force of the Lisbon Treaty only: it was originally an 'independent specialized organization of Community law'.[1] It is the only institution whose decision-making bodies can adopt legal acts without the direct involvement of Member States' representatives and without any prior authorization being required: as is further examined below, in the Governing Council, (euro area) National Central Bank (NCB) governors participate in their personal capacity. Those governors thus wear a 'supranational hat' when they sit in the Governing Council thereby endorsing then a role similar to the one played by Commissioners in the European Commission, which is also a supranational institution like the ECB.[2] Contrary to those, they can however rely on, and benefit from, the knowledge and the expertise of their NCBs whereas Commissioners primarily rely on Commission administrative services, which are also supranational. In other words, the importance of the role played by national administrations in the system of the European System of Central Banks (ESCB) is greater than the one played by national administrations in 'standard EU' areas in which the Commission commonly operates. Among the reasons for the ECB's unique status are also its strong independence,[3] its standing

* This chapter is the outcome of research conducted in the framework of the research project IMPACTEBU, a project that received funding from the European Union's Horizon 2020 research and innovation programme under the Marie Sklodowska-Curie grant agreement No 895841.

[1] Chiara Zilioli and Martin Selmayr, 'The European Central Bank: An independent specialized organization of Community law' (2000) 37 CML Rev 591.

[2] That is, that both the European Commission and the ECB represent and act in the interest of the Union as a whole, as opposed to, for example, the Council and the European Council, which are intergovernmental organs, meaning that Member States government representatives come together and represent the various national interests.

[3] Consolidated version of the Treaty on the Functioning of the European Union [2012] OJ C326/47 (hereafter TFEU), Art 130.

Diane Fromage, *Assessing and (Re-)situating Today's ECB in the EU's Institutional Landscape* In: *The New European Central Bank*. Edited by: Thomas Beukers, Diane Fromage, and Giorgio Monti, Oxford University Press. © Diane Fromage 2022. DOI: 10.1093/oso/9780198871231.003.0013

in-between the EU27, the euro area, and since 2013, the European Banking Union (EBU).[4]

While some of these characteristics stem from the ECB's original design as it was included in the Maastricht Treaty, others are rather the result of subsequent evolutions observable in law and practice within the EU. Against this background, this chapter first seeks to examine how the ECB's institutional design has evolved over the past twenty years. Much ink has, for instance, already been spent on the consequences of the creation of the EBU for the ECB's governance structure. However, very little is known generally about the preparatory organs of the ECB (ie the ECB's Committees). Furthermore, the institutional logic—and thus also the relationship between EU and national authorities—that underpins the governance structure in the area of monetary policy arguably differs from the one in place in the area of banking supervision. This chapter's second objective is hence to evaluate how today's ECB compares to the other EU institutions, while also outlining the balance between national and supranational components in the various ECB bodies and procedures. In so doing, it outlines the tensions that arise from the dual—national and European—nature of the NCBs and their governors. In fact, the national component or dimension that exists within the ECB may take different forms, including for instance that of representation, influence, or interests. This analysis pursues to highlight them rather than to strictly categorize them, a task which the secrecy that characterizes part of the functioning of the ECB makes impossible. This chapter finally asks what the implications of these evolutions might be for the accountability structures in place.

To this end, this chapter firstly considers how the ECB's institutional structures have evolved over time (II). It then proceeds to ask how national influence within the E(S) CB's structures has evolved over time (III). Today's ECB institutional structures are subsequently compared to those of other EU institutions and bodies (IV). The final part concludes (V).

It is undeniable that the ECB has been submitted to important shifts since its creation. These include, for example, the fact that the divide between euro area and EU27/ internal market where the ECB is involved in EU27-matters in a variety of instances and capacities never vanished (and likely never will), contrary to what had originally been planned. As a consequence, today's ECB stands in-between the EU27, the EBU (twenty-one Member States since October 2020), and the euro area (nineteen Members). The participation of non-euro area Member States in the EBU also has important consequences for the ECB as the relationship it entertains with the Competent Authorities of those Member States differs from the one that exists between it and the Competent Authorities of euro area Member States. Finally, as a consequence of the co-existence of the internal market and the EBU, and of the different levels of integration achieved within them, important questions related to the divide of responsibilities between, on the one hand, the EU-wide European Banking Authority and European Commission and, on the other, the euro area-focused ECB have arisen over time. Although they are significant and bear important consequences for the ECB, these developments are not considered in the present chapter, which more modestly

[4] On the ECB's role in the EBU, see chapter 7 by Kern Alexander, and chapter 8 by Federico Della Negra and Gianni Lo Schiavo, in this volume.

focuses on the ECB's institutional structures and how these compare to the structures of other EU institutions and bodies.[5]

II. The ECB's Institutional Structures: From Maastricht to Lisbon Today

This section first examines what the ECB's original institutional structure was (A). Subsequently, the structures in place in the area of banking supervision are considered (B). The next section focuses on the evolution of these structures and asks how the share of the national component have evolved over time both *de jure* and *de facto* (C).

A. The ECB's original institutional architecture

The ECB's institutional architecture is contemplated both in the core of the EU Treaties (today in the Treaty on the Functioning of the EU (TFEU)), and in Protocol No 4 on the System of European Central Banks and the European Central Bank (ESCB Statute), annexed to the Treaties. These provisions provide for the existence of organs for EU-wide, as well as for Euro-area specific decision-making bodies (1), and for the establishment of preparatory bodies (ECB Committees) (2).

(1) ECB decision-making bodies: Balancing EU-wide representation and euro area-specific interests

As noted, the ECB's institutional architecture was first defined in the Maastricht Treaty,[6] and is thus the result of the negotiations that preceded its adoption. On '[t]he Road to Maastricht',[7] national preferences, and especially French and German ones, shaped the ECB's characteristics. As is well-known, the ECB's independence was a pre-condition to Germany's agreeing to the creation of the EMU,[8] but a national dimension in the ECB's structure and functioning were advocated by the French government. Then French minister of Economy and Finance, Pierre Bérégovoy, believed that 'the more operational functions passed to the ECB, the more the market operators would shift their business to its location', and he wanted to protect the French financial markets in the event that the ECB would not be established in France.[9] Hence, he called for the ECB's operation to be decentralized.[10] Also, the French (unsuccessfully)

[5] See nonetheless the other chapters included in this edited volume as well as its introduction, which examine individual aspects of these questions, for example chapter 6 by Jonathan Bauerschmidt, chapter 7 by Kern Alexander, and chapter 8 by Federico Della Negra and Gianni Lo Schiavo, in this volume.

[6] Treaty establishing the European Community [2002] OJ C325/33, Arts 105–109b and Consolidated version of the Treaty on the Functioning of the European Union, Protocol (No 4) on the Statute of the European System of Central Banks and of the European Central Bank [2016] OJ C202/230 (hereafter ESCB Statute).

[7] Kenneth Dyson and Kevin Featherstone, *The Road to Maastricht. Negotiating Economic and Monetary Union* (OUP 1999).

[8] This was for instance stated by the then governor of the *Bundesbank* in a speech he gave in Paris on 16 January 1990; ibid 386–87.

[9] ibid 211.

[10] ibid 210.

suggested that members of the Governing Council be accountable to both the European Parliament and national parliaments.[11] Solidarity among Member States (as opposed to two-speed integration dividing those Member States participating in Stage 3 of EMU from those that did not) was dear to the French as well: they called for the establishment of both a euro area-only Governing Council and an EU-wide General Council to 'facilitat[e] co-operation between 'ins' and 'outs'.[12]

The Maastricht Treaty—like the Lisbon Treaty still does too—defined three decision-making bodies: the Governing Council, the Executive Board, and the General Council whereby the former two have, however, a significantly more important role to play within the ESCB. This is evidenced both by the tasks assigned to these bodies examined further below, as well as by their standing in the Treaties. Indeed, Article 129(1) TFEU unequivocally provides that '[t]he ESCB shall be governed by the decision-making bodies of the European Central Bank which shall be the Governing Council and the Executive Board'. By contrast, Article 141(1) TFEU clearly points to the temporary character of the General Council in stating that '[i]f and as long as there are Member States with a derogation [from their belonging to the Euro area foreseen in the Treaties], and without prejudice to Article 129(1), the General Council of the European Central Bank referred to in Article 44 of the Statute of the ESCB and of the ECB shall be constituted as a third decision-making body of the European Central Bank'.

The main decision-making body of the ECB is thus the Governing Council composed of governors of the NCBs whose currency is the euro, who participate in their personal capacity, and the members of the ECB's Executive Board.[13] The balance between supranational and national representation has evolved over time to the benefit of the latter since the number of euro area Member States went from twelve to nineteen since the euro was first introduced. Hence, balance which was originally one to two in favour of national representation is now one to three, and no mechanism is foreseen with a view to compensating for this,[14] except perhaps for the. This combination of national and supranational representation has been viewed as a sign of the federal character of the ESCB.[15] The Governing Council 'adopt[s] the guidelines and take[s] the decisions necessary to ensure the performance of the tasks entrusted to the ESCB under these Treaties and this Statute ... shall formulate the monetary policy of the Union ... and shall establish the necessary guidelines for their implementation'.[16] The Executive Board, which comprises six members (the President of the ECB, its Vice-President, and four other members),[17] '*implement[s]* monetary policy in accordance with the guidelines and decisions laid down by the Governing Council'.[18] It also prepares the meetings of the Governing Council,[19] and additional powers may

[11] ibid 242.
[12] ibid 242.
[13] TFEU (n 3) Art 283(1) and ESCB Statute (n 6) Art 10.
[14] Chiara Zilioli, 'Art. 283 AEUV' in Hans von der Groeben, Jürgen Schwarze, and Armin Hatje (eds), *Europäisches Unionsrecht* (Nomos 2015), para 4.
[15] Ulrich Palm, 'Art. 283 AEUV' in Eberhard Grabitz, Meinhard Hilf, and Martin Nettesheim (eds), *Das Recht der Europäischen Union: EUV/AEUV* (CH Bech 2021), para 7.
[16] ESCB Statute (n 6) Art 12.1.
[17] TFEU (n 3) Art 283(2) and ESCB Statute (n 6) Art 11.
[18] ESCB Statute (n 6) Art 12.1 (emphasis added).
[19] ibid Art 12.2.

be delegated to it if the Governing Council so decides.[20] Lastly, the General Council allows for EU-wide participation as it is composed of the President and the Vice-President of the ECB, and of the governors of all EU NCBs. Although the other members of the Executive Board may participate as well, they have no voting rights.[21]

As mentioned, NCB Governors sit in their personal capacity on the Governing Council (this derives from the strict independence they are submitted to). Nonetheless, they are arguably still (and perhaps even increasingly) influenced by their status as the Governors of a *national* institution even when they sit on the Governing Council (see also Section IV below). NCBs indeed remain primarily national institutions, even if they now belong to the Eurosystem, which is composed of the ECB and the NCBs from euro area Member States and which 'conduct[s] the monetary policy of the Union'.[22] This means that they have become *national Europeanized institutions* in so far as their actions are strongly influenced by European integration[23] and as they—and not the ECB—shall 'carry out the operations which form part of the tasks of the ESCB' wherever possible,[24] but also with the consequence that (some) of their institutional features are governed by EU rules. For instance, NCBs have to be guaranteed a status of independence,[25] and the duration of the mandate of NCB Governors may not be inferior to five years. Those Governors are also protected from severe national injustices due to their dual status as NCB Governors and members of the Governing Council as is examined more in detail subsequently. The ECB is to be consulted on national legislation in its fields of competence, and it may thus have influence on NCBs by this means.[26] And, of course, NCBs have the duty to implement Governing Council decisions.

All this notwithstanding, NCBs in their quality as *national* institutions play a key role too. The ECB heavily relies on them to gain the information that underpins its monetary policy decisions, and NCBs are strongly involved in the ECB's preparatory bodies considered in the following subsection.

(2) Uncovering the unknown: ECB preparatory bodies

As mentioned in the introduction, only scarce information is available on the three kinds of Committees that exist within the ECB (Eurosystem/European System of Central Banks (ESCB) committees, *ad hoc* Committees established by the Governing Council, Audit Committees), and they have attracted close to no academic attention to date.

[20] ibid Art 12.1.
[21] TFEU (n 3) Art 141 and ESCB Statute (n 6) Art 44.
[22] TFEU (n 3) Art 282(1).
[23] Each Member State indeed has a duty to 'ensure that its national legislation including the statutes of its central bank is compatible with the Treaties and the Statute of the ESCB and of the ECB'; TFEU (n 3) Art 131 and ESCB Statute (n 6) Art 14.1.
[24] ESCB Statute (n 6) Art 12.1.
[25] TFEU (n 3) Art 130.
[26] ibid Art 127(4). See, for instance, Opinion of the European Central Bank of 30 November 2020 on amendments to the Law on Parliament [2020] (CON/2020/30) concerning the Swedish NCB and Opinion of the European Central Bank of 21 July 2020 on the amendment of the appointment criteria of Banco de Portugal's Governor and other members of the Management Board [2020] (CON/2020/19).

The existence of the ESCB Committees is recognized in the ECB's Rules of Procedure,[27] and their task is to 'assist in the work of the decision-making bodies of the ECB':[28] they hence 'provide expertise in their fields of competence and facilitate the decision-making process and implementation of decisions'.[29] They report to the Governing Council via the Executive Board, which has the capacity to establish and dissolve them. In the committees, NCBs and the ECB are set on an equal footing being each represented by up to two representatives selected by the NCB governors and the Executive Board, respectively. They are chaired by one of the ECB representatives, and the ECB provides secretarial support.

Both the Governing Council and the General Council may request studies to the Committees, this latter possibility being specifically recognized and further detailed in the General Council's Rules of procedures with a view to defining the involvement of non-euro area NCB representatives. Indeed, the General Council may 'request studies of specific topics by [the ESCB] committees'.[30] Furthermore, '[t]he national central bank of each non-participating Member State may appoint up to two staff members to take part in the meetings of a committee whenever it deals with matters falling within the field of competence of the General Council and whenever the chairperson of a committee and the Executive Board deem this appropriate'.[31] Beyond this, the possibility exists to involve representatives of other EU institutions and bodies and other third parties under the same circumstances.[32]

Considering that only limited information on these Committees is available publicly,[33] the information on the existing committees presented here corresponds to the list published by the Slovenian NCB, and was valid as of 31 December 2016.[34]

There are seventeen committees which deal both with substantive issues linked to central banking and banking supervision (Accounting and Monetary Income Committee (AMICO), Financial stability Committee (FSC), Market Operations Committee (MOC), Monetary Policy Committee (MPC), Market Infrastructure and Payments Committee (MIPC), Risk Management Committee (RMC)), and with more organizational aspects (Banknote Committee (BANCO), Committee of Controlling (COMCO), Eurosystem/ESCB Communications Committee (ECCO), Information Technology Committee (ITC), Internal Auditors Committee (IAC), International

[27] Decision of the European Central Bank of 19 February 2004 adopting the Rules of Procedure of the European Central Bank (ECB/2004/2) [2004] OJ L80/33, Art 9 (hereafter ECB Rules of Procedure).

[28] ibid Art 9.1.

[29] Hanspeter K Scheller, *The European Central Bank: History, Role and Functions* (European Central Bank 2004) 64.

[30] ECB Rules of Procedure (n 27) Art 9.2 and Decision of the European Central Bank of 17 June 2004 adopting the Rules of Procedure of the General Council of the European Central Bank (ECB/2004/12) [2004] OJ L230/61, Art 8 (hereafter Rules of Procedure of the General Council).

[31] ibid.

[32] ECB Rules of Procedure (n 27) Art 9.4.

[33] This state of affairs was confirmed by a request for information to the ECB. Exceptions to this are nonetheless the sections of the ECB's website dedicated to the Audit Committee and Internal Auditors Committee <https://www.ecb.europa.eu/ecb/orga/governance/html/index.en.html> accessed 21 November 2021, and the information on the Ethics Committee: European Central Bank, *Institutional Provisions: Statute of the ESCB and of the ECB, Rules of Procedures, Ethics Committee, Implementation of Separation* (ECB 2015).

[34] National Bank of Slovenia, 'Committees' <https://www.bsi.si/en/about-us/eurosystem/committees> accessed 21 November 2021.

Relations Committee (IRC), Legal Committee (LEGCO), Organisational Development Committee (ODC), Statistics Committee (STC), Budget Committee (BUCOM), Human Resources Conference (HRC)). Note that the Governing Council may also 'decide to establish ad hoc committees in charge of specific advisory tasks'.[35]

As is evidenced by the above summary, the existing permanent Committees cover very different areas including both substantive and organizational issues. Consequently, they may be expected to fulfil different functions, and may thus be viewed as contributing to a varying (ie more or less important) degree to the ECB's fulfilling its tasks, and to the ESCB's overall functioning. It is nonetheless impossible to draw more meaningful conclusions amid the absence of more detailed publicly available information.

The Committees' existence arguably corresponds to the need for the ECB's decision-making bodies to receive input from, and coordinate their actions with, the NCBs, which, according to the structure of the ESCB, and as already noted, play a decisive role in the implementation of ECB decisions and in its operations generally. Committees contribute to the channelling of national preferences and, more neutrally, they may be expected to allow for the exchange of information and best practices among NCBs and with the ECB. They do not, as such, a priori respond primarily to other needs, which could include shortage of staff on the ECB's side, but are rather the sign that Governing Council meetings need preparing, and that ECB decisions are largely implemented by NCBs. In view of the important role they play, it would therefore be desirable for more information to be made publicly available. It is indeed understandable that some of the data shared within some of the Committees is sensitive and cannot easily be disclosed, as such disclosure could have adverse economic effects or could constrain the ECB in the conduct of its monetary policy. But it is hard to comprehend why at least the list of committees that currently exist, as well as the list of the topics discussed, would not be published on the ECB's website, particularly because the ECB has been adamant and indeed pro-active in its efforts to increase transparency on its activities.

B. The adaptation of the ECB's institutional design to the EBU: increased national influence in the functioning of the ECB?

Following the decision made by the Member States in 2013 to rely on the possibility opened by Article 127(6) TFEU to confer some supervisory tasks upon the ECB,[36] the ECB became the main supervisor of EBU credit institutions as part of the Single Supervisory Mechanism (SSM). Nonetheless, it is to fulfil this function in complete independence from its monetary policy and other functions.[37] Its institutional structures thus had to be adapted to allow it to perform this new function whilst guaranteeing that this happened independently from the performance of is monetary policy

[35] ECB Rules of Procedure (n 27) Art 9a.

[36] Council Regulation (EU) No 1024/2013 of 15 October 2013 conferring specific tasks on the European Central Bank concerning policies relating to the prudential supervision of credit institutions [2013] OJ L287/63 (hereafter SSM Regulation).

[37] ibid Art 25.

functions. This resulted in the creation of the Supervisory Board (1), in the establishment of Joint Supervisory Teams (2), whilst Common services also exist (3).

(1) Supervisory Board
The Supervisory Board in charge of preparing supervisory decisions is an ECB internal organ established by secondary law[38] (as opposed to the decision-making organs whose basis is found in the Treaties). It is composed of NCA representatives (one per participating Member State), but the participation of those NCBs that are not NCAs is also foreseen.[39] Where that is the case, the national representatives involved share the vote allocated to the Member State in question, but two representatives sit at the table. National representation is hence significantly superior to ECB (ie supranational) representation which is only ensured by the Chair, the Vice-Chair, and the four additional members. The imbalance between national and supranational representation is even more pronounced than in the Governing Council. Board members shall act in the interest of the Union as a whole,[40] thus they do not seek the individual interests of the Member State they represent. It remains the case that, on the one hand, the voting system in place is less supranational than the one in place today within the Governing Council, and that, on the other hand, NCAs' independence is less strictly guaranteed than the independence of NCBs. Generally, the characteristics of their institutional set up are more left up to the individual Member States than those of NCBs which are in part defined in EU primary law. For what concerns the applicable voting arrangements, each member of the Supervisory Board has one vote. Furthermore, 'decisions shall be taken by a simple majority of its [the Supervisory Board's] members.... In case of a draw, the Chair shall have a casting vote'.[41] In contrast to this, each member of the Governing Council has one vote too (so there is no weighing mechanism either in most cases). However, since the total number of members of the Governing Council now exceeds twenty-one, a rotating system is in place.[42] As to the NCAs' requirement of independence and institutional settings, they are defined in Article 19 SSM Regulation (independence), the ECB Code of Conduct for the Members of the Supervisory Board,[43] and in the Capital Requirements Directive (CRD IV).[44] As such, NCAs, too, have become *national Europeanized institutions*. However, the applicable rules are less stringent than those defining the characteristics applicable to NCBs. In accordance with Article 4(4) CRD IV, 'Member States shall ensure that the competent authorities have the expertise, resources, operational capacity, powers and independence necessary to carry out the functions relating to prudential supervision, investigations and penalties set out in this Directive and in Regulation (EU) No 575/2013'.

38 ibid Art 26.
39 ibid Art 26(1).
40 ibid Art 26(1).
41 ibid Art 26(6).
42 ESCB Statute (n 6) Art 10(2).
43 Code of Conduct for the Members of the Supervisory Board of the European Central Bank [2015] OJ C93/2.
44 Directive 2013/36/EU of the European Parliament and of the Council of 26 June 2013 on access to the activity of credit institutions and the prudential supervision of credit institutions and investment firms, amending Directive 2002/87/EC and repealing Directives 2006/48/EC and 2006/49/EC [2013] OJ L176/338, Art 4 (hereafter CRD IV).

They 'shall ensure that the functions of supervision pursuant to this Directive and to Regulation (EU) No 575/2013 and any other functions of the competent authorities are separate and independent from the functions relating to resolution',[45] and adequate cooperation between NCAs and National Resolution Authorities shall be guaranteed.[46] However, these provisions leave ample margin of (national) discretion to the Member States. Whilst this is certainly in line with the duty set on the Union to respect its Member States' constitutional identities recognized in Article 4(2) Treaty on European Union (TEU), and allows Member States to define their institutional structures in the way that is most suitable to their individual institutional setting and (political) traditions, this is also likely to lead to important differences and perhaps even to some shortcomings. For instance, the limited independence of the Austrian and the German NCAs, FMA and BaFin, from their government could be criticized,[47] and in any case confirms that the national component is stronger within the Supervisory Board than it is within the Governing Council. The fact that numerous NCBs—that are shaped by more stringent EU obligations—act as NCAs may not be obviated. As a consequence of this, the attribution of supervisory tasks to the ECB following the establishment of the SSM points to the ECB's institutional structure having arguably become less supranational, or at least more prone to national influence, than had previously been the case when it was only in charge of the conduct of the EU's monetary policy even if in this domain as well, the national component has become stronger as a result of the growing number of NCB governors sitting on the Governing Council. This numerical superiority does not necessarily mean that the influence of the single governors has been reinforced however. The rotating system could point in the opposite direction, and the secrecy of the deliberations within the Governing Council makes it impossible to draw definite conclusions in this regard. We also observe varying dynamics because of the attribution of supervisory powers to the ECB: on the one hand, the centralization of supervisory tasks with the ECB is a clear sign of supranationalization within the EU. On the other hand, however, compared to the ECB's internal bodies devoted to monetary policy, the internal institutional structure of the ECB in the supervisory pillar is arguably less supranational, in the sense that it could be more prone to national influence.

This tendency is confirmed by the composition of the Steering Committee, which is tasked with supporting the Supervisory Board's activities.[48] Indeed, it is formed by the Supervisory Board's Chair, its Vice-Chair, one ECB representative, and five NCA representatives designated on a rotating basis; the national component is stronger than it is in the Executive Board, which supports the Governing Council, as the latter is composed of six supranational representatives, that is, NCB representatives do not take part in it. This difference may nonetheless be justified by the fact that the conduct of the EU's monetary policy has been attributed to the Union in full, whereas banking

[45] ibid Art 4(7).
[46] ibid Art 4(8).
[47] On this, see European Banking Authority, 'EBA Report on the Supervisory Independence of Competent Authorities' (EBA Report no 29, 18 October 2021) <https://www.eba.europa.eu/sites/default/documents/files/document_library/Publications/Reports/2021/1022092/EBA%20report%20on%20supervisory%20independence%20of%20competent%20authorities.pdf> accessed 21 November 2021.
[48] SSM Regulation (n 36) Art 26(10).

supervision is a shared competence that is exercised jointly by EU and national authorities, as examined in the next paragraph.

(2) A strong role for NCAs: Joint Supervisory Teams

As noted above, the SSM is composed of both the ECB and the NCAs, which play an important role in its functioning. This is the case for two main reasons. First, NCAs remain primarily responsible for the fulfilment of certain tasks (for instance, they supervise Less Significant Institutions (LSIs) and may be instructed by the ECB to perform certain tasks).[49] Second, they participate in Joint Supervisory Teams (JSTs).[50]

These teams are composed of both ECB and NCA officials.[51] They were created with a view to supporting the ECB, which, arguably, could not exercise the day-to-day supervision of all SIs directly and on its own, both on the ground of insufficient staffing and on the ground of insufficient knowledge of the individual banking sectors and supervisory cultures. Their tasks include, *inter alia*, the conduct of the Supervisory Review and Evaluation Process (SREP) for SIs, the participation 'in the preparation of a supervisory examination programme to be proposed to the Supervisory Board', the implementation of said programme and any ECB supervisory decision, the coordination with on-site inspections teams in the implementation of the programme, and the liaison with the NCAs.[52]

JSTs allow the ECB to benefit from the NCAs' national experience,[53] thereby insufflating a national dimension to the SSM, one that comes in addition to the already significant national dimension inherent in the SSM's institutional structure within the ECB outlined above. This notwithstanding, it remains the case that the ECB keeps the upper hand (as it should be in view of the ultimate responsibility it bears for the prudential supervision of SIs): even if NCAs may appoint the person(s) of their choosing to become part of a particular JST,[54] the ECB keeps the control over this as it 'may require the NCAs to modify the appointments they have made if appropriate for the purpose of the composition of a joint supervisory team'.[55] This provision interestingly leaves ample margin of discretion to the ECB in its application, and the Supervisory Board's Rules of procedure do not shed any light on this aspect.

(3) ECB decision-making bodies and shared services

Despite the creation of specific independent structures for the conduct of prudential supervision within the ECB, the separation between the supervisory and the monetary

[49] For a critical stance on the allocation of supervisory powers between the ECB and the NCAs within the ECB, see Raffaele D'Ambrosio, 'Single Supervisory Mechanism: Organs and Procedures' in Mario P Chiti and Vittorio Santoro (eds), *The Palgrave Handbook of European Banking Union Law* (Palgrave Macmillan 2019) 165 ff.

[50] See also chapter 8 by Federico Della Negra and Gianni Lo Schiavo, in this volume.

[51] Regulation (EU) No 468/2014 of the European Central Bank of 16 April 2014 establishing the framework for cooperation within the Single Supervisory Mechanism between the European Central Bank and national competent authorities and with national designated authorities (SSM Framework Regulation) (ECB/2014/17) [2014] OJ L141/1, Arts 3 and 4 (hereafter SSM Framework Regulation).

[52] ibid Art 3(2).

[53] Gianni Lo Schiavo, 'Il ruolo della BCE' in Mario P Chiti and Vittorio Santoro (eds), *L'Unione bancaria europea* (Pacini Giuridica 2016) 218.

[54] SSM Framework Regulation (n 51) Art 4(2).

[55] ibid Art 4(3).

policy functions is nonetheless not absolute (and rightfully so). This is so because the Governing Council remains in charge of approving the Supervisory Board's decision following a non-objection procedure, but also because some of the services of the ECB are shared between both functions.

As noted above, the decision-making bodies of the ECB are defined in the Treaties such that the Supervisory Board alone could not make supervisory decisions. The euro area-wide dimension brought about by the consent procedure by the Governing Council may nonetheless be viewed as limited, considering that it is not a decision-*making* procedure proper, but one that essentially takes the Governing Council's consent as the course of action by default. Hence, the Supervisory Board has been viewed as having 'a certain *de facto* decision-making power in the field of banking supervision'.[56]

On the other hand, shared services 'providing support to both the monetary policy and the supervisory function [may be established] in order to ensure that these support functions are not duplicated, thus helping to guarantee the efficient and effective delivery of services'.[57] Despite being shared services, '[d]ivisions dedicated to supervisory tasks have been established within several 'shared service' business areas'.[58] The existence of these shared services hence corresponds to an attempt to minimize unnecessary bureaucratic structures, and does not affect the supranational nature of the ECB (support) services in question.

In summary, whereas the creation of these shared services or the involvement of the Governing Council in supervisory decisions may not necessarily significantly affect the balance between the national and the supranational components within the ECB, the same may not hold true of the addition of the supervisory pillar itself and the creation of the Supervisory Board and the JSTs it has demanded. In fact, other developments witnessed over the past two decades beg the question whether the national component has not grown significantly within the ECB; the next section is thus devoted to this matter.

III. Has the National Component within the Supranational ECB Grown Larger?

Having now mapped the features of the ECB's institutional structures in both the area of monetary policy as well as in supervisory matters, and thus how the ECB's institutional structure generally has evolved since it started to function two decades ago, the question that remains is whether, on the whole, the ECB (and perhaps also the ESCB) should be viewed as having become more or less supranational an EU institution (or

[56] Raffaele D'Ambrosio, 'Single Supervisory Mechanism: Organs and Procedures' in Mario P Chiti and Vittorio Santoro (eds), *The Palgrave Handbook of European Banking Union Law* (Palgrave Macmillan 2019) 159.

[57] Decision of the European Central Bank of 17 September 2014 on the implementation of separation between the monetary policy and supervision functions of the European Central Bank (ECB/2014/39) [2014] OJ L300/57, Art 3(4).

[58] ibid Recital 11.

a system) over time, in the sense that the balance between national and supranational influence has shifted in favour of the former.

As is shown in the next subsections, what emerges is rather a mixed picture for there are arguments that point both to the ECB's having become more nationally oriented and to its being more (or as equally as ever) supranational. This is the result of the representation of national interests having become stronger within the ECB's institutional structures (A), and of its national component having become more salient in practice (B). The reinforcement of the ECB's supranational character by means of recent EU judicial decisions nonetheless stands in stark contrast to these tendencies speaking in favour of enhanced national influence (C).

A. Enhanced representation of national interests in the ECB's institutional structure proper

In terms of the elements that point to the ECB's institutional structure having allowed for national interests to become more strongly represented,[59] the first element that bears mentioning is the enlargement of the euro area and the subsequent growth in the number of NCB governors who now very significantly outnumber Executive Board members in the Governing Council. Second is the addition of the supervisory pillar. As shown, the creation of the banking supervision pillar has undoubtedly brought about an influx of national positions. This is so because of the structural features mentioned above (ie the composition of the Supervisory Board and NCAs' characteristics; the composition of the Steering Committee; and the existence and the importance of the JSTs), but also because of the idea that the Supervisory Board appears to abide by a logic that is closer to that of an EU agency (ie the coordination of national positions) than is the case within the supranational Governing Council. As has been noted, '[t]he SSM constitutes a "system of financial supervision composed by the ECB and national competent authorities of participating Member States" (Article 2 para. 9 of Council Regulation 1024/2013 [SSM Regulation]). This administrative network is comparable to those coordinated by some European agencies (the EFSA, the ECHA, the ESAs and the Single Resolution Board [SRB]), but its organisation is, due to the strong powers of intervention of the ECB vis-à-vis the [individual] national authorities, certainly more hierarchical than that of the latter.'[60]

In any case, the (necessary and welcome) existence of the JSTs composed of both ECB and national officials, on which the ECB is dependent in the conduct of its supervisory tasks are means for the Member States to channel their preferences in a way that is stronger than the influence NCBs can exercise in the conduct of monetary policy, not least because of the important differences that still exist among the single national supervisory cultures, and because of the high degree of differentiation of all

[59] At least collectively. As noted previously, whether this is true of individual NCBs or Member States is unclear.

[60] Paul Weismann, 'The Supervisory Board of the ECB: An Agency-Like Body to Stabilise the Banking Sector?' in Johannes Pollak and Peter Smolinski (eds), *The Role of EU Agencies in the Eurozone and Migration Crisis: Impact and Future Challenges* (Palgrave Macmillan 2021) 80.

kinds that remains within the EBU, for instance vertically as NCAs supervise LSIs autonomously.[61] This strong national character of the SSM characterized by the fact that decisions are made for individual (national) credit institutions also justifies, for instance, the original democratic accountability mechanisms in place, whereby national parliaments may directly hold ECB representatives to account by inviting them to appear before them under certain circumstances together with a representative of their respective NCA.[62] This possibility represents the first time ever that a *national* institution may directly exercise accountability functions on an *EU* institution.

A further illustration of the (controversial yet undoubtedly important) role national institutions possess within the SSM can be found in the outcome of the judicial disputes brought before the Court of Justice and the German Federal Constitutional Court whose main object is yet to be fully settled.

On the occasion of the *L-Bank case*,[63] the General Court stated that 'exclusive competences [have been] delegated to the ECB [by the Council, and that these have] to be implemented within a decentralised framework, rather than having a distribution of competences between the ECB and the national authorities in the performance of the tasks referred to in Article 4(1) of that regulation [SSM Regulation]'.[64] This interpretation was later confirmed by the Court of Justice which unequivocally found on appeal that 'the ECB is 'exclusively competent' to carry out, for prudential supervisory purposes, the tasks listed in Article 4(1) in relation to 'all' credit institutions established in the participating Member States, without drawing a distinction between significant institutions and less significant institutions', and that '[t]he national competent authorities . . . assist the ECB in carrying out the tasks conferred on it by Regulation No 1024/2013, by a decentralised implementation of some of those tasks in relation to less significant credit institutions'.[65] By contrast, the *Bundesverfassungsgericht*, while generally agreeing with the Court of Justice's interpretation and not finding the creation of the EBU to be unlawful, still came to a more ambiguous conclusion in the *European Banking Union case*.[66] It bears the potential for a new conflict between the Federal Constitutional Court and the EU to arise in the future, and thus deserves to be quoted at length here. The Federal Court indeed posited that:

[61] On this, see especially Chiara Zilioli and Karl-Philipp Wojcik (eds), *Judicial Review in the European Banking Union* (Edward Elgar Publishing 2021); Chiara Zilioli and Karl-Philipp Wojcik, 'European Banking Union: A Giant Step towards European Integration and a Challenge for Judicial Review' in Chiara Zilioli and Karl-Philipp Wojcik (eds), *Judicial Review in the European Banking Union* (Edward Elgar Publishing 2021) 1–15.

[62] SSM Regulation (n 36) Art 21. On the use of this mechanism in practice, see Diane Fromage, *Changing Parliaments in a Changing European Union: The Role of National Legislatures in Larger Member States* (Hart Publishing forthcoming).

[63] Case T-122/15 *Landeskreditbank Baden-Württemberg—Förderbank v European Central Bank* [2017] EU:T:2017:337 (hereafter Landeskreditbank case (2017)) and Case C-450/17 P *Landeskreditbank Baden-Württemberg—Förderbank v European Central Bank* [2019] EU:C:2019:372 (hereafter Landeskreditbank case (2019)).

[64] Landeskreditbank case (2017) (n 63) para 54 later confirmed by the Court of Justice.

[65] Landeskreditbank case (2019) (n 63) paras 37 and 41.

[66] BVerfG, Judgement of the Second Senate of 30 July 2019 no 2 BvR 1685/14 ECLI:DE:BVerfG:2019:rs20190730.2bvr168514.

> Even with regard to the SSM Regulation, the national supervisory authorities ultimately retain important tasks and powers relating to banking supervision ... They carry out these tasks based on Member State competences and not as a result of a re-delegation of competences that had been conferred on the ECB ... According to the allocation of tasks between the ECB and the national supervisory authorities as laid down in the SSM Regulation, the latter remain competent for significant elements of the supervision of individual credit institutions ... All tasks and powers not conferred on the ECB remain with the national authorities ... A re-delegation of EU administrative tasks would require that all supervisory tasks had been fully conferred on the ECB, which is evidently not what the SSM Regulation provides; otherwise, it would amount to an ultra vires act ... Under Art. 127(6) TFEU, it is only possible to confer 'specific tasks' relating to banking supervision on the ECB. Thus, the ECB's competences are limited to precise and clearly defined areas of banking supervision. Art. 127(6) TFEU does not allow a full conferral of banking supervision ... ; consequently, the Member States retain the competence for all tasks and powers that are not conferred on the ECB under the SSM Regulation ... A re-delegation of EU administrative tasks would require that all supervisory tasks had fully been conferred on the ECB, which is specifically not what the SSM Regulation provides.[67]

As is obvious, the Court of Justice's and the Constitutional Court's views on the role and standing of national authorities and the ECB within the SSM differ, although the Court of Justice's interpretation is naturally the only valid one within the EU legal order. In particular, according to the Court of Justice, the creation of the SSM has led to prudential supervision being the sole responsibility of the supranational ECB, although national influence remains strong. In contrast, according to the Federal Constitutional Court national influence is strong, not only because of the role NCAs play within the ECB and the JSTs but also because NCAs themselves remain primarily responsible of the supervision of Less Significant Institutions. In any event, these judicial disputes both confirm the key role played by NCAs in the SSM, a role which may further be inferred from the fact that the ECB's authority vis-à-vis NCAs is more limited than the authority it possesses vis-à-vis NCBs in the area of monetary policy.

The addition of the supervisory pillar may thus be viewed as having increased the national component inherent to the ECB's structures. Beyond this, it may be argued that also in the field of monetary policy practice over the past decade has pointed towards the emergence of publicly expressed discrepancies with the supranational decision taken by the Governing Council; this trend is considered next.

B. The potential reinforcement of the national dimension in practice

Before looking into this issue, it must admittedly first be acknowledged that the supranational character of the ECB in the field of monetary policy was strengthened during

[67] ibid paras 183–87.

the euro area crisis when decisions started to be taken by majority voting whereas consensus had been the norm until then. It was also undoubtedly, and strongly, reinforced following the change in the applicable voting rule within the Governing Council that intervened after the accession of the nineteenth euro area Member State.

As has been noted:

> Following long debates,[68] '[i]n another evolutionary step transforming the ECB's initial setup [of the Treaty of Maastricht, which had established the principle of 'one member, one vote'], the Treaty of Nice therefore called for a revision of the Governing Council's decision-making procedures. In March 2003, the Governing Council introduced a rotation system, in which NCB governors would receive voting weights as a function of their economic significance, once the number of governors (or, equivalently, euro area countries) reached 15. In December 2008, the ECB decided to postpone the actual implementation of the reform until the number of governors reached 18.'[69]

This reform responded to the need to ensure that decisions could still be made by the Governing Council as it was deemed that the group of thirty-three representatives that would have eventually been able to cast a vote (six members of the Executive Board and twenty-seven NCB governors) would have been unable to come to an agreement.[70] The introduction of the rotating system in place today undeniably makes the structure of the main decision-making body of the ECB more supranational. At the same time however, it should not be forgotten that personal and even critical views on the ECB's monetary policy are now regularly made public by individual NCB governors indeed.[71] Admittedly, these may be the expression of disagreements on the way in which the monetary policy is conducted in general, or discontent inspired by the impact of the euro area monetary policy on the Member State of respective governors. The question may naturally also be asked whether the rise in the (public) opposition expressed by some Governing Council members was provoked by the reform of the voting rules that resulted in more supranationalism being the rule.[72] It is certainly hard to determine what may have prompted this trend, especially considering that it intervened at a time when the ECB was called to play a much more active and indeed political role to preserve the common currency after the outbreak of the Global Financial Crisis. This is also a period characterized by a significant change in the way in which it conducts its monetary policy,[73] whereby the ECB has had to resort

[68] Peter Stella and Jerome Vandenbussche, 'Governance and Monetary Policy Decision-Making at the ECB' in Jakob de Haan and Helge Berger (eds), *The European Central Bank at Ten* (Springer 2010) 143.

[69] Jakob de Haan and Helge Berger, 'Introduction' in Jakob de Haan and Helge Berger (eds), *The European Central Bank at Ten* (Springer 2010) 8.

[70] ibid.

[71] A recent illustration of this phenomenon may, for example, be found in Bundesbank's governor statement in favour of a potential tightening of the ECB's monetary policy: Jens Weidmann, 'Erfolgsgeschichte Soziale Marktwirtschaft—mit Rat und Tat in die Zukunft' (Speech at the 70th anniversary of the German Economic Institute, Frankfurt am Main, 27 May 2021) <https://www.iwkoeln.de/fileadmin/user_upload/Institut_der_deutschen_Wirtschaft/Veranstaltungen/2021/70_Jahre_IW_Festrede_Jens_Weidmann.pdf> accessed 21 November 2021.

[72] This remark is owed to Klaus Tuori whom I thank for it (as well as for the discussion on this topic).

[73] See also chapter 2 by Vestert Borger and chapter 3 by Klaus Tuori, in this volume.

to unconventional monetary policy instruments. These, in turn, have significant economic effects, which have adversely affected the various Member States resulting in controversies and judicial disputes.[74] Regardless of what the trigger for the public expression of disagreements may have been, that is whether it is the change in the voting arrangements within the Governing Council or whether it is the resort by the ECB to unconventional monetary policy and its more active and less neutral role, it remains the case that the recurrent public expression of disagreements, or at least of public opinions, constitutes a very dangerous development. This is so because it goes counter to the principle of ECB independence, which justifies the non-publicity of Governing Council proceedings. As has been noted, 'the [ESCB] Statute does not permit publication of the individual voting of the members of the Governing Council because, rather than contribute to further transparency, this would jeopardise the independence of its members, since they would then be more likely to come under national or other pressure'.[75] In expressing their opinion publicly, Governing Council members de facto risk jeopardizing the protection afforded to them by the ESCB Statute. This, in turn, may lead to the renationalization of the debate on the (euro area-wide) monetary policy, and could for example incentivize national parliaments or governments to try and exercise influence on their individual governors. We shall return to this issue in the conclusion of this chapter.

C. The Eurosystem's and the ECB's supranational character (still) reinforced by recent judicial developments

In stark contrast to the trend towards an overall stronger national dimension in the structure and the operation of the ECB outlined in the two previous subsections stand two recent important decisions of the Court of Justice, which have strongly reinforced the supranational character of the Eurosystem and the ECB's powers within it.

The first of these two cases is the *Rimšēvičs case*,[76] in which the Court of Justice was called to interpret Article 14 ESCB Statute on NCBs for the first time. This provision sets an obligation on Member States to guarantee that their legislation including the statutes of their NCBs is compatible with the Treaties. NCB Governors' mandates must be longer than five years and a 'Governor may be relieved from office only if he no longer fulfils the conditions required for the performance of his duties or if he

[74] As illustrated most notably by the *Gauweiler* and *Weiss* judgments (Case C-62/14 *Gauweiler and Others v Deutscher Bundestag* [2015] EU:C:2015:400 and Case C-493/17 *Proceedings brought by Heinrich Weiss and Others* [2018] EU:C:2018:1000, respectively). The question whether the way in which the ECB conducts its unconventional monetary policy is governed by a supranational euro area-wide logic or by a logic that also leaves significant room for national preferences is beyond the scope of the present analysis. Suffice it to note for the purpose of the present analysis that the way in which the Public Sector Purchase Programme operates has a very limited supranational component in as far as the ECB purchases only a limited share of national bonds, which are in their majority held by the NCBs of the respective Member States.

[75] European Central Bank, 'The institutional framework of the European System of Central Banks' (ECB Monthly Bulletin July 1999) 57 <https://www.ecb.europa.eu/pub/pdf/mobu/mb199907en.pdf> accessed 21 November 2021.

[76] Joined Cases C-202/18 and C-238/18 *Rimšēvičs and European Central Bank v Republic of Latvia* [2019] EU:C:2019:139. For a discussion of this case, see chapter 12 by Takis Tridimas, in this volume.

has been guilty of serious misconduct. *A decision to this effect may be referred to the Court of Justice by the Governor concerned or the Governing Council on grounds of infringement of these Treaties or of any rule of law relating to their application*' (emphasis added).

In the case at hand, the Latvian Anti-Corruption Office had temporarily prohibited Mr Rimšēvičs from performing his duties as Governor of the Central Bank of Latvia. This case provided an opportunity for the Court of Justice to clarify the status of NCBs within the ESCB and to reinforce its supranational character since it set the emphasis on the importance of and the consequences that derive from the fact that NCBs are part of the ESCB even if they remain national institutions. The Court forcefully found that:

> [t]he ESCB represents a novel legal construct in EU law which brings together national institutions, namely the national central banks, and an EU institution, namely the ECB, and causes them to cooperate closely with each other, and within which a different structure and a less marked distinction between the EU legal order and national legal orders prevails ... Article 14.2 of the Statute of the ESCB and of the ECB reflects the logic of this highly integrated system which the authors of the Treaties envisaged for the ESCB and, in particular, of the dual professional role of the governor of a national central bank, who is certainly a national authority but who acts within the framework of the ESCB and sits, where he is the governor of a national central bank of a Member State whose currency is the euro, on the main decision-making body of the ECB.[77]

Owing to the ESCB's highly integrated nature, the Court of Justice went as far as annulling directly the national decision that prevented Mr Rimšēvičs from exercising his functions within the ESCB. This should be viewed as a signal to the Member States that their NCBs are part of a supranational system, the ESCB, and not only national institutions which they manage as they please. The Court could arguably have reached the same outcome without taking such a drastic measure. However, in my view, it is likely that the Court wanted to make a point. It wanted to stress the NCB's character as *Europeanized* national institution, but it probably also wanted to use this case as an example in the hope that it could strengthen both the NCBs' and the NCAs' independence as it has very limited tools to protect the NCAs' independence.[78]

The Court's findings in the recent *ECB v Slovenia* case[79] regarding the inviolability of Union archives may, too, be viewed as having reinforced the *dual national-European nature* of NCBs. It indeed clarified the scope of the protection afforded to the ECB, and

[77] ibid paras 69 and 70 (emphasis added).

[78] For a discussion on the potential of spillover of this area of banking supervision (or the absence thereof), see René Smits, 'A National Measure Annulled by the European Court of Justice, or: High-level Judicial Protection for Independent Central Bankers' (2020) 16 EuConst 120, 139 ff. Although I fully share René Smits' view that the remedy provided for under ESCB Statute (n 6) Art 14(2) is unique under the Treaties and that, therefore, possibilities for similar judicial actions to protect national authorities involved in other national-EU procedures are inexistent, I still believe that this case sends a strong warning to the Member States. Furthermore, as noted above, in a majority of Member States the NCA functions are, in fact, assumed by the NCBs such that NCAs could indirectly be protected by this provision.

[79] Case C-316/19 *European Commission v Republic of Slovenia* [2020] EU:C:2020:1030.

considered that a Member State is not entitled to unilaterally seize ECB documents located at the premise of an NCB without the ECB's authorization.[80] The ECB's independent nature as a supranational EU institution was re-confirmed, even if it heads the ESCB composed also of the (Europeanized) NCBs led by (Europeanized) governors, and even if it heavily relies on the NCBs in the conduct of its monetary policy.

As noted in the introduction to this section, contradictory trends that point both towards the national component within the ECB having become stronger and towards its supranational character having become reinforced exist, thus making any assessment uneasy. They are likely to fluctuate over time in as far as these developments at least partly relate to evolutions observable in practice as opposed to resulting from changes to the legal framework in place. Additionally, the factors that play a role in these changes are particularly varied.[81] For instance, the euro area crisis was only one element that triggered direct change. The expansion of the euro area was also a factor, as was the creation of the Banking Union and arguably the maturing process of a still particularly young central bank and currency Union. Contradictory tendencies coupled with limited information make an assessment of the balance between supranationalism and national influence difficult, arguably more so than in other EU institutions. The next section seeks to compare today's ECB with the other EU institutions and bodies.

IV. Re-situating the ECB in the EU's Institutional Landscape: How Do the Institutional Logics that Govern Today's ECB Compare to Those of other EU Institutions and Bodies?

To try and evaluate the ECB's institutional structure and the supranational and nationally oriented logic(s) that underpin it, a comparison with the other EU institutions and bodies that exist may be useful, even if both types of influences are admittedly always present, only in different proportions. Furthermore, in view of the limited space available, it is only a modest attempt that is made here to shed some light on the ECB's structure.

In the area of monetary policy, the ECB with its supranational Governing Council operating on a collegial basis and with NCBs governors participating in their personal capacity and thus following a supranational logic may be viewed as resembling the European Commission.[82] Indeed, the Commission is independent, and like NCB Governors are too when they participate in the Governing Council, Commissioners are expected to act in full independence.[83] Contrary to what is prescribed regarding

[80] ibid paras 100ff.

[81] On this, see further the introduction to this edited volume.

[82] As noted above, NCB governors' influence may nonetheless also lead to stronger national influence if their policy stance were to be dictated by the impact of the euro area monetary policy in their own Member State. See also Manuela Moschella and Nicola M Diodati, 'Does Politics Drive Conflict in Central banks' Committees? Lifting the Veil on the European Central Bank Consensus' (2020) 21 European Union Politics 183.

[83] Consolidated version of the Treaty on European Union [2012] OJ C326/01, Art 17(3).

the Commission where, unless the Member States decide otherwise (as they have) not all of them should have 'their' Commissioner, it is not foreseen that at some point in time some NCB Governors cease to be members of the Governing Council.[84] However, it remains that the rotating voting system in place within the Governing Council may be viewed as pursuing the same goal of efficiency whilst being underpinned by the same supranational logic.

As noted in the introduction to this chapter, there nonetheless exists a crucial difference between the ECB's and the Commission's structures, which affects their supranational nature. Commissioners are supported by supranational Commission Directorate Generals and services, whereas the Governing Council is supported by supranational ECB services too, but individual NCB Governors rely on the administrations of their NCBs as well.

In this context, how should ECB preparatory committees be assessed? These do not appear to fulfil the same function as the committees traditionally involved in the comitology procedure, for these committees of national representatives are called to voice an opinion on an implementing act proposed by the Commission, whereas ECB preparatory committees contribute to the preparation of the decisions subsequently made by the ECB decision-making bodies. As such, the ECB committees rather appear to fulfil a function similar to that of the Council Working Groups, in whose framework national representatives discuss and prepare the decisions made by the Council of the EU.[85]

In view of these characteristics, the ECB's institutional structures may be viewed as corresponding to an institutional logic that may best be qualified as hybrid in as far is it is partially similar to that of the supranational Commission, and partially similar to that of the intergovernmental Council. The departure from the collegial logic that would demand for the (common) decisions of the Governing Council to remain uncontested by its members might point towards the more nationally focused logic that governs ECB Committees affecting the supranational Governing Council too. The relationship between the ECB and the NCBs within the ESCB has nonetheless remained unaffected over time, meaning that, for example, its hierarchical nature whereby NCBs have to implement the decisions at the EU level has not been compromised (even if the findings of the German Federal Constitutional Court in the *Weiss* case threatened this). If anything, the integrated and supranational nature of the ESCB has only been reinforced over time, as shown by the recent *Rimšēvičs* and *ECB v Slovenia cases*. Notwithstanding this, as illustrated in this chapter, it is undeniable that tensions have arisen as a result of the dual national and European nature of NCBs and their governors, a characteristic that has over time given rise to evolving and sometimes contradictory dynamics between national and supranational dimensions.

In the area of Banking Supervision, the corresponding ECB internal organs and institutional structures function in a radically different way, although the SSM too, like the ESCB, is a system composed of the ECB and national authorities. The Supervisory Board's and the Steering Committee's compositions, and the JSTs that

[84] ibid Art 17(5).

[85] On these organs, see Jonathan Bauerschmidt, 'Council of the European Union: Internal Organisation' in Laurence Gormley and others (eds), *EU Encyclopedia* (OUP forthcoming).

assist in the supervision of SIs, have a much stronger national component than the Governing Council and the Executive Board do. The division of tasks and the collaboration between the ECB and the NCAs also operate differently than they do between the ECB and the NCBs, and they rather resemble the system in place between the Commission and the National Authorities in the area of competition law—although the Commission admittedly does not participate in the day-to-day supervision, contrary to the ECB within the SSM.[86] In fact, '[t]his model of integration has [been found to have] functioned very well and has served as a template in other cases, such as the European Public Prosecutor's Office'.[87] The SSM's structures however also present similarities with those of EU agencies, as already noted above.

Even if the system of cooperation between national and EU authorities and the model for their representation as they exist within the SSM may therefore be qualified as unique (as opposed to their being identical to other institutional structures in other areas of EU law), it is beyond doubt that they differ significantly from those in place in the area of monetary policy, as is only logical in view of the different types of EU competences and of the various types of decisions involved.

V. Conclusion

This chapter has shown that the ECB's institutional structures and logics of functioning have significantly evolved both *de jure* and *de facto* since its creation two decades ago, pointing to its having become a 'new ECB'. It has also highlighted that parts of this structure (ie its committees) are still largely unknown up until today. Furthermore, it has highlighted that the dual *national* and *European* nature of NCBs and their governors have given rise to tensions and varying dynamics.

The institutional structure of today's ECB is to be viewed as situated somewhere between the supranational Commission, the intergovernmental Council of the EU, the coordinated systems that underpin the coordination among national authorities within EU agencies such as the European Supervisory Authorities, and the multilevel or composite systems of administrative cooperation as they exist for example in the field of competition law.

Considered as a whole, the ECB's institutional framework and functioning has shifted towards less supranational logics in the sense that national influence has grown over time. In the area of banking supervision, this is less problematic as it is an area in which harmonization is still limited and in which individual decisions are made that have a significant impact on the single national economies. Although it is a policy area in which, too, independence is key, banking supervision is commonly assumed

[86] On the role and divide between the Commission and the National competition authorities, see Giorgio Monti, 'Independence, Interdependence and Legitimacy: The EU Commission, National Competition Authorities, and the European Competition Network' (2014) EUI Department of Law Research Paper No 2014/01 <https://cadmus.eui.eu/handle/1814/29218> accessed 21 November 2021.

[87] Chiara Zilioli, 'Twenty years of building bridges: the process of legalisation of European central banking' in European Central Bank, 'Building bridges: central banking law in an interconnected world' (ECB Legal Conference 2019) 11 <https://www.ecb.europa.eu/pub/pdf/other/ecb.ecblegalconferenceproceedings201912~9325c45957.en.pdf> accessed 21 November 2021.

by institutions other than NCBs that are less independent. As such, the strong national component that exists is perhaps unavoidable as long as higher levels of integration are not achieved.

The partial shift towards renationalization visible in the field of monetary policy as illustrated by the recurring expression of dissenting views is arguably more concerning for it goes against the ECB's independence, and for this is an EU exclusive competence in which euro area-wide decisions are made. At the same time, considering the activism that has characterized the way in which monetary policy has been conducted since the euro area crisis, and especially considering the ECB's resort to unconventional monetary policy instruments that have had a significant economic impact (economic policy being an area which is only meant to be coordinated among Member States at the EU level), this shift was perhaps difficult to avoid. As noted, there is nonetheless an inherent danger to the renationalization of the debate and the ensuing shift to the background of the general European interest, as evidenced by the very launching of, and the findings in, the *Weiss* case of the German Federal Constitutional Court and the procedure on the Pandemic Emergency Purchase Programme pending before the same court.

In conclusion, mention should also be made of the fact that these shifts, and the undeniable increase in the level of complexity they have provoked over the past two decades, arguably raise important issues of accountability.[88]

The ECB's supranational character alongside the fact that monetary policy is a competence that is exclusively exercised at the EU level arguably calls for administrative, democratic, and judicial accountability to be solely guaranteed at the EU level. It follows that only the European Court of Auditors may control the ECB's actions in the area of monetary policy (with due observance of the existing limitations), that only the Court of Justice may assess the legality of the ECB's actions (which arguably calls for easier individual access to the Court to be created), and that democratic accountability can, at present, only be guaranteed by the European Parliament (even though another organ in which the euro area alone would be represented should arguably be involved in parallel to ensure that the chain of legitimacy which the relationship between (affected) voters and representatives is not broken like it is at present with the participation of all MEPs regardless of whether they are elected in euro area Member States or not). The informal relationships that have developed between the ECB and national parliaments in the area of monetary policy over the past decade may be viewed as one that fulfils a radically different function for it serves information purposes more than accountability proper. The same applies to the relationships between NCB governors and national parliaments: considering the significant impact ECB decisions have on the Member States and their economies, it is undoubtable that national parliamentarians should be duly informed, also because these decisions should influence the decisions they make in areas in which they do have powers (contrary to the situation in the field of monetary policy because of central bank independence and monetary policy being an EU exclusive competence).

[88] On the ECB's accountability regime generally, see chapter 11 by Fabian Amtenbrink and Menelaos Markakis, in this volume.

The evolution of the ECB that leads it to become subject to stronger levels of national influence may, though, call for the redefinition of the accountability mechanisms in place, as has already been done in the field of banking supervision where original mechanisms of accountability between the ECB and national parliaments exist. But the intrinsic supranational nature of the accountability mechanisms in place should be preserved, and any renationalization of the debates regarding the ECB's policies avoided if the ECB is to remain capable of achieving its objective to maintain price stability.

14

The ECB in the New Normal

Organizing Fiscal Support for Monetary Policy

Ad van Riet[*]

I. Introduction

When the European Economic and Monetary Union (EMU) was set up, the European Central Bank (ECB) was given exclusive competences for the conduct of monetary policy, with the primary objective to maintain price stability for the euro area as a whole and otherwise to support the general economic policies in the European Union (EU).[1] Awaiting further political integration, EMU was designed without a fiscal counterpart to the ECB that in turn could assist monetary policy with stabilizing the euro area economy. The Member States adopting the euro instead faced more stringent requirements for their economic policies and public finances to ensure the proper functioning of EMU.[2]

The ECB's 'institutional loneliness'[3] at the euro area level turned out to be a serious weakness of the EMU architecture when a powerful common fiscal response was required to increase the efficacy of monetary policy in times of economic crisis, fragmented financial markets, and constraints on interest rate management (Section II). This chapter therefore reviews how euro area governments could cooperate to establish fiscal framework conditions in support of monetary policy that are more similar to those found in other currency areas.

First, member countries could create a central fiscal capacity to establish a euro area economic policy stance consistent with the orientation of monetary policy (Section III). Second, they could introduce a safe sovereign asset for the euro area to anchor

[*] The views expressed in this chapter are those of the author and should not be reported as representing an official position of UNU-CRIS. Comments and suggestions by the editors of this volume are gratefully appreciated.

[1] See the 'Consolidated Version of the Treaty on the Functioning of the European Union' [2016] OJ C202/47 (hereafter 'TFEU'), Arts 127 and 130. The responsibility for euro area monetary policy lies with the Eurosystem, which is made up of the ECB and the National Central Banks (NCBs) of the euro area countries.

[2] The Member States of the EU are obliged to treat their economic policies as a matter of 'common concern' and to coordinate them within the EU Council (TFEU (n 1) Arts 119, 120, 121, and 126). The Treaty of Lisbon of 2009 introduced a power to adopt measures specific to the euro area countries to strengthen the coordination and surveillance of their budgetary discipline and to set out economic policy guidelines for them (TFEU (n 1) Art 136).

[3] See Tommaso Padoa-Schioppa in Christa Randzio-Plath and Tommaso Padoa-Schioppa, 'The European Central Bank: Independence and Accountability' (2000) University of Bonn Center for European Integration Studies (ZEI) Working Paper No B–16, 37 <https://www.econstor.eu/bitstream/10419/39496/1/325873607.pdf> accessed 1 December 2020.

Ad van Riet, *The ECB in the New Normal* In: *The New European Central Bank.* Edited by: Thomas Beukers, Diane Fromage, and Giorgio Monti, Oxford University Press. © Ad van Riet 2022. DOI: 10.1093/oso/9780198871231.003.0014 financial integration, secure an even monetary transmission, and facilitate the implementation of monetary policy (Section IV). Third, euro area governments could provide an *ex ante* fiscal backstop to their own National Central Bank (NCB) and (indirectly) the ECB to underpin the credibility of large-scale monetary policy operations (Section V). A new normal of fiscal support for monetary policy could strengthen the EMU architecture and support confidence in the euro (Section VI).[4]

II. The Institutional Loneliness of the ECB

The lack of an EMU institution in charge of euro area economic policy and the concerns about fiscal sustainability in some member countries constrained the efficacy of monetary policy in recent years.

First, the Great Financial Crisis of 2008 demanded a forceful fiscal expansion alongside the ECB's credit easing measures to stabilize financial markets, support the banking sector, and counter the unavoidable recession. Since the EU budget is targeted at economic convergence and market integration rather than macroeconomic stabilization,[5] the bulk of any fiscal stimulus has to come from the Member States. However, they must operate within the margins of flexibility of the Stability and Growth Pact (SGP), which at that moment did not include a general escape clause.[6] Moreover, the countries with a high public-debt-to-gross domestic product (GDP) ratio (notably Greece and Italy) had little if any fiscal space, and those with more sustainable public finances thus made the largest contribution to the collective response.[7]

Second, the sovereign debt crisis of 2010–12, which spilled over to fragile banks and threatened to break up the euro, triggered a fragmentation of financial markets along national lines of creditworthiness and was accompanied by a common fiscal austerity drive which suppressed euro area output growth. The ECB continued with enhanced credit easing for banks to relax private financing conditions and tried to stabilize disrupted national bond markets to enable its monetary stimulus to reach the whole euro area. An ECB promise of unlimited outright market interventions to address non-fundamental sovereign spreads was necessary to restore investors' confidence in the future of the euro. Given the implied mutualization of national sovereign risk, proposals for a euro area treasury issuing eurobonds to implement a common fiscal policy and overcome the market fragmentation failed to gain political momentum.[8]

[4] A fully fledged fiscal union would go much further, because it entails a central government with fiscal policy competences to provide for common public goods, redistribute public resources, and promote system-wide stabilization, while raising taxes and issuing public debt to finance these tasks.

[5] The EU budget plays only a modest role in cushioning economic shocks since it is small (about 1 per cent of EU gross national income) and must be in balance every year (TFEU (n 1) Art 310).

[6] Member States must adhere to a structural budgetary position that is close to balance or in surplus (based on TFEU (n 1) Art 121) and avoid an excessive deficit (TFEU (n 1) Art 126 and Protocol No 12). The SGP comprises the secondary legislation which provides for the relevant multilateral surveillance and coordination procedures.

[7] See Ad van Riet (ed), 'Euro area fiscal policies and the crisis' (2010) ECB Occasional Paper Series No 109 <https://www.ecb.europa.eu/pub/pdf/scpops/ecbocp109.pdf> accessed 1 December 2020.

[8] See Ad van Riet, 'Safeguarding the euro as a currency beyond the state' (2016) ECB Occasional Paper Series No 173 <https://www.ecb.europa.eu/pub/pdf/scpops/ecbop173.en.pdf?58b212353f0ff17de8938 11907b60667> accessed 1 December 2020.

Third, the corridor of the ECB's key interest rates reached the zero lower bound in July 2012. Given the constraints on lowering the deposit facility rate (too far) into negative territory, the ECB implemented a series of non-standard measures—including a large-scale public sector purchase programme (PSPP) as from March 2015—to provide additional monetary accommodation in its fight against too low inflation.[9] Meanwhile, the aggregate fiscal stance of the euro area was broadly neutral, whereas the further monetary stimulus—as pointed out by the ECB—could have been more effective with a coordinated fiscal expansion.[10] Moreover, the pursuit of low-for-long interest rates had (unintended) side-effects, since it also eased the governments' intertemporal budget constraint, kept unviable firms alive, increased financial risk-taking, and redistributed income and wealth.[11] Furthermore, the Eurosystem accepted ever-more financial risks related to its growing balance sheet. Large losses on its monetary policy operations might deplete its reserves and capital. An unavoidable recapitalization of the NCBs and the ECB could be a vehicle for fiscal transfers between the euro area countries and violate the budget rights of national parliaments.[12] This experience suggested that a common fiscal policy should relieve the stabilization task of monetary policy, especially in an environment of ultra-low interest rates and fragmented financial markets.

Similar constraints on the efficacy of monetary policy arose after the outbreak of the coronavirus disease (COVID-19) in 2020. As some of the hardest-hit countries (again) had little fiscal space to counter its socio-economic consequences, Europe put in place supranational safety nets. However, euro area leaders could not agree on issuing common 'coronabonds' to collectively raise additional budgetary resources in the capital market for a sizeable common fiscal stimulus alongside the ECB's large-scale pandemic monetary easing. The political compromise on an EU-wide recovery plan, paid for by substantial EU borrowing guaranteed by the EU budget, was a momentous step forward in terms of fiscal integration. Yet, it remained an exceptional response to an emergency situation and missed a permanent euro area dimension.

[9] See Ad van Riet, 'Twenty Years of European Central Bank Monetary Policy: A Keynesian and Austrian Perspective' (2019) 239 Journal of Economics and Statistics 797 (hereafter van Riet, 'Twenty Years ECB'). See also chapter 2 by Vestert Borger and chapter 3 by Klaus Tuori, in this volume.

[10] See Mario Draghi, 'Unemployment in the Euro Area' (Luncheon Address at the Federal Reserve Bank of Kansas City Symposium on 'Re-Evaluating Labor Market Dynamics', Jackson Hole, 22 August 2014) <https://www.ecb.europa.eu/press/key/date/2014/html/sp140822.en.html> accessed 1 December 2020; Peter Praet, 'The ECB's monetary policy: past and present' (Speech at the Febelfin Connect event, Brussels/Londerzeel, 16 March 2017) <https://www.ecb.europa.eu/press/key/date/2017/html/sp170316.en.html> accessed 1 December 2020.

[11] See Ad van Riet, 'The ECB's Fight against Low Inflation: On the Effects of Ultra-Low Interest Rates' (2017) 5 International Journal of Financial Studies 1, Art 12; van Riet, 'Twenty Years ECB' (n 9).

[12] Going against the European Court of Justice, the German Federal Constitutional Court even concluded that the ECB exceeded its monetary policy competences, because the PSPP had significant side-effects which in its view were equivalent to economic policy. See 'Case C-493/17 *Heinrich Weiss and Others*' [2018] EU:C:2018:1000; BVerfG (German Federal Constitutional Court) 5 May 2020, 2 BvR 859/15 DE:BVerfG:2020:rs20200505.2bvr085915, paras 1–237.

III. A Euro Area Fiscal Capacity

Economic theory pointed early on to the advantages of a central fiscal capacity for stabilizing a monetary union (apart from financing common public goods and redistributing public revenues). First, it can contribute to an area-wide monetary-fiscal policy mix that maintains both internal and external macroeconomic balance in the face of common shocks. Second, a central budget can be employed to help individual member countries to address large domestic shocks or common shocks with strong asymmetric effects that overburden national fiscal policy and could spillover to the rest of the monetary union. Third, common budgetary resources could be used to promote economic convergence and market integration and thus a more synchronized business cycle among the member countries around a similar path for potential growth. Hence, there should ideally be a common treasury as counterpart to the common central bank to share the stabilization burden.[13]

The construction of EMU without a central fiscal capacity implies that the task of managing the euro area economy falls in essence on the ECB. The member countries on their part are expected to maintain a high degree of economic flexibility as well as sound and sustainable public finances as necessary to successfully adjust to domestic shocks. The objective of economic policy coordination is to ensure their structural resilience and budgetary discipline, both in their own interest and that of euro area stability. In addition, multilateral surveillance should sustain their economic convergence and market cohesion.[14]

This EMU architecture appeared appropriate for the first decade of the euro when the economy experienced mostly upside inflation risks and national financial markets were integrating. However, the more complex economic and financial environment in the euro's second decade demanded a more active fiscal policy coordination to support the ECB in its fight against too low inflation, especially when its key interest rates reached the zero lower bound and financial markets became fragmented.[15]

Since the sovereign debt crisis, the Eurogroup finance ministers explicitly discuss the euro area fiscal stance resulting from the draft budgetary plans of the euro area countries in the context of the European Semester for economic policy coordination.[16] However, the flexibility embedded in the EU's fiscal rules cannot bridge the gap between strong and weak national public finances when on aggregate a countercyclical

[13] See Peter B Kenen, 'The Theory of Optimum Currency Areas: An Eclectic View' in Robert A Mundell and Alexander K Swoboda (eds), *Monetary Problems of the International Economy* (Chicago University Press 1969) 41–60; Paul de Grauwe, *Economics of Monetary Union* (13th edn, OUP 2020).

[14] See also nn 2 and 6.

[15] See Ad van Riet, 'The European Central Bank as the Only Game in Town: How Could Fiscal Policy-Makers Play Along?' (2018) 51 Credit and Capital Markets 93.

[16] 'Regulation (EU) 473/2013 of the European Parliament and of the Council of 21 May 2013 on common provisions for monitoring and assessing draft budgetary plans and ensuring the correction of excessive deficit of the Member States in the euro area' [2013] OJ L140/11 requires euro area countries to submit a draft budgetary plan to the European Commission and the Eurogroup. The Commission adopts opinions on whether these plans comply with SGP requirements and conducts an overall assessment of the euro area fiscal stance in preparation of a discussion in the Eurogroup. The European Fiscal Board (EFB) gives independent advice to the Commission on the fiscal stance appropriate for the euro area.

fiscal expansion would be warranted. Given the provisions of the SGP, only member countries with a nearly balanced budget or a surplus in structural terms and low risks to fiscal sustainability could be expected to contribute with a fiscal impulse on a voluntary basis—unless it would destabilize their own economies. Countries without such fiscal space should first restore sound and sustainable public finances in line with SGP requirements. The organization of an appropriate euro area fiscal stance is therefore handicapped by the need for governments to find a balance between their fiscal contribution to area-wide macroeconomic stabilization and domestic requirements for achieving and maintaining fiscal sustainability.[17]

This fiscal sustainability constraint on coordinated action could be overcome with a euro area fiscal capacity of sufficient size to complement the aggregate fiscal stance when needed to dampen strong area-wide output fluctuations in concert with the ECB, as well as to assist the recovery of individual member countries hit by a large asymmetric shock, subject to common decision-making and parliamentary accountability.[18] In addition, the SGP could be amended to reduce the pro-cyclical bias in national fiscal policies and enhance the incentives for governments to undertake structural reforms and improve the quality of public finances in the interest of future output growth.[19] Assuming full respect of the ECB's statutory independence, a more balanced overall monetary-fiscal policy mix could accelerate the euro area recovery and the return to price stability. If successful, it would shorten the time needed for the ECB to pursue negative interest rates and large-scale open-market operations.

Following up on the five EU presidents' report on completing EMU by 2025,[20] the European Commission reflected on options for enhancing euro area macroeconomic stabilization and fostering economic convergence of the member countries, within the EU framework. As part of an EMU-related package of proposals for the post-2020 EU budget, it suggested that a European Minister of Economy and Finance could be given the task to strengthen economic policy coordination in support of monetary policy.[21] This coordination task could be facilitated by new budgetary instruments for a stable euro area, in particular a European Investment Stabilisation Function (EISF) and a

[17] See Krzysztof Bańkowski and Marien Ferdinandusse, 'Euro area fiscal stance' (2017) ECB Occasional Paper Series No 182 <https://ec.europa.eu/info/sites/info/files/ecb_-_euro_area_fiscal_stance.pdf> accessed 1 December 2020.

[18] On the design options for a euro area fiscal shock absorber, see Gilles Thirion, 'European Fiscal Union: Economic rationale and design challenges' (2017) Centre for European Policy Studies Working Document 1 <https://papers.ssrn.com/sol3/papers.cfm?abstract_id=3047087> accessed 1 December 2020. For a thought experiment on how it could be embedded into the EU fiscal framework, see Christophe Kamps and Nadine Leiner-Killinger, 'Taking stock of the functioning of the EU fiscal rules and options for reform' (2019) ECB Occasional Paper Series No 231 <https://www.ecb.europa.eu/pub/pdf/scpops/ecb.op231~c1ccf67bb3.en.pdf> accessed 1 December 2020.

[19] See European Fiscal Board, 'Assessment of EU fiscal rules with a focus on the six- and two-pack legislation' (EFB 2019) <https://ec.europa.eu/info/publications/assessment-eu-fiscal-rules-focus-six-and-two-pack-legislation_en> accessed 1 December 2020.

[20] See Jean-Claude Juncker, 'Completing Europe's Economic and Monetary Union' (European Commission, Report in close cooperation with Donald Tusk, Jeroen Dijsselbloem, Mario Draghi, and Martin Schulz, 22 June 2015) <https://wayback.archive-it.org/12090/20191231140925/https://ec.europa.eu/commission/sites/beta-political/files/5-presidents-report_en.pdf> accessed 1 December 2020.

[21] See European Commission, 'Further steps towards completing Europe's economic and monetary union: a roadmap' (Communication) COM(2017) 821 final and European Commission, 'New budgetary instruments for a stable euro area within the Union framework' (Communication) COM(2017) 822 final.

Reform Support Programme (RSP), which would be accessible for Member States that complied with the EU economic governance framework.[22] The EISF would enable the Commission to borrow capital and extend loans to individual euro area countries (with the members of the European Exchange Rate Mechanism (ERM II) free to join in) in the event of a large asymmetric shock, so as to stabilize public investment at a time when their fiscal capacity was stretched. The RSP would draw on EU budget resources and provide financial incentives and technical support for growth-sustaining administrative, institutional, and structural reforms.[23]

Trying to advance the political discussion, the French and German governments (supported by Spain) reached an agreement in the course of 2018 on creating a euro area budget within the EU framework with the objective to foster convergence, promote competitiveness, and contribute to stabilization of the member countries, under strategic guidance from the Euro Area Summit. A separate European Unemployment Stabilisation Fund could lend money to the social-security systems of member countries facing an economic crisis.[24]

The 'New Hanseatic League' of eight smaller member countries led by the Netherlands strongly resisted in particular the stabilization element of a euro area budget, because they feared that entering into public risk-sharing without previous public risk-reduction could undermine fiscal discipline and lead to permanent budgetary transfers.[25] As a result, the Eurogroup and the Euro Summit of December 2018 restricted the scope of the agreement to a euro area budgetary instrument for convergence and competitiveness (BICC), to be anchored within the EU budget for 2021–27.[26] Under the BICC, which was to become part of the European Semester, all euro area countries (as well as the ERM II members wishing to join in) could receive grants for undertaking ambitious structural reforms and public investments, subject to the fulfilment of agreed milestones and targets.[27] The EU budget envelope of €25

[22] See European Commission, 'Proposal for a Regulation of the European Parliament and of the Council establishing a European Investment Stabilisation Function' (Communication) COM(2018) 387 final and European Commission, 'Proposal for a Regulation of the European Parliament and of the Council on the establishment of the Reform Support Programme' (Communication) COM(2018) 391 final.

[23] The back-to-back EISF loans of up to €30 billion, guaranteed by the EU budget, could be coupled with a grant to cover the interest costs. The RSP comprised three elements, with an overall tentative budget of €25 billion: (1) a Technical Support Instrument as follow-up to the Structural Reform Support Programme; (2) a new Reform Delivery Tool; and (3) a new Convergence Facility for non-euro area countries.

[24] See 'Meseberg Declaration: Renewing Europe's Promises of Security and Prosperity' (Declaration adopted during the Franco-German Council of Ministers, Meseberg, 19 June 2018) <https://www.diplomatie.gouv.fr/en/country-files/germany/events/article/europe-franco-german-declaration-19-06-18> accessed 1 December 2020 and the French-German 'Proposal on the architecture of a Eurozone Budget within the framework of the European Union' (16 November 2018) <https://www.consilium.europa.eu/media/37011/proposal-on-the-architecture-of-a-eurozone-budget.pdf> accessed 1 December 2020.

[25] See, eg, 'Northern Member States Unite on Euro-Zone Reform' *The Economist* (London, 8 December 2018).

[26] See Council of the EU, 'Term sheet on the budgetary instrument for convergence and competitiveness (BICC)' (Council Press Releases 466/19 and 642/19, Brussels, 14 June 2019 and 10 October 2019) <https://www.consilium.europa.eu/en/press/press-releases/2019/06/14/term-sheet-on-the-budgetary-instrument-for-convergence-and-competitiveness/pdf> and <https://www.consilium.europa.eu/en/press/press-releases/2019/10/10/term-sheet-on-the-budgetary-instrument-for-convergence-and-competitiveness-bicc/pdf> accessed 1 December 2020.

[27] See European Commission, 'Proposal for a Regulation of the European Parliament and of the Council on a governance framework for the budgetary instrument for convergence and competitiveness for the euro area' (Communication) COM(2019) 354 final. The BICC would be integrated within the Reform Support

billion reserved for the BICC (of which €17 billion was allocated to the euro area countries for reform delivery) could only be increased by voluntary national contributions in line with a new intergovernmental agreement among the participating countries. Technical discussions on adding a stabilization function to this remit would continue.

Progress with the BICC was overtaken by the EU's comprehensive economic response to the COVID-19 pandemic in tandem with the ECB's massive monetary support aimed at stabilizing financial markets and countering the macroeconomic fall-out from the Great Lockdown. The common fiscal response, as also called for by the ECB,[28] emerged from the political willingness of the Member States to act together in the fight against a common adversary and to avoid the mistakes made during the sovereign debt crisis.[29]

To start with, the normal budgetary requirements under the SGP were temporarily suspended in view of the expected severe economic downturn affecting the euro area as a whole and the need to coordinate a supportive fiscal stance.[30] This general escape clause—which was introduced in the SGP as a lesson from the Great Financial Crisis of 2008—allowed Member States to deviate from their budgetary adjustment paths to tackle the health emergency and address its negative socio-economic consequences. Yet, the SGP also states that taking all necessary budgetary measures should not endanger fiscal sustainability in the medium term.

Governments that entered the COVID-19 recession with healthy public finances were in a much better position to meet this condition than those that already had a high public-debt-to-GDP ratio. The lack of fiscal space in the hardest-hit countries (in the first instance Italy and Spain) constrained them in taking sizeable countermeasures, which in turn could lead to a sustained economic divergence that undermined the cohesion of the internal market and the stability of the euro. Following an appeal to their solidarity and self-interest, however, Member States were quick to establish common safety nets for firms, workers, and sovereigns with a total value of €540 billion.

For example, the European Investment Bank (EIB) created a European guarantee fund of €25 billion to provide up to €200 billion in loans—in partnership with local lenders and national promotional banks—to companies. Furthermore, it activated emergency funds of up to €40 billion to bridge short-term financing needs of small and medium-sized enterprises. The European Commission received approval to give

Programme. The governance framework provided for the EU Council with only the euro area countries having a right to vote to set *ex ante* strategic orientations on the reform and investment priorities for the euro area as a whole and to give country-specific guidance. On this basis, euro area countries could submit proposals for reform and investment packages to be supported under the BICC.

28 Christine Lagarde, 'Opening remarks' (Online Edition of the State of the Union conference organized by the European University Institute, Florence, 8 May 2020) <https://www.ecb.europa.eu/press/key/date/2020/html/ecb.sp200508~81cd924af6.en.html> accessed 1 December 2020.

29 See Council of the EU, 'Report on the comprehensive economic policy response to the COVID-19 pandemic' (Council Press Release, Brussels, 9 April 2020) <https://www.consilium.europa.eu/en/press/press-releases/2020/04/09/report-on-the-comprehensive-economic-policy-response-to-the-covid-19-pandemic/> accessed 1 December 2020.

30 European Commission, 'The activation of the general escape clause of the Stability and Growth Pact' (Communication) COM(2020) 123 final.

Member States facing a sudden severe increase in public expenditure related to employment protection temporary access to EU debt-financed financial support of up to €100 billion to mitigate unemployment risks in an emergency (SURE), that is, for national short-time work schemes.[31] Euro area governments enabled the European Stability Mechanism (ESM) to offer a new credit line on which fiscally constrained member countries could draw to receive Pandemic Crisis Support of up to 2 per cent of their GDP, specifically to cover the healthcare costs related to the coronavirus outbreak. These 'timely, targeted and temporary' supranational measures *de facto* performed the stabilization role that a central fiscal capacity for the euro area would be expected to play, complementing the ECB's monetary stimulus. But further common initiatives were called for to protect the EU's future growth potential.[32]

Building on a Franco-German initiative[33] and on European Commission proposals,[34] the European Council reached a political agreement to offer further financial assistance to the hardest-hit countries and regions by redirecting EU budget resources for 2020 and putting together a revamped EU budget of €1074 billion (in 2018 prices) for 2021–27. European leaders further agreed on an ambitious 'Next Generation EU' recovery plan worth €750 billion (in 2018 prices) for 2021–23 that involved substantial Commission borrowing in the capital market with a partial repayment through new EU taxes. Member States thus received access to guarantees, grants, and loans, channelled through EU programmes, in particular to promote green and digital investments, finance structural reforms, and strengthen the resilience to future emergencies.

A handful of 'frugal' countries around the Netherlands questioned in particular the need for grants (which ease national fiscal constraints) as opposed to loans (which further increase governments' debt) and tried to tighten the governance framework.[35] The political compromise split the EU recovery funds into a maximum of €390 billion in conditional grants and up to €360 billion in concessional loans. Each Member State was given the right to ask the European Council in exceptional cases to verify that the receiving country shows a satisfactory fulfilment of the milestones and targets of its agreed national recovery and resilience plan, a procedure which would delay but could not automatically stop the Commission's decision on the payment.[36] This

[31] The SURE instrument, created by 'Council Regulation (EU) 2020/672 of 19 May 2020 on the establishment of a European instrument for temporary support to mitigate unemployment risk in an emergency (SURE) following the COVID-19 outbreak' [2020] OJ L159/1, is the emergency operationalization of the European Unemployment Reinsurance Scheme.

[32] European Fiscal Board, 'Assessment of the fiscal stance appropriate for the euro area in 2021' (EFB 2020) <https://ec.europa.eu/info/publications/assessment-fiscal-stance-appropriate-euro-area_en> accessed 1 December 2020.

[33] See the 'French-German Initiative for the European Recovery from the Coronavirus Crisis' (Paris, 18 May 2020) <https://www.diplomatie.gouv.fr/en/coming-to-france/coronavirus-advice-for-foreign-nationals-in-france/coronavirus-statements/article/european-union-french-german-initiative-for-the-european-recovery-from-the> accessed 1 December 2020.

[34] European Commission, 'The EU budget powering the recovery plan for Europe' (Communication) COM(2020) 442 final.

[35] See 'Non-paper on EU support for efficient and sustainable Covid-19 recovery' (Published by the Office of Austrian Chancellor, Sebastian Kurz, on behalf of Austria, Denmark, the Netherlands and Sweden, Vienna, 23 May 2020) <https://www.politico.eu/wp-content/uploads/2020/05/Frugal-Four-Non-Paper.pdf> accessed 1 December 2020.

[36] See the conclusions adopted by the Special European Council (Brussels, 17–21 July 2020) <https://www.consilium.europa.eu/en/meetings/european-council/2020/07/17-21/> accessed 1 December 2020. Payment of EU funds was made dependent on the fulfilment of the economic conditions to ensure their

political agreement was hailed as a historical breakthrough for European fiscal integration, since for the first time it combined substantial EU public debt issuance and some EU taxes with a fiscal redistribution scheme, albeit with mutual oversight of spending.

An open question is whether the EU's economic response to the COVID-19 crisis qualifies as an alternative to a euro area fiscal capacity. The various common safety nets introduced during the pandemic were conducive to macroeconomic stabilization in a time of crisis but were not designed to address ordinary business cycle fluctuations at the euro area level. The objective of Next Generation EU, in particular the Recovery and Resilience Facility,[37] is to support national reforms and public investments, similar in spirit to the BICC. But it is a temporary budgetary instrument designed for EU purposes. The contribution of the Eurogroup would have to be expressed through the EU Council's recommendation on the economic policy of the euro area that is addressed to the euro area countries individually and collectively in the European Semester.

A permanent euro area fiscal capacity embedded in the EU framework—funded with regular national contributions, allocated tax revenues, or euro area borrowing—is still needed to secure an appropriate monetary-fiscal policy mix, assist individual member countries faced with a large asymmetric shock, and reward national structural reforms that strengthen economic convergence and competitiveness. The ECB would gain a more effective monetary policy, because a central budgetary instrument can be employed to ensure a consistent economic policy stance that supports more synchronized output growth in the member countries, an even monetary transmission across integrated markets, and a stabilization of the euro area business cycle, conducive to price stability.

IV. A Safe Sovereign Asset for the Euro Area

Apart from a euro area fiscal capacity, the single monetary policy would also benefit from a single safe sovereign asset available in sufficient supply that effectively anchors the euro area financial system.

First, a common sovereign asset for the euro area regarded as safe would serve as a stable benchmark for pricing both public and private debt securities, mitigate the risk of volatile intra-area capital flows between safe and risky member countries, and promote financial integration. A more unified capital market supports an even

effectiveness as well as on the respect of the rule of law to protect the EU's financial interests. On the rule of-law mechanism, see the later European Council conclusions (Brussels, 10–11 December 2020) <https://www.consilium.europa.eu/en/meetings/european-council/2020/12/10-11/> accessed 18 December 2020.

[37] The proposed Regulation for a Reform Support Programme, which included the BICC, was withdrawn and its content was replaced by the Recovery and Resilience Facility (with revised objectives and an adjusted reform delivery mode) and a separate Technical Support Instrument. Hence, the proposed Regulation for a governance framework for the BICC was also withdrawn. See European Commission, 'Proposal for a Regulation of the European Parliament and of the Council establishing a Recovery and Resilience Facility' (Communication) COM(2020) 408 final.

transmission of monetary policy across the euro area and reduces the need for the ECB to stabilize national sovereign bond markets.[38]

Second, a common public debt security would meet the financial industry's rising demand for high-quality and liquid assets to comply with EU and national prudential requirements. A safe euro area public debt security is also an effective tool to break the negative feedback loop between vulnerable governments and systemic banks holding national sovereign debt on their balance sheet which could decline in value in a fiscal crisis.[39] A more resilient euro area banking system enhances financial stability and facilitates monetary policy.

Third, common public debt would function as reliable collateral for secured inter-bank lending. Banks could also pledge it in credit operations with their NCB if it is accepted as eligible collateral. The ECB could itself buy and sell common public debt securities as part of outright monetary policy operations in the euro area money and/or capital market instead of having to use a basket of national public sector securities of variable quality and liquidity. A safe euro area sovereign instrument could further be held as a reserve asset by other central banks, which would facilitate foreign exchange swaps and market interventions and enhance the international role of the euro.[40]

Since the Great Financial Crisis of 2008, many proposals have been put forward in the quest for a safe sovereign asset for the euro area, with or without mutualization of national public debt.[41] The majority of European leaders always excluded the option of issuing genuine eurobonds under joint and several liability of the countries participating in EMU, because public debt pooling could in their view only be envisioned as part of a future fiscal union. Until that time, the ultimate safety of common public debt must therefore be secured as much as possible through other means.

European supranational institutions like the EIB and the ESM issue public debt securities—also denominated in other currencies than the euro—to acquire funds to fulfil a specific mandate. They enjoy the highest credit rating thanks to their strong capital base, as provided by the participating EU countries. The European Commission regularly accesses the capital market to borrow modest sums—guaranteed by the own resources of the EU budget to secure a top credit rating—which are passed on as rescue loans to Member States and third countries. Since the COVID 19 crisis, this borrowing activity also covers temporary financing of the SURE instrument of up to €100 billion, which is backed up by at least €25 billion of bilateral guarantees voluntarily committed by Member States to the EU budget. To finance Next Generation EU, the Commission will further tap the capital market in 2021–26 at a range of maturities for a maximum of €750 billion (in 2018 prices, or €806 billion in current prices) to

38 See Ad van Riet, 'Addressing the safety trilemma: A safe sovereign asset for the eurozone' (2017) ESRB Working Paper Series No 35 <https://www.esrb.europa.eu/pub/pdf/wp/esrbwp35.en.pdf> accessed 1 December 2020.

39 See Markus K Brunnermeier and others, 'ESBies: safety in the Tranches' (2017) 32 Economic Policy 175 (hereafter Brunnermeier and others, 'ESBies').

40 See European Central Bank, 'The International Role of the Euro' (ECB 2019) <https://www.ecb.europa.eu/pub/ire/html/ecb.ire201906~f0da2b823e.en.html> accessed 1 December 2020.

41 See the review by Fabian Amtenbrink, René Repasi, and Jacob de Haan, 'Is there Life in the Old Dog Yet? Observations on the Political Economy and Constitutional Viability of Common Debt Issuing in the Euro Area' (2016) 12 Review of Law & Economics 605.

cover Member States' requests for funding their recovery from the pandemic.[42] The steady repayment of this EU debt with accrued interest until 2058, in particular the part that is used for grants to Member States, is secured by a temporary increase in the own-resources ceiling, as well as by the introduction of EU taxes.

Most of the Commission's enlarged borrowing activity derives directly from the EU's economic response to the COVID-19 emergency. The restrictions in terms of size, duration, and scope that apply to this EU debt make it less suitable for fulfilling all the aforementioned monetary policy functions of a safe sovereign asset for the euro area. Euro area governments could also charge, for example, a European Public Debt Office (or the ESM) with the task to issue and refinance an adequate amount of common public debt securities backed up by a diversified portfolio of national sovereign bonds. Given the different risk profiles of euro area countries, flanking measures are required to ensure that investors perceive this sovereign bond-backed common security as a safe asset at all times.

One option to achieve this objective is to structure the euro area security into a junior tranche which carries all the credit risks on the underlying portfolio of national sovereign bonds and a senior tranche of European Safe Bonds (ESBies) with a very low probability of default.[43] The ultimate safety of the senior tranche could be guaranteed by adding a modest reserve fund to cover credit losses if ever the absorption capacity of the junior tranche was fully exhausted.[44] Alternatively, the ESM could be mandated to issue so-called 'E-bonds' and use the proceeds to construct a portfolio of national sovereign bonds. E-bonds could be secured either by an increase in the ESM's capital base or by the financial returns from its status as a senior investor who always gets paid before other creditors. Creating a common safe asset for the euro area should thus be feasible without asking the member countries to assume an undue common liability to guarantee its safety.[45]

A political decision to introduce a single sovereign asset that unifies and stabilizes the euro area financial system and can serve as a tool for monetary policy requires several disciplinary and regulatory issues to be addressed. For example, to contain moral hazard, a country's participation in the scheme could be made conditional on full compliance with the EU's economic governance rules. Alongside, the preferential treatment of national sovereign bonds in EU prudential legislation for credit institutions as risk-free assets—which gives governments easier access to funding than

[42] See European Commission, 'On a new funding strategy to finance NextGenerationEU' (Communication) COM(2021) 250 final.

[43] See Brunnermeier and others, 'ESBies' (n 39). The European Commission came with a 'Proposal for a Regulation of the European Parliament and of the Council on sovereign bond-backed securities (SBBS)' (Communication) COM(2018) 339 final, to enable a private market-led development of SBBS, remove regulatory impediments, and create a level playing field with national sovereign bonds. Euro area countries feared, however, that their own sovereign debt would become subordinated to the SBBS.

[44] See Alexandra MD Hild, Bernhard Hertz, and Christian Bauer, 'Structured Eurobonds: Limiting Liability and Distributing Profits' (2014) 52 JCMS 250.

[45] For some legal and practical issues, see Álvaro Leandro and Jeromin Zettelmeyer, 'Creating a Euro Area Safe Asset without Mutualizing Risk (Much)' (2019) Peterson Institute for International Economics Working Paper No 19-14 <https://papers.ssrn.com/sol3/papers.cfm?abstract_id=3432533> accessed 1 December 2020; Sebastian Grund, 'The Quest for a European Safe Asset—A Comparative Legal Analysis of Sovereign Bond-Backed Securities, E-Bonds, Purple Bonds, and Coronabonds' (2020) 6 Journal of Financial Regulation 233.

corporations—could be carefully phased out for euro area governments.[46] At the global level, the Basel Committee on Banking Supervision should allow supervisors to grant this regulatory privilege to the new common public debt security (as is the case already for EIB, ESM, and EU debt) to recognize its quality as a safe asset for investors and to ensure that the euro area can compete for funds in international capital markets at the same level as third countries.

V. A Fiscal Backstop for the Eurosystem

The financial independence of the ECB and the NCBs enables the Eurosystem to define monetary policy without having to consider the expected profits and losses on its market interventions. Still, the acquired monetary assets and the accepted collateral must be sufficiently secure and the net monetary liabilities it assumes must be covered by adequate capital and reserves, both to sustain its operational capacity and the public's trust in its activities. Moreover, a sudden need for fresh capital may lead politicians to impose conditions. The Eurosystem therefore closely monitors and carefully manages the financial risks associated with its monetary policy actions.[47]

The net income accruing to the euro area NCBs as a result of their monetary policy function is in principle pooled at the Eurosystem level before it is allocated to them in proportion to their paid-up shares in the capital of the ECB. As shareholders, the euro area NCBs also receive their share of the ECB's profits after its financial buffers have been replenished.[48]

Over the past decade, the financial risks related to this net monetary income have been affected by two opposing factors. On the one hand, non-standard monetary easing targeted at reducing economic risks increased the risk-bearing capacity of other economic sectors. For the Eurosystem, this risk-reduction also made significant losses on its monetary operations less likely. On the other hand, the pursuit of low-for-long interest rates created incentives for (excessive) financial risk-taking and debt accumulation, both in the private sector and the public sector. Moreover, the Eurosystem substantially increased its risk exposure over time as it intensified its monetary accommodation. Large financial losses occurring in a severe stress scenario could in theory exhaust its reserves and capital base.

[46] 'Regulation (EU) 575/2013 of the European Parliament and of the Council of 26 June 2013 on prudential requirements for credit institutions and investment firms and amending Regulation 648/2012' [2013] OJ L176/1 (the so-called Capital Requirements Regulation) as amended, allows banks under certain conditions to assign claims on central governments a zero-risk weight without exposure limit and to consider them as high-quality liquid assets. See also Ad van Riet, 'The Preferential Treatment of Government Debt in Financial Law: The Case of Europe' in Emilios Avgouleas and David C Donald (eds), *The Political Economy of Financial Regulation* (CUP 2019) 385–418.

[47] See European Central Bank, 'The financial risk management of the Eurosystem's monetary policy operations' (ECB 2015) <https://www.ecb.europa.eu/pub/pdf/other/financial_risk_management_of_eurosystem_monetary_policy_operations_201507.en.pdf> accessed 1 December 2020 and chapter 4 by Jens van 't Klooster, in this volume.

[48] See TFEU (n 1), 'Protocol (No 4) on the Statute of the European System of Central Banks and of the European Central Bank' [2016] OJ C202/230 (hereafter 'ESCB/ECB Statute'), Arts 32.5 and 33.1.

The main financial risks to net monetary income arise from five sources. First, the Eurosystem provided sizeable refinancing to its counterparties at longer maturities than usual to support bank lending to the economy, while accepting a wider range of lower-rated financial instruments than normal as eligible collateral, especially in stressed money market conditions.[49] Early in the COVID-19 crisis, it adopted an emergency package of collateral easing measures, adding Greek sovereign debt instruments as eligible collateral and grandfathering the collateral eligibility of marketable assets that fell below the minimum credit quality requirements. Collateral valuation haircuts, variation margins, and other risk controls were still applied, but the risk tolerance level was increased during the pandemic.[50]

Second, the interest rate that the Eurosystem receives on credit given to the banking sector normally exceeds the interest rate that it pays on deposited bank reserves. However, the net positive effect of these dual interest rates on monetary income was diminished over time. As from June 2014, the ECB's deposit facility rate was cut below zero and reduced further in several steps to -0.5 per cent in September 2019. Starting with the Targeted Longer-Term Refinancing Operations (TLTROs) of June 2016, banks meeting the condition of sufficiently expanding their net lending to the private sector (excluding loans for house purchases) could borrow from the Eurosystem at a negative interest rate as low as the deposit facility rate. This credit subsidy offered the participating banks a partial offset for the tax implied by the negative interest rate on their deposited reserves.

Third, starting end-October 2019, a two-tier remuneration system applicable to bank reserves came into effect.[51] Minimum reserves as well as excess reserves held by banks in the deposit account continued to be taxed at the negative deposit facility rate. However, the part of excess reserves held in a current account with the Eurosystem (up to six times their minimum reserves) was remunerated at 0 per cent. This two-tier system reduced the average interest costs for the banking sector of holding excess reserves and was meant to support the bank-based transmission of monetary policy. During the COVID-19 crisis, the Eurosystem kept the deposit facility rate constant at -0.5 per cent but the lowest interest rate applicable to TLTROs was reduced in two steps to -1.0 per cent (and the access conditions were eased). In the following TLTRO of end-June 2020 it allocated some €1300 billion of credit with a three-year maturity to the participating banks (or about €550 billion after subtracting repayments of maturing loans). Since this additional liquidity could be parked at 0 per cent on a current account or at -0.5 per cent on a deposit with the Eurosystem, this operation entailed significant positive net interest transfers at the expense of net monetary income.

[49] See 'Guideline 2014/528/EU of the European Central Bank of 9 July 2014 on additional temporary measures relating to Eurosystem refinancing operations and eligibility of collateral and amending Guideline ECB/2007/9 (ECB/2014/31)' [2014] OJ L240/28 (hereafter 'Guideline ECB/2014/31'). See also chapter 4 by Jens van 't Klooster, in this volume.

[50] See 'Guideline (EU) 2020/515 of the European Central Bank of 7 April 2020 (ECB/2020/21)' [2020] OJ L110I/26 and 'Guideline (EU) 2020/634 of the European Central Bank of 7 May 2020 (ECB/2020/29)' [2020] OJ L148/10 both amending Guideline ECB/2014/31 (n 49).

[51] See 'Decision (EU) 2019/1743 of the European Central Bank of 15 October 2019 on the remuneration of holdings of excess reserves and of certain deposits (recast) (ECB/2019/31)' [2019] OJ L267/12.

Fourth, the Eurosystem assumed substantial credit risks on its balance sheet as a result of monetary operations in stressed private and public debt markets, although it also took risk containment measures. Focusing on public debt, it created a limited Securities Markets Programme (SMP) and purchased from May 2010 to March 2012 for about €220 billion in sovereign bonds of Greece, Ireland, Portugal, Italy, and Spain.[52] Although the SMP was not subject to conditionality, the ECB took note of, or requested, fiscal measures and economic reforms by these crisis-hit countries that would reduce its exposure to sovereign risk.[53] The ECB replaced the SMP in September 2012 by a commitment to undertake unlimited Outright Monetary Transactions (OMTs) in disrupted sovereign bond markets to counter currency redenomination risk premia related to fears of the reversibility of the euro. Activation of this monetary backstop was made conditional on strict and effective compliance with a full EU adjustment programme, preferably with IMF involvement, to reduce the likelihood of a sovereign default.[54]

Fifth, the Asset Purchase Programme (APP) as well as the Pandemic Emergency Purchase Programme (PEPP)—both covering eligible public and private sector debt instruments—significantly increased the Eurosystem's interest income, but also its exposure to corporate and sovereign defaults. The (expanded) APP for quantitative easing was implemented from October 2014 to December 2018, restarted in November 2019, and temporarily scaled up during the COVID-19 crisis to reinforce the accommodative impact of the ECB's monetary policy rates.[55] The principal payments from the maturing APP securities are reinvested for as long as necessary to restore price stability. The ECB launched the PEPP in March 2020 to stabilize financial markets and deliver extra monetary accommodation in direct response to the COVID-19 pandemic and implemented it until the end of March 2022.[56] The principal payments of maturing PEPP securities are reinvested until at least the end of 2024. By December 2021, the Eurosystem had acquired in total about €4,000 billion of public sector securities under the APP and the PEPP (of which 90 per cent were issued by central, regional, and local governments as well as recognized public agencies of euro area countries and 10 per cent were issued by European supranational institutions; see Figure 14.1) and about €685 billion of private sector securities.

The benchmark for the country allocation of public sector asset purchases under the APP and the PEPP (which only take place in the secondary market) is in principle the ECB's capital key instead of the proportion of national public debt outstanding

[52] See 'Decision 2010/281/EU of the European Central Bank of 14 May 2010 establishing a securities markets programme (ECB/2010/5)' [2010] OJ L124/8.

[53] Whereas Greece, Ireland, and Portugal had agreed to an EU/IMF adjustment programme, the ECB president (Trichet) sent (leaked) letters in August 2011 to the governments of Italy and Spain, co-signed by the respective NCB governors, urging them to step up fiscal consolidation and structural reforms.

[54] See 'Technical features of Outright Monetary Transactions' (ECB Press Release, Frankfurt am Main, 6 September 2012) <https://www.ecb.europa.eu/press/pr/date/2012/html/pr120906_1.en.html> accessed 1 December 2020.

[55] In particular, see 'ECB announces expanded asset purchase programme' (ECB Press Release, Frankfurt am Main, 22 January 2015) <https://www.ecb.europa.eu/press/pr/date/2015/html/pr150122_1.en.html> accessed 1 December 2020.

[56] See 'Decision (EU) 2020/440 of the European Central Bank of 24 March 2020 on a temporary pandemic emergency purchase programme (ECB/2020/17)' [2020] OJ L91/1, as amended.

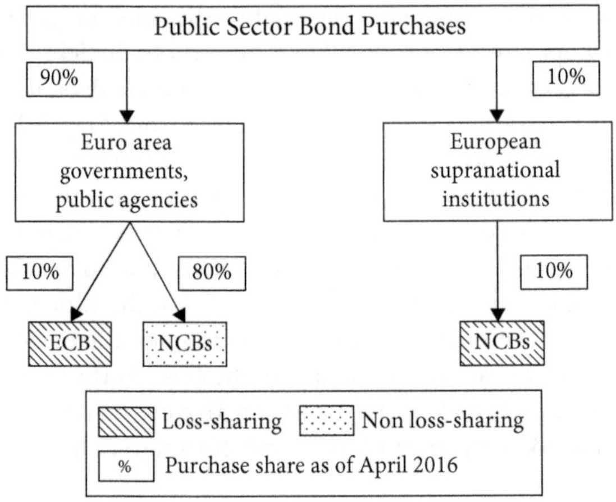

Figure 14.1 Public Sector Bond Purchases under the APP and the PEPP
Source: Created by the author based on ECB information (see nn 55, 56, and 57).

in the capital market. The total amount of these purchases is furthermore subject to issue share and issuer ceilings, which prevent the ECB and NCBs from getting a blocking minority in a public debt restructuring and becoming a dominant creditor of public institutions, respectively.[57] However, to preserve sufficient flexibility during the COVID-19 pandemic, these self-imposed limits were less strictly maintained for the PEPP and could be revised if necessary.

Considering eligible assets, both the APP and the PEPP were restricted to debt instruments with a minimum credit quality of investment-grade. Government bonds of euro area countries receiving EU/IMF financial assistance, which were rated below investment-grade, benefited from a waiver, provided that their adjustment programme was on track. Greek government bonds were not (yet) eligible for the APP but were accepted for the PEPP. Certain losses were so far only incurred on corporate sector bonds that after a credit downgrade to below the investment-grade threshold had to be sold again at a lower price.

The public sector bond portfolio acquired through the APP and PEPP is subject to a special loss-sharing regime which allocates most of the national sovereign risks to the respective NCBs (Figure 14.1). The financial results on the supranational bonds acquired by NCBs and on the national public sector bonds purchased by the ECB (each covering 10 per cent of the total since April 2016) are fully shared within the Eurosystem. Profits and potential losses on the remaining 80 per cent are for the sole account of the NCBs which bought the public sector bonds of their own country. The decision that each NCB will carry itself most of the direct financial consequences of a possible default by its own country is meant to prevent the mutualization of

[57] See 'Decision (EU) 2020/188 of the European Central Bank of 3 February 2020 on a secondary markets public sector asset purchase programme (recast) (ECB/2020/9)' [2020] OJ L39/12.

national sovereign risk as well as monetary financing of the failing government via the Eurosystem's balance sheet.[58]

A euro area NCB that incurs major financial losses in excess of its buffers has two main options to replenish its capital. First, it may decide to record the remaining loss on its balance sheet and carry it forward until retained future profits enable it to restore the statutory capital base. Second, a distressed NCB may be able to borrow in the capital market or from other NCBs and the ECB to cover the gap, using as collateral its share in future net monetary income.[59] These options avoid the political complication for the NCB of having to ask its shareholder(s) (mostly the national government) *ex post* for a recapitalization.

As for the ECB, any loss that it incurs in a financial year may be offset against its general risk provision and the general reserve fund. Should its financial buffers ever be exhausted, the ECB may ask the euro area NCBs to cover the shortfall with a contribution from their net monetary income in proportion to their paid-up shares in the ECB's capital.[60] The ECB may record any remaining negative difference on its balance sheet as a loss carried forward. Future seigniorage revenues and other net income would then be used to offset this loss and to replenish its capital and the financial buffers before resuming dividend payments to the euro area NCBs.[61] Still, a prolonged financial constraint could undermine the credibility of monetary policy.[62]

The ECB could also, if necessary, make a call on the NCBs to contribute extra capital within the limits and under the conditions set by the EU Council.[63] Already in the year 2000, following an ECB recommendation, the EU Council approved that at some point in the future it could request further capital of up to €5 billion beyond its initial subscribed capital of €5 billion.[64] Amid the sovereign debt crisis in 2010, the Governing Council decided to make full use of this option and increased the ECB's subscribed capital from €5.76 billion to €10.76 billion, paid-up by the euro area NCBs.[65] A further recapitalization of the ECB could be complicated to agree *ex post* in a political setting whereby the EU Council must consult with the European Parliament and the European Commission, and preferably all Member States should give their blessing.

Confidence in the ability of the ECB and the NCBs to perform their monetary policy tasks could therefore benefit from an explicit fiscal backing that could be

[58] See Peter Praet, 'Public sector security purchases and monetary dominance in a monetary union without a fiscal union' (Speech at the Conference 'The ECB and Its Watchers XVI', Frankfurt am Main, 11 March 2015) <https://www.ecb.europa.eu/press/key/date/2015/html/sp150311_1.en.html> accessed 1 December 2020.

[59] See Willem Buiter, 'The Eurosystem: An accident waiting to happen' *VoxEU* (London, 1 October 2020) <https://voxeu.org/article/eurosystem-accident-waiting-happen> accessed 1 December 2020.

[60] See ESCB/ECB Statute (n 48) Art 33.2.

[61] See Daniela Bunea and others, 'Profit distribution and loss coverage rules for central banks' (2016) ECB Occasional Paper Series No 169 <https://www.ecb.europa.eu/pub/pdf/scpops/ecbop169.en.pdf> accessed 1 December 2020.

[62] See Francesco Chiacchio, Grégory Claeys, and Francesco Papadia, 'Should We Care about Central Bank Profits?' (2018) Bruegel Policy Contribution 13 <https://www.bruegel.org/wp-content/uploads/2018/08/PC-13_2018.pdf> accessed 1 December 2020.

[63] See ESCB/ECB Statute (n 48) Art 28.1.

[64] See 'Council Regulation (EC) 1009/2000 of 8 May 2000 concerning capital increases of the European Central Bank' [2000] OJ L115/1.

[65] See 'Decision 2011/20/EU of the European Central Bank of 13 December 2010 on the increase of the European Central Bank's capital (ECB/2010/26)' [2011] OJ L11/53.

activated in a severe crisis.[66] The related EMU-specific coordination challenge could in principle be overcome with democratically legitimized fiscal guarantees that respect national budget rights.[67] The member countries could each make an unconditional fiscal commitment when necessary to indemnify or recapitalize their own NCB for monetary policy-related losses and to put it in a financial position to respond positively to an ECB call for additional capital. These *ex ante* fiscal guarantees would demonstrate to the public that euro area governments are collectively responsible for the financial risks that the Eurosystem takes with its much-expanded balance sheet.[68] A euro area fiscal capacity and a common safe asset can be effective tools to facilitate the task of monetary policy and reduce the chance that this fiscal backstop for the Eurosystem might ever be needed, which in turn could make it acceptable to all member countries.

VI. Conclusion

The EMU architecture relies above all on the single monetary policy to stabilize the euro area, whereas on several occasions since 2008 it became evident that fiscal assistance was warranted. Learning from the EU's cooperative economic response to the COVID-19 pandemic, euro area governments acting together could enhance the efficacy of ECB monetary policy in three complementary fiscal areas.

First, they could establish a permanent euro area fiscal capacity within the EU framework with the objective to stabilize output movements at the supranational and/or national level. Giving member countries financial rewards for structural reforms could further help to raise their potential growth and promote economic convergence. A supportive euro area economic policy stance would shorten the time needed for the ECB to pursue negative interest rates and to undertake large-scale open-market operations. Second, euro area countries could introduce a common public debt security that is backed up by a portfolio of national sovereign bonds and a reserve fund. A safe sovereign asset for the euro area that is available in sufficient supply would anchor financial integration, secure an even monetary transmission, and facilitate monetary policy. Third, euro area governments could make an unconditional fiscal commitment to indemnify or recapitalize their own NCB as

[66] During the COVID-19 pandemic, some major central banks received a full or partial indemnity from their government, which created an equity cushion to absorb exceptionally large losses. See Bank for International Settlements, 'Annual Economic Report 2020' (BIS, Basel, 30 June 2020) <https://www.bis.org/publ/arpdf/ar2020e.htm> accessed 1 December 2020.

[67] See Gerhard Illing and Philipp J König, 'The European Central Bank as Lender of Last Resort' (2014) 4 DIW Economic Bulletin 16.

[68] As an exception, in 2013 the Nederlandsche Bank received an *ex ante* guarantee from the Dutch State to cover the gap between the crisis-related increase in risk exposures and the available financial buffers until these risks had returned to normal. This fiscal backstop was available (but never called in) from 1 March 2013 to 1 March 2018 and covered up to €5.7 billion, with the effect that during this period the NCB did not have to make special risk provisions that would reduce its regular dividend payments to the State. See the letter of the Dutch Minister of Finance to the Chair of the House of Representatives on the proposal to grant a guarantee to the Nederlandsche Bank (Session 2012–2013, Document 33 548 No 8, 15 February 2013 (in Dutch)).

well as (indirectly) the ECB, if ever needed. This fiscal safeguard for the Eurosystem would recognize the importance of its financial independence for a credible monetary policy geared towards price stability.

Looking ahead, a new normal of fiscal support for monetary policy could also pave the way for the formal establishment of a euro area treasury as fiscal counterpart to the ECB that would address its institutional loneliness with full respect for its statutory independence.

PART IV
A CONTEXTUAL ANALYSIS OF THE ECB

Part 4 takes stock of all of the transformations discussed earlier to offer cross-cutting reflections on the nature of today's ECB as well as where the ECB could or should be heading. This calls for a comparison of the ECB's mandate with the mandate of other central banks, an analysis of the role of EU constitutional law for the ECB, and a reflection on the ECB's future path.

15

The ECB Mandate—a Comparative Constitutional Perspective

*Christy Ann Petit**

I. Introduction

The turmoil of the financial, banking, and sovereign debt crises (all crises are commonly grasped under the term 'Great Financial Crisis', GFC hereinafter) triggered different—creative and proactive—responses from central banks globally. Central banks face mutually reinforcing structural and cyclical challenges. Indeed, the low interest rates environment worldwide has reduced their leverage to use interest rate cuts as a policy tool.[1] Low inflation and slow, declining growth (with declining labour productivity and ageing population) co-occur with the pressing concerns for climate change risks, globalization, and digitalization. All those challenges influence central bank actions.

During the GFC, the fear of reaching the effective lower bound[2] crystallized amongst central bankers as a major constraint on their ability to use the policy rate to conduct monetary policy. This fear triggered the use of new monetary policy tools:[3] large-scale purchases of assets and securities in quantitative easing, and statements to put forward the predictions on interest rates, called forward guidance, which was introduced in support of accommodative monetary policy amongst several central banks to reduce long-term interest rates.[4]

* An earlier version was presented at the ADEMU 'A Dynamic Economic and Monetary Union' Conference, 'The New ECB in Comparative Perspectives' (September 2017, Florence). The author is grateful to Diane Fromage, Giorgio Monti, Thomas Beukers, Michal Krajewski, and Elena Sedano Varo for comments on earlier versions, and Fabian Amtenbrink for his comments during the 2021 ICON-S Mundo Conference. All errors and omissions remain the author's responsibility.

[1] Ben Bernanke, Michael T Kiley, and John M Roberts, 'Monetary Policy Strategies for a Low-Rate Environment' (2019) Finance and Economics Discussion Series 2019-009 <https://www.federalreserve.gov/econres/feds/files/2019009pap.pdf> accessed 13 July 2021. See also Klaus Tuori in this volume on conventional and unconventional monetary policy by the European Central Bank.

[2] See Carlo Altavilla and others, 'Is there a zero lower bound? The effects of negative policy rates on banks and firms' (2019) ECB Working Paper No 2289 <https://www.ecb.europa.eu/pub/pdf/scpwps/ecb.wp2289~1a3c04db25.en.pdf?2ce8cbb75e8750c3e82f7847c63591e9> accessed 13 July 2021 and Florian Heider, Farzad Saidi, and Glenn Schepens, 'Life Below Zero: Bank Lending under Negative Policy Rates' (2019) 32 Review of Financial Studies 3728.

[3] Ben Bernanke, 'The New Tools of Monetary Policy' (2020) 110 American Economic Review 943.

[4] Simon M Potter and Frank Smets, 'Unconventional Monetary Policy Tools: A Cross-Country Analysis' (2019) Bank for International Settlements CGFS Papers No 63, 32–35 <https://www.bis.org/publ/cgfs63.pdf> accessed 13 July 2021 (hereafter Potter and Smets, Unconventional Monetary Policy Tools), short-term policy rates were moved in negative territory, for instance, for the European Central Bank (ECB) since mid-2014: see Miguel Boucinha and Lorenzo Burlon, 'Negative Rates and the Transmission of Monetary Policy' (2020) ECB Economic Bulletin Issue 3/2020 <https://www.ecb.europa.eu/pub/economic-bulletin/

Christy Ann Petit, *The ECB Mandate—a Comparative Constitutional Perspective* In: *The New European Central Bank*.
Edited by: Thomas Beukers, Diane Fromage, and Giorgio Monti, Oxford University Press. © Christy Ann Petit 2022.
DOI: 10.1093/oso/9780198871231.003.0015

In a context of institutional flexibility and political necessity,[5] central banks' responses to the GFC (COVID apart) further shaped the scope of their mandate. These responses sparked criticism about stretched boundaries of such mandate. Looking more closely at the framework of central banks, the word 'mandate' is oftentimes inexistent in statutory sources. Generally, a mandate is analysed together with the objectives and tasks (or functions)[6] of a central bank. In order to better understand the concept of central bank 'mandate', and more specifically the relationship between mandate, objectives, and tasks, two different approaches to a mandate can be distinguished: a functional and a purposive approach.

Firstly, central banks' mandates are defined functionally where the bundle of functions or tasks assigned to them differs across central banks including in their organization. One common denominator is the combination of monetary policy and means of settlement within one entity.[7] Moreover, modern central banks can be responsible for financial stability, for an effective payment system, liquidity management, and the related function of Lender of Last Resort (LOLR), for the financial system infrastructure, services to the government, and other public good functions.[8] Second, a central bank's mandate may be defined purposively, that is by focusing on its objectives. In an abstract and broad approach, central banks would have the following objectives: maintaining price stability, high employment and output stability, economic growth, financial stability (including microprudential and macroprudential policies), interest rates stability, and stability in foreign exchange markets[9] (and an ongoing active debate on climate change actions). Central banks' objectives often serve as an indicator to evaluate the performance of the central bank entrusted with such objectives. Again, there is no universal model for the objectives of central banks and different situations exist: multiple objectives within a same function, distinct objectives for different functions,[10] and a common objective diffused across different functions. Therefore, the mandate encompasses objectives and tasks,[11]as an umbrella, which

articles/2020/html/ecb.ebart202003_02~4768be84e7.en.html> accessed 13 July 2021. See also chapter 2 by Vestert Borger and chapter 3 by Klaus Tuori, in this volume.

[5] See Alan Blinder and others, 'Necessity as the Mother of Invention: Monetary Policy after the Crisis' (2017) 32 Economic Policy 707, including a forward-looking perspective on the central banks' mandates. See also Thomas Beukers, 'The New ECB and its Relationship with the Eurozone Member States: Between Central Bank Independence and Central Bank Intervention' (2013) 50 CML Rev 1579, 1591.

[6] Bank for International Settlements, 'Issues in the governance of central banks' (Report from the central bank governance group, May 2009), 17 <https://www.bis.org/publ/othp04.pdf> accessed 13 July 2021 (hereafter BIS Report).

[7] ibid 21.

[8] ibid 28–49.

[9] Frederic S Mishkin, *The Economics of Money, Banking, and Financial Markets* (10th edn, Pearson 2013) 435, another objective may include to support the state's financing needs in times of crisis. However, in normal times, such objective is to prevent the misuse of state's financial powers, see Charles AE Goodhart, 'The changing role of central banks' (2010) BIS Working Papers No 326, 1 <https://www.bis.org/publ/work326.pdf> accessed 13 July 2021 (hereafter Goodhart, 'The changing role of central banks').

[10] François Gianviti, 'The Objectives of Central Banks' in Mario Giovanoli and Diego Devos (eds), *International Monetary and Financial Law: The Global Crisis* (OUP 2010) 450 (hereafter Gianviti, 'The Objectives of Central Banks').

[11] The difference between objectives and functions is thin; the BIS Report uses the chicken and egg metaphor (n 6) 18.

justifies following both a purposive and a functional analysis of central banks' mandate in a comparative perspective.

The comparative analysis in this chapter puts the European Central Bank (ECB) under central focus with other selected central banks—the Federal Reserve System (FED), the Bank of Canada (BoC) and the Bank of England (BoE). The latter three central banks are older than the ECB/European Union constituency, so they undeniably benefit from a longer experience and yet all those four major central banks in Western economies mostly converged in policy measures during the GFC as will be examined. In constitutional terms, the EU Treaties give exclusive competence to the European Union (EU) for monetary policy.[12] Since 2014, the ECB has been conferred by secondary legislation the responsibility for banking supervision in a system including the ECB and national competent authorities within the 'Single Supervisory Mechanism' (SSM).[13] If the monetary policy function was dominant in the common perception of central bank mandates until the GFC, since then, there has been a significant shift to financial stability as an objective of different functions of central banks.[14]

This chapter will examine in turn the formal sources and implementation of the mandate. The mandate is a separate concept from central banks' *objectives*, *tasks* and the policy *measures* used to achieve them. However, as a theoretical construct not expressly worded in the black letter of the statutes, the mandate is generally inferred from the central banks' objectives as specified by the applicable legal framework. The comparative examination of formal sources will show that central banks' objectives and their priority in the central bank mandate suffer from some misconceptions, sometimes due to the flexibility used, and how they have been interpreted following specific policy actions. Beyond formal sources, the implementation of the mandate may stretch, and ultimately, shape its scope. Diverse sources—constitutional, statutory, and legal acts—allow a systematic analysis (objectives and tasks), together with policy statements and institutional documents (including speeches and agreements on the strategy and implementing measures) that support the examination of the mandate's implementation.

The ECB, the youngest central bank in the sample, may learn from its peers, and lead by example in some instances. The 'new' ECB questions our preconceptions and understanding of its mandate, the scope of objectives and tasks, in a comparative

[12] Michael Waibel, 'Monetary Policy: An Exclusive Competence Only in Name?' in Sacha Garben and Inge Govaere (eds), *The Division of Competences between the EU and the Member States: Reflections on the Past, the Present and the Future* (Hart Publishing 2017).

[13] Legally based on the Consolidated Version of the Treaty on the Functioning of the European Union [2012] OJ C326/47, Art 127 (6) (hereafter TFEU) and Protocol No 4 on the Statute of the European System of Central Banks and of the European Central Bank [2016] OJ C202/230, Art 25.2 (hereafter ESCB and ECB Statute), to the exception of insurance undertakings. See also Council Regulation (EU) no 1024/2013 of 15 October 2013 conferring specific tasks on the European Central Bank concerning policies relating to the prudential supervision of credit institutions [2013] OJ L287/63, Art 1; Case C-450/17 P *Landeskreditbank Baden-Württemberg—Förderbank v European Central Bank* [2019] ECLI:EU:C:2019:372. See further chapter 7 by Kern Alexander, and chapter 8 by Federico Della Negra and Gianni Lo Schiavo, in this volume.

[14] Rosa María Lastra, *International Financial and Monetary Law* (2nd edn, OUP 2015) 55–64; Paul Davies, 'Financial Stability and the Global Influence of EU Law' in Marise Cremona and Joanne Scott (eds), *EU Law beyond EU Borders: The Extraterritorial Reach of EU Law* (OUP 2019); Gianni Lo Schiavo, *The Role of Financial Stability in EU Law and Policy* (Kluwer 2017). See chapter 5 by Agnieszka Smoleńska and Thomas Beukers, in this volume.

perspective in law and in action. How has the ECB's mandate been implemented in comparison to other central banks since the GFC? How does the ECB's mandate compare to other central banks? The purposive and functional analysis will elaborate on the current legal frameworks of central bank mandates (Section II.A). The implementation of the mandates, via diverse policy actions since the GFC, have reshaped the scope of central bank mandates in giving different priority among objectives, adding or reinforcing some objectives and tasks (Section II.B). The chapter will elaborate on the reasoning behind departing from the single-dual mandate grid for central banks. The traditional distinction 'single versus dual' mandate can indeed be nuanced, namely with another distinction between a broad, twin, and hierarchical mandate.

II. Central Bank Mandates: Formal Sources and their Implementation

The mandates are first examined through their constitutional, statutory, and legal sources. Monetary policy is a traditional central banking task, associated with a price stability objective. The latter exists alongside other objectives that reflect economic policies' direct or indirect considerations, such as financial stability, employment, growth, economic, and financial welfare, with a growing concern for climate change-related and environmental risks. Across central banks, these other objectives are pursued with a different priority ranking, ranging from equal to price stability, to 'below' it (secondary or contributory objectives in EU jargon), and are not always clearly associated with corresponding other central bank functions than monetary policy. In this regard, the dichotomy between single versus dual mandate is not always straightforward at the statutory level as will be examined in A. This leads to a complex set of circumstances: a single objective or multiple objectives for the same function (ie monetary policy examined hereinafter), or multiple objectives for different central bank functions (possibly as many as enumerated in the introduction).[15]

Turning to the implementation, extra-statutory elements, such as an inflation target framework or an agreement between the central bank and another government body, exhibit how central banks' price stability objective translates the mandate into policy actions. Furthermore, secondary sources complement primary sources (using the EU parlance). Hence, central bank mandates should not be examined only through statutory sources because this would give only a static analysis or even inconclusive results (as we will see, statutes may remain silent on the interplay of objectives and functions). Non-statutory elements and post-GFC practices that have transformed central banks as we know them are decisive in leading a systematic analysis (B).

[15] Gianviti, 'The Objectives of Central Banks' (n 10) 454; and on the Tinbergen rule of one instrument per policy target, see Kenneth J Arrow, 'Tinbergen on Economic Policy' (1958) 53 Journal of the American Statistical Association 89.

A. Legal sources of central bank mandates, objectives, and tasks

This subsection identifies the mandate of the four central banks, their underlying objectives, and the applicable priority ranking. A brief functional analysis, based on the tasks (or functions) assigned to the central banks in statutory constitutional and legal sources, elaborates further the systematic approach to the central bank mandates. The analysis starts with the ECB (1) and compares it subsequently with the three other central banks examined on the same analytical grounds (ie focusing first on objectives (2), and secondly on tasks (3)). Table 15.1 summarizes these objectives and their ranking following statutory sources.

(1) ECB's mandate and hierarchized multiple objectives

The European System of Central Banks (ESCB) and the ESCB/Eurosystem differ from one another because derogations still apply to some Member States,[16] as was the case for the UK during its membership of the EU. The ESCB/Eurosystem is the focus of the analysis here even if the shortcut 'ECB' is sometimes used. Some elements of the ESCB/Eurosystem's mandate are stated or referred to in its statutory sources. The EU Treaties set a primary objective and other objectives (commonly referenced as secondary and contributory) while secondary law activated, via Treaty legal bases, a competence for prudential supervision and some macroprudential responsibilities that assign other objectives under supervisory tasks and responsibilities.

Starting with the purposive analysis, objectives are a component of the central banks' mandate, next to its tasks (examined hereinafter). The ESCB/Eurosystem has a constitutional and statutory-anchored primary objective underlying the definition of its monetary policy. This primary objective is to maintain price stability, in accordance with the Treaty on the Functioning of the European Union (TFEU) and the Statute of the ESCB and the ECB.[17] Moreover, the letter of the foundational texts sets the ESCB/Eurosystem other objectives, which include the support to the general economic policies in the Union, acting in accordance with the principle of an open market economy with free competition.[18] The TFEU legal basis refers to broader contributory objectives set in the Treaty on the European Union (TEU) insofar as the ESCB/Eurosystem is to contribute to the objectives of the Union, namely, a sustainable development of Europe based on balanced growth and price stability, aiming at full employment and social progress.[19] The ECB shares these Union objectives with the other EU institutions and the Member States. Moreover, the ESCB/Eurosystem is also expected to contribute to the smooth conduct of policies relating to the prudential supervision of

[16] TFEU (n 13) Art 139 (2). Due to Member States having a derogation, in some articles in the remit of the ESCB's mandate, the reference to Member States must be read instead as Member States whose currency is the euro. The objectives and tasks of the ESCB as set forth in TFEU (n 13) Art 127(1) to (3) and (5) do not apply to Member States with a derogation (TFEU (n 13) Art 139 (2)(c)).

[17] TFEU (n 13) Arts 119(2), 127(1) and 282(2) and ESCB and ECB Statute (n 13) Art 2.

[18] TFEU (n 13) Art 127(1).

[19] TFEU (n 13) Art 127(1) refers to Consolidated Version of the Treaty on European Union [2012] OJ C326/01, Art 3(3).

Table 15.1 Central bank objectives and their ranking based on statutory sources

	ESCB/ Eurosystem	BoE	BoC	FED
Mandate	Hierarchical mandate	Twin mandate	Broad mandate	Dual mandate
Statutory source (mandate)	Article 127(1) TFEU, Article 3(3) TEU	Sections 2A and 11, BoE Act (amended)	Preamble BoC Act	Section 2A Monetary Policy Objectives Federal Reserve Act
Objectives (or goals)	Price stability—primary objective for monetary policy Without prejudice to the objective of price stability, support general economic policies—secondary objectives Objectives of the Union (sustainable development, growth, employment, and social progress)—broader contributory objectives Safety and soundness of credit institutions and stability of the financial system (since 2014, in a supervisory system)	Price stability—primary objective for monetary policy Subject to price stability: growth and employment Support to the economic policy of the government—secondary objectives Financial stability objective (shared with other entities)	Objectives listed with reference to several macroeconomic variables (production, trade, prices, and employment) Objectives: to regulate credit and currency, to control and protect the external value of money, to use external value of money, within the scope of monetary action, to mitigate fluctuations in production, trade, prices, and employment	Two goals *de facto*: maximum employment and stable prices Financial stability mission reinforced (since the GFC), with involvement in the FSOC
Priority or ranking among objectives	Hierarchized objectives, primary price stability objective	Hierarchized objectives, primary price stability objective But twin objective when considering financial stability	Not explicitly indicated in statutory sources	Equal objectives

credit institutions and the stability of the financial system,[20] which adds to the above contributory objectives. As indicated in the introduction, the ECB is responsible for banking supervision in the euro area, together with the NCAs within the SSM. In this regard, secondary law defines the ECB's objectives within banking supervision, namely, to ensure the safety and soundness of credit institutions and to contribute to the stability of the financial system within the Union and each Member State.[21]

That said, objectives are unquestionably hierarchized within the monetary policy function, with an overriding importance of the price stability objective over the other objectives, which have been called in the literature secondary and within those, contributory objectives, despite early disagreement from the ECB on the term 'secondary' that was publicly disclosed recently.[22] If the general mandate of the ESCB/Eurosystem includes a primary objective for price stability, it is questionable not to call its other objectives of a 'secondary' nature given that they are indirectly pursued, or a 'second element in the ECB's mandate'.[23] This chapter does not enter in the debate of the economic merits of secondary objectives within the monetary policy function. The legal bases, part of a living constitution, are however left with room for interpretation, used in the GFC context, and for which the broader economic context and interactions with fiscal and economic policies matter (see Section III). Therefore, even though monetary policy is not defined in the EU Treaties,[24] the prominence of the price stability objective within its monetary policy function, and across functions, is expressly set and justifies designating its mandate as 'hierarchical', while the financial stability objective has been reinforced since the GFC (B).

From a functional perspective, the mandate is carried out through the ESCB with four 'basic tasks':[25] the definition and implementation of the Union monetary policy,[26] the conduct of foreign-exchange operations, the responsibility of the official foreign reserves of the Member States,[27] and the promotion of the smooth operation of

[20] TFEU (n 13) Art 127(5) and ESCB and ECB Statute (n 13) Art 3.3. The omission reflects the fact that 'competent authorities' within the euro area corresponds indeed to the ECB and National Competent Authorities within the Single Supervisory Mechanism.

[21] '[W]ith full regard and duty of care for the unity and integrity of the internal market based on equal treatment of credit institutions with a view to preventing regulatory arbitrage' as per Council Regulation (EU) 1024/2013 of 15 October 2013 conferring specific tasks on the European Central Bank concerning policies relating to the prudential supervision of credit institutions [2013] OJ L287/63, Art 1 (hereafter SSM Regulation). See Pierre Schammo, 'The European Central Bank's Duty of Care for the Unity and Integrity of the Internal Market' (2017) 42 EL Rev 3; Marco Lamandini, David Ramos and Javier Solana, 'The European Central Bank (ECB) as a Catalyst for Change in EU Law. Part 1: The ECB's Mandates' (2016) 23(1) Columbia Journal of European Law 1 (hereafter Lamandini and others, 'The European Central Bank').

[22] European Central Bank, 'Clarifying the Nature of ECB Support for General Economic Policies in the Community' (Directorate General Economics, DMP/1120/01, 29 January 2002), 2 <https://www.ecb.europa.eu/ecb/access_to_documents/document/pa_document/shared/data/ecb.dr.par2021_0007_clarifyingmonpol2002.en.pdf> accessed 13 July 2021.

[23] ibid 5.

[24] Case C-370/12 *Pringle v Government of Ireland and Others* [2012] ECLI:EU:C:2012:756, para 53.

[25] Pursuant to TFEU (n 13) Art 127(2) and ESCB and ECB Statute (n 13) Art 3.1.

[26] The Eurosystem is in charge of the *conduct* of the monetary policy (TFEU (n 13) Art 282(1), emphasis added).

[27] The ESCB/Eurosystem responsibility is to hold and manage the official foreign reserves of the Member States, without prejudice to the holding and management of foreign-exchange working balances by the Member States' governments: see TFEU (n 13) Art 127(2) and (3). This started with the NCBs' transfer of foreign reserve assets to the ECB, in accordance with ESCB and ECB Statute (n 13) Art 30. Foreign reserves include US dollar, Japanese yen, Chinese renminbi, gold, and IMF Special Drawing Rights. See Livia Chițu,

payment systems. In addition to those tasks, as previously said, the ECB was conferred specific tasks concerning policies relating to the prudential supervision of credit institutions and other financial institutions.[28] Following the above purposive analysis, EU secondary law gives additional objectives within those supervisory tasks that are now exerted within the SSM as a system. The legal basis in the Treaties for this (Article 127(6) TFEU) has been activated with the creation of the Banking Union supervisory pillar that gives the ECB a responsibility to contribute to the stability of the financial system,[29] as well as for microprudential supervision. The ECB has been given some macroprudential responsibilities by the same secondary legislation which are shared responsibilities of the ECB and national authorities within the Banking Union.[30] The ECB's objectives within banking supervision, that is, the safety and soundness of credit institutions and the stability of the financial system, seem to be coequal objectives with no hierarchy or at least left undetermined by EU secondary law wording.

This list of tasks sheds light on the complex institutional arrangements between the ESCB/Eurosystem's tasks, the ECB's responsibilities to implement those tasks on its own or through the National Central Banks (NCBs)[31] forming the Eurosystem for the conduct of the monetary policy, and the ECB's responsibilities in the system for banking supervision and for systemic risks within the European System of Financial Supervision. Therefore, both the ESCB/Eurosystem's mandate 'strictly' speaking, and the ECB's mandate including those new responsibilities must be taken into account when examining the implementation of the mandate (B). The purposive analysis will shed light on the nature of the objectives and their interplay across the three other central banks.

(2) Other central banks' objectives in their statutory sources

The statutory sources of the three other central banks also emphasize price stability in their objectives, but their priority ranking differs or is undetermined. The analysis below follows this order: the BoE, the BoC, and the FED.

The mandate of the BoE can be reconstructed through the different objectives stated in the BoE Act. The objectives of the BoE are to maintain price stability, and subject to that, to support the economic policy of the government, including its objectives for growth and employment.[32] This ranks those objectives with a priority given to price

Joaquim Gomes, and Rolf Pauli, 'Trends in central banks' foreign currency reserves and the case of the ECB' (2019) ECB Economic Bulletin Issue 7/2019 <https://www.ecb.europa.eu/pub/economic-bulletin/articles/2019/html/ecb.ebart201907_01~c2ae75e217.en.html> accessed 13 July 2021.

[28] TFEU (n 13) Art 127(6) and ESCB and ECB Statute (n 13) Art 25.2.

[29] TFEU (n 13) Art 127(5). The SSM Regulation (n 21) in its recital 55 reads: 'The conferral of supervisory tasks implies a *significant responsibility* for the ECB to safeguard financial stability in the Union' (emphasis added). See Gianni Lo Schiavo, *The Role of Financial Stability in EU Law and Policy* (Kluwer 2017) 46–57 and Jennifer Payne, 'The Institutional Design of Financial Supervision and Financial Stability' in Fabian Amtenbrink and Christoph Herrmann (eds), *EU Law of Economic & Monetary Union* (OUP 2020).

[30] SSM Regulation (n 21) Art 5 'Macroprudential tasks and tools'. Note also the establishment of the European Systemic Risk Board for macroprudential oversight in the EU (hosted at the ECB and part of the European System of Financial Supervision), contributing to the prevention and mitigation systemic risks to financial stability, since 2010. See also chapter 8 by Federico Della Negra and Gianni Lo Schiavo, in this volume.

[31] ESCB and ECB Statute (n 13) Art 9.2.

[32] Bank of England Act 1998, s 11.

stability over the other 'supportive' objectives. The BoE has been conferred responsibility for monetary policy,[33] which is formulated and implemented by the Monetary Policy Committee (MPC) that interacts with the Financial Policy Committee (FPC).[34] This leads to a primary objective for price stability and supportive objectives geared towards economic policy support, resembling the case of the ECB. Furthermore, the BoE has a statutory financial stability objective that has been reinforced since 1998 and even more so since the GFC,[35] with the support of the Financial Stability Committee (FSC), to protect and enhance the stability of the financial system of the UK. The financial stability objective is a collective responsibility, as the BoE must work with other bodies to this end, including the supervisors (see 3). Notably, it has been argued that the strengthening of the financial stability objective at a statutory level during and in the aftermath of the GFC changed the BoE's mandate to a 'twin' mandate.[36] The word twin is different from dual insofar as it has the effect of putting two objectives on an equal footing but within two different central bank functions (ie BoE's monetary policy strategy is determined separately from financial stability strategy, as will be examined in the functional approach in 3). In contrast, the FED dual mandate, examined hereinafter, includes two objectives within monetary policy.

At the BoC however, the statutory sources of the mandate include multiple objectives. The BoC's mandate is indicated in broad terms in the preamble of the BoC Act, which has been unchanged since 1934. The central bank has been established 'generally to promote the economic and financial welfare of Canada'.[37] This excerpt of the preamble is designated as its mandate by the BoC itself.[38] Another part of the preamble highlights more specific objectives: 'to regulate credit and currency in the best interests of the economic life of the nation, to control and protect the external value of the national monetary unit and to mitigate by its influence fluctuations in the general level of production, trade, prices and employment, so far as may be possible within the scope of monetary action'.[39] In this quote, it is worth noting the account for the general level of prices considered together with other macroeconomic variables, that is, production (or growth), trade, and employment. Their fluctuations can be influenced by monetary policy actions. The level of prices is a close sibling to price stability mentioned earlier for the ECB and the BoE. The BoC preamble adds the level of trade to the more specific objectives listed above, that is, geared towards price

33 The FPC and the MPC have the common objective to support the economic policy of the government, including growth and employment concerns: Bank of England Act 1998, pt II and in particular s 13 for the MPC.

34 Beyond the supportive objective as phrased in Bank of England Act 1998, s 11. For the FPC, s 9 (c)(1) and (4).

35 Bank of England Act 1998, s 2A, as amended by the Banking Act 2009, the Financial Services Act 2012, and the Bank of England and Financial Services Act 2016.

36 Rosa Maria Lastra and Kern Alexander, 'The ECB Mandate: Perspectives on Sustainability and Solidarity' (2020) Directorate General for Internal Policies, Policy Department for Economic, Scientific and Quality of Life Policies PE 648.813, 8 <https://www.europarl.europa.eu/RegData/etudes/IDAN/2020/648813/IPOL_IDA(2020)648813_EN.pdf> accessed 13 July 2021 (hereafter Lastra and Alexander, The ECB Mandate).

37 Bank of Canada Act, RSC, 1985, c B-2.

38 Bank of Canada, 'Bank of Canada Annual Report 2019', 7 <https://www.bankofcanada.ca/wp-content/uploads/2020/03/AR-2019-EN.pdf> accessed 13 July 2021 (hereafter Bank of Canada Annual Report 2019).

39 Bank of Canada Act, RSC, 1985, c B-2, Preamble.

stability, growth, and employment. Therefore, the BoC's preamble encompasses economic policy objectives that were mentioned for its counterparts but go beyond these. Such emphasis should however not mislead the reader, as there is also a constraint or safeguard: 'within the scope of monetary action' that closes the preamble in its formal wording.

Furthermore, the BoC Act has a focus on Canadian 'economic and financial welfare', which can cover monetary policy and macroprudential policies (economic policy). The Minister of Finance is consulted by the governor on monetary policy and its relation to general economic policy,[40] and the Minister's opinion overrides the Governor's in case of difference of opinion concerning the monetary policy to be followed (this is exceptional but it happened in the 'Coyne affair' that led to the Governor's resignation in 1961).[41] The BoC also has the responsibility for the oversight of payments and other clearing and settlement systems, for the purpose of controlling systemic risk in accordance with another legal act.[42] Thus, the BoC's mandate stands out in its broad terminology and the shared responsibilities with the government it establishes. But only through its policy implementation does the BoC give priority to price stability as Canadian monetary policy follows an inflation-control target framework agreed between the BoC and the Minister of Finance.[43]

The FED's mandate is commonly described as dual, while there are three objectives written in the Federal Reserve Act: 'to promote effectively the goals of maximum employment, stable prices, and moderate long-term interest rates.'[44] 'Dual' is justified insofar as only in a stable macroeconomic environment do the long-term interest rates remain low.[45] During the GFC, the financial stability mission of the FED has been reinforced, with the creation of the Financial Stability Oversight Council (FSOC) by the Dodd-Frank Act.[46] The latter has three purposes: to identify risks to the financial stability of the United States, to promote market discipline, and to respond to emerging threats to the stability of the financial system.[47] This evolution in the legal framework has widened the mandate of the FED, even if the Federal Reserve Act has not been amended (in contrast with the BoE Act).

Formally, the FED's dual mandate including stable prices and maximum employment is specific in comparison with that of the other central banks. Those two

[40] ibid s 14 (1).

[41] After consultation with the Governor and with the approval of the Governor in Council, the Minister of Finance may give a written directive concerning monetary policy, in specific terms and applicable for a specified period; ibid s 14(2).

[42] Payment Clearing and Settlement Act, SC 1996, c 6, Sch, in particular subs 11.09.

[43] This agreement adopted in 1991 is discussed in B.

[44] 12 USC s 225a (23 December 1913, ch 6, para 2A), as added by act of 16 November 1977 (91 Stat 1387) and amended by acts of 27 October 1978 (92 Stat 1897); 23 August 1988 (102 Stat 1375); and 27 December 2000 (114 Stat 3028).

[45] Frederic S Mishkin, 'Monetary Policy and the Dual Mandate' (Speech at Bridgewater College, Bridgewater Virginia, 10 April 2007) <https://www.federalreserve.gov/newsevents/speech/mishkin20070410a.htm> accessed 13 July 2021.

[46] Shared involvement of the FSOC, the FED Board of Governors, the Commodities Futures Trading Commission, the Securities & Exchange Commission, and the Federal Deposit Insurance Corporation. See the Dodd-Frank Act, Title VIII 'Payment, Clearing, and Settlement Supervision'. Dodd–Frank Wall Street Reform and Consumer Protection Act, Public Law 111–203, 21 July 2010, HR 4173 (hereinafter 'Dodd-Frank Act').

[47] Dodd-Frank Act (n 46) paras 111 and 112.

objectives have an equal status in the FED's statute. In other words, growth, employment, and support for economic policies are not secondary or supporting objectives as they are for the ECB or the BoE. However, the financial stability mandate, given, by a legal act, to manifold actors among which the FED, echoes the evolution observed for the ECB and the BoE. First, the ECB has some microprudential and macroprudential responsibilities in the EU (that give more teeth to the contribution to the stability of the financial system it is called to make according to the Treaties), and the BoE formally has a statutory financial stability objective. In this regard, the preamble of the BoC Act is so broadly phrased that financial stability could be considered to fall within 'the promotion of the economic and financial welfare of Canada'.

Finally, the hierarchy of objectives is clearly set in the statutes for the ESCB with a primary objective for price stability, as well as for the BoE in relation to its monetary policy function (yet, as per statute, the BoE has monetary policy and financial stability objectives). However, the relationship of the price stability objective with other objectives within the monetary policy function has a different degree. 'Without prejudice to the objective of price stability' (for the ECB) differs in its wording from 'subject to [maintaining price stability]' (for the BoE). The first expresses price stability as a necessary condition for the ESCB/Eurosystem contribution to other objectives, and the second, the BoE's support to economic policy. Literally, notwithstanding a different wording, the two express a hierarchy, which comparatively prove that the other second level, contributory or supportive, objectives are theoretically broader for the ESCB than in the BoE's case. In contrast, the hierarchy of objectives is not the same for the other two central banks. Indeed, the FED has, formally, objectives of equal status (employment and stable prices), while it is left undetermined for the BoC at the statutory level. The latter case could be interpreted in both ways (equal objectives without any priority, or hierarchized, in case the constraint expressed in the preamble to fall within the scope of BoC's monetary action means to strictly follow the main road of monetary policy, that is, inflation control, see B).

(3) Functional perspective on the mandate

This subsection examines the mandate of central banks, as set forth in the statutory sources, from a functional perspective. Again, central banks use different terminologies, that is, tasks and functions, considered here interchangeably. The basic tasks of the ESCB are set forth in the Treaties and its Statute and were upgraded in EU secondary legislation with post-financial crisis microprudential and macroprudential reforms. A comparison of the ECB's tasks with those of the other central banks examined, puts into perspective the central banks' roles and responsibilities, in their statutory sources, and allows to better grasp and situate the mandate and objectives just examined in a systematic approach. The same order applies: the BoE, the BoC, and the FED.

The BoE functions are entrusted to several competent committees within the central bank which are responsible not only for monetary policy, but also for macroprudential and microprudential supervisory functions to preserve financial stability. The FPC contributes to the BoE's financial stability objective by ensuring the protection and enhancement of the UK financial system's resilience.[48] By contributing to the financial

[48] Bank of England Act 1998, ss 9 (c)(1) and 9 (c)(2).

stability objective, the FPC is a macroprudential entity which coexists beside the MPC as a price stability entity within the BoE.[49] Alongside the FPC, the Prudential Regulation Authority (PRA; a subsidiary of the BoE) and the Financial Conduct Authority (FCA)[50] are also involved from a microprudential supervision perspective. The PRA's functions are exercised through yet another Committee, the Prudential Regulation Committee (PRC), which aims at promoting the safety and soundness of PRA-authorized persons (recalling one of the objectives of banking supervision in the euro area). This committee structure reflects a functional split between concerns for price stability (MPC), financial stability (FPC) with a further divide between macroprudential (FPC), and microprudential concerns (PRC at the BoE together with other entities). This functional approach illustrates how the BoE pursues a price stability objective as well as a financial stability objective within its mandate, which corroborates the appellation 'twin' mandate—of a different nature than the FED dual mandate. The BoE also has a payment systems oversight responsibility with a dedicated statutory framework.[51]

The same trend of reinforcing the microprudential and macroprudential functions can be observed in Canada, but it started earlier than in the other central banks, that is, before the GFC, but with a different institutional setting. The BoC is responsible for monetary policy, and another independent institution, the Office of the Superintendent of Financial Institutions (OSFI) created in 1987, is in charge of regulating banks and other financial institutions as a microprudential supervisor. The OSFI and the BoC conduct macro stress-tests together.[52] Furthermore, under the BoC Act (but outside the preamble), the BoC also contributes to the promotion of the stability of the Canadian financial system.[53] In this regard, the Minister of Finance is responsible for financial stability with the support of other federal agencies whose mandates contribute to financial stability, including the BoC, the OSFI, and the Canada Deposit Insurance Corporation (CDIC).[54] The supervisory tasks are, however, separated and conferred to a distinct entity—OSFI, an office of the government over which the Minister presides and keeps responsibility.[55] Therefore, the BoC does not have extensive supervisory tasks on its own, only the conduct of stress tests together with the OSFI. This institutional arrangement is a distinct feature of the BoC if compared to the ECB and the BoE, which are both entrusted with microprudential and macroprudential tasks (with organizational arrangements, and a separation from

[49] Tamarah Shakir and Matthey Tong, 'The Interaction of the FPC and the MPC' (2014) Bank of England Quarterly Bulletin 2014 Q4, 400–01 <https://www.bankofengland.co.uk/quarterly-bulletin/2014/q4/the-interaction-of-the-fpc-and-the-mpc> accessed 13 July 2021.

[50] The PRA has the status of Company, but wholly owned subsidiary. Section 7AA introduced by s 137 (3) of the Financial Services (Banking Reform) Act 2013, for the FCA: see Bank of England and Financial Services Act 2016

[51] See pt 5 in Banking Act 2009, c 1.

[52] The governor of the Bank of Canada is in the OSFI Committee together with the Superintendent, the Commissioner of the Financial Consumer Agency of Canada, the CEO of the Canada Deposit Insurance Corporation and the Deputy Minister of Finance. See Office of the Superintendent of Financial Institutions Act, RSC, 1985, c 18 (3rd Supp), pt I, s 18 (hereafter OSFI Act).

[53] Bank of Canada Act, RSC, 1985, c B-2, s 18(g).

[54] The CDIC is the federal deposit insurer and resolution authority since amendments to its mandate in 2017.

[55] OSFI Act (n 52) s 4 (1).

other functions of the central banks that do not fall within the scope of this chapter). Moreover, the BoC may act as a fiscal agent for the government of Canada in the payment of interest and principal of the public debt, and generally for the management of the public debt of Canada, when required to do so by the Minister,[56] which corresponds to a fiscal agent function. This constitutes another distinctive feature of the BoC insofar as the BoE has ceased to be responsible for the debt management of the government since 1997[57] and as, constitutionally, this falls outside of the Treaties' scope for the ESCB (with the explicit prohibition of monetary financing in Article 123 TFEU).

Within its mandate, the FED covers functions other than monetary policy, and among those, banking supervision. The official title of the Federal Reserve Act makes it clear that the act is 'to establish a more effective supervision of banking in the United States'. The FED is generally responsible for the regulation and supervision of different financial entities. However, depending on where the institution chooses to operate and to be chartered (either at federal or state level), and which authority (either federal or state) grants the permission for the business operations, the supervisory and regulatory responsibility might be exerted by other federal regulators in addition to the supervision of the chartering state.[58] Therefore, the FED shares part of its functions in banking supervision at the federal level (with the Office of the Comptroller of the Currency), and with individual state banking departments at the state level. Regardless of these differing organizational dimensions, the FED's involvement in micro and macroprudential tasks brings this central bank close to the ECB and the BoE. As previously examined, they had both their prudential tasks reinforced within respectively a hierarchical and twin mandate. The FED is not so far from the latter considering its role in banking supervision, albeit shared and with a complex institutional apparatus. Furthermore, regarding the payment systems function, the FED is partly involved in supervisory and regulatory functions for financial market utilities' infrastructures designated as systemically important by the FSOC following the Dodd-Frank Act.[59] This function is also present in the ESCB/Eurosystem, the BoC, and the BoE.

In conclusion, if the statutory sources somehow circumscribe the mandate of the central banks, the concept 'mandate' is inexistent in all statutory sources and shows the necessity of examining objectives and tasks systematically. The ESCB/Eurosystem's mandate is found in the EU Treaties (and Statute of the ESCB and ECB) as well as EU secondary legislation that activated the legal basis for microprudential supervision and contribution to the stability of the financial system. Formally, the status of primary objective for price stability, expressly provided at primary law level, justifies the use of hierarchical mandate, to some extent. The BoE's twin mandate stems from

[56] Bank of Canada Act, RSC, 1985, c B-2, s 24(2).

[57] A Debt Management Office operates as the executive agency of the Treasury, following the independence of the BoE.

[58] For example, the Office of the Comptroller of the Currency (OCC) supervises institutions chartered at the federal level, whereas the Federal Deposit Insurance Corporation (FDIC) supervised institutions that are not members of the FED. For a practitioners' overview, see Reena A Sahni and Timothy Byrne, 'Banking Regulation 2021' (Global Legal Insights, March 2020) <https://www.globallegalinsights.com/practice-areas/banking-and-finance-laws-and-regulations/usa> accessed 13 July 2021.

[59] Dodd-Frank Act (n 46) Title VIII.

its objectives as stated in different parts of the BoE Act (as amended). The FED's dual mandate is provided for in the Federal Reserve Act (monetary policy objectives) while the Dodd-Frank Act reinforces the financial stability function, which slightly tilts the FED mandate to a twin situation. Those sources are statutory, either with a constitutional or legal status. In most cases, other than the Bank of Canada, the objectives help to further define and circumscribe the central bank's mandate. The BoC finds its mandate in the preamble of the BoC Act written in broad terms with multiple goals that have prevailed differently over time as will be examined.

The evolution of central bank objectives since the GFC signals more emphasis on financial stability at the statutory level for most central banks (ie the BoE Act as amended, the FED involved together with the FSOC as a result of the Dodd-Frank Act, microprudential and macroprudential tasks at the ECB stemming from EU secondary legislation). The BoC's mandate stands out as its macroprudential function was reinforced before the GFC: the central bank acts together with other entities (OSFI and CDIC) to safeguard financial stability.[60]

When the formal mandates are silent or left undetermined as to the priority of objectives or interactions among functions, a systematic analysis putting together the functional and purposive analyses gives some insightful perspectives across central banks. Moreover, the implementation of the mandate informs on its scope 'in action', and how an interpretative reading of formal sources partly unveils and explains some preconceptions about central bank mandates and the flexibility used from the frameworks.

B. Implementation of central bank mandates: a purposive and functional approach since the GFC

The objectives that are part of central bank mandates are implemented through frameworks for monetary policy strategy, stemming from extra-statutory elements. The concerns for the stability of the financial system, as set in the statutory sources across central banks, have been (re)interpreted and/or reinforced post-GFC, not only through some amendments examined above but also through practice. Central banks do not self-determine their objectives formally (as they stem from statutory mandates), but they do shape the substance of those objectives and their interplay, in particular when the interplay among several objectives (and functions) is left undetermined by the mandate. They do so through monetary policy-making, in other words adopting monetary policy strategy, implementing measures, and procedures.[61]

The findings across the four central banks help to reflect upon the place and the scope of the price stability objective within central bank mandates. In particular,

[60] Payment Clearing and Settlement Act (PCSA) revised several times since the GFC, for example the introduction of the concept 'payments system risk' and the broadening of the definition of systemic risk in 2014: PCSA, SC 2014, c 39, s 360.

[61] Adam Čáp, Mathias Drehmann, and Andreas Schrimpf, 'Changes in Monetary Policy Operating Procedures over the Last Decade: Insights from a New Database' (2020) BIS Quarterly Review <https://www.bis.org/publ/qtrpdf/r_qt2012c.pdf> accessed 13 July 2021 (hereafter Čáp, Drehmann, and Schrimpf, 'Changes in Monetary Policy Operating Procedures').

they shed some light on whether the statutory priority of one objective or the equal rank between several objectives is confirmed or may, on the contrary, prove flexible in crisis times. The ECB's monetary policy strategy is first examined with yardsticks (1) that are then used to compare it with its peers (2). Moreover, the GFC triggered the use of new monetary policy measures, so-called 'unconventional', and illustrated with forward guidance, the Lender of Last Resort (LOLR) function,[62] and quantitative easing (QE), whose principle will be discussed within common and distinct features of central banks implementing their formal mandate (3). LOLR and QE will not be examined in detail because of their technical terms and quantitative scale across the examined central banks. All in all, mandates of central banks might formally differ in their scope, but their implementation might in practice converge in times of crisis and let us have a critical eye on formal mandates that are identified and categorized as a hierarchical, twin, dual or broad mandate. This refines the usual 'single vs dual' mandate distinction.

(1) ECB monetary policy strategy: whatever it takes within the mandate

Extra-statutory sources detail the ECB's price stability objective in a 'strategy'. The TFEU does not define monetary policy per se but refers to its objectives, examined in Section II, without laying down any qualitative or quantitative definition of price stability. The ECB's stability-oriented monetary policy strategy was initially further elaborated in the first Eurosystem's strategy publication, which indicated its main elements and a numerical reference. A 1998 press release defined the price stability objective, which was clarified in 2003 to strike out deflation and streamlined in a new 'ECB's monetary policy strategy statement' in July 2021.[63] The former definition (revised only once) at that time read: 'from a year-on-year increase in the Harmonised Index of Consumer Prices (HICP) for the euro area of below 2% to rates below, but close to, 2% over the medium term'.[64] By setting this numerical target through an extra-statutory press release, the ECB wanted to ensure its credibility and to anchor expectations of economic agents. In addition, the strategy follows a medium-term orientation that allows the Governing Council to account for real economy prospects, in other words, in line with the other objectives identified above in the statutory sources. Concretely, employment and growth are variables taken into account in this medium-term orientation, despite the ECB's 'hierarchical mandate with price stability at the top'.[65] The new definition from the first ECB's monetary policy strategy statement in July 2021 is

[62] The LOLR is an important function of modern central banking: see Goodhart, 'The changing role of central banks' (n 9) and Lamandini and others, 'The European Central Bank' (n 21) 19–22.

[63] European Central Bank, 'A stability-oriented monetary policy strategy for the ESCB' (ECB Press Release, 13 October 1998) <https://www.ecb.europa.eu/press/pr/date/1998/html/pr981013_1.en.html> accessed 13 July 2021. European Central Bank, 'The ECB's monetary policy strategy statement', <https://www.ecb.europa.eu/home/search/review/html/ecb.strategyreview_monpol_strategy_statement.en.html> 8 July 2021, accessed 13 July 2021.

[64] The addition of 'but close to' corresponds to the clarification: European Central Bank, 'The ECB's monetary policy strategy' (ECB Press Release, 8 May 2003) <https://www.ecb.europa.eu/press/pr/date/2003/html/pr030508_2.en.html> accessed 13 July 2021.

[65] Christine Lagarde, 'The Monetary Policy Strategy Review: Some Preliminary Considerations' (Speech at the 'ECB and its Watchers XXI' conference, Frankfurt am Main, 30 September 2020) <https://www.ecb.europa.eu/press/key/date/2020/html/ecb.sp200930~169abb1202.en.html?utm_source=cl_twitter> accessed 13 July 2021.

more specific and easier to communicate on: 'The Governing Council considers that price stability is best maintained by aiming for two per cent inflation over the medium term' (para 5). Hence, the inflation target is more straightforward than in the previous phrasing, while the medium-term orientation remains included. The reference to the HICP is being adapted with the inclusion of owner-occupied housing, following consultations held in the process of the Strategy Review. During and in the aftermath of the GFC, several unconventional measures have been adopted[66] described as a way to 'secure the ECB mandate'.[67] In response to concerns expressed about the fulfilling of the ECB's mandate, monetary policymakers repeatedly used the 'transmission' of the single monetary policy as a justification for unconventional measures. Those measures were, among others, negative deposit facility rates, targeted longer-term refinancing operations (TLTROs), and an expanded asset purchase programmes (APPs) as part of its QE.[68] The sovereign debt crisis triggered measures that raised controversies and legal challenges.[69] In addition, the ECB relied on forward guidance for the first time in the summer of 2013 for its policy rate, and again in January 2015 in relation to its operations within its APPs.[70] The most well-known forward guidance is former ECB President Mario Draghi's message of 'whatever it takes' that aimed at dissipating 'unfounded fears' of the reversibility of the euro in 2012.[71] Therefore, unconventional tools served a monetary policy strategy whose effectiveness was put under threat by the consequences of the GFC.

The exercise of the function of LOLR can also be interpreted as part of the unconventional measures conducted by the ECB in the realm of monetary policy. What is striking from a constitutional perspective is that this function is not expressly stated in the Treaties and ESCB and ECB Statute. Yet, the practice does witness a certain LOLR role for the euro area[72] that can be considered falling under a transversal objective of

[66] The OMT programme was never activated. See consequences at the constitutional level: Michael Ioannidis, 'Europe's New Transformations: How the EU Economic Constitution Changes during the Eurozone Crisis' (2016) 53 CML Rev 1237; Takis Tridimas and Napoleon Xanthoulis, 'A Legal Analysis of the Gauweiler Case: Between Monetary Policy and Constitutional Conflict' (2016) 23 MJ 17; Klaus Tuori, 'Monetary Policy (Objectives and Instruments)' in Fabian Amtenbrink and Christoph Herrmann (eds), *The EU Law of Economic and Monetary Union* (OUP 2020) 668–775 (hereafter Tuori, 'Monetary Policy').

[67] Mario Draghi, 'The interaction between monetary policy and financial stability in the euro area' (Keynote Speech at the First Conference on Financial Stability organised by the Banco de España and Centro de Estudios Monetarios y Financieros, Madrid, 24 May 2017) <https://www.ecb.europa.eu/press/key/date/2017/html/ecb.sp170524_1.en.html> accessed 13 July 2021.

[68] Philippine Cour-Thimann and Bernhard Winkler, 'The ECB's Non-Standard Monetary Policy Measures: The Role of Institutional Factors and Financial Structure' (2012) 28 Oxford Review of Economic Policy 765 (hereafter Cour-Thimann and Winkler, 'The ECB's Non-Standard Monetary Policy Measures'). See also Isabel Schnabel, 'Going negative: the ECB's experience' (Speech at the Roundtable on Monetary Policy, Low Interest Rates and Risk Taking at the 35th Congress of the European Economic Association, Frankfurt am Main, 26 August 2020) <https://www.ecb.europa.eu/press/key/date/2020/html/ecb.sp200826~77ce66626c.en.html> accessed 13 July 2021 (hereafter Schnabel, 'Going negative: the ECB's experience') and chapter 3 by Klaus Tuori, in this volume.

[69] See Tuori, 'Monetary Policy' (n 66) 653–86, and chapter 12 by Takis Tridimas, in this volume.

[70] Potter and Smets, 'Unconventional Monetary Policy Tools' (n 4) 32.

[71] Reiterated in both the statement and Q&A: see Mario Draghi and Vitor Constâncio, 'Introductory statement to the press conference (with Q&A)' (ECB Press Conference, Frankfurt am Main, 6 September 2012) <https://www.ecb.europa.eu/press/pressconf/2012/html/is120906.en.html> accessed 13 July 2021.

[72] A *de facto* Lender of Last Resort action: see Carlos Garcia-de-Andoain and others, 'Lending-of-last-resort is as lending-of-last-resort does: Central bank liquidity provision and interbank market functioning

financial stability. The LOLR function is partly within the ESCB/Eurosystem's mandate and partly within the Eurosystem NCBs' responsibilities (the latter with limitations to safeguard the single monetary policy and its 'transmission'). Even though the adoption of emergency lending measures was common among the central banks studied in this chapter, the LOLR split within the ESCB/Eurosystem stands out when compared to the three other central banks (3).

Let us first distinguish the credit and monetary approach to LOLR[73] and then identify the responsibilities within the ESCB/Eurosystem. In the LOLR function, macro level and micro level liquidity supply should be distinguished,[74] related respectively to monetary policy operations and liquidity provision to individual institutions. In the GFC context, the liquidity shock within the system was addressed in the first—monetary—approach to LOLR, the so-called classical approach.[75] To cope with this liquidity shock, the ECB had turned the LTROs from three-months long to six-months long (2008) and even to three years (2011).[76] The nature of the responsibilities undertaken in this macro level LOLR function gives more prominence to the safeguarding of financial stability. In contrast, the liquidity stress and issues faced by solvent credit institutions fall under the second—credit—approach, notably through emergency liquidity assistance (ELA). Thus, ELA intervened outside of 'normal' Eurosystem monetary policy operations with micro level liquidity supply that could be, as some argued, part of the prudential supervisor tasks insofar as its objectives are not only the safety and soundness of banks but also the contribution to the stability of the financial system within the Union and *each* Member State. In fact, the ELA measures adopted for banks in Ireland, Greece, Cyprus, and Portugal were significant, all the more for Greek banks considering their size and duration.[77]

The micro level LOLR function was exercised by the NCBs within their remaining functions in accordance with Article 14.4 ESCB and ECB Statute. An 'ELA agreement' adopted in 2017[78] clarified *ex post* the ECB's role in the provision of ELA by the Eurosystem NCBs. This confirmed that the 'credit approach' to LOLR remains at the national level formally, provided there is no interference with the ESCB/Eurosystem's mandate (ie objectives and tasks).[79] NCBs' Governors have a duty to watch other

in the euro area' (2016) ECB Working Paper Series No 1886 <https://www.ecb.europa.eu/pub/pdf/scpwps/ecbwp1886.en.pdf> accessed 13 July 2021.

[73] Peter Praet, 'The ECB and its role as lender of last resort during the crisis' (Speech at the Committee on Capital Markets Regulation conference on the lender of last resort—an international perspective, Washington, DC, 10 February 2016) <https://www.ecb.europa.eu/press/key/date/2016/html/sp160210.en.html> accessed 13 July 2021 (hereafter Praet, 'The ECB and its role as lender of last resort during the crisis').

[74] Armin Steinbach, 'The Lender of Last Resort in the Eurozone' (2016) 53 CML Rev 361, 365.

[75] Praet, 'The ECB and its role as lender of last resort during the crisis' (n 73).

[76] A length considered unusual for monetary policy, see Tuori, 'Monetary Policy' (n 66) 651.

[77] Marcel Magnus and Aspasia Xirou, 'Emergency Liquidity Assistance—Moving Away from "Constructive Ambiguity"?' (2017) Directorate General for Internal Policies, Economic Governance Support Unit PE 587.395 <https://www.europarl.europa.eu/RegData/etudes/BRIE/2017/587395/IPOL_BRI(2017)587395_EN.pdf> accessed 13 July 2021.

[78] European Central Bank, 'Agreement on emergency liquidity assistance' (17 May 2017) <https://www.ecb.europa.eu/pub/pdf/other/Agreement_on_emergency_liquidity_assistance_20170517.en.pdf> accessed 13 July 2021 (hereafter European Central Bank, 'ELA agreement'), revised in November 2020.

[79] ibid s 3.3 and s 3.2(b), on the matter of information sharing.

NCBs notifying their ELA not to undermine single monetary policy. This showcases an interaction between the formal mandate and extra-statutory sources that give further clarity on this unusual split within the ESCB, and substantively, the tensions between single monetary policy and safeguarding financial stability.

Overall, the ECB has flexibility in defining and quantifying its price stability objective, but such flexibility remains limited in the interplay with other objectives. This is so because, formally, the hierarchy of objectives within the mandate will not change apart from the unlikely event of a Treaty amendment in that direction. A hierarchical mandate is embedded in the ECB legal and policy strategy frameworks due to the existence and operations of single monetary policy for a longer time than the other tasks more fiercely established since the GFC, and despite some changes in secondary sources that activated part of the mandate of the ECB (supervisory and macroprudential tasks). As public discourse has shown, the ECB has used unconventional measures to sustain the singleness of its monetary policy (including its transmission) although they have had a broader reach, in particular in terms of safeguarding the financial system stability. The full LOLR function falls more neatly within other central bank mandates as will be examined (3) following the comparison of monetary policy strategy frameworks that determine price stability within monetary policy strategy (2).

(2) Price stability determined within monetary policy strategy

The price stability objective of central banks is translated in a monetary policy strategy, which is not part of the statutory sources, and captures the implementation side of the mandate. The comparison puts into the mix: press releases, statements, and agreements. Table 15.2 summarizes some of the findings. It will be shown that the formal texts conferred the necessary flexibility for the adoption of unconventional measures in the context of the GFC (3 below). The comparison of the ECB's price stability objective framework with the other central banks will be made in the same order as above: BoE, BoC, and FED.

Within the BoE's monetary policy mandate, price stability is defined by the inflation target of 2 per cent expressed in annual rate of inflation based on the consumer prices index. The target is announced each year by the Chancellor of the Exchequer in the annual budget statement. The MPC sets the monetary policy and its main instruments to meet this target, including the Bank Rate, 'in a way that helps to sustain growth and employment' as published in several Monetary policy summaries.[80] The rhetoric is also one of economic policy consideration, in line with the BoE's mandate (ie maintaining price stability, and *subject to that*, supporting the economic policy, including its objectives for growth and employment). Moreover, the balancing between the monetary policy objective and the more economic ones for growth and employment depends on the interaction between the MPC and the FPC with their respective objectives as previously examined. The GFC provoked such balancing exercise. At the June and August 2017 monetary policy meetings, the summaries stated: 'the MPC's

[80] In accordance with the BoE Statute, and as reaffirmed in BoE statements, for example Bank of England, 'Monetary Policy Summary and minutes of the Monetary Policy Committee meeting ending on 4 August 2020' (6 August 2020) <https://www.bankofengland.co.uk/-/media/boe/files/monetary-policy-summary-and-minutes/2020/august-2020.pdf> accessed 13 July 2021.

Table 15.2 Determination of price stability objective and relationship with other central banks' objectives in practice

	ESCB/ Eurosystem	BoE	BoC	FED
Price stability determined in monetary policy strategy	Monetary policy strategy as defined in 1998 and 2003, revised in the ECB's monetary policy strategy statement on 8 July 2021, to be re-assessed in 2025	Inflation target with a yearly revision	Inflation-control target agreement (2016–21)	FOMC statement on Longer-Run Goals and Policy Strategy (since 2012), reviewed in August 2020
Extra statutory text	Press releases; monetary policy strategy statements from 2021	Annual budget statement, target announced by the Chancellor of the Exchequer	Joint agreement between the BoC and the government	FOMC Statement
Priority or ranking among objectives in practice	Financial stability 'subordinate' to price stability	Monetary policy trade-offs with the employment objective, due to the economic conditions (in crisis times) Financial stability objective of equal status with price stability	Price stability under the 2016–2021 joint agreement	Equal footing between stable prices and maximum employment Adapted in August 2020 with average inflation targeting, and maximum employment goal preceding stable prices (as per the FED Act wording)

remit specifies that, in exceptional circumstances, the Committee must balance any trade-off between the speed at which it intends to return inflation sustainably to the target and the support that monetary policy provides to jobs and activity'.[81] This statement softened the priority given to the inflation objective over economic-driven objectives in 'exceptional circumstances', as the BoE's forward guidance corroborates.

[81] Bank of England, 'Monetary Policy Summary and minutes of the Monetary Policy Committee meeting ending on 14 June 2017' (15 June 2017) <https://www.bankofengland.co.uk/-/media/boe/files/monetary-policy-summary-and-minutes/2017/minutes-june-2017.pdf?la=en&hash=8DA98529B834BD78381A312F9E23052AA5CA464E> accessed 13 July 2021 (hereafter Bank of England 2017a), and Bank of England, 'Monetary Policy Summary and minutes of the Monetary Policy Committee meeting ending on 2 August 2017' (3 August 2017) <https://www.bankofengland.co.uk/-/media/boe/files/monetary-policy-summary-and-minutes/2017/august-2017.pdf?la=en&hash=ACAEA347E695260F8E0AFF090DACA15E20768058> accessed 13 July 2021 (hereafter Bank of England 2017b).

A post-GFC statement of the MPC signalled an inversion of priorities where the employment objective is privileged, in such exceptional circumstances. The monetary policy instrument (Bank Rate) was not changed at least until the unemployment rate (measured with the Labour Force Survey headline) had reached a certain threshold,[82] considering the significant threat to financial stability posed by the stance of monetary policy.[83] The BoE had recourse to forward guidance to foster the common understanding on the balance the MPC seeks between its monetary policy task ('returning inflation promptly to the target') and the broader supportive objective within the BoE's mandate ('providing support to the economic recovery').[84] The exceptional circumstances expressed in these terms lasted until May 2018[85] and related to economic policy as well as supervisory considerations.[86] This change happened when CPI inflation reached above the 2 per cent target provoking a slight tightening of monetary policy.[87]

Compared with a yearly announcement for the BoE, the timeframe is different for other central banks. The BoC price stability objective is further determined, every five years, in an inflation-control target agreement between the federal government and the BoC. In the BoC's agreement renewed in 2016, the approach is the following: 'the primary objective of Canada's monetary policy is to promote the economic and financial welfare of Canadians, by contributing to sustained economic growth, rising levels of employment and improved living standards.'[88] This framework echoes the statutory mandate in repeating some of the macroeconomic variables that are in the BoC Act Preamble. Moreover, it guides the interest rate setting (target for the overnight rate), which aims at low and stable inflation, within a flexible exchange rate. The BoC inflation target has been 2 per cent, the midpoint of the 1 to 3 per cent inflation-control range, for fifteen years. Despite a broad phrasing of the mandate in the BoC preamble, restated in this agreement, the BoC mandate is operationalized in setting

[82] A threshold of 7 per cent; see Bank of England, 'Monetary policy trade-offs and forward guidance' (Bank of England Monetary Policy Committee, 2013), ch.5 <https://www.bankofengland.co.uk/-/media/boe/files/inflation-report/2013/monetary-policy-trade-offs-and-forward-guidance.pdf> accessed 13 July 2021 (hereafter Bank of England 2013), 34–35.

[83] Namely, the FPC judged that that threat cannot be contained by the substantial range of mitigating policy actions available to the FPC, the FCA, and the PRA in a way consistent with their objectives. However, the price stability objective priority was still formally included in the following terms: 'until the margin of slack within the economy has narrowed significantly, it will be appropriate to maintain the current exceptionally stimulative stance of monetary policy, provided that such an approach remains consistent with its primary objective of price stability and does not endanger financial stability': ibid 5.

[84] ibid 6.

[85] Bank of England, 'Monetary Policy Summary and minutes of the Monetary Policy Committee meeting ending on 21 March 2018' (22 March 2018) <https://www.bankofengland.co.uk/-/media/boe/files/monetary-policy-summary-and-minutes/2018/march-2018.pdf?la=en&hash=2CE0A37B662DBE4F3F604D0A186CD0168E340996> accessed 13 July 2021 (hereafter Bank of England 2018). The summary in May 2018 attached the exceptional circumstances 'presented by Brexit' 10 May 2018.

[86] See, eg, the 2017 August Monetary policy summary: the exceptional circumstances mentioned new international trading arrangements, weaker real income growth likely to accompany that adjustment over the next few years, and taking into account the effects of the recent prudential decisions of the FPC and the PRA: Bank of England 2017b (n 81).

[87] Bank of England 2018 (n 85), and 2 August 2018 when an increase of BoE's Bank Rate was adopted.

[88] Bank of Canada, 'Joint Statement of the Government of Canada and the Bank of Canada on the Renewal of the Inflation-Control Target' (24 October 2016) <https://www.bankofcanada.ca/wp-content/uploads/2016/10/Joint-Statement.pdf> accessed 13 July 2021 (hereafter Bank of Canada 2016).

a target for controlling inflation. Over time the mandate has been interpreted differently depending on the macroeconomic conditions and policy thinking.[89] Various governors adopted different monetary policy stances. For instance, a monetarist period between 1975 and 1982 had the main objective to fight inflation. The abandonment of monetary targeting in 1982 was followed in 1988 with the idea defended by Governor Crow to consider price stability as the only objective of the BoC.[90] This idea was translated into BoC monetary policy framework with numerical inflation targets in 1991. Therefore, it is argued that the BoC has followed inflation targeting as its 'sole, *de facto* official objective' within its monetary policy since 1991.[91] This reflects a policy choice of one objective amongst the multiple objectives that are within the BoC Act preamble and the importance of policy strategy implementing a formal mandate.

However, this implementation of the BoC's mandate has been reshaped by the GFC. As acknowledged in the 2016 renewal, the mandate is exercised while monetary authorities have 'dramatically extended the limits of their policy toolkits to combat persistent weakness, guard against deflation, repair financial system functioning, and restore confidence'.[92] And as argued by some economists, the BoC pursued other policy objectives than price stability in sustaining the economy, as one could observe the persistence of low interest rates while inflation was in the target range.[93] This shifted the BoC closer to its multiple objectives provided for in the formal mandate. Interestingly, the Bank of Canada Report for 2019 highlighted the research and examination of a dual mandate (low inflation and maximum employment) in view of the 2021 renewal.[94] *A contrario*, one can read the BoC is not yet there: it is not dual, nor single, or hierarchical, hence 'broad' is an adequate terminology, not only considering central banks' statutory sources but also in light of the BoC policy strategy that eventually determines a priority among multiple objectives stated in its formal mandate.

The FED's statutory mandate and related objectives can be interpreted thanks to the different Statements on Longer-Run Goals and Policy Strategy of the Federal Open Market Committee (hereinafter 'FOMC Statement' in short). This extra-statutory document has stated since January 2012 the longer-run goals and constitutes the foundation to the FED's policy actions.[95] The first 2012 FOMC statement specified that 'inflation at the rate of 2 percent, as measured by the annual change in the price index for personal consumption expenditures, is most consistent over the longer run with the

[89] Marc Lavoie and Mario Seccareccia, 'Reciprocal Influences: A Tale of Two Central Banks on the North American Continent' (2013) 42 International Journal of Political Economy 63, 70–71 (hereafter Lavoie and Seccareccia, 'Reciprocal Influences').

[90] ibid 70, 72.

[91] ibid 73.

[92] Bank of Canada 2016 (n 88).

[93] Mario Seccareccia and Najib Khan, 'The Illusion of Inflation Targeting: Have Central Banks Figured Out What They Are Actually Doing Since the Global Financial Crisis?' (2019) 48 International Journal of Political Economy 364, 368.

[94] Bank of Canada Annual Report 2019 (n 38) 15, and possible commitment to full employment: see Carolyn A Wilkins, 'Choosing the Best Monetary Policy Framework for Canada' (Speech at the McGill University Max Bell School of Public Policy, Montréal, 20 November 2018) <https://www.bankofcanada.ca/wp-content/uploads/2018/11/remarks-201118.pdf> accessed 13 July 2021.

[95] Federal Reserve System, 'Transcript of Chair Powell's Press Conference' (29 July 2020) <https://www.federalreserve.gov/mediacenter/files/FOMCpresconf20200729.pdf> accessed 13 July 2021.

Federal Reserve's statutory mandate'.[96] The accompanying press release in 2012 stated the dual mandate as follows: 'Consistent with its statutory mandate, the Committee seeks to foster maximum employment and price stability … To support a stronger economic recovery and to help ensure that inflation, over time, is at levels consistent with the *dual* mandate, the Committee expects to maintain a highly accommodative stance for monetary policy.'[97] The dual mandate, to promote maximum employment and stable prices, is explicit as in the FED Act. The 2012 FOMC Statement clearly mentioned a balanced approach in promoting them,[98] maximum employment standing on an equal footing with price stability as an objective of monetary policy.[99]

The interplay between price stability and maximum employment has, however, a different colour with the August 2020 revision (in the context of the review of the FED Monetary Policy strategy). Indeed, the revised Statement adopted unanimously by the FOMC, accounted for the monetary policy conduct in the past decade,[100] therefore inherited from the GFC consequences. The maximum employment and inflation goals are now divided in two distinct paragraphs: employment is stated before inflation. It is a reversed order in comparison with previous FOMC Statements. The new approach is an average inflation target, while for employment the FED bases its policy decisions on 'assessments of the *shortfalls* of employment' instead of '*deviations*' from its maximum level.[101] This subtle change reflected the FOMC view that 'a robust job market can be sustained without causing an outbreak of inflation'.[102] Therefore, high employment will not raise policy concerns provided there are no hikes in inflation or other (financial stability) risks impeding the achievement of the FED's goals.[103] In this reading, the two objectives' complementarity confirmed the flattening of the Phillips

[96] Rosa M Lastra, 'The Role of Central Banks in Monetary Affairs: A Comparative Perspective' in Thomas Cottier and others (eds), *The Rule of Law in Monetary Affairs* (CUP 2014) 87 (hereafter Lastra, 'The Role of Central Banks in Monetary Affairs'); Federal Reserve System, 'Federal Reserve issues FOMC statement of longer-run goals and policy strategy' (Federal Reserve System Press Release, 25 January 2012) <https://www.federalreserve.gov/newsevents/pressreleases/monetary20120125c.htm> accessed 13 July 2021.

[97] Emphasis added; Federal Reserve System, 'Federal Reserve issues FOMC statement' (Federal Reserve System Press Release, 25 January 2012) <https://www.federalreserve.gov/newsevents/pressreleases/monetary20120125a.htm> accessed 13 July 2021.

[98] Historically though, alternative periods shift emphasis on one objective over the other: see Aaron Steelman, 'The Federal Reserve's "Dual Mandate": The Evolution of an Idea' (2011) The Federal Reserve Bank of Richmond Economic Brief No 11–12 <https://www.richmondfed.org/publications/research/economic_brief/2011/eb_11-12> accessed 13 July 2021 (hereafter Steelman, 'The Federal Reserve's "Dual Mandate": The Evolution of an Idea').

[99] Federal Reserve System, 'Transcript of Chairman Bernanke's Press Conference' (25 January 2012), 2 <https://www.federalreserve.gov/mediacenter/files/fomcpresconf20120125.pdf> accessed 13 July 2021.

[100] Federal Reserve System, 'Federal Open Market Committee announces approval of updates to its Statement on Longer-Run Goals and Monetary Policy Strategy' (Federal Reserve System Press Release, 27 August 2020) <https://www.federalreserve.gov/newsevents/pressreleases/monetary20200827a.htm> accessed 13 July 2021.

[101] Federal Reserve System, 'Statement on Longer-Run Goals and Monetary Policy Strategy' (Adopted effective 24 January 2012, amended effective 27 August 2020) <https://www.federalreserve.gov/monetarypolicy/review-of-monetary-policy-strategy-tools-and-communications-statement-on-longer-run-goals-monetary-policy-strategy.htm> accessed 13 July 2021.

[102] Jerome H Powell, 'New Economic Challenges and the Fed's Monetary Policy Review' (Speech at 'Navigating the Decade Ahead: Implications for Monetary Policy', Jackson Hole, Wyoming, 27 August 2020) <https://www.bis.org/review/r200827d.pdf> accessed 13 July 2021 (hereafter Powell, 'New Economic Challenges and the Fed's Monetary Policy Review').

[103] Or low unemployment rate also known as NAIRU—non-accelerating inflation rate of unemployment: see Federal Reserve System, 'Review of Monetary Policy Strategy, Tools, and Communications.

Curve, described as 'gone' by FED Chair J Powell.[104] Furthermore, he stressed that the changes 'really *codif[y]* the way we're already acting with our policies',[105] which acknowledges the unconventional era triggered by the GFC becoming conventional and expressly part of FED strategy.

This codification through a FOMC statement can be seen as an extension of the statute of the FED.[106] In this review, the statutory mandate of the FED has been taken as a given, 'as well as the FOMC's previously articulated longer-run inflation objective of 2 percent'.[107] Overall, the inversion in the FOMC Statement put the objectives in the same literal order (maximum employment before stable prices) as the wording of section 2A of the Federal Reserve Act (formal source of the FED dual mandate). Prior to the GFC, two other acts from the US Congress steered the FED in interpreting and implementing the goals from the FED Act (ie the Employment Act of 1946, amended by the Full Employment and Balanced Growth Act in 1978, known as the Humphrey-Hawkins Act). Without going into details, as it precedes the GFC, the Humphrey-Hawkins act shifted emphasis on the employment goal as the most important objective.[108] This sequence shows that what happened between 2012 (when inflation targeting discussions in the US built upon prior moves from the Reserve Bank of New Zealand and the Bank of Canada since the early 1990s) and the summer of 2020 (revised FOMC statement) is not unusual in the implementation of the FED mandate. Those shifting priorities happened in specific socio-political and economic contexts (post-second world war, hikes in oil prices, and the consequences of both the GFC and COVID-19 crises for 2020).

Considering those four monetary policy strategy frameworks, the ranking of central banks' objectives examined according to the statutes is more precise for the BoE and the FED. In particular, the BoE did use flexibility after the GFC in assessing the trade-offs among monetary policy objectives (ie price stability and subject to that, growth and employment supportive objectives) by including in the balance the support of monetary policy to jobs and activity. The practice has already evolved under the FED's dual mandate, that is, the FOMC Statement interpreted the underlying goals of maximum employment and price stability, without any changes in the FED Act wording. Thus, the same order (maximum employment being before stable prices) shows that the coequal objectives may have different weight in the interpretation of the formal dual mandate, and therefore in the policy actions of the FED. In practice,

Q&As' <https://www.federalreserve.gov/monetarypolicy/review-of-monetary-policy-strategy-tools-and-communications-qas.htm> accessed 13 July 2021.

[104] Sage Belz, David Wessel, and Janet Yellen, 'What's (Not) Up with Inflation?' (The Brookings Institution, Hutchins Center on Fiscal & Monetary Policy, 2020) 8–10; I want to thank Giorgio Monti for this point. See Yun Li, 'The Fed Chairman Says the Relationship between Inflation and Unemployment Is Gone' (*CNBC*, 11 July 2019) <https://www.cnbc.com/2019/07/11/the-fed-chairman-says-the-relationship-between-inflation-and-unemployment-is-gone.html> accessed 13 July 2021.

[105] Powell, 'New Economic Challenges and the Fed's Monetary Policy Review' (n 102).

[106] Richard H Clarida, 'A presentation on US monetary policy' (Peterson Institute for International Economics, virtual event, 31 August 2020) <https://www.piie.com/events/fed-vice-chair-richard-h-clarida-us-monetary-policy> accessed 13 July 2021.

[107] Powell, 'New Economic Challenges and the Fed's Monetary Policy Review' (n 102).

[108] Steelman, 'The Federal Reserve's "Dual Mandate": The Evolution of an Idea' (n 98).

it is also a matter of balance with other economic policies (ie the Humphrey-Hawkins Act). As for the BoC, the joint inflation-control target agreement unveils its alignment towards price stability concerns like other central banks, even though the BoC's broad mandate is restated in this agreement and thus cannot lead to conclude that a priority will be always given to price stability in this jurisdiction (regardless of the renewed 2021 agreement that is extra-statutory). For the ECB, the primary objective of price stability remains, and notwithstanding the strengthening of a financial stability objective, it is still subordinate to price stability.

(3) Common and distinct features in implementing the central bank mandates

If mandates differ in central bank statutes (a broad, twin, dual, or hierarchical mandate), they somehow converge in the implementation of the price stability objective, as is shown by an examination of their monetary policy strategy frameworks (eg in statement, agreement, or press release publication). The other objectives have a different ranking, which is sometimes left undetermined. The financial stability function and objective of central banks have been consolidated particularly in the aftermath of the GFC (at constitutional level or in legal acts, for example the frameworks created or adapted in the Banking Act for BoE; PCSA for BoC; micro and macroprudential tasks at the ECB, and with the Dodd-Frank Act at the FED). The financial stability objective feeds into several central banking functions (either explicitly or implicitly via risks taken into account for monetary policy). This results from monetary policy frameworks that used the flexibility from the formal sources for their interpretation.

Furthermore, during and post-GFC, similar unconventional measures were adopted within monetary policy reactions,[109] from forward guidance to emergency lending, including massive asset purchases. The mandate and interplay of objectives, determined 'in action', targeted not only price stability objective but also the financial stability objective.

Forward guidance was used by all central banks in a context of lower bound interest rates.[110] Even if at different times over the GFC (first the FED in December 2008, the BoC in April 2009,[111] then the ECB and the BoE in summer 2013[112]), it gained in clarity with several elements captured.[113] Insofar as it upgrades communications and

[109] Bank for International Settlements, 'A Monetary Lifeline: Central Banks' Crisis Response' (2020) BIS Annual Economic Report, 55 <https://www.bis.org/publ/arpdf/ar2020e2.pdf> accessed 13 July 2021; and Daniel Gros and others, 'Crisis Response of Central Banks—The ECB Policy in Comparison to the Policy of the FED and the Bank of England' (2012) Directorate General for Internal Policies, Policy Department A: Economic and Scientific Policy PE 475.117, 35–47, 78 <https://www.europarl.europa.eu/cmsdata/107822/topic_2_jul.pdf> accessed 13 July 2021.

[110] Karyne Charbonneau and Lori Rennison, 'Forward Guidance at the Effective Lower Bound: International Experience' (2015) Bank of Canada Staff Discussion Paper No 2015-15, 2–3 <https://www.bankofcanada.ca/wp-content/uploads/2015/11/dp2015-15.pdf> accessed 13 July 2021.

[111] Michael Ehrmann and others, 'Can More Public Information Raise Uncertainty? The International Evidence on Forward Guidance' (2019) ECB Working Paper Series No 2263, 9 <https://www.ecb.europa.eu/pub/pdf/scpwps/ecb.wp2263~d433238380.en.pdf> accessed 13 July 2021 (hereafter Ehrmann and others, 'Can More Public Information Raise Uncertainty?'); and it retreated in 2014: Robin Harding, 'Bank of Canada Retreats from Forward Guidance' *Financial Times* (Washington, 15 October 2014) <https://www.ft.com/content/6322f51e-53aa-11e4-929b-00144feab7de> accessed 13 July 2021.

[112] Bank of England 2013 (n 83).

[113] Potter and Smets, 'Unconventional Monetary Policy Tools' (n 4) 33; time-contingent, or state-contingent thresholds with related economic conditions, and sometimes left open-ended: see Ehrmann and others, 'Can More Public Information Raise Uncertainty?' (n 111) 9–10.

clarity of monetary policy actions, the examined central banks tend to keep using it except for the central bank of Canada (although it returned to it in the course of 2020).[114] The FED, which initiated it, innovated with a new way to communicate policy intentions. Indeed, from January 2012 onwards, the FED Summary Economic Projections included FOMC participants projections for the federal funds rate, that is, the policy rate.[115] Later on, the FED connected its forward guidance on policy rates to its APPs like the ECB but did so a year earlier (2014 instead of 2015 for the ECB). The new ECB's monetary policy strategy statement from July 2021 is itself a refined tool for the ECB's forward guidance, which specifically insists on its communications through both traditional and new products. Forward guidance is considered an effective tool in a context of effective lower bound,[116] and constitutes a third line, a sort of policy-making translation of the frameworks for monetary policy strategy (that are themselves an extension of the Statute).

The LOLR function within the ESCB/Eurosystem stands out when compared to that of other central banks due to the split between the ESCB/Eurosystem functions and the NCBs' remaining functions, without undermining the tasks and objectives of the ESCB/Eurosystem. In comparison with this approach to LOLR (where we distinguished between a monetary approach—adopted by the ECB—and a credit approach—adopted by NBCs), the BoE has followed them both in pursuing LOLR function in open monetary operations (monetary approach) and institutionalized with lending against collateral (credit approach). The BoE has different applicable frameworks that testify that the nature of its LOLR function has changed since the GFC.[117] Moreover, the BoC's LOLR function also covers both the monetary and credit approach, under specific conditions, including having a credible recovery and resolution framework.[118] Lastly, the FED saw its LOLR powers limited by the Dodd-Frank Act.[119] This evolution went in the opposite direction to the BoE, which has witnessed

[114] See Bank for International Settlements, 'Monetary Policy Frameworks and Central Bank Market Operations' (23 June 2020) <https://www.bis.org/mc/compendium.htm> accessed 13 July 2021; Theophilos Argitis, 'Bank of Canada Adopts Forward Guidance to Spur Recovery' (*BNN Bloomberg*, 15 July 2020) <https://www.bnnbloomberg.ca/bank-of-canada-adopts-forward-guidance-to-spur-recovery-1.1465782> accessed 13 July 2021.

[115] Potter and Smets, 'Unconventional Monetary Policy Tools' (n 4) 33.

[116] Čáp, Drehmann, and Schrimpf, 'Changes in Monetary Policy Operating Procedures' (n 61) 36; Potter and Smets, 'Unconventional Monetary Policy Tools' (n 4) 40–44.

[117] Michael Anson and others, 'The Bank of England as Lender of Last Resort: New Historical Evidence from Daily Transactional Data' (2017) Bank of England Staff Working Paper No 691 <https://www.bankofengland.co.uk/-/media/boe/files/working-paper/2017/the-bank-of-england-as-lender-of-last-resort-a-new-historical-evidence-from-daily-transactional-data.pdf?la=en&hash=173967C0B9499B9B2E3792E82D484863C7DF3760> accessed 13 July 2021; Ian Plenderleith, 'Review of the Bank of England's Provision of Emergency Liquidity Assistance in 2008-09' (Report presented to the Court of the Bank of England, 2012) 76–79 <https://www.bankofengland.co.uk/-/media/boe/files/news/2012/november/the-provision-of-emergency-liquidity-assistance-in-2008-9> accessed 13 July 2021, and for the frameworks: a Discount Window Facility framework, which in simple terms provides facilities for liquidity insurance, provided conditions set in the framework are met (eg in terms of eligible collateral) and the 2019 BoE's revised Sterling Monetary Framework.

[118] Christopher Graham, Natasha Khan, and Alexandra Lai, 'Recent Changes to the Bank of Canada's Emergency Lending Assistance Policy' (2016) Bank of Canada Review <https://www.bankofcanada.ca/wp-content/uploads/2016/11/boc-review-autumn16-graham.pdf> accessed 13 July 2021.

[119] The FED can provide emergency loans only through broad-based facilities and cannot help an individual troubled firm (ie non-bank institutions). William Nelson, 'Lessons from Lender of Last Resort Actions during the Crisis: The Federal Reserve Experience' (2014) BIS Papers No 79, 76–77 <https://

a broadened scope of its LOLR function. However, the BoC and the ECB do have a common feature in the adoption of an agreement to frame emergency lending. The framework for Canadian emergency lending assistance exists within an agreement, similarly to the ELA agreement of the ECB, so in extra-statutory sources that give more prominence to other concerns than price stability. The publication of ELA frameworks departs from the 'constructive ambiguity' that used to be dominant across central banks, and that partly explains the relative absence from the statutes (and resistance to publish data and terms on the use of ELA in order to avoid moral hazard and financial stability risks).[120] Distinguishing monetary and credit approaches may however become challenging[121] and the use of ELA during the GFC reached novel dimensions in scope, also in its interaction with financial assistance programmes on the brink of fiscal policy measures that raises broader question on the policy mix framework. Different avenues for changes have been advocated, that is, recognizing an exclusive competence to the ECB or assigning those responsibilities within its supervisory pillar.[122]

Thirdly, QE is another widespread unconventional measure across central banks apart from the BoC. The latter did announce that it could use outright purchases of assets that would change the balance sheet composition and size, in other words through quantitative/credit easing, but has not had recourse to it.[123] Therefore, the unconventional measures activated by the BoC were much more limited than in the case of the ECB, the BoE, and the FED, and meant to address market volatility propagated from the US. Among the reasons explaining this difference, there is the Canadian banking system's history (concentrated, with a centralized oligopolistic structure with branch-banking, in comparison with a more decentralized 'unit banking' model in the US)

www.bis.org/publ/bppdf/bispap79d.pdf> accessed 13 July 2021; Stanley Fischer, 'The Lender of Last Resort Function in the United States' (Speech at 'The Lender of Last Resort: An International Perspective', Washington, 10 February 2016) <https://www.federalreserve.gov/newsevents/speech/fischer20160210a.htm> accessed 13 July 2021; Hal S Scott, 'The Federal Reserve: The Weakest Lender of Last Resort Among Its Peers' (2015) 18 International Finance 321.

[120] Christos V Gortsos, 'Other Specific Tasks and Competences of the European Central Bank Relating to Financial Stability' in Christos V Gortsos (ed), *European Central Banking Law: The Role of the European Central Bank and National Central Banks under European Law* (Springer International Publishing 2020) 388.

[121] The circumstances of a crisis blur the distinction between 'ordinary' liquidity assistance and the LOLR liquidity assistance: Rosa M Lastra, 'The Role of Central Banks in Monetary Affairs: A Comparative Perspective' in Thomas Cottier and others (eds), *The Rule of Law in Monetary Affairs* (CUP 2014) 87.

[122] Also calls for harmonizing and centralizing ELA arrangements: see International Monetary Fund, 'Euro area policies: Financial Sector Assessment Program-Technical Note-Systemic Liquidity Management' (2018) IMF Country Report no 18/229, 30 <https://www.imf.org/en/Publications/CR/Issues/2018/07/19/Euro-Area-Policies-Financial-Sector-Assessment-Program-Technical-Note-Systemic-Liquidity-46103> accessed 13 July 2021, and earlier, René Smits, *The European Central Bank: Institutional Aspects* (Kluwer Law International 1997) 269–71.

[123] The FED started its Asset Purchases Programme in November 2008, the BoE in January 2009, and the ECB in January 2015. See Cour-Thimann and Winkler, 'The ECB's Non-Standard Monetary Policy Measures' (n 68) and Klaus Tuori in this volume. See also Bank of Canada, 'Monetary Policy Report. Annex' (Governing Council of the Bank of Canada, April 2009), 26 <https://www.bankofcanada.ca/wp-content/uploads/2010/03/mpr230409.pdf> accessed 13 July 2021. A 3-page Framework for Conducting Monetary Policy at Low Interest Rates is still applicable (see Bank of Canada, 'Framework for Monetary Operations and Liquidity Provision' <https://www.bankofcanada.ca/markets/market-operations-liquidity-provision/framework-market-operations-liquidity-provision/#framework> accessed 13 July 2021).

and its institutional foundations, banking supervision, and regularly reviewed regulations and charters.[124] It is notable that, for the ECB, the APP and its public sector component raised judicial reviews to question the boundaries of its mandate that led to much debated discussions with the resistance of the German Federal Constitutional Court towards the Court of Justice.[125] Overall, the common and distinct features, grasped from the viewpoint of central bank statutes and extra-statutory elements could have both exogenous and endogenous parameters, and among which: 'different market structures, players, practices and economic conditions'[126] which go beyond the comparative constitutional analysis of this chapter.

Section II examined the statutory sources and the frameworks for price stability determination. The BoC and the FED have more leeway to reinterpret their mandate, because it is broad for the BoC and dual for the FED. The BoE, with a 'twin' mandate, has reinforced the financial stability objective. The ECB has had a single monetary policy with a primary objective for price stability for more than twenty years, which was most of the time captured by a hierarchical, sometimes simplified as 'single', mandate and could well enter in the twin mandate club, should the new microprudential function and macroprudential responsibilities from the post-GFC reforms be assumed more openly and firmly. A twin mandate does not invalidate a hierarchical structure between objectives assigned to different functions. However, a dual mandate is out of question in the current EMU structure.

The distinction between single and dual mandates is thus too restrictive and a first scheme following this small sample of central banks includes dual, hierarchical, twin, and broad mandates. The examined central banks have their mandate enshrined in statutory sources. Though, as the 'm' word is literally missing in those Statutes, central banks' objectives and tasks enshrined in formal sources are taken systematically together and interpreted in action. In dealing with the GFC, the scope of central banks' actions evolved through diverse, innovative measures to achieve central bank objectives in an unusual, unconventional way. Most of them required the adoption or interpretation of extra-statutory texts 'operationalizing' the monetary policy frameworks. This policy action puts an emphasis on the implementation of the mandate as well as the flexibility of such frameworks while it still relies on statutory sources (letter and spirit). In other words, central banks follow and design their monetary policy strategy to implement their mandate and underlying objectives in a flexible manner, which shows a thin separation between central bank's principles and the 'operational targets it sets for itself'.[127] One can observe policy flexibility, here illustrated with measures

[124] Michael D Bordo, Angela Redish, and Hugh Rockoff, 'Why Didn't Canada Have a Banking Crisis in 2008 (or in 1930, or 1907, or ...)?' (2015) 68 Economic History Review 218; Renée Haltom, 'Why Was Canada Exempt from the Financial Crisis?' (2013) Econ Focus 22; Lavoie and Seccareccia, 'Reciprocal Influences' (n 89) 64–65.

[125] In particular the litigation that started in Germany regarding the Public Sector Purchase Programme of the ECB, and the following saga in the *Weiss* case: see Fabian Amtenbrink and René Repasi, 'The German Federal Constitutional Courts Decision in Weiss: A Contextual Analysis' (2020) 45 EL Rev 757; and, Editorial comments, 'Not Mastering the Treaties: The German Federal Constitutional Court's PSPP Judgment' (2020) 57 CML Rev 965.

[126] Čáp, Drehmann and Schrimpf, 'Changes in Monetary Policy Operating Procedures' (n 61) 28.

[127] Ricardo Reis, 'Central Bank Design' (2013) 27 Journal of Economic Perspectives 17, 19 (hereafter Reis, 'Central Bank Design').

adopted in exceptional times. An unchanged mandate for price stability (due to constitutional rigidity) goes hand in hand with this policy flexibility exerted within the implementation of the objectives underlying central banks' mandate, or even a different reading of the objectives (eg the FED with stable prices and maximum employment of equal importance but was formerly inverted in the FOMC Statement until August 2020).

III. Conclusions

A systematic approach to formal central bank mandates included a purposive and functional analysis. Furthermore, the implementation of mandates since the GFC has witnessed important evolutions in central bank policy and measures, with a feedback loop on the mandate due to their magnitude, the interpretation, and actions led via extra-statutory sources. They had an instrumental role in addressing major issues in the banking, financial markets, and the real economy—all defended by the four central banks as falling within their mandate. Three major lessons can be drawn from the analysis carried in this chapter.

First, if the objectives are formally stated, their priority may be shifted in practice. When examining central bank mandates, the constitutional, statutory, or legal objectives cover price stability for all central banks studied, as well as, for some central banks, other objectives: the objective of maximum employment or employment (the FED's coequal objective and the BoE's supportive objective, respectively), the objective of growth (the BoE's supportive objective), or objectives under economic and financial welfare (the BoC's multiple objectives), while the ESCB/Eurosystem includes some of those within its secondary and contributory objectives, under a strict hierarchy where the price stability objective takes priority formally. All these central banks are also in charge of an objective relating to the stability of the financial system, admittedly with different wording (for instance financial stability for the ECB and a specific toolbox)[128] and shared responsibility with other agencies or bodies. Other legal acts and/or policy statements for some of the central banks give prominence to more economic driven objectives. The latter objectives have different levels of priority within the monetary policy function: equal to price stability, secondary, supportive, or contributory objectives.

Following the functional analysis, the objectives are more or less clearly associated with central bank functions in formal and extra-statutory sources. This association takes different shapes: multiple objectives within the monetary policy function, which was extensively examined for unpacking the formal and *de facto* priority of objectives and the strengthening of the financial stability objective across several functions, in law and in action. The formal mandate of the ECB has remained unchanged in primary law but reinforced in secondary law that activated the EU Treaties' legal basis to confer microprudential and macroprudential tasks upon the ECB. This evolution, together with ECB monetary policy actions to curb the GFC consequences, reinforced

[128] See chapter 5 by Agnieszka Smoleńska and Thomas Beukers, in this volume.

financial stability as a shared objective of several functions. And yet, a systematic analysis does not always resolve the lack of formal directions as to the interplay of objectives for achieving central bank tasks.[129]

Second, this chapter examined how the hierarchy has been operationalized through monetary policy actions post-GFC. In those cases, monetary policy strategy determined via extra-statutory sources highlight and determine the reasoning for an inversion of objectives, or a policy shift that emphasizes one specific objective within the monetary policy function. Thus, the ranking of objectives may evolve through central bank decision-making, as the symbolic inversion of the dual objectives of the FED proved; the policy actions within monetary policy objectives trade-offs by the BoE between maintaining price stability, and, supportive growth and employment objectives, and, the changes in the approach of the BoC within its broad mandate over time. The FED example showcased that having coequal objectives in the formal mandate of the central bank gives room for policy flexibility, including in the adoption of adequate actions in specific circumstances (ie the Congress Acts to steer towards the maximum employment objective). In contrast, the ECB has seemingly a more restrained margin of manoeuvre to do so because of detailed primary sources (in comparison with its peers), hierarchized objectives, and enumerated tasks. It is not a single but hierarchical mandate, which could better acknowledge its post-GFC sibling in micro and macroprudential tasks.

Thirdly, another lesson drawn from the comparative analysis in this chapter, the ECB has the most detailed formal sources for objectives and tasks of the four examined central banks. However, there is a thin line between deciding on other objectives 'below' price stability, and this leading to reinterpret the scope of this primary objective. The GFC triggered a reinforced objective for financial stability even though it is said to be 'subordinate' to price stability. In this regard, the other mandates of the BoE (twin with monetary and financial stability), the BoC (broad with multiple objectives), and FED (dual with maximum employment and price stability),[130] make the hierarchical mandate of the ECB formally more rigid and with less room for actions in theory.

There is a degree of discretion in the hands of central banks when leading their policy actions. However, any significant trade-offs that occur among several objectives should be decided democratically (eg if the 'green' mandate is put ahead of employment, both contributory objectives within the EU, or if climate change risks are integrated within the scope of the price stability objective or secondary objectives). The central bank mandate, in its wording, reflects social preferences in a given society. A political choice is expressed *ex ante* and submitted to diverse legal safeguards to shield the central banks from *a posteriori* changes (to some extent). Most of the central bank statutory acts, as well as their amendment, require an action outside the remit of central banks as non-majoritarian independent institutions, that is in the hands of the parliament, the government, and/or the people (if submitted to a referendum), as with some legal acts adopted and implemented since the GFC examined in this chapter.

[129] Reis, 'Central Bank Design' (n 127) 19.

[130] New Zealand and Australian central banks have an objective targeting respectively sustainable and full employment besides inflation.

A more significant overhaul across central banks will rely on a new design and implementation of frameworks that cannot be made in isolation from economic policy. As extra-statutory sources showed, the definition and delimitation of monetary policy transpose the mandate, but one cannot isolate inflation from other real economy objectives that are, according to some central bank mandates' wording and/or spirit, only indirect concerns. With the COVID-19 outbreak, measures adopted on the fiscal and economic front paved the way to fiscal stimulus together with significant monetary stimulus. Unconventional monetary policy tools were indeed reactivated fiercely and in the ongoing strategy reviews, the ammunitions that were (re)used to resort to monetary policy firepower cannot be ignored by policymakers and central bankers when redesigning and adapting central bank monetary policy frameworks. The first ECB's monetary policy strategy statement following the ECB Strategy Review acknowledged expressly unconventional instruments beyond the policy rates, that is, forward guidance, asset purchases, and LTROs, and the possibility to adopt new policy instruments to achieve the price stability objective.[131]

Beyond a 'codification' of practices, negative side effects of unconventional measures[132] (negative interest rates, forward guidance, and asset purchases) might still undermine the effective transmission of monetary policy[133] and question its legitimacy whenever it enters fiscal policy grounds. This shows an evident policy mix taking place at EU level with reliance on national recovery plans. This policy mix has been assumed in other jurisdictions (to different degrees with the BoC, the BoE, and the FED).

It is open to debate whether the conference on the future of Europe may trigger a revision of the EMU chapter (as the legal bases for monetary policy must be revised hand in hand with those for economic policy). Concretely, an overhaul of economic/fiscal policies that would affirm the objectives of sustainability and maximum employment drive us back to the revision of Treaty primary sources. Last but not least, regardless of treaty changes, some policies adopted within the overarching European Union agenda already influence central banking in action (as observed with the implications of climate change for monetary policy and central banking within the ECB mandate).[134]

Once the strategy reviews are concluded across several central banks, legal scholars should work on the definition of modern central banking to represent the realities of the post-crisis world in central banking comparative law. If monetary policy was considered the 'queen function' of central banks in the twentieth century,[135] what will be the master function in the twenty-first century? Will handling sustainability

[131] European Central Bank, 'The ECB's monetary policy strategy statement' (n 63) para 8.

[132] See, for example, the risks of reaching the 'reversal rate' in a negative interest rates environment and the higher banks' risk-taking: Schnabel, 'Going negative: the ECB's experience' (n 68).

[133] Some of the unconventional measures could have 'diminishing effectiveness' and still have some limitations: Claudio Borio, 'When the Unconventional Becomes Conventional' (Speech at the 'ECB and Its Watchers XXI' conference, Frankfurt am Main, 30 September 2020) <https://www.bis.org/speeches/sp200930.pdf> accessed 13 July 2021.

[134] European Central Bank, 'ECB presents action plan to include climate change considerations in its monetary policy strategy' (ECB Press Release, 8 July 2021), <https://www.ecb.europa.eu/press/pr/date/2021/html/ecb.pr210708_1~f104919225.en.html> accessed 13 July 2021 and European Central Bank, 'The ECB's monetary policy strategy statement' (n 63) para 10.

[135] Lastra, 'The Role of Central Banks in Monetary Affairs' (n 96) 80.

and financial stability risks[136] be the new generation of twin functions in a post-GFC and post-COVID crisis world? In such case, statutory texts may need some adaptations and (re)interpretations, in particular if the fight against climate change and unemployment scale their status up in the ranked (or unranked) objectives across central bank mandates. The breadth of the changes observed in central banking will have to be reflected in statutory sources in the longer run for democratic and legitimacy reasons and to better account for an upgraded policy mix.

136 Lastra and Alexander, 'The ECB Mandate' (n 36) 20.

16
The Role of Constitutional Law for the ECB
Past, Present, and Future

Marijn van der Sluis

I. Introduction

Seen from a distance, it appears that the Maastricht Treaty utterly failed to achieve its goals. Over the years, the legal pillars of the Economic and Monetary Union (EMU) seem to have been circumvented, or ignored. The first of these, the 3 per cent-rule, was flouted by France and Germany, which later enabled Greece (which was not supposed to have been allowed in the euro area in the first place for it failed to respect the requirements set to this end) to run enormous deficits which would then become one of the causes of the euro area crisis. During the euro area crisis, the no-bailout clause, anchored in the Treaties to incentivize Member States to maintain sound finances, was ignored, as some Member States were bailed out by others. The prohibition of monetary financing was flouted by the European Central Bank (ECB) through the large-scale purchase of sovereign bonds it started in 2010. Moreover, the ECB ignored its mandate by trying to keep the euro area together. At critical moments, law appears to have failed in securing the outcome intended by the drafters of the Maastricht Treaty.

This chapter offers a constitutional perspective on the development of EMU, in particular the ECB. In doing so, it will displace the narrative that the Maastricht Treaty was a failure.[1] It will argue that the Maastricht Treaty actually succeeded in most of its goals on EMU. Key to this understanding of the development of EMU is that the goals of the Maastricht Treaty were not only of an economic nature, but also political in that they concerned the overall organization of European integration. By laying down the main rules of EMU in a Treaty, rather than for example using only a simple enabling clause, the Member States sought to keep themselves, as a collective, in charge of the overall process of (monetary) integration. By contrast, the institutions were only given specific tasks with regard to EMU. The aim of this chapter is then to assess the development of the ECB from a broader perspective. In effect, this chapter argues that the question whether there is a 'new' ECB requires an examination of the constitutional context in which the ECB operates.

A distinct benefit of examining the broader aims of the rules of EMU is that it also leads to a better understanding of the law. If we take the no-bailout clause as an

[1] The arguments in this chapter build on my PhD thesis, defended in 2017 at the European University Institute. Marijn van der Sluis, 'In Law We Trust: The Role of EU Constitutional Law in European Monetary Integration' (PhD thesis, European University Institute 2017) (hereafter Van der Sluis, 'In Law We Trust').

Marijn van der Sluis, *The Role of Constitutional Law for the ECB* In: *The New European Central Bank*. Edited by: Thomas Beukers, Diane Fromage, and Giorgio Monti, Oxford University Press. © Marijn van der Sluis 2022.
DOI: 10.1093/oso/9780198871231.003.0016

example, the question arises how we can explain the discrepancy between its name and economic purpose, and the actual text. If the clause were truly meant to prevent bailouts, to prohibit Member States from offering financial assistance to other Member States in times of economic malaise, why write such a convoluted provision that does not actually speak about bailouts? The ambiguity of the clause is even more disconcerting when one realizes that the economic rationale of the clause ultimately depends on judges stepping up in a moment of crisis to prevent a Member State from helping another Member State where a larger crisis is on the horizon. If a Treaty provision is meant to have such a drastic outcome, one may have expected the drafters of the Treaty to provide for this in much clearer terms. A purely economic perspective is thus insufficient to explain the creation and application of the clause. Something is missing. Any proper account of the history of EMU must square the economic narrative with the legal text.

Engaging with the legal history of EMU has gained in importance since the Court of Justice of the European Union (CJEU) in its landmark cases *Pringle* and *Gauweiler* on euro area crisis law invoked the *travaux préparatoires* of the Maastricht Treaty.[2] For previous treaties, these documents were not always publicly available. Unfortunately, the use of historical documents for the interpretation of the Treaties in *Pringle* and *Gauweiler* was not particularly convincing as the Court failed to engage with the economic narratives that had dominated the explanations for the legal provisions of EMU until then.

This chapter builds on the argument presented by de Witte a couple of years ago.[3] He argued that the euro area crisis had not led to a constitutional mutation of the EU. Rather, he saw increased institutional variation, where changes in how EMU is governed had not spilled over to the general constitutional architecture of the EU. A distinct aspect of de Witte's argument is that change is a rather constant factor of EU law.[4] His scepticism of grand narratives of 'constitutional mutation' reflects a more general constitutional wisdom, namely that the meaning of constitutional provisions evolves as a matter of course. Whilst this might generally be true for all legal rules, it is especially relevant for rules that have a constitutional character and are thus difficult to amend. The focus then shifts from the substance of the rules to the constitutional framework in which the exact meaning of the rule is determined. In this perspective, it is hardly interesting to note that the rules governing the ECB have evolved.[5] What is far more interesting is the process through which that happened. Which institutions were involved, what legal claims did they make, and what types of opposition to those claims could reasonably be organized?[6]

2 Case C-370/12 *Pringle v Government of Ireland and Others* [2012] ECLI:EU:C:2012:756, para 135 (hereafter Case C-370/12 *Pringle*) and Case C-62/14 *Gauweiler and Others v Deutscher Bundestag* [2015] ECLI:EU:C:2015:400, para 100 (hereafter Case C-62/14 *Gauweiler*). On these judgments, see also chapter 2 by Vestert Borger, in this volume.

3 Bruno de Witte, 'Euro Crisis Responses and the EU Legal Order: Increased Institutional Variation or Constitutional Mutation?' (2015) 11 EuConst 434.

4 ibid 435.

5 The evolution of the rules of EMU may of course be relevant for other reasons.

6 There is already quite a body of scholarship that examines the organization of the response to the euro area crisis, often with an emphasis on the inter-governmental nature of the decision-making process. What is often not discussed in these analyses is the extent to which this organization flows from the Maastricht Treaty itself. See, eg, Jürgen Habermas, *The Crisis of the European Union: A Response* (Polity Press 2012);

Perhaps surprisingly for a legal analysis, the conclusion that the Maastricht Treaty was rather successful should not be mistaken for a normative assessment. I believe the ECB to be an institution without democratic legitimacy. Economic and monetary policy choices do not belong in international treaties that have constitutional characteristics.[7] The fact that all Member States ratified the Treaty does not automatically lend the ECB democratic legitimacy. The Maastricht Treaty should not have been adopted, but that does not mean it was unsuccessful.

Section II of this chapter discusses what is meant with a constitutional perspective of EMU, and what its added value is regarding our understanding of the development of the euro. Section III then highlights the position of the ECB regarding its legal framework. The argument is that the independence of the ECB was constructed as a form of isolation. Due to this isolation, the ECB has significant discretion in the interpretation of the legal framework that governs it. Section IV contrasts the reinterpretative process of the no-bailout clause with how a new interpretation of the mandate of the ECB came about. Whereas for the no-bailout clause political negotiations and compromises led to a new interpretation of the clause before a ruling of the CJEU on the topic, no such process could emerge regarding the mandate of the ECB. The penultimate, Section V highlights the difficulties of courts to engage with the legal framework of the ECB. Section VI concludes.

II. A Constitutional Approach to EMU

The constitutional approach, as applied in this chapter, concerns an examination over time of the legal rules that govern the relations between public institutions.[8] Within states, such an approach would usually focus on the relations between courts, parliaments, and governments.[9] Within the EU, and for this chapter in particular, this also covers the ECB and the Member States (acting individually and collectively[10]).[11] The

Federico Fabbrini, *Economic Governance in Europe: Comparative Paradoxes and Constitutional Challenges* (OUP 2016).

[7] Marijn van der Sluis, 'EU Law for a New Generation?' (2016) 14 ICON 480. See also Richard Bellamy and Albert Weale, 'Political Legitimacy and European Monetary Union: Contracts, Constitutionalism and the Normative Logic of Two-Level Games' (2015) 22 JEPP 257, 268: '... legal constitutionalism presupposes that there can be agreement on the basis of the constitutional essentials of a European monetary order, although the epistemic conditions do not exist to establish that agreement.' On European over-constitutionalization beyond the area of EMU, see Dieter Grimm, *The Constitution of European Democracy* (OUP 2017) ch 5.

[8] This approach overlaps with historical institutionalism, which was developed within political science to understand how institutions create path dependency and respond to or are altered by critical junctures. Institutions are seen as both giving shape to events and being shaped by them. This chapter nonetheless focuses on the constitutional approach to EMU, as it finds the primary 'institution' to be the set of rules on EMU of the Maastricht Treaty. For a description of how historical institutionalism can be used for legal analysis, see Rogers M Smith, 'Historical Institutionalism and the Study of Law' in Gregory A Caldeira, Daniel R Kelemen, and Keith E Whittington (eds), *The Oxford Handbook of Law and Politics* (OUP 2008).

[9] See eg Mark A Graber, *A New Introduction to American Constitutionalism* (OUP 2014).

[10] Luuk van Middelaar, *The Passage to Europe: How a Continent Became a Union* (Yale University Press 2014) (hereafter Van Middelaar, *The Passage to Europe*).

[11] For a historical-institutionalist perspective on the early years of the euro area crisis, see Ledina Gocaj and Sophie Meunier, 'Time Will Tell: The EFSF, the ESM, and the Euro Crisis' (2013) 35 European Integration 239.

assumption is that changes to the legal rules are at least in part the result of how those relations are structured. Constitutional rules organize the political arena, and constitutional rules are changed, neglected, or interpreted differently as a result of political struggles and decisions taking place in that arena. This approach allows for an examination of the interaction between law and politics where neither is seen as dominant. It would be a mischaracterization to see constitutional law only as the framework within which politics takes place, because politics also directly affects constitutional law, either because judges have a certain political preference, or because institutions more generally shape our understanding of constitutional law. Conversely, there is a misconception that in crises politics trump law. What can be seen in this chapter is that during crises the interpretation of *certain provisions* might quickly and significantly change. However, as we will also see, the institutions involved in those reinterpretations are still creatures of law. Their composition, voting arrangements, institutional relations, etc are products of legal rules. Politics takes place in an environment shaped by law, even if law is itself shaped by politics.

For EMU, understanding the evolution of the legal rules that shape the relations between institutions (in a broad sense) is impossible without taking account of the nature of those rules as Treaty rules. The embedding of EMU within the Maastricht Treaty was a distinct choice that reflected not only a certain view on how EMU should function on a day-to-day basis,[12] but also of the process of European integration more broadly. Regarding the former, when EMU was proposed in the 1970s, the Werner Report saw the need for a treaty mostly in light of the need to transfer certain competences, not for locking in a specific economic view. Hence, the transfers of competences were not linked to the achievement of specific goals. This was, of course, fully in line with the predominant Keynesian view on economics, which stresses flexibility in decision-making and the need for coordination between monetary and economic policies. Legal rules then primarily served to enable political control of economic and monetary policy. As is well known, the economic ideas that permeated the negotiations of the Maastricht Treaty were more sceptical of political interventions and sought to restrict as much as enable.[13] However, that change in economic ideas does not suffice to understand the Maastricht Treaty. Equally important was that the choice for an extensive treaty reflected a specific vision of European integration, whereby institutions would be given specific tasks, but the overall responsibility for integration stayed with the Member States collectively.[14]

The Maastricht Treaty is thus the confluence of two mutually supportive ideas: namely that rules are central to macro-economic policy-making and that the Member States should maintain control over the process of European integration, especially in the area of EMU. Both ideas shaped the rules of EMU. Whilst the economic background of EMU is well known, the perspective of the Maastricht Treaty as a tool to structure integration can perhaps best be explained through an examination of the Treaty rules on economic governance (now Articles 121 on multilateral surveillance

[12] Van der Sluis, 'In Law We Trust' (n 1) ch 2.

[13] On the history of those political-economic ideas, see Nancy MacLean, *Democracy in Chains: The Deep History of the Radical Right's Stealth Plan for America* (Penguin 2017).

[14] For a description of the Member States as a collective, see Van Middelaar, *The Passage to Europe* (n 10).

and 126 of the Treaty on the Functioning of the European Union (TFEU) on the excessive deficit procedure). For these provisions, their inclusion in the Treaties had the effect of protecting the Member States from an overly intrusive EU. They aimed to limit European action as much as to promote it. By creating two procedures that specify how, and to what extent, the Union may interfere with Member States economic policies, the Member States reduced the opportunities for the Union institutions to promote integration. Moreover, the Treaty protects the political discretion of the Council in the Excessive Deficit Procedure (EDP) to make an 'overall assessment' of the situation in a Member State.[15] If the EDP is seen in this light, the German proposal for a 'Stability Pact' becomes the first attempt to overthrow the compromises of the Maastricht Treaty, as it would have introduced strict numerical rules that Member States would have to abide by.[16] This attempt was thwarted by France and the Commission, and the Stability & Growth Pact (SGP) then merely implemented the provisions of the Treaty. Where there have been complaints about the SGP being 'toothless', this should be seen as an affirmation of the strength of the Treaties as a tool to protect the discretion of the Member States.[17] Crucially, the SGP left intact the discretion of the Council to determine what an excessive deficit is and what steps need to be taken to remedy an excessive deficit. Only in cases where the Council was deprived of the opportunity to make a proper assessment of the (economic) situation in a Member State, can one reasonably speak of a failure of the Maastricht Treaty. In other words, the EDP largely worked as may have been expected, with minimal limits to the discretion of the Member States and with a sufficient number of veto players that could block further integration.

A constitutional perspective on the development of economic governance at least until the euro area crisis would thus stress the lack of evolution in the interpretation of the Treaty provision as being the result of the institutional set-up of economic governance. In the absence of a crisis in which a new consensus could be forged, disagreement between the Member States would prevent them from acting as a collective thereby preventing a significant evolution of the meaning of the clause. In 2009, Hodson also noted that EMU had not (yet) led to deepened integration in the economic sphere, contrary to what certain theories of integration had expected.[18] Of course, the euro

[15] Consolidated Version of the Treaty on the Functioning of the European Union [2012] OJ C326/47, Art 126 (6) (hereafter TFEU).

[16] For an analysis of the SGP from this perspective, see Matthieu Segers and Femke van Esch, 'Behind the Veil of Budgetary Discipline: The Political Logic of the Budgetary Rules in EMU and the SGP' (2007) 45 JCMS 1089.

[17] It can also be observed that France and Germany could not have broken the legal rules of the corrective arm of the SGP, since the pertinent legal obligations applied to the Commission and the Council, not to the Member States. The legal argument could perhaps be made that France and Germany violated their Treaty obligation to avoid excessive deficits. The Council had found that these Member States indeed had excessive deficits. However, this would ignore the point of the excessive deficit *procedure*, which is to monitor and remedy such deficits. As a German negotiator of the SGP (and later ECB Executive Board Member) Jürgen Stark stated, the procedure is not about the sin, but the failure to repent. As the Council later found that Germany and France had resolved the situation, the procedure was thus successful. Jürgen Stark, 'Genesis of a Pact' in Anne Brunila, Marco Buti, and Daniele Franco (eds), *The Stability and Growth Pact: The Architecture of Fiscal Policy in EMU* (Palgrave Macmillan 2001).

[18] Dermot Hodson, 'EMU and Political Union: What, If Anything, Have We Learned from the Euro's First Decade?' (2009) 16 JEPP 508. See also Andrew Moravcsik, 'The European Constitutional Settlement' in

area crisis then 'corrected' this situation, partially on the basis of a new treaty article (Article 136 TFEU, introduced by the Lisbon Treaty in 2009) that had introduced ambiguity about the scope of EU economic governance.[19] However, the fact that the euro area crisis led to a rapid deepening of integration does not explain why economic governance had functioned with such stability for a decade.

The discussions above about the no-bailout clause and economic governance show that a constitutional approach to EMU is not about simply adding a new element to the interpretation of the rules of EMU, but about examining the interaction between the economic and political goals of the rules. For the no-bailout clause, this meant that its economic goals can be part of a more comprehensive analysis that also includes some political motivations. For economic governance it is clear that the political goals stood in distinct contrast to the economic goals. The chapter now turns to the ECB and examines how the institutional set-up (meaning here its relations with other actors) of the ECB affected the re-interpretation of the mandate of the ECB. The mandate is the set of rules that govern what the ECB is allowed or obliged to do and what it is excluded from doing. This concerns primarily the objectives and tasks of the ECB as well as the prohibition of monetary financing. Where this chapter is not concerned with the substance of the evolution of the mandate of the ECB, but with the process, it suffices to note here that the primary objective of the ECB has broadened, as it for example now includes the objective of maintaining the integrity of the euro area, and that the prohibition of monetary financing has been interpreted very narrowly.[20]

III. The ECB as a Constitutional Interpreter

The set-up of the ECB is often compared to that of the German Bundesbank, prior to its inclusion in the Eurosystem. Of course, for Germany the ratification of the Maastricht Treaty required that the ECB would resemble its own central bank, which had built a strong reputation as protector of the national currency.[21] Whilst the legal

Sophie Meunier and Kathleen R McNamara (eds), *Making History: European Integration and Institutional Change at Fifty* (OUP 2007).

[19] TFEU (n 15) Art 136 is ambiguous as it appears to offer a broad enabling clause for EMU ('In order to ensure the proper functioning of economic and monetary union'), only to limit action to what is already possible under the Treaties, but then tailored to euro area Member States ('in accordance with the relevant provisions of the Treaties, the Council shall [take action], in accordance with the relevant procedure from among those referred to in Articles 121 ... '). If the purpose of the clause was only to allow measures specifically for euro area Member States, the broad language about the proper functioning of EMU was not necessary.

[20] For a more thorough analysis of the development of the mandate of the ECB, see Kaarlo Tuori and Klaus Tuori, *The Eurozone Crisis: A Constitutional Analysis* (CUP 2014) (hereafter Tuori and Tuori, *The Eurozone Crisis*); Marijn van der Sluis, 'Similar, Therefore Different: Judicial Review of Another Unconventional Monetary Policy in Weiss (C-493/17)' (2019) 46 LIEI 263 (hereafter Van der Sluis, 'Similar, Therefore Different'). See also chapter 2 by Vestert Borger, chapter 3 by Klaus Tuori, and chapter 15 by Christy-Ann Petit, in this volume.

[21] For the history of the negotiations of EMU and the ECB in particular, see Harold James, *Making the European Monetary Union: The Role of the Committee of Central Bank Governors and the Origins of the European Central Bank* (Harvard University Press 2012). On the negotiations of the Maastricht Treaty, see Kenneth HF Dyson and Kevin Featherstone, *The Road to Maastricht: Negotiating Economic and Monetary Union* (OUP 1999).

framework of the ECB, as laid down in the Maastricht Treaty, indeed resembles that of the Bundesbank, the legal environment in which those sets of provisions are meant to be applied is significantly different.[22] Whereas the Bundesbank was independent from the government, but not from politics in a more general sense, as its independence and mandate could be revoked by law, the ECB's independence was configured as a form of isolation from all other EU institutions and to a certain extent from the Member States.[23] This isolation also affected the development of the interpretation of the Treaties, as it became a key aspect in the resolution of conflicts about monetary policy.

Two elements of the set-up of the ECB in particular made for an isolated entity. Firstly, the independence and mandate of the ECB are an integral part of the Treaties. Not only the independence and mandate themselves are explicitly mentioned several times in EU primary law, but they are also flanked by numerous provisions that further develop those rules. Especially regarding the ECB's independence, the Treaties describe the personal, financial, and institutional aspects in quite some detail.[24] Particularly relevant here is the distance that is created between the ECB and the institutions of the EU in charge of designing and adopting secondary legislation. Even though the European Court of Justice ruled in the early years that the ECB could be bound in general by secondary legislation, it also upheld the broad construction of the independence of the ECB to decide on monetary policy.[25] For example, in recent discussions on the democratic 'accountability' of the ECB, the suggestion has been made that the European Parliament (EP) should offer a clear interpretation of the secondary mandate of the ECB, describing which economic policies in the Union it finds most important.[26] Obviously, such action cannot legally bind the ECB, as there is no legal basis on which the EP can make such determination *and* because it would violate the independence of the ECB.[27] Secondary legislation is of little help in guiding the interpretation of EMU primary law regarding the ECB, save certain exceptions.[28]

[22] Giandomenico Majone, 'Rethinking European Integration after the Debt Crisis' (2012) University College London Working Paper No 3/2012 <https://www.ucl.ac.uk/drupal/site_european-institute/sites/european-institute/files/working-paper-debt-crisis.pdf> accessed 1 March 2021.

[23] On the lack of political embeddedness for the ECB, see Amy Verdun, 'The Institutional Design of EMU: A Democratic Deficit?' (1998) 18 Journal of Public Policy 107 (hereafter Verdun, 'The Institutional Design of EMU').

[24] On the ECB's independence, see chapter 10 by Alexander Thiele, in this volume.

[25] Case C-27/04 *Commission v Council* [2004] ECLI:EU:C:2004:436.

[26] Gregory Claeys and Marta Domínguez-Jiménez, 'How Can the European Parliament Better Oversee the European Central Bank?' (2020) Directorate General for Internal Policies, Policy Department for Economic, Scientific and Quality of Life Policies PE 652.747 <https://www.europarl.europa.eu/RegData/etudes/IDAN/2020/652747/IPOL_IDA(2020)652747_EN.pdf> accessed 1 March 2021.

[27] The secondary mandate is furthermore concerned with the economic policies *in* the Union, not those *of* the Union. This suggests that the ECB should primarily take into account the policies of the Member States.

[28] See TFEU (n 15) Art 125(2), regarding the power of the Council to specify definitions for the application of the prohibition of monetary financing. It should also be noted that parts of the ESCB/ECB Statute can be amended through the ordinary legislative procedure. This has created limited opportunities for the institutions to wield influence over the ECB. See, for example, the conflict between the ECB and the Council over the regulation of central counterparties: Jim Brunsden and Claire Jones, 'ECB Scraps Clearing Powers Request in Feud with European Capitals' *Financial Times* (Brussels and Frankfurt am Main, 20 March 2019). Another exception is the power of the Council to confer the power to conduct prudential supervision of financial institutions. In this area, the Council and EP (as the ECB applies other secondary legislation in the conduct of prudential supervision) have significant influence on the behaviour of the ECB. See further

The accountability measures put in place vis-à-vis the EP and the Council were also designed in such a way as to avoid the appearance of a hierarchical relationship towards the ECB. Given that the EP lacks the power to sanction the ECB, it may even be doubted that these procedures can be qualified as accountability mechanisms.[29] The members of the Executive Board of the ECB may be heard by the ECON Committee of the EP, but this does not encompass a competence of that committee or of the EP as a whole to instruct the ECB to take certain actions. Nor is the ECB President obliged to offer substantive answers in response to questions from MEPs. It is this lack of tools of the EP vis-à-vis the ECB that explains the creation and flourishing of the 'monetary dialogue' whereby the ECB President appears regularly before the EP. Appearing before the EP gives the ECB a safe venue to explain its policy choices whilst also giving the appearance of democratic legitimacy.[30]

Also relevant in this regard was that the CJEU has not developed a distinct vision on the functioning of the institutions of the EU. The notion of 'institutional balance' has been employed in the reasoning of the Court to delineate between the tasks of various institutions, but the notion appears to be based primarily on the text of the Treaties.[31] In other words, the jurisprudence of the CJEU did not stand in the way of a constitutionally independent central bank. Whereas on the national level, it would be unusual to place the statute of the central bank on the same level as the constitution,[32] the EU Treaties are rich in detail about economic policies and institutional configurations.[33] The democratic difficulty of elevating an independent central bank to the treaty level was discussed by the German Constitutional Court in its judgment on the Maastricht Treaty.[34] It accepted the ECB as a modification of the principle of democracy due to scientific evidence and the experience with the Bundesbank, notwithstanding the fact that neither concerned a constitutional level of independence. For the CJEU, the

on the ECB's role in prudential supervision: chapter 7 by Kern Alexander, and chapter 8 by Federico Della Negra and Gianni Lo Schiavo, in this volume.

[29] A commonly used definition of accountability as mechanism is found in Mark Bovens, 'Two Concepts of Accountability: Accountability as a Virtue and as a Mechanism' (2010) 33 West European Politics 946. On the ECB's democratic accountability, see further chapter 11 by Fabian Amtenbrink and Menelaos Markakis, in this volume.

[30] Marijn van der Sluis, 'Maastricht Revisited: Economic Constitutionalism, the ECB and the Bundesbank' in Maurice Adams, Federico Fabbrini, and Pierre Larouche (eds), *The Constitutionalization of European Budgetary Constraints* (Hart Publishing 2014) (hereafter Van der Sluis, 'Maastricht Revisited'). Most literature on the monetary dialogue is less sceptical; see, for example, Stefan Collignon and Sebastian Diessner, 'The ECB's Monetary Dialogue with the European Parliament: Efficiency and Accountability during the Euro Crisis?' (2016) 54 JCMS 1296; Fabian Amtenbrink and Kees van Duin, 'The European Central Bank before the European Parliament: Theory and Practice after Ten Years of Monetary Dialogue' (2009) 34 EL Rev 561; Diane Fromage and Renato Ibrido, 'The "Banking Dialogue" as a Model to Improve Parliamentary Involvement in the Monetary Dialogue?' (2018) 40 Journal of European Integration 295.

[31] Merijn Chamon, 'The Institutional Balance, an Ill-Fated Principle of EU Law?' (2015) 21 European Public Law 371.

[32] Compare Art 106 of the Dutch Constitution, which reads (in full, translated): 'The monetary system shall be regulated by Act of Parliament.'

[33] Gareth Davies, 'Democracy and Legitimacy in the Shadow of Purposive Competence' (2015) 21 ELJ 2.

[34] BVerfG Judgment of the 2nd Chamber of 12 October 1993 2 BvR 2134/92, 2 BvR 2159/92 Official Court Report 89, 155, para 154.

independence of the ECB would not prima facie be an issue.[35] Counterfactually, the CJEU could also have developed a view on the institutional relations in the Union which prioritizes democracy. That could then have led to the view on central bank independence as an exception to the principle of democracy, which would therefore need to be construed very narrowly.

A second aspect of the set-up of EMU that made for an isolated central bank was the lack of a central economic/fiscal policy-maker on the European level.[36] Due to the lopsided nature of EMU, there would be a strong monetary policy-maker on the European level, with no obvious counterweight for economic policy. On the national level, even independent central banks would engage with and, to a certain extent, co-ordinate with the government to avoid contradictory policies.[37] Economic and fiscal policies obviously affect the environment in which central banks seek to achieve their monetary policy goals and vice versa. Economic/fiscal policy-makers and monetary policy-makers thus have strong interests in each other's policies. As noted by Jean-Victor Louis, the lack of a single European economic policy also makes the ECB vulnerable to critique, as there is no other institution available to take responsibility for the economic situation in the euro area.[38] Sustained criticism from the public and from politicians might then hamper the credibility of the ECB in the conduct of monetary policies. The restrictive character of the rules on economic governance—discussed above—is thus also relevant for the ECB. The launch of the Eurogroup was an attempt to create a counterweight to the ECB, but especially prior to the euro area crisis the lack of economic policy tools on the European level prevented the Eurogroup from engaging with the ECB as a unified actor. As economic policy remained a national responsibility in EMU, the Eurogroup as a whole held insufficient sway over euro area economic policy to influence the ECB. Only during the euro area crisis, when the Eurogroup (politically) decided on the allocation of financial assistance and on conditionality, was there a unified actor that could sway policy in the euro area to such an extent that it gained influence over the monetary policies of the ECB, for example in relation to the timing of policies.[39]

The result of the isolated position of the ECB is that there is no obvious political interlocutor for the interpretation of the EMU provisions regarding the ECB. In other words, in most instances it will be the ECB that determines the meaning of the rules on monetary policy. An obvious example is the interpretation of 'price stability' as meaning a level of inflation below or close to 2 per cent in the medium term, as the

[35] For a rare discussion on the involvement of the CJEU in EMU, especially in relation to the ECB, see Paul Craig, 'EMU, the European Central Bank and Judicial Review' in Paul R Beaumont and Neil Walker (eds), *Legal Framework of the Single European Currency* (Hart Publishing 1999).

[36] On this point, see chapter 14 by Ad van Riet, in this volume.

[37] For a more elaborate discussion of this issue, see Marijn van der Sluis, 'Contesting the Monetary Policies of the European Central Bank' in Alessandra Arcuri and Florin Coman-Kund (eds), *Technocracy and the Law: Accountability, Governance and Expertise* (forthcoming) (hereafter Van der Sluis, 'Contesting the Monetary Policies of the European Central Bank').

[38] Jean-Victor Louis, 'The Euro-Group and Economic Policy-Coordination' in Jean-Victor Louis (ed), *The Euro in the National Context* (British Institute of International and Comparative Law 2002) 365–66. Also see Verdun, 'The Institutional Design of EMU' (n 23).

[39] See further Van der Sluis, 'Contesting the Monetary Policies of the European Central Bank' (n 37). See on the interaction between the ECB and the Member States chapter 2 by Vestert Borger, in this volume.

ECB stated in 2003.[40] Another example of this *de facto* authority of the ECB is the definition of its monetary policy task. As stated in its Annual Report of 1999, the ECB saw emergency liquidity assistance (ELA) falling outside its purview. ELA is generally offered by central banks to banks in moments of crisis, where general doubts about the health of the financial system affect all or most banks.[41] Although this task was generally seen as a core competence of central banks, the ECB found that ELA fell outside its own mandate, because ELA is more oriented towards financial than price stability. As a result of this determination, Member States needed legislation authorizing their NCBs to offer ELA on their own account, that is, as part of the tasks they may still fulfil outside of those that flow from their belonging to the European System of Central Banks.[42] In those instances in which those NCBs would offer ELA on their own account, the Governing Council could nonetheless intervene.[43]

The issue here is not that the decision to restrictively interpret the mandate was particularly controversial or unreasonable, but that there was no institution that could effectively challenge the decision made by the ECB through another route than through the courts. The ECB in many cases has few alternatives than to follow its own view on the Treaties. Political consultation with the EP, the Council, or the Commission will quickly give the impression that the ECB is subjecting itself to their opinion. As the ECB is shielded from political pressure, the political process is unable to aid the ECB in its task of constitutional interpretation.

In the previous section, it was argued that the creation of EMU through an extensive treaty containing the foundational pillars of the single currency served to strengthen the role of the Member States in the process of European integration. In this section, it was shown that the ECB was given considerable leeway in interpreting the boundaries of its own powers. These two points appear contradictory. The power to interpret the boundaries of one's own powers goes a long way in determining one's own political future (as the Bundesverfassungsgericht keeps reminding us). Especially because within EMU the ECB takes such a prominent position, the ability of the ECB to interpret its own legal framework would appear to be the most relevant aspect regarding the future of the euro. Furthermore, stressing the 'auto-interpretation' of the ECB legal framework raises a question of timing: why did the reinterpretation of the mandate of the ECB only occur after a decade of monetary union?

Two features of EMU prevented, and to some extent still prevent, the ECB from becoming the central player in deciding the future of EMU. The first is that the central banking community is built around a set of shared beliefs on the proper organization of central banking.[44] In this view, political involvement in monetary policy brings in the wrong incentives. Instead, independent central bankers with a narrow mandate

[40] Van der Sluis, 'Maastricht Revisited' (n 30). This definition was recently amended.

[41] Nicholas Anthony Lee, 'Fluid Dynamics: Emergency Liquidity Assistance during the Eurocrisis' (LLM thesis, European University Institute 2016).

[42] See, eg, Andres Tupits, 'Legal Framework for the Eurosystem National Central Bank' (PhD thesis, University of London 2010) 176–77.

[43] Protocol No 4 on the Statute of the European System of Central Banks and of the European Central Bank [2016] OJ C202/230, Art 14.4 (hereafter ESCB/ECB Statute).

[44] Amy Verdun, 'The Role of the Delors Committee in the Creation of EMU: An Epistemic Community?' (1998) EUI Working Paper of the Robert Schuman Centre No 1998/44 <http://diana-n.iue.it:8080/handle/1814/69999?show=full> accessed 1 March 2021.

would set a policy that would benefit the economy as a whole. As these beliefs allowed the central bankers to be part of the core of the negotiations on the Maastricht Treaty, the central banking community would not easily discard them after the launch of the euro, limiting their willingness to take an expansive view on their own monetary powers. A second aspect of EMU, and central banking in general, is that monetary policy is only part of a broader set of policies that affects the success or viability of a currency. As described above, monetary policy and (other) economic policies affect each other, leading economic policy-makers and monetary policy-makers to interact and, depending on the institutional environment in which this interaction occurs, influence each other. A single currency requires many supportive economic policies to function, such as the free movement of capital.[45] Even an expansionist view on the powers of the ECB could not lead to the conclusion that the central bank could on its own decide the future of the euro.

IV. The ECB during the Euro Area Crisis

As mentioned in the introduction, the so-called no-bailout clause found in Article 125 TFEU is a textually straightforward clause that is disconnected from the economic reasoning behind it. A no-bailout clause seeks to prevent moral hazard by stating that in case of a crisis, support may not be offered. The aim is to induce 'good behaviour' in order to prevent crises. The credibility of the clause depends in part on the perceived willingness of a court to enforce the clause. During the negotiations of the no-bailout clause, the Commission observed that a no-bailout clause might not actually prevent bailouts, given the interests involved within the EU.[46] Hence, the Commission sought to weaken the text of the clause, whilst emphatically stressing the name (and thus the economic rationale) of the clause. The disconnect between legal text and economic reasoning was purposeful. The aim of the no-bailout clause was to give the impression of the existence of a no-bailout clause, not to actually prohibit bailouts. The legal history of the no-bailout clause is thus more complex than the CJEU makes it seem in *Pringle*.[47]

The ambiguity of the clause was rediscovered during the crisis. Suddenly, the emphasis was on the text of the provision and on the requirements for offering financial support.[48] Two criteria emerged: first, strict conditionality was discussed as a *legal requirement* of aid, not just as a way to secure the quality of the loans, but as an alternative route to provide for the proper economic and fiscal policies in EMU. Secondly,

[45] See also, for example, the economic framework necessary for a single currency as described in the Committee for the Study of Economic and Monetary Union, 'Report on the Economic and Monetary Union in the European Communities' (17 April 1989) <https://ec.europa.eu/economy_finance/publications/pages/publication6161_en.pdf> accessed 1 March 2021.

[46] European Commission, 'One market, one money. An evaluation of the potential benefits and costs of forming an economic and monetary union' (Directorate-General for Economic and Financial Affairs, European Economy no 44, 1990), 110–111 <https://ec.europa.eu/economy_finance/publications/pages/publication7454_en.pdf> accessed 1 March 2021. See also Van der Sluis, 'In Law We Trust' (n 1) 118–20.

[47] Case C-370/12 *Pringle* (n 2) para 135.

[48] See, eg, Jean-Victor Louis, 'Guest Editorial: The No-Bailout Clause and Rescue Packages' (2010) 47 CML Rev 971.

financial assistance could only be given if the stability of the euro area as a whole was in danger. In negotiating the provision of financial assistance through the crisis, it was the Member States of the euro area that collectively shaped the future of the euro. They set the conditions for assistance and although that brought the euro to the brink of collapse, the Member States in the end collectively agreed on the provisions of financial assistance and the conditions.[49]

Although the emphasis in the legal literature is on the judgment by the CJEU on this topic,[50] the reinterpretation of Article 125 TFEU was primarily the product of an intense period of negotiations between the Member States.[51] At first, the economic rationale of the clause was simply ignored by emphasizing the text of the clause. However, especially for Germany it was beneficial to introduce conditionality as a legal requirement, in light of a possible involvement of the German Constitutional Court *and* towards Member States that would seek financial assistance. As the institutional framework in which assistance was renegotiated, for example in the transition from the European Financial Stability Framework to the European Stability Mechanism, multiple opportunities arose to negotiate the *legal* requirements under which assistance could be offered, ultimately leading to the amendment of Article 136 TFEU. The *Pringle* judgment of the CJEU is then noteworthy for its lack of innovation. Whereas it may have been expected that the Court would endorse in broad terms the political consensus, it had several possibilities to enforce a more 'European' perspective on the organization of financial assistance, for example with regard to the respect for the Charter of Fundamental Rights or the use of EU economic governance as the basis for conditionality.[52] However, the CJEU accepted in whole the view on the legality of bailouts that was developed by the Member States over the course of several months. Only in later judgments did the CJEU take small steps with regard to bringing conditionality under the umbrella of EU law.[53]

For the reinterpretation of the mandate of the ECB, no such process could emerge. Due to the isolation of the ECB (which was only partially lifted during the crisis) there was no structured interaction with other institutions to create a broad, and publicly supported, compromise on the new terms of the ECB. Obviously the Member States and the other institutions did have opinions about the evolution of the understanding of the mandate, and the ECB was cognizant of the sensitivities in the different Member

[49] The fact that the Member States agreed collectively on financial assistance and conditionality hides the inequalities between the Member States. This is one of the reasons why the creation of the European Stability Mechanism (ESM) outside the EU legal order has been criticized.

[50] See, eg, Tuori and Tuori, *The Eurozone Crisis* (n 20); Matthias Goldmann, 'The European Economic Constitution after the PSPP Judgment: Towards Integrative Liberalism?' (2020) 21 German Law Journal 1058.

[51] For an extensive analysis of how the Member States cooperated in this period of the crisis, see Vestert Borger, 'The Transformation of the Euro: Law, Contract, Solidarity' (thesis, Leiden University 2018), and chapter 2 by Vestert Borger, in this volume.

[52] See, eg, Regulation no 472/2013 of the European Parliament and the Council of 21 May 2013 on the strengthening of economic and budgetary surveillance of Member States in the euro area experiencing or threatened with serious difficulties with respect to their financial stability [2013] OJ L140/1, Art 7.

[53] René Repasi, 'Judicial Protection against Austerity Measures in the Euro Area: Ledra and Mallis' (2017) 54 CML Rev 1123.

States in reshaping its understanding of the legal framework.[54] It is highly doubtful that the ECB would have been able to reinterpret its mandate in the crisis if there had been persistent opposition from the collective of Member States.[55] However, the political consensus that emerged on the actions of the ECB was based on an acquiescence of a new status quo that was tentatively being shaped by the ECB, rather than on compromises that politicians had to publicly defend both in Brussels and in their home state. When the ECB started taking an expansive view on its own mandate, most importantly through the invocation of protecting the monetary policy transmission mechanism and the integrity of the euro area as goals of its policies, it moreover neglected to highlight any new boundaries to the new interpretation. Introducing hard limits in its view on the legal framework might have hampered its credibility to intervene in the markets.

Whereas it was impossible to reinterpret the mandate of the ECB through a political process, the ECB strategically sought to mitigate its isolated position vis-à-vis the Member States.[56] This strategy is visible in relation to the timing of the launch of several programmes, and their characteristics. Regarding timing, the ECB left it to the Member States to take the lead in the euro area crisis; the evolution of ECB crisis management can be traced back to the timing of the steps taken by the Member States. This pattern was visible from the 'start' of the crisis in May 2010, with the ECB launching its Securities Markets Programme (SMP) immediately after the agreement on bilateral loans from the other Member States to Greece. The replacement of the SMP with the Outright Monetary Transactions (OMT) programme was facilitated by the decision of the Member States to launch the Banking Union in 2012.[57] By waiting to launch these transformative programmes, the ECB was able to defend its programmes by reference to the groundbreaking compromises reached by the Member States. It also minimized the risk of being accused of allowing the Member States to avoid difficult decisions, especially during the early stages of the crisis.[58] Substantively, the ECB sought to strengthen the approach of the Member States in the euro area crisis. Key was the replacement of the Securities Markets Programme with the OMT programme. Under the SMP, the ECB interfered in the sovereign bond markets of specific Member States, leading to fraught interactions not only with the individual Member States whose bonds were bought, but also with the rest of the Member States. As the ECB bought

[54] One example is the visits of ECB President Draghi to some national parliaments. See Tobias Tesche, 'Instrumentalizing EMU's Democratic Deficit: The ECB's Unconventional Accountability Measures during the Eurozone Crisis' (2018) 41 Journal of European Integration 447.

[55] One way in which the Member States collectively could have tried to correct the course of the ECB was through appointments to the Executive Board, especially after the resignations of Jürgen Stark and Sabine Lautenschläger.

[56] On the ECB as a strategic actor, see C Randall Henning, 'The ECB as a Strategic Actor: Central Banking in a Politically Fragmented Monetary Union' (2015) School of International Service Research Paper No 2015-1 <https://papers.ssrn.com/sol3/papers.cfm?abstract_id=2548333> accessed 1 March 2021; Francisco Torres, 'The EMU's Legitimacy and the ECB as a Strategic Political Player in the Crisis Context' (2013) 35 Journal of European Integration 287.

[57] Nicolas Véron, 'Europe's Radical Banking Union' (2015) Bruegel Essay and Lecture Series <https://www.bruegel.org/2015/05/europes-radical-banking-union/> accessed 1 March 2021.

[58] Jonathan Yiangou, Mícheál O'keeffe, and Gabriel Glöckler, '"Tough Love": How the ECB's Monetary Financing Prohibition Pushes Deeper Euro Area Integration' (2013) 35 Journal of European Integration 223. The three authors were employed by the ECB.

bonds of specific Member States only, it brought down their borrowing costs, without any negotiated conditionality. Under the Public Sector Purchases Programme (PSPP), the ECB had the National Central Banks buy the bonds of their own Member State, but without sharing the risks associated with these purchases.[59] The effect is that the risks remain at the national level, and a sovereign default would not immediately affect the other NCBs.

V. The Judicialization of EMU

Previous sections have alluded to the involvement of the courts in controlling the boundaries of the power of the ECB to (re)interpret its own mandate. This section then discusses the difficulties of courts in controlling the mandate of the ECB: being deferential towards the ECB is problematic as it would allow the ECB to determine the boundaries of its own competences. Equally problematic is strict supervision, given the inexperience and inherent inabilities of courts with controlling the exercise of monetary policy powers. This section therefore suggests that the problem stems from the role of constitutional law in the set-up of EMU.

It is important to note that at the launch of EMU, there were few concrete expectations about *how* the European and/or the national courts would become involved in EMU, in particular in monetary policy. This is at least partly visible in the lack of academic discussion on the topic at the time. Although EMU would be 'rules-based', it would not, or at least not immediately, be judicialized. One reason for this is the general lack of examples of judicialization of monetary policy. Even in Germany, the Constitutional Court had not been involved in setting the boundaries of the independence of the Bundesbank. When it outlined the importance of the rules of the Maastricht Treaty for the participation of Germany in EMU, it did so without having the experience of applying a similar set of rules to central banking within Germany. Historically speaking, the intervention of courts, and especially of highest courts and constitutional courts, in monetary policy is an anomaly.[60] Yet, during the euro area crisis, a dialogue 'erupted' between the German Constitutional Court and the CJEU on the definition of monetary policy and the role of the judiciary in controlling the ECB. After central bankers had successfully kicked out the politicians from the monetary policy arena through the Maastricht Treaty,[61] judges climbed back in during the euro area crisis. The question then is whether the involvement of the judiciary in EMU significantly limits the discretion of the ECB in interpreting its mandate. This section therefore examines the circumstances of the judicialization of EMU.

Despite its historical significance, the discussion of monetary policy in the *Gauweiler* judgment hardly feels innovative from an EU law perspective. The CJEU examined the competences of the institution and highlighted certain characteristics

[59] See chapter 2 by Vestert Borger, and chapter 3 by Klaus Tuori, in this volume.

[60] For an overview of cases before the US Supreme Court in the nineteenth and early twentieth centuries, see Richard H Timberlake, *Constitutional Money: A Review of the Supreme Court's Monetary Decisions* (CUP 2013).

[61] Strictly speaking, the politicians allowed themselves to be kicked out.

of the policy area that require a specific judicial approach. The Court also highlighted the principle of proportionality, another staple of EU law. Perhaps also unsurprisingly from an EU law perspective, the ECB is found not to have acted outside its competences. One reason why the reasoning in this case was so familiar is because the CJEU has been an important actor in many different policy areas in European integration, first and foremost the economic aspects of European integration. Especially in competition law, the CJEU often engages with economic theory and arguments, even if it does not fully embrace them.[62] From an EU law perspective, the involvement of the Court is therefore not particularly surprising, which might also explain the lack of academic interest in the *process* of judicialization of EMU, seeing it as a natural part of European integration.[63]

In certain circumstances, the European courts indeed have no difficulty in examining the behaviour of the ECB. An example is *UK v ECB* of the General Court, on policy regarding central counterparties (CCPs).[64] The General Court agreed with the UK that the ECB's decision to require CCPs to be located in the euro area went beyond its competence to promote the smooth operation of payment systems. In this case, the decision of the ECB upset a privileged applicant under Article 263 TFEU, namely a Member State. As many CCPs in the EU were located in the UK, it was foreseeable that the decision would be challenged in Luxembourg. The ECB also became more vulnerable to judicial challenges through a limited localization of its monetary policies, meaning that during the euro area crisis the ECB took many monetary policy decisions that affected certain Member States more directly than others. Besides the fact that this brought the ECB into direct contact with national politics,[65] it also increased the likelihood that certain decisions would directly affect individuals, as was the case in *Accorinti*.[66] Here, individuals brought an action for damages based on non-contractual liability after the ECB swapped its bonds with the Greek government to avoid the restructuring of government bonds. These cases show the Courts' willingness to examine the claims made by the ECB about its legal framework in rather straightforward disputes under EU law.

However, when it concerns core issues of EMU, the judges in Luxembourg have taken a notably deferential approach, as was already shown in the two landmark cases *prior* to the euro area crisis. In *Commission v Council*, the CJEU was asked to assess the legality of the Council's refusal to continue the Excessive Deficit Procedure against France and Germany.[67] Even though the Court in its judgment mentioned the importance of the efficacy of the procedure, a standard move to provide an expansive reading of EU law, it offered no further indication of what was required of the institutions other than the straightforward application of the Treaties.[68] Hence, the Council could

[62] Anne C Witt, 'The European Court of Justice and the More Economic Approach to EU Competition Law—Is the Tide Turning?' (2019) 64 Antitrust Bulletin 172.

[63] Fabbrini offers an account of judicialization of EMU that focuses on the developments of the crisis, largely neglecting the developments prior to the crisis: Fabbrini, *Economic Governance in Europe* (n 6) ch 2.

[64] Case T-496/11 *United Kingdom v European Central Bank* [2015] ECLI:EU:T:2015:133.

[65] Thomas Beukers, 'The New ECB and its Relationship with the Eurozone Member States: Between Central Bank Independence and Central Bank Intervention' (2013) 50 CML Rev 1579.

[66] Case T-79/13 *Accorinti and Others v European Central Bank* [2015] ECLI:EU:T:2015:756.

[67] Case C-27/04 *Commission v Council* [2004] ECLI:EU:C:2004:436.

[68] ibid para 74.

not be obliged to follow the assessments of the Commission regarding the situations in France and Germany. The same strategy was applied in the *OLAF* case, concerning the application of the OLAF-regulation to the ECB.[69] Also in this case the CJEU shied away from offering a substantive vision of EMU, confirming that the ECB would independently set monetary policy, but without offering the ECB a special position in relation to secondary law. With the Court clearly not interested in charting a course for the development of EMU, no other major cases arrived at the Court before the euro area crisis.

Whereas in these cases the CJEU was able to resolve the conflict without constructing an overall view on EMU, the references from the German Constitutional Court during the euro area crisis required a more substantive response, which brought to light the difficulty of judicial supervision of the ECB.[70] Critics rightly point out that the CJEU *de facto* follows the ECB's own assessment of the legality of the programmes.[71] Where in *Gauweiler* the CJEU at least stated that a programme may not have the foreseeable result of unduly harmonizing interest rates,[72] something that can be determined relatively easily by a court, the CJEU quietly dropped this requirement in *Weiss*.[73] The approach of the German Constitutional Court towards the ECB can in turn be criticized as unrealistic; it requires a balancing between economic and monetary effects, without giving any indication of which effects should be taken into account and how these should be weighed. Nor does it explain how judges can make such assessments.[74]

Both courts thus struggle with the judicial supervision of the ECB. The difficulty of both courts to construct a convincing approach towards the ECB flows from a single source, namely the lack of an overarching normative account of the role of law and of courts in EMU that considers the special legal construction of EMU as a form of constitutional law *and* which incorporates the institutional particularities of courts supervising central banks in the EU.[75] For the reinterpretation of Article 125 TFEU, this problem was less pronounced, as the CJEU could follow the interpretation of the Member States acting collectively, which was also supported by the ECB and the EP. For the reinterpretation of the mandate of the ECB, the CJEU could not build upon the

[69] Case C-11/00 *Commission v European Central Bank* [2003] ECLI:EU:C:2003:395.

[70] See also chapter 10 by Alexander Thiele, and chapter 12 by Takis Tridimas, in this volume.

[71] For critical discussions of *Weiss*, see Mark Dawson and Ana Bobić, 'Quantitative Easing at the Court of Justice—Doing Whatever It Takes to Save the Euro: Weiss and Others' (2019) 56 CML Rev 1005; Van der Sluis, 'Similar, Therefore Different' (n 20).

[72] Case C-62/14 *Gauweiler* (n 2) para 113. The full requirement is that 'the programme in question cannot be implemented in a way which would bring about a harmonisation of the interest rates applied to the government bonds of the Member States of the euro area regardless of the differences arising from their macroeconomic or budgetary situation'.

[73] Van der Sluis, 'Similar, Therefore Different' (n 20).

[74] Ana Bobić and Mark Dawson, 'Making Sense of the "Incomprehensible": The PSPP Judgment of the German Federal Constitutional Court' 57 CML Rev 1982; Marijn van der Sluis, 'Duits Constitutioneel Hof Zet Verhoudingen in de Europese Rechtsorde Op Scherp over de Bevoegdheden van de ECB' (2020) 69 Ars Aequi 972.

[75] Van der Sluis, 'Similar, Therefore Different' (n 20). For another issue with the judicial control of the ECB, see Jacopo Alberti, 'Challenging the Evolution of the EMU: The Justiciability of Soft Law Measures Enacted by the ECB against the Financial Crisis before the European Courts' (2018) 37 Yearbook of European Law 626.

opinion of the Member States and subsequently struggled more to provide a convincing narrative on the judicial supervision of the mandate of the ECB.

VI. Conclusion

The behaviour of the ECB during the euro area crisis, and now during the COVID-19-crisis has shocked many observers in especially northern Member States. Law was supposed to keep the ECB in check. A high level of independence, coupled with a narrow mandate, would provide for a stability-oriented and conservative central bank. From a constitutional perspective, it is obvious that these expectations were unrealistic. If law is made the primary tool to keep a central bank in check and the legal instrument in question is not amenable to change through a viable political process *and* there is no single political institution that controls the economic environment in which monetary policy is implemented, of course the meaning of those laws will start to shift based on the opinions of the central bank itself. When there is then no attention paid to how courts may effectively intervene, either with regard to process or substance, it should not come as a surprise that judicial supervision also fails to effectively circumscribe the powers of the central bank.

Seen from a constitutional perspective, the process through which EMU evolved is thus in line with the institutional framework created by the Maastricht Treaty. The Member States took control of the overall direction in which EMU would evolve, which then allowed the ECB to take the lead with regard to the reinterpretation of its own mandate. Hence, the conclusion is that despite the fact that the euro area crisis has led to significant innovations in the day-to-day governance of EMU, the constitutional environment in which the ECB operates has not significantly changed. This means that the ECB continues to have significant discretion in the interpretation of its own mandate, and that the constraints on this discretion remain weak and are often intangible.

The connections between the analytical view on the role of law and the normative views on the law in EMU are paradoxical. The—incorrect—analysis that the Maastricht Treaty failed to achieve its goals is often accompanied by a plea to strengthen the euro as a 'rules-based' currency. Prior to the COVID-19 crisis, the debate over another 'overhaul' of economic governance was heating up once again. What economic rules on fiscal policy would contribute to a successful currency? And how could enforcement of such rules be guaranteed? The analysis that the Maastricht Treaty actually succeeded in structuring the process of European integration, must, in my opinion, lead to the conclusion that the euro and the ECB must be deconstitutionalized. The manner in which the substantive rules of the euro were reformed during the crisis does not offer a healthy model for further reform.

17

The ECB's E-ROAD Ahead

René Smits

I. Introduction

Twenty years after its establishment, the European Central Bank (ECB) is an institution in a world entirely different from the one it found itself in at its inception. Since 1998, major technological and societal changes have occurred, with important new challenges for the ECB. Let me only mention the following developments, later indicating which chances for renewal they may bring. For ease of reference, and without pretending academic rigour in the enumeration, I classify these chances and challenges under five headings, each starting with a different letter (R, O, A, D, and E), thus making: the E-ROAD ahead. But first, the changes and developments:

1. The world in 2021 is one of rising illiberal regimes where *democracy is under attack* not just from populists and conspiracy advocates but, perhaps even more menacingly, from the influence of big money and powerful *lobby groups* whose impact is sometimes documented and disseminated by non governmental groups and think tanks but often occurs behind closed doors. Democratic transitions are fought tooth and nail not only by dictators who have been in power for thirty (Uganda) or fifty (Togo) years or otherwise since independence (Zimbabwe) but also in vested democracies such as the United States of America (Trump, 2020 elections). Or transitions are prevented from threatening the cosy exercise of power by ever more restrictions on free media, adopted even by Member States of the EU itself. Political opponents are branded 'enemies of the people' (UK, US) or hunted down abroad (China, Saudi Arabia), poisoned at home or abroad (Russia) or driven into exile (Rwanda). This picture of the world of politics informs central banks about the far more dangerous place they need to operate in than a quarter of a century ago, when the recent liberation from communism after the fall of the Berlin Wall promised an era of freedom and democracy. The ECB's fellow central bankers from outside the EU may be confronted with such developments domestically but even within its own ranks; one of its governing bodies, the General Council, includes Governors from Member States considered illiberal (Hungary and Poland).[1] The influence of lobbying

[1] See Case C-824/18 *A.B. and Others v Krajowa Rada Sadownictwa* [2021] EU:C:2021:153 on the independence of the Polish judiciary, with references to earlier case law, and Case C-78/18 *Commission v Hungary* [2020] EU:C:2020:476. See also Marija Pejčinović Burić, 'Letter of the Secretary General of the Council of Europe to the Government of Hungary on the state of emergency in Hungary' (Strasbourg, 24 March 2020) <https://rm.coe.int/orban-pm-hungary-24-03-2020/16809d5f04> accessed 27 October 2021 and the European Parliament (EP) resolution of 16 January 2020 on ongoing hearings under Art 7(1) of

René Smits, *The ECB's E-ROAD Ahead* In: *The New European Central Bank.* Edited by: Thomas Beukers, Diane Fromage, and Giorgio Monti, Oxford University Press. © René Smits 2022. DOI: 10.1093/oso/9780198871231.003.0017

and worse, (alleged) corruption, has seeped into the Eurosystem's functioning as the court cases concerning Mr Rimšēvičs, Governor of the Latvian central bank, make clear.[2] Also, the Single Supervisory Mechanism (SSM) is confronted with allegations about use of domestic banking systems by oligarchs and mafiosi elements in Cyprus,[3] Latvia,[4] and Malta.[5] The importance of ethics in finance, and the need to include anti-money laundering (AML) and countering terrorist financing (CTF) in the ECB's prudential tasks,[6] adopted in the wake of the Great Financial Crisis cum sovereign debt crisis, form major new challenges which the less dangerous world of 1998 may not have held. The political and business environment in which an independent central banking system needs to operate has become ever more harsh and confrontational. The loss of one central bank

the TEU regarding Poland and Hungary [2020] 2020/2513(RSP). On this EP Resolution, see Case C-650/18 *Hungary v European Parliament* [2020] EU:C:2020:985, Opinion of AG Bobek. See also chapter 4 by Jens van 't Klooster, in this volume.

[2] See Joined Cases C-202/18 and C-238/18 *Ilmārs Rimšēvičs and European Central Bank v Republic of Latvia* [2020] EU:C:2019:139. On this, see René Smits, 'A National Measure Annulled by the European Court of Justice, or: High-level Judicial Protection for Independent Central Bankers: ECJ 26 February 2019, Cases C-202/18 *Ilmārs Rimšēvičs v Republic of Latvia* and C-238/18 *European Central Bank v Republic of Latvia* ECLI:EU:2019:139' (2020) 16 EuConst 120.

[3] See Nektaria Stamouli and Drew Hinshaw, 'U.S. Takes on Russia's Favorite Money Haven: Cyprus, Washington regulators crack down on money laundering in the tiny Mediterranean island in a bid to check Moscow's power in Europe' *Wall Street Journal* (Nicosia, 30 September 2018) <https://www.wsj.com/articles/u-s-takes-on-russias-favorite-money-haven-cyprus-1538316001> accessed 27 October 2021; Paul Tugwell and Georgios Georgiou, 'Cyprus No Longer Mediterranean Haven for Russian Businesses' *The Moscow Times* (Moscow, 10 January 2019) <https://www.themoscowtimes.com/2019/01/10/cyprus-no-longer-mediterranean-haven-for-russian-businesses-a64097> accessed 27 October 2021; Michael Peel, 'Moscow on the Med: Cyprus and its Russians' *Financial Times* (London, 15 May 2020) <https://www.ft.com/content/67918012-9403-11ea-abcd-371e24b679ed> accessed 27 October 2021. On the SSM generally, see also chapter 7 by Kern Alexander, and chapter 8 by Federico Della Negra and Gianni Lo Schiavo, in this volume.

[4] See Organized Crime and Corruption Reporting Project, 'The Russian Laundromat Exposed' (20 March 2017) <https://www.occrp.org/en/laundromat/the-russian-laundromat-exposed/> accessed 27 October 2021. Also, a Latvian commercial bank, ABVL Bank, saw its licence withdrawn in 2018 after the US Treasury accused it of money laundering and circumventing sanctions against the People's Republic of Korea. See Financial Crimes Enforcement Network, 'Proposal of Special Measure Against ABLV Bank, AS as a Financial Institution of Primary Money Laundering Concern' (Department of the Treasury, Federal Register vol 83 no 33, 16 February 2018) <https://www.fincen.gov/sites/default/files/federal_register_notices/2018-02-16/2018-03214.pdf> accessed 27 October 2021.

[5] *The Malta Independent*, 'Money from Sicilian mafia operation passed through Maltese banks—report' *The Malta Independent* (Saint Julian, 18 January 2020) <https://www.independent.com.mt/articles/2020-01-18/local-news/Money-from-Sicilian-mafia-operation-passed-through-Maltese-banks-report-6736218548> accessed 27 October 2021; Claire Farrugia, 'Authorities to look into reports mafia used Malta banks in EU funds scam' *The Times of Malta* (Birkirkara, 16 January 2020) <https://timesofmalta.com/articles/view/authorities-looking-into-reports-mafia-used-malta-banks-in-eu-funds.763932> accessed 27 October 2021.

[6] In spite of recitals 28 and 29 in the preamble to the SSM Regulation (Council Regulation (EU) No 1024/2013 of 15 October 2013 conferring specific tasks on the European Central Bank concerning policies relating to the prudential supervision of credit institutions [2013] OJ L287/63 (hereafter SSM Regulation)) which seem to exclude AML/CTF from the ECB's supervisory mandate, the ECB has explained how it takes AML/CTF issues into account in the authorization (or withdrawal of authorization) of a credit institution, in assessing the suitability of its shareholders and the fit and proper nature of the members of a bank's management, in the supervisory review and evaluation process (SREP) and in prudential administrative measures and penalties: see European Central Bank, 'Anti-money laundering' <https://www.bankingsupervision.europa.eu/banking/tasks/anti-moneylaundering/html/index.en.html> accessed 27 October 2021.

as a shareholder since the ECB's start brought this home: due to Brexit, the Bank of England left the group of National Central Bank (NCB) parents of their joint subsidiary, the European Central Bank.

2. *Technological developments* have been phenomenal. The internet has become *the* source of connection and information at a global level. Online shopping and banking had changed commerce for good, even before the COVID-19 pandemic altered consumer behaviour still more rapidly than before. Big Tech rules the lives of many of the Earth's 7.9 billion inhabitants: through WhatsApp messaging, Instagram sharing, or Facebook posting; Facebook is so branched out across the globe that it challenged the central banks by announcing, in 2019, a new global 'currency', initially labelled *Libra*, now *Diem*.[7] The use of distributed ledger techniques and the development of crypto-assets[8] are game-changers. Closer to central banks, the issue of digital currencies (on which more below) is getting underway.[9] In mobile communication Apple, albeit not considered a monopoly, is firmly in the lead. The world's richest man owns a delivery service, Amazon, that stretches out far beyond the United States. Microsoft is *the* computer brand. And everywhere people who like to find information turn to Google. Using these firms' 'free' services, human beings find themselves traced and confronted with personalized advertisements. The omnipresence of commercials and online ads, often even before playing music, listening to a podcast, or viewing a video at YouTube, and the availability of products 24/7 through home delivery, make this world a much more (e-)commerce-driven place than it was when the ECB started functioning. This has had an impact on banks: non-traditional providers of payment services have sprouted, regulated in the Payment Services Directive No. 2 (PSD2),[10] impacting the European System of Central Banks (ESCB)'s exercise of its fourth 'basic task' which is 'to promote the smooth operation of payment systems'.[11] The Commission's proposal[12] to regulate crypto-assets has already led the ECB to suggest, in its Opinion on the draft legislation, that any authorization to offer asset-referenced tokens (with an EU currency as reference) be subject to a binding opinion of the ECB, or the relevant non-euro area central bank, so as to prevent an impingement of the central bank's monetary

[7] See the Diem Association's website at <https://www.diem.com/en-us/> accessed 27 October 2021 (hereafter 'the Diem Association's website').

[8] Erroneously called crypto-'currencies': see, for instance, Bitcoin's website at <https://bitcoin.org/en/ > accessed 27 October 2021, and Ethereum's website at <https://ethereum.org/en/> accessed 27 October 2021, among others.

[9] By way of example, see eNaira, 'Design Paper for the eNaira' (2021) <https://www.enaira.gov.ng/about/design> accessed 27 October 2021.

[10] Directive (EU) 2015/2366 of the European Parliament and of the Council of 25 November 2015 on payment services in the internal market, amending Directives 2002/65/EC, 2009/110/EC and 2013/36/EU and Regulation (EU) No 1093/2010, and repealing Directive 2007/64/EC [2015] OJ L337/35.

[11] Consolidated Version of the Treaty on the Functioning of the European Union [2012] OJ C326/47, Art 127(2) fourth indent (hereafter TFEU) and TFEU Protocol No 4 on the Statute of the European System of Central Banks and of the European Central Bank [2016] OJ C202/230, Arts 3.1 fourth indent and 22 (hereafter ESCB Statute).

[12] Commission, 'Proposal for a Regulation of the European Parliament and of the Council on Markets in Crypto-assets, and amending Directive (EU) 2019/1937' COM (2020) 593 final.

policy and payments systems prerogatives.[13] Commercial banks, the traditional counterparties for central banks in their operations, are becoming endangered as the preferred conduits for capital allocation, whether through economic developments or as a result of evolutions stimulated by public authorities (the EU's capital market union).[14]

3. As if these developments had not changed the setting in which the ECB is operating sufficiently, the outbreak of the *COVID-19 pandemic* in 2020 upset the world completely.[15] It led to the propagation of a 'new normal' of social distancing (vastly diminishing social interaction and the warmth and intimacy thereof), home work (denting commuting times and massively diminishing or completely eliminating hours at the office for those jobs that allow online work), and online teaching (with 'home schooling' for pupils attending primary, secondary, and tertiary school). The pandemic, whose spread provided evidence of the interconnectedness of the global society, also led to severe economic downturns, in many places the worst recessions since the 1930s, the reduction in output often surpassing the figures for the Great Financial Crisis cum sovereign debt crisis a decade earlier. This required immediate action by public authorities, at the fiscal level (budget stimuli, the introduction of furlough schemes, and an expansion in employment benefit eligibility) and at the level of monetary authorities and prudential supervisors.[16] They pumped money into the economy, helped banks carry on in spite of increased (expected) losses, and encouraged them to keep lending to the real economy to mitigate the disastrous economic fall-out of COVID-19. The ECB's Pandemic Emergency Purchasing Programme (PEPP)[17] and the other ECB measures in the face of the pandemic made clear how reliant the European economy has become on swift and decisive action by the only federal institution of the EU with 'fire power'. And, while restrictive measures, vaccinations, and medicines may lead the world to overcome the current pandemic (albeit in very uneven terms of availability across the globe of

[13] Opinion of the European Central Bank of 19 February 2021 on a proposal for a regulation on Markets in Crypto-assets, and amending Directive (EU) 2019/1937 [2021] OJ C152/1.

[14] See Commission, 'Communication from the Commission, to the European Parliament, the Council, the European Economic and Social Committee and the Committee of the Regions on A Capital Markets Union for people and businesses-new action plan' (Communication) COM (2020) 590 final.

[15] An insightful perspective is given by Yuval Noah Harari in the weekend edition of the *Financial Times*: Yuval Noah Harari, 'Lessons from a year of Covid' *Financial Times* (London, 26 February 2021) <https://www.ft.com/content/f1b30f2c-84aa-4595-84f2-7816796d6841> accessed 27 October 2021.

[16] For an overview of the actions by the ECB, on both monetary policy and prudential supervision, see René Smits, 'The European Central Bank's pandemic bazooka: mandate fulfilment in extraordinary times' (2020) EULawLive <https://eulawlive.com/op-ed-the-european-central-banks-pandemic-bazooka-mandate-fulfilment-in-extraordinary-times-by-rene-smits/> accessed 27 October 2021, elaborated in René Smits, 'The European Central Bank's pandemic bazooka: mandate fulfilment in extraordinary Times' in Dolores Utrilla and Anjum Shabbir (eds), *EU Law in Times of Pandemic—the EU's Legal Response to COVID-19* (Editorial Comares forthcoming) (hereafter Smits, 'The European Central Bank's Pandemic Bazooka: Mandate Fulfilment in Extraordinary Times').

[17] Decision (EU) 2020/440 of the European Central Bank of 24 March 2020 on a temporary pandemic emergency purchase programme (ECB/2020/17) [2020] OJ L91/1, recently amended by Decision (EU) 2021/174 of the European Central Bank of 10 February 2021 amending Decision (EU) 2020/440 on a temporary pandemic emergency purchase programme (ECB/2021/6) [2021] OJ L50/29 (hereafter 'ECB Decision of 10 February 2021 on a temporary pandemic emergency purchase programme').

remedies and of the hardship resulting from lockdowns and downturns), there is every reason to expect similar outbreaks of global infectious diseases[18] in the years to come.

4. From an environmental point of view, a welcome side effect of the pandemic has been the reduction in CO_2 emissions and other health-affecting substances, such as nitrogen, into the atmosphere. Yet, when the recovery underway does not to lead to 'building back better', after the pandemic, *climate change and biodiversity loss* will be confronting humankind in all seriousness.[19] The twenty years of almost unmitigated growth in CO_2 emissions have set the world on a dangerous slippery slope towards global warming. The four years of confrontation instead of cooperation in this area during the previous US presidency have led to even greater risks, including President Trump's withdrawal of the United States from the Paris Agreement,[20] reversed by his successor President Biden. Beyond climate change, the loss of biodiversity undermines the 'liveability' of the Earth. In the context of international agreements to combat the twin dangers to the planet, it should be recalled that such norms are also in existence, or in preparation, for biodiversity. The 1993 Convention on Biological Diversity,[21] ratified by the European Union,[22] is scheduled to be followed up by a convention in 2022 at the Kunming Biodiversity Conference.[23] In a resolution[24] of January 2020, the European Parliament called for this follow-up agreement to contain 'legally binding targets'. The EU's own Biodiversity Strategy[25] for 2030 is part of the European Green Deal,[26] which shows the close connection between the climate change and biodiversity objectives. Central banks have begun to address these

[18] See, as a recent instance, European Centre for Disease Prevention and Control, 'Ebola virus disease outbreak in North Kivu, Democratic Republic of the Congo' (Risk assessment, Stockholm, 22 February 2021) <https://www.ecdc.europa.eu/en/publications-data/ebola-virus-disease-outbreak-north-kivu-democratic-republic-congo-2021> accessed 27 October 2021.

[19] At the time of writing, the 26th UN Climate Change Conference of the Parties (COP26) in Glasgow is about to start; see <https://ukcop26.org/> accessed 27 October 2021.

[20] Paris Agreement [2016] UNTC No 54113 (hereafter Paris Agreement).

[21] Convention on Biological Diversity [1993] OJ L309/3. See also Convention on Biological Diversity [1993] UNTC No 30619 (hereafter UN Convention on Biological Diversity).

[22] See the list of parties of the UN Convention on Biological Diversity (n 21) at <https://www.cbd.int/information/parties.shtml> accessed 27 October 2021.

[23] See United Nations Environment Programme, 'UN Biodiversity Conference' (online, 11–15 October 2021—Kunming, 25 April–8 May 2022) <https://www.unenvironment.org/events/conference/un-biodiversity-conference-cop-15> accessed 27 October 2021.

[24] European Parliament resolution of 16 January 2020 on the 15th meeting of the Conference of Parties (COP15) to the Convention on Biological Diversity [2020] 2019/2824(RSP) OJ C270/94, para 25 (Parliament 'calls on the Commission and the Member States to strengthen the implementation mechanisms of the CBD and to actively pursue the development of ambitious legally binding targets, detailed timelines, clear performance indicators, tracking instruments, and peer review/reporting mechanisms based on common standards—ideally in cooperation with sub-national governments—to ensure full transparency and accountability for the Parties and the overall effectiveness of the next Global Biodiversity Strategy plan').

[25] See Commission, 'Communication for the Commission to the European Parliament, the Council, the European Economic and Social Committee and the Committee of the Regions on EU Biodiversity Strategy for 2030' (Communication) COM (2020) 380 final.

[26] Commission, 'Annex to the Communication from the Communication for the Commission to the European Parliament, the European Council, the Council, the European Economic and Social Committee and the Committee of the Regions on The European Green Deal' COM (2019) 640 final.

issues: an ever-increasing membership of central banks and supervisors explores the issues of greening finance and their roles in this process: the Network for Greening the Financial Sector,[27] enthusiastically chaired by Frank Elderson. The monetary policy review[28] undertaken by the ECB also provided ample space for including these issues.

What can the ECB do to face the major changes and developments arising in its fields of competence and adjacent areas in the years ahead? I see four ways forward by which the ECB may address some of the issues which these developments bring forth. It is clear that the ECB cannot alone, by itself, address the issues—collaboration with other actors and reliance on, or alignment of, policies adopted by governments and pursued by private enterprise will be required. Other agencies, public or private in nature, face similar issues and need to adapt to the Great Global Transition we undergo (or, phrased in a less passive manner: which we are all agents in). Below, I identify four approaches (Reform, Open up, Address, and Develop) which the ECB may (in my mind: should) take. And this always in the context of: Europe. Hence, as said, the E-ROAD ahead. Naturally, there is overlap, and no academic distinction, between several of these concepts: to 'address' may also be labelled 'to develop'. This loose use of words is employed as an easy-to-remember mantra to distinguish between the forms of action that I recommend.

II. Open Up

The democracy-under-attack issue and the growing populism and the accompanying lack of respect in the public discourse, identified above as the first of the four major changes since 1998, requires a more open, transparent, 'listening' central bank. Technological developments, mentioned as the second such major development, may empower the Central Bank to develop into such an authority.

The transparency that has been initiated under President Mario Draghi (monetary policy accounts)[29] and reinforced under President Christine Lagarde should be stepped up. Based on a bedrock of principled openness,[30] the idea would be to avoid any unnecessary secrecy. Such translucency would enable the ECB's stakeholders, ultimately the 342 million inhabitants of the euro area, to see what the guardian of their currency and the overseer of their banks is undertaking to fulfil its public mandate. Naturally, such openness should respect the law and the justified interests of

[27] For more details on the Network for Greening the Financial System, see <https://www.ngfs.net/en> accessed 27 October 2021.

[28] European Central Bank, 'ECB launches review of its monetary policy strategy' (ECB Press Release, 23 January 2020) <https://www.ecb.europa.eu/press/pr/date/2020/html/ecb.pr200123~3b8d9fc08d.en.html> accessed 27 October 2021. For more on the review, see European Central Bank, 'Strategy review' at <https://www.ecb.europa.eu/home/search/review/html/index.en.html> accessed 27 October 2021.

[29] See European Central Bank, 'Monetary policy accounts' at <https://www.ecb.europa.eu/press/accounts/html/index.en.html> accessed 27 October 2021.

[30] Even in the face of a provision that requires '[t]he proceedings of the meetings' of the Governing Council to be confidential, allowing the Governing Council to 'make the outcome of its deliberations public' (ESCB Statute (n 11) Art 10.4).

counterparties and other persons.[31] So, there would still be confidentiality of the individual dealings in financial markets, and of the interaction between the ECB and the banks it supervises, their shareholders and relevant third parties, as secrecy would continue to apply when market operations are conducted or prudential decisions are taken.[32] The interaction between NCBs and national competent authorities, on the one hand, and the ECB, on the other, would also remain confidential. And there would be differences in transparency between the various functions of the ECB (prudential supervision relying on a bond of trust between supervisor and supervised which requires confidentiality)[33] and in accordance with the market sensitivity and business secrets involved. But the ECB would be completely transparent wherever it could, and it would plead for transparency in the legal provisions applying to it. To give a couple of examples:

Its website would be much more easily navigable for interested citizens, for instance to easily find the questions of MEPs[34] and the ECB's answers,[35] to know of the workings of the Eurosystem's preparatory committees,[36] and to know of any undertaking engaged in with third parties in the area of supervision and resolution (Memorandums of Understanding (MoUs)). It's good to see that transparency is being enhanced ever more: following earlier suggestions,[37] the ECB is now publishing its MoUs.[38]

[31] On ECB transparency, see Deirdre Curtin, '"Accountable Independence" of the European Central Bank: Seeing the Logics of Transparency' (2017) 23 EL Rev 28.

[32] Relevant in this context are recent decisions in cases concerning the ECB's preparatory act of declaring Banco Popular to be failing or likely to fail (FOLTF); see Case T-15/18 *Organización de Consumidores y Usuarios (OCU) v ECB* [2021] EU:T:2021:661 and Case T-827/17 *Aeris Invest Sàrl v ECB* [2021] EU:T:2021:660. See EULawLive, 'General Court dismisses request to give full access to ECB documents on Banco Popular's assessment' (2021) <https://eulawlive.com/general-court-dismisses-request-to-give-full-access-to-ecb-documents-on-banco-populars-assessment/> accessed 27 October 2021.

[33] For an exposition of this trust issue, see Case C-15/16 *Bundesanstalt für Finanzdienstleistungsaufsicht v Baumeister* [2017] EU:C:2017:958, Opinion of AG Bot.

[34] Fortunately, a recent improvement is a link to the European Parliament's listing of questions to the ECB at the top of the page with the ECB's answers; see European Parliament, 'European Parliament website—Questions to the ECB' <https://www.europarl.europa.eu/committees/en/econ/documents/search?committeeMnemoCode=ECON&textualSearchMode=TITLE&textualSearch=&documentTypeCode=QUCB&reporterPersId=&procedureYear=&procedureNum=&procedureCodeType=&peNumber=&aNumber=&aNumberYear=&documentDateFrom=&documentDateTo=&meetingDateFrom=&meetingDateTo=&performSearch=true&term=9&page=0&pageSize=10> accessed 27 October 2021.

[35] Still available under the misnamed header 'Publications on International and European Co-operation', which is not where one would look.

[36] It is not the ECB's own website but that of one of the NCBs, *Banka Slovenije*, which carries a list of these committees as of 31 December 2016 (!), under 'About us' and subtab 'Eurosystem', choosing 'Committees', available at <https://www.bsi.si/en/about-us/eurosystem/committees> accessed 27 October 2021.

[37] René Smits, 'SSM and the SRB accountability at European level: room for improvements?' (2020) Directorate-General for Internal Policies, Economic Governance Support Unit PE 645.726 <https://www.europarl.europa.eu/RegData/etudes/STUD/2020/645726/IPOL_STU(2020)645726_EN.pdf> accessed 27 October 2021 (hereafter Smits, 'EP accountability paper'). Earlier, see René Smits, 'Reflections on Euro Area Banking Supervision: Context, Transparency and Culture from an Institutional Law Perspective' in Gianni Lo Schiavo (ed), *The European Banking Union and the Role of Law* (Edward Elgar Publishing 2019).

[38] European Central Bank, 'ECB publishes supervisory Memoranda of Understanding' (ECB Press Release, 19 February 2021) <https://www.bankingsupervision.europa.eu/press/pr/date/2021/html/ssm.pr210219~ae49c81a2a.en.html> accessed 27 October 2021. See also European Central Bank, 'Memoranda of Understanding' <https://www.bankingsupervision.europa.eu/legalframework/mous/html/index.en.html> accessed 27 October 2021.

The ECB would publicly come out in favour of greater access to the files, also supervisory files, after the need for secrecy has diminished or evaporated. It would stand for opening up its archives to academic and journalistic scrutiny instead of invoking secrecy every time a difficult question comes up.[39] The ECB would adopt the argument that cross-sector legislation protecting supervisory files can be loosened somewhat, along the lines case law cautiously adopted and academic proposals made in this field,[40] acknowledging the need for transparency of public action and accountability of prudential supervisors.[41] Also, the ECB would rely less in court proceedings on confidentiality provisions[42] and thus to some extent 'open up'.

It would ideally seek an amendment of Article 10.4 ESCB Statute in a next round of Treaty change to achieve a standard which, while allowing notes of the policy-setting meetings of the Governing Council to be divulged after a reasonable time, still would protect the confidentiality of an open conversation among colleagues from across Europe. In this context, one may recall that the confidentiality imposed by Article 10.4 ESCB Statute was born out of the more secretive times but, also, that one of the reasons for the strict confinement of proceedings of the Governing Council was to avoid situations in which NCB governors would be taken to task by media and politicians in their home State for the lack of defence of 'the national interest'. All members of the Governing Council, Executive Board members, and NCB Governors alike, are to serve the European interest.[43] Practice has shown that such protection against openness of the debate does not actually work: NCB Governors themselves have been keen to tell their national audiences about their policy stances,[44] whereas ECB

[39] See Päivi Leino-Sandberg, 'Public access to ECB documents: are accountability, independence and effectiveness an impossible trinity?' in European Central Bank, 'Building bridges: central banking law in an interconnected world' (ECB Legal Conference 2019) 203 <https://www.ecb.europa.eu/pub/pdf/other/ecb.ecblegalconferenceproceedings201912~9325c45957.en.pdf?258d648ffcf1be39f9d927e5c13f393f> accessed 27 October 2021 (hereafter ECB Legal Conference 2019).

[40] René Smits and Nikolai Badenhoop, 'Towards a Single Standard of Professional Secrecy for Supervisory Authorities—A Reform Proposal' (2019) 44 EL Rev 295.

[41] Michael W Taylor, Marc G Quintyn, and Eva HG Hüpkes, 'The Accountability of Financial Sector Supervisors: Principles and Practice' (2005) IMF Working Paper No 05/51 <https://www.imf.org/en/Publications/WP/Issues/2016/12/31/The-Accountability-of-Financial-Sector-Supervisors-Principles-and-Practice-18018> accessed 27 October 2021.

[42] See, eg, Case T-730/16 *Insolvent Estate of Espírito Santo Financial Group SA v ECB* [2019] EU:T:2019:161 and, on appeal, Case C-396/19 P *ECB v Insolvent Estate of Espírito Santo Financial Group SA* [2020] EU:C:2020:845; Case T-798/17 *Fabio De Masi and Yanis Varoufakis v ECB* [2019] EU:T:2019:154 and, on appeal, Case C-342/19 P *Fabio De Masi and Yanis Varoufakis v ECB* [2020] EU:C:2020:1035.

[43] On the limits of 'regional influence [in] the decision-making process . . . permissible for defining monetary policy', see René Smits, *The European Central Bank—Institutional Aspects* (Kluwer Law International 1997) 172.

[44] Reference is made to the brief submitted by the *Bundesbank* in the proceedings before the German Constitutional Court in Case C-62/14 *Gauweiler and Others v Deutscher Bundestag* [2015] EU:C:2015:400, in which the ECB's OMT were challenged: Deutsche Bundesbank, 'Statement to the Federal Constitutional Court, with a particular focus on the OMT programme and the matter of TARGET2 balances' (21 December 2012) <https://www.bundesbank.de/resource/blob/799688/a6e46b9d71e86f076c2aa07e1cd24b7a/mL/201.2-12-21-omt-data.pdf> accessed 27 October 2021. Reference is also made to the press release of Dutch central bank Governor Klaas Knot of 13 September 2019 speaking out against the ECB's monetary policy decisions of that month: De Nederlandsche Bank, 'Klaas Knot reageert op monetairbeleidsmaatregelen van de ECB' (De Nederlandsche Bank Press Release, 13 September 2019) <https://www.dnb.nl/actueel/algemeen-nieuws/persberichten-2020/klaas-knot-reageert-op-monetairbeleids-maatregelen-van-de-ecb/> accessed 27 October 2021 (English version not found). Bundesbank President Jens Weidmann aired his dissent in an interview with BILD Zeitung; see Deutsche Bundesbank, 'Weidmann: ECB Governing Council

Executive Board members have left office prior to the end of their mandate due to policy disagreements.[45]

Information that needs no protection, including on income of staff or fees for outside experts, would be publicly available, naturally effectively protecting the privacy of natural persons.

An idea to explore is that of town hall meetings across Europe, in simulation of a practice once instituted by the Reserve Bank of India which itself serves a subcontinent-wide country with a multitude of languages, religions, and ethnicities.[46]

Thus, an opening up of the ECB would pave the way to even more intense interaction with the people and business it is intended to serve. In the context of the changes indicated above, this reinventing of its identity by the ECB is, in my view, beneficial to its mandate fulfilment in the current era: a central bank as an expert technocracy is no longer a tenable model and what is suggested here is about the way a central bank should rethink its openness and its identity. This is also the core of the next point.

III. Reform

On all of the recommended paths to go down, the ECB would best be served when undertaking a reform of its operational functioning. The new times, with accelerating changes in technology and sociology, and faced with risks of breath-taking urgency, call for a mindset that is not made in the mould of old-fashioned central bankers. A combination of expertise and technical savvy in complex areas, coupled with a mindset to serve the public cause (price stability, financial stability) has usually characterized central bankers. These qualities need to be expanded with more visionary thinking and a real connection with the entrepreneurial spirit prevalent among

has gone too far' (Deutsche Bundesbank Press Release, 14 September 2019) <https://www.bundesbank.de/en/tasks/topics/weidmann-ecb-governing-council-has-gone-too-far-806968> accessed 27 October 2021. The new Governor of the Oesterreichische Nationalbank, Robert Holzmann, criticized the decisions taken in the September 2019 meeting of the ECB's Governing Council in an interview with Bloomberg; see Alessandro Speciale, Boris Groendahl, and Maria Tadeo, 'ECB's Newest Policy Maker Says Latest Stimulus May Be a Mistake' *Bloomberg* (New York, 13 September 2019) <https://www.bloomberg.com/news/articles/2019-09-13/ecb-s-newest-policy-maker-says-latest-stimulus-may-be-a-mistake> accessed 27 October 2021. See also chapter 13 by Diane Fromage, in this volume.

[45] It has been reported that two, or perhaps three, German Board members (Jürgen Stark [2006–11], Jörg Asmussen [2012–14], Sabine Lautenschläger [2014–19]) left office early due to disagreements over the ECB's unconventional monetary policy measures. It has been alleged that among the 'personal reasons' for leaving the function of President of the Deutsche Bundesbank, Jens Weidman was unhappy to be the perennial 'nay-sayer' or 'hawk' among his colleagues on the Governing Council; see Deutsche Bundesbank, 'Statement by Bundesbank President Dr Jens Weidmann' (Deutsche Bundesbank Press Release, 20 October 2021) <https://www.bundesbank.de/en/press/press-releases/statement-by-bundesbank-president-dr-jens-weidmann--877830> accessed 27 October 2021. The *Financial Times*, reporting on this statement wrote: . . . colleagues said he was tired of opposing ECB policies and expected these frustrations to increase as the economy recovers, inflation rises and the ECB's generous stimulus becomes harder to justify'; see Martin Arnold and Guy Chazan, 'End of an era as Bundesbank chief Jens Weidmann steps down' *Financial Times* (Frankfurt am Main and Berlin, 20 October 2021 <https://www.ft.com/content/d8b413f1-818c-4afc-8007-714209e5d66b> accessed 27 October 2021.

[46] See René Smits, 'The ECB and the rule of law' in ECB Legal Conference 2019 (n 39) s 6 subs 'Direct exposure to citizens: EU and India'.

younger generations. And with a truly global outlook, not only see(k)ing connections in the world of central bankers but way beyond. A slow but steady move towards such reform of the organization seems to be underway already.

Europe's central bank is staffed by dedicated professionals many of whom started working there for a purpose, beyond earning a living and making a career. There is no questioning their devotion and loyalty. Yet, as with any organization that is powerful and rather secluded from scrutiny by political or market forces, tendencies may develop that encourage group thinking or, judging from the architectural style of the new headquarters,[47] a siege mentality: safely working from well-protected towers must have an impact on even the most open-minded of people. Therefore, it would befit the central bank were it to actively seek to become an 'accountable organization organizing itself in a manner which reinforces *independent thinking and accountable behaviour*'.[48] Pro-actively organizing '*auto-correction against biases and tunnel vision*'[49] and fostering an open culture in which dissent[50] for the common good is encouraged would make the ECB fit for times of enormous challenge and deep technological and societal change.

Again, this is not to say that the ECB's current organization is not fit at all for these changes. Some of the recommended approaches may very well be practised but are shielded from outside view (which is a reflection of the state of affairs under the 'O' of 'open up', mentioned above). Yet, the technological changes require state-of-the-art knowledge-at-the-vanguard to be widely represented among staff and penetrable at management level and above. Also, the age of populism and undermining of expertise demand an ever more responsive attitude on the part of the expert centre for monetary, payments, and supervision matters that the ECB is. Thus, an open attitude and an inquisitive mind are as much prerequisites of personnel as technical expertise. This goes beyond diversity in terms of gender, language, background, education, and ethnicity, although these elements of variety among staff are important in themselves and should inform the hiring process of staff (and the appointment process of members of the Executive Board, the Governing Council, and the Supervisory Board).[51] What I refer to here is what I have labelled the 'colour' of an organization in terms of organization and cooperation. I include here a Box (Box 1) from my report to the European Parliament:[52]

'Adaptability' and 'openness' are keywords here. I would argue that staff members should be encouraged to adopt different attitudes to issues before a decision is adopted;[53] and *to stimulate creative and original thinking*. As I wrote in the Spring of

[47] See the section 'The ECB's main building' on the ECB's website at <https://www.ecb.europa.eu/ecb/premises/html/index.en.html> accessed 27 October 2021.

[48] Smits, 'EP accountability paper' (n 37) 40 (emphasis in the original).

[49] Ibid.

[50] Dissent can also be organized by having two opposing teams prepare a policy measure: one team presenting a measure which is contemplated and the other team a different one (or none). Of course, members of both teams should be conscious of their own biases.

[51] Diversity and agility as requirements for the members of these collective bodies concern the national authorities who nominate or appoint them: the lack of women in the Governing Council reflects in part their absence among the ranks of NCB Governors.

[52] See Smits, 'EP accountability paper' (n 37) 40–41.

[53] Reflecting the observation by Israeli historian/philosopher Yuval Noah Harari: '... discord in our thoughts, ideas and values compel us to think, re-evaluate and criticise. Consistency is the playground of

Box 1 Colour perspectives on problem solving and organisation

One example is the ordering by social psychologist and change management consultant Léon de Caluwé of modes of thinking[a] that are prevalent and that may assist in understanding, or fostering, change: 'blue' for management, planning and control, 'red' for motivation and a sense of togetherness (the 'soft side' of an organisation), 'yellow' for politics and power play, 'green' for reflection on changes and sharing knowledge, with 'white' standing for openness to change.

Another example of 'colouring' is from Eduardo de Bono's *Six thinking hats*[b] in which the author proposes that one can consciously adopt a certain 'thinking mode' to approach a problem: 'blue' for the big picture, 'white' for factual information, 'red' for an emotional perspective, 'black' for critical judgment, 'yellow' and 'green' for welcoming new ideas and solutions; a sequence of 'thinking modes' may help solve an issue the organisation faces.

A further example is from Frederic Laloux's *Reinventing Organisations*,[c] in which the author labels organisations (in business, government, or health care) as 'red' when characterised by a top-down command structure, as 'amber' where conformism and discipline prevail, as 'orange', when characterised by entrepreneurial effectiveness as a? norm, as 'green' where relationships trump outcomes as organisational value, and as 'teal' for self-managed organisations.[d]

a Hans Vermaak and Léon de Caluwé, 'The Colors of Change Revisited: Situating and Describing the Theory and its Practical Applications' in Rami AB Shani and Debra A Noumaie (eds), *Research in Organizational Change and Development* (vol 26, Emerald 2018).

b Reference is made to Edward de Bono, *Six Thinking Hats* (Little Brown and Company 1985). See also his website at <https://www.debono.com> accessed 27 October 2021.

c Frederic Laloux, *Reinventing Organizations: A Guide to Creating Organizations Inspired by the Next Stage of Human Consciousness* (Nelson Parker 2014). See also Frederic Laloux, 'The Future of Management Is Teal—Organizations are moving forward along an evolutionary spectrum, toward self-management, wholeness, and a deeper sense of purpose' (2015) 80 Strategy + Business <https://www.strategy-business.com/article/00344?gko=30876> accessed 27 October 2021.

d Along the lines of Ricardo Semler's democratic management style, epitomized in Ricardo Semler, *Maverick! The Success Story Behind the World's Most Unusual Workplace* (Warner Books 1993).

2020, information about these practices may give the European Parliament an insight into how 'open' and 'reflective' the ECB is, and how responsive it is to suggestions from the citizens of Europe, supervised entities, and bodies which are to hold the ECB accountable.[54]

dull minds': see Yuval Noah Harari, *Sapiens—A Brief History of Mankind* (Dvir Publishing 2011) 184 (hereafter Harari, *Sapiens—A Brief History of Mankind*). See Yuval Noah Harari's website at <https://www.ynharari.com/> accessed 27 October 2021.

[54] First and foremost, the European Parliament (TFEU (n 11) Art 284(3), ESCB (n 11) Art 15.3, SSM Regulation (n 6) Art 20) but, also, the Council (TFEU (n 11) Art 284(1), (2), (3), ESCB Statute (n 11) Art 15.3, Interinstitutional Agreement 2013/694/EU between the European Parliament and the European Central Bank on the practical modalities of the exercise of democratic accountability and oversight over the exercise of the tasks conferred on the ECB within the framework of the Single Supervisory Mechanism [2013] OJ L320/1) and national parliaments (SSM Regulation (n 6) Art 21). On the ECB's accountability, see chapter 11 by Fabian Ambtenbrink and Menelaos Markakis, in this volume.

Naturally, responsiveness and accountability do not equate to submission: the central bank must take its own decisions in independence and always be wary of listening to interest groups without balancing their views with those of others and making up its own mind. The outcome must be reasoned and explained. My guess is that a slight further pendulum swing in the direction of responsiveness from independence-hand-in-hand-with-traditionalism, may be good for the ECB.

IV. Develop

Two major developments sketched above that the ECB needs to address these days are the issue of climate change and biodiversity loss in the context of its monetary policy and its prudential supervision (while not excluding that these matters are also relevant for other functions, including in the payments area) and the development of a digital currency.

A lot has already been said about the twin issues of climate change and biodiversity loss where I submit the ECB is not only *competent* to reassess its operations in a manner that conforms with the EU's adopted Green Deal and proposed Climate Law[55] but is *mandated* to do so.[56] Any reliance on an alleged 'principle of market neutrality,[57] that does not exist in law, is a spurious defence of undefendable activities by a central banking system with a multitrillion-euro balance sheet (€8,368,278,000,000 in October 2021, that is, more than eight times 10^{12}),[58] in the face of calamitous actions affecting nature. The principle of an open market economy with free competition,[59] favouring an efficient allocation of resources,[60] which does exist, does not oppose the 'greening' of monetary policy either. Rather, it informs policy-makers of the injunction of the Treaty authors to 'favour an efficient allocation of resources' which, in the current state of affairs, implies deviating from the outcome of the 'market' which is distorted in functioning and effects.[61] Nor does any imputed lack of democratic legitimacy form sufficient grounds for avoiding a greening of monetary policies. With

[55] Regulation (EU) 2021/1119 of the European Parliament and of the Council of 30 June 2021 on establishing the framework for achieving climate neutrality and amending Regulations (EC) no 401/2009 and (EU) 2018/1999 (European Climate Law) [2021] OJ L243/1; see Commission, 'Proposal for a Regulation of the European Parliament and of the Council on establishing the framework for achieving climate neutrality and amending Regulation (EU) 2018/1999 (European Climate Law)' COM (2020) 80 final (hereafter Commission, 'Proposal for a European Climate Law') and Council of the European Union, 'Amended Proposal for a Regulation of the European Parliament and of the Council on establishing the framework for achieving climate neutrality and amending Regulation (EU) 2018/1999 (European Climate Law)' COM (2020) 563 final.

[56] See René Smits, 'Elaborating a Climate Change-Friendly Legal Perspective for the ECB' (2021) University of Amsterdam—Amsterdam Center for Law & Economics <https://papers.ssrn.com/sol3/papers.cfm?abstract_id=3913653> accessed 27 October 2021.

[57] See chapter 4 by Jens van 't Klooster, in this volume.

[58] European Central Bank, 'Consolidated balance sheet of the Eurosystem as at 22 October 2021' <https://www.ecb.europa.eu/press/pr/wfs/2021/html/ecb.fst211026.en.html> accessed 27 October 2021.

[59] TFEU (n 11) Art 119(1) and (2).

[60] ibid Art 127(1), last sentence.

[61] Isabel Schnabel, 'Never waste a crisis: COVID-19, climate change and monetary policy' (Virtual roundtable on 'Sustainable Crisis Responses in Europe' organized by the INSPIRE research network, 17 July 2020) <https://www.ecb.europa.eu/press/key/date/2020/html/ecb.sp200717~1556b0f988.en.html> accessed 27 October 2021; Isabel Schnabel, 'When markets fail—the need for collective action in tackling climate change' (European Sustainable Finance Summit, Frankfurt am Main, 28 September 2020) <https://

the Union's politicians (European Council,[62] Commission,[63] and Parliament[64]) clearly choosing an active pro-climate stance, the Eurosystem is Treaty-bound to support these preferences so long as this can be matched with providing price stability, its primary objective. After all, the ECB and the National Central Banks are *to support the economic policies in the EU with a view to contributing to the Union's objectives*,[65] several of which clearly relate to sustainability issues, including: sustainable development, a high level of protection and improvement of the quality of the environment, and solidarity between generations.[66] (In so far as the 'democracy argument' relates to a green taxonomy, which is for the political institutions to develop, and for central banks to follow, reference is made to the overview of taxonomy legislation shown in Box 2 below.[67]) The question whether other Union objectives need to be served by the Eurosystem depends in part on the policies adopted by the Union political institutions: any emphasis on employment and social policies should, in my view, be heeded by the central bank, always respecting its primary mandate of price stability. Even in the absence of political decisions in a given area, the Eurosystem would—again, from my perspective—be wise to take the Union's objectives into account and to elaborate reasoning as to why an objective translates, or does not translate, in central bank policies. To give an example: equality between women and men may relate primarily to the staffing and remuneration of the ECB and NCBs, whereas more economic-policy related objectives may translate in central banking policy choices. Having reasoning on which objectives to follow, and which not to give precedence to, ready and available when asked, or pro-actively, may assist the ECB to better explain its conduct.

www.ecb.europa.eu/press/key/date/2020/html/ecb.sp200928_1~268b0b672f.en.htm> accessed 27 October 2021.

[62] See European Council, 'European Council meeting (12 and 13 December 2019)—Conclusions' (EUCO XT 20027/19, Brussels, 13 December 2019) <https://www.consilium.europa.eu/media/41796/13-euco-art50-conclusions-en.pdf> accessed 27 October 2021 ('EU leaders endorsed the objective of making the EU climate-neutral by 2050, in line with the Paris Agreement. They underlined that the transition to climate neutrality will bring significant opportunities for economic growth, markets, jobs and technological development'); and European Council, 'European Council meeting (10 and 11 December 2020)—Conclusions' (EUCO 22/20, Brussels, 11 December 2020) <https://www.consilium.europa.eu/media/47296/1011-12-20-euco-conclusions-en.pdf> accessed 27 October 2021 ('To meet the objective of a climate-neutral EU by 2050 in line with the objectives of the Paris Agreement, the EU needs to increase its ambition for the coming decade and update its climate and energy policy framework. To that end, the European Council endorses a binding EU target of a net domestic reduction of at least 55 per cent in greenhouse gas emissions by 2030 compared to 1990. It calls on the co-legislators to reflect this new target in the European Climate Law proposal and to adopt the latter swiftly').

[63] See Commission, 'Annex to the Communication from the Commission to the European Parliament, European Council, the Council, the European Social and Economic Committee and the Committee of the Regions. The European Green Deal' COM (2019) 640 final, and Commission, 'Proposal for a European Climate Law' (n 55).

[64] See the European Parliament resolution of 12 February 2020 on the European Central Bank Annual Report for 2018 [2020] 2019/2129(INI) OJ C294/33.

[65] TFEU (n 11) Art 127(1), second sentence; ESCB Statute (n 11) Art 2, second sentence. Both provisions refer to Consolidated Version of the Treaty on European Union [2012] OJ C326/1 (hereafter TEU) Art 3.

[66] TEU (n 65) Art 3.

[67] See also Willem Bovenschen and René Lieshout, 'EU Taxonomy, action plan & supervisory developments on sustainable finance: what uses may these have for the E(S)CB?' in European Central Bank, 'ESCB Legal Conference 2020. 11 September—2 November 2020' (February 2021) <https://www.ecb.europa.eu/pub/pdf/other/ecb.escblegalconferenceproceedings2020~4c11842967.en.pdf> accessed 27 October 2021.

Box 2 Overview of EU green taxonomy legislation

- Taxonomy Regulation: Regulation (EU) 2020/852 of the European Parliament and of the Council of 18 June 2020 on the establishment of a framework to facilitate sustainable investment, and amending Regulation (EU) 2019/2088, [2020] OJ L198/13;
- Sustainable Finance Disclosure Regulation (SFDR): Regulation (EU) 2019/2088 of the European Parliament and of the Council of 27 November 2019 on sustainability-related disclosures in the financial services sector [2019] OJ L317/1;
- Non-financial Reporting Directive (NFRD): Directive 2014/95/EU of the European Parliament and of the Council of 22 October 2014 amending Directive 2013/34/EU as regards disclosure of non-financial and diversity information by certain large undertakings and groups [2014] OJ L330/1;
- Benchmark Regulation & Benchmark Regulation Amendment: Regulation (EU) 2019/2089 of the European Parliament and of the Council of 27 November 2019 amending Regulation (EU) 2016/1011 as regards EU Climate Transition Benchmarks, EU Paris-aligned Benchmarks and sustainability-related disclosures for benchmarks [2019] OJ L317/17.
- Proposed: Corporate Sustainability Reporting Directive (CSRD), COM/2021/189 final.

Beyond the secondary objective in its mandate,[68] there are valid grounds for basing a 'greening' of monetary policy[69] on the first leg of the mandate, as Isabel Schnabel[70] and Frank Elderson[71] have made clear.[72] Further arguments for greening the ECB's

[68] See Nik de Boer and Jens van 't Klooster, 'The ECB's neglected secondary mandate: an inter-institutional solution' (Positive Money Europe, 2021) <http://www.positivemoney.eu/wp-content/uploads/2021/10/The-ECBs-neglected-secondary-mandate_v6.0.pdf> accessed 27 October 2021.

[69] I refrain from specifying the kind of monetary policy measures that would result. Reference is made to Dirk Schoenmaker, 'Greening Monetary Policy' (2021) 21 Climate Policy 581; Jens van 't Klooster and Rens van Tilburg, 'Targeting a sustainable recovery' (2020) Positive Money Europe Paper September 2020 <http://www.positivemoney.eu/wp-content/uploads/2020/09/Green-TLTROs.pdf> accessed 27 October 2021.

[70] See her speeches in the summer of 2020 mentioned in (n 61). And, more recently, her statement 'the question is not whether the ECB should incorporate climate change and other aspects of environmental protection into its monetary policy decisions, but how and to what degree this should be done' in Isabel Schnabel, 'From green neglect to green dominance?' ('Greening Monetary Policy—Central Banking and Climate Change' online seminar, organized as part of the "Cleveland Fed Conversations on Central Banking", 3 March 2021) <https://www.ecb.europa.eu/press/key/date/2021/html/ecb.sp210303_1~f3df48854e.en.html> accessed 27 October 2021.

[71] Frank Elderson, 'Greening monetary policy' (*The ECB Blog*, 13 February 2021) <https://www.ecb.europa.eu/press/blog/date/2021/html/ecb.blog210213~7e26af8606.en.htm> accessed 27 October 2021.

[72] See also one of the background papers to the ECB's monetary policy strategy review: Michael Ioannidis, Sarah Jane Hlásková Murphy, and Chiara Zilioli, 'The mandate of the ECB: Legal considerations in the ECB's monetary policy strategy review' (2021) ECB Occasional Paper Series No 276 <https://www.ecb.europa.eu/pub/pdf/scpops/ecb.op276~3c53a6755d.en.pdf?34605304c0df6620b17a6a7b32fed3cf> accessed 27 October 2021.

function are based on Article 11 TFEU (environmental consistency)[73] and Article 216(2) TFEU[74] (the binding nature of the Paris Agreement).[75]

I consider it noteworthy that, contrary to the conclusion of the earlier monetary policy review (2003), the ECB, in its monetary policy statement[76] of 8 July 2021, included a reference to its secondary mandate, specifying:

> Without prejudice to the price stability objective, the Eurosystem shall support the general economic policies in the EU with a view to contributing to the achievement of the Union's objectives as laid down in Article 3 of the Treaty on European Union. These objectives include balanced economic growth, a highly competitive social market economy aiming at full employment and social progress, and a high level of protection and improvement of the quality of the environment.

Upon concluding its monetary policy review,[77] the ECB already took bold steps towards incorporating climate change into the implementation of its mandate. The ECB announced[78] a climate change action plan including a roadmap[79] which would see the central bank include climate change considerations in its monetary policy framework and operations ('in the areas of disclosure, risk assessment, collateral framework and corporate sector asset purchases'). This would see the ECB incorporate climate change into macro-economic modelling, 'introduce disclosure requirements for private sector assets as a new eligibility criterion or as a basis for a differentiated treatment for collateral and asset purchases', take climate risks on board when assessing collateral, and incorporate climate change criteria into the Corporate Sector Purchasing Programme (CSPP).[80] The current steep rise in energy prices, a phenomenon that is bound to become exacerbated when the transition to a carbon-free economy takes shape, may become an issue for the ECB when measuring inflation.

[73] 'Environmental protection requirements must be integrated into the definition and implementation of the Union's policies and activities, in particular with a view to promoting sustainable development'. See Javier Solana, 'The Power of the Eurosystem to Promote Environmental Protection' (2019) 30 EBLR 547.

[74] 'Agreements concluded by the Union are binding upon the institutions of the Union and on its Member States'; see TFEU (n 11) Art 216(2).

[75] Paris Agreement [2016] OJ L282/4, 4. It includes these obligations: 'Holding the increase in the global average temperature to well below 2°C above pre-industrial levels and pursuing efforts to limit the temperature increase to 1.5°C above pre-industrial levels ...' (Art 2(1)(a) and 'Making finance flows consistent with a pathway towards low greenhouse gas emissions and climate-resilient development' (Art 2(1)(c)).

[76] European Central Bank, 'The ECB's monetary policy strategy statement' (2021) <https://www.ecb.europa.eu/home/search/review/html/ecb.strategyreview_monpol_strategy_statement.en.html> accessed 27 October 2021.

[77] See European Central Bank, 'An overview of the ECB's monetary policy strategy' (2021) <https://www.ecb.europa.eu/home/search/review/html/ecb.strategyreview_monpol_strategy_overview.en.html> accessed 27 October 2021 (hereafter ECB, 'An overview of the ECB's monetary policy strategy').

[78] European Central Bank, 'ECB presents action plan to include climate change considerations in its monetary policy strategy' (ECB Press Release, 8 July 2021) <https://www.ecb.europa.eu/press/pr/date/2021/html/ecb.pr210708_1~f104919225.en.html> accessed 27 October 2021.

[79] European Central Bank, 'Detailed roadmap of climate change-related actions' (2021) <https://www.ecb.europa.eu/press/pr/date/2021/html/ecb.pr210708_1_annex~f84ab35968.en.pdf> accessed 27 October 2021.

[80] Notably omitting to mention the Public Sector Purchasing Programme (PSPP), which is much bigger and where requiring green bonds would have a major impact but also, in view of the still limited issuance of green bonds by EU sovereigns, severely restrain the PSPP.

Beyond the issue of climate change, the new monetary policy strategy moved to 'aiming for two per cent inflation over the medium term', away from the pervious, somewhat more hawkish '*below but close to* 2%'.

On the digital currency, I see developing and introducing such a modern-day variant to banknotes with legal tender status[81] as the primary challenge facing central banks and, notably, the ECB. This challenge relates to the technological developments, classified as the second such major development which the ECB faces mentioned earlier in this chapter. Considering the advances already made by other central banks and the need not to allow the People's Bank of China to be the first major monetary authority with the patents and software to introduce such a currency in time, or to allow Facebook to introduce a 'cryptocurrency' to serve the 'unbanked',[82] the ECB's task is to move forward fast. Its exploration of issues,[83] shown in Box 3 below,[84] is a good starting point, indicating as it does, potential legal bases for introducing a digital currency:[85]

Other central bank(-related) preparatory reports[86] provide fertile ground for the exploration and introduction of a CBDC in Europe. The ECB is well-advised to be open on the varied options available and not to remain too closely associated with the current set-up of the banking and payment systems, from an understandable but potentially critical wish to preserve the banks as conduits for the provision of legal tender to the economy. It may be that the electronic developments and artificial intelligence progress we face at dazzling speed allow for, nay clamour for, openness to direct distribution of a payment instrument to the citizens and companies of Europe, thus providing a democratic example to the world. More generally, one may perceive a tendency towards 'democratization' of finance. My urging to proceed does not imply a need to hasten unwisely. There are major consequences tied to each of the choices in Box 3. These should be widely researched and discussed,[87] and are likely to involve political decision-making.[88]

[81] On the concept of legal tender and the extent of the EU's exclusive competence in the monetary sphere, see Case C-422/19 *Johannes Dietrich and Norbert Häring v Hessischer Rundfunk* [2021] EU:C:2021:63.

[82] See 'the Diem Association's website' (n 7).

[83] European Central Bank, 'Report on a digital euro' (October 2020) <https://www.ecb.europa.eu/pub/pdf/other/Report_on_a_digital_euro~4d7268b458.en.pdf> accessed 27 October 2021 (hereafter ECB, 'Report on a digital euro').

[84] Taken from the ECB, 'Report on a digital euro' (n 83).

[85] As with green monetary policy measures, I refrain from elaborating on these legal bases. Legal writing on this issue is sure to develop soon.

[86] The central banking community is developing its reflections on the issue as these reports make clear: Wouter Bossu and others, 'Legal Aspects of Central Bank Digital Currency: Central Bank and Monetary Law Considerations' (2020) IMF Working Paper No 2020/254 <https://www.imf.org/en/Publications/WP/Issues/2020/11/20/Legal-Aspects-of-Central-Bank-Digital-Currency-Central-Bank-and-Monetary-Law-Considerations-49827> accessed 27 October 2021. See, following, International Monetary Fund and others, 'Digital Money Across Borders: Macro-Financial Implication' (2020) IMF Policy Paper No 2020/050 <https://www.imf.org/en/Publications/Policy-Papers/Issues/2020/10/17/Digital-Money-Across-Borders-Macro-Financial-Implications-49823> accessed 27 October 2021; Bank for International Settlements and others, 'Central bank digital currencies: foundational principles and core features' (2020) BIS Innovation Hub Other Report No 1 <https://www.bis.org/publ/othp33.pdf> accessed 27 October 2021.

[87] For an early assessment, see Seraina Grünewald, 'Public money post COVID-19: The case for Central Bank Digital Currency' (11th FLC Online Symposium 'Sustainable recovery in the post-covid financial sector', 5 February 2021) <https://www.onlineseminar.nl/allenovery/webinar/62c57ae9-f620-4c08-8720-e9f6bef2cccf/11th-flc-symposium-sustainable-recovery-in-the-post-covid-financial-sector/#watch-player> accessed 27 October 2021.

[88] Notably when TFEU (n 11) Art 133 is activated: 'Without prejudice to the powers of the European Central Bank, the European Parliament and the Council, acting in accordance with the ordinary legislative

Box 3 Types of Central Bank Digital Currency (CBDC) and their possible legal bases

1. *127(2) TFEU + 20 ESCB Statute ('other instruments of monetary control')*
   CBDC for central bank counterparties only
2. *127(2) TFEU + 17 ESCB Statute +? (accounts with the Eurosystem)*
   CBDC in hands of households, private entities
3. *127(2) TFEU + 22 ESCB Statute (clearing and payment systems)*
   CBDC as settlement medium for eligible participants
4. *128 TFEU + 16 ESCB Statute (issuance of bank notes) + 133 TFEU*
   CBDC issued as an instrument equivalent to a banknote

On the issue of technological developments, there is no need for the ECB to replicate what is developed on a global scale by the 'central banks' central bank', the Bank for International Settlements (BIS) which established a BIS Innovation Hub[89] in 2019. This is a collaborative 'space' (spread out over Hong Kong, Singapore, Switzerland, London, and Stockholm)[90] to work on 'innovation priorities of the central bank community'. The collaborative and inclusive[91] approach to the technological challenges is epitomized by the BIS Innovation Summit to be held in March 2021.[92] What I plead here is for the ECB to be closely involved in the innovation undertakings at central bank level.

V. Address

For the maturing central bank that the ECB is, addressing grievances and dealing with an often-perceived lack of understanding of the functioning of the monetary authority (evidenced by the populist discourse about central bankers acting not in the public interest) is vital to fulfil its mandate to maintain price stability and foster financial stability. In an era when technical expertise is spurned and fundamental misunderstandings and misgivings about the financial system are widespread, listening to these stories and addressing them is core to the survival of a technocratic body. This test of its capacity to take heed of societal developments may be the biggest challenge arising out of the four developments identified above and concerns the issue of 'Openness'. It requires the openness of mind and the diversity in spirit that I mentioned above as ingredients for the ECB's long-term success.

procedure, shall lay down the measures necessary for the use of the euro as the single currency. Such measures shall be adopted after consultation of the European Central Bank'.

[89] Bank for International Settlements, 'About the BIS Innovation Hub' <https://www.bis.org/about/bisih/about.htm> accessed 27 October 2021.

[90] Centres are also foreseen for Toronto and Frankfurt/Paris.

[91] Speakers include experts who work at the frontline of technological advances.

[92] See Bank for International Settlements, 'Bank for International Settlements to hold inaugural BIS Innovation Summit on 22-25 March' (BIS Press Release, 25 February 2021) <https://www.bis.org/press/p210225.htm> accessed 27 October 2021.

The ECB's recommendation, in the conclusion of its monetary policy review, of moving towards a Harmonised Index of Consumer Prices (HICP) that includes the costs of owner-occupied housing (OOH)[93] is a sign of the willingness to address the critique that housing has been unjustifiably excluded from measuring inflation. The huge increases in house prices in many Member States have certainly cost the consumer cum citizen dearly in purchasing power; this effect would in the future be taken on board when assessing inflation.

The same term, 'addressing', is applicable to another aspect of today's world: the lack of ethics in finance and the pervasiveness of money laundering and the financing for greed and gluttony. The first, coupled with the financing of terrorist activity, is already covered by numerous norms.[94] AML/CTF has been included among the fields of competence of the European Banking Authority (EBA).[95] Recent calls for a dedicated agency[96] have resulted in legislative proposals[97] which include directly applicable

[93] 'To further enhance the representativeness of the HICP and its cross-country comparability, the Governing Council has decided to recommend a roadmap to include owner-occupied housing (OOH) in the HICP'; see ECB, 'An overview of the ECB's monetary policy strategy' (n 77).

[94] Including emanating from the Financial Action Task Force (Financial Action Task Force's website at <https://www.fatf-gafi.org> accessed 27 October 2021) and the EU's AML/CTF Directives, notably Directive (EU) 2015/849 of the European Parliament and of the Council of 20 May 2015 on the prevention of the use of the financial system for the purposes of money laundering or terrorist financing, amending Regulation (EU) No 648/2012 of the European Parliament and of the Council, and repealing Directive 2005/60/EC of the European Parliament and of the Council and Commission Directive 2006/70/EC [2015] OJ L141/73, as amended.

[95] See, notably, Regulation (EU) 1093/2010 of the European Parliament and of the Council of 24 November 2010 establishing a European Supervisory Authority (European Banking Authority), amending Decision No 716/2009/EC and repealing Commission Decision 2009/78/EC [2010] OJ L331/12 (so-called EBA Regulation) Arts 9a and 9b, as amended by Regulation of the European Parliament and of the Council of 18 December 2019 amending Regulation (EU) 1093/2010 establishing a European Supervisory Authority (European Banking Authority), Regulation (EU) 1094/2010 establishing a European Supervisory Authority (European Insurance and Occupational Pensions Authority), Regulation (EU) 1095/2010 establishing a European Supervisory Authority (European Securities and Markets Authority), Regulation (EU) 600/2014 on markets in financial instruments, Regulation (EU) 2016/1011 on indices used as benchmarks in financial instruments and financial contracts or to measure the performance of investment funds, and Regulation (EU) 2015/847 on information accompanying transfers of funds [2019] OJ L334/1. The EBA is now 'solely responsible for leading, coordinating and monitoring AML/CFT efforts across the entire EU financial sector'. See also European Banking Authority, 'Opinion of the European Banking Authority on the future AML/CFT framework in the EU' (EBA/OP/2020/14, 10 September 2020) <https://www.eba.europa.eu/sites/default/documents/files/document_library/Publications/Opinions/2020/931092/Opinion%20on%20the%20future%20AML%20CFT%20framework%20in%20the%20EU.pdf> accessed 27 October 2021. Finally, see European Banking Authority, 'Guidelines on money laundering and terrorist financing risk factors' (EBA/GL/2021/02, 1 March 2021) <https://www.eba.europa.eu/sites/default/documents/files/document_library/Publications/Guidelines/2021/963637/Final%20Report%20on%20Guidelines%20on%20revised%20ML%20TF%20Risk%20Factors.pdf> accessed 27 October 2021.

[96] See Communication from the Commission on an Action Plan for a comprehensive Union policy on preventing money laundering and terrorist financing 2020/C 164/06 [2020] OJ C164/21, and European Banking Authority, 'Response by the European Banking Authority to the European Commission's public consultation on an AML/CFT Action Plan and the establishment of an EU level AML/CFT Supervisor' (2020) <https://www.eba.europa.eu/sites/default/documents/files/document_library/Publications/Other%20publications/2020/923773/EBA%20response%20to%20the%20consultation%20on%20the%20Commission%27s%20AMLCFT%20action%20plan%20final%20for%20publication.pdf> accessed 27 October 2021.

[97] See European Commission, 'Anti-money laundering and countering the financing of terrorism legislative package' (20 July 2021) <https://ec.europa.eu/info/publications/210720-anti-money-laundering-countering-financing-terrorism_en#amla> accessed 27 October 2021.

AML/CTF-related rules[98] and the establishment of an EU Authority for anti-money laundering and countering the financing of terrorism (AMLA).[99] Furthermore, AML/CTF has been included in the approach to its supervisory functions[100] in spite of the apparent exclusion of such concerns evidenced in recital 28 of the preamble to the SSM Regulation.

The wider issue of ethics in the financial sector pertains not only to the greening of finance—that is, to a transition to a carbon-free circular economy[101]—but, also, to such questions as:

- Do current private banking practices increase income disparity and lead to expulsion of people to the sidelines of the economy?
- Does the financial sector serve the 'unbanked' and 'unbankable', those who cannot afford a bank account or are not admitted to financial literacy, or to literacy for that matter?
- How servant are banks and other financial services providers to the achievement of the Sustainable Development Goals (SDGs),[102] the globally agreed set of objectives to be achieved by 2030?

Whereas the ECB cannot take up the role that is reserved for market participants, its approach to these issues will influence their conduct. Thus, addressing these issues belongs to the ECB's task of 'contributing to the safety and soundness of credit institutions and the stability of the financial system'[103] and is befitting of the monetary authority of a Union professing to be a community of values, as set out in Article 2 TEU:

> The Union is founded on the values of respect for human dignity, freedom, democracy, equality, the rule of law and respect for human rights, including the rights of persons belonging to minorities. These values are common to the Member States in a society in which pluralism, non-discrimination, tolerance, justice, solidarity and equality between women and men prevail.

VI. Europe

The approaches to undertake, recommended above, would allow the ECB to emerge as a central bank serving Europe (the 'E' in the title of this chapter) and as a stronger

[98] See Commission, 'Proposal for a Regulation of the European Parliament and of the Council on the prevention of the use of the financial system for the purposes of money laundering or terrorist financing' COM (2021) 420 final.

[99] Commission, 'Proposal for a Regulation of the European Parliament and of the Council establishing the Authority for Anti-Money Laundering and Countering the Financing of Terrorism and amending Regulations (EU) No 1093/2010, (EU) 1094/2010, (EU) 1095/2010' COM (2021) 421 final.

[100] See (n 6).

[101] Recalling the undertaking in the Paris Agreement (n 20): 'Making finance flows consistent with a pathway towards low greenhouse gas emissions and climate-resilient development'.

[102] UN General Assembly Resolution 70/1 of 25 September 2015 'Transforming our world: the 2030 Agenda for Sustainable Development' (A/Res/70/1, 21 October 2015).

[103] SSM Regulation (n 6) Art 1.

participant in the Union's development. There is no questioning that the ECB cannot act alone. Even stronger: it cannot continue to be the sole strong federal actor at EU level, in crises and beyond. The interplay between the Commission and the ECB[104] in the years of the Great Financial Crisis and, again, in the face of the COVID-19 pandemic cannot remain the institutional set-up of the Union. In the recent, and ongoing, pandemic crisis, the EU's response[105] was to a certain extent also fiscal in nature, with the SURE mechanism.[106] SURE ('Support to mitigate Unemployment Risks in an Emergency') is to support Member States in the amount of up to 100 billion euros, funded through bonds issued by the Commission,[107] with almost 90 billion euros in support disbursed at the time of writing.[108] The bonds issued are 'social bonds':[109] a special EU SURE Social Bond Framework in accordance with the ICMA Social Bond Principles.[110] Yet, the only real 'bazooka' the EU could muster was a Pandemic Emergency Purchasing Programme, initiated by the ECB,[111] announcing a potential monetary stimulus of, ultimately, 1.85 billion euros.[112] Although, on the fiscal side, a Recovery and Resilience Facility (RRF) adopted by the European Parliament and the Council[113] in February 2021, a 672.5 billion euro facility which forms part of the larger (750 billion euro) Next Generation EU (NGEU) plank in the EU's multi-annual budget[114] exists, this is a stimulus that is still to come, a year and a half after the beginning of the pandemic and the steep recession it caused. Such imbalance between fiscal and monetary policy capabilities cannot last.[115] The current debate on a rethinking of

[104] For a discussion of their interplay in the financial crisis, see René Smits, 'European Supervisors in the Credit Crisis: Issues of Competence and Competition' in Mario Giovanoli and Diego Devos (eds), *International Monetary and Financial Law. The Global Crisis* (OUP 2010).

[105] Member States' fiscal stimuli, coordinated to a certain extent, were far more forceful than what the EU could muster, without a swiftly adaptable budget and without a budgetary instrument for the euro area, discussed at length, diminished in size and effectiveness, and ultimately shelved.

[106] Council Regulation (EU) 2020/672 of 19 May 2020 on the establishment of a European instrument for temporary support to mitigate unemployment risks in an emergency (SURE) following the COVID-19 outbreak [2020] OJ L159/1.

[107] By 27 January 2021, the Commission had issued 53.5 billion euros in social bonds: see Commission, 'SURE. The European instrument for temporary Support to mitigate Unemployment Risks in an Emergency' <https://ec.europa.eu/info/business-economy-euro/economic-and-fiscal-policy-coordination/financial-assistance-eu/funding-mechanisms-and-facilities/sure_en> accessed 27 October 2021.

[108] ibid.

[109] See Commission, 'EU SURE Social Bond Framework' (7 October 2020) <https://ec.europa.eu/info/sites/info/files/about_the_european_commission/eu_budget/eu_sure_social_bond_framework.pdf> accessed 27 October 2021.

[110] See Internal Capital Market Association, 'Social Bond Principles—Voluntary Process Guidelines for Issuing Social Bonds' (June 2020) <https://www.icmagroup.org/assets/documents/Regulatory/Green-Bonds/June-2020/Social-Bond-PrinciplesJune-2020-090620.pdf> accessed 27 October 2021.

[111] See 'ECB Decision of 10 February 2021 on a temporary pandemic emergency purchase programme' (n 17).

[112] See Smits, 'The European Central Bank's Pandemic Bazooka: Mandate Fulfilment in Extraordinary Times' (n 16).

[113] Regulation (EU) 2021/241 of the European Parliament and of the Council of 12 February 2021 establishing the Recovery and Resilience Facility [2021] OJ L57/17.

[114] See Council of the European Union, 'A recovery plan for Europe' <https://www.consilium.europa.eu/en/policies/eu-recovery-plan/> accessed 27 October 2021.

[115] See Isabel Schnabel, 'Unconventional fiscal and monetary policy at the zero lower bound' (Third Annual Conference organized by the European Fiscal Board on 'High Debt, Low Rates and Tail Events: Rules-Based Fiscal Frameworks under Stress', Frankfurt am Main, 26 February 2021) <https://www.

the excessive deficit procedure (EDP) and the Stability and Growth Pact (SGP)[116] is likely to reinforce recurrent ECB calls for smart coordination of fiscal and monetary policies, while fully respecting the independence of the central bank.[117]

Stronger executive powers for the Commission, the introduction of a European Minister of Finance, and the creation of fiscal powers of intervention at EU level are called for. For the ECB, as long as the euro area does not overlap completely with the EU,[118] a fiscal capacity at euro area level is what counts. Political agreement on a euro area budget may be far off but is needed. Relying for too long on the Central Bank as Lender of Last Resort, beyond its liquidity providing function to commercial banks, may in the long run undermine the ECB rather than strengthen it. To shoulder the burden of adequate and effective action alone,[119] without meaningful prompt response at federal level by the governments together or by the Union's executive leads to expectations that cannot always be met. And it leads to an ever-present questioning of the limits of the Eurosystem's mandate,[120] and disputes on the side-effects of monetary policy that do nothing to enhance its legitimacy. But the wider development

ecb.europa.eu/press/key/date/2021/html/ecb.sp210226~ff6ad267d4.en.html> accessed 27 October 2021 (hereafter Schnabel, 'Unconventional fiscal and monetary policy at the zero lower bound').

[116] On which the European Stability Mechanism (ESM)'s staff have opined with ideas to raise the reference value for public indebtedness from 60 per cent to 100 per cent of GDP; see European Stability Mechanism, 'EU fiscal rules: reform considerations' (2021) ESM Discussion Paper Series No 17 <https://www.esm.europa.eu/sites/default/files/document/2021-10/ESMDP17.pdf> accessed 27 October 2021.

[117] See, for instance, Isabel Schnabel, 'A new strategy for a changing world' (Speech at the virtual Financial Statements series hosted by the Peterson Institute for International Economics, Frankfurt am Main, 14 July 2021) <https://www.ecb.europa.eu/press/key/date/2021/html/ecb.sp210714~0d62f657bc.en.html> accessed 27 October 2021.

[118] Of the currently twenty-seven EU Member States, Denmark has an opt-out (TFEU (n 11) Protocol No 16 on certain provisions relating to Denmark [2016] OJ C202/287) to the TFEU (n 11) on certain provisions relating to Denmark, while eight other Member States enjoy a derogation under TFEU (n 11) Art 140 or their respective accession treaties. Thus, 9 out of the 27 current EU Member States are not part of the Euro Area.

[119] Allow me to quote Isabel Schnabel once again: 'it will be difficult for monetary policy alone to stabilise the economy satisfactorily'—a citation from Schnabel, 'Unconventional fiscal and monetary policy at the zero lower bound' (n 115).

[120] A judicial challenge of the PEPP did not succeed in Germany, where the sequel to the 5 May 2020 decision of the German Constitutional Court in respect of the PSPP was dismissed. See BVerfG, Order of the Second Senate of 29 April 2021 2 BvR 1651/15 ECLI:DE:BVerfG:2021:rs20210429.2bvr165115, and Bundesverfassungsgericht, 'Unsuccessful applications for an order of execution relating to the judgement of the Second Senate on the ECB's asset purchase programme PSPP' (Bundesverfassungsgericht Press Release no 38/2021, 18 May 2021) <https://www.bundesverfassungsgericht.de/SharedDocs/Pressemitteilungen/EN/2021/bvg21-038.html> accessed 27 October 2021, confirms the impressions given by then Bundesbank President Jens Weidman in the Frankfurter Allgemeine Zeitung on 3 August 2020: see Christian Siedenbiedel, 'Weidmann sieht Forderungen des Verfassungsgerichts als erfüllt an' *Frankfurter Allgmemeine Zeitung* (Frankfurt am Main, 3 August 2020) <https://www.faz.net/aktuell/finanzen/jens-weidmann-verfassungsgerichtsurteil-zur-ezb-erfuellt-16887907.html> accessed 27 October 2021 [Weidmann considers demands of the constitutional court to have been fulfilled], with a reference to the ECB's 3–4 June monetary policy account which included lengthy considerations on the proportionality of the asset purchasing programmes; see European Central Bank, 'Account of the monetary policy meeting of the Governing Council of the European Central Bank held in Frankfurt am Main on Wednesday and Thursday, 3–4 June 2020' <https://www.ecb.europa.eu/press/accounts/2020/html/ecb.mg200625~fd97330d5f.en.html> accessed 27 October 2021. See also Dolores Utrilla, 'Three months after Weiss: Was nun?' (2020) EULawLive <https://eulawlive.com/three-months-after-weiss-was-nun/> accessed 27 October 2021. Apparently, the ECB has submitted documents to the German government and parliament through the Bundesbank on its proportionality assessment. See also chapter 14 by Ad van Riet, in this volume.

of the Union, including how to approach ever more disturbing developments concerning the rule of law, notably in several Member States,[121] is beyond the scope of this contribution.

VII. Final Words

*R*eform, *O*pen-up, *A*ddress, *D*evelop for *E*urope: combining these changes or, as I see them, injunctions for the ECB at this age and at this stage of its development, make for a clear signpost: the E-ROAD to take. The democracy-under-attack issue (1) requires a more open, transparent, 'listening' central bank; the technological developments (2) empower the central bank to do so and drive it towards a CBDC; (3) COVID-19 leads to conclusions on a stronger (fiscal) Europe and the need for better fiscal-monetary interplay, and (4) the climate change and biodiversity loss issues[122] require greening of the ECB's policies[123] and regularly simulating climate

[121] Concerning the situation in Poland and Hungary, reference is made to the following select developments: European Parliament, 'Parliament prepares legal proceedings against Commission over rule of law mechanism' (Statement by the President of the European Parliament, Strasbourg, 20 October 2021) <https://the-president.europarl.europa.eu/en/newsroom/parliament-prepares-legal-proceedings-against-commission-over-rule-of-law-mechanism> accessed 27 October 2021; Case C-650/18 *Hungary v European Parliament* [2021] EU:C:2021:426; European Commission, 'Rule of Law: Commission adopts next step in the infringement procedure to protect judicial independence of Polish judges' (European Commission Press Release, 27 January 2021) <https://ec.europa.eu/commission/presscorner/detail/en/ip_21_224> accessed 27 October 2021; Case C-791/19 *Commission v Poland* [2021] EU:C:2021:596. See also Case C-204/21 R *Commission v Poland* [2021] EU:C:2021:878, Order of the Vice-President of the Court ordering Poland to pay the European Commission a daily penalty payment of €1 million as long as it has not suspended the application of the provisions of national legislation on the Disciplinary Chamber of the Supreme Court. See Court of Justice of the European Union, 'Order of the Vice-President of the Court in Case C-204/21 R Commission v Poland' (CJEU Press Release No 192/21, 27 October 2021) <https://curia.europa.eu/jcms/upload/docs/application/pdf/2021-10/cp210192en.pdf> accessed 27 October 2021. The rule of law is also at issue in other Member States; see, for example, Ingrid Leijten, 'Constitutional Review in Sight?, The Venice Commission on the Dutch Childcare Allowance Scandal' (*Verfassungsblog on Matters Constitutional*, 25 October 2021) <https://verfassungsblog.de/constitutional-review-in-sight/> accessed 27 October 2021. See also (n 1) and Rule of Law, 'Everything you need to know about the rule of law in Poland' <https://ruleoflaw.pl/> accessed 27 October 2021.

[122] See Network for Greening the Financial System, 'Biodiversity and financial stability: building the case for action' NGFS Occasional Paper—Study Group interim report October 2021 <https://www.ngfs.net/sites/default/files/medias/documents/biodiversity_and_financial_stablity_building_the_case_for_action.pdf> accessed 27 October 2021.

[123] And strengthening the prudential legislation. See the call by Frank Elderson for a legal requirement for banks to draft transition plans, based on the assessment that 'European banks may be largely misaligned with the economic transition path towards carbon neutrality by 2050': Frank Elderson, 'Overcoming the tragedy of the horizon: requiring banks to translate 2050 targets into milestones' (Keynote speech at the Financial Market Authority's Supervisory Conference, Vienna, 20 October 2021) <https://www.ecb.europa.eu/press/key/date/2021/html/ecb.sp211020~03fba70983.en.html> accessed 31 October 2021. On 27 October 2021, the Commission submitted a banking package with proposals containing implementation of global banking Standards (Basel III) and an—at first sight—moderate strengthening of the rules relating to banks' exposure to environmental, social, and governance (ESG) risks. It includes reporting of ESG risks to supervisors and ensuring that 'misalignment of the [banks'] business model and strategy with the relevant Union policy objectives or broader transition trends towards a sustainable economy in relation to [ESG] factors' is part of bank management's strategy and becomes embedded in the Supervisory Evaluation and Review Process. Banks would thus be expected to align their business plans with the EU objective towards a carbon-free economy. See European Commission, 'Banking Package' (2021) <https://ec.europa.eu/info/publications/211027-banking-package_en> accessed 27 October 2021.

change and transition policy developments in stress tests such as the one already undertaken.[124]

Simplistic perhaps, to suggest working with such first letters combined, but potentially appealing to a general public, a part of which needs convincing that an independent central bank is a good thing to have, that a single currency for a single market is a friendly concept, not an inimical one, and that money, in paper or digital form, '*is the most universal and most efficient system of mutual trust ever devised; a symbol of trust among humans*'.[125] Trust and connection[126] are what is needed in these times. By reforming, opening up, addressing, and developing for Europe, the ECB may have profoundly challenging yet also fulfilling tasks in the years ahead.

[124] Luis de Guindos, 'Shining a light on climate risks: the ECB's economy-wide climate stress test' (*The ECB Blog*, 18 March 2021) <https://www.ecb.europa.eu/press/blog/date/2021/html/ecb.blog210318~3bbc68ffc5.en.html> accessed 27 October 2021.

[125] Yuval Noah Harari, 'The Scent of Money' in Harari, *Sapiens—A Brief History of Mankind* (n 53).

[126] Vivek H Murphy, *Together: The Healing Power of Human Connection in a Sometimes Lonely World* (Harperwave 2020). Published in Dutch as De kracht van verbinding, this book by the 19th Surgeon General of the United States combines the personal and the societal in a forceful plea for connection.

Index

For the benefit of digital users, indexed terms that span two pages (e.g., 52–53) may, on occasion, appear on only one of those pages.

Tables and boxes are indicated by *t* and *b* following the page number

accountability and democratic legitimacy of the ECB 265–91
accountability gap 2, 22, 270
weak democratic legitimacy 2
accountability relationship between ECB/ national parliaments 22
monetary dialogue 41–42, 272–73, 278–79, 288–89, 399
evolution of 273–87
COVID-19 pandemic, ECB and 285–87
ECB's role as crisis manager 274–79
expanded ECB powers, and 16, 19
inception of ECB 267–73
political influence, insulation of ECB from 269–70
rationale for accountability 265–66
SSM 152–53
strengthening all dimensions of ECB legitimacy, 287–91
input legitimacy 288–89
output legitimacy 290–91
throughput legitimacy 289–90
AML/CTF 426–27
Asset Purchase Programme (APP) 62–63, 285–86, 353–55
PEPP, and 72–73
quantitative easing 90
size 64, 90

Bank for International Settlements (BIS) 209–10
BIS Innovation Hub 425
BIS Innovation Summit 425
ECB as full member 218, 222
promoting cooperation on monetary policy among central banks 222
banking licences 199–200
banking supervision *see* EBU, ECB's role in
banking union *see* EBU, ECB's role, in
Basel Committee on Banking Supervision (BCBS)
attendance at 224
ECB, and 209–10, 224
BICC 345–46, 348
biodiversity loss 413–14, 420–21
ECB mandated to act 420–21
EU Biodiversity strategy 413–14
BoC
deflation, and 381
inflation, and 370, 371, 380–81
LOLR 385–86
mandate 369–70, 371
functional perspective on 372–74
implementation 384–87
QE 386–87
BoE 238–39
inflation, and 378–80
no goal independence 247–48
LOLR 385–86
mandate 368–69, 371
functional perspective on 371–72, 373–74
implementation 384–87
QE 386–87
Budgetary Instrument for convergence and competitiveness (BICC) *see* BICC

central banks
Bank of Canada *see* BoC
Bank of England *see* BoE
BIS, and 222
Committee of Central Bank Governors 34–35
digital currency *see* digital currency
duties and objectives 238–40, 247–48, 362–63, 365–74
European Central Bank *see* ECB
European System of Central Banks (ESCB) *see* ESCB

central banks (*cont.*)
expansion of role 239–40
Federal Reserve System *see* FED
implementation of mandates: purposive and functional approach 374–88
common and distinct features in implementing central bank mandates 384–88
ECB monetary policy strategy 375–78
price stability determined within monetary policy strategy 378–84
intervention in Member State economic policy-making 16
justification of central bank independence 238–47
economic background 238–43
German democratic theory 243–47
legal sources of central bank mandates, objectives, and tasks 365–74
ECB's mandate and hierarchized multiple objectives 365–68
functional perspective on the mandate 371–74
implementation of mandates 374–88
other central banks' objectives in their statutory sources 368–71
mandates 362–63, 364
legal sources of mandates, objectives, and tasks 365–74
manifestations of independence 247–49
goal independence 247–48
goal-choice independence 248
instrumental independence 249
national central banks *see* NCBs
political factors 239–40, 241–42, 251–53, 268
quantitative easing
central bank practice, in 66–71
central banks' use of 53–54
central counterparties (CCPs) 107, 121–22
ECB oversight 121–23, 295–96, 304, 406
Charter of Fundamental Rights of the EU 146, 303, 403
climate emergency
COVID-19, beneficial effects of 412–13
ECB, and 245–46, 250–51
action plan 3, 24
ECB mandated to act 420–24
ECB, banking regulation, and sustainability 170–72
environmental impact of ECB monetary policy operations 93–94
inflation, and 160–61
NGFS *see* NGFS
physical risks 92–93
pricing risks
ECB ensuring institutions price climate and environmental risks 93–94
environmental sustainability risks, mispricing of 161–62
pro-carbon bias of ECB operations 93–94
risk management, and 92–93
seriousness of 413–14
shaping ECB policy making 20
stranded assets 181–82
transition risks 92–93
collateral framework of ECB (1990s-present) 80–102
ECB risk management before 2010 82–89
banks needing sufficient collateral to secure refinancing transactions 84
CEPH 87–88
collateral eligibility 80–81, 82, 84, 85–87
credit quality requirements 87–88
ECAF, and 87–88, 88*t*
ECB's mandate placing few constraints on risk management strategy 85
Eurofed 83
risk of counterparty default 83–84
setting interest rates 83
Single List of Eligible Collateral 81, 87–89
two-tiered system of eligible collateral 86*t*, 86–87
ECB risk management since 2010 89–94
banks having sufficient collateral to secure refinancing transactions 89
ECB lowering ECAF credit quality requirement 89
ECB's purchase programmes 90
effects of euro area crisis 89–91
environmental impact, 92–94
financial stability, and 90–92
nature of risk attached to outright purchases 90
environmental and climate-related considerations 81
environmental impact of ECB monetary policy operations 93–94
risk management, and 92–93

failures of European financial markets to adequately price risk 81
future of ECB risk management 94–101
coordinating with EU political institutions 100–1
developing internal credit rating facilities 98–100
market attentiveness instead of market neutrality 97–98, 102
revising objectives of risk management 95–97
risk efficiency 95
risk equivalence 97
Committee of Central Bank Governors 34–35
Committee of European Banking Supervisors (CEBS) 116
common currency *see* euro/currency union
Common Eurosystem Pricing Hub (CEPH) 87–88
competences
asymmetry of 137–38
delineation of competences by CJEU 139–41
ECB competences and tasks as a bank supervisor 164–67
Conference on the Future of Europe 3, 390
constitutional law's role for the ECB 392–408
constitutional approach to EMU 394–97
ECB as a constitutional interpreter 397–402
ECB during euro area crisis 402–5
judicialization of EMU 405–8
see also Court of Justice of the EU (CJEU)
Corporate Sector Purchase Programme (CSPP) 72–73
Court of Justice of the EU (CJEU) 292–317
application of national law by ECB 313–14
CJEU interpreting national law 314
national case law 314
delineation of competences 139–41
financial stability 109–10
fines 314–16
application of 314–15
proportionality 315
publication 316
reasons 315–16
increasing numbers of challenges 3, 292
independence of the ECB
importance of 294
intensity of judicial control, and 259–63
judicial accountability of ECB 293–94, 295–96
judicial review of new ECB 52–57
judicial scrutiny and standard of review 303–4
principles of judicial review 303–4
process requirements 306–7
reasons 305, 307, 315–16
standard of scrutiny 304–6
judicialization of EMU 405–8
legality of the ESM 49
nature of challenges 292–93, 294
objectives v effects: boundaries of monetary policy 296–302
Gauweiler 298–99, 302–3
German Federal Constitutional Court 298–303
objectives-based reasoning 297–99
Pringle 296–99
Weiss 299–300, 302–3
OMT Programme see *Gauweiler*
proportionality 302–3
fines 315
proportionality review 305
prudential supervision 308–13
composite procedures and hybridity 310–13
Crédit mutuel Arkéa v ECB, 310
Landeskreditbank 308–9
prudential supervision: composite procedures and hybridity 310–13
ABLV Bank 312
Fininvest 310–12
PSPP see *Weiss*
see also constitutional law's role for the ECB
COVID-19 2, 22
constraints on efficacy of monetary policy 342
crisis coordination, and 127–28
deflation, and 158–59
economic difficulties caused by 71
economic policy response, ECB 71, 285–87, 346–48, 412–13
budgetary requirements under the SGP temporarily suspended 346
ECB role 71
EIB's guarantee fund 346–47
EU Recovery Plan 162–63
LTROs 20, 285–87

COVID-19 (*cont.*)
monetary policy measures 72
Pandemic Crisis Support 346–48
pandemic emergency longer-term refinancing operations 72
PEPP *see* Pandemic Emergency Purchase Programme (PEPP)
inflation, impact on 74, 390
significant effects of 412–13
reduction in emissions 413–14
currency union *see* euro/currency union

deflation 67
COVID-19 158–59
ECB concerns about 76, 375–76
meaning of 158–59
PSPP tackling 53, 65, 66
QE, and 77
democracy
democratic legitimacy *see* accountability and democratic legitimacy of the ECB
under attack 409–11
digital currency 424, 430–31
digital euro
ECB advocating 24
ECB competence in area of payment systems 119–20
impact on financial stability 119–20
possibility of 3, 24, 420
primary challenge facing central banks, as 424
types of central bank digital currency 425*b*
duty of cooperation in good faith 203, 204–5, 206

EBA 216, 319–20
AML/ CTF, and 426–27
assessments of materiality of sustainability risks 170–71
Basel Committee, observer at 224
Board of Supervisors, ECB on 115
colleges of supervisors 168
more harmonized system of supervision, promoting 169
power to issue recommendations or guidelines 293–94
regulatory and technical implementing standards, promulgating 167, 215–16
EBRD 222
EBU, ECB's role in 7, 11, 25, 156–83
ECB's mandate 157–63
ECB's secondary objectives 160–63
price stability 157–60
pillars of the EBU *see* EDIS; SRM; SSM
promoting European integration 156
purpose of EBU 156
SRM, Banking Union and 175–81
ECB/SSM coordination with SRB 179–81
SRB *see* SRB
SRM 176–79
SSM, banking union and 163–75, 279–85
accountability 280–85
ECB, banking regulation, and sustainability 170–72
ECB competences and tasks as a bank supervisor 118, 164–67
ECB executive role 152–53
ECB primary task of price stability and new supervisory role 172–75
legal basis of ECB supervision 163–64
national parliaments, scrutiny by 284–85
reporting requirements 281
Supervisory Board 167–70
ECAF
credit quality requirements 88*t*
euro area sovereign debt crisis, and 92
lowering credit quality requirement 87–88, 89
Single List of Eligible Collateral, as core of 87–88
ECB
accountability *see* accountability and democratic legitimacy of the ECB
actions contested in courts *see* Court of Justice of the EU (CJEU)
Banking Union, and *see* EBU, ECB's role in
changes to 1
climate change, and *see* biodiversity loss; climate emergency
collateral framework *see* collateral framework of ECB from1990s-present
constitutional law, role of *see* constitutional law's role for the ECB
COVID-19, and *see* COVID-19
creation and inception of 267–73
ESRB, and *see* ESRB

evolution *see* evolution of the ECB
financial stability *see* financial stability and the ECB
fluctuating popular support for 3
future developments *see* future road ahead
GFC, and *see* Great Financial Crisis 2008 (GFC)
inflation *see* inflation
institutional structures *see* institutional structures of the ECB
international dimensions *see* international arena, ECB in
judicial review *see* Court of Justice of the EU (CJEU)
Member States, and *see* Member States
independence *see* independence of the ECB
mandate *see* mandate of the ECB
monetary policy *see* monetary policy of the ECB
NGFS, and 92–93, 171
objectives *see* monetary policy of the ECB; price stability; secondary objectives of the ECB
politics/political institutions, and 14–17, 271–73
monetary dialogue 41–42, 272–73, 278–79, 288–89, 399
price stability *see* price stability
prudential regulation *see* prudential regulation
prudential supervision *see* prudential supervision
quantitative easing *see* quantitative easing (QE)
risk management *see* collateral framework of ECB (1990s-present)
sovereign debt, and *see* sovereign debt/sovereign bond markets
Economic and Monetary Union *see* EMU
economic integration, ECB and 136–55
asymmetry between monetary policy and economic policy 136
budgetary stability: economic policy coordination and financial assistance 142–47
European Stability Mechanism, ECB and 144–47
strengthening of Stability and Growth Pact 142–44
cunning of European integration 153–55
delineation of competences 139–41
financial stability: new forms of supervision for the internal market 147–53
macroprudential supervision in the ESRB 147–49
microprudential supervision in SSM 118
EDIS 156, 157
EFSF 4–5, 43, 274–75
ECB, and 209–10, 275
safeguarding stability of euro area 2, 227
EIB
COVID-19 Guarantee fund 346–47
legal status 218
public debt securities 349–51
Emergency Liquidity Assistance (ELA) 36–37, 112, 125–26, 377, 400–1
ECB involvement in ELA provision by NCBs 125–26
falling within purview of NCBs, interpreted by ECB as 124
liquidity assistance to banks, as 123–24
mitigating risk of contagion 124
NCBs as LOLRs to individual institutions 123–26
EMU
asymmetry of competences 137
constitutional approach to 394–97
Delors Report 270
ECB prominence in 2
financial stability
law of economic and monetary union, and 108–10
overriding objective, as 8, 12
judicialization of 405–8
more active fiscal policy coordination needed 343
'no-bailout' clause as founding principle 37–38
no central fiscal capacity 343
perspectives on EMU change 7–9
weaknesses shown in GFC 1, 2
ESCB 60, 63, 85, 125, 371
buying and selling, lending and borrowing 85
contributing to conduct of prudential supervision 34–35, 108–9, 138, 161
contributing to supervisory policy 150

ESCB (*cont.*)
ECB, and 119, 124, 213–14, 271–72
ESCB Committees 322–24
financial stability, and 34–35, 108–9, 115, 133
governance 321–22, 332–33, 416–17
integrated and supranational nature 336
international representation of 213–14
monetary policy, and 137–38, 289, 367–68
monetary tasks 213
national administrations, importance of role of 318–19
nature of role 108–9
NCBs, and 334, 336
payments system, promoting smooth functioning of 135, 304
price stability 298–99, 371
primary objective 158
prohibited from engaging in monetary financing 138
respect for market economics 161–62
secondary objectives 160, 303
SSM, and 150
supporting general economic policies of EU 138, 300–1, 303
ESCB/Eurosystem 365–68, 371, 373–74, 385–86, 388
LOLR 376–78
ESFS 185, 187–88, 204–5, 368
duty of cooperation 206
ESM 2, 4–5, 43, 209–10, 274–75
adjustment programmes 45–46, 51–52, 274–75, 353, 354
conditionality 45–46, 64–65, 78–79
creation of 144
direct recapitalization 44–45
E-bonds 350
ECB, and 144–47, 275, 277, 303
ECB's role and tasks 11, 21, 145–46, 227, 230–31
ESM-related tasks 227–29
influence in practice 228–29
no formal role in adoption of measures 277
role-splitting 145–46
financial stability, and 109–10
inflation 296–97
intergovernmental organization, as 2, 227–28, 349–50
measure of economic policy, as 49, 139
no-bailout clause, and 50–51
Pandemic Crisis Support 346–48
permanent assistance fund, as 44
precautionary programmes 45–46
Pringle see *Pringle*
safeguarding stability of euro area 49, 139, 227, 296–97
Troika, as part of 11
ESRB 116, 173
composition and governance 148, 149
creation of 116, 117
ECB, and 116–18, 155
macroprudential supervision 116–17, 147–49
no legal personality 148
organisation 148, 149
task of 147
warnings and recommendations 148–49
'act or explain' 148–49
European Parliament, and 149
ethics in the financial sector 427
euro/currency union
digital euro *see* digital currency
euro area crisis *see* euro area sovereign debt crisis
enlargement of EU, and 21, 329
fiscal capacity, need for 343–48
advantages of 343
COVID-19 pandemic response 346
economic policy coordination ensuring economic resilience 343
EMU-related package of proposals 344–45
euro area budget within the EU framework, agreement on 345
Eurogroup finance ministers discussions 343–44
fiscal sustainability constraint on coordinated action 344
more active fiscal policy coordination, need for 343
New Hanseatic League 345–46
permanent euro area fiscal capacity, need for 348
task of managing euro area falling on ECB 343
launch of common currency 1, 60
only coordinating role for EU institutions initially 18–19
operation of euro area payment systems 120–21

original set-up of currency union, ECB in 31–36
safe sovereign asset for euro area, need for 348–51
benefits of 348–49
ensuring investors perceive as safe 350
moral hazard, containing 350–51
euro area sovereign debt crisis 4–5, 10, 20, 29, 33–36
ECAF, and 92
ECB in original set-up of currency union 31–36
narrow conception of stability 33–36
stability paradigm 31–33
new stability conception *see* new stability conception
pressure on ECB 14
'whatever it takes' pledge by Draghi 2, 45–46, 132, 139–40, 375–76
see also Great Financial Crisis 2008 (GFC)
Euro Summit (2012) 44
Euro Summit (2018) 345–46
Eurogroup 43–44
budgetary instrument for convergence and competitiveness (BICC) 345–46
COVD-19, response to 2
ECB, and
cooperation with 229–30
ECB submitting report to Eurogroup 281
Eurogroup as counterweight to ECB 400
euro area fiscal stance, discussions on 343–44
euro area sovereign debt crisis 400
Eurogroup+ 281–82
European Semester, and 348
G7 meetings 224
influence of 221–22
recapitalization assistance for Spain 43–44
Supervisory Board, and 281–82
SURE 2
European Anti-Fraud System (OLAF) *see* OLAF
European Bank for Reconstruction and Development (EBRD) 222
European Banking Authority (EBA) *see* EBA
European Banking Union (EBU) *see* EBU
European Central Bank *see* ECB
European Commission 319–20, 355
borrowings 349–50
CCPs 122–23
euro area macroeconomic stabilization 344–45
financial assistance 347–48
assessing financing needs of Member States 275
computation of financing needs 145
SURE 346–47
G7 meetings 224
G20 meetings 224
'green' bonds 101
IMFC, and 222–23
SSM 165, 167, 190, 192–93
State aid control 109–10
stronger executive powers for 429–30
supranational institution, as 318–19, 335–36
Sustainable Finance Action Plan 170–71
Troika, part of 209–10
Eurosystem Credit Assessment Facility (ECAF) *see* ECAF
European Deposit Insurance System (EDIS) *see* EDIS
European Financial Stability Facility (EFSF) *see* EFSF
European Investment Bank (EIB) *see* EIB
European Investment Stabilisation Function (EISF) 344–45
European Monetary Institute (EMI) 81
European Monetary Union *see* EMU
European Parliament 101, 112–13
biodiversity 413–14
democratic accountability 338
ECB, and 152, 270–72
ECB reporting to 253–54
'green' monetary actions 245–46
holding ECB to account 289–90
Interinstitutional Agreement 280, 281, 289
meaningful relationship, legal arrangements providing for 270
monetary dialogue 41–42, 272–73, 278–79, 288–89
NGFS 171
secondary objectives of ECB 398
SSM 280–85
ESRB warnings and recommendations, and 149
international agreements 211–12
RRF 427–29
strengthening democratic control 149

European Semester 348
budgetary coordination 186–87
budgetary instrument for convergence and competitiveness (BICC), and 345–46
economic policy coordination 142, 343–44
reviews and timetable 142
Stability and Growth Pact, and 142
European Stability Mechanism (ESM) *see* ESM
European System of Central Banks (ESCB) *see* ESCB
European System of Financial Supervision (ESFS) *see* ESFS
European Systemic Risk Board (ESRB) *see* ESRB
European Unemployment Stabilisation Fund *see* SURE
Eurosystem 62–63, 86–87, 98, 126–27, 148, 214–15
aims and objectives 95
blocking minority 63–64
composition of 322, 368
defining monetary policy 15, 351
ECB, and 267
ECB's exclusive external competence, and 214–15
ELA 124
ESCB/Eurosystem 365–68, 371, 373–74, 385–86, 388
LOLR 376–78
Eurosystem oversight policy 121–22, 304
financial risks, and 342, 351–52, 353, 354–56
fiscal backstop for Eurosystem, need for 351–56
improving market functioning 95–96
payment and securities settlement systems 119, 120
PSPP 299–300
repo facility 127–28
secondary government bond markets, intervening in 45–46
Single List of Eligible Collateral 87–89
supranational character 333–35
evolution of the ECB 7–22
causes and factors of 17–22
changing ideas 18–19
discretion in mandate of an independent institution 20–21
events 19–20
new relations with old and new institutions 22
personalities 22
political decisions 21
treaty change 17
central bank intervention in Member State economic policy-making 16
ECB mandate 9–11
ECB's relationship to sovereign debt 12–14
establishment of ECB 1
future developments and challenges 22–25
perspectives on EMU and ECB change 7–9
politics, ECB relationship with 14–17
transformation of the ECB 7
excessive deficit procedure 138, 395–96, 406–7, 427–29
Expanded Asset Purchase Programme (EAPP) 53

FED
goal-choice-independence 323
inflation, and 381–84
mandate 370–71
functional perspective on 373–74
implementation 384–88
price stability 269
QE 386–87
financial crisis *see* Great Financial Crisis 2008 (GFC)
financial stability
conventional use of an economic concept 107–8
definition 34–35, 107–8
financial stability linked to condition of the financial system 107
objective of financial stability 107
resilience of the financial sector 107–8
digital euro, and 119–20
ECB, and *see* financial stability and the ECB
EMU, and *see* EMU
ESRB *see* ESRB
importance of 8, 105
interest rate increases 23–24
law of the economic and monetary union, and 108–10

pervasive nature of financial stability concerns since GFT 109–10
references to financial stability in EU Treaties 108–9
LOLR *see* Lender of Last resort (LOLR)
measuring 108
policy instruments of 110–12
risk management consequences for 90–92
sovereign debt crisis *see* sovereign debt/ sovereign bond markets
SSM *see* SSM
state aid, and 109–10
stranded assets 181–82
supranational public good, as 105–6, 109–10
systemic risk *see* systemic risk
tools for maintaining 110–12, 111*t*
financial stability and the ECB 105–35
financial stability as ECB objective 12, 19, 24, 47, 50, 52, 161
monetary policy tools as secondary policy instrument of financial stability 128–34
distinction between preventive and remedial instruments 134
ECB standard monetary policy 130
ECB's unconventional monetary policy measures 130–32
unconventional monetary policy and financial stability 132–33
policy instruments of financial stability 110–12
preventive policy instruments of financial stability 112–23
macroprudential supervision 115–18
microprudential supervision 115–16, 118
payment systems 118–23
prudential regulation 112–15
prudential supervision 115–18
remedial policy instruments of financial stability 123–28
crisis coordination 126–28
ELA: NCBs as LOLRs to individual institutions 123–26
Financial Stability Board (FSB) 224
ECB's enhanced position in 224, 230–31
fines *see* Court of Justice of the EU (CJEU)
fit and proper authorizations 202
Friedman, Milton 18, 83, 136, 155, 240–42, 252–53
future road ahead 409–31
addressing ethical issues in financial sector 426–27
anti-money laundering actions 426–27
ethical issues in private banking 427
addressing grievances/criticisms 425–26
challenges 409–31
climate change and biodiversity loss 413–14
COVID-19 pandemic, effects of 412–14
democracy, attacks on 409–11
lobbying and alleged corruption 409–11
technological developments 411–12
climate change and biodiversity loss, addressing 420–25
greening' of monetary policy 420–23
overview of EU green taxonomy legislation 422*b*
digital currency 424–6
ECB as central bank serving Europe 427–30
ECB as stronger participant in EU development 427–29
fiscal capacity at euro area level 429–30
stronger executive powers for Commission 429–30
opening up 414–17
archives and files, greater access to 416
confidentiality maintained only where needed 414–15, 416–17
openness of debate 416–17
non-private information, publication of 417
principled openness and transparency 414–15
website improvements 415
reform 417–20
adaptability and openness in staff approaches 418–19
creative and original thinking, encouragement of 418–19
diversity in hiring staff 418
reasoned and explained outcomes 420
reform of ECB operational functioning 417–18

G7 209–10, 224

G20 209–10, 222, 224, 230
Gauweiler 10
CJEU approving OMT programme 10, 30, 48–53, 58, 133, 139–40, 298
competence 140–41, 302, 405–6
deferential approach of CJEU 25, 277–78, 316–17
ECB barred from purchasing government bonds 12
functional independence of ECB 15
price stability as objective 146
proportionality review 278, 302, 305
travaux préparatoires of Maastricht Treaty, use of 393
Germany
democratic theory 243–47
German Federal Constitutional Court 298–303, 330–31
reunification 18, 32
goal independence
ECB, and 15, 247–48, 250–51, 275–76
meaning 247–48
goal-choice independence 248
Great Financial Crisis 2008 (GFC) 1, 4–5, 8, 10, 14, 136
bulk of fiscal support from Member States 341
constraints on efficacy of monetary policy 341
contributing causes 161
crisis coordination, and 126–28
ECB independence, and 14
EMU, and *see* EMU
leading to greater powers for ECB 1
origins 20
single currency creating economic constraints 138
sources of financial instability overlooked in Maastricht Treaty, showing 147
see also euro area crisis

Harmonised Index of Consumer Prices (HICP) *see* HCIP
HCIP
owner-occupied housing 375–76, 426
price stability, and 9, 158

independence of the ECB 8, 14–17, 19, 40, 237–64
banking supervision 152–53
challenges to 250–55
duties to cooperate 254–55
duties to report to European institutions 253–54
public criticism 250–53
CJEU, and 294
discretion in mandate of an independent institution 20–21, 22–23, 25
euro crisis, and 14
functional independence 15
goal independence 15, 247–48, 250–51, 275–76
independence in times of crisis 237–38
independent monetary policy, threats to 255–63
bond purchases 257–59
fiscal and wage policy of Member States 255–57
intensity of judicial control 259–63
inflation, and 20–21, 32, 247–48, 257–58
instrumental independence 15, 250–51, 252–53
justification of central bank independence 238–47
economic background 238–43
German democratic theory 243–47
manifestations of independence 247–49
goal independence 247–48
goal-choice independence 248
instrumental independence 249
monetary independence 152–53
nature of 14
threats to 15–16, 19
inflation 14
BoC, and 370, 371, 380–81
BoE, and 378–80
COVID-19, impact of 74, 390
deflation, and 65
ECB, and 34–35, 77–78, 250–51, 288–89
independence, and 20–21, 32, 247–48, 257–58
interest rates, and 80, 157–58, 172
low inflation rate 250–51, 257–58, 342, 343, 361
measuring 20–21, 249, 423, 426
monetary policy, and 21, 40, 65–66, 159, 267–68
price stability, inflation rate for 34–35, 53–54, 60, 80, 126, 158–59, 174, 182, 247–48, 375–76, 400–1, 424

PSPP 65–66, 69–71, 300
public investment 263–64
QE 53, 66–68, 77
unconventional' measures, use of 75–76, 390
energy prices, and 61–62, 69–70
environmental mitigation polices, and 160–61
ESM, and 296–97
FED 381–84
higher transparency in forecasts, and 172–73
independence, and 18, 242–43, 247–48, 249, 268
inflation culture of a society 242–43
inflationary environment, factors in 239–41, 256–57, 268
rising 2
trade-off' between inflation and employment 31–32
institutional structures of the ECB 318–39
adaptation of ECB's institutional design to EBU 324–28
ECB decision-making bodies and shared services 327–28
JSTs 327
Supervisory Board 325–27
ECB's original institutional architecture 320–24
ECB decision-making bodies 320–22
ECB preparatory bodies 322–24, 336
institutional logics governing ECB 335–37
hybrid nature of 336
institutional loneliness of ECB 341–42
Maastricht to Lisbon to today 320–28
adaptation of ECB's institutional design to EBU 324–28
ECB's original institutional architecture 320–24
national component within ECB, size of 328–35
enhanced representation of national interests 329–31
Eurosystem/ECB supranational character reinforced by CJEU 333–35
potential reinforcement of national dimension in practice 331–33
instrumental independence 249, 256–57
ECB, and 15, 250–51, 252–53
international arena, ECB in 209–33
critical appraisal of ECB's international dimension 229–32
'borrowing' of ECB should be enshrined in Treaties 231
ECB's derived international legal personality 232
ECB's evolving international dimension 230–31
ECB international cooperation instruments should pertain only to cooperation 232
mismatch between ECB's internal powers and its halfway international capacity 230
technocratic ECB not able to be fully in charge of international dimension 229–30
ECB's close cooperation with international institutions 209–10
evolution of ECB's international dimension 220–29
Article 219 TFEU practice 220–21
'borrowing' of ECB outside EU Treaty framework 227–29
ECB's international cooperation instruments 224–27
relationship with international organizations and for a 221–24
legal framework of ECB's international dimension 211–16
ECB's international cooperation on role within SSM 215–16
ECOFIN, role of 214–15
parallelism between internal-external powers 213
price stability as central objective 212–13
special institutional balance in field of EMU external relations 213–14
specific institutional balance in field of EU external relations 211–12
tricky international legal status of ECB 216–20
ECB's international legal personality 219–20
ECB's legal personality 218
international legal personality 217–18
International Monetary and Financial Committee (IMFC) 222–23

International Monetary Fund (IMF) 11, 39, 145, 222, 230
assistance packages 39, 354
ECB, and 209–10, 213, 218, 222–23
financial stability, indicators of 108
membership and representation 222–23
significance of 222–23
Troika, part of 209–10

joint supervisory teams (JSTs) 168, 195–96, 327, 329–30, 336–37
judicial review *see* Court of Justice of the EU (CJEU)

Keynesianism
permanent trade-off' between inflation and employment 31–32
shift towards monetarism 31–32

Lender of Last Resort (LOLR)
ECB as LOLR 12–13, 38, 50, 52, 376–78
enhanced credit support 131
sovereign bond buying 131–32, *see also* sovereign debt/sovereign bond markets
ELA: NCBs as LOLRs to individual institutions 123–26
ESCB/Eurosystem 376–78
intentional obscurity of function 18–19
lack of EU-wide LOLR 2
macro-level LOLR function incorporated into ECB monetary policy 124
nature of function 123–24
quantitative easing, and 78–79
systemic risk, and *see* systemic risk
less significant institutions (LSIs) 330
NCAs supervising 163, 166, 188–89, 327, 329–30, 331
Listens Portal, ECB 287
Longer-Term Refinancing Operations (LTROs) 10, 61, 285–87
aim of supporting government bond markets 61
COVID-19, and 20
enhanced credit support 131
liquidity used in carry-trade to buy sovereign debt 13

Macroeconomic Imbalance Procedure 142–44
macroeconomics, QE in 66–68
ECB, and 105, 116–17
ESRB *see* ESRB
macroprudential supervision 115–18
meaning of 116
macroprudential supervision 115–18
ESRB, in 147–49
mandate of the ECB 2, 9–11, 361–91
climate change and biodiversity loss, addressing 420–24
euro area crisis, and 402–5
financial stability *see* financial stability
hierarchized multiple objectives, and 365–68
implementation: purposive and functional approach 375–78
common and distinct features in implementing central bank mandates 384–88
price stability determined within monetary policy strategy 378–84
limits to ECB's Treaty mandate 2
market neutrality 85
new tasks assigned to ECB 11
price stability *see* price stability
risk management strategy 85
secondary objectives of the ECB 160–63
supporting general economic policies of EU 11
market neutrality 249
ECB's mandate, in 85
free competition, and 158–59, 161–62, 249, 365–67, 420–21
legal rationale 161–62, 420–21
market attentiveness instead of market neutrality 97–98, 102
normative justification for 97
potential limitations of 161–62
proportionality, and 174–75
risk equivalence, and 94, 97
Member States
central banks *see* central banks
Commission assessing financing needs of 275
ECB, and 2
ECB becoming LOLR to 78–79
fiscal and wage policy, independence and 255–57
GFC, support during 341
national parliaments, ECB and 22
accountability relationship 22
SSM, scrutiny role and 284–85

NCAs *see* NCAs
NCBs *see* NCBs
QE 78
SMP, and 37–40
SPG, operating within 341, 343–44
Supervisory Board, and 325–26
microprudential supervision 115–16, 118
SSM, in 149–53, 189–93
monetarism 31–32
focus on price stability 31–32
Keynesianism to monetarism 31–32
shift towards 18–19, 34–35
monetary dialogue 41–42, 272–73, 278–79, 288–89, 399
monetary policy of the ECB
constraints on efficacy of 340
ECB focus on 34–35, 161, 212–13
environmental objectives, and *see* climate emergency
financial stability *see* financial stability
future of monetary policy increasingly contested 2, 3
GFC, and 10
goal independence 15
'greening' of 420–24
independent monetary policy, threats to 255–63
bond purchases 257–59
fiscal and wage policy of Member States 255–57
intensity of judicial control 259–63
inflation, and 21, 40, 65–66, 159, 267–68
initial consensus model central bank 60–61
interest rates 60–61
stability-oriented monetary policy strategy 60
interest rates 9, 60–61, 75–76
macro-level LOLR function incorporated into 124
monetary policy tools as secondary policy instrument of financial stability 128–34
distinction between preventive and remedial instruments 134
ECB standard monetary policy 130
ECB's unconventional monetary policy measures 130–32
unconventional monetary policy and financial stability 132–33
new monetary policy 75–79
new monetary toolbox 23
unconventional measures 75–79
price stability *see* price stability
quantitative easing *see* quantitative easing (QE)
unconventional monetary policy measures 75–79, 130–32
adoption of 10, 11, 75–76
enhanced credit support: ECB as LOLR to banking system 131
financial stability, and 132–33
first phase 76
second phase *see* quantitative easing (QE)
sovereign bond buying: ECB as LOLR to sovereigns 131–32, *see also* sovereign debt/sovereign bond markets
SSM as start of 61
whatever it takes within the mandate 375–78

national central banks *see* NCBs
National Competent Authorities (NCAs) *see* NCAs
national parliaments, ECB and 22
accountability relationship 22
SSM, scrutiny role and 284–85
NCAs 7
ECB, and 11, 22, 168–69, 327
JSTs, and 327
national Europeanized institutions, as 325–26
SSM, and
NCA tasks, powers, and responsibilities 193–95
oversight of SSM functioning, NCAs duty of assistance in 206–7
SSM authorizations, role in 198–204
fit and proper authorizations 202
other SSM authorizations for SIs 202–4
SSM common procedure 199–201
SSM banking supervision of significant institutions, role in 195–98
JSTs 195–96, 327, 329–30, 336–37
SEP: off-sit and on-site supervision 196–97
SREP 197–98
Supervisory Board, membership of 325–26

NCBs
ECB decisions, and 324
ELA: NCBs as LOLRs to individual institutions 123–26
ECB's involvement in ELA provision by NCBs 125–26
ELA falling within purview of NCBs 124
Eurosystem, and *see* Eurosystem
monetary policy 137–38
PSPP, and 63, 64–65
Supervisory Board, membership of 325–26, 329
Network for Greening the Financial System (NGFS) *see* NGFS
new stability conception 36–46
OMT *see* Outright Monetary Transactions (OMT)
SMP *see* Securities and Market Programme (SMP)
reconciling with the law 46–52
mandate 46–50
prohibition on monetary financing 50–52, 61–62
Next Generation EU 155, 348, 427–29
financing 162–63, 349–50
nature and purpose 347, 348
RRF 2, 155, 348, 427–29
NGFS 92–93
ECB as member 92–93, 171
ensuring adequate pricing of risk as objective 92–93
'no-bailout' clause of TFEU 32–33, 36–37, 138, 144, 297–98
EMU, and 392–93, 394, 397
euro area crisis 402–5
founding principle of EMU, as 37–38
reinterpretation 12, 16–17

OECD 224, 230
OLAF 254–55, 304, 406–7
ECB, and 253–54
OMT 2, 10, 36–37, 41–46, 51–52, 74–75
ESM recapitalization 44–45
last resort instrument, as 53
not activated 46
providing liquidity 12–13
purchasing government bonds 29
structural reform through SSM 44–45
traditional model of central banking, ending of 61
'whatever it takes' pledge by Draghi 2, 45–46, 132, 139–40, 375–76
see also *Gauweiler*
open market economy *see* market neutrality
Optimal Currency Area (OCA) theory 18–19
Outright Monetary Transactions (OMT) *see* OMT

Pandemic Emergency Purchase Programme (PEPP) *see* PEPP
payment systems 118–23
digital euro introduction as ECB competence in 119–20
ECB's actions 119
functions and importance of 118–19
operation of euro area payment systems 120–21
scope of ECB's financial market infrastructure oversight 121–23
TARGET2 120–21
technological transformation, effects of 119–20
PEPP 2, 10, 57, 285–87, 353–55
challenge to 57
Covid-19, and 20, 71–75
nature of 72–73, 76
flexibility 72–73, 74–75
influenced by exceptional nature of COVID-19 crisis 76–77
OMT programme, as successor of 76
unique pandemic QE programme, as 73
providing liquidity 12–13
quantitative easing 71–75
Member States' fiscal responsibility, and 78
objectives and effects of PEPP 74–75
PEPP as pandemic quantitative easing 72–74
size of 90
price stability 157–60, 375–78
definition 9, 158
ECB failure since 2001 to achieve 159
ECB independence, and 14, 146–47, 159–60
inflation rate for 34–35, 53–54, 60, 80, 126, 158–59, 174, 182, 247–48, 375–76, 400–1, 424
monetary policy strategy, determined within 378–84

monetary policy tools, achieving price stability by 158
primacy of ECB's price stability objective 8, 9, 10–11, 14, 146–47, 157–58, 172–75, 212–13
PSPP, and *see* Public Sector Purchase Programme (PSPP)
stability, narrow conception of 33–36
stability paradigm 31–33
tools for maintaining 110–12, 111*t*
'undefined legal term', as 20–21
Pringle 51–52, 139, 140, 141, 228–29, 403
conferring new tasks on ECB 227–28
delineating boundary between economic and monetary policy 139–40
discretion to entity undertaking the action 298–99
effect of decision 229, 231
indirect effect on price stability, monetary policy and 152
interpretation of no-bailout clause 144, 297–98
legality of ESM 49, 50–52, 139, 144, 296–97
maintaining financial stability of the monetary union 109–10, 296–97
non-binding international cooperation instruments, ECB and 227–29, 231
objectives-based reasoning 297–98
prohibition on monetary financing 51
stability of the euro area as matter of economic policy 140
travaux préparatoires of Maastricht Treaty, invoking 144, 393
proportionality
CJEU 302–3, 305
ECB focus on 22
fines 315
market neutrality, and 174–75
prudential regulation 112–15
ECB advisory role in the legislative process 113–14
ECB contributing to prudential supervision of credit institutions 115, 116
ECB influence over prudential rule-making 115
microprudential measures 112–13
resilience oriented approach 113–14
setting of *ex ante* rules to prevent instability 112–13
prudential supervision 11, 115–18
absence of centralized supervision for euro area 116
CJEU, and *see* Court of Justice of the EU (CJEU)
ESRB *see* ESRB
less contested than monetary policy choices 3
macroprudential supervision 115–18
microprudential supervision 115–16, 118
nature of 115–16
PSPP 10, 342
Asset Purchase Programme (APP), extension of 62–63
deflation, and 53, 65, 66
economics of 65–66
inflation, and 65–66, 69–71, 300
legal form and basis 63
monetary policy instrument, as 69–71
providing liquidity 12–13
quantitative easing 61–66
first QE programme proper in the euro area 62–63
main features of the PSPP 63–65
main programme, PSPP, as 76
Member States' fiscal responsibility, and 78
purchases in secondary markets 63–64
stated aims of the PSPP 65–66
quantitative easing and PSPP in economic theory and central bank practice 66–71
macroeconomics, QE in 66–68
size of 90
see also *Weiss*
Public Sector Purchase Programme (PSPP) *see* PSPP

qualifying holding authorizations 199, 200–1
quantitative easing (QE) 19, 23–24, 59–79, 386–87
APP *see* Asset Purchase Programme (APP)
becoming key feature of ECB monetary policy 76
boom and bust cycles, creating 77
central bank tool for the ECB, as 69–71
central banks' use of 53–54
deflation, and 77

quantitative easing (QE) (*cont.*)
ECB becoming a creditor of countries receiving financial assistance 145
ECB becoming LOLR to Member States 78–79
ECB utilization later than other central banks 76
effects of QE going beyond traditional reach of monetary policy 77–78
inflation, and 53, 66–68, 77
macroeconomics, QE in 66–68
Member States' fiscal responsibility, and 78
nature of 53
PEPP *see* Pandemic Emergency Purchase Programme (PEPP)
price stability, and 77
PSPP *see under* Public Sector Purchase Programme (PSPP)
reasons for 77
relationship with potential objectives of monetary policy 77–79
unconventional impact on economy and particular asset prices 78

Recovery and Resilience Facility (RRF) 2, 155, 348, 427–29
Reform Support Programme (RSP) 344–45
risk management *see* collateral framework of ECB (1990s-present)

Scelle, George 145–46
secondary objectives of the ECB 23, 160–63
climate change mitigation *see* climate emergency
definition 160
environmental sustainability 10–11, 161–62
financial stability *see* financial stability
market neutrality *see* market neutrality
supporting general economic policies of EU 11, 24, 160–61
Securities and Market Programme (SMP) *see* SMP
SEP: off-site and on-site supervision 196–97
significant institutions (SIs) 212–13, 330
authorization powers of ECB 198
fit and proper authorizations 202
ECB and NCAs role in supervision of 195–98, 212–13, 327
JSTs 195–96, 327, 329–30, 336–37
SEP: off-site and on-site supervision 196–97
SREP 197–98, 327
Single List of Eligible Collateral 87–89
Single Resolution Board (SRB) *see* SRB
Single Resolution Mechanism (SRM) *see* SRM
Single Supervisory Mechanism (SSM) *see* SSM
Six-Pack 142, 143–44
SMP 10, 29, 36–40
accountability 152–53
executive role of ECB 153
Member States support, and 37–40
political decisions, and 21
providing liquidity 12–13
purchasing government bonds 29, 36–37, 40
separation of supervisory and monetary functions 151–52
size 90
unconventional measures, start of 61
sovereign debt/sovereign bond markets 12–14, 29–58, 341
collateral, ECB treating sovereign debt as 13–14
constraints on efficacy of monetary policy 341
ECB as LOLR to sovereigns 131–32
ECB barred from purchasing government bonds 12, 50–52
ECB in original set-up of currency union 31–36
narrow conception of stability 33–36
stability paradigm 31–33
ECB's role as crisis manager 274–79
EFSF *see* EFSF
ESM *see* ESM
fragmentation of financial markets 341
implied mutualization of national sovereign risk 341
LTROs as monetary financing 13
new stability conception *see* new stability conception
sovereign debt crisis 29, 33–36
transformation of ECB 29–30, 58
SPG 18–19, 43, 138, 427–29
amendments to reduce pro-cyclical bias in national fiscal policies 344
budgetary stability, nature of 142

complaints about 395–96
European Semester, and *see* European Semester
fiscal sustainability 346
general escape clause 341, 346
Member States operating within 341, 343–44
strengthening of 142–44
Six-Pack 142, 143–44
suspension of normal budgetary requirements 346
SRB 149, 175, 329
ECB, and 177
ECB/SSM coordination with 179–81
jurisdiction 176
NCAs, consulting with 176, 180
recommendation on resolutions 178–79
requiring changes to organizational structures 180
resolution plans 180–81
role 156, 178
Single Resolution Fund 156, 175
SRM operating through 156, 175
SREP 197–98, 327
SRM 176–79
aims of 176
Banking Union, and *see* EBU, ECB's role in
ECB/SSM coordination with SRB 179–81
operating through SRB 156
pillar of EBU, as 156
SRB *see* SRB
SSM 72, 121
accountability of ECB 152–53
Banking Union, and *see* EBU, ECB's role in
common procedures, SSM 199–201
banking licences 199–200
qualifying holding authorizations 199, 200–1
decision-making 152
determining whether measure pursues financial or price stability 152
ECB and NCAs role in supervision of significant institutions 195–98
JSTs 195–96, 327, 329–30, 336–37
SEP: off-site and on-site supervision 196–97
SREP 197–98
ECB as microprudential supervisor in 150, 155
ECB tasks, powers, and responsibilities 189–93
ECB supervising systemically important banks 149, 150, 163–75, 184–85
ECB competences and tasks as a bank supervisor 164–67
ECB's executive role 152–53
legal basis of ECB supervision 163–64
effectiveness 185
ESCB, and 150
financial stability as objective 151
ECB, and 151
jurisdiction 170
membership 169–70
microprudential supervision in 147, 149–53
oversight of functioning of the SSM, role of ECB in 204–7
ECB's responsibility for oversight 204–6
NCA's duty of assistance 206–7
pandemic relief measures 72
pillar of EBU, as 156
purpose 163, 188
rationale and organization 186–89
relationship between ECB and NCAs in the SSM 184–208
ECB tasks, powers, and responsibilities 189–93
NCA tasks, powers, and responsibilities 193–95
overview 186–95
role of ECB and NCAs in SSM authorizations 198–204
role of ECB and NCAs in supervision of significant institutions 195–98
role of ECB in oversight of functioning of the SSM 204–7
SSM authorizations, role of ECB and NCAs in 198–204
fit and proper authorizations 202
other SSM authorizations for SIs 202–4
SSM common procedures 199–201
strict separation of supervisory and monetary functions required 151
structural reform through 44–45
stability
EFSF *see* EFSF
ESM *see* ESM
financial *see* financial stability
narrow conception of stability 33–36

stability (*cont.*)
  new stability conception *see* new stability conception
  price *see* price stability
  stability paradigm 31–33
Stability and Growth Pact (SPG) *see* SPG
stagflation 18, 157–58
state aid
  financial stability, and 109–10
Supervisory Board 167–70, 325–27
  Chairman
    appointment and removal 283–84
    role of 281–82, 326–27
  composition and representation 325–27
  ECB, and 173, 325–26
  ECB Code of Conduct 325–26
  governance 173
  joint supervisory teams (JSTs) 168, 195–96, 327, 329–30
  Steering Committee 326–27, 329
  tasks and responsibilities 167–68, 169, 325–26
  voting 325–26
Supervisory Review and Evaluation Process (SREP) *see* SREP
Support to mitigate Unemployment Risks in an Emergency (SURE) 2
SURE 2, 345, 346–47, 349–50, 427–29
systemic risk 204–5, 207–8
  banking sector 183
  ESRB *see* European Systemic Risk Board (ESRB)
  European System of Financial Supervision, in 368
  identifying systemic risks 108
  LOLR, and 36, 134
  macroprudential tools, ECB's limited competence to use 183
  meaning of 34–35
  preventing 34–35, 36
  stranded assets 181–82
  Supervisory Board, and *see* Supervisory Board

TARGET2 78, 119
  purpose and nature of 120–21
  systemic dimension 121
targeted longer-term refinancing operations (TLTROs) *see* TLTROs
technological developments 411–12
  payment systems 119–20, 411–12
time inconsistency problem 239–40, 268
TLTROs 83, 285–86, 352, 375–76
Treaty mandate *see* mandate of the ECB
Troika 11, 21, 209–10, 227, 228–29, 243–45

Weiss 10, 52–57, 243–45, 307, 407
  CJEU approval of PSPP 10, 299–300
  competence 140–41, 302
  deferential approach of CJEU 25, 277–78, 316–17
  ECB acting ultra vires 3
  ECB barred from purchasing government bonds 12
  ECB's goal independence 15, 275–76
  objectives-based test 300–1
  proportionality review 248, 302, 305